The Art and Science of
Culinary Preparation c.\

A Culinarian's Manual

Jerald W. Chesser, CEC, CCE

The Educational Institute of the American Culinary Federation, Inc.

St. Augustine, Florida

This book has been developed, written and designed specifically for the apprentices registered in the National Apprenticeship Training Program for Cooks, Registry N-90093, U.S. Department of Labor, a program of The Educational Institute of the American Culinary Federation, Inc. It is meant to be used by all who would study the culinary arts.

Published by The Educational Institute of the American Culinary Federation, Inc.
P.O. Box 3466
10 San Bartola Road
St. Augustine, FL 32085-3466

Printed in the United States of America

Library of Congress Catalog Card Number # 91-076371

ISBN 0-9631023-1-1

First Edition, 1992

Dedication

This text is dedicated to the memory of Alec Cline, CEC and the many other chefs who exhibited the highest level of professionalism in and out of the kitchen, encouraging others to pursue knowledge and sharing their knowledge with others without regard to personal gain or glorification.

The Team

Author
Jerald W. Chesser, CEC, CCE

Senior Editors
Stephen C. Fernald, CWC
William B. Jacoby, MS

Food Science Editor
Cornelia Price, MS

Contributing Editors
Roland Henin, CMC, CCE
David Kellaway, CMC, CCE
Keith Keogh, CEC
Hans J. Schadler, CEC
Casey Sinkeldam, CMPC, CEC

Research Editors
Jeffrey C. Labarge, CEC, CCE
Michael Robins, CMC

Nutrition Review
The Nutrition Projects Committee of
The Educational Institute of the American
Culinary Federation

Book Design
Pamela Shanholtzer, Robin Shepherd Studios

Cover and Section Heading Art
Robin Shepherd, Robin Shepherd Studios

Illustrations
Mike Barnhart

*On behalf of the
future chefs and cooks of America
who will benefit, the members
of the American Culinary Federation
are pleased to thank*

KRAFT FOODSERVICE, INC.
and

THE KRAFT GENERAL FOODS FOUNDATION

*for the financial support
which has made possible
the development of this book.*

Table of Contents

Section I
GENERAL INFORMATION

1   What is the Art and Science 1

2   Background Skills and Knowledge for Culinary Preparation 15

Section II
ESSENTIAL KNOWLEDGE FOR UNDERSTANDING CULINARY PREPARATION

3   Temperature and its Application to Culinary Preparation 27

4   Emulsion 41

5   How Foods are Flavored and Seasoned 47

6   Elements of Presentation 61

7   Fats and Oils 67

8   Dairy Products 79

9   Eggs 87

Section III
HOT FOOD PREPARATION

10   Fruits 95

11   Vegetables. 103

12   Potatoes and other Tubers. 127

13   Farinaceous Cookery 139

14   Stock. 159

15   Soups 171

16   Hot Sauces 201

17   Meat (Beef, Veal, Lamb and Pork) 235

18   Poultry. 263

19   Game 273

20   Seafood and Freshwater Fish. 285

21   Breakfast Cookery 311

Section IV
GARDE MANGER

22   Cold Sauces 327

23   Salads. 339

24   Gelatin and Aspic Jelly 363

25   Forcemeat and Mousse 385

26   Pate, Terrines, and other Garde Manger Products 399

27   Hors D'oeuvres and Appetizers 411

28   Charcuterie. 433

29   Sandwiches 447

Section V
BAKING

30 Principles of Baking 465

31 Yeast Bread and Rolls 477

32 Quick Breads 489

33 Pastry Dough 499

34 Fillings 515

35 Cakes 523

36 Frostings and Toppings 535

37 Basic Decorative Items 545

38 Sorbet, Ice Cream, and Frozen Desserts 553

Preface

The year 1929 brought tragedy, trauma and general depression for the United States and the World, yet there was one group which looked to the future of the nation and the future of the profession that it would come to represent. It was in this year in New York City that a group of individuals came together to form the foundation of the American Culinary Federation (ACF). The continuation of this faith in the future of the professional chef has led to this text. The road leading to this work has a long history. In 1963, the first edition of Manual for Culinarians was published by the American Culinary Federation Educational Institute (ACFEI) as a reference for the apprentices involved in the ACFEI apprenticeship program. A revised version of the manual was printed in 1982. In 1989, the ACFEI discerned the need for a new text for the apprentice program. This would be a text which would continue the tradition of excellence in presenting culinary information established by the previous manuals yet endeavor to address in greater depth the issue of why ingredients and processes are used, as well as the many changes which have occurred in the preparation of food over the years. The Art and Science of Culinary Preparation is the result.

Understanding and learning how to produce food allows the culinarian to produce quality products based on established procedures. This is accomplished by the study of theory and by practicing skills basic to the production of food. This type of information is presented throughout this text. When this information is combined with supervised hands-on training, the culinarian will have achieved the preliminary level of understanding necessary to produce quality dishes.

Movement beyond the preliminary level of culinary preparation requires inquiry into why ingredients and processes are used. The chef does not just produce dishes based on established procedures. The goal of the culinarian is to create and innovate. Why things are done in a particular manner, how ingredients interact in the dish, the effect of temperature and a variety of other factors are the keys that unlock the realm of limitless possibilities in culinary preparation which is the art and science of culinary preparation. It is the realization that for food to be attractively or even artistically presented is not sufficient. The presentation needs to be supported by desirable flavors, textures and colors which are a result of the keys in preparation. These issues are addressed throughout the text in relation to the various types of production being discussed.

I consider culinary preparation to be the pursuit of excellence in its most pleasing, enjoyable and satisfying form. It is hoped that the ACFEI apprentice and other aspiring culinarians will find that the information contained in this text, combined with instruction and training, both academic and professional, will open the broad vistas of culinary preparation. Culinary preparation is a time-honored and honorable profession within which I wish you the brightest and most productive of futures. Remember that humankind requires food for both the body and mind in order to grow and I encourage you to pursue both types of sustenance.

Acknowledgments

A text of this scope requires extensive research and deliberation. It is not the result of the work of one single individual, but the synthesis of the combined efforts of many individuals. It is this synthesizing of facts, theories and opinions that brings validity and strength to the final text. This text is the outgrowth of the effort of many people. Roland Henin, CMC, CCE; Keith Keogh, CEC; Casey Sinkeldam, CMPC, CEC; David Kellaway, CMC, CCE; Hans Schadler, CEC; Steve Fernald, CWC; Jeffrey Labarge, CEC, CCE, and Michael Robins, CMC, assisted in researching and formulating the content of this text. Cornelia Price provided research assistance and guidance in the area of food preparation and its relationship to food science. The Nutrition Committee of the ACFEI reviewed the text regarding nutritional concerns. Kevin Kerstein, Kevin Hickey, Jeffrey Igel and Ines Ifarraguerri plus many other students from the University of Wisconsin-Stout, Johnston and Wales (Rhode Island) and University of Central Florida provided input from a student perspective regarding the text. Encouragement and assistance in many forms was provided by William Jacoby, Jeff Larson, Edwin Brown and the Officers and Staff of the ACF and ACFEI. A special thanks goes to the Kraft Foundation for its support of this text from its inception to its completion.

J.W. Chesser

Purpose

The purpose of <u>The</u> <u>Art</u> <u>and</u> <u>Science</u> <u>of</u> <u>Culinary</u> <u>Preparation</u> is to present the basic knowledge needed to understand and become skillful in basic food preparation, and at the same time to discuss why ingredients and procedures are used. Organization of the material is consistent with this goal. The text is laid out in five sections: General information, essential knowledge for understanding culinary preparation, hot food preparation, garde manger and baking. The first section is an introduction to culinary preparation and general information which the aspiring culinarian will need to understand food preparation and the profession of professional chef. The second section is a presentation of basic and background information necessary to all food preparation. The culinarian who understands this section will be better prepared to study the material presented in the last three sections of the text.

The grouping of the last three sections of the text are necessarily arbitrary and consistent with the current division of labor in the modern kitchen. This does not, however, mean that the information presented in each section has no bearing on later sections. Previous material is often referred to in later chapters or the reader is directed back to previous chapters for a fuller explanation of particular items and issues. Divisions are used to assist in separating the information into more easily managed units for learning and instruction.

Recipes are an integral part of the presentation of basic culinary knowledge. However, they necessarily represent an individual's interpretation of a particular dish or item. It is for this reason that the recipes presented in this text are minimal in comparison to other culinary texts. The recipes included are presented to assist the reader in understanding the facts, theories and concepts presented. Aspiring culinarians will draw upon the knowledge of the instructor/chef and the multitude of recipe books available for the variety of other dishes prepared in the kitchen and will eventually begin to create their own recipes.

The effectiveness of any text as a teaching tool lies with the instructor/chef. No singular text can address all of the variations of preparation techniques and application of processes and ingredients. The instructor/chef will find it necessary to discuss the variations that occur from kitchen to kitchen, region to region, and country to country in order to broaden the meaningfulness and usefulness of the information presented in this text. These discussions will be effective in reinforcing the continuity of the science of culinary preparation while clarifying the individuality and artistry of culinary preparation. Realizing the need for this type of discussion, it is assumed that other references will be used in conjunction with the material contained in this text to present the aspiring culinarian with as complete a body of knowledge as possible. The bibliography included in this text is a guide to other quality references in this field of study.

The study of fact, theory and concept is not sufficient to educate a culinarian. The individual must have the opportunity to see the skills, processes and ingredients in action, and to practice them. Whether in the ACFEI apprentice program or other culinary arts programs, it is this combination of theory and practice which will lead to sound, functional knowledge. This text is designed to blend with a practical instruction component developed by the chef/instructor. The apprentice/student who is assisted in the combining of the study of this text, auxiliary materials and appropriate practical components will have a thorough grounding in the art and science of culinary preparation.

Section I
General Information

What is the Art & Science?
Background Skills & Knowledge
for Culinary Preparation

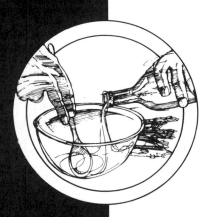

Chapter 1

CHAPTER OBJECTIVES

- To introduce the historical progression leading to modern cookery.
- To discuss the organization of the classical and modern kitchen.
- To discuss the responsibilities of the executive chef in the modern kitchen.
- To discuss the interaction of service and preparation.
- To discuss the factors contributing to the development of a cuisine.
- To introduce the factors affecting menu planning.
- To discuss the importance of balancing a menu.
- To discuss the relationship of art and science in culinary preparation.

Art and Science

Human beings eat to survive, so it must be assumed that from the beginning of time the gathering, preparation and consumption of food has been the primary focus of humanity. Our concern as culinarians lies with the preparation of the food.

Humankind, in the beginning, ate to survive. Today, we still eat to survive; however, in most areas of the world, effort has been made to make the food, whether bountiful or not, more enjoyable. This includes the cooking of meats to make them more easily eaten and digested; cooking vegetables to improve flavor and provide a variety of textures, and combining various food stuffs to create exciting flavor combinations and appealing color mixtures. These efforts go beyond the preparation needed to prepare food for the survival of those who eat it. This is the art associated with the preparation of food.

It is not solely the artful manipulation and combination of food which results in good tasting food. Development of pleasing textures and flavors involves the interaction of the various foods and preparation methods used. The preparation we discuss in this text, in one sense, goes far beyond the preparation of food stuffs needed for humankind to survive. In another sense, our discussions will touch on nutritional aspects of preparation which are important to the survival of the consumer. The nutritional value of the food prepared must be considered. This part of food preparation can be considered to be the science. Balancing the art and science is the goal of the culinarian. Producing food which is nutritious and good tasting requires both art and science.

A BRIEF HISTORY OF CULINARY PREPARATION

The phrase "a brief history of culinary preparation" is, at best, misleading and, at worst, a bald-faced lie. It is not possible to do justice, in a brief manner, to a subject which is equivalent to the history of the human race. This art and science began more than 300,000 years ago when, according to carbon dating, man began to use fire for the preparation of food. There have been very few discoveries or inventions of humanity since fire that have not affected, in some manner, the preparation of food.

When was salt first used in food preparation? How did various spices and herbs begin to be used? These and many other questions concerning the history of food preparation cannot be answered. However, as archaeology has slowly uncovered the ancient civilizations around the world, it has unearthed an increasingly large body of knowledge concerning the development of cuisine the world over.

When humans first used herbs and spices is not known, but their importance in the ancient world is known. The acquisition of these and other food stuffs was a prime factor in the development of trade routes throughout both the Western and Eastern Hemispheres. Alexander the Great brought to Greece spices from the Orient and melons and other fruits from Persia. The trade routes begun by Alexander were later used by the Ptolemys of Egypt and by the Roman Empire. Spices and herbs hold a special place in the history of mankind, having been as eagerly sought as gold, silver and jewels.

A less glamorous culinary cousin of spices, grain, has always been the key to the might of nations. The treasures of Africa were not simply gold, ivory and jewels for Rome. Africa was far more important as the breadbasket of the Empire. The pound of grain, which was the right of every citizen of Rome, came from the fertile fields of North Africa. It was to protect these shipments of grain that the Roman Empire cleared the Mediterranean Sea of pirates and built a system of roads, many parts of which are still in use today.

Historically, the procuring of various foods has always been of great significance. For the Roman Empire it was

Cooking with an open fire required great strength as well as cooking skill.

(From Bartolomeo Scappi, *Dell arte dell cucinare* [On the Arts of Cooking] 1643. Artwork courtesy New York Public Library, Rare Book Division)

grain, for the English Empire tea and sugar. Today it is foods of all types for third world nations which cannot feed their populations, while other countries have more than they can use. Each of these developments has contributed to the development of culinary preparation in the world.

Culinary development initially was tied to developments within an individual country or region; however as each region came into contact with people from other areas, ideas were exchanged. The result was a traceable progression in the development of food preparation from the Egyptians, to the Assyrians, to the Chaldeans, to the Babylonians, to the Hebrews, to the Persians, to the Greeks, to the Romans, to the Gallo-Romans and then to the Franks, the direct forerunners of the French kitchen. The French kitchen is the cornerstone for most historians of the beginning of modern dining in the western world.

A pattern of refinement and development of culinary preparation began with the early Egyptian rulers and continued to the time of the Persians. The techniques of preparation and the combination of ingredients moved beyond that necessary to ensure survival. This tradition of refined, even exquisite, culinary preparation was further developed by the Greeks. They not only refined preparation techniques, but also the tools and equipment used. The cauldron, gridiron and frying pan are all Greek contributions to the kitchen.

The citizens of early Rome were admirers of all things Greek. This included their art, law and letters. This admiration was also extended to include food preparation. They imported from Greece not only the ideas for preparation and tools, but also the cooks. Rome's appreciation of fine food was evidenced in many ways. It was during the era of Roman greatness that Apicius, a rich merchant, published the first comprehensive book on cookery. This work, Romanae Artis Coquinariae Leber (The Roman Cookery Book), was a compilation of the many recipes and bits of information about food Apicius collected during his extensive travels. The prominent Roman gourmet, Lucullus, sent emissaries and explorers to new countries to seek out new entrees, spices, seasoning and exotic foods. This search for culinary adventure was pursued with a passion by the elite of the Roman Empire.

The development of cuisine in the region of Rome is an example of how cuisines have developed in regions all over the world. In the Roman Empire there were two levels of culinary development taking place simultaneously. The one most often discussed is that of the ruling elite. However, there was also development within the lower class of society in the countries which Rome controlled. Combinations of foods at this level of society were very different from that of the elite. They could best be described as working fare or farm food. The dishes were far simpler and utilitarian, definitely reflective of the economic status of the individual. As time progressed, there was integration of the discoveries of the very rich into the foods of the lower classes. It is from this mingling of higher and lower level cuisine that the cuisine considered representative of a region today has developed.

The Romans are credited with introducing to the rest of Europe a sense of culinary art. When Rome conquered the Franks and Gauls, they brought with them their appreciation of fine food. There was a melding of the culinary traditions already existing in the conquered lands with that of the Roman rulers. Emperor Charlemagne, the first broadly recognized ruler in Europe after the fall of the Roman Empire, laid the foundations for the type of culinary preparation and service that would develop in Europe. He invested his feasts with all the pomp and ceremonies he could design.

It was from this rich history, from

this infusion of culinary expertise from all over the Western Hemisphere by virtue of the rule of Rome and Charlemagne that the future crown jewel of the culinary arts developed. At the age of fourteen, in 1326, a young man by the name of Guillaume of Tirel was a kitchen boy (he turned the huge roasts on the spit in front of the open fire) in the kitchens of Queen Jeanne of France. This young boy was destined to be a founder of the movement toward the modern French kitchen. As an apprentice he was given the nickname of Taillevent, a name which has become famous. It was his book Le Viandier which set the tone for cookbooks to come in the future. The work of Apicius, while important, was the work of a philosopher. The work of Taillevent was that of a practitioner.

The work of Taillevent was still not refined in the modern sense. It was typical of the medieval chef. The foods were pureed and pounded almost into oblivion and then served with heavy sauces which disguised flavors. It was the work of Italian chefs such as Martino of Como in the 1400's and Bartolomeo Scappi in the 1500's, which began the move to dishes using more whole pieces of meat. They creatively used combinations of fruits and vegetables and experimented with pastry making in what was then thought of as the Arabic manner. It was the marriage of Catherine de Medicis to Henry II of France that brought Italian cooks to France. The refinements of the Italian

cooking were to become the basis for a shift in the French kitchen.

Francois Pierre de la Varenne, in his book Le Cuisinier François, brought into focus the changes in the French kitchen from Taillevent to the middle of the 1600's. The shift was away from the heavy banquets and unbalanced use of spices. A concern for balance and harmony in the meal began to come to the forefront. There was no doubt, however, that it was still only a *culinary art*. There was little movement toward anything *scientific* until the great chef and scholar Antonin (Marie-Antoine) Careme founded the "Classical French Cookery."

Chef Careme was born in Paris in 1784. He was self-taught in the arts and sciences, with emphasis on architecture. These skills he transferred to his creations in foods. Although Careme's work was reflective of the opulent, heavy meals of the 18th century, he was the first to begin recording recipes in a standard manner. He also began to streamline menus.

A major change which occurred in the 1850's was the introduction by Urbain Dubois and Emile Bernard of *service a la russe*. Careme had been introduced to this type of service when in Russia, but preferred the traditional *service a la francaise* which allowed for more showmanship. *Service a la francaise* was the presentation of a large number of dishes at the same time. These might be changed two or three times during the meal resulting in three or four courses. This type of service was a link

Careme's view of confectionary as a branch of architecture is displayed in these illustrations

Artwork courtesy Edward B. Page and P. W. Kingsford.

to the cooking and presentation of the medieval kitchen.

Service a la russe is the serving of dishes individually instead of all at once. This style of service was well established and preferred by the master chef, Maitre Auguste Escoffier. It was the turn of the 20th century when Escoffier created the "French School of Culinary Arts - La Cuisine Classique." Escoffier's culinary career was supremely brilliant. He was regarded as the Emperor of the World's Kitchens. His changes in the kitchen were in the menu, the food preparation and the kitchen itself.

It is Escoffier who shaped the modern menu. The streamlined menus were designed for the *service a la russe* which had been pushed into the forefront by Dubois and Bernard. Although his menus were still quite heavy in comparision to those served today, they were indeed light fare compared to those of even a century before. The change in style of service and streamlining of the menu made it possible for restaurants to begin to flourish.

The menu and service were not the only concerns Escoffier had about culinary preparation during his time. The low esteem in which the profession of cookery was held at the time deeply disturbed him. He was aware that in a large part the laxity of many of the individuals in the profession and the poor working conditions of the kitchen contributed to the problem of low esteem.

Escoffier pledged himself to reform the kitchens as much as possible. He thereby began the changes which have resulted in the modern kitchen. A few of the many firsts attributed to Escoffier included:

1. ALL COOKS WERE REQUIRED TO WEAR THE NEWLY FASHIONED CHECKERED TROUSERS AND WHITE JACKET.
2. HE REQUIRED HIS COOKS TO BATH REGULARLY.
3. HE INSISTED THAT HIS COOKS ACQUIRE SCHOOLING SO THEY COULD BETTER THEMSELVES.
4. HE WAS THE FIRST TO MOVE THE KITCHEN OUT OF ITS TRADITIONAL LOCATION IN THE UNVENTILATED BASEMENT.
5. HE DISCOURAGED SMOKING AND DRINKING ALCOHOL BY MEMBERS OF HIS STAFF.
6. ONE OF HIS GREAT ACHIEVEMENTS WAS THE DEVELOPMENT OF THE KITCHEN BRIGADE. THIS DIVISION OF THE KITCHEN INTO STATIONS ELIMINATED MUCH OF THE CONFUSION TRADITIONAL IN THE KITCHEN UP TO THE TIME OF ESCOFFIER.
7. HE BEGAN THE PROCESS OF STANDARDIZING RECIPES AND MENUS.

The innovations of Escoffier began to make culinary preparation an art and a science. The emphasis of the preparation became quality, not quantity.

While it is true that Escoffier set the stage for the development of the modern French kitchen, the changes have not stopped there. The twentieth century has brought tremendous changes in equipment and fuels available for food preparation. The preservation of food has changed the face of the professional culinarian's work. Refrigerated shipping and storage, vacuum packaging and inert gas packaging have all had an impact on not only the preparation of food in the commercial kitchen, but also the organization and manpower requirements.

In his introduction to the first edition of <u>Le Guide Culinaire</u>, Escoffier said, "These men of genius (Dubois and Bernard), although admirers of the great Careme, nevertheless did not hesitate to change those parts of his work which no longer agreed with current trends." These words, printed in November of 1902, are not only applicable to those who preceded Escoffier, but also to those who came after. This was, and still is, particularly true in the United States. The constant influx of immigrants from all over the world combined with the bountiful quantity and variety of foods available in the United States has brought about the creation of a wide variety of dishes. While these dishes are anchored in the traditional cuisine of the native country from which the immigrant comes, they are often changed by the foods available. What has evolved are a variety of types of cuisine which both are and are not unique to the United States or its various regions.

Throughout the twentieth century the kitchen and menu have been streamlined. Preparations have come to be viewed from the standpoint of nutritional value as well as taste. The culinarian has been faced with many choices regarding speed of preparation and quality of product. As culinarians we live in a world which is blessed with many modern conveniences and just as many paradoxes regarding how each will ultimately impact the dish we prepare. There is no question that the history of culinary preparation has just begun, whether the issue is kitchen organization, style of service, cuisine or many, yet to be raised, issues.

KITCHEN ORGANIZATION

The organization of the hotel and restaurant kitchen will depend upon the size of the operation and type of menu and service. The classical kitchen brigade system established by Escoffier was designed for a large operation utilizing complex menus. The classical brigade included a *chef* (*executive chef*) who was responsible for all activities in the kitchen. The second in command in the kitchen was the *sous chef* (*second chef*) who was directly in charge of production.

Production in the kitchen was divided into stations which were overseen by *chefs de partie*. This included:

1. The *saucier* who was responsible for sauces, stews, stocks, hot hors d'oeuvres and saute.
2. The *potager* was responsible for soups; stocks for soups, and chowders.
3. The *poissoner* was responsible for fish dishes.
4. The *entremetier* prepared vegetables, starches and eggs.
5. The *rotisseur* was responsible for roasted and braised meats and for meat gravies.
6. The *grillardin* prepared broiled items, and possibly deep-fried meats and fish.
7. The *garde manger* was responsible for cold foods; including salads, dressings, pates, cold hors d'oeuvres, and buffet items.
8. The *patissier* prepared pastries and desserts with a baker responsible for breads and rolls.
9. The *tournant* acted as swing or relief cook.

The various *chefs de partie* were assigned *commis* which were cooks or helpers. Standard were the *premier commis* or *station cook*, *deuxieme commis* or *cook's helper*, and *troisieme commis* or *cook's helper assistant*.

Larger modern kitchens still use a version of the classical brigade organization. The major change is a collapsing of positions and changing of titles. The titles used and the positions in the classical brigade that are collapsed into these are :

1. *Executive chef*, this individual is still responsible for the overall kitchen operation.
2. *Sous chef*, one is appointed for each shift the kitchen is open and for semi-independent operations within a hotel property.
3. *Garde manger chef*, this person is considered the pantry supervisor and works with the pantry person as an assistant.
4. *Second cook* has the combined responsibilities of all the chef de parties in the classical brigade except the garde manger, patissier and baker. The second cook is assisted by station cooks in the various stations throughout the kitchen.
5. *Short-order cook/broiler-cook*, this is a new position which reflects the changes in service and preparation.

This position is responsible for preparation of items to order and working the line (the final plating area in the kitchen). This individual normally has minimal involvement in preparation of more complex items. In some operations this individual may also act as saute cook.

6. *Pastry chef* , this individual plans the dessert menu and prepares pies, cakes and other desserts.
7. *Baker*, this person is responsible for breads and rolls.
8. *Cook's helpers* are assigned to the various stations to assist with preparatory work. This is considered to be a training position.

The medium size modern kitchen will still use an abbreviated form of the brigade; however, the baker and patissier positions are deleted. In this size operation there will normally be only minimal baking done on site. Baking, in this kitchen, is delegated either to the second cook or to the chef. This size operation will have what is termed a working chef. This chef performs administrative duties in addition to assuming a production station in the kitchen.

The position of second cook will have the combined responsibilities of a sous chef and second cook. The short-order cook will be the main line supervisor and will be involved in overall preparation and production. The pantry cook will prepare all cold food items and ice cream desserts. The cook's helper position will still be a training position; however, it will have a greater role in actual preparation.

The small restaurant normally does no baking on site with the exception of quick-breads or items which are purchased ready to "proof and bake." The lead position will again be a working chef who works directly with the short-order cook and pantry cook. In this type of operation the cook's helper will normally also be the pot and dish washer.

The complexity of the staffing of a property will be in proportion to the complexity of the property itself. The number of staff members does not necessarily reflect the quality of the food served by the establishment. The one item which remains constant from the classical brigade to the more modern versions is the importance of the position of the chef, whether an executive or working chef.

The executive chef sets the tone and tempo of the kitchen. This individual is the administrative head of the entire kitchen. The responsibilities of the executive chef include planning, purchasing, supervision, training, preparation and service. There is truth in the statement, "a well organized executive chef means a well organized kitchen." The executive chef delegates responsibility and authority to subordinates, but overall responsibility remains this person's domain. As the technology of the 20th century evolves into the technocracy of the 21st century, demand will become even greater for executive chefs who can truly function as effective administrators.

To qualify as an executive chef, a cook must have many talents and years of experience in food preparation and service. The chef is, in effect, a food production manager and purchasing agent as well as a skilled cook. To operate their kitchen at a profit, they must be well versed in the varied and detailed functions of each position and station. Few people outside of the profession are fully aware of the responsibility of the executive chef. The chef is one of the most important administrators in the establishment, often with more than one hundred cooks, assistant cooks, helpers and apprentices on his staff.

The AMERICAN CULINARY FEDERATION EDUCATIONAL INSTITUTE (ACFEI) certifies the competency level of chefs and cooks. Certification is awarded at the following levels:

Cook
Pastry Chef
Sous Chef
Working Pastry Chef

Chef de Cuisine
Executive Chef
Executive Pastry Chef
Master Chef
Master Pastry Chef

These certification levels cannot be assumed to be equal in all respects to those titles used within the various foodservice establishments in the United States. The certification levels awarded by the ACFEI require the individual to document prior training, education and experience. Positions assigned similar titles in industry may require a greater or lesser degree of training, education and experience. An example would be a Certified Master Chef who is executive chef for a major hotel, restaurant or club. The title of executive chef as used in this discussion of kitchen organization indicates the level of responsibility the title entails, not the level of certification.

The U.S. Department of Labor maintains a *Dictionary of Occupational Titles*. In Volume I, listed in the definition of titles, is the definition for executive chef shown in Figure One.

SERVICE

It is not possible to prepare food properly without considering the type of service that will be used. The types of service most commonly associated with commercial food service are: French, Russian, English, American and buffet-style. French-style service allows for a great deal of showmanship by the chef and members of the staff. When French service is used, the item is prepared partially in the kitchen, this is a matter of thorough *mise en place*, and finished by the chef or members of his staff on a gueridon cart in the dining room. There are few establishments which can command a sufficient check average to make this type of service feasible.

Russian service is still used, on a limited basis, for special banquets in a few restaurants. This type of service calls for the kitchen to arrange the food on large platters or serving vessels. These are then presented and served to the guest by the serving staff. Although not as impressive as French service, this type of presentation does allow for showmanship on the part of the service staff. The kitchen's responsibility for plating is greatly reduced with this service.

English service is the presentation of the food in large serving dishes. Traditionally the host of the party then serves the other guests. This service is rarely

"Executive Chef (hotel and restaurant) 187.111 chef de cuisine, chef, head and manager of food production. -- Supervises and coordinates activities of chefs, cooks and other kitchen workers engaged in preparing and cooking foods in large hotels and restaurants to insure and efficient and profitable food service. Plans or participates in menu planning and utilization of food surpluses and leftovers, taking into account probable number of requests, marketing conditions, popularity of various dishes and recency of menus. Estimates food consumption and purchases or requisitions food ingredients and kitchen supplies. Reviews menus, analyzes recipes, determines food, labor policy to control costs. Supervises cooking, and other kitchen personnel and coordinates their assignments to insure economical and timely food production. Observes methods of food preparation and cooking, sizes of portions and garnishing of foods to insure food is prepared in prescribed manner. Devises special dishes and develops recipes. Hires, trains and discharges employees. Maintains time and payroll records. May be responsible for profitable operation of food department. May supervise or cooperate with steward in matters pertaining to the kitchens, pantry and storerooms. Is responsible for the training of apprentices."

Figure 1

used in the United States in its pure form. Family-style service, however, is used in some restaurants. The food is placed on the table in large serving dishes for the guests to pass and serve themselves. This informal style is not appropriate in many settings, but, when appropriate, can reduce the labor required for plating in the kitchen.

American-style service requires the individual plating of all items in the kitchen. Although it requires more labor for plating, it allows for the tightest control of portion sizes and greater efficiency of service. The reduction of staff produced by this type of service occurs in the dining room. The duty of the server is reduced to the presentation of the plated food and service of other required items, such as beverages and condiments.

Buffet-style service is the presentation of the food in large quantities on a service line, which may be either portable (using chafing dishes) or permanent (using permanently installed hot and cold service tables). Guests are either served or serve themselves at the buffet. Normally beverages are served by the wait staff at the guest's table. This style of service has become very popular for holiday service (Easter or Thanksgiving) and for special banquets where a less formal service style is suitable.

Each of these styles of service has a different effect on the staff required in both the kitchen and dining room. In addition the service has an impact on the preparation of the food itself. The key issue in the relationship of service and preparation is whether or not the food is cooked to order. When food is prepared to the order, as in American service, it is cooked and immediately served to the customer. This is also the manner in which French service is done. Russian service and English service, depending on the number of guests, can be cooked to order.

Webster's dictionary defines *buffet* as "a meal set out on a buffet table for ready access and informal service." This type of service requires the preparation of food in advance and holding it until service. The science of cooking is particularly important in the preparation of foods for buffet-type service. As will be discussed in the chapter on application of heat, the effects of heat and lack of heat play a critical role in the final product. It would not be advisable to serve items on a buffet which become unstable after extended exposure to heat.

The type of service an establishment uses will be determined by the guest served. Once the type is set then the kitchen may organize itself to function accordingly. Proper adaptation of the preparation methods in the kitchen requires an understanding by the cook of the important relationship between preparation and service of food. The goal of the culinarian is to balance the preparation method with the service style in a manner that delivers to the guest the highest quality product.

CUISINE

Understanding kitchen organization and types of service begins the novice cook on the long road to quality food preparation. An additional factor that must be addressed is that of cuisine. A basic definition of cuisine is -- food and the manner and style in which it is prepared. Escoffier is credited with the establishment of "La Cuisine Classique" or classic cuisine. This can be defined as food prepared in the style and manner of the school of thought established by Escoffier, which is an extension of the classical French cookery begun by Careme. To prepare food in this manner is to accept the guidelines established by the chefs of this school of thought.

The discussion of individual types of cuisine can include volumes of information; however, there are basic factors which contribute to the development of a cuisine. Typically when a style of food preparation is labeled a cuisine, it represents either a particular country (geographic region) or philosophy (religious or cultural).

The geographical region has played a major part in the creation of a cuisine due to climate. The combination of foods available was, and in many third world countries still is, related to the climate. In the warmer climates, where food became tainted rapidly due to lack of refrigeration, the creation of spicy dishes which masked the often off flavors of the various ingredients was common.

This same use of spices and herbs in a particular manner may be attributed to the economic status of the region. A poor country, where the people regularly consume varietal meats such as stomach and intestine, will create combinations of spices, herbs and acidic fruits and vegetables which mask the flavor of the meats used. The warmer climates also have the greatest availability of spices and herbs; therefore, it is common for dishes from these regions to be more complex and highly flavored than those from cooler regions.

Religion plays an important role in the establishment of cuisine, particularly by limiting the types of food stuffs which may be eaten. The manner in which food is processed or the combination of food items for particular holidays place many restrictions on the development of foods eaten. The Kosher foods of the strict observers of the Jewish faith are an excellent example of this. The restrictions in Kosher cuisine are not limited to simply the exclusion of pork. There are strict rules concerning the slaughter of animals, as well as a total ban on dairy products at certain meals.

This infusion of religious and cultural beliefs and attitudes gives a particular cuisine its own distinctive character. The Chinese, for example, believe that the cook should be ready to adapt to whatever ingredients are available. This attitude can be attributed to the recurring food shortages in China over many centuries. Survival depended on the individual's ability to utilize what food was available. Possibly it was this same concern for survival that made food a distinctive part of the Chinese philosophy of life. Part of what makes Chinese cuisine unique is the manner in which flavors are delicately layered in the various dishes which make up a meal.

The broadest method for categorizing cuisine is by country and possibly religion. The use of country in particular fails to consider the shifts in types of foods and methods of preparation which can occur even within one country. The accomplished cook must discern the finer distinctions within the maze of cuisine. To assume that Italian cuisine is characterized by tomato-based sauces is to ignore Northern Italian cuisine which utilizes tomato only minimally and in a far different manner.

Regional cuisine within a country or region of the world is what will give true insight into the variety of flavor combinations available to the cook. A brief contemplation of the differences between the meal served in an Oklahoma cafe and a Maine cafe will serve up a prime example of the variation that can exist within a single country. Another error is to believe that cuisines are no longer developing. American cuisine (the foods which are considered to have been created in the United States) is a perfect example of a cuisine which is still changing each and every day. It is drawing upon the huge variety of nationalities who have come to reside within its borders.

American cuisine is a reflection of the rich variety of foods which are available to the cook in the United States and the cultural heritage of its population. You will find parts of German, French, Mexican, Italian, Indian, Chinese, Russian, Scandinavian, Spanish and many other cuisines reflected in what is termed American cuisine.

As the world continues to shrink due to improved transportation and shipping, there will be a continued change of cuisine within all regions of the world. The cook who appreciates the factors which help to determine the character of a cuisine will be better able to understand the effect gained from the ingredient combinations involved in the cuisine. This appreciation and understanding will also result in a greater ability to create unique yet complementary blends of cuisine in menu development.

MENU

The menu is the cornerstone upon which the total food service establishment is built. Ultimately it will determine what the image of the operation is; the staff needed; the equipment needed, and the price which is to be charged. Does the guest decide the menu or the menu decide the guest? The menu remains at all times a compromise between the menu-maker and the guest. The ideal situation would be to have the perfect dish for every taste; but this is an impossible task. The menu is composed so that it pleases enough people to compensate the chef's staff for its efforts.

The menu has a different meaning to each person, depending on the part played in the complex relationship of guest, server, cook and administrator. For the culinarian it is the working plan, yet eventually it is also the written description of the food which is offered to the guest. As the working plan, proper menu development involves many factors.

The capabilities of each crew member play an important role in the operation's ability to produce a menu. Chefs must consider the equipment available to assure proper and timely preparation. A knowledge of foods and their characteristics, combined with a knowledge of the availability and cost of foods is required to construct a menu appropriate to the needs of the customer and the establishment. Possibly of the greatest importance, the chef must be familiar with the guests in order to cater to their needs and tastes -- in some estab-

lishments a very difficult task, in others, a very simple one.

Menu planning is an intricate crossword puzzle. All the pieces must be put together so that they fit the particular operation. The ability to plan a menu properly comes from the necessary knowledge and practice. Even a wizard in menu-making will see weak spots in a menu revealed once it is put into use. When the weak spots are revised as the usage continues, the result will be a menu that serves the needs of the guest and therefore the establishment. Consistency in planning and evaluation is the secret of a successful menu.

Prior to actually choosing the items to be included in the menu, the chef/menu planner must first find the answers to the following questions:

What is the targeted market? (This is simply another way of asking, "Who is the customer?") As has already been stated, the tastes of the guest will ultimately determine what items are included on the menu. It serves little purpose for a chef to serve items which are not desired by the guest.

In order to gauge the tastes of the guests, it will be necessary to have some knowledge of their cultural background. The tastes of an individual from the midwestern United States are definitely different from those of someone from the northeastern United States. An appreciation for and understanding of regional cuisines is a cornerstone in this balance between the menu and the guest. This is not to say that the only foods served to guests are those with which they are familiar. However, when the chef introduces new dishes, a knowledge of the types of dishes normally eaten by the guest can help in selection of dishes which will not be greeted by immediate rejection.

What is the price range of the proposed menu? The price range of the menu will be a deciding factor in the type of items included in the menu. Price range is most often established by the type of property in which the menu is to be used. The type of service is as major a factor as the food stuffs used in determining the actual price range needed to meet profit expectations.

What type of meal and service is the menu being designed for? The major meal designations used in the United States today are breakfast, lunch and dinner. There is a market for mid-afternoon, early evening and late night which some properties, particularly those in clubs and hotels, will have to accommodate. The room service menu of the hotel will require a slightly different mix of items than will that in the main dining room. The banquet menus for the restaurant or hotel will differ often from those offered in the rest of the operation. It may be that a large hotel or resort will have a number of different types of food facilities operating in the same property offering a wide range of types of food and service from fast food to formal dining. Service will be a major factor to consider in choosing items for the menu.

What are the regional conditions which may affect product availability and price? To place items on the property's menu which are only available for limited periods during the year may not always be in the best interest of the operation. It may prove wiser to choose food stuffs which are more readily available. To feature fresh strawberries on a menu in Minnesota year-round is possible, but during at least nine months of the year expensive. The chef/menu planner must know the market and plan accordingly. How much of a limitation regional conditions are to purchasing for the menu will, as with all aspects of menu planning, be decided by the guest.

What are the staff and equipment limitations of the establishment? The chef cannot chose menu items requiring steaming if the kitchen does not have a steamer. It serves no purpose, other than frustration for both the guest and the staff, to offer a finely finished saute dish on the menu when neither the amount of staff nor the skill level of the staff are adequate to allow production of a quality product. The items chosen to make up the menu must be appropriate to the equipment and staff available.

What are the nutritional requirements and expectations of the guest for the establishment? The chef should always be aware of the nutritional consequences of menu development. The items selected and the preparation methods chosen determine the nutritional value of the menu; however, the customer determines what level of nutritional balance the establishment must strive for.

It is only after these questions are answered that the chef/menu planner can then proceed to make a selection of the items which will comprise the menu.

Once the process of item selection begins, the greatest degree of culinary knowledge is required. A menu is more than simply a compilation of items. Escoffier compared a meal to a symphony. A symphony builds one movement upon another until a grand finale is achieved. The progression of the meal is not identical to this but extremely similar.

Even in the simplest menu it must be remembered that the items must complement and meld gracefully to give the customer a complete sensory experience and yet provide nutritional balance. To achieve this the chef must strive for balance of flavor, color, texture and shape, as well as ingredients. This requires more than appreciation of food, it demands a knowledge of how flavors are created and nutritional value preserved. The art allows for the innovative combination of dishes and the creation of beauty in the food. The development of a menu which allows the guest to choose from a wide variety of items, yet achieve a meal which is balanced in both flavor and nutrition, requires science.

The components of a menu vary widely and are only limited by the guest they serve. The traditional classical menu for a formal meal can be seen in Figure Two. This is a far more complex selection than that served in the average restaurant in the United States. The restaurant menu in the United States is compressed to normally four items served in two courses with a dessert optional. This is, to a great extent, the manner in which society now views meals.

The classical menu is reflective of a more elaborate age and is currently used only for those who can afford it. The modern menu in the United States is more suitable for the broader section of the population who are able to enjoy eating out. Again, it must be stated that there is still a market for the more elaborate type of menu and presentation. It is however, a relatively narrow one.

The progression in the classical menu, which could extend to as many as thirteen courses, was created to serve a definite purpose: a pleasant layering of flavors on the palate that allows each to be distinctive in its own right. The distinctive characteristics of each dish complement and enhance the flavor of that which comes before and after. If a particular dish is so heavy in flavor as to overpower what comes after

it, then a palate cleanser will be needed. This normally is a citrus based sorbet or sherbet and is not meant to add bulk to the meal but to simply cleanse the mouth in preparation for the next dish. In the shortened menus utilized so much in the operations of today, a palate cleanser is not normally used because of both time and cost. This being the case, it is necessary for the modern chef to balance the flavors even more carefully, since there is no opportunity to cleanse the mouth between dishes.

CONCLUSION

This chapter is addressed to the question of what is culinary art and science. Various areas have been touched upon in an effort to convey the complexity of the issue with which this text is dealing. That issue to many people is simply considered cooking, plain and simple. However, culinary preparation, in its fullest sense, is neither plain nor simple. It requires a combination of passion and knowledge on the part of the practitioner. The following chapters will provide the knowledge. It is the hope of those who have contributed to this text that you, the reader, will provide the passion.

TEN-COURSE MENU

Cold Hors d'oeuvres
Soup
Fish or Hot Hors d'oeuvres
Main Dish
Hot Entree
Cold Entree
Sorbet
Roast with Salad
Vegetable
Sweet Dish or Dessert

SEVEN-COURSE MENU

Cold Hors d'oeuvres
Soup
Fish
Sorbet
Hot Entree w/Vegetable
Salad
Sweet Dish or Dessert

AMERICAN RESTAURANT MENU
Salad or Soup
Main Dish with vegetable
Dessert (optional)

Figure 2

REVIEW QUESTIONS

1. What was important about the work of Chefs Careme and Escoffier?
2. What position has remained constant from the Classical Brigade to the organization of the modern kitchen?
3. Why did Escoffier create the Classical Brigade and why is a version of it still used today?
4. What are the responsibilities of the modern Executive Chef?
5. What effect does the type of service have on preparation?
6. What factors contribute to the development of a cuisine?
7. What factors affect menu planning?
8. What does balancing a menu mean?
9. Define the art and science of culinary preparation.

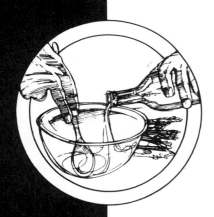

Chapter 2

Background Skills

KNOWLEDGE AND THE CULINARIAN

Culinary preparation, as both an art and science in the modern kitchen, requires more than just a knowledge of the food being prepared and the methods of preparation. Adherence to sanitary standards and the ability to communicate in the common language of the kitchen are a must. It is through a knowledge of basic skills, terminology and rules of the kitchen that the final goal, preparation and service of quality food, is achieved.

- **To discuss the importance of sanitation in food preparation.**

- **To introduce the concept of HACCP.**

- **To explain the importance of being familiar with the various forms of kitchen language.**

- **To show the importance of mise en place.**

- **To introduce the U.S. and metric measurement systems.**

- **To discuss the proper use of the recipe.**

- **To introduce the knife as a primary tool in the kitchen.**

SANITATION AND THE CULINARIAN

THE MODEL CULINARIAN IS IN GOOD HEALTH; HAS CLEAN PERSONAL HABITS; HANDLES FOOD SAFELY, AND APPRECIATES THE NEED FOR SANITARY PRACTICES.

It is not possible to overemphasize the importance of sanitation in the process of food preparation. Of all the responsibilities the food handler has, there is no responsibility greater than that of protecting the people who eat the food prepared.

Whether cook, baker, chef, butcher, dishwasher or server, the professional food handler is the recipient of the public's trust that the food served is wholesome, which means "fit for human consumption."

The confusion which arises in discussing sanitary food preparation is based on a misinterpretation of this term. It is not necessary for food to be well seasoned or expertly prepared to be considered wholesome by definition. It is quite possible that food which has been prepared using the finesse of a true artist in the area of spices and herbs is still not wholesome.

The artistry is only meaningful when acting in concert with the science of sanitary handling methods. Food stuffs must not be allowed to become contaminated, whether by exposure to incorrect temperatures or cross-contamination. It is not the purpose of this text to provide a thorough discussion of sanitation in the food service operation. It will be addressed here primarily from the standpoint of the food handler as the primary contributor to improper sanitation in the kitchen and serving area.

BASIC RULES OF SANITARY FOOD HANDLING

A pathogen, or specific causative agent of disease, is most often transmitted, or allowed to grow due to improper handling, by the kitchen worker. The World Health Organization concurs that the food handler must be considered one of the primary agents of food related illness. Part 2.3 of *Health Surveillance and Management Procedures for Food Handling Personnel*, a report published by the World Health Organization in 1983, dealing with the Food Handler is shown in Figure One.

The ability of the food handler to ensure the wholesomeness of the food prepared and served will depend upon following a few basic rules of personal hygiene and good food handling. These rules can be divided into three groups, the first being GENERAL PERSONAL HYGIENE. The basic rules for this area are as follows:

Food handling personnel play an important role in ensuring food safety throughout the chain of production, processing, storage and preparation. Mishandling and disregard of hygienic measures on their part may enable pathogens to come into contact with food and in some cases, to survive and multiply in sufficient numbers to cause illness in the consumer. Occasionally, food handling personnel may transfer pathogens that they are carrying in or on their bodies, and such pathogens may survive and may multiply in the food and subsequently cause disease.

The sequence of events whereby a food handler may contaminate food in such a way as to cause food-borne disease is as follows:

1. Pathogens are shed in feces, urine or discharge from the nose, ears or other areas of exposed skin in sufficient quantity.
2. Pathogens are transferred to the hands or exposed parts of the body which come into direct or indirect contact with the food.
3. The organisms survive long enough to be transferred to food.
4. The food that is contaminated is not treated in such a way as to destroy the organisms before they reach the consumer.
5. Either the number of organisms on the food constitutes an effective dose or the nature of the food and its conditions of storage are such as to allow the organisms to multiply and produce an effective dose or to produce toxins in quantities sufficient to cause illness.

Figure 1

1. The food handler should bathe daily.
2. The food handler should wear a clean, neat uniform. A clean uniform is not only a sign of good sanitation practices, it is also a sign of personal pride.
3. Hair should be restrained by either a hat or hair net to reduce the possibility of contamination of the food.
4. Fingernails should be short, clean and free of nail polish.
5. Open sores, cuts or burns should be carefully checked for infection and covered with an antiseptic bandage and waterproof protector. Food should never come into contact with open or infected sores, cuts or burns.
6. A complete physical examination is recommended for all food handlers to ensure that they have no communicable diseases.
7. Smoking or chewing of tobacco products should never take place in the food preparation or serving area.

The second group is concerned with the importance of having clean hands when handling food, and is titled, CLEAN HANDS: HEALTHY FOOD. The following actions require immediate hand washing before continuing work.

1. Contact with infected or otherwise unsanitary areas of the body.
2. Use of a handkerchief or tissue.
3. Hand contact with unclean equipment and work surfaces, soiled clothing or cleaning towels.
4. Handling raw food, particularly meat, poultry and fish items.
5. Clearing away soiled dishes and utensils.

The third group is GENERAL RULES OF SANITARY FOOD HANDLING.

1. Tasting or sampling of food should always be done using two spoons. Never taste anything from a stirring utensil.
2. Perishable food should be kept out of the TEMPERATURE DANGER ZONE. This is

a temperature range of **45°-140° F**, in which bacteria multiply most rapidly. KEEP HOT FOODS HOT, above 140°F and KEEP COLD FOODS COLD, below 45°F.

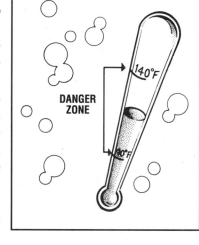

3. Clean and disinfect surfaces and utensils after processing raw food items, in order to prevent cross-contamination.
4. Thaw foods under refrigeration, not at room temperature.
5. Cook potentially hazardous foods (meats, fish, poultry, eggs and dairy products) to the recommended internal temperature to prevent the growth of bacteria.
6. FIFO - - FIRST-IN-FIRST-OUT: Food received first should be used first.
7. Always use wholesome food from approved sources.
8. Discard questionable food. WHEN IN DOUBT, THROW IT OUT!

Clean hands: healthy food

There is no question that the preparation of food is ultimately expected to result in an experience of exciting and satisfying flavors. However, the culinarian can never forget that there is always an unstated expectation of wholesomeness. The culinarian who follows the basic rules for sanitary food preparation will truly be protecting a public trust.

HACCP

HACCP is an acronym, or abbreviation, for HAZARD ANALYSIS CRITICAL CONTROL POINTS. This is a complex name for a vital part of kitchen management. A critical control point is a point during the processing of a food item when a mistake in the storage, preparation, handling, cooking or service of the item can result in the illness or even death of a customer.

HACCP is the process of food personnel constantly watching for health problems associated with the food they are serving. An important part of this process is the inspection of all products for potential problems at the first critical point of control, before they enter the kitchen. However, knowing the proper procedures for keeping food fresh and wholesome during its journey to the table is equally important.

WHY SHOULD WE BE CONCERNED?

We make decisions in the kitchen everyday that affect the wholesomeness of the food we serve. It is essential that you recognize the critical control points and how to avoid hazards. The primary weapon against food-borne illness is heat and the removal of heat, cooling. In 1988, 87% of all food-borne illness from foodservice establishments was due to improperly stored food. These food-borne illnesses could have been successfully avoided by someone with a knowledge and understanding of the effects of temperature on microorganisms.

METHODS OF CONTROL

Microbes are, in general, an enemy in the kitchen. Fortunately, most of them grow slowly at refrigerator temperatures. Most of them can be killed if brought up to a high enough temperature. For this reason, controlling the environment of the food is the primary weapon against microbes.

COLD

Keeping cold foods at or below 40°F will maintain most potentially lethal bacteria at a minimum level. Keeping food at the correct temperature does not preclude the need for visual inspection before it is used. Some pathogenic bacteria, such as Lysteria, Yersinia and others, do continue to multiply at 40°F. Always inspect food for abnormalities before using.

HEAT

Heat can be used to destroy bacteria that are present in the food. It is for this reason that a KILL STEP is sometimes used in the preparation of foods. Bringing soups and sauces to a boil for a few minutes before holding them on the service line will reduce the number of bacteria that may be growing in them. This step is similar to the pasteurization of milk products.

It must be remembered that the KILL STEP reduces the number of bacteria, but will not make a spoiled food wholesome. Most toxins produced by bacteria are not destroyed by the temperatures at which foods are cooked. As the old saying goes, "When in doubt, throw it out."

THE LANGUAGE OF THE KITCHEN

Visitors to a foreign country have a difficult time comprehending the culture and the people, if they do not know at least a small amount of the language. To understand the art and science of culinary preparation, it is also necessary to know the language. Many of the terms used in the kitchen are familiar to everyone, however, they may have different, or additional, definitions in the kitchen.

Many of the more specialized terms will be dealt with in the individual chapters throughout this text. The terms for the bakery and pastry shop in particular will be discussed in the section on baking. A glossary of common kitchen terms is provided in this text. You need to review these to start on the road to a full comprehension of the language of the kitchen. This is a language which does not recognize the boundaries of one country or dialect.

The purpose of the language of the culinarian is much the same as that of the accountant or the physician. It allows those who produce food to communicate in a common form. This need for a common language encompasses more than just a conglomeration of terminology. It also includes application of certain principles and philosophies. Of vital importance in this area are MISE EN PLACE, WEIGHTS and MEASURES, and the RECIPE.

MISE EN PLACE

Mise en place, in the broadest sense, means a constant state of efficient readiness. Certified Master Chef Roland Henin states that it is "a general name given to those elementary preparations which are constantly resorted to during the various stages of all culinary preparation." It is this organizing of one's self and station that allows for timely preparation and service.

Mise en place varies with the specific objectives of the kitchen and the individual. However, the goal remains the same. It is the organization and completion in advance of all the preliminary tasks involved in the preparation of a meal. Whether the *mise en place* is carried out for a conventional kitchen, preparation kitchen or finishing kitchen, the preliminary work, pre-prep, must be completed methodically and carefully before further work in the kitchen can be executed.

Basic *mise en place* for the various stations and departments in the kitchen should be put in writing to insure consistency. However, the individual preparing items must always determine the *mise en place* necessary for the various duties and recipes assigned in the kitchen. The saying "a good *mise en place* is half the cooking", applies to small kitchens as well as large preparation and finishing kitchens.

Simplification of the cooking process is the goal. Before cooking and service begins, allow yourself time to check carefully your *mise en place*. In this manner, cooking and, ultimately, service can be completed in an organized and timely fashion.

Mise en place for service should always include a number of reserve items. These should be of comparable quality to the original menu items. This step will allow unexpected orders to be filled easily and promptly. This reduces customer dissatisfaction and staff

---

U. S. STANDARD

WEIGHTS & MEASURES	EQUIVALENTS
POUND (LB OR #)	16 OZ = 1 #
OUNCE (OZ)	
NOTE: FL OZ IS FLUID OUNCE, A MEASUREMENT	
WHICH IS RELATIVE TO OUNCE, A WEIGHT,	
ONLY IN RELATION TO WATER.	
TEASPOON (TSP)	3 TSP = 1 T
TABLESPOON (T) (1/2 FL OZ)	16 T = 1 C
CUP (C) (8 FL OZ)	2 C = 1 PT
PINT (PT) (16 FL OZ)	2 PT = 1 QT
QUART (QT) (32 FL OZ)	4 QT = 1 GAL
GALLON (128 FL OZ)	
INCH (IN)	12 IN = 1 FT
FOOT (FT)	3 FT = 1 YD
YARD	
MILE	5280 FT = 1 MI

Figure 2

frustration. Cleaning and closing the work station or total kitchen is also part of *mise en place*. Taking inventory of supplies on hand, planning for the next day, clearing and cleaning all food service areas are duties that must be performed each day.

Each function in the kitchen is dependent on other functions. A complete interaction of all functions is necessary to have a complete *mise en place*. The general term, *mise en place*, in the larger sense means everything from arranging the utensils and linen to preparing a goulash in the preparation kitchen. Within this larger application is the smaller form of *mise en place* that must be performed for every action in the total food service establishment. These come together to make the large *mise en place* that yields effective preparation and service.

WEIGHTS & MEASURES

Currently the majority of kitchens in the United States adhere to non-metric measurement. Figure Two shows the U.S. measurements used today and their equivalents.

Since the Metric Conversion Bill (HR 8674) established the U. S. Metric Board there has been talk of converting U. S. kitchens to metric measurements. When, or if, this conversion will take place, is a question which cannot currently be answered. This does not change the need for the novice culinarian to develop the ability to use metric measure and convert measurements from one system to the other. Figure Three shows the basic metric measurements.

The influx of a greater number of foreign companies into the American marketplace will bring about a natural increase in the use of metrics. Figure

---

METRIC MEASUREMENT

The metric system uses three Latin prefixes to indicate measurements which are less than the base measure..

      DECI means 1/10 (.100)
      CENTI means 1/100 (.010)
      MILLI means 1/1000 (.001)

Three Greek prefixes are used to indicate more than the base measure.

      DECA means 10
      HECTO means 100
      KILO means 1000

The base measures in metrics are Liter (l) for liquid; Meter (m) for distance; Gram (g) for weight.

Use of the metric system itself is very simple. Deciliter equals .010 of a liter and Kilogram equals 1,000 grams. It is the conversion of U.S. standard measurements to metric, and vice versa, that becomes slightly more complicated. Listed below are the conversion factors needed to accomplish the most common conversions.

ENGLISH TO METRIC	METRIC TO ENGLISH
1 inch = 2.54 centimeters (cm)	1 cm = 0.3937 inch
1 foot = 30.5 centimeters (cm)	1 cm = 0.0328 foot
1 yard = 0.914 meter (m)	1 m = 1.094 yards / 39.37 inches
1 mile = 1.609 kilometers (km)	1 km = 0.6214 mile
1 quart = 0.9464 liter (l)	1 l = 1.06 quarts
1 ounce = 28.35 grams (gm)	1 gm = 0.0353 ounce
1 pound = 0.4536 kilogram (kg)	1 kg = 2.2 pounds

Figure 3

Four shows the related conversion factors for metric measurements. It will be necessary for the culinarian to become thoroughly familiar with both types of measurement in order to function in the kitchen.

THE RECIPE

The most widely used communications tool in the kitchen is the recipe. This is a set of instructions for making a food dish from various ingredients. It is a vitally important part of the language of the kitchen. We have all seen chefs portrayed as people who simply add a variety of items to a mixture and miraculously end up with a glorious dish. This is not, however, really the case.

The preparation or creation of good food is rarely an accident. Whether consciously or subconsciously, good food is almost always the result of established mixtures and methods or a knowledge of what the interactions are of various food items.

It is the recipe, sometimes called formula, that makes it possible for a particular dish to be recreated by someone other than the original creator. The more detailed and specific the recipe, the more assurance there is that the reproduction will be similar to the orig-

inal. Recipes do not stifle the creativity of the chef. They make it possible for that creativity to gain immortality.

RECIPE STRUCTURE

The structure of a recipe can be broken into four parts.

1. NAME OF DISH
2. YIELD (NUMBER OF PORTIONS OR TOTAL QUANTITY PRODUCED)
3. INGREDIENTS AND AMOUNT OF EACH
4. METHOD OF PREPARATION

The name of a dish not only makes it possible to differentiate between recipes, it is also a guide to the origins of the recipe. The yield is very important. This makes it possible to determine how many servings can be expected from the mixture and what the cost will be.

The listing of ingredients and their amounts must be done very carefully. The broad variety of food items available makes it necessary to be very specific when listing ingredients. To state that onions are needed is to leave a great deal to the interpretation of the reader. Are the onions used to be yellow, red, white or green. How much effect the use of one type and not another will have on the final product can only be decided by the creator of the recipe and those who use it.

It is also of great importance that standard weights and measures be used. The old recipes that called for so many handfuls of an item or a teacup full of milk may have been acceptable when the recipe was taught by its creator to an apprentice. However, when the creator cannot personally pass the recipe on, thereby insuring consistency of amount, these units of measure are unreliable.

It is also best to give ingredient amounts by weight whenever possible. A recipe that calls for three onions, leaves open for interpretation the actual amount of onion used. Were those to be three small, medium, large or jumbo onions?

The method for preparing the item is just as important as the ingredients and their amounts. These instructions should be clear and concise. It should not be assumed that the reader will automatically know what to do. The terminology used must be correct and clearly understandable. Style of cooking and temperatures for cooking should be given.

USING A RECIPE

The recipe acts as a road map for the novice culinarian. Through the preparation of a variety of recipes it is possible for you to experience the expertise of many great chefs and benefit from their triumphs and mistakes. For the experience to be meaningful the recipe must be followed.

Measure carefully, use the ingredients called for and closely adhere to the instructions for preparation. If you do, the end product can truthfully be said to be a reproduction of the creator. If the product is not what was expected or wanted, then either you try another recipe or adjust the one being used. If you begin adjusting the recipe before seeing what it will produce when followed closely, you will have never produced the intended product.

2 oz. for 4 portions = ? oz. for 20 portions

The majority of this text is devoted to discussing why particular foods and methods of preparation are used. The sum of these discussions is that each ingredient and nuance of preparation ultimately effects the final product. Therefore, when you adjust the recipe you have changed the final product.

CONVERTING RECIPES

It is often necessary to produce a smaller or larger quantity of a recipe. When these occasions arise, there is a simple method available for accurately adjusting the amounts of ingredients used without changing their percentage of the total ingredients used. This is the determination of a MULTIPLIER.

If the current recipe being used yields 24 - 6 oz portions and what is needed is 60 - 6 oz portions it is necessary to find the multiplier. Since the weight of the individual portions has remained the same it is only necessary to divide the new number of portions needed by the original number the recipe produced. In this case we divide 60 by 24 and this gives a multiplier of 2.5. We can now multiply the amount of each ingredient by 2.5 and know how much is needed to produce the quantity needed.

The process for determining a multiplier requires one more step when the portion size changes. For example if the original recipe produced 24 - 6 oz portions, but now we need 48 - 12 oz portions, we need to add a step. First we must determine the total quantity produced by the recipe and that needed for the new production. Multiplying 24 by the 6 oz tells us that the original recipe produced a total of 144 oz. The new amount needed is 48 portions times 12 oz, or 576 oz total. Now we simply proceed as we did before. Divide the new amount needed, 576 oz, by the original recipe amount, 144 oz and the recipe multiplier will be 4.

PERCENTAGES IN RECIPES

The use of a multiplier in recipe conversion is to ensure that the proportion represented by each ingredient in a recipe remains constant. In other words, in the process of increasing or decreasing the overall quantity of a recipe, the relationship of one ingredient to all other ingredients remains the same.

An ingredient's proportion to the total of all ingredients in a mixture is more reliable than the actual weights and measures in a recipe. For this reason bakers, in particular, often use percentages in calculating formulas. There are two methods for calculating the percentage represented by each ingredient in a recipe: TRUE PERCENTAGE and BAKER'S PERCENTAGE.

The baker's percentage is widely used, but less accurate. In this method, flour represents 100% of the formula. The percentage of each ingredient in the recipe is calculated in relation to the amount of flour in the recipe. The formula is:

TOTAL WEIGHT OF AN INGREDIENT
÷ TOTAL WEIGHT OF FLOUR
= INGREDIENT PERCENTAGE

EXAMPLE: 2 LB SUGAR ÷ 5 LB FLOUR = 40%

The best method for figuring percentages is true percentage. This is based on the total weight of all ingredients in the recipe, the total being 100%. The formula is:

TOTAL WEIGHT OF AN INGREDIENT
÷ TOTAL WEIGHT OF ALL INGREDIENTS
= INGREDIENT PERCENTAGE

EXAMPLE: RECIPE USES 2 LB SUGAR,
5 LB FLOUR, 8 OZ EGGS, 2 OZ BAKING
POWDER, 1 OZ SALT, 5 OZ BUTTER,
THE TOTAL WEIGHT OF THE RECIPE IS 8 LB.
2 LB SUGAR ÷ 8 LB = 25% SUGAR CONTENT

This method of calculation yields the proportion of any ingredient in a recipe accurately.

THE KNIFE: A CHEF'S TOOL

The knife is considered by most culinarians to be their most valuable and versatile tool in the kitchen. It is a tool worthy of respect and, when handled properly by an individual proficient in its use, can appear to be a thing of wonder. Actually there is no magic in a knife, no matter where it is made. It is the person wielding the knife that makes it so valuable.

Proper knife usage begins with good safety practices. A few basic rules of safe knife usage include the following:

1) A sharp knife is safer than a dull knife.

2) Use the right knife for the job.

3) When carrying a knife, hold it parallel to and tight against your leg as you walk.

4) The handle of a knife should always be kept dry and clean.

5) Always cut on a cutting board or similar surface.

6) Always cut away from yourself.

The primary rule of knife safety is a simple one. KEEP YOUR MIND ON WHAT YOU ARE DOING!

The type of knife chosen for a particular job in the kitchen will depend on the type of work being done. There are a number of different kinds of knives, each designed for a particular purpose. The basic types include:

1) FRENCH KNIFE: Probably the most popular all-around knife in the kitchen. It is particularly well designed for general cutting and chopping.

2) PARING KNIFE: This knife is small and easy to handle for peeling and coring fruits and vegetables.

3) BONING KNIFE: This knife is designed to bone out meat, poultry and fish. It is available with varying degrees of blade flexibility to allow for the most delicate fish bone and the harder more resilient bones of large cattle.

4) CARVING KNIFE: This is a finely edged knife designed for slicing and carving of meat.

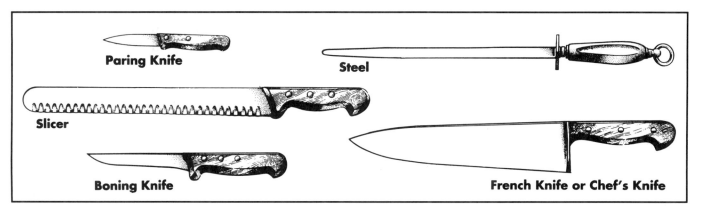

Paring Knife

Steel

Slicer

Boning Knife

French Knife or Chef's Knife

The knife, as a tool, is of little use unless it is sharp. To maintain it in proper condition, it is necessary to tone the blade. This is done by using a STEEL, a steel post with a slightly roughened surface which is magnetized to remove burrs from the blade. It is used by holding the knife blade at a 20° point angle to the steel and making long even strokes the length of the steel on both sides of the blade. The purpose is to return the cutting edge to a sharp V and remove burrs. This process removes very little actual metal from the blade.

A blade will require sharpening from time to time. This differs from use of the steel. If done manually, a three-sided stone is normally used. The coarse side is used to work thick heavy blades, such as cleavers, and to remove large nicks. The medium side is used for medium weight blades, such as butcher knives. The fine side is used for light blades, such as boning knives, and to do fine honing of blades. These are used by holding the knife blade at a 20° point angle to the stone and making long figure 8 passes over the stone. This process wears away the metal of the blade and therefore is not used to replace the use of the steel.

There are a number of mechanical knife sharpeners available. Many of these do a superior job of sharpening blades. However, there are those which remove excessive amounts of metal. Choose mechanical sharpeners carefully and regularly inspect them to insure the guides angling the blade to the stone are set correctly.

MANUAL OR MECHANICAL CUTTING

It is necessary at times to choose between mechanical food processing equipment and hand cutting of food items needed in preparation of various dishes. This choice is usually based on the time available, quantity needed and the exactness of the cut desired. The electric slicer and various other food processors are quicker than even the most proficient knife handler when dealing with large quantities. However, they do not normally deliver as exact a cut. The exception to this would be the use of the electric slicer for the slicing of cold meats.

In mass production, where labor cost is of major importance, the machine produced product may be considered adequate for the purpose. In the fine service operation, where a more refined level of product is the goal and menu prices allow for more labor cost, the hand cut item will more often be the choice.

The production of a wide variety of dishes requires a familiarity with the various cuts used in advanced culinary preparation. The group of cuts which act as the base for kitchen prep are termed the Classical Cuts. These cuts and their measurements include the following:

1) ALLUMETE (Matchstick) - 1/16" x 1/16" x 2"

2) **JULIENNE (Double Matchstick)** - 1/8" x 1/8" x 2"

3) **BATONETTE (French Fry)** - 1/4" x 1/4" x 2"

4) BRUNOISE (Square Allumete) - 1/16" x 1/16" x 1/16"
5) MACEDOINE (Square Julienne) - 1/8" x 1/8" x 1/8"
6) **SMALL DICE (Square Baton)** - 1/4" x 1/4" x 1/4"
7) **MEDIUM DICE** - 1/2" x 1/2" x 1/2"
8) **LARGE DICE** - 3/4" x 3/4" x 3/4"
9) **SLICE** - To Cut into Uniform Cross Cuts
10) PAYSANNE - 1/2" diameter spheres or triangles
11) PARISIENNE - Round Shaped
12) OLIVETTE - Olive Shaped
13) NOISETTE (Toulenee or Turned) - Small seven-sided barrel
14) CHATEAU - Large Barrel Shape
15 CONCASSE - Roughly Chopped
16) **CHOP** - Cut into Irregularly Shaped Pieces
17) **MINCE** - Chop into Very Fine Pieces
18) **EMINCER** - Cut into Very Thin Slices
19) **SHRED** - Cut into Very Thin Strips (This can be done with a French knife, but is most often done with the coarse blade of a hand held grater or food processor.)

* A chart of common cuts is on page 26.

Although each of the nineteen various cuts listed has a distinctly different purpose in a dish, the cuts which are most commonly called for in the kitchen are those whose names are printed in bold letters. These are also the cuts which best lend themselves to machine production. The beginning cook must first master these ten common cuts in order to begin learning culinary preparation.

CONCLUSION

The basic knowledge needed for proficient performance in the kitchen is not limited to that of sanitation, knife usage or the kitchen language dealt with in this chapter. *Mise en place* and recipe usage are central to success in the kitchen, but alone they do not guarantee it. What is discussed in this chapter is only part of the body of information needed to succeed in the kitchen. The information presented here is the foundation upon which the aspiring culinarian will continue to build in the chapters that follow.

REVIEW QUESTIONS

1. List three basic rules of personal hygiene for the food handler.
2. Why is sanitation an important component in the production of quality food?
3. What is the importance of the language of the kitchen?
4. List the basic U. S. weights and measures and their metric equivalents.
5. Discuss the concept of HACCP as it applies to food preparation.
6. List three rules for safe knife handling.
7. Define *mise en place* and discuss its importance in the kitchen.
8. What information should a recipe contain?
9. Why is it important to follow a recipe carefully?
10. What are the four basic types of knives and their usages?
11. What are the factors that determine the choice between hand cutting and machine cutting of food items?
12. What are the ten basic common cuts and their measurements?

CLASSICAL CUTS

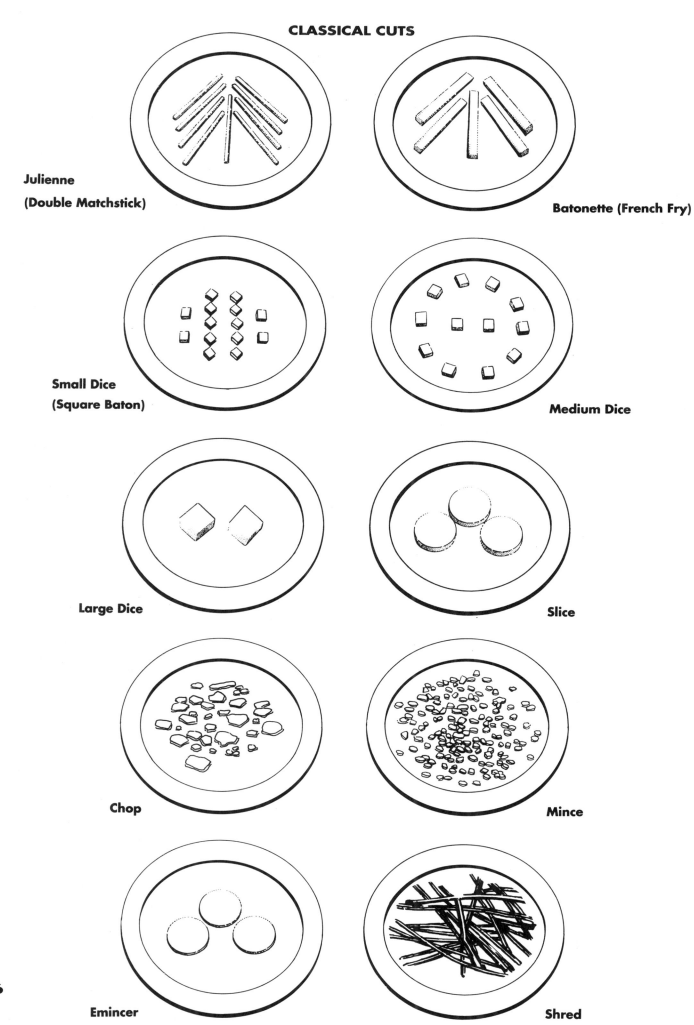

Julienne (Double Matchstick)

Batonette (French Fry)

Small Dice (Square Baton)

Medium Dice

Large Dice

Slice

Chop

Mince

Emincer

Shred

Section II
Essential Knowledge for Understanding Culinary Preparation

Temperature & its Application
  to Culinary Preparation

Emulsion

How Foods are Flavored & Seasoned

Elements of Presentation

Fats & Oils

Dairy Products

Eggs

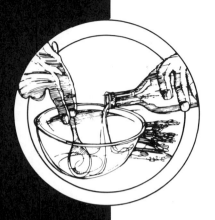

CHAPTER OBJECTIVES

- **To introduce the concept of heat transfer and its relation to food preparation.**

- **To explain BTU, phase change, heat capacity, and thermal conductivity as integral parts of food preparation.**

- **To show how and why heat removal affects food preparation.**

- **To discuss the effects of heating food.**

- **To list and discuss various cooking methods.**

Chapter 3

Temperature

In this chapter we will discuss the variety of ways in which temperature affects food. This includes a discussion of the effects of not only an increase in temperature of the food, but also decreases in the food temperature. To begin, we will discuss temperature as a factor in the service of wholesome food.

HEAT TRANSFER

The transference of heat is of great importance to the culinarian. It is this movement of heat from one surface, product, etc., to another that is a determining factor in the quality of any product produced. In order to understand how to gain positive effects from the transfer, you need an understanding of what heat is.

Heat

Simply put, heat is a form of energy. When a substance gets hot and absorbs energy, the molecules have more energy than when cold. The molecules then vibrate and bounce off of one another and expand in volume. This is what happens when you open the door to a steamer too quickly. The steam, high in energy, expands rapidly and bounces off your face, thereby transferring its energy to you. It is also the force that blows pan lids off boiling pots and causes a souffle to rise.

Like water, many substances exist as a solid, liquid or gas, depending on the amount of energy absorbed. Solid water, ice, has very little stored energy

and must absorb energy in order to melt. Gaseous water, steam, contains a great deal of energy as heat. When it comes into contact with something cooler than itself, it loses heat energy to that substance.

Physics

There are two basic rules that govern how heat works. First, heat moves in the direction towards cold. In this manner, heat energy is absorbed by something cold. Secondly, the amount of heat absorbed by the cold substance is limited by two factors:

1) HEAT ENERGY, LIKE ELECTRICITY, MUST BE CONDUCTED THROUGH A BARRIER IN ORDER TO MOVE FROM AREAS OF HOT TO COLD.
2) HEAT ENERGY WILL SEEK TO REACH EQUILIBRIUM WITH ITS SURROUNDINGS, UNLESS SOMETHING PREVENTS THIS.

These two basic rules explain why a warm item placed in a refrigerator will become cold. It loses its heat to the surrounding atmosphere. The temperature of the item drops, loses heat energy, until its temperature closely

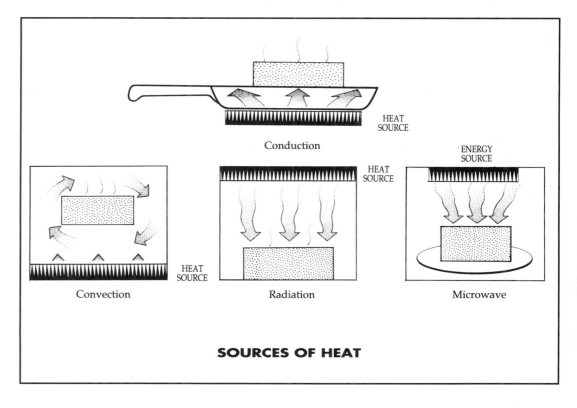

Conduction

Convection

Radiation

Microwave

SOURCES OF HEAT

matches that of the surrounding air. At this point it has reached equilibrium.

The fact remains that a barrier can change the amount of heat transferred. If you place the warm item in a styrofoam container, close the lid, and then put it in the refrigerator the item cools far more slowly. Why? Styrofoam is a terrible conductor of heat and prevents the heat energy from transferring into the cooler surrounding air. The styrofoam inhibits the process of equalization.

How Foods Are Heated

There are three ways that heat travels from one place to another.

CONDUCTION: This is the same way that electricity flows through a wire. Energy is passed from one molecule or atom to an adjacent molecule or atom without moving. The energy is simply passed along the conductor.

CONVECTION: This is the way fluids, liquids and gases, pass on their energy. Heated molecules move through cooler molecules and pass on their heat. In a pan of water, hot water from the bottom of the pan rises to the top, yielding its heat to cooler water in the pan. This process is continued until most of the water has the same heat energy. This is also what happens in a convection oven when air is forced through the heating chamber. Molecules of air exchange their heat with cooler air and the item being cooked. The cooking process speeds up because the air next to the food is constantly being exchanged with warmer air rather than the oven slowly conducting heat through the air to the product as happens in a regular oven.

RADIATION: Nothing gets hot until energy is absorbed. Energy radiating from a source, whether it is hot coals, the sun or a salamander, is absorbed by something else. At this point a temperature change occurs. Radiation energy can be conducted to something else; absorbed by whatever the radiation collides with, or reflected away to something else.

Radiation comes in different forms. Each is dependent on the length of wave that delivers it. For example, a very long wave is a radio wave. Shorter waves include infrared (heat), visible light, ultraviolet, and x-rays (a very short wave). These are all components of what is called the electromagnetic spectrum.

The type of waves used by microwaves are closest in length to radio waves. They are so close that the wavelengths used have to be licensed by the Federal Communications Commission. The waves used oscillate rapidly. The net effect is a reversal of the electromagnetic field surrounding the food at a rate of many times per second.

Certain molecules have their own magnetic field, with water being the most prevalent. When the electromagnetic field is reversed back and forth many times a second, the water molecules flip back and forth inside the food, trying to align themselves within this field. This violent flipping of the water molecules results in a direct transfer of energy to the food, so it gets hot.

BTU

To understand what is happening in the cooking process, the concept of heat units must be introduced. A British Thermal Unit, BTU, is the amount of heat energy needed to raise one pound of water one degree Fahrenheit. This unit can be used to measure what happens when a substance goes from one physical state to another, such as solid to liquid or liquid to gas.

The heat of fusion of water is the energy required to change ice into liquid water. This is equal to 144 BTU's per pound of ice. The heat of vaporization of water is the energy required to change liquid water into a gas/steam. This is equal to 971 BTU's per pound of water. Notice that the higher the energy level, the more BTU's are needed to cause a change in the compound.

Heat Of Fusion

This is the energy needed to melt or freeze ice. Ice melts at 32°F, it also freezes at this temperature. When it melts, it absorbs 144 BTU's per pound at 32°F. As it freezes it yields the same amount of energy to its surroundings.

Heat of fusion is an important concept in the making of ice cream. During the making of a frozen dessert, the chilled liquid mixture is stirred inside a metal container. This container is rotated in a mixture of ice and salt. Why is not just ice used? If only ice was used, the liquid would seek to reach equilibrium with the ice at about 32°F. This could take a long time. By adding salt, the ice is forced to melt, requiring the uptake of 144 BTU's per pound of ice melted. The energy needed for this comes from the heat in the water from the melted ice. This allows the temperature to drop to around 27°F, since only pure water freezes at 32°F.

Conduction through the wall of the ice cream container transfers heat from the mix to the ice and salt mixture. This melts more ice, making the ice and salt mixture colder. The net result is that the ice cream goes from a liquid to a solid.

Heat Vaporization

One of the most important transfers of heat is that which takes place when steam cools. Just as it takes 971 BTU's to turn water into steam, when steam turns to liquid water, condensation, there are 971 BTU's released to something else. For example, water is brought to a boil in a stove top steamer and broccoli is placed in the steamer and the lid closed. The broccoli is cooler than the steam in the kettle so the steam condenses on the vegetable. The broccoli gets wet, but more importantly it absorbs 971 BTU's per pound of steam that condenses on it.

This can be compared to cooking broccoli in liquid water. If you use one pound of boiling water and add the broccoli the temperature drops 1°F. This means you have added only one BTU to the vegetable and it will take a long time for it to cook. If you use one pound of steam and it all condenses on the broccoli you have added 971 BTU's to it.

You can see why cooking with steam can be a much more efficient method of cooking foods. Often the cooking time will be shorter and much more efficient. Commercial steamers operate under pressure and therefore can raise the temperature of the steam well above the 212°F boiling point and the number of BTU's that the steam can carry per degree F. This is why commercial steamer units cook foods so quickly.

ABOUT WATER

Water is a peculiar solvent in the world of chemical solvents. It plays such a major role in our food system that a few of its properties are worth mentioning. It is known as the UNIVERSAL SOLVENT because it dissolves so many compounds, especially those that are considered polar. Polar means that the molecule has areas that are considered to be negatively or positively charged.

Water is polar. That is why it flips back and forth in the alternating electromagnetic fields of a microwave. This polarity also gives it the ability to dissolve sugars, salts, some vitamins, and minerals. Fats and oils are nonpolar. This is why oil and water just don't mix.

Almost all substances expand when heated, and so does water. However, most substances contract when they get cold and are at their greatest density when frozen. Water on the other hand is at its densest at slightly above the freezing point. Unlike most substances, when frozen, water's volume expands. This is why beer and wine bottles left in the freezer for a quick chill, will explode if left too long.

PHASE CHANGE

A phase change is when a compound goes from a liquid state to a solid or gas state, or from a solid to a liquid or gas, or from a gas to a liquid. A property of all compounds is that when going through a phase change the temperature will remain constant until that phase change occurs. This means that it is extremely easy to bring pure water up to 212°F at sea level and keep it there. However, you cannot get it any hotter until you turn it into steam.

HEAT CAPACITY

Heat capacity is the number of BTU's that must be added to a substance in order to raise its temperature 1°F. This calculation is relative to water, with the heat capacity of water being 1.00. An analysis of Figure One will show that you must add more than twice as much heat to water to change its temperature than you do to oil. This plays an important part in the recovery of cooking temperatures.

THERMAL CONDUCTIVITY

Thermal conductivity is a measure of how many BTU's can travel through a substance per hour, per degree F, given a surface of one square foot. An analysis of Figure Two shows how poorly foods conduct energy in comparison to metals. This is why we have such problems with carry-over cooking. The heat is held in the food and keeps on cooking even though the heat source is removed. This is also why we have to cool liquid foods in a water bath before placing them in the refrigerator. If we did not, the center would stay hot because the food acts as an insulator.

Note that copper is a terrific conductor of heat. That is why it is so highly prized in the kitchen. Heat is rapidly conducted from the heat source to all parts of the copper in the pan and then radiated to the food in the pan in even amounts. Stainless steel is only a fair conductor of heat. This means that it will not spread the heat out evenly to all sections of the steel. The heat is passed more directly

HEAT CAPACITY		
SUBSTANCE	% WATER	HEAT CAPACITY
BROTH	88	0.71
BUTTER	15	0.50
VEGETABLE OILS	0	0.40
CREAM	35	0.75
SKIM MILK	91	0.95
LEAN BEEF	72	0.82
MUTTON	90	0.93
LEAN PORK	57	0.73
VEAL	63	0.77
WATER	100	1.00

Figure 1

CONDUCTIVITY	
MATERIAL	THERMAL CONDUCTIVITY
ICE (32°F)	1.28
WATER (32°F)	0.32
WATER (200°F)	0.40
AIR (68°F)	0.01
PEANUT OIL	0.10
VEGETABLES (AVERAGE)	0.25
STAINLESS STEEL	9.40
COPPER	230.00
PYREX GLASS	0.05

Figure 2

to the food. This uneven distribution of heat results in "hot spots" in pans made of stainless steel.

This may seem like a great deal of technical information that is only marginally relevant to the culinarian. However, a minimal understanding of these principles can lend terrific insight to the processes used to prepare foods. These concepts are simple rules that allow us to make more informed judgments in the kitchen. In the discussion of different cooking methods used we will refer back to these tables.

HEAT REMOVAL - COOLING

Now that the process of heating foods has been addressed, we will discuss what happens when foods are cooled. Removing heat from a product is as important as adding heat. It promotes longer shelf life and can add another dimension to the culinary experience. Remember, some dishes are expected to be served cold.

Why Cool Foods?

The primary reason to cool foods is to inhibit spoilage. As mentioned in Chapter 2, some microbes can grow at cooler temperatures. However, cooler temperatures slow down the growth.

Enzymatic and other chemical reactions also progress more slowly at reduced temperatures. Many fruits and vegetables are still living plants when they arrive at the door of the walk-in. They are still producing gases and heat. Apples are a good example of these. Refrigeration retards this process and allows these products to be kept for much longer periods of time. Chemical changes in lipids, the fats and oils, and in meats and poultry are slowed at lower temperatures. Microbial activity in cheese, yogurt, bread dough and other products is slowed to a minimal level.

How Food Is Cooled

Heat transfer, the process by which food in the refrigerator is cooled, depends upon four things.

1. QUANTITY OF AIR CIRCULATION AROUND A PRODUCT.
2. SIZE OF THE PRODUCT.
3. TYPE OF CONTAINER THE FOOD IS IN.
4. HOW COOL THE PRODUCT WAS WHEN PLACED IN THE REFRIGERATOR.

Note in Figure Two, that air is a terrible conductor of heat. Because of this, the removal of heat from a food product is dependent on other factors.

1. IT MUST BE IN A CONTAINER THAT IS A GOOD CONDUCTOR OF HEAT.
2. THE CONTAINER MUST NOT BE SO LARGE AS TO IMPEDE TRANSMISSION OF HEAT, UNLESS IT IS ALREADY COOL WHEN PLACED IN THE REFRIGERATOR.
3. THERE MUST BE ADEQUATE AIR CIRCU-

LATION IN THE REFRIGERATOR SO THAT WARM AIR IS MOVED AWAY FROM THE PRODUCT AND IS SUBSEQUENTLY COOLED. NOTE: THIS REQUIRES PROPER SPACING OF ITEMS ON THE SHELVES IN THE REFRIGERATOR, ALLOWING FOR CIRCULATION BETWEEN ITEMS.

Prior to refrigeration, liquid foods such as soups and sauces must be cooled. In Figure Two you will notice that water and ice are the best conductors of heat that you have readily available in large amounts. Foods that are high in fat, cream based soups, sauces, and others, are very difficult to cool down because of their poor conduction qualities. It is extremely important that these types of foods be cooled in a circulating water bath prior to refrigeration, otherwise the center of the food will not cool. This can cause the product to spoil before you have a chance to use it.

Freezing Foods

Freezing does more to preserve food than refrigeration does. However, there are some added considerations that are often overlooked. We tend to think that once a food is frozen it is safe and nothing can happen to it. Unfortunately this is not true. There is no hard and fast rule as to how long a frozen product will last. Knowledge of the factors involved can help you make the best decisions in particular situations.

Chemical reactions are slowed by cooling and are slowed even further by freezing. These reactions do not come to a complete stop until you get near -460°F! Most are slowed to a point where they do not concern us any more, but others do not. One of the major reactions that is of concern is the process of lipid oxidation. This is when fats and oils in a product are attacked by oxygen in the atmosphere, resulting in a rancid smell and other off flavors. This is a major problem in frozen meat and some fatty fish.

Problems Associated With Freezing And Thawing

Meat or other food items that are to be frozen need to be wrapped to prevent moisture loss and to retard the entrance of atmospheric oxygen into the package. When the food is improperly wrapped, the tissue dries out through a process called sublimation. This is when a solid (ice) goes directly to a gas (vapor) without turning into a liquid first. The frozen item never has to thaw in order to dry out. It just has to be exposed to the dry air of the freezer. The result of this slow drying is that the fat oxidizes; off flavors and odors develop, and the product is reduced in quality. This process is called FREEZER BURN.

Another process that can occur while food is frozen is the migration of ice crystals. This occurs when the freezer is not cold enough or the product has been stored too long in a freezer that has been opened and closed too many times. The length of time a product can be stored is dependent on the type of product being stored; how it is wrapped, and how cold the freezer is.

Pure water freezes at 32°F, but water that has substances dissolved in it, such as salts, sugars, or others, will freeze at a much lower temperature. Inside the cells of meat, fish, vegetables, or the gel matrix of a frozen dessert there exists water of this type. So, even though the product is frozen there is a minuscule amount of liquid water.

Over a period of time these droplets of water tend to attract each other. They come together and freeze as a new grouping of droplets, expanding in the process. This ruptures the frozen tissue around the new ice crystal. When the product is thawed you can see a network of small holes throughout the product.

This allows water to leach out quickly and the result is a product that is dry and tough.

In some cases liquid water has the effect of concentrating certain solutes (salts, sugars, minerals) as it moves through the product. This presents a special problem in ice creams where lactose can be concentrated to the point of precipitation. In other words, ice cream that has been handled poorly in storage can develop lactose sugar crystals that make the mixture feel grainy in the mouth.

These problems are prevented by rotation of frozen foods so that they are used in a timely manner. In addition, use a separate freezer to store foods at well below zero for long term storage.

Thawing Foods

Thawing a food item is best done at refrigerator temperatures. However, this method is not without its problems. In Figure Two you will notice that ice has four times the thermal conductivity of water. When you thaw a food product, the outer layer melts quickly due to the conducting effect of the ice. Once the outer layer of ice is melted though, the interior of the product is insulated from heat transfer by the water in its tissues. Furthermore, the temperature near the edge of the ice front is not far from 32°F and is perfect for the migration of ice crystals. These can still coalesce, freeze, expand and cause damage to the frozen tissue.

Other than cooking or serving the item while still frozen, there are two major alternatives to thawing foods in the refrigerator. One is to thaw the food at room temperature, which is definitely not recommended. The center of the item will remain frozen while the outside will spoil in the heat of the kitchen.

The other method is better for small items that you need quickly. Wrap the item well in plastic and submerge it in a recirculating cold water bath until the item is sufficiently thawed out. This works because water is a better conductor of heat than air and the water is kept cold and moving across the surface of the item. The cool water also reduces the chances of microbial contamination.

A food allowed to thaw in the refrigerator over a period of time will be of higher quality than one that has been quickly thawed. This may be because the water is not drawn out of it by the excessive heat of the kitchen or the osmotic pressure differential in the water bath. Osmotic pressure differential is the difference between the salts in the solution inside the tissues of the product being thawed and the water it is being thawed in. The saltier solution will leach out into the "purer" water and the result is a loss of much of the product's natural juices.

HEATING OF FOODS

Chemical Changes

There are many dramatic changes that occur during the heating of foods. Although current research does not make it possible to identify all that happens when a food is heated, we will discuss what is known. Protein molecules unwind and open up from their natural state. As a consequence they are made more digestible; form gels; participate in browning reactions, or interact with other compounds to form the chemicals responsible for the flavor of the final product.

Complex carbohydrate molecules, such as starches, react with water and heat, acting as thickeners and gel formers. Simple carbohydrates, such as the many different types of sugars found in foods, can react with other compounds to form other flavor molecules. Examples would be those responsible for the flavors of jams and fresh fruit pie fillings. Simple carbohydrates also act as sweeteners for the foods they are mixed with.

Fats and oils may turn rancid more quickly under the effect of heat and water. They do, however, add body to heated foods and act as flavor carriers for flavoring ingredients that do not dissolve well in water. Garlic is a prime example of this. These are but a few of the chemical reactions that occur when food is heated.

Flavor Development

The development of flavor that results from heating food is of special interest. One of the most important reactions is the browning reaction called MAILLARD BROWNING. It is the chemical reaction of free amino acids with sugars to form hundreds of different compounds ranging from sour organic acids to aldehydes and ketones. A few of these are carcinogens, but most are responsible for flavors and odors that we associate with things like fresh baked bread, pies, popcorn and even cooking meats.

The biggest problem with browning reactions that take place in cereal products is that they use up lysine. This is an important amino acid necessary to our diet which is already in short supply in cereal products. On the other hand, it is what makes bread brown when it bakes, a magic that is worth the loss of a few amino acids!

CARAMELIZATION of sugars takes place at high heat, 300°+F. It plays a small part in the color of baked grain products, unless there is a high concentration of sugar on the outside of the product where the high temperature of the oven can affect it. Caramel rolls are an example of this, where the sugar in the pan is allowed to caramelize around the dough as it bakes in a hot oven. As with maillard browning, sugar that is allowed to caramelize creates many acids,

aldehydes, ketones and other chemical compounds. These are responsible for the color and flavor of what we have come to know as caramel.

Both browning reactions proceed at a faster rate at higher temperatures. However, even at room temperature they will proceed. These reactions are responsible for the color, and to a certain extent, flavor of maple syrup and honey. They are equally responsible for the aromas of chocolate, tea, coffee and many other common food items that are brown in color.

Many of the browning reactions that take place are a combination of these two processes. The list of chemical compounds that are formed are many and varied. The main difference between the two reactions is that caramelization happens to sugars in the absence of amino acids. Maillard browning happens in the presence of sugars and free amino acids, but many of the end products are the same.

Another browning reaction that plays a part in cooking is retarded by heat. This is called ENZYMATIC BROWNING, where the contents of a cell are exposed to oxygen in the air and the result is a darkening of the flesh. This is the reaction that makes sliced apples turn dark when left out in the open. Covering them with a little water and lemon juice will slow this reaction, but cooking the apple slices will destroy the enzyme, a protein, that is responsible.

Temperature & Flavor

There are many effects of heat on the aroma and flavor characteristics of food. Some of the chemicals responsible for the typical aroma or flavor of a food can be formed when the food is heated. Some of these molecules are very small in size and when heat energy is added they volatilize or turn to gas. This gas can be detected by the nose at one part per billion or less! By maintaining the boiling point of these compounds for too long, you can deplete your supply of them if you are not careful.

Fruit fillings, for instance, when heated form delightful fruit ester compounds. These are the molecules believed to be responsible for the aroma of cooked fruit, yet, prolonged heating will also evaporate many of these. The trick is to apply just enough heat to prepare the fruit while leaving enough of the fruit esters for the customer to enjoy. This same principle applies to cooking with herbs where the delicate aroma and flavor compounds can easily be lost.

The aromas of a hot food are much more pronounced than are those of a cold food. The chemicals responsible for the aroma are more easily volatilized in the hot dish. In order to be detected by the nose, the chemicals must be a gas and able to travel through the air. Therefore if you want to impress your customer with a terrific aroma, you serve your hot food HOT!

Flavor changes are less pronounced at different temperatures but still occur. The compounds that are responsible for flavor are formed in much the same way that aroma compounds are, but are not driven off by heat as quickly. Food that we actually taste is in its liquid phase and is a bit more resistant to volitilization of flavor compounds. Some compounds are sensitive to temperature changes and their flavors will change depending on the service temperature. Honey for instance is not as sweet when hot as it is when at room temperature.

METHODS OF COOKING

Now that the basics have been addressed, let's pull this all together and look at some specifics.

Saute

SAUTE literally means to jump. You must limit the amount of food in the pan so that it can be tossed or flipped. The purpose of saute is to cook the food quickly in order to minimize water loss and vitamin destruction, yet maximize browning and flavor development.

The food is cut into small pieces, so that the surface area of the pieces is greatest. The heat is fairly high to allow browning to take place and flavor to develop. There is also a small amount of fat in the pan to keep the food from sticking and to act as a heat conductor.

If too much food is placed in the pan at one time, the heat that is stored in the pan and fat is rapidly conducted to the food. This cools the pan and fat and heats the food. But, if due to too large a quantity, the heat is not enough to sear the food then the heat imparted to the food only heats the water in the food. The heated water expands and in this case leaches out into the pan.

Looking at Figure One, you will remember that it takes twice as much energy to heat water as it does oil. You now have a quantity of water in the pan from the food you were trying to saute. Therefore it will take twice as long to bring the pan back up to temperature.

Looking at Figure Two, you will notice that the thermal conductivity for water is greater than for oil. The result is that not only will the water take longer to heat up, but the heat will tend to remain in that free water, rather than entering into the food itself.

The food which was to be sauteed is now stewing in its own juices. You are boiling your food and the flavor compounds that you were trying to form are not forming, because they are not browning. If the item is meat, it will lose most of its moisture and become tough and gray. If the food is vegetables, you might as well have boiled them in the first place. This slow boiling will only destroy the vitamins and color.

The importance of sauteing small portions at a time can easily be seen in light of the hazards of overloading the pan. Sauteing a small portion in a small amount of fat over a high heat will sear the outside of the food so that the water will remain inside the food. This water will absorb heat across the seared barrier and conduct it into the center of the product. There it will cook or denature the proteins in meats or soften the tissues of vegetables. As you can see, this must be done quickly in order to retain nutritional integrity, as well as to ensure proper browning and/or flavor development of the food.

Braise

BRAISING takes place at a lower temperature, on the whole, than sauteing. The pieces of meat and vegetables used are often much larger. When braising, the meat is often seared first in hot fat. This prevents the loss of water and flavor during the cooking process. It also serves to brown the outside of the meat and to form flavor compounds that will determine the final flavor of the dish. (Refer to the discussion of browning reactions earlier in this chapter.)

The meat used is often from an older animal or from what is termed an 'inferior' cut, the tougher pieces of meat. These cuts contain more connective tissue that can only be dissolved by long slow cooking with moist heat.

Once the meat has been seared and browned, liquid and sometimes vegetables are added. The pot is then covered and brought up to approximately 210°F in a slow oven. The moist heat is drawn completely into the piece of meat. It is allowed to stay there until the connective tissue that holds the muscle fibers together dissolves.

During this exposure to the moist heat, the proteins which make up the muscle fibers are denaturing or unwinding a bit. This exposes chemical groups on the protein that attract and hold water. When the process is complete, the connective tissue has melted into the liquid and will give the sauce made from the braising liquid a gelatin shine. The meat will be tender and very juicy from the absorbed water. The flavors introduced throughout the cooking process will be successfully married.

Broiling & Grilling

These two cooking methods are really the same, with the only difference being gravity. Both methods depend on transfer of heat through the air in order to brown and heat a food. The major flavor compounds are developed through the browning of the food and any marinade used before the heating of the food.

As with saute, the transfer of heat to the center of the product is through the conduction of heat across the surface of the food into the center of the food. The more tender cuts of meat are used for these methods, because there is no time to break down any connective tissue present.

Deep Fat Frying

This process is at the same time quite complex and extremely simple. It is complex in that rules of frying must be followed, but beyond that you can fry almost anything, including ice cream.

Water is very easy to maintain at 212°F, but oil is very difficult to maintain without a working thermometer and an even heat source. Remember, we usually cook in water at or near the temperature of a phase change. Fortunately and unfortunately, oil does not go through a phase change until a much higher temperature is attained. Fortunately, because we do not want to work with boiling oil. Unfortunately, because it makes keeping the temperature constant very difficult. Frying temperatures are often in the range of 325-400°F. These temperatures are difficult to maintain, but in order to cook food evenly it must be done.

Oil is a relatively poor conductor of heat, but, as with other fluids, it will transfer heat by conduction. This means that, as oil heats at the bottom of the kettle, it rises to the surface. In the process of rising it transfers its heat to the rest of the oil in the kettle. This happens until all the oil is at the same temperature.

When a food is fried in oil, it is completely surrounded by heat and so cooks evenly. Since such high temperatures can be attained in deep fat frying, browning reactions take place at an accelerated rate. These are responsible for the flavor and aroma of fried food coatings.

The temperature drop due to the introduction of the food is compensated by the fact that the heat capacity of the oil is fairly low. It will maintain the desired temperature by absorbing heat rapidly from the source. (Refer to Figure One.) This is true unless the amount of product intro-duced is out of proportion with the amount of fat. The principle here is the same as overloading the saute pan.

In deep fat frying the oil must be protected from the food and the food from the oil. There is always a certain amount of evaporation of the water from the food that takes place during the frying process, but too much will dry out the food and destroy the oil. A coating on the fried food will help to seal in that moisture and protect the oil. More importantly the water will turn to steam and cook the product inside the coating.

The rate of conduction of heat across the coating barrier will depend on the type of coating used. If you will remember, air is a terrible conductor of heat (Refer to Figure Two.). A batter that has large amounts of air whipped into it slows the conduction of heat from the oil to the product. For a batter that contains mostly starch and liquid, the thickness of the batter will determine how fast heat is transferred into the center of the food.

The best tasting fried foods are those that are sealed into their own casings by the frying process. These foods are in turn cooked in their own steam, which is fueled by the heat of the oil used to fry the food.

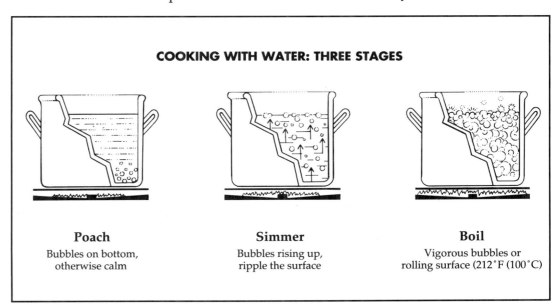

COOKING WITH WATER: THREE STAGES

Poach
Bubbles on bottom, otherwise calm

Simmer
Bubbles rising up, ripple the surface

Boil
Vigorous bubbles or rolling surface (212°F (100°C)

Baking And Roasting

BAKING is the cooking of a food with dry heat that surrounds the item being cooked. This is a method of delivering heat at an even rate to all sides of a food, so that all parts cook at the same rate. This differs from roasting in that the temperature used is often lower and the term baking applies to items other than meat.

The rate of heat transfer is dependent on the type of container the food is in, since conduction of heat plays a large part in the heating process. (Refer to Figure Two.) Convection can speed this type of heat transfer because of the constant replacement of heated air at the surface of the food or the container it is in. Since there is a concentration of heat at the surface of the product, where all heat must enter the product, and temperatures of 325°+F are used, the browning reaction proceeds at an accelerated rate.

ROASTING, on the other hand, is the cooking of meats at high enough temperatures that the browning process is greatly accelerated on the surface of the meat. This is possibly due to the amount of protein and amino acids present in the meat, but also because of the fats present. There are fewer sugars than, say, in a cake, but they react at the high heat to give the wonderful smell of roasting meat.

Boiling And Steaming

There are similarities between boiling food and frying foods in deep fat. The water is heated by convection, hot water rising through the pan to heat the other water molecules. Since there is an excess of hot water to the amount of food, the food cooks at an even rate. Unfortunately this is where the similarity to deep fat frying ends.

Boiling water reaches a maximum temperature of 212°F and the nearer you get to that temperature, the more agitation of the food you get. The result can be broken pieces of food which can be very unattractive. For this reason, food is rarely boiled. Instead it is simmered at a lower temperature, or steamed at a higher temperature.

STEAMING of foods can achieve higher temperatures without the agitation of boiling. The use of steam under pressure makes it possible to even reach the temperatures used in deep fat frying and baking.

Steam under pressure can reach very high temperatures because there is no air present. However, too much pressure is undesirable in cooking because it tends to compress foods that are unprotected. Lower pressure is generally used. One drawback is that in a commercial steamer you cannot easily visually inspect the food as it is cooking so overcooking can be a problem.

Although steam can reach high temperatures, the browning reactions that occur with other methods of heating do not occur as readily. In order for maillard browning or caramelization to occur there must be a lower water content for the molecules to find each other and react. The water present in the steam acts as a barrier to many of the chemical reactions that result in browning.

CONCLUSION

The control of heat transfer is a key to the production of good food. When this control is exercised with care and finesse, the result can be marvelous. When done carelessly, all other efforts are wasted.

REVIEW QUESTIONS

1. What is heat transfer?
2. List and discuss three ways in which foods are heated.
3. Define BTU, phase change, heat capacity and thermal conductivity as they relate to food preparation.
4. Discuss the effects freezing has on food items.
5. List three factors which affect the removal of heat from a food product.
6. What is the difference between enzymatic browning, maillard browning and caramelization?
7. List and discuss four methods of cooking food.

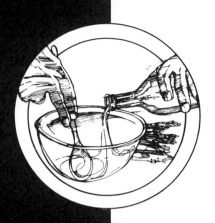

Chapter 4

- **To introduce emulsions as a part of culinary preparation.**
- **To define emulsion.**
- **To discuss emulsifiers and how emulsions are stabilized.**
- **To discuss why emulsions breakdown.**

Emulsion

The preparation of food is truly a matter of bringing together the physical properties of various ingredients to create a good tasting mixture. However, not all ingredients blend together easily. When ingredients used are immiscible (do not mix together), it is often necessary to force them to form a stable homogeneous solution. It is the purpose of this chapter to familiarize the culinarian with examples of emulsions and how they are formed. This is at once a very simple, yet complex procedure that is used in many sauce preparations. It is essential to understand the basics of what is happening, although it is not our intention to turn you into a food scientist. By understanding the basics it will be easier to avoid potential problems during the making of these types of sauces.

Homogenization decreases the size of the larger fat globules in milk, and thereby prevents them from rising to form a separate layer of cream at the top of the bottle. Homogenization is a process of breaking up larger fat droplets and forming a stable emulsion where the butterfat will remain in solution.

WHAT IS AN EMULSION?

An emulsion is the even dispersal of one liquid throughout another immiscible liquid. If the drops of the dispersed liquid are small enough and well separated from each other, the mixture will be thicker than either liquid and will remain in solution, for a time. The amount of time for which the emulsion is stable depends upon what is preventing the dispersed phase from coming together (pooling) and separating from the other liquid.

HOW IS AN EMULSION STABILIZED?

There are several methods used to prevent the dispersed phase from pooling and some of them work better than others. It is the natural tendency of like molecules to attract each other. For instance, if you shake oil and vinegar in a jar it will form what is known as a temporary emulsion. Very temporary. At first the drops of oil in the jar slowly begin to attract each other. As the drops get bigger, they grow faster, incorporating more drops of oil until there is only one very large drop of oil, the upper phase of the jar.

The way to make a more stable emulsion is physically to prevent the drops from being able to get together. This is accomplished in one of several ways. The use of emulsifiers, finely divided (powdered) solids, polysaccharides, proteins or even thick liquids can help stabilize an emulsion. Each of these ingredients can be important in different situations.

Emulsifiers have the unique physical property of having two distinctly different areas on one molecule. Each of these areas would prefer to be dissolved in a different substance. This is known as the hydrophilic/lipophilic (water loving/fat or oil loving) balance. This sounds confusing, but in reality is quite simple. For instance, lecithin, which is found in egg yolks, is the primary emulsifier in both mayonnaise and hollandaise. It works because one part of the lecithin molecule attracts the oil or fat and the other part attracts the water and water compatible parts of the emulsion. This means that surrounding each oil or fat droplet there is a coating of lecithin where each lecithin molecule is acting like a miniature staple, holding the two phases together.

Finely divided solids or powders can stabilize an emulsion by absorbing oil and water at the interface (the point where the oil and water meet). Very finely ground dried herbs fit into this category. Polysaccharides, such as certain gums, can also interfere with the pooling process of the dispersed phase. While it is common in the processed food industry to add gums to food, it is not quite so common in the restaurant industry. This does not mean that gums are not important. Pectins are present in jams, jellies and other fruit products. While they are not usually thought of as an emulsion stabilizer, they can act as such.

Other examples of polysaccharide gums are agar (also known as kosher gelatin), guar gum, carrageenan, locust bean gum (also known as carob) and xanthan gum. These work by interfering with the pooling process of the dispersed phase or by forming a matrix that traps the dispersed droplets. Many of these are found in processed foods and are used infrequently in today's kitchens. Cooked starch solutions can also act to stabilize emulsions by interfering with the pooling effect, but acids (such as lemon juice) in the system can break down the starch over time, making the stabilizer ineffective. An example of an emulsion stabilized by this method is a demi-glace that is mounted with butter just prior to serving.

Gelatin is an example of a protein that can act as a stabilizer in much the same manner as described above. Proteins that are naturally present in foods can make very effective emulsifiers because they, too, have hydrophilic and lipophilic properties. Since they are such large molecules, they also interfere with the pooling of the dispersed phase. It is protein that is responsible for holding the fat in suspension in the meat emulsions in bologna and frankfurters. Salad dressings can be stabilized by using egg whites in the same way one would make mayonnaise because of the protein (albumen, etc.) in the egg whites.

Another method of stabilizing an emulsion is to add a thick liquid to the two immiscible liquids. A fruit salad dressing may contain citrus juice, oil, and herbs but it will form only a very temporary emulsion when mixed. By adding honey the mixture is sweetened and more stable.

WHAT IS THE CONTRIBUTION OF OTHER INGREDIENTS?

Many flavoring agents are added to emulsified sauces. Some serve only to add flavor. Others, such as vinegars and citrus juices (acids), can also change the physio-chemical properties of the emulsifier. Proteins can be denatured and therefore unfolded, creating a greater barrier between the dispersed droplets. Further, in the case of mayonnaise and hollandaise, the acid changes the chemical properties

of the emulsifier so that it can take up more lipid (fat or oil) before becoming saturated.

Plant particulates for the most part are too large to act as a barrier between the dispersed phase droplets. They are effective in the initial breaking up of the droplets when the mixture is whisked or blended and they do act as flavoring ingredients. This group includes chopped herbs, crushed garlic, chopped onion, citrus peel and others.

WHY DO EMULSIONS BREAKDOWN?

We have discussed what emulsions are and what tends to stabilize them. Now we will talk about why emulsions break, separate or never form in the first place. There are three main reasons that emulsions separate:

1) LIQUID IS ADDED TOO QUICKLY.
2) THE MIXTURE BECOMES SATURATED.
3) TEMPERATURE.

Improper Mixing

When the liquid that is to be dispersed is added too quickly, the emulsion may never form or may quickly separate. This occurs because there is not sufficient time for the liquid to disperse fully. The tiny drops cannot form, and pools of the liquid are created instead. This is why the recipes for mayonnaise and hollandaise call for the oil to be added in a slow, thin stream. As the old chef said, "If too much butter is added too fast, the eggs will be swimming in it, not gathering it up."

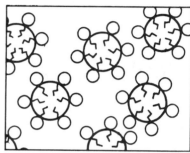

Long molecules like starch and proteins stabilize emulsions by getting in between droplets and interfering with coalescence. Soap-type emulsifiers actually embed themselves partly in the fat droplets and leave their electrically charged heads projecting into the water phase. Coated in this way with a shell of negative charge, the droplets actually repel each other.

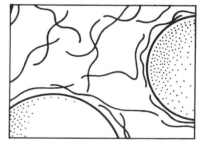

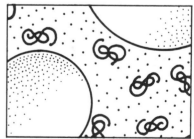

The proteins in egg white produce a long-lived foam by unfolding at the interface between liquid and air and bonding to each other. A solid network of reinforcement is the result (i.e.: whipped egg-whites). This is the same mechanism that allows egg whites to be made into a mayonnaise – instead of an air bubble being protected by the proteins, a drop of oil is sequestered.

There are two solutions for this problem. One is to slow down the stream of liquid, giving it time to disperse into the continuous phase. The second solution is to increase the speed of mixing the item.

Saturation

When an emulsified mixture becomes saturated, it is similar to when the liquid is added too quickly. The difference is that no amount of whisking will incorporate all of the liquid. For example, in the first instance cited above, the oil in the mayonnaise never had a chance to disperse. With saturation, there is simply too much oil.

The basic ratio for an emulsion using egg yolk as the emulsifier is one large egg for each six ounces of oil or melted fat (butter). This is true for emulsions such as mayonnaise and hollandaise. This is based on the fact that, when you add seven ounces of oil, the egg yolk becomes saturated. That is, it is too full to hold more oil. A towel can only hold a certain amount of water without dripping. When it becomes totally saturated with water, it begins to release some. This is exactly what happens in an emulsion when too much of the liquid to be dispersed is added.

When saturation occurs, the solution is to put some of the continuous ingredient into a separate mixing bowl and slowly add the broken emulsion to it. In the case of mayonnaise or hollandaise, place some beaten egg yolk in a mixing bowl and begin to whisk the broken emulsion into it. This decreases the proportion of dispersed phase, oil or butter, to the water and water soluble solids contained in the egg yolk.

When the emulsified mixture nears saturation it is easier to break it by over-whisking. This is because the kinetic energy involved in stirring or mixing causes collisions between the dispersed droplets. Without a sufficient amount of emulsifier present to keep the droplets apart the collisions can start a chain reaction that results in the pooling of the dispersed phase. Adding a small amount of acid, in the form of lemon juice or vinegar can make the emulsifier hold more liquid and therefore increase the saturation point of the mixture.

Temperature

Temperature abuse is a major cause of broken emulsions. In the kitchen, the most common emulsion is between oil or fat and a water based solution (vinegars, fruit juices, wines, stock, etc.). Often the emulsifier is a protein or is part of a protein system.

Proteins are relatively large molecules that exist in their native state folded in a certain configuration. (This allows them to fulfill their biological purpose, whatever that may have been.) When the protein is exposed to heat, acid or agitation it can be unfolded. This unfolding (a change in shape) is called denaturation. This exposes different parts of the molecule which changes its chemical properties. As stated earlier, proteins often act as emulsifiers because of lipophilic and hydrophilic portions of the molecule. When the protein is denatured, these groups can be exposed.

In hollandaise, you whisk eggs and acid (wine, lemon juice, etc.) over heat to denature the proteins deliberately. When the egg mixture is fully cooked, the butter is slowly added to the mixture. The matrix formed by the proteins in the egg yolks acts to separate the butter droplets and acts as an emulsifier in conjunction with the lecithin.

In the case of mayonnaise, the proteins present in the egg yolk are partially responsible for emulsification. These proteins can be destabilized by excessive heat (high room temperature), excessive agitation (over-whisking in the mixer) and acids used (flavoring agents such as vinegar, lemon juice, etc.). A little bit of denaturation can act to stabilize your emulsion, but working your mixture too much can destroy the mixture.

Excessive heat, agitation or acid can catalyze chemical reactions that can destroy the protein molecule in terms of its emulsifying properties. Furthermore, the energy input (heat and agitation) in the presence of acids can also act to destroy some of the other emulsifiers such as the lecithin in egg yolk. This is why it is important to know when to be careful when making an emulsion and to learn to recognize the warning signs of imminent breakage.

Another problem is that of thickness. When oil gets cold, it gets thick. When it gets hot, it becomes thin. Water does not do this to any noticeable extent. This presents a problem in making an emulsion because, not only are you trying to combine two immiscible substances, you are often trying to mix two solutions that are of different thicknesses. If you are trying to make a mayonnaise in a very cold room, you encounter the problem trying to incorporate a thick oil into a relatively thin egg mixture. When this happens, the oil molecules are stiff and inflexible and tend to remain clumped together. For a good emulsion to form, the oil droplets must be only a few microns in diameter (a bacteria is a micron across) and if the oil is clumping together, it will not be able to disperse effectively. This is also a problem in the making of hollandaise, if you are trying to add butter that is too cool.

Butter sauces (*buerre blanc*, etc.) are emulsions that are formed utilizing the proteins and natural emulsifiers found in the fresh whole butter (strengthened by acid in wine or citrus juice). This emulsion is very temperature dependent in that, if it is allowed to cool and is reheated, it will break. The

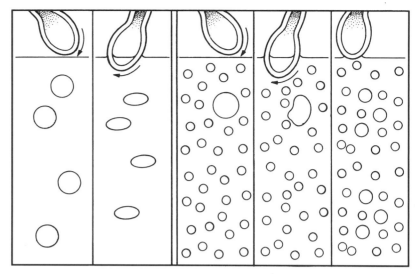

When oil droplets are sparse, they easily evade the whisk, and are hard to divide. When after much work they are smaller and more numerous, the droplets themselves become obstacles to new drops of oil, and help break them up.

long term stability of the sauce is dependent on the stability of the emulsifiers present, especially the proteins. Acids in the wine or citrus juice will eventually break down the emulsifiers present, creating flavor changes as well as destabilizing the emulsion. This means that it is nearly impossible to hold a butter sauce for more than six hours at room temperature (in a working kitchen this is quite warm) without experiencing flavor reversion. Also, it is extremely difficult, if not impossible, to reheat a butter sauce that has been allowed to chill for the same reasons given for making mayonnaise in a cold room, the fat is too thick in comparison to the water soluble components of the sauce.

WHY STUDY EMULSIONS?

We need to understand emulsions because they affect nearly every area of food preparation. Even the "mother sauces" (major family of hot sauces) are emulsions of a sort. In each there is a small amount of fat present that is not noticeable because it is held in solution by various means. Examples are sauces that are mounted with butter just prior to service, hollandaise and mayonnaise. Even common ingredients that we use every day are emulsions and, if we handle them incorrectly, they will separate.

Whipping cream is an example of an oil-in-water emulsion. If you over whip it, the butterfat falls out of solution. Butter and margarine are examples of water-in-oil emulsions. Again, if you expose them to too much heat, they will separate. Chocolate is an emulsion stabilized in part by the temperature at which it is held. When melting it, certain rules must be adhered to or else it, too, will separate.

The list goes on and on. However, this discussion has been limited to the problems associated with the making of emulsion sauces. These causes usually push the limits of the emulsifier in how much oil or fat can be held in suspension without the sauce breaking. This is what makes the sauce thick, rich and worth the extra effort to master.

REVIEW QUESTIONS

1. What is an emulsion?
2. What is a stabilized emulsion?
3. How is an emulsion stabilized?
4. What is lecithin, where does it come from and how is it used in the kitchen?
5. What is the importance of vinegar in the preparation of an emulsion sauce?
6. List and discuss the three major reasons an emulsion breaks.
7. What does the culinarian need to study emulsions?

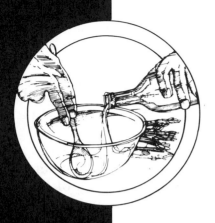

Chapter 5

CHAPTER OBJECTIVES

- **To discuss the distinction between seasoning and flavoring.**
- **To discuss seasoning.**
- **To introduce the primary seasoning agents.**
- **To discuss storage and handling of seasonings.**
- **To discuss flavoring.**
- **To introduce the primary flavoring agents.**
- **To discuss storage and handling of flavoring agents.**

Flavoring Foods

Eating is essential for life, yet the enjoyment of eating good food is dependent on good flavor. Humans have traveled the globe, often at great risk, in search of fine flavors and methods for preserving foods, seeking, primarily, what we refer to as "spices."

In the thirteenth century, spices were so precious that they were accepted as currency along with gold. Little was known of the trade routes to India and the Middle East at this time. Possession of these secrets commanded fame and fortune. The search for spices drove Columbus and Magellan to travel the seas and discover new continents.

Today, spices are readily available, yet those individuals who possess in-depth knowledge of them and their value command respect. This chapter will discuss how seasoning and flavorings relate to culinary application. This requires definition of the various types and forms of items available as well as the different functions they serve. To begin, we must discuss the basic taste sensations, so that we can better understand seasoning and flavoring.

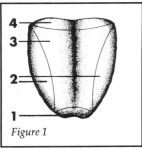

Figure 1

1. **Sweet**
2. **Sour**
3. **Salty**
4. **Bitter**

TASTE SENSATIONS

Of the five senses humans have, smell and taste are directly related. They are detected simultaneously because the mouth and nose share the same airway. The eighteenth century French gastronome, Brillat-Savarin enlightened the issue of taste and smell when he stated, "Smell and taste form a single sense, of which the mouth is the laboratory and the nose is the chimney; or, to speak more exactly, of which one serves for the tasting of the actual bodies and the other for the savoring of their gases."

The human body identifies basic taste sensations through the tongue. The map of the tongue shown in Figure One highlights areas that are most sensitive to particular sensations. There are four major sensations: sweet, sour, bitter and salty.

SWEET sensations come from sugars and sweeteners. These are detected at the tip of the tongue. Sweetness is also the primary sensation that the body prefers. When drinking lemonade, for example, it is natural to desire the sweetness of sugar over the sourness of lemon. Too much lemon dominates the lemonade and the mouth rejects the sourness by puckering. The body, within limits, will tolerate an overabundance of sweet substances and allow you to swallow them. When something that is extremely sour, bitter or salty is eaten, the body protests. The body perceives it as a potentially toxic danger, and the result is one's inability to swallow easily.

SOUR sensations come from acids and are detected on the sides of the tongue. Citrus juices, such as lemon and lime, tomato products and vinegars are all acidic foods. The tongue reacts in varying degrees to acids, depending on the concentration. A small amount is pleasing to the palate. A heavy concentration causes the mouth to pucker.

SALTY sensations come from sodium chloride and other salts such as sodium glutamate and potassium chloride. This sensation is detected at the front of the tongue. Salt is actually an essential nutrient and is desirable in small quantities. Overuse of salt results in a physiological need to drink large quantities of water, causing a loss of appetite.

BITTERNESS is a reaction to alkaloids which are bitter. This sensation is detected at the back of the tongue. Quinine and caffeine are examples of bitter alkaloids. Although the body rejects high concentrations of alkaloids, we have become accustomed to low concentrations. Examples are those found in coffee and tonic water.

Few sensations are encountered in complete isolation. For this reason, they are at times difficult to define or detect. Temperatures also affect our sensitivity to taste. Foods that are too hot or too cold seem to lose flavor only because our taste buds cannot easily detect flavors at extreme temperatures.

The interaction of taste and temperature varies from compound to compound. Sucrose and hydrochloric acid have optimum taste at 35°-50°C. However, each acid will be different, due to its own chemical properties. Sugars also differ in the same manner. Fructose, the major component of honey, and some other monosaccharides exhibit poor sweetening ability when hot, yet are very sweet when cold. This change is related to the amount of energy the molecule has and thereby its shape. The molecule has to have the right shape to match up with the taste bud.

The reaction of salt (table salt) to temperature is very important in food preparation. It can actually taste bitter at 10°C. The amount of salt in a dish can be more easily detected at lower temperatures than at higher temperatures. In view of this fact, it is advisable to season a dish at the temperature at which it is to be served. Otherwise you risk the dish being too salty. Quinine is another substance which is far more discernible at lower temperatures. This well tested, bitter substance is much more bitter at lower temperatures. This is also true for other alkaloids like caffeine.

It is important that the taste sensations of various compounds are considered when seasoning and flavoring foods. Mixing and matching sensations is truly challenging and exciting. Seasoning and flavoring are what stimulate the taste sensations. Therefore the culinarian needs to understand the difference between seasoning and flavoring. In addition, how these apply to cooking must be known.

SEASONING

TYPES & DEFINITIONS

Seasoning can be defined as the enhancement of the natural flavor of food without drastic alteration of this flavor. Salt, in its various forms, is the primary seasoning agent. There are two primary types of salt available:

ROCK SALT is mined from deposits on land. This salt is very coarse in texture and is often refined and sold as table salt, normally with iodine added, or pickling salt, which does not contain iodine.

SEA SALT is produced by the evaporation of sea water. Sea salt is an impure salt, containing natural iodine and other compounds. It is considered more natural because it comes from the ocean.

From the two primary salts there are also derived flavored salts and soy.

FLAVORED SALTS are refined salt combined with other natural flavorings. Garlic salt, celery salt and seasoned salt are examples of flavored salts. These salts can be used in cooking and work well in marinades.

SOY, in its various forms of paste or sauce, comes from the orient where it is derived from soy beans fermented in a salt brine. It is dark brown in color. In liquid form it can provide a very subtle seasoning. However, it will alter the color of the food because of its dark color. Soy will vary widely in salt content. Add less than recommended by a recipe and taste before adding more.

An example of a secondary source of seasoning is MONOSODIUM GLUTAMATE, also called MSG, the sodium salt of glumatic acid. This is a white powdery compound which is produced naturally by both plants and animals. The MSG which is used as a seasoning in today's kitchen may be derived from a number of natural sources, including wheat gluten, seaweed, and beet or cane sugar. It is extracted through a process of fermentation and drying which eventually results in the fine white crystals known as MSG. It has only a slightly salty taste of its own. Its purpose is to bring out the natural flavors of the food. Even though MSG is a sodium, it contains only 1/3 of the sodium of normal table salt. MSG is very common in oriental cooking and, if used in proper amounts, can reduce the need for salt.

CHARACTERISTICS

The characteristics and benefits of using salt in food preparation are many. Salt is an essential nutrient that is very desirable in small quantities. It also has, as previously stated, a specialized taste sensation for detecting it. Salt, like sugar, is a crystal which will dissolve in water. This enables it to blend in with most foods easily and quickly, but not with fats.

Salt also has an incredible capacity to absorb water. Salt, when placed on food, can draw water out and in turn, penetrate into the food where the water once was. The withdrawing of the water can enhance the natural flavor of the food.

An example of this practice is illustrated when a piece of fish is lightly salted before being baked in the oven. Although the heat from the oven draws much of the moisture out of the fish, the salt aids this process and can be tasted throughout the fish.

A more extreme example of salt's absorptive power is evident in a salt-cured country ham. In this case, salt acts as a preservative by drawing almost all of the moisture from the ham. This helps to eliminate bacterial growth.

The benefits of using salt can quickly be undone if it is not used with restraint. Its incredible absorptive ability can completely dry out the product if too much salt is exposed to the product for too long. To recover food which has had too much salt added is very difficult and often impossible.

Some basic guidelines for seasoning foods are as follow:

1. SEASONING, AS WELL AS FLAVORING, IS INTENDED TO ENHANCE THE MAIN INGREDIENT, NOT TO HIDE ITS FLAVOR OR COVER UP POORLY PREPARED FOOD.

2. MOST SEASONING FOR LIQUID PRODUCTS IS DONE TOWARD THE END OF THE COOKING PROCESS, ESPECIALLY IF THE LIQUID WILL BE REDUCED.

3. LIQUIDS THAT REDUCE CAUSE SEASONINGS TO CONCENTRATE, INTEN-SIFYING THE SEASONINGS TASTE. TO GAIN THE RIGHT BALANCE OF SEASONING:

    A) COOK YOUR LIQUID PRODUCT FOR THREE-QUARTERS OF ITS TOTAL COOKING TIME.

    B) TASTE IT TO SEE WHAT SEASONING, IF ANY, IS NEEDED.

    C) ADD A SMALL AMOUNT OF SEASONING AND ALLOW THE LIQUID TO FINISH COOKING. REMEMBER, YOU CAN ALWAYS ADD MORE, IF NEEDED.

    D) TASTE AGAIN AND ADJUST SEASONING, IF NEEDED.

4. WHEN PREPARING SOLID PIECES OF FOOD IT IS BEST TO SEASON AT THE BEGINNING OF THE COOKING PROCESS. THIS ALLOWS THE SEASONING TO BE ABSORBED AND BLEND INTO THE FOOD. IT ALSO ALLOWS TIME FOR THE SEASONING TO BRING OUT THE NATURAL FLAVORS OF THE FOOD ITSELF.

5. NOTE, BECAUSE SALT DRAWS WATER OUT, WHEN ATTEMPTING TO BROWN MEATS IT MAY NOT BE ADVANTAGEOUS TO SALT THE MEAT BEFORE COOKING. THE WATER EXTRACTED BY THE SALT MAY RETARD THE BROWNING PROCESS.

6. SEASONING MAY ALSO BE ADDED AFTER COOKING. THIS CAN BE VERY EFFECTIVE IF THE COOKED FOOD HAS LITTLE FLAVOR OF ITS OWN. FRENCH FRIES ARE A SIMPLE, BUT CLASSIC EXAMPLE. MANY PEOPLE ENJOY THE FRENCH FRY MORE FOR THE SALT THAN THE POTATO.

NUTRITION TIPS

Nutritionally there are a number of considerations when using sodium derivatives such as salts and MSG in food preparation. There is some evidence that salt contributes to high blood pressure and heart disease. Many food service operations offer low sodium menu items for health conscious customers. These establishments use alternatives to salt such as lemon juice, vinegar and sherry. Each of these enhances the flavor of food, but also, unlike salt, they add flavor of their own.

The use of MSG is also an area of concern nutritionally. There is ongoing research of a possible link between MSG and allergic reactions in some people. Whether MSG is used in food preparation will depend upon the customers being served. Future trends seem to point toward lower sodium diets. Therefore, the developing culinarian will be wise to explore alternatives to salt and MSG. The ability to evaluate and correct seasoning, and flavor as well, is a cook's most valuable attribute. This ability is the result of knowledge and experience, both of which take time.

STORAGE & HANDLING

Storage of seasoning agents and salts requires a dry, cool place. They should be stored out of direct sunlight and in sealed containers. Exposure to moisture will cause salt to cake, making it difficult to work with. It may be necessary to place rice or some other absorptive agent

Poppy - Pavot

1. Longitudinal section of the seed capsule
   (a) Empty seed chamber
   (b) Filled seed chamber

2. Seed capsule (cross-section)

3. Whole seed capsule

in the salt to prevent caking. This is not as necessary as it was in years past because of the addition of anti-caking agents by the salt fabricator.

FLAVORING

Flavoring, as opposed to seasoning, is the addition of a new flavor to a food. This results in an alteration of the original natural flavor. The various types of flavoring agents can be categorized as spices, herbs, concentrated flavoring agents, wines, vinegars and marinades.

Without flavor, there is little distinction from one recipe to the next. It is flavor, in most cases, which defines international cuisine. The chili pepper of Mexico, the fermented soy bean sauce of the Far East, the turmeric and cardamom mixture of Indian curry, as well as the oregano and basil flavored tomato sauce of Italy, all provide strong distinctive flavors.

It is extremely helpful for today's chef to be familiar with the various flavors associated with international cuisines. This familiarity, along with a working knowledge of seasoning and flavoring principles, will enable a chef to use flavors successfully in new and unexpected combinations.

It should be noted that there are dominant flavors and undertones. The dominant flavor should be limited to one or two elements, such as the main ingredient and possibly one additional ingredient or flavor agent. Any additional flavoring should be very subtle, so as not to take attention away from the dominant flavor.

A particular recipe may call for five or six herbs and/or spices. One or two of these should be dominant. The other agents should combine to form subtle undertones. These undertones may often not even be recognizable, yet persistent enough in the overall flavor to be classified as "the secret ingredient." An example would be the addition of a very minute amount of ground cinnamon or nutmeg, which can add great complexity to the flavor of a cream sauce, yet be virtually undetectable.

SPICES
TYPES & DEFINITIONS

The term *spice* comes from Latin and, roughly translated, means "fruits of the earth". Spices, as distinguished from herbs, are derived from various parts of the plant. For example, the bark (cinnamon), the buds (cloves), the flowers (saffron), the fruit (allspice), the root (ginger) and the seed (mustard). Spices can be categorized as either whole or ground.

Saffron

Whole spices are in their natural forms: seeds, nuts, bark, roots, flowers, leaves, buds or fruit. The advantage of a whole spice is its longer shelf life in comparison to a ground spice. Some spices contain antioxidants, components which slowdown the removal of their essence by the introduction of oxygen. These antioxidants are still intact in a whole spice, allowing them to be stored for three to six months without loss of flavoring power. It is also easier to remove whole spices from food when desired. When left in the food, they provide an interesting texture. The disadvantage is the increased time needed to release their full flavoring power.

Ground spices are ones which have been reduced to a selected size by a food mill or other grinding method. The advantage of the ground spice is its ability to incorporate more uniformly into foods. Spices in this form will also release their flavor more easily into foods. Due to the increase in surface area and, therefore, more interaction with oxygen in the atmosphere, ground spices have a much shorter shelf life. At best, they can be held three months.

CHARACTERISTICS

Spices, as well as herbs, contain "volatile" elements, meaning "elements which evaporate when exposed to heat." These volatile elements make up a large part of the overall flavor profile of a spice or herb. When flavoring foods it is best to add spices and herbs towards the end of the cooking process. Sufficient time must be allowed for full release of flavor by the spice or herb, yet not enough time to allow the volatile elements to evaporate.

Spices have a virtually unlimited variety of usages in the kitchen. There are some spices and herbs which are associated with specific regional cuisines, such as curry in Indian cuisine and coriander in Thai cuisine. This association no longer means that these are only to be used in the production of dishes relative to each cuisine, or that dishes associated with a particular cuisine cannot contain other flavoring agents. Many chefs are adding surprising twists to regional favorites by adding unlikely spices and herbs. This bringing of new life to traditional foods is considered by many to be the wave of the future.

STORAGE & HANDLING

Spices should be handled with care. The larger the particle size, the more durable it will be for storage. Remember that whole spices will resist flavor deterioration better than ground spices. All spices should be kept in tightly sealed containers, and should be resealed immediately after use. When buying spices, purchase no more than can be used in three months, and date each container for proper rotation. Due to the volatile nature of the spices' flavor, they should always be stored at less than 68°F., at a humidity of 55 percent or less. They should not be stored in direct sunlight.

Artemisia

HERBS AND SPICES

NAME	TYPE	CHARACTERISTICS	EXAMPLE USE
Allspice	Whole or Ground spice	Small brown berry. Flavor resembles a combination cinnamon, clove & nutmeg. Native to W. India.	Sausages, braised meats, poached fish, cooked fruits, puddings, pies, relishes.
Anise	Whole or ground spice	Licorice flavor, native to Spain, China, Syria.	Cookies, pastries, bread.
Basil	Herb leaf; fresh or dried	Aromatic green leaf, member of mint family. Can be grown fresh in warm weather.	Tomato dishes, pesto, egg dishes, salads, marinades, fish, compound butters.
Bay Leaf	Whole leaf herb.	Stiff, dark green, oblong leaf. Pungent aroma. Reminiscent of sassafras. Comes from Laurel tree.	Stocks, sauces, soups, stews, braised meats.
Bouquet Garni	Flavoring mix	A personal selection of herbs, vegetables and occasionally spices, often tied with a string	Stocks, soups, sauces
Caraway	Whole spice, seed.	Dark brown, curved seed. Grown in Northern Europe.	Rye bread, cabbage, sauerkraut, Eastern European cuisine.
Cardamom	Whole pod or ground seed spice.	Tiny brown seeds, white on green pods. Sweet & aromatic, expensive. Native of India & Guatemala.	Pickling, danish pastries, curries.
Cayenne	Ground spice, seed.	Ground hot red pepper. Very powerful. Native of French Guiana.	In small amounts: soups, sauces, fish, eggs.
Celery Seed	Whole or ground spice, seed.	Tiny brown seed, with strong celery flavor. Too much can create a "hot" spice effect.	Salads, dressings, pickling, tomato dishes, marinades.
Chervil	Herb leaf, fresh or dried.	Mild flavor of parsley and tarragon.	Soups, salads, sauces, egg dishes, chicken, fish, dressings.
Chili Powder	Ground spice, blend.	Blend of ground cumin, chili pepper, oregano, allspice. Can be mild or hot.	Chili, stews, sauces, ground meats.
Chives	Fresh, dried, frozen herb.	Fine, hollow, green top of a very small onion.	Salads, egg & cheese dishes, fish soups, sauces.

NAME	TYPE	CHARACTERISTICS	EXAMPLE USE
Cilantro	Leaf herb, dried or fresh.	Light green aromatic leaf. Shape of flat parsley but much more pungent flavor. Leaf from coriander seed.	Salads, salsa, sauces, soups, eggs, dressings.
Cinnamon	Stick or ground spice.	Aromatic bark from cinnamon or cassia tree. Reddish brown color. Native of East India.	Preserves, stewed fruits, breads, pastries, desserts, ham, hot beverages.
Clove	Whole or ground spice.	Dried flowerbud of tropical clove tree, pungent, sweet in flavor. Native of Indonesia.	Whole: Marinades, stocks, sauces, braised meats, hams, and pickling. Ground: Pastries, fruits and cakes.
Coriander	Whole or ground spice.	Round, light brown seed. Slightly aromatic flavor. Native to Argentina and Morocco. Seed to cilantro leaf.	Pickling, sausage, stocks, pork, curries, gingerbread, salsa, dressings.
Cumin	Whole or ground seed, spice.	Small seed resembling caraway, but lighter in color. Grown in Mexico and Syria.	Ingredient in chili and curry powder blends. Sausage, meats, salsa, egg & cheese dishes.
Curry	Ground blend, spice.	Mixture of approx. 20 spices, peppery, yellow in color. Includes tumeric, cumin, coriander, ginger, clove, cinnamon. Can vary from mild to very hot.	Curry dishes, vegetables, soups, sauces, fish, meat, rice.
Dill	Whole seed or "dill weed" which are leaves. Leaf fresh or dried.	Herb and seed with "dill pickle" flavor. Seed more pungent than herb.	Seed: Pickling, soups, sauerkraut, marinades. Herbs: Salads. soups, fish & shellfish, vegetables, sauces, vinegars.
Fennel	Whole seed.	Greenish brown seed, similar in flavor to anise. Grown in S. America, Asia, and Africa.	Sausage, tomato, sauces, marinades, fish, pickling.
Fine Herbes	Herb blend.	Generally a bouquet blend of three or more herbs used to enhance various dishes. Finely chopped herb mixture--chives, tarragon, parsley, basil, savory, etc.	Herb sauce, compund butters broiled meats, fish, cold sauces.
Garlic	Fresh, whole bulb. Dried: Granulated, powder, or mixed with salt.	Strong, aromatic member of onion family.	Used widely in cooking.
Ginger	Spice, fresh whole, dried powder, candied crystallized, or pickled.	Light brown knobby root from tropical plant.	Baked goods, desserts, fruits, curry dishes, pickling, chutney, Chinese, Caribbean & Japanese cuisine.
Juniper Berry	Whole spice.	Slightly soft, purple berry. "Piney" flavor. Principle flavor of gin.	Marinades, game dishes, sauerkraut.
Mace	Whole "blade" or ground spice.	Made from outer covering of nutmeg. Orange red in color. Aromatic, similar to nutmeg in flavor but milder.	Baked goods, desserts, fruits, sausage, fish, vegetables, preserves.
Marjoram	Dried herb leaf.	Grey green herb from mint family. Similar to oregano but milder.	Beef, veal, lamb, sausage, pates, poultry, stews, soups, vegetables, salads, sauces.
Mint	Herb leaf, fresh or dried.	Aromatic herb with cool flavor. Spearmint and peppermint are most common.	Lamb, fruits, tea, fruit beverages, peas, carrots, potatoes, jellies, soups, sauces.
Mirepoix	Flavoring mix	Mixture of vegetables, herbs, and spices used to enhance the flavor of meat, fish and shellfish dishes. Common ingredients are--onion, celery, carrot, leek, garlic, peppercorns, bay leaf, clove, thyme and rosemary.	Stocks, soups, sauces, roasts.

NAME	TYPE	CHARACTERISTICS	EXAMPLE USES
Mustard Seed	Whole and ground seed.	Very pungent seed--white, yellow or brown.	Blended w/vinegar to make prepared mustard. Pickling, sauces, salsa, Prepared: Sandwiches, sauces, dressings, ham.
Nasturtium	Leaf and seed.	Plant with yellow, orange, and red flowers, with sharp casting leaves and seeds with pungent odor.	Salads, pickling, mustard.
Nutmeg	Whole or ground spice.	Sweet, aromatic kernel of nutmeg fruit. Grown in Netherlands and East & West Indies.	Baked goods, pies, cream sauces, soups, chicken, veal, vegetables, desserts, breads.
Oregano	Leaf or ground herb, fresh or dried.	Pungent herb, similar to marjoram, but stronger. Native to Italy and Mexico, grown domestically.	Italian & Mexican dishes, tomato sauces, soups, sauces, stews, meats, salads, marinades.
Paprika	Ground spice.	Ground from dried sweet red pepper. Spanish: Bright & mild. Hungarian: Darker & more pungent.	Asset to bland pale food. Fish, seafood, meats, salads, sauces, dressings, garnish.
Parsley	Fresh leaf herb in bunches. Dried.	Green leaf, curly or flat, with delicate sweet flavor. Excellent source of vitamin C.	Garnish, fried, stews, sauces, salads, vegetables, potatoes.
Pepper	Whole "peppercorns" black, white, or green cracked, medium or fine ground.	Small hard berry. Black: Pungent, aromatic. White: What is left when black outer casing is removed, milder. Adds sharp tang to all foods. Green: Packed in mild brine.	Widely used with just about all foods including green in sweets.
Poppy Seeds	Whole spice.	Tiny blue black seeds with crunchy nut like flavor. It is a product of the opium poppy, but does not contain opium.	Garnish for breads, rolls, pastry, fillings, cookies, cakes, salsas, dressings.
Rosemary	Whole leaf herb, fresh or dried.	Light green leaf resembling pine needles. Very aromatic. Once grown, very healthy and strong, even in cold weather.	Lamb, fish, beef, sauces, soups, stews, salads, marinades.
Sachet Bag	Spice mix.	Various spices tied in a small cheesecloth sack.	Braised meats, game stews, pickling, soups, sauces.
Saffron	Whole "threads", spice.	Only the stigmas from the saffron crocus are used. Very expensive. Gives bright yellow color to foods. Mild distinctive flavor.	Flavor and color baked goods, rice, potatoes, soups, sauces, curry, meats.
Sage	Whole, rubbed, or ground herb leaf, fresh or dried.	Pungent grey green herb with fuzzy leaves, oblong shape.	Stuffings, meat, poultry, soups, stews, salads, fish.
Savory	Fresh or dried herb leaf.	Fragrant herb of mint family. Summer preferred to winter.	Salads, eggs, vegetables, stuffings, soups, meats, fish, sauces.
Sesame	Whole (hulled or unhulled) seed.	Small yellowish seed with nutty taste. High oil content. Imported from Asia, East and Central America.	Can be roasted. Bread & roll garnish, salads, oriental candy.
Tarragon	Fresh, dried, pickled herb leaf.	Delicate green herb that is both mint & licorice-like. Small oblong leaf.	Bearnaise sauce, tarragon vinegar, chicken, fish, salads, dressings, eggs.
Thyme	Fresh or dried herb leaf, crushed or ground.	Tiny brownish green leaf, very aromatic.	Soups, chowders, stocks, sauces, meats, poultry, salads, dressing.
Turmeric	Ground spice.	Intense yellow root of ginger family. Mild but peppery flavor.	Curry powder, pickles, relish, salads, eggs, rice, chow-chow.

HERBS
TYPES & DEFINITION

The second category of flavoring agents encompasses herbs, which comes from Latin meaning "grass." Herbs are defined as the leaves and stems of soft stemmed, non-woody plants. The types of plants from which the common herbs originate primarily grow in temperate climates. Herbs and their use can be traced back to ancient Egypt, Greece and China. It would seem that they were originally gathered for culinary purposes. It has been said that medicine developed as a byproduct of cooking. Whether this is true or not, herbs were used in the ancient world for both culinary and medicinal purposes. This duality of purpose still exists for many herbs today. Many herbs are still used in medicine and provide vital substances for drugs used in pharmaceutical production.

Herbs can be categorized as either fresh, dried, pickled or frozen.

FRESH herbs are, as the name denotes, those which are used without alteration, freshly picked. This does not necessarily mean the cook picks them from the garden. They are available packaged, as are fresh cut flowers, from many suppliers.

DRIED herbs are the same as fresh herbs, except they have had the water removed, which concentrates the flavor. After the herbs have been picked, they are tied in bunches and hung in a dry room or placed in a very slow oven to dry. Once dried they are removed from the stem, if necessary, and placed in airtight containers.

PICKLED herbs are fresh herbs which have been stored in brine.

FROZEN herbs may be either directly frozen at between 0-10°F or blanched and then frozen. Those which are blanched first will have a longer shelf life, approximately six months. Those frozen directly have a shelf life of approximately 6-8 weeks in the freezer. Freeze-dried herbs are also available.

These are fresh herbs which have been freeze-dried and then vacuum packed.

CHARACTERISTICS

Savory

Fresh herbs are always preferred over dried herbs because the flavor tends to be more complex and complete. Unlike spices, many herbs can be grown fresh in a garden or window box during warmer months. Dried herbs, which are not stale, deliver a more concentrated flavor. The rule of thumb is: one teaspoon of dried herbs is roughly equivalent to three teaspoons of fresh herbs. A frozen herb has a flavoring power similar to that of fresh.

It should be noted that when working with cold foods, the product should sit at least one hour in the refrigerator after the addition of either herbs or spices to allow for full release and combination of flavors. In the preparation of hot foods, flavoring can be added at the beginning, middle or end of the cooking process. Which is best will be determined by the type of flavoring and type of food.

Most flavorings need heat and time to release their flavor so that they can blend in fully. Fresh herbs take a very short amount of time to release their flavor. These should be added at the end of the cooking process. Ground spices and dry herbs require more time for their flavor to be released and should be added at the middle of the cooking process.

As with spices, herbs are recognized by their traditional culinary application. This application is often related to the cuisine of a particular region, such as basil and oregano in tomato sauces as part of Italian cuisine. But, as stated, herbs can grow fresh all over the globe today. This has caused a revolution of new flavor combinations and trends. "Regional Cuisine" has become very popular, now that many restaurants can truthfully boast of local brook trout, for example, with freshly picked basil and chives. Because fresh herbs are more subtle in flavor than dried, the end result can be much more delicate. Fresh herbs can truly make the difference between a good meal and an outstanding meal.

NUTRITIONAL TIPS

Spices and herbs have very little nutritional value themselves. They do allow us to decrease fat and salt content in products, yet still maintain a good flavor. Reducing fat and salt content can leave food very bland, but spices and herbs bring it back to life. Instead of sauteing a chicken breast in butter with salt, flour, egg wash and breading, a nutritional and flavorful alternative would be to rub the raw breast with fresh rosemary. It can then be poached in a flavorful vegetable stock. Once cooked, the breast could be seasoned with fresh lemon juice and a touch of lemon zest.

STORAGE & HANDLING

To store fresh herbs, it is best to pick them right before they bloom. It is at this point that their flavor is strongest. Each type should be separately wrapped in a slightly damp paper towel, placed in a plastic bag and stored under refrigeration. Fresh herbs are very delicate and should be handled with great care. If fresh herbs begin to turn brown, they can be chopped finely and combined with sufficient oil to keep them moist. This mixture can be stored in a jar in the refrigerator, and will keep well for at least two weeks.

Dried herbs should be dated and stored in airtight containers. Dried herbs should last approximately six months, before they start to lose their flavor. Frozen herbs should also be dated, and they should be stored in sealable heavy plastic bags. Maintaining

a temperature of -10°F or less, is essential to proper holding of any frozen food.

CONCENTRATED FLAVORING AGENTS
TYPES & DEFINITIONS

Flavoring agents are concentrated in one of two ways: Extraction (oleoresins) or distillation (essential oils). Essential oil is a stem distillation of the flavor and aroma compounds in an herb or spice. It has the advantage of being colorless and very concentrated. The disadvantage of essential oils is that they lack some flavor compounds present in the final oil.

Oleoresins are extracts from herbs and spices that are usually subjected to vacuum. In vacuum the extract is concentrated and most or all solvent (such as alcohol) is removed. It is not uncommon to add essential oils to oleoresins to improve the flavor characteristics, since a great amount of flavor is lost from an oleoresin when the solvent is evaporated away.

Cooking oils, such as olive oil, walnut oil, sesame oil, avocado oil and coconut oil, can also be used as flavoring agents. They work well in salads, marinades, salsas, braised meats and dressings, to name just a few applications. Refer to Chapter 7, "Fats & Oils," for more detailed information regarding the use of oils.

WINES
TYPES & DEFINITIONS

Wines have become a staple flavoring ingredient in almost all culinary repertories. Wine is defined as the liquid produced from fermented fruits. The types vary widely in color and flavor, resulting in usages ranging from desserts to sauces to saute.

There are two basic categories of wine: Table wines and fortified wines. TABLE WINES are usually the fermented juice of grapes, although fruits such as elderberry, peach and orange can be used, and even non-fruits like rhubarb and rice.

Red table wines include Claret, Cabernet Sauvignon, Pinot Noir, Burgundy, Merlot, Zinfandel, Concord and various blends.

White table wines include Chablis, Chardonnay, Riesling, Sauternes, Moselle and Graves to name a few.

Champagnes, or sparkling wines, are normally made from white or rose wine in which a second fermentation process is used to create the sparkling characteristics.

FORTIFIED WINES are table wines which have had spirits added during or after fermentation in order to give them their distinct flavor. Varieties of fortified wine include Sherry, Port, Marsala, Madeira, Malaga and California Tokay. Many of these wines are similar in flavor but native to different countries or regions.

CHARACTERISTICS

Wines have unlimited uses in the kitchen. They contribute not only flavor to dishes, but also acidic value, sugar and salt. The alcohol content of the wine contributes little to the flavor of the item, yet is a major consideration for the stability of sauces and dressings. Wines are normally reduced prior to addition to mixture, particularly those containing eggs and dairy products. Reduction of the wine evaporates most of the alcohol and reduces the acid level, leaving the flavor profile intact. The alcohol and acid in raw wine creates a natural heat which can cause coagulation of the proteins in an egg. In these instances the product is in danger of breaking.

Wine reductions are essential for soups and sauces, as well as for braising, deglazing and sauteing. Wines contribute a great deal of flavor to marinades, salads, and salad dressings. In most cooking applications it is not necessary to use the finest quality wine available. An inexpensive grade is more than adequate for most uses. A fine quality wine may be preferred, however, for a very delicate sauce or dessert. The contribution of wines to sorbets, desserts and pastries is major.

NUTRITIONAL TIPS

Wine is high in calories. Ounce for ounce, alcohol has nearly twice the calorie content of table sugar. If consumed in large quantities, wine can be detrimental to one's health. The American Heart Association suggests that no more than one or two glasses be consumed daily. This should be kept in consideration when cooking. Many of today's restaurant customers are very health conscious. However, remember that much of the caloric content is the alcohol and much of this evaporates in reduction.

STORAGE & HANDLING

Wines should be stored away from high heat and direct sunlight. A cool, dark room is best for storage of unopened wine. Reseal wine bottles immediately after use and refrigerate once opened. Wine which has been opened begins to deteriorate immediately and within two to three days the change is very noticeable. Fortified wines, as a result of their higher alcohol content, usually have a longer shelf life than table wines after opening.

VINEGARS
TYPES AND DEFINITIONS

Vinegar is technically a byproduct of fermented wine. The word *vinegar* comes from French meaning "sour wine." Commercially distilled vinegars generally contain around 5 percent acetic acid, which is what gives vinegar its flavor characteristics.

CIDER vinegar is made from apples and is native to America. It should be amber in color and is good for general cooking purposes.

DISTILLED vinegar is colorless and very strong. It is often used in pickling.

MALT vinegar is made from malted

barley and is caramel colored. It is used for pickling; as a seasoning on its own, and is a key ingredient in Worcestershire sauce.

RICE vinegar is inherent to Japan and China. It can be red, white or black in color. It is most notably known for flavoring soups such as "sweet and sour."

WINE vinegar can be derived from red, white, rose wine or sherry. The finest wine vinegars are made in oak vats.

FLAVORED vinegars are vinegars to which herbs, fruits, or spices have been added. These are particularly valued in the production of cold dressing and certain special sauces. Examples of flavored vinegars include rosemary, dill, tarragon, lemon, raspberry, rose petal and horseradish.

CHARACTERISTICS

Vinegar was originally used as a preservative, however, it has become increasingly sought after as an aromatic complement to foods. Wine vinegars work well with herbs, spices and fruits. A good rule of thumb to follow in using vinegars is cider or wine vinegars for general cooking purposes; wine, rice, sherry and herb vinegars for salads, and distilled or malt vinegars for pickling. When flavoring with vinegar be sure to taste your product constantly to avoid overseasoning. In hot foods, add vinegar toward the end of the cooking process, so as not to lose the flavor because of evaporation.

The acidic quality of vinegar can be a plus as well as a minus in cooking. The true culinarian will strive to understand the relationship between both the sweet and the sour flavors of food. A delicate balance of sweet and sour, as with salt and sweet, can be delightful in a dish. The acid of the vinegar increases the potency of the sweet when the balance is just right. However, this is a truly delicate balance which will require a great deal of tasting and testing. Vinegars have great value in the kitchen when used with understanding and caution.

STORAGE AND HANDLING

Vinegars, with the exception of flavored vinegars, do not require refrigeration after opening. They should be stored at a moderate temperature, room temperature, away from direct sunlight. Reseal vinegars after use and minimize introduction of foreign particles to the vinegars. As a vinegar is opened and exposed to air and foreign particles, there is sometimes the formation of what is called the "mother." This is a cloudy mass which will not harm the vinegar, but should be removed before use.

RAW MARINADE FOR GROUPER: INGREDIENTS AND PURPOSE

OLIVE OIL:	PROVIDES A LIQUID BODY
HONEY:	SEASONS SLIGHTLY WITH SWEETNESS AND PROVIDES AN AGENT THAT WILL ENABLE HERBS AND SEASONING TO STICK TO THE FISH BETTER
SALT:	SEASONING AND FLAVOR ENHANCEMENT
BLACK PEPPER:	CRACKED, TO PROVIDE FLAVOR
CAYENNE PEPPER:	FOR A TOUCH OF PEPPERY BITE; JUST A TOUCH
FRESH THYME/FRESH CILANTRO:	PROVIDE AROMATIC FLAVOR
CHOPPED FRESH GARLIC:	PUNGENT FLAVOR

Figure 2

MARINADES
TYPES AND DEFINITIONS

The final flavoring agent is the marinade, a seasoned liquid in which a product is soaked for the purpose of either flavoring, or tenderizing, or both. There are three primary kinds of marinade and three primary types of marinades. The primary kinds of marinade are cooked, raw and instant. The three primary types are oil, acid and flavor.

COOKED marinade is first prepared over heat, then cooled before the product is added.

RAW marinade is a mixture used without being cooked, thereby requiring longer exposure of the product and is used to change the texture of the product. Figure Two describes a raw marinade.

INSTANT marinade is primarily used for flavoring a product and is formulated for a relatively short marination time.

OIL-BASED marinades are used to preserve moisture in a product.

ACID-BASED marinades are used to help tenderize a product. They are normally based on vinegars, wines, lemon juice or other acid type liquids.

FLAVOR marinades are herbs, spices and vegetables. The purpose is to flavor the product by extended exposure.

CHARACTERISTICS

A marinade will be of one of the three kinds mentioned, but may be a combination of all three types, depending on the final product desired. A cooked marinade, because it is heated, allows spices to release their full flavor, resulting in a full flavored final product. Raw marinades are best for marination under refrigeration for longer periods of time. When acid-based, they will result in a tenderizing of the product.

When marinating for longer periods of time it is recommended that oil be used in the marinade to prevent moisture loss. The thicker the product, the longer it will take for the marinade to penetrate. Marinades are particularly helpful in removing the "game" flavor from venison or lamb. There is a great deal of room for experimentation with marinades. Start with smaller quantities, like a single chicken breast, before moving on to a larger item, such as a whole beef loin. An example of a simple raw marinade for brushing on a grouper filet before grilling is given in Figure Two. Included is the purpose for each component.

STORAGE AND HANDLING

A cooked marinade is best stored under refrigeration, and has a very long shelf life. Both raw and instant marinades should also be stored under refrigeration. All marinades should be stored in sealed containers. All marination should be done under refrigeration, unless the product is cooked immediately.

CONCLUSION

Seasoning and flavoring are the cornerstones of culinary excellence. If time is taken to understand the principles and elements, along with the theory and practice, simple dishes can be masterpieces. A sign of inexperience is overseasoning or flavoring. The aspiring culinarian should constantly work various flavor combinations to develop a greater understanding of the interactions. Traditional boundaries have been relaxed in recent years, allowing the taking of a classical dish and adding a subtle twist. In this manner the culinarian develops a personal style. One of the greatest assets of culinary art and science is that it is limited only by the imagination of the practitioner.

REVIEW QUESTIONS

1. Define *seasoning* and *flavoring*.
2. What is the primary seasoning? List the four primary types.
3. Define and discuss *MSG*.
4. What do volatile elements have to do with cooking?
5. What are the advantages and disadvantages of whole spices?
6. What is the difference between an herb and a spice?
7. When should seasonings and flavorings be added to food?
8. Why are fresh herbs considered better?
9. What is the difference between an essential oil and an oleoresin?
10. What role does wine play in the flavoring and seasoning of food?
11. Why must you be cautious when using vinegars?
12. What are the kinds and types of marinades?

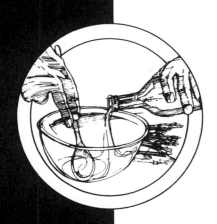

Chapter 6

CHAPTER OBJECTIVES

- **To discuss the importance of proper presentation of food.**

- **To introduce the basic factors involved in presentation.**

- **To discuss and define garnish.**

- **To explain the principles of garnishing foods.**

- **To introduce the guidelines for arranging plates and platters.**

Presentation

How food is presented is almost as important as how it is prepared. Poor presentation of well prepared food lowers its value. Throughout history humankind has adorned and decorated food. Whether this was done to the extreme or in a very simple manner, the intent was to make it more appealing.

Presenting food properly requires a high level of skill, knowledge and imagination. It is far more than placing a sprig of parsley beside the steak or chicken on the plate. The key word in food presentation is balance. It is a balance of color, flavor, texture, size, shape and temperature. The food presented must be appropriate for the occasion. It should be matched to the likes and beliefs of the guest. Presentation must complement the food, not disguise or hide it. Failing to do these things will doom to failure the best of dishes.

BASIC FACTORS
OF PRESENTATION

TEMPERATURE

Good presentation of food means nothing if the food is not at the correct serving temperature. To ensure the quality of hot food, serve it on hot plates and platters. All the food should be at the correct temperature before placement on the plate or platter. Hot food should be covered with warm plate covers, to retain heat. It is vital that hot food be served to the customer immediately.

Cold food is to be served on chilled plates, platters and serving dishes. It should be thoroughly chilled before serving. It should be refrigerated or held on ice, if it is to be held before plating. As with hot food, cold food should be served immediately after plating.

The most basic factor in food presentation is temperature. HOT FOOD SHOULD BE SERVED HOT! COLD FOOD SHOULD BE SERVED COLD! Successful coordination of food temperatures requires good planning and execution. Bearing in mind these primary rules, we can begin to talk about the other factors of presentation.

FLAVOR

A plate of food is intended to be eaten. This means everything on the plate. When the guest begins to eat, they do not eat the meat on the plate first, then the vegetable and then the potato. They take bites of each. At any point, the mouth of the guest contains the flavor of every food presented on the plate. If the combined flavors of these items are not pleasing, then the meal is a failure.

No matter how well each item on a dinner plate is prepared, if the flavors are not complementary, the effect is not pleasing. It is not enough to ensure good preparation. You must also ensure a good, balanced presentation of flavors. Escoffier said that a meal is like a symphony. It begins softly, gradually building to a grand finish. Escoffier knew that it is the melding of the flavors in the mouth, which determines the pleasure of a meal.

To place shrimp in cream sauce on the same plate with sweet and sour cabbage is to create an unpleasant flavor for the guest. As they eat the shrimp with the cream sauce, and then take a bite of the cabbage, an unpleasant taste sensation occurs in the mouth. The acid in the cabbage dish curdles the cream in the shrimp dish as they meld in the mouth. It is this mismatching which should be avoided. Both the shrimp and the cabbage may have been well prepared. Both may have been excellent dishes by themselves. Yet, when served together, the effect is undesirable.

Balancing flavors on the plate will become easier as you become familiar with food. To begin, remember, that normally, rich is served with lean; sweet with spicy, and sweet with sour. Your goal is to produce a pleasing, not overpowering, taste experience for the guest. To make everything on a plate highly seasoned or sweet would be overwhelming for the taste buds. Your mouth needs a somewhat bland or mild item to accompany the highly flavored one.

If the entire symphony was the crash of the cymbal and boom of the timpani, it would only give you a headache. Yet when the smooth, soothing sounds of the clarinet and flute are followed by these in proper balance, it wakes you up. It allows enjoyment of both to their fullest. Food presentation, whether on a plate or as a huge buffet, is the same.

Remember that it is flavor which makes food enjoyable. However, flavor is not always obvious to the eye. To create eye appeal in presentation requires you to think about other things.

COLOR

Although a plate of fried fish, hush puppies and french fries may taste good, it has minimal eye appeal. It is all brown in color and crisp in texture. It offers little variety or excitement for the eye. The simple addition of a scoop of fresh cole slaw on a bright green leaf of lettuce can change this. It improves not only the flavor and mouth feel of the total meal, it also provides color contrast to the eye. It is a bright spot on a stark landscape.

In presenting food, hot or cold, remember that multiple colors are more appealing to the eye. However, too many colors can create the effect of confusion. The colors used in food presentation should be natural. Artificial or non-food colors are never appropriate. Color should not just be put on a plate or platter. It should be derived from something which has a purpose. The sprig of parsley may brighten the plate, but serves no useful purpose.

The use of fruits and vegetables with meat dishes will always improve the color of the presentation, but should be appropriate for the dish. The goal is to create a plate with eye appeal. However, the plate should be empty when the guest finishes eating. Color on the plate should be part of what is to be eaten.

★ NOTE: *It is the color of fruits and vegetables which contribute the most to eye appeal. You must work to protect these natural colors in preparation. It does little good to put green pepper in a dish for color and then cook it until the color is washed out and dull.*

SHAPES

Eye appeal is gained not only through color, but through the shape of the food. As with color, variety is the key. A plate of meatballs, new potatoes, and brussels sprouts may taste good, and have pleasing color, yet it is boring.

Everything is round. Try replacing the brussels sprouts with green beans and the new potatoes with mashed potatoes. You now have not only a variety of colors, but of shapes. The effect is pleasing to the eye.

The possibility of shapes is limited only by your imagination. Be careful though! What you create must be produced for many people. You can carve miniature leaves from zucchini that will look great and add color to the plate. However, do you really want to carve five hundred of them?

There are a great many possible cuts of vegetables and fruits which can be done without huge effort. Make good use of the simple cuts. Use a variety of long thin cuts, rounds, triangles, half rounds, slices, squares and rectangles. These will improve your presentation greatly, without great effort.

Choose foods whose natural shapes complement each other. A poached baby apple with a spiced fruit chutney served with a natural broiled chicken breast and asparagus spears will result in a plate with balanced flavor, color and shape. Little effort is required. The shapes were created by nature.

TEXTURE

Texture in food presentation takes two forms. One is the way food feels in the mouth: Soft, firm, crunchy. The second form is the exterior appearance of an item. Does it look soft and yielding, or hard and unyielding? Is it liquid, solid or in between? Is it dull, shiny, wet or dry? Texture is all of these. If you question the importance of texture in food think about the junk food advertisements on television. We sell potato chips because they crunch. A soda is poured in a stream out of a can, looking cool, wet and appetizing.

As with flavor, color and shape, variety is the key to using texture. Think about how a plate of macaroni and cheese, mashed potatoes, and jello feels in your mouth as you eat it. Most people would say they wanted something they could sink their teeth into. Food presented as a group must be balanced in texture. If it is together on a plate, there should be soft, firm and preferably crunchy food. This will give the balance which satisfies the urge to bite into something.

This can be done by using a variety of preparation methods as well as foods. With a nice crisp fried chicken, a mashed potato is fine. A poached chicken breast would go much better with julienne carrots and snow peas. A variety of textures, both physical and visual, should be present on each plate.

1. Physical
   a. smooth
   b. coarse
   c. solid
2. Visual
   a. pureed
   b. speckled
   c. patchy

GARNISH

Food presentation is often referred to as GARNITURE. This is defined as the process of GARNISH. The term garnish originated from the French term *decorer* which means "to adorn or to furnish." In English the term is more generalized. The term GARNI is also used to mean garnish. History shows that these terms have been used for a variety of preparations and dishes over the centuries.

In classical French kitchens, the terms *garni* and *garniture* had a long history. It was unthinkable to write a classical menu without the classical garniture of each particular dish. The French kitchen had many simple and elaborate garnishes which had developed over the years. Most of these were related to famous diplomats, politicians, historical events and regions of particular agricultural products. Recipes for these dishes required very specific ingredients and knowledge. Examples of these are shown in Figure One.

Many of these classical garnishes are used in today's kitchens. They act as a base for developing new and different presentations. Keeping in mind the basic guidelines for presentation, use the classical garnishes to begin your exploration of garniture.

MODERN PLATE GARNISH

Today the word garnish is widely misused. A sprig of parsley or an orange slice, or even a crabapple on a curly lettuce leaf, is placed on a plate next to a slice of prime rib or fried chicken. Although this adds color to the plate, such garnishes are not functional. They contribute little to the flavor or texture of the dish and are rarely eaten by the guest. Use imagination and thought before applying a garnish.

CLASSICAL GARNITURE

A. TOURNEDO ROSSINI (GARNISH FOR MUSICIAN) GARNISHED WITH GOOSE LIVER, TRUFFLES AND SAUCE MADEIRA.
B. ARGENTEUIL (GARNISH FOR REGION) - GARNISHED WITH ASPARAGUS.
C. BORDELAISE (GARNISH FOR REGION) - GARNISHED WITH BEEF MARROW AND RED WINE SAUCE.
D. DORIA (GARNISH FOR DIPLOMAT) - GARNISHED WITH CUCUMBER.

Figure 1

should be APPROPRIATE TO THE FOOD, FUNCTIONAL and EDIBLE.

Currently, there is a shift to smaller portion sizes with good nutritional balance. Plates are balanced, yet not overcrowded. The plate is best when simple and elegant to the eye.

PLATE & PLATTER ARRANGEMENT

A plate or platter should present a combination of foods working together. It should not be several separate components that happen to be on the same plate. Harmony and unity is a combination which pleases the eye. It is one in which no particular item is overbearing. This does not mean that one item may not be dominant, but that the others present complement it.

Of primary importance is that the

If a plate has the proper balance of the five basic factors, no garnish is necessary. In most cases, refer back to the classical garniture. These provide balance for proper presentation. Where there is poor contrast, such as steak and baked potato, a simple garnish may be needed for balance. However, this

---

PLATE & PLATTER ARRANGEMENT.

1. KEEP FOOD OFF THE RIM OF THE PLATE. THE WELL OF THE PLATE IS WHERE THE FOOD IS MEANT TO BE. IF THERE IS TOO MUCH FOOD FOR THE WELL OF THE PLATE, GET A LARGER PLATE OR REDUCE THE AMOUNT OF FOOD.

2. ARRANGE THE FOOD IN UNITY. THE PLATE SHOULD LOOK LIKE ONE MEAL MADE UP OF SEVERAL ITEMS. DO NOT HAVE THE FOOD SPREAD TO ALL PARTS OF THE PLATE. THE CUSTOMER'S EYE SHOULD FOCUS ON THE CENTER OF THE PLATE, NOT THE EDGE.

3. PLACE FOOD ON THE PLATE IN THE MOST ATTRACTIVE MANNER. FOR EXAMPLE:
   A. THE BEST SIDE OF THE MEAT FORWARD.
   B. THE BACK PART OF DUCK OR CHICKEN HALF SHOULD FACE AWAY FROM THE CUSTOMER.
   C. THE BONE OF A CHOP SHOULD FACE AWAY FROM THE CUSTOMER.

4. SAUCES CAN IMPROVE PLATE PRESENTATION WHEN USED PROPERLY. IN ARRANGING THE PLATE DO THE FOLLOWING:
   A. SERVE SAUCE AROUND OR UNDER FOOD.
   B. PRODUCTS THAT ARE SERVED IN THE SAUCE SHOULD NOT BE DISGUISED OR MASKED BY THE SAUCE.
   C. IF SAUCE IS TO BE PUT ON TOP OF A MEAT OR VEGETABLE, NAP IT WITH A THIN RIBBON FOR COLOR AND SERVE ADDITIONAL SAUCE ON THE SIDE.
   D. BE CAREFUL NOT TO OVERSAUCE. SAUCE IS MEANT TO COMPLEMENT AND ENHANCE THE FLAVOR OF FOOD, NOT HIDE THE FLAVOR.
   E. SAUCES SHOULD BE KEPT LIGHT AND MORE NATURAL, NOT THICK AND PASTY.

5. REFRAIN FROM USING THE SAME PATTERN OVER AND OVER AGAIN. PARTICULARLY FOR BUFFET PRESENTATION, VARIETY IN PLATTER ARRANGEMENT IS AS IMPORTANT AS COLOR VARIATION.

6. GARNISH ONLY WHEN NECESSARY. A GARNISH IS ONLY ADDED TO A PLATE OR PLATTER FOR BALANCE AND MUST BE FUNCTIONAL.

7. SIMPLICITY IS THE KEY. IN FOOD PRESENTATION IT IS MORE ATTRACTIVE TO HAVE A SIMPLE PLATE PRESENTATION RATHER THAN AN OVERWORKED, COMPLEX ONE. ELABORATE DESIGNS OFTEN CAUSE CONFUSION. THEY ARE TIME CONSUMING AND UNPLEASANT TO THE EYE, IF NOT DONE PROPERLY. IT IS SIMPLE, ELEGANT GARNITURE WHICH REQUIRES AND REFLECTS THE HIGHEST LEVEL OF CULINARY SKILL.

Figure 2

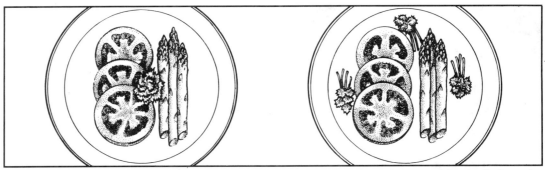

Garnishing with parsley sprigs in the center of the plate pulls this salad together. Placing them around the edge dissipates the attention and creates a busy effect even though it fills out the plate.

portion size match the plate or platter size. It should not be crowded, nor look sparse. The portion size of each item should logically balance with the other. For example, on a meat entree plate it would be wrong for the vegetable portion to be larger than the meat. The central focus of the plate is the meat. The accompanying items should highlight the meat, not overshadow it.

Some simple, basic guidelines for plate arrangement are given in Figure Two. These must be used in concert with the five basic factors already given.

CONCLUSION

Presentation of food requires skill and practice. It is not just a matter of putting the food on a plate or platter and sending it out to the customer. The time and effort spent on preparation can be wasted through sloppy presentation and service. We recommend that you adhere closely to the guidelines presented here.

There is a great deal of opportunity for creativity and originality within them. Experiment, develop, originate your own signature for your dishes. Use the classical garnishes to good effect. And, above all, serve your food in the finest manner possible. Balance is the key and, if achieved, quality is the result. The meals you serve your guests will be symphonies of food and will be long remembered.

REVIEW QUESTIONS

1. Why is proper presentation of food important?
2. List two basic rules for dealing with food temperature in presentation.
3. Discuss flavor as a factor in presentation.
4. What effect does color have on presentation?
5. How is eye appeal affected by shape?
6. What is the importance of texture in presentation?
7. Name three basic guidelines for garnish.
8. Discuss proper plate and platter presentation.

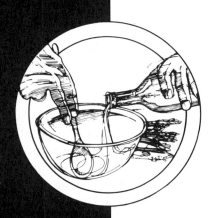

Chapter 7

CHAPTER OBJECTIVES

• **To define fat and oil.**

• **To discuss saturated and unsaturated fats.**

• **To introduce the various types of fats and oils and discuss their extraction.**

• **To discuss the effect of temperature on fats and oils.**

• **To discuss nutritional concerns associated with fats and oils.**

Fats and Oils

The intent of placing fats and oils in a separate chapter in this text is to discuss some of the facts, falsehoods and controversies related to this important part of our food. Many claims relating to health issues are made regarding the various properties of different fats and oils. The attitude of the customer varies according to these claims. It is important to know a few facts about the fats and oils you will be using in the kitchen, as well as the foods you will be preparing that contain some of these. This knowledge is necessary to make wise decisions in satisfying the demands of your customers.

DEFINITION

The difference between fats and oils is that fats are solid at room temperature and oils are liquid at room temperature. Bearing this in mind, and to simplify this discussion, we will refer to both as *fats*.

Chemically, fats are made up of a glycerine molecule and three fatty acids. This is why they are sometimes called a triglyceride or even a tri-acyglycerol. The key to learning about this often puzzling part of our foods is the fatty acids. These are, for the most part, made up of two types of molecules: Carbon and hydrogen. These molecules are joined in specific configurations which determine their type as a fatty acid.

Stated simply, the fatty acid is basically a chain of carbon atoms. Each of these carbon atoms can attach itself to something else in four positions. In Figure One are drawings of stearic and oleic acids in chemical shorthand. In this shorthand, C stands for a carbon atom, H for a hydrogen atom, and O for an oxygen atom. The fatty acid is attached to the glycerine molecule at the OH end of the molecules. This type of bond can be easily broken, allowing free fatty acids to exist in a product. This will be discussed more later in this chapter.

It is important to note that each of these molecules has 18 carbon atoms and each carbon atom is attached to something else in four positions. The stearic acid molecule is said to be saturated because the carbon atoms are attached to as many hydrogen atoms as they can possibly hold onto. The difference between the stearic acid and oleic acid molecule is that there are two hydrogen atoms missing from the oleic acid and there is a double bond (=) between two of the carbon atoms. Oleic acid is said to be monosaturated. A poly-unsaturated fatty acid is one where there is more than one double bond in the fatty acid chain (this is also shown in Figure One) and there are more hydrogen atoms missing at the rate of two per double bond. The degree of saturation of a particular fat molecule with hydrogen will determine the characteristics of that fat.

A fat contains three fatty acids attached at one end to a three-carbon molecule called glycerine (or glycerol). The three acids can be all the same, all different or any mixture in between. When a plant or animal makes the fats it contains, it takes a glycerine molecule and any three fatty acids that it has available in its system and puts them together. Each type of plant or animal only makes certain kinds of fatty acids.

Figure 1

LINOLEIC AND LINOLENIC ARE POLYUNSATURATES AND ARE ESSENTIAL IN THE DIET. (LINOLENIC IS AN OMEGA-3-FATTY ACID.)

These fatty acids are used to make the fats needed for energy storage or other uses. This is important to remember in trying to determine how the oil from a particular plant or animal is, for example, 25 percent saturated fat when you know that there are three fatty acids per triglyceride. This can be seen by comparing the fatty acid chains as shown in Figure One.

The degree of saturation in a fat determines some of its properties and uses in the kitchen. A fat that is high in saturated fatty acids is a solid at room temperature, in other words, a true fat. A fat that is high in unsaturated fatty acids will tend to be liquid at room temperatures, in other words, an oil. This means that you normally tell how saturated a fat is by the temperature at which it solidifies.

Alaskan salmon would be in big trouble if their flesh did not contain high amounts of unsaturated fats because they would solidify in the icy waters in which they live. In fact, the fats in salmon, and many other oily fish, contain long chained fatty acids and have many double bonds. These are Omega-3-fatty acids which have many double bonds. According to some health experts these are beneficial in fighting heart disease. However, other experts disagree.

Tropical fruit, such as bananas, contain some saturated fatty acids and this poses a problem when you freeze them. The fats harden in the cold temperatures and cause cells in the fruit to rupture. This releases enzymes that darken in the fruit. Some deep-sea creatures, like orange roughy, do not contain triglycerides at all. They have two unsaturated fatty acids stuck together end-to-end, which act like a natural antifreeze.

Milk fat is mostly palmitic, oleic and stearic acid, but also contains some very short chained fatty acids, too. This is important in the process of ripening cheese and the souring of milk. The short chained fatty acids are removed from the glycerol backbone at the OH end and, since they are so small, they evaporate easily. This is one of the reasons why a well aged cheese or old milk smells the way it does.

Oils and fats such as olive oil, canola (rapeseed) oil, lard, beef tallow and peanut oil contain high amounts of monounsaturated fatty acids such as oleic. Oils, such as safflower, sunflower, corn, soybean and cottonseed oil contain high amounts of polyunsaturated fatty acids such as linoleic (two double bonds) and linolenic (three double bonds).

Vegetable fats, sometimes referred to as butters or tropical oils, are derived from tropical plants or fruits such as cocoa, coconut and palm. These contain high amounts of saturated fats. These butters are unusual in that at least one of the fatty acids in the triglycerides is unsaturated. This causes all of the fat to melt within a very narrow temperature range. This characteristic is valuable in confectionery work where they can be used to give a very specific mouth feel to a product. For instance, chocolate "melts in your mouth." It does so because, when it reaches body temperature, the chocolate melts, all of it. If you substituted lard for cocoa butter, the chocolate product would melt over a wide range of temperatures, leaving a greasy feel in the mouth.

Figure Two lists a few of the types of fatty acids found in foods. It also tells you how long the fatty acids are and what their importance is. This list is by no means complete, but it may give you an idea of the kinds of fatty acids that are present in our food. The sources listed are merely examples of where you might find some of these acids as triglycerides.

Why does the culinarian study

SOME EXAMPLES OF FATTY ACIDS

NAME	SOURCES	ADDITIONAL INFORMATION	# OF CARBONS	SATURATED
Buteric and Capric	Dairy "	Gives some cheese its own distinctive flavor and aroma.	4 6	Yes "
Lauric	Palm and Coconut		12	Yes
Oleic and Linoleic	Vegetables and oils	Essential in the diet.	18	No
Palmitic and Stearic	Primarily animal fats	Present in great numbers in hard fats.	16 18	Yes Yes
Arachidonic	Marine oils	An Omega-3 fatty acid with four double bonds.	20	No

Figure 2

something which is obviously food chemistry? The answer is that, by knowing a little bit of the chemistry and structure of fats you are using, you will be able to make wiser decisions concerning their use and purchase.

TYPES & EXTRACTION METHODS

The oils and fats used in the kitchen are extracted in some manner from plants or animals. The methods used affect the quality of the product and how it can or should be used in the kitchen.

OIL EXTRACTION METHODS

Oils used for cooking are extracted from fruit (olives); seeds (canola, sunflower); grains (corn); legumes (peanut); nuts (walnut), and many other sources. Extraction and refining processes determine, in part, how the oil can be used. Oils that are pressed from the source will contain other chemical compounds besides oil that will add flavor, aroma and tastes that may or may not be welcome. Further,

since these compounds are present, the oils cannot achieve as high a temperature without burning the impurities or being broken down by these impurities.

Some oils are chemically extracted with solvents like hexane before being further refined. Once the oil has been extracted from the source, the solvent is removed by evaporation, further purifying the oil. The oil is treated first with acids and then with bases to get rid of unwanted compounds that the solvent also extracted. The oil is then bleached to remove soaps and pigments. Finally, it is steam cleaned in a vacuum in order to remove undesirable flavors and odors. The final product is light in color and nearly odorless.

OLIVE OIL

Olive oil is an example of an oil that would be ruined by an extraction procedure that employed chemical solvents. The final product would probably be suitable for deep fat frying, but the flavor, color and aroma so highly prized in this oil would be absent. This is why olives are pressed to remove the oil.

Olive oil is used widely in cooking and has been used since the beginning of written history. The method of processing determines the type of oil produced and, consequently, the flavor and color of the oil. As with all other oils, if the label states that it is olive oil, it must be pure olive oil.

EXTRA VIRGIN OLIVE OIL is from the first cold pressing of the olives. It will be deep green in color and have a definite olive oil flavor and aroma.

VIRGIN OLIVE OIL is from the second cold pressing of the oil or is a mixture of the first and second pressing. It has a lighter color and a milder flavor.

REFINED OLIVE OIL may be a third or fourth pressing of the olives or it may be a heat extracted oil. In either case, it will have inferior qualities, lacking in the flavor, aroma, and color of olives.

Grades for olive oil are A, B and C. These are indicators of the oil's flavor, color and purity. The grading of olive oil is not required and may not be present at the point of purchase.

FAT EXTRACTION METHODS

Fats from meat or poultry used for cooking have traditionally been extracted in the kitchen. This is still true to some extent. Poultry, pork or beef kidney fat (suet) is still sometimes dry rendered in the kitchen. *Dry rendered* means it is heated slowly in a pan until it is melted and then strained. Sometimes fats that rise to the surface in the cooking of stocks or sauces (a type of wet rendering) are reserved for cooking purposes. In either case, this is often the only way to procure these types of fats. Each has unique characteristics in flavor, usage and storage properties.

LARD

Lard is the fat from clean, fresh and sound fatty tissue of hogs in good health. There are three basic types of lard based on where the fat comes from

on the hog. *Leaf lard* is from the fat that surrounds the kidneys. It has the highest degree of saturation (it is the hardest fat on the pig) and is considered to be the highest quality. *Lard* (unspecified) is from fat other than leaf fat. It has a lower degree of saturation. Finally, *pork fat* is the fat from the bones, head, ears, etc. This type is salvaged from parts of the hog that are not generally used for much else. This type cannot be termed *lard*.

Extraction methods used by the food processors in order to supply lard commercially include wet and dry rendering of fatty tissues. *Wet rendering* is where fatty tissues are heated in water or in steam under pressure. Fat is skimmed from the surface; water is removed from the fat, and the lard is deodorized in a manner similar to the deodorization of oils.

Dry rendering is where fatty tissues are heated slowly under a vacuum. The water evaporates quickly at a lower temperature under the vacuum, minimizing fat hydrolysis. The fat is finally filtered off and deodorized. *Low temperature rendering*, an additional form of rendering, uses finely chopped meat tissue that is heated slowly until the fat is liquid. The fat is removed by centrifugal force before being filtered. It is then deodorized.

Lard quality is based on three criteria: Color, texture and flavor. Lard should be a light golden color when melted and not grainy. Harsh flavors or odors are a result of poor processing techniques.

BEEF FAT

Beef fat is processed in a manner similar to that of lard, but it is not its equivalent. As with lard, the highest quality fat is the fat surrounding the kidneys. This is termed *leaf fat* or *true suet*. Beef fat can also be derived from fat deposits elsewhere in the animal. This is termed *carcass fat* and is of secondary quality to suet. *Shop fat* is from the trimmings of the animal, and is the lowest quality fat. These types of fat are processed in the same manner as lard.

Beef fat quality is judged on color, flavor and texture. It should be white to off white when cold and will have a mild flavor if processed correctly.

VEAL KIDNEY FAT

Veal kidney fat is the leaf fat from the veal carcass and is highly prized in many kitchens for its mild flavor. Due to its short supply, this fat will have to be rendered in your own kitchen.

POULTRY FAT

Poultry fats are used in some kitchens because they have a very distinctive flavor and aroma. These fats are not commonly available commercially and will need to be rendered in your own kitchen. Goose or chicken fat is sometimes used in patés to enhance the flavors of the other ingredients. Roux from chicken fat is also common in the making of a velouté to use with chicken or turkey dishes.

WINTERIZED

Fat is sometimes winterized to assure a certain level of saturation. Liquid pork or beef fat is allowed to cool slowly. As the cooling takes place, triglycerides that contain higher numbers of saturated fatty acids will form crystals first. These crystals are removed at certain stages; re-melted and filtered, then deodorized. The first crystals will have most of the double bonds. This means that you can order beef or pork fat with a certain degree of saturation. This fat will have relatively little flavor or odor but will have the advantage of being able to achieve high frying temperatures because of its purity. This procedure is also sometimes used on some oils such as corn oil.

SHORTENING

Shortening is a type of fat that has additives that enhance its usage in baked goods or as a frying fat.

FRYING SHORTENING is hydrogenated vegetable oil or winterized animal fat to which an anti-foaming agent is added (often methyl silicone). It is often a mixture of fats, such as all-vegetable shortening. A shortening may or may not contain antioxidants. These are compounds that lessen the impact of oxygen molecules on those double bonds in the unsaturated fats by acting as oxygen scavengers.

ALL-PURPOSE SHORTENING is a vegetable oil that has been hydrogenated to the point of plasticity so that it can be spread or will cream smoothly when beaten. It, too, may contain antioxidants.

EMULSIFIED OR BAKER'S SHORTENING is also hydrogenated to the point of plasticity but also contains emulsifiers. These allow more liquid and sugar to be incorporated into a baked good. The addition of emulsifiers makes this a bad shortening for frying foods because it will break down faster. However, it is excellent when used for its intended purpose.

A COMPOUND SHORTENING is one which is made from a combination of vegetable and animal fats.

BUTTER

Butter is the finest fat available in terms of flavor, mouth feel and richness. There is nothing that can duplicate it. However, some people actually prefer the taste of margarine. Butter must be at least 80 percent milkfat in order to meet federal laws regulating the product. Normally it is around 81 percent milkfat, 0.1 percent milk solids, 1.5-2.0 percent salt and 16 percent water. Notice that butter is not a pure fat. When replacing it with a shortening in a recipe, the moisture content must be considered.

High quality raw butter will be creamy and without grain. When cooked, it will be pale to deep yellow in color. The flavor of raw butter should be rich and mellow and, when cooked, nutty in flavor. Butter is scored on 100 possible points that include color, flavor, texture, body and salt distribution (if salted). Government grades are AA (score = 93+), A (score = 92), B (score = 90+), and C (score = 89). Butter is available in a number of sizes and in several forms, such as whipped, salted, unsalted, pats, bulk, etc.

MARGARINE

Margarine is used as a substitute for butter in many kitchens, but it is not the same thing. It is a mixture of vegetable oils that is hydrogenated to the point of being plastic in form. It may or may not be mixed with cream to create a butter facsimile. As with butter, margarine must contain no less than 80 percent fat. It must also contain 16,000 IU (international units) of vitamin A per pound. This makes the product similar to butter in vitamin content. Although similar, this product is not butter and truth-in-menu laws demand that, if margarine is substituted, the consumer must be informed.

Margarine should have a straw yellow color and should be free of off aromas and flavors. Because it has less dairy product and therefore fewer short chained free fatty acids present, margarine has a higher smoke point. The smoke point differs from brand to brand. The product should have a texture similar to butter. This will vary depending on the amount of hydrogenation that has taken place and the amount of air that has been whipped into it. Flavor will vary depending on the ingredients used in the product. Consumer acceptance of the product will vary accordingly.

Some consumers have grown up with this product in the home and have come to prefer its flavor. Other consumers eat margarine because they wish to avoid cholesterol. Only the animal fats contain cholesterol, therefore a margarine made from pure vegetable oils will not have any cholesterol in it.

TEMPERATURE AND ITS EFFECT ON FATS AND OILS

As previously stated, heat can destroy fat or oil over a period of time. Since one of the major uses of fats, however, is in the cooking of foods, such as frying, sauteing, etc., it would not be logical to try to keep all of our fats and oils cold and dry all the time. Frying fats are oils or fats of high purity that will hold up to high heat for a reasonable amount of time.

In choosing the right kinds of fat to cook with, there are some facts that you need to keep in mind. Unsaturated fats are more susceptible to oxidation. The more saturated a fat is, the easier it is to oxidize. In other words, the double bonds in the fatty acids are targets for attack by oxygen molecules. This can cause a rancid flavor; possible odor or color changes, and an increase in thickness. Factors that can accelerate rancidity include:

1. OXYGEN.
2 HEAT.
3. LIGHT.
4. METALS SUCH AS COPPER OR IRON.
5. PIGMENTS SUCH AS CHLOROPHYLL (FOUND IN GREEN VEGETABLES) OR MYOGLOBIN (FOUND IN MEAT TISSUE).
6. THE DEGREE OF UNSATURATION.

Many commercially available fats and oils contain a small amount of an antioxidant, like BHA, BHT, or Gallate, in order to offset the problem of rancidity. There are also fats and oils which contain only monounsaturated and saturated fats which are not susceptible to oxidation. Another method of assuring that there is a low number of polyunsaturated fatty acids, and therefore relatively few oxidation targets, is the process of hydrogenation.

Hydrogenation is the process whereby unsaturated fatty acids are made more saturated by artificially adding hydrogen atoms to the fatty acids. The hydrogen is chemically forced onto the carbon chains where there are double bonds present. This accomplishes two things. First, it inhibits oxidative rancidity by reducing the number of targets available for attack. Secondly, it makes the oil solidify at a higher temperature. This is how margarine is made. Oils high in unsaturated fatty acids are hydrogenated until they contain more saturated fatty acids and therefore are solid at room temperature. Partially hydrogenated soybean oil is also an example of hydrogenation.

Another problem is that of fat HYDROLYSIS. This means that a water molecule reacts with the glycerol part of the fat molecule and causes the fatty acid to break off. Eventually this results in the lowering of the *smoke point* of the fat and, subsequently, the *flash point*. These two points are the temperature at which the fat begins to smoke and the point at which fat catches fire, respectively. Hydrolysis can be accelerated by foreign particles or water that come into contact with hot fat.

Combining the two principles of hydrolysis and oxidation together, you can see why it is important to take care of your fat. In order to avoid oxidative rancidity, store your oils in a cool, dark place. Avoid storing or cooking with them in either iron or copper pots. If you use fats to fry, minimize the surface area of the fat by frying in a deep rather than a shallow pot to avoid contact with oxygen.

Fats that are high in mono-unsaturated fatty acids, such as olive oil, are not quite as susceptible to rancidity as polyunsaturates. (Figure Three lists the fatty acid composition of some of the more common fats used for cooking.) Impurities, however, in the olive oil, such as chlorophyll, can react with the oil to turn it rancid. The impurities may also hydrolyze the fatty acid from the glycerol backbone under the right conditions, such as heating.

Figure Four lists some fats and their smoke points for the sake of comparison. This data was compiled by *Consumer Reports* magazine (June,

FAT COMPOSITION

FAT/OIL	% SATURATED	% MONO-UNSATURATED	% POLY-UNSATURATED
Beef Tallow	52	44	4
Butter Fat	66	30	4
Canola Oil	6	58	6
Coconut Oil	92	6	2
CornOil	13	25	62
Cottonseed Oil	27	19	54
Lard	41	47	12
Olive Oil	14	77	9
Palm Oil	51	39	10
Peanut Oil	18	48	34
Safflower Oil	9	13	78
SoybeanOil	15	24	61
Sunflower Oil	11	20	69

Figure 3

FATS AND SMOKE POINTS

FATS	SMOKE POINT (F)
Oils	
Corn	400-450
Peanut	400-425
Safflower	450 +/-
Soybean	425-450
Sunflower	450+/-
Olive	325-400
Shortenings	
All Vegetable	350-450
Vegetable/Animal Mix	390-450

Figure 4

1985) using clean, new oils, and repetitions were averaged. It points out two things. One, the smoke point for a highly refined fat or oil (one that contains almost pure fat or oil) is in excess of 400°F. Secondly, fats or oils that contain pigments; like olive oil and butter, or emulsifiers; like baker's shortening, will have lower smoke points.

Hydrolysis of fats generally occurs when the fat has been heated. This is because a certain amount of energy is needed to break the bond between the glycerol and the fatty acid. While this is not always the case (bacterial enzymes work well in the cold during the ripening of cheese), for the most part hydrolysis requires some heat. Water, in some form, is also necessary.

This is why clarified butter has such a low smoke point. It is nearly impossible to remove all of the water from the butter and there is also the problem of pigments present and some salt. Further, a small amount of acid from the milk has had time to work on the butterfat which may have already freed some of the fatty acids.

Clear butter has a smoke point of around 400°F initially, but hydrolysis proceeds rapidly lowering the smoke point. This means that clear butter may be great for sauteing an escallop of veal where the butter becomes a part of the sauce, but it makes a lousy fat for deep frying. It simply breaks down too quickly. By now, you can see why whole butter is not at all suitable for most types of frying, since it has around 3 percent solids and 11 percent water. The solids will burn at a fairly low temperature and the water will hydrolyze the fats, lowering the smoke point.

PROTECTING YOUR FRYING FATS AND OILS

When frying foods, it is important to take the time to filter your fat at the end of each day, or shift, if possible. This removes water absorbing particles as well as salts that get into your fat during the frying process.

It is important to have the proper amount of breading on a frying item. In addition, the breading should not be too wet. Not enough breading can result in the leakage of water or other foreign substances, including oils, into the frying fat. Some evaporation of water into the oil during frying is unavoidable, but a properly breaded product will minimize this. Meat items, such as bacon or sausage, even though they contain a high amount of fat, should not be deep fat fried without a protective coating. The salts, water and

CALORIES FOUND IN FOOD CONSTITUENTS	
FOOD CONSTITUENT	APPROXIMATE CALORIES/GRAM
PROTEIN	4
CARBOHYDRATES	4
ALCOHOL	7
FAT/OIL	9

Figure 5

myoglobin present in the meat can accelerate the hydrolysis of the fats.

Water, salts, unstable oils and/or breading can start the chain of events that leads to hydrolysis of your fat. Filtering of the fat and care in breading will not make your fat last indefinitely, but it will maximize the shelf life of an expensive cooking medium.

NUTRITIONAL CONCERNS

From a nutritionist's point of view, fats contain more calories per gram than all the other macronutrients. Figure Five lists the caloric values for comparison.

This points out one very good reason to reduce the amount of fat in your diet, especially if you are trying to lose weight. You should not, however, lose sight of the fact that fats are important in the diet for many reasons. First of all, they are a cooking medium allowing for even heat transfer from the heat source to the food. (This is discussed more fully in Chapter 3.) Secondly, they are important in the sensory qualities of the food.

Some flavoring agents, garlic for instance, are more easily dispersed in fats. Some fats themselves have flavor compounds in them and are, in turn, used to flavor other foods. Goose fat, olive oil, unrefined sesame seed oil and bacon grease are just a few of these. Fats also often contribute to what is termed "mouth feel." It is the fat that gives premium ice cream its smooth consistency, *fois gras* its creaminess, and salmon mousse its silky texture. Also, the fat in a dish can be thought of as juiciness, as, for example, in a juicy steak or sausage.

It is neither practical nor possible to eliminate fat from your diet totally, if you are still eating food. All foods contain some fat, with the possible exception of ingredients such as sugar or salt, which are pure chemical compounds. Some fats are important in that they form vitamins in the body. Vitamin E is fat soluble and is found in many whole grains and in wheat germ. Two essential fatty acids (your body does not produce these) are linoleic and linolenic acids. These fatty acids are needed in minute quantities and are found in many types of food, but are extremely important in the diet.

The controversies surrounding the types of fats used in cooking are complex and will not be quickly resolved. The American Heart Association recommends that you limit your fat intake to only 30 percent of your total dietary intake. This advice is being followed as evidenced by the growing popularity of low fat items served in many restaurants.

CHOLESTEROL is not a fat, but is associated with meat and dairy foods which are high in saturated fat. Cholesterol is manufactured by the body using saturated fatty acids as the building blocks. Therefore, many experts feel that saturated fats should be avoided. Some experts believe that cholesterol itself should be minimized in the diet in order to avoid possible heart disease later on. (Other experts say that this is an ineffective method of controlling cholesterol in your body.)

What is generally agreed on by the experts is that the amount of fat consumed in your diet should be lowered to 20 or 30 percent maximum and the amount of fiber eaten should be increased. (Certain types of fiber actually pull cholesterol out of your body.) While fats of all types should be limited, saturated fats are thought of as "evils," because they are associated with foods lower in fiber.

Cholesterol is manufactured by animals (including humans) and is, therefore, found in the fat and flesh of all animals. It is not made by plants and is, therefore, not found in any oils of plant origin. Examples of foods containing cholesterol include butter, meat, poultry, eggs and some fish. Saturated fats that can act as building blocks for cholesterol are found in all foods but are in the highest concentrations in tropical oils, butter and hard margarine, meats and egg yolks.

Monounsaturated fatty acids found in olive and other oils are currently getting a lot of attention. Some studies have demonstrated a link between a low incidence in coronary heart disease with the consumption of oils high in this type fatty acid. Other studies have found that diets high in Omega-3 fatty acids, found in salmon and other fish, also may lower the chance for heart disease. All the studies may be wrong or they may all be right. At this time nothing is clear, because there are too many experts saying different things.

Artificial fats have been developed that the FDA is currently investigating. One, Simplesse, has been approved in certain food categories. The company that developed it, Nutrasweet, has applied for its use in a number of other categories. Simplesse is a protein and therefore contains four calories per gram instead of the nine that a fat would have. It is made from egg whites and milk protein that is chopped up so finely (micro-particulated) that your tongue is fooled into thinking that it is a fat. It is currently being used in some ice creams and bakery goods. Since it is a protein, it cannot be used to fry foods, but it does show promise as a fat substitute.

Another synthetic fat that may or may not be approved by the FDA is called Olestra. This compound is actually a sugar molecule with 6 or more fatty acid chains attached to it. It forms a huge molecule that cannot be absorbed by your intestine and therefore contributes no calories to the diet. Supposedly it can be used to fry foods. The FDA is considering the merits of allowing this fat substitute to be used in the marketplace.

One thing is clear, if your customer wants to eat margarine instead of butter, low fat yogurt instead of double cream, and scrambled egg whites instead of whole eggs, then the customer is right. The customer is always right.

CONCLUSION

As you can see, fats are an important ingredient in the kitchen. The selection of the appropriate fat or oil has an effect not only on the quality of the product, but on many other issues as well. Is it necessary for the culinarian to be extremely familiar with the chemistry of a food to be able to prepare good food? The answer is "No," with qualifications. Because the chemistry of the food does affect the characteristics of the final product in terms of quality (flavor, color, texture) and customer acceptance (quality, value and nutrition combined), culinarians must strive to have at least a minimal understanding of this often ignored facet of our enterprise. This understanding will be gained by staying abreast of the developments in food science, manufacturing, preparation and nutritional application.

REVIEW QUESTIONS

1. Discuss the chemical makeup of fats and oils.
2. What is the difference between saturated, monounsaturated, and polyunsaturated fatty acids? Give an example of each.
3. Discuss what *saturated* and *unsaturated* means.
4. Discuss the extraction methods for oils.
5. Discuss the different types of olive oil.
6. Discuss how lard is extracted and the various types of lard.
7. Discuss how suet is extracted.
8. Define *winterized*.
9. Define *shortening* and discuss the various types of shortening.
10. Discuss the difference between butter and margarine.
11. Define *oxidation* and *hydrolysis* and discuss how they affect fats and oils.
12. Define *smoke point* and *flash point*.
13. Discuss the importance of fat in the kitchen.
14. Discuss the dietary concerns associated with fat in the diet.

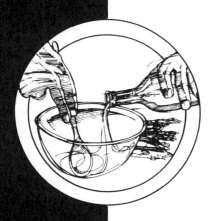

Chapter 8

CHAPTER OBJECTIVES

- **To introduce dairy products as primary and secondary ingredients in culinary preparation.**

- **To discuss the various types of milk available.**

- **To discuss cream and its characteristics.**

- **To discuss fermented and processed milk products used in the kitchen.**

- **To discuss cooking with milk.**

- **To explain the various forms of butter used in culinary preparation.**

- **To discuss the various types of cheeses and cooking with cheese.**

Dairy Products

Dairy products of all types are among the most widely used ingredients in cooking and baking. Whether acting as a primary or secondary component in a dish, they contribute in many ways to the character of the finished product. You need to know the various products available; what they contribute to cooked foods, and how they are best prepared. This chapter will discuss much of this, concentrating heavily on milk, cream and cheese.

MILK

FRESH WHOLE MILK is what the cow gives naturally. To be termed fresh whole milk the most that can be added to it is vitamin D. Nothing can be taken away. It contains a minimum of 3.25 percent butterfat (also termed milk fat), 8.5 percent nonfat milk solids, and 88 percent water. This is one of the many truly wonderful gifts of nature. It is one of the most nutritious and wholesome natural products available. It can be purchased in many forms, all of which are various forms of fresh whole milk after processing.

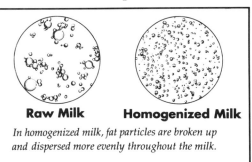

Raw Milk　　**Homogenized Milk**

In homogenized milk, fat particles are broken up and dispersed more evenly throughout the milk.

PASTEURIZATION and HOMOGENIZATION are processes commonly used in milk production. Pasteurized milk has been heated to kill most bacteria present and then cooled. Most commercial milk and cream products are pasteurized. Homogenized milk is forced through a series of extremely small holes. This separates the fat particles into such small pieces they will remain suspended in the milk or cream. The result is milk or cream which does not readily separate. It gives a better cooking and drinking quality. It is common for milk purchased in the United States to be both pasteurized and homogenized.

RAW MILK is sold in some states and has not been pasteurized or homogenized. This type of milk is rarely used in commercial kitchens. Certified milk is also rarely used. Produced by herds of dairy cattle certified to be disease-free and kept under strict sanitary conditions, this milk may be sold either raw or pasteurized.

FORTIFIED MILKS are also common in today's kitchen. Commonly these have vitamins A and/or D and, possibly, extra non-fat milk solids added to them. Other vitamins may be added to the milk, but all additions must be listed on the label.

SKIM/NONFAT MILK has most or all of the fat removed. It contains less than 0.5 percent fat. LOW-FAT MILK contains 0.5-2 percent fat. Skim and low-fat milk cannot be considered an equal to whole milk. The reduction of butterfat content will change the character of the item being prepared. Butterfat gives not only richness of flavor, but body and mouth feel.

FLAVORED MILKS, chocolate for example, have flavoring ingredients and, possibly, sugar added. FLAVORED MILK DRINKS, such as chocolate flavored milk drink, are skim or partially skim milk which have sugar and other ingredients added. These types of milks are rarely used for cooking. When they are used to replace whole milk, you must consider the reduced butterfat content, increased sugar content and, in the case of milk drinks, any other additives. These are best suited for drinking.

CREAM

Cream is a form of milk. The fat globules are more concentrated in it than in whole milk. Cream provides a richness and body in items prepared with it that is not readily available otherwise. It is not uncommon in institutional cooking to use whole milk in place of cream. When this is done there must be the addition of a thickening agent to replace the body that the cream would have given the dish. A thickening agent will help replace the texture, but cannot normally replace the rich flavor. Cream is less likely to form a skin when heated or boiled and is far more stable than milk in cooked sauces and soups.

Cream is available in three market grades. The name of each indicates its butterfat content. The replacement of one fat with another must be based on understanding this content. To replace heavy cream with half and half would

BUTTERFAT CONTENT OF CREAM

MARKET GRADE	BUTTERFAT CONTENT
HEAVY WHIPPING CREAM	36-40% BUTTERFAT.
LIGHT WHIPPING CREAM	30-36% BUTTERFAT.
LIGHT CREAM	18-30% BUTTERFAT.
HALF AND HALF	A COMPOSITE OF MILK AND CREAM. IT MUST CONTAIN AT LEAST 10.5% BUTTERFAT.

Figure 1

greatly change the character of the dish being prepared. Figure one shows the butterfat content of the various grades of cream.

Cream is often whipped and used as a topping for dishes or as an ingredient for dishes. Whipping creams develop a stable foam when whipped. Their butterfat content creates a supporting structure, encapsulating air and holding it. While it is possible to whip lighter creams and even skim milk, they will have very little stability. If a whipped milk product which will hold and stand is needed, whipping cream should be used.

To properly whip cream and gain as much stability as possible follow the guidelines listed below.

1) THE EQUIPMENT AND CREAM SHOULD BE AS COLD AS POSSIBLE.

2) OFTEN SUGAR IS ADDED TO WHIPPED CREAM TO INCREASE THE SWEETNESS. THIS SHOULD NOT BE DONE UNTIL IT IS WHIPPED, OTHERWISE IT WILL DECREASE THE STABILITY OF THE FINISHED PRODUCT. POWDERED SUGAR IS PRE-FERRED, BECAUSE IT HAS A LESS NEG-ATIVE EFFECT ON THE STABILITY.

3) DO NOT OVERWHIP THE CREAM. STOP WHEN STIFF PEAKS FORM. IF WHIPPED TOO LONG IT BECOMES GRANULAR AND THEN TURNS TO BUTTER.

FERMENTED MILK PRODUCTS

Cooking uses a variety of milk products produced from fermented or soured milk. These add a stronger, more pronounced, flavor to dishes. They also add acid to the dish. This acid, when used properly, is beneficial to many preparations. In later chapters these products will be mentioned frequently and their properties discussed in relation to various preparations.

SOUR CREAM is one of the most commonly used of these products. It has been cultured (Bacteria has been intentionally added in order to ferment the product.) or fermented by the addition of lactic acid bacteria to cream. The bacteria grows in the cream and makes acid as a byproduct, giving the cream a tangy flavor and thick texture. Sour cream has about 18 percent butterfat content. It is used widely in cooking and baking.

BUTTERMILK is fresh liquid milk (whole, low-fat, or 1 percent) cultured by the addition of bacteria. It has a rich, thick texture, and a tangy acid taste. It is often used with baking powder to create leavening in baked goods. Buttermilk can be used in recipes calling for soured milk.

YOGURT is milk cultured with a special bacteria. The result is a milk product which has a custard-type texture. Sometimes additional milk solids or flavorings, fruits or sweetners are added. Yogurt has long been associated with Middle Eastern cookery. However, it is becoming more widely used in the kitchen today.

PROCESSED MILK PRODUCTS

Milk is available in forms other than those which must be kept refrigerated. The ones most commonly used in the kitchen are those from which all or part of the water has been removed. EVAPORATED MILK can be made from whole or skim milk and contains a minimum of 7.5 percent butterfat. It has 60 percent of the water removed. Evaporated milk is sterilized by exposure to high heat and canned. The product has a somewhat cooked flavor. It is used in baking and some other recipes.

CONDENSED MILK is made from whole milk with 60 percent of the water removed. The reduced milk is heavily sweetened with sugar and must contain a minimum of 8.5 percent butterfat. It is available canned or in bulk quantities. Condensed milk cannot replace other milk products unless the sugar content of the recipe is adjusted.

Dried milks have all moisture removed, creating a powder. They are available as either dried whole milk made from whole milk, or dried non-fat milk made from skim milk. The original type of dried milk is called REGULAR. It is not easily dissolved, making it difficult to use. INSTANT dried milk dissolves more easily and is commonly used in the kitchen. These types of milk are often called for in baking formulas. Non-fat dry milk is also termed NONFAT DRY MILK SOLIDS in many recipes.

COOKING WITH MILK & CREAM PRODUCTS

In cooking, milk and cream products are preferred to some vegetable oil and animal fat products because of their flavor and richness. However, they require care in preparation to ensure a quality end product.

CURDLING is a problem when using these products. Milk curdles when milk proteins solidify and separate from the whey. WHEY is the mixture of water, salt and other solids present in the milk. If you have left a glass of milk setting out overnight and have seen the clotted, unappetizing milk the next day, you know what curdling is. The goal of the cook is to prevent this from happening in the preparation of a dish containing milk.

The enemies of milk in normal cooking are acids, salt and heat. When cooking food, we commonly expose it to all three of these at the same time. Protecting milk products from these requires a certain amount of caution and

---

PREVENTING CURDLING

1. AVOID COMBINING MILK OR CREAM WITH STRONG ACIDS, UNLESS STARCH IS PRESENT. WHEN MILK IS STABILIZED WITH A STARCH, SUCH AS FLOUR IN ROUX OR WAXY MAIZE, IT HELPS TO STABILIZE AND PROTECT THE MILK PROTEINS FROM SEPARATING.
2. REMEMBER THAT HEAT IS A NATURAL ENEMY OF MILK. REDUCING HEAT AND COOKING TIMES, WHEN POSSIBLE, CAN HELP TO PREVENT CURDLING.
3. TEMPER MILK AND CREAM BEFORE ADDING TO A HOT LIQUID. TEMPER MEANS TO EQUALIZE THE TEMPERATURE OF AN ITEM. THIS IS DONE BY ADDING SMALL AMOUNTS OF HOT LIQUID TO A COLD ONE, STIRRING VIGOROUSLY. WHEN THE COLD LIQUID BECOMES WARM IT IS THEN ADDED BACK TO THE REMAINING HOT LIQUID.
4. MILK SCORCHES EASILY. IT IS BEST HEATED IN A DOUBLE BOILER OR STEAM KETTLE, NOT ON DIRECT HEAT. THE SCORCHING PROBLEM IS CAUSED BY THE PROTEINS, NATURAL SUGARS AND THICKNESS OF THE MILK. THIS PRECAUTION SHOULD BE TAKEN WITH ANY THICK PRODUCT. THE POSSIBILITY OF SCORCHING IS NOT LESSENED AFTER STARCH IS ADDED.
5. RECONSTITUTED DRY MILK WILL CURDLE QUICKER THAN FRESH MILK. EXTREME CAUTION IS NEEDED WHEN USING IT.
6. HEATED MILK SAUCES WILL FORM A SCUM ON TOP IF LEFT EXPOSED TO AIR. THIS CAN BE PREVENTED BY COVERING THEM WITH A THIN COATING OF MELTED BUTTER.

Figure 2

planning. Figure Two lists basic guidelines for preventing curdling when cooking with milk and milk products.

BUTTER

Butter is discussed in more than one place in this text. It is both a dairy product and a fat by definition. Butter is composed of 80 percent butterfat, in some types slightly higher, and the remainder is milk solids and water. Valued as a flavoring agent and lubricant for culinary preparations, butter gives a richness and flavor to foods which is difficult to duplicate. It is one of the most widely used fats in the kitchen. Chapter 6 discussed grades and composition of butter in detail, as well as nutritional aspects.

Most butter on the market is lightly salted. However, SWEET OR UNSALTED BUTTER is also available. It is more perishable than salted butter, yet has a fresh, sweeter taste. Butter is purchased commercially in one of three forms.

1. PATTIES ARE INDIVIDUAL SERVINGS WHICH VARY FROM 48 TO 96 PER POUND. THE PURCHASER SPECIFIES SIZES NEEDED.

2. PRINTS ARE BUTTER PACKAGED IN ONE POUND BLOCKS. THEY CAN EITHER BE FOUR QUARTER-POUND PIECES PACKED TOGETHER, OR ONE 1 POUND BLOCK. THESE ARE USED IN KITCHENS WHICH NEED BUTTER IN SMALLER AMOUNTS OR HAVE IT DISTRIBUTED AT A VARIETY OF DIFFERENT STATIONS.

3. TUBS OR BULK BUTTER ARE USUALLY 40-64 POUNDS IN WEIGHT. THESE ARE GOOD IN LARGE KITCHENS, WHERE BUTTER IS RAPIDLY USED IN LARGE QUANTITIES.

Some foodservice operations also use WHIPPED BUTTER. This is butter which has been expanded in volume by the incorporation of air and sometimes gelatin. It has a softer consistency and improved spreadability. Although it has certain uses, remember that you are paying for air.

CLARIFIED BUTTER, butter from which the milk solids have been removed, is widely used in cooking. Frying or making roux with whole butter is not recommended. The solids in the butter burn far too easily when frying. The water incorporated into a roux made with whole butter can cause separation in sauces.

All butters should be stored tightly wrapped or covered and refrigerated. The flavor of butter is delicate and readily absorbs other flavors. Butter will turn rancid when stored at room temperature. The best temperature for storage is 35^0F or below.

CHEESE

Cheese is a food produced by separating milk solids from whey by curdling, causing the proteins to coagulate. This is done by the introduction of selected bacteria or RENNET, an enzyme, into the milk. The curds are then drained, processed and cured or aged in a variety of ways. The large variety of cheeses result from various processing techniques and the type of milk used. There are over 300 types of cheese known in the world. The type of cheese is determined by five factors listed below.

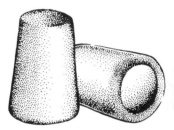

Sap Sago

1. TYPE OF MILK USED (COW, GOAT OR SHEEP'S MILK).

2. METHOD OF CURDLING AND TEMPERA-TURE DURING THE CURDLING PROCESS.

3. HOW CURDS ARE CUT AND DRAINED.

4. THE WAY THE CURDS ARE HEATED, PRESSED OR HANDLED.

5. CONDITIONS OF RIPENING.

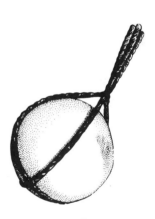

Provolone

Cheese is composed of three major components: Water, fat and protein. The protein in cheese is derived from the milk solids. All cheeses are high in protein. Water content of cheese will vary with the type. A fresh, soft cheese, such as cottage cheese, has 80% water. This is at the top range of water content. A very hard, aged cheese, such as parmesan, is at the low end with 30 percent water.

Fat content of cheese will vary with the type of milk used. Double creme cheese has at least 60 percent fat and triple creme has at least 75 percent. These are the richest cheeses.

The flavor and texture of a cheese is not only dependent on its composition, but also on how it is ripened. Ripening is the process of converting freshly made curds into distinctive, flavorful varieties. Flavors are developed by the introduction of certain molds or bacteria during processing.

Cheeses are classified according to the ripening agent used and whether it ripens from the inside or the outside.

1. CHEDDAR, SWISS, GOUDA, AND PARMESAN ARE <u>BACTERIA</u>-<u>RIPENED</u> <u>FROM</u> <u>THE</u> <u>INSIDE.</u>

2. LIMBURGER AND LEIDERKRANZ ARE <u>BACTERIA</u>-<u>RIPENED</u> <u>FROM</u> <u>THE</u> <u>OUTSIDE.</u>

3. BLEU CHEESE, INCLUDING ROQUEFORT AND STILTON ARE <u>MOLD</u>-<u>RIPENED</u> <u>FROM</u> <u>THE</u> <u>INSIDE</u>

4. BRIE, CAMEMBERT AND ST. ANDRE ARE <u>MOLD</u>-<u>RIPENED</u> <u>FROM</u> <u>THE</u> <u>OUTSIDE.</u>

5. COTTAGE CHEESE AND BAKER'S CHEESE ARE <u>UNRIPENED.</u>

TYPES OF CHEESE

With the wide variety of cheeses it is not possible to discuss each one. However, cheeses are divided into large groupings. We will discuss the characteristics of the cheese in these groupings.

UNRIPENED CHEESES are soft, white, freshly made cheeses. These include cottage, baker's, ricotta, cream, neufchatel and mozzarella.

SEMI-SOFT CHEESES are more developed than unripened, but still have a generally buttery texture. These include fontina, bel paise, munster and brick.

SOFT-RIPENED CHEESES are ripened from the outside toward the center. When young, they are firm and compact, with little flavor. As they mature they soften, and when fully ripe, may be runny. These include brie, camembert, leiderkranz and both double and triple creme cheese.

HARD-RIPENED CHEESES are cured cheeses which have a firm texture. They have varying degrees of mildness or sharpness of flavor, depending on their age. These include cheddar, colby, monterey jack, domestic swiss, gruyere and jarlsburg cheese.

BLUE VEINED CHEESES owe their flavor and appearance to the blue and green mold which is variegated throughout the cheese. These cheeses include rouquefort, stilton, gorgonzola and blue.

HARD GRATING CHEESES owe their flavor to a long aging period, as high as two years. These cheeses include parmesan and romano, which are often sold already grated.

GOAT CHEESES are made from goats' milk and produced in a variety of forms in France called *chevre*. Fresh, unaged chevre is the most popular, having a mild flavor, and very white color, with a dry texture. This cheese has a distinctively peppery flavor, which is slightly acidic. The most widely available French chevre is montrachet.

PROCESSED CHEESE

Processed cheeses are manufactured by grinding one or more natural cheeses. The ground cheese is then heated and blended with emulsifiers and other ingredients. The mixture is poured into molds to solidify. Processed cheese is a uniform product that does not age or ripen like natural cheese. It has a mild flavor and gummy texture. The benefit of processed cheese is its good holding and melting quality and its low price. It is often used in cooking. There three basic types of processed cheese.

AMERICAN CHEESE usually refers to processed cheese made from cheddar. This is very popular for sandwich making.

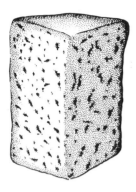

Blue Cheese is mold-ripened from the inside.

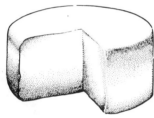

Ricotta is an unripened cheese.

PROCESSED CHEESE SPREAD and FOOD contain a lower percentage of cheese. The bulk is replaced by moisture, such as milk or water. This product contains a higher level of moisture than is allowed in a product labeled processed cheese.

COLD PACK or CLUB CHEESE is not heated and pasteurized like processed cheese. It is simply ground and mixed with flavoring and seasonings to a spreadable consistency.

COOKING WITH CHEESE

The flavors derived from the use of various cheeses in cooking can be great. However, it is necessary to handle them carefully. As with milk, cheese can be ruined by heat.

1. USE LOW HEAT. CHEESE IS HIGH IN PROTEIN WHICH BECOMES TOUGH AND STRINGY WHEN EXPOSED TO EXCESSIVE HEAT.
2. SAUCES CONTAINING CHEESE SHOULD NOT BE BOILED.
3. GRATE CHEESE FOR FASTER AND MORE EVEN MELTING.
4. AGED CHEESES MELT AND BLEND INTO FOODS MORE EASILY THAN YOUNG CHEESES.
5. AGED CHEESE ADDS MORE FLAVOR TO FOODS THAN YOUNG, MILD CHEESE, SO LESS IS NEEDED.

Cheddar, Swiss and parmesan are the three varieties of cheeses used most widely in cooking. Cheddar is most frequently used in the United States. It is used especially in sauces, melted onto foods or for gratinee. Swiss is used more often in European-type dishes. These include mornay sauce, souffles and quiche. Parmesan is used as a grated topping for prepared foods and as a seasoning or flavoring in dishes.

When properly exposed to heat, wondrous changes take place in many cheeses. The flavor of a brie becomes even more mild and the texture creamier. The feta becomes sweet and moist. The flavor of the cheddar becomes mild yet distinct. Experiment to find the balance of heat needed for the cheese you have chosen to use and watch your guests enjoy the results.

STORAGE & SERVICE

The holding qualities of cheese vary widely. In general, the firmer, more aged the cheese, the longer it will keep. For example, a cottage cheese must be used in a week. A parmesan may keep for a year or longer. Soft-ripened cheese, such as camembert and brie deteriorate rapidly once they have fully ripened. In general, store cheese under refrigeration. Oxygen is an enemy of cheese. It will change drastically once it is cut. Cheeses will also dry out rapidly when exposed to the air. Wrap cheese tightly with heavy plastic wrap for storage.

Serve cheese, except unripened cheeses, at room temperature. Only at room temperature do the flavors fully develop. Cheese should be cut just prior to service to prevent drying and flavor loss.

Cheddar　　　　**Swiss**

Cheddar and Swiss Cheese are bacteria-ripened from the inside.

REVIEW QUESTIONS

1. List and discuss the types of milk used in cooking.
2. Discuss the different types of cream.
3. Define *sour cream, buttermilk* and *yogurt.*
4. Discuss the difference between evaporated and condensed milk.
5. List five guidelines for preventing curdling in milk.
6. Discuss the differences between whipped butter and clarified butter.
7. Discuss what determines a type of cheese.
8. Discuss cooking with cheese.

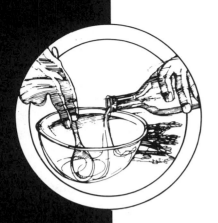

Chapter 9

CHAPTER OBJECTIVES

- **To introduce the egg as an ingredient.**
- **To discuss the composition of the egg.**
- **To explain the various government egg grades.**
- **To discuss quality factors associated with purchasing eggs.**
- **To introduce the various available forms of eggs.**
- **To discuss the preparation characteristics of eggs.**
- **To introduce the nutritional value of the egg.**

Eggs

Certain foods play a major role in cooking. One of these is the egg. It can be served as a main dish, as an accompaniment to other dishes or as an ingredient in an item. Due to its versatility, the egg is considered a primary ingredient in culinary preparation, providing moisture, structure and richness in dishes. It is also an emulsifier and aerator when properly handled and used. It is important that you, the future culinarian, become familiar with this important food source.

In cooking, the term EGG refers to the oval, thin shelled ovum of a bird, used as food. There are many types of eggs, such as goose, duck and turkey. In this chapter we are most concerned with those of the domesticated fowl called a chicken. The other types can be and sometimes are, used in the modern kitchen, but the chicken egg is most common. Recipes calling for egg are referring to chicken eggs, unless another type is named. The term egg in this chapter will mean the egg of a chicken.

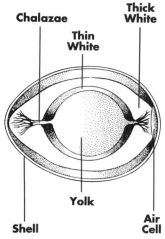

Chalazae
Thin White
Thick White
Yolk
Shell
Air Cell

COMPOSITION

A whole egg is made up of a yolk, white and shell. A membrane lines the shell and forms an air cell at the large end of the egg. Mother Nature has worked very hard to create the right package for the contents of the egg. The yolk is held centered in the egg by the CHALAZAE. These are the two white strands which are present when an egg is broken.

The SHELL, or outer covering of the egg, may be white or brown. Shell color has no effect on the quality, cooking properties or nutritive value of the egg. Color of the shell is determined by the breed of chicken.

Composed primarily of calcium carbonate, the shell is very fragile. It is porous, which allows it to breathe. The porous nature of the shell allows loss of moisture even if unbroken.

The WHITE is the food and moisture source for the embryo in a fertilized egg. It accounts for 67 percent of the liquid weight of the egg. Egg white is made up of two parts. A thick white surrounds the yolk. A thinner, more liquid part is between the membrane and the thicker white. Albumin protein is the major component of the white. It also contains sulphur.

The white is clear and soluble when raw. It is white and firm when coagulated. Albumin in the egg white is valued by the cook and baker for its ability to hold air when beaten. Beaten egg whites provide light fluffy texture for souffles, chiffon pies, angel food cakes and other food items.

The YOLK is the unfertilized embryo in the egg. Yellow in color, the depth of color will vary with the feed of the hen. The yolk is high in fat and protein, and contains iron. A large yolk has approximately 59 calories. The yolk is valued for the richness and texture which it provides in both cooking and baking.

CRITERIA FOR SELECTION

Selection of eggs is both simple and complicated. It is complicated by the many factors affecting the quality of an egg. It is simplified by the standards established by the United States Department of Agriculture (USDA). When purchasing from an approved and inspected supplier, it is possible to depend on the USDA grades for quality and size. Your decision becomes one of what size and quality of egg do you need?

BUOYANCY TEST FOR FRESHNESS
(Place the egg in water)

An egg newly laid is heavy.
It sinks and lies flat.

As the egg ages, an air pocket expands and adds buoyancy.
A week-old egg begins to rise.

A three week-old egg stands upright as the air pocket expands further.

(The spread test for freshness is on page 91.)

GRADING EGGS

The grading of eggs is based on a number of factors. There are three grades of eggs which the cook and baker are concerned with: AA, A and B. Age and handling of the egg are the primary determinants of quality. As an egg ages, the white becomes thin and the air cell between the membrane and the shell enlarges. The yolk membrane becomes thinner as the egg ages. This results in a yolk which spreads more and will break more easily. The yolk will be off center in the white and flat instead of tall and rounded. Figure One shows the difference in the appearance of the various eggs.

Appearance is not the only thing affected as the egg ages. When the white thins the albumin protein has lost part of its ability to build and maintain structure. It will not develop as great a volume when beaten. The stability of the beaten white will be less. The thickening and emulsifying power of the yolk is also reduced.

Grade AA eggs, when broken, have only a small amount of spread and the yolk will be in the center of the white. The white is thick and stands high. The chalazae is prominent in the white. The yolk is firm, round and high. These eggs are the best. They are suitable for any type of use. They are definitely preferred for poaching, frying and cooking in the shell.

Grade A eggs, when broken, have a moderate amount of spread. The white is reasonably thick and stands fairly high. The chalazae are prominent in the white. The yolk is firm and stands fairly high. This is the most commonly used grade of egg. It is suitable for all types of use.

Grade B, when broken, spread greatly, having only a small amount of thick white. The white, in general, appears weak and watery. The chalazae are small or completely absent. The yolk is flat and broad. These eggs are normally purchased already broken in a variety of forms. They are suitable for scrambling or baking and as an ingredient with other foods. Grade B eggs should be used only when the appearance of the whole egg is not important. They are not suitable for use when the egg is to provide a high level of structure in an item.

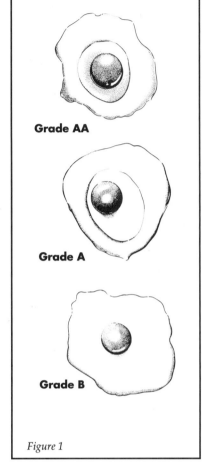

Grade AA

Grade A

Grade B

Figure 1

EGG SIZES

CLASSIFICATION	MINIMUM WEIGHT PER DOZEN
JUMBO	30 OZ.
EXTRA LARGE	27 OZ.
LARGE	24 OZ.
MEDIUM	21 OZ.
SMALL	18 OZ.
PEE WEE	15 OZ.

Figure 2

SIZING EGGS

Although eggs are graded for quality, this does not address the issue of size. The grade of an egg does not relate to the size of the egg. Eggs are classified as JUMBO, EXTRA LARGE, LARGE, MEDIUM, SMALL and PEE WEE. These names indicate the minimum weight per dozen for each of the sizes. In cooking and baking, this becomes important. Replacement of a jumbo egg with a pee wee egg will cause problems in the item being made. The amount of moisture has been reduced by half. The reverse would cause similar problems. Refer to Figure Two for the weight of the various sizes.

The most commonly used size in commercial and home cookery is large. The jumbo and extra large are sometimes used for breakfast eggs, poaching or frying. This size may also be preferred for scrambled eggs if the price is comparable to large eggs. Medium, small and pee wee eggs are rarely used in commercial cooking. They simply increase handling and can create problems in recipe production. Large eggs are the standard for recipes calling for a set number of eggs. If a larger or smaller egg is needed it will be stated.

SHELL QUALITY

The shape and surface quality of the shell is considered when eggs are graded. A grade AA or A egg has a shell which is oval in shape. It should be free of feces, and generally clean. Rough spots which do not effect the shell strength are permitted. The shell of all eggs must be unbroken when shipped and received.

PURCHASING FACTORS

Purchase only the quantity of eggs needed for one or, at most, two weeks. Accept only eggs which are clean, sound and odor free. There are various methods of preserving eggs, such as oiling, wrapping and refrigeration. However, the preferred method is refrigeration. Exposure to temperatures above 55°F shortens the life of the egg. Higher temperatures hasten breakdown of egg white and yolk. You should accept only eggs delivered under refrigeration.

Fresh eggs should be properly boxed. The best packaging for the commercial kitchen is fiberboard boxes. Eggs should be packed in the carton in snug-fitting trays. This will reduce the breakage. Polyurethane-urethane cartons are common in the supermarket. However, they are an unnecessary expense and a handling problem for commercial kitchens.

Check the grade of eggs delivered to you. The carton should be clearly marked with the grade and size. It is advisable to break a few eggs at random to see if they meet the specifications for the grade ordered. This will also help to determine if they have been properly handled by the supplier.

MARKET FORMS

Eggs are currently available in a number of forms. Which form you choose will depend on the intended use of the egg. It is common for a large kitchen to have a wide variety of types available at all times. The convenience forms may not be suitable for breakfast cookery, yet can save a great deal of labor in other types of cooking and baking.

FRESH OR SHELL EGGS

This is the preferred form for most breakfast cookery. In many kitchens fresh eggs are used for all production. Although the fresh flavor is very desirable, for many types of preparation they create extra labor through handling. They also require more storage space.

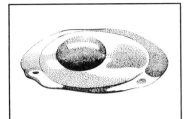

NEWLY LAID:
• Yolk compact
• Dense white
• Slight fluid outer layer

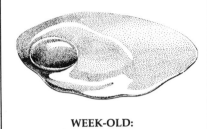

WEEK-OLD:
• Yolk moves off center
• White loosens and becomes more fluid

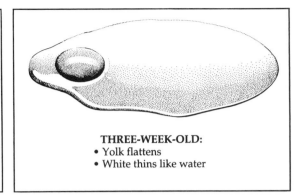

THREE-WEEK-OLD:
• Yolk flattens
• White thins like water

FROZEN EGGS

Frozen eggs are of high quality and available in a number of forms. They are pasteurized in processing, reducing concerns about bacterial growth. Available as whole eggs, yolks, whites or whole eggs with extra yolks added, they can be purchased in 30# cans or 5# cartons. These should be thawed under refrigeration, which requires 2 days. Frozen eggs are excellent for many types of baking; scrambling; omelettes, and use in other types of cooking requiring broken eggs. Normally these are grade A eggs. However, you should check with your supplier.

DRIED EGGS

These are available as whole eggs, yolks or whites. They are used primarily for baking. Dried eggs are not recommended for breakfast cookery. This dried product is not shelf stable. Store refrigerated or frozen, and tightly sealed.

SPECIALTY EGG PRODUCTS

The variety of specialty egg products is rapidly expanding. A few of the specialized products available include whole eggs with extra yolks, whole eggs with corn syrup and sugared egg yolks. All of these come frozen and are used primarily in the bakery. Also available are frozen salted egg yolks and hard cooked egg yolks. Whole, peeled, hard boiled eggs are available in five gallon pails, refrigerated.

PREPARATION

The primary purpose of exposing eggs to heat is the coagulation of the proteins. The cook and baker who understand when this occurs will be able to produce a superior product.

1) **WHOLE EGGS AFTER BEING BEATEN WILL COAGULATE AT 156°F (68°C).**

2) **WHITES WILL COAGULATE AT BETWEEN 140°F (THIN WHITE) - 152°F (THICK WHITE) (60-66°C).**

3) **YOLKS COAGULATE AT 144-160°F (62-70°C).**

4) **WHOLE EGGS COMBINED WITH LIQUID, SUCH AS IN CUSTARD, COAGULATION OCCURS AT 175-185°F (79-85°C).**

Exposure of an egg to higher temperatures than those necessary to coagulate the proteins may achieve a more suitable serving and eating temperature. However, it toughens the cooked egg. Extended exposure to heat can result in discoloration and off flavors. When cooking eggs, avoid high temperatures and long cooking times.

A common occurrence in eggs which are cooked and held for long periods of time is development of a green color. This is particularly common in scrambled eggs held in hot tables. This is a result of the iron in the egg yolk reacting with the sulphur in the egg white. Iron sulfide is formed causing the discoloration.

Egg whites are often beaten before being used. The purpose is to create a light, airy mass which will lighten the item it is part of. This requires proper handling to achieve the final goal. All egg yolk, which is high in fat, must be removed prior to beating. Contact with any fat should be avoided before and during beating. All equipment must be clean and fat-free. It is recommended that equipment be wiped with a towel slightly dampened with acid, such as lemon juice or vinegar, prior to beating egg whites.

Egg whites foam better at room temperature. Remove them from the refrigerator one hour before beating. The addition of a mild acid, such as lemon juice or cream of tartar, can increase the foaming of the egg whites, improving the volume. The normal proportion to add is two teaspoons of cream of tartar per pound of egg whites.

It is important that you not overbeat the whites. They will lose their lifting ability and will look dry and curdled. A properly beaten white will look moist and shiny.

STORAGE AND HANDLING

Protection of the egg is of great importance. When improperly handled, its properties as an ingredient and independent food item are impaired. Remember that eggs lose quality quickly at room temperature. They should always be stored at 36° to 40°F.

Eggs have porous shells, which allow air to enter the shell. They should be stored away from foods that may pass on undesirable odors. Eggs are best stored in the case to prevent moisture loss. Eggs should only be frozen out of the shell and when not needed immediately.

NUTRITION TIPS

Nutritionally eggs are important. They contain vitamins A, D, E, K and B-complex. They are high in iron and one egg equals one ounce of lean meat, fish or poultry. One large egg provides 15% of the USDA recommended daily allowance for protein. Eggs are low in saturated fat and one large egg is approximately 80 calories. The major concern with eggs is cholesterol. One large egg averages 213 mg. of cholesterol. For many people with various health problems, cholesterol is restricted as part of their diet. Although there is no effort to stop cooking with eggs, there is a need to find ways to reduce the cholesterol content of prepared foods. One of the ways is to use egg whites instead of whole eggs, since the cholesterol is in the yolk. This requires consideration of the effects that the yolk had on the item, but will prove to be worth the effort.

CONCLUSION

The egg is unquestionably one of the best food sources, yet it requires thought and consideration. As a culinarian, your goal must be to make the best possible use of any food source. In the case of the egg this means handling it properly to protect against bacteria growth and nutritional degradation. It also means choosing how, and in what manner, to use it nutritionally.

REVIEW QUESTIONS

1. Define the term *egg*.
2. List and discuss the three parts of the egg.
3. Discuss what occurs as an egg ages.
4. List and discuss the sizes and grades of eggs.
5. List five available forms of eggs.
6. Discuss coagulation of egg protein and the temperature at which it occurs.
7. List four guidelines for properly beating egg whites.
8. Discuss methods for gaining increased volume when producing egg white foam.
9. State the proper method for storage of fresh eggs.
10. Discuss the nutritive value of an egg.

Section III
Hot Food Preparation

Fruits
Vegetables
Potatoes & other Tubers
Farinaceous Cookery
Stock
Soups
Hot Sauces
Meat - Beef, Veal, Lamb & Pork
Poultry
Game
Seafood & Freshwater Fish
Breakfast Cookery

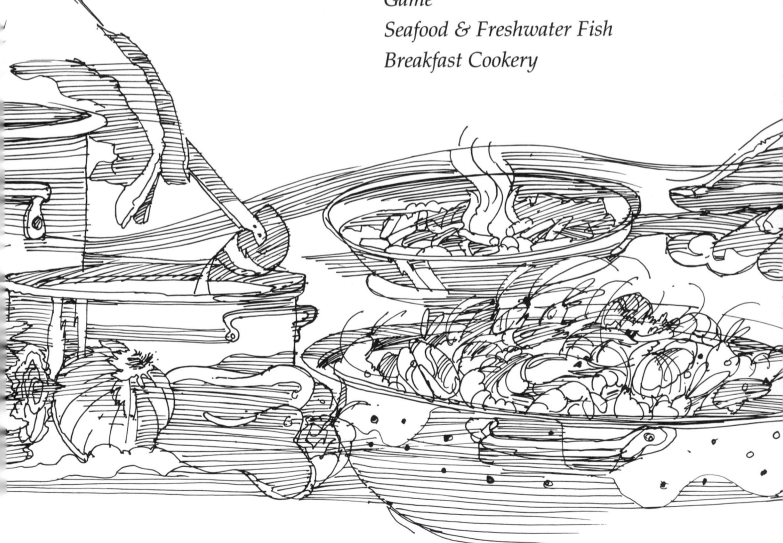

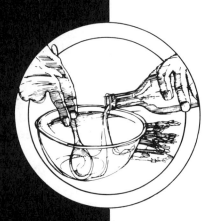

Chapter 10

CHAPTER OBJECTIVES

- **To introduce fruit as a primary ingredient in culinary preparation.**
- **To discuss the characteristics of fruit.**
- **To discuss the preparation of fruit.**
- **To discuss the selection and handling of fruits.**

Fruits

Fruits of all types are used in a wide variety of ways in the kitchen. They are served raw, marinated and cooked. Fruits are often used as a source of flavor, texture and color variation in dishes. They are also widely used in the preparation of delectable sauces and condiments. These luscious food items are often the perfect complement to the flavor of meats, poultry and vegetables. As jellies, jams and preserves, they make the consumption of bread and cakes more enjoyable.

What is this food called *fruit?* It is defined as the usually edible reproductive body of a seed plant, especially one which has a sweet pulp associated with the seed. These are the result of a transformation of a flower to a seed with the formation of some adjacent edible tissues. Structural differences within the various fruit-yielding flowers are reflected in the fruits themselves.

A simple bloom produces a simple fruit, such as the apple, peach, banana or orange. Technically nuts and grains also belong to this group. Flowers with many stamens and pistils, the reproductive organs of the plant's flower, yield an aggregate fruit with a cluster of sections. This is true of the strawberry, blackberry and loganberry. Others are formed by the merging of several flowers thereby forming a collective fruit. This is true of the pineapple and fig.

A discussion of fruit is complicated by the sheer magnitude of the subject. The apple, as a single variety of fruit, has over 8,000 known varieties. It is not possible, and would not be practical, to discuss every fruit type here. We will discuss the preparation and usage of fruits as a group.

Decorative sectioning of pineapple

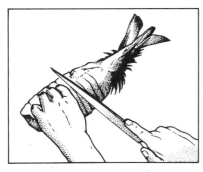

CHARACTERISTICS OF FRUIT

FLAVOR

The flavor of fruits is the result of their content of sugars, organic acids, mineral salts and aromatic compounds. Among the fruits valued for their sweetness are apples, melons, pears, peaches, apricots and figs.

The acids that contribute to the flavor of fruits are primarily malic and citric, with tartaric present in some fruits, such as grapes. These are all non-volatile acids. It is malic acid which predominates in apples, apricots, cherries, pears, plums, peaches and bananas. Citric acid is the primary acid present in oranges, grapefruit, lemons, loganberries, raspberries and tomatoes. Although these acids do contribute to the flavor of the fruits, the total acid content of fruits in general is not considered high. Apples contain 0.60 percent or less acid and lemons 6.0 percent when calculated (malic acid in the apple and citric acid in the lemon) as a percentage of the edible portion of the fruit.

TEXTURE

The texture of fruits is largely determined by the cellulose, which forms the walls of the plant cells, in combination with pectin and other substances. It is the water content within the cells of the plant that determines the crispness of the tissue. When water is lacking, the cells begin to contract, wilting the structure. It is for this reason that many fruits, as well as green vegetables, should be stored in a very humid environment.

The cellulose, which forms the structure of the fruit, is softened by cooking. This alteration is retarded by the presence of acids within limits and accelerated by the presence of alkaline substances.

METHOD OF PREPARATION

The primary goal in the preparation of any food item is to make it more palatable and in the process to preserve as much of its nutritional value as possible. The preparation of fruit is far more concerned with the latter part of this goal than the former. Fruit of most types are prized for their sweet succulent flavor and luscious texture. The greater challenge in handling fruits is the preservation of its natural flavor and nutritional value.

Fresh fruit, depending on the type, can offer a menu item which is low in fat and lower in carbohydrates than most prepared desserts. Fruit is naturally high in vitamins, minerals and fiber and low in sodium. You must make every effort to preserve the fruit's natural attributes. You need to remember that vitamins and minerals are volatile when exposed to excessive heat, acid, alkali (such as baking soda) or light.

PREPARATION OF FRESH FRUIT

Fruit is often served fresh and uncooked. This is one of the best ways to enjoy to the fullest the flavor and texture of fruits. This does not mean, however, that it is not prepared for service to the customer. Whether served fresh as a singular item or as part of a dish or presentation, it must be processed properly. The method of preparation can vary from fruit to fruit, depending on individual characteristics.

SOFT FRUIT

Preparation of soft fruits, such as strawberries and raspberries, requires careful handling. All fruits should be washed before use to remove dirt, chemicals and insects. However, extended washing or other exposure to liquid will remove the natural wax coating on the berry. This will cause it to *bleed* and lose shape. These fruits are not peeled in any manner before being eaten.

The softer types of fruits should be rinsed and then <u>gently</u> shaken to remove excess water. If necessary they may be carefully dried. Soft berries should be washed as close to use as possible, to minimize softening.

These types of fruit will also lose their shape quickly when sugared. To prevent them from becoming excessively mushy, sugar them just far enough in advance to allow the sugar to dissolve and form a smooth, nongranular liquid.

FRUITS SUSCEPTIBLE TO ENZYMATIC BROWNING

Apples, pears, bananas and peaches are some of the fruits susceptible to enzymatic browning. (This browning effect is discussed in Chapter 3.) After they are peeled and cut, it is necessary to protect them from the air as much as possible.

If they are to be held for anything other than a very short period of time, it may be necessary to treat them with citric acid or a light salt solution. This treatment will inhibit browning and will help to preserve the fresh color of the fruit. A solution of one cup water with one teaspoon of lemon juice is sufficient to slow the browning process. Be careful with the amount of lemon or other citrus juice used. Otherwise the natural flavor of the fruit will be over-powered by that of the citrus. A light salt solution may be used for this purpose, but is not as effective.

Immersing some fruits in an acid solution prevents browning.

NOTE: Do not soak any fruit in either a citrus juice or salt solution for an extended period. If you do, the fruit will acquire an acidic or salty taste.

Fruits of this type may also be marred when cut with carbon steel knives. Their natural acid content may react to the blade, causing a black smear or streak to appear on the surface of the cut fruit. This is also true of citrus fruits. It is best to cut all fruit with stainless steel knives. In addition, a sharp knife will minimize cell damage to the fruit which in turn releases less of the enzyme/substrates that cause browning. This means that less browning will take place. As with all food production, the knives and other tools used must be cleaned and sanitized before use.

SEEDING FRUITS

With the exception of those fruits whose seeds are considered inseparable from the fruit itself such as bananas, strawberries, kiwis and raspberries, fruits should be seeded before service. This is even true for raspberries and the like when they are served other than whole, when they are pureed for example.

It is not acceptable in quality food service for the guest to find a lemon seed or cantaloupe seed in their dish. Although it is difficult to remove the seeds of fruits such as watermelon, it is necessary for certain types of service. An example is the use of watermelon in a fresh fruit compote at brunch. In this case, the melon should be cut into small pieces or balled and the seeds removed. If the watermelon is served sliced, it is acceptable to leave the seeds and not mar the integrity of the slice.

The seeds of the apple are poisonous in large amounts and should always be removed unless the fruit is served fresh and whole. Although the seeds of the orange and grapefruit are harmless, they should be removed from the fruit segments when they are used in a salad combination.

PARING FRUITS

Whether a fruit needs to be pared will depend on the type of fruit and the manner of presentation. In a Waldorf salad the red color of the apple's peel is attractive in a rather colorless mixture and the texture of the peeling adds interest to the bite. However, to put unpared apple slices into a pie and bake it, may not add the same positive aspect to the dish.

Although the decision to pare a fruit depends on the type and service of the fruit, there are some basic guidelines to paring fruit.

1. A GREAT DEAL OF THE NUTRITIVE VALUE OF FRUITS SUCH AS APPLES AND PEACHES IS CONTAINED IN THE SKIN AND THE FLESH CLOSE TO THE SKIN OF THE FRUIT. FOR THIS REASON THEY SHOULD BE CAREFULLY PARED TO REMOVE AS LITTLE FLESH AS POSSIBLE. FROM THE STANDPOINT OF WASTE THIS IS ALSO TRUE WITH ALL OTHER FRUITS. WHENEVER POSSIBLE THEY SHOULD BE WASHED WELL AND USED WITH THE SKIN INTACT.

2. THE SKIN OF CITRUS FRUITS, PARTICULARLY LEMONS, LIMES AND ORANGES ARE GOOD FLAVORING AGENTS IN THEMSELVES. HOWEVER,

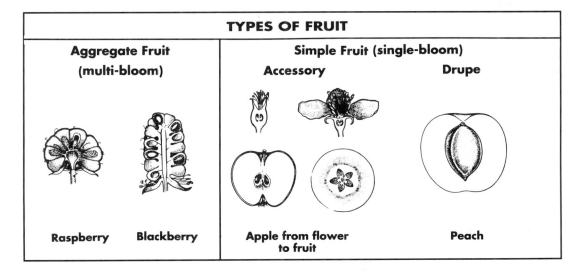

TYPES OF FRUIT		
Aggregate Fruit (multi-bloom)	Simple Fruit (single-bloom)	
	Accessory	Drupe
Raspberry　　Blackberry	Apple from flower to fruit	Peach

WHEN USED FOR THIS PURPOSE, IT IS BEST THAT THEY BE USED AS ZEST, EXTREMELY SMALL THIN STRIPS. ALBEDO, OR *PITH* ASSOCIATED WITH THE SKIN IS OFTEN BITTER. THE ZEST, OR COLORED PART OF THE SKIN, CONTAINS MUCH OF THE FLAVOR.

3. CANTALOUPE AND OTHER MELONS, AS WELL AS GRAPEFRUIT, ARE OFTEN SERVED WITH THE RIND INTACT. THIS IS ACCEPTABLE IF THE FLESH IS LOOSENED WITHIN THE RIND FIRST.

4. IT IS NECESSARY TO LEAVE AS MUCH FLESH INTACT AS POSSIBLE WHEN PARING. HOWEVER, THE FLESH OF MELONS CLOSE TO THE RIND IS OFTEN BITTER OR SOMETIMES TASTELESS. HOW CLOSE ONE TRIMS TO THE OUTER FLESH MUST ALSO TAKE INTO ACCOUNT THE FLAVOR CHARACTERISTICS OF THE FRUIT AND HOW RIPE THE FRUIT IS.

COOKING FRESH FRUIT

Fruits are cooked in a variety of ways and used in a wide array of dishes in the kitchen. If the goal of the cooking is to impart a new flavor to the fruit but retain as much of the fruit's original shape, texture and nutritive value as possible, the cooking should be done quickly. Extended cooking will cause fruits to soften and lose shape.

Loss of shape can be reduced by cooking the fruit in a sugar medium. Sugar also assists in retaining more of the natural flavor and color of the fruit. It is for this reason that fruits canned in syrup, particularly heavy syrup, have brighter colors, firmer texture and fresher flavors.

Poaching is one of the more common methods for cooking fruits to accompany other dishes. The lower temperature reduces the agitation of the liquid and does not distort the shape of fruit like boiling can. With poaching it is possible to blend the flavor of the fruit with another complementary flavor. The result is a flavorful and colorful fruit that is an excellent accompaniment for a variety of meat dishes or cream based desserts.

Poached Pears
In Red Raspberry Juice

INGREDIENTS	AMOUNTS
BARTLETT PEARS	12
RED RASPBERRIES	4 CUPS
WATER	3 QUARTS
SUGAR	6 CUPS
VANILLA BEAN, SPLIT LENGTHWISE	1
NUTMEG	1/2 TEASPOON
RASPBERRY LIQUOR	1 CUP

METHOD

1. PUREE ONE HALF OF THE BERRIES IN A PROCESSOR OR BLENDER.

2. STRAIN THE PUREE THROUGH A FINE-MESHED SIEVE, OVER A BOWL, USING A WOODEN SPOON TO SQUEEZE ALL OF THE JUICE OUT. THERE SHOULD BE ONE AND ONE-THIRD CUPS OF RASPBERRY JUICE.

3. POUR THE WATER INTO A LARGE PAN; ADD THE SUGAR, NUTMEG, THE VANILLA BEAN HALVES, THE RASPBERRY JUICE AND THE RASPBERRY LIQUOR.

4. PLACE THE PAN OVER MEDIUM HEAT.

5. STIR THE MIXTURE WITH A WOODEN SPOON UNTIL THE SUGAR HAS COMPLETELY DISSOLVED, BRING IT TO A BOIL AND BOIL FOR A FEW MINUTES.

6. AS THE SYRUP BOILS, PEEL THE PEARS, REMOVE THE STEMS, AND CORE THEM WITH AN APPLE CORER. SUBMERGE THE PEARS IN MIXTURE OF 2 QUARTS WATER WITH 1/4 CUP LEMON JUICE TO PREVENT ENZYMATIC BROWNING.

7. LOWER THE HEAT UNDER THE SYRUP TO A SIMMER AND DROP THE PEARS INTO IT.

8. COOK THIS MIXTURE FOR 16 MINUTES, ADD THE REMAINING RASPERRIES AND TURN THE HEAT OFF. LET THE PEARS AND THE RASPBERRIES COOL IN THE SYRUP.

9. PLACE THE MIXTURE INTO A SERVING DISH. CHILL WELL BEFORE SERVING. THIS WOULD SERVE AS EITHER A DESSERT OR MEAT ACCOMPANIMENT. IF SERVED AS A DESSERT IT COULD BE SERVED WITH ICE CREAM, WHIPPED CREAM OR CUSTARD SAUCE WITH CRISP COOKIES. APPLES OR PEACHES COULD BE USED INSTEAD OF PEARS, AND BLACK CURRANTS OR GOOSEBERRIES COULD BE USED INSTEAD OF RED RASPBERRIES.

Fruits may also be quickly sauteed, such as in flambe desserts. The texture of fruit is altered as little as possible, yet the natural flavor is highlighted by the sugars, caramelized or not, and liqueurs, etc., incorporated with the fruit.

Many fruits are pureed, raw or cooked, and used either by themselves or blended with other ingredients as sauces. When cooked prior to being pureed, the fruits are brought to a boil and then reduced to a simmer until the liquid is reduced to *au sec* (practically dry). In this manner the flavor of the other ingredients can be blended with that of the fruit, yet, when pureed, there should be little need for additional binding of the mixture.

Raw, pureed fruit may be blended into other mixtures to add both color and flavor. They make a particularly good addition to salad dressings and sauces used for game.

FRUIT PREPARATIONS AS CONDIMENTS

There are a number of condiments commonly used in food service which are, to a large extent, a blending of the flavor of fruits with other ingredients. The Indian chutney is a good example. This combination of fruits, spices, sugars and vinegars is served as an accompaniment with a broad range of Indian dishes. Many varieties of the Chinese sweet and sour sauce contain fruits of various kinds, along with the balance of sugar and vinegar.

Possibly the best known fruit condiments are jellies, jams and preserves. Once a standard production item, these are rarely made in today's commercial kitchen. They are now normally purchased from commercial distributors. Nonetheless, they are fruit condiments.

Jelly is prepared strictly from the juice of the fruit, often extracted from the whole fruit or berry; jam includes small pieces of flesh, and preserves contain larger, recognizable pieces of the fruit. All of these condiments contain sugar for sweetness and gel strength and have pectin added to insure they gel.

SELECTION & HANDLING OF FRUIT

SELECTION

It is not possible in this text to discuss the selection criteria for all the various fruits. However there are some basic criteria for selection of any fruit.

1. THE QUALITY OF FRUIT CHOSEN WILL BE GUIDED BY THE INTENDED END USE. IF THE FRUIT IS TO BE PRESENTED TO THE CUSTOMER WHOLE, OR IN A MANNER THAT MAKES THE APPEARANCE OF THE SKIN IMPORTANT, THEN THE PURCHASE OF THE HIGHEST QUALITY AVAILABLE IS IMPORTANT. HOWEVER, IF THE FRUIT IS TO BE COOKED OR PEELED AND CUT INTO SMALL PIECES, THE EXTERIOR APPEARANCE MAY NOT BE AS IMPORTANT. LESS ATTRACTIVE AND LESS EXPENSIVE FRUIT MAY SERVE THE PURPOSE ADEQUATELY.

2. FRUIT SHOULD ALWAYS BE CHOSEN THAT HAS A TEXTURE CONSISTENT WITH THE STANDARD FOR THE FRUIT BEING PURCHASED. OVERLY RIPE FRUIT WILL QUICKLY LOSE ITS FIRMNESS AND THE FLAVOR WILL CHANGE. FRUIT WHICH IS NOT RIPE MAY BE HARD AND WILL NOT HAVE FULLY DEVELOPED FLAVOR.

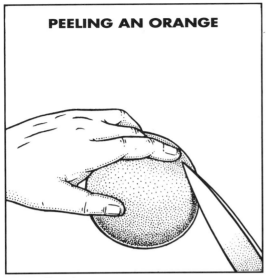

PEELING AN ORANGE

Slice off ends.

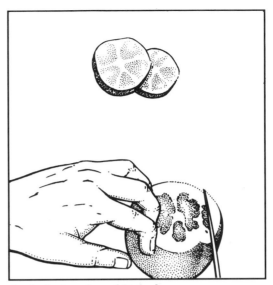

Cut in just under white pulp.

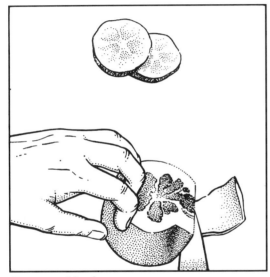

Cut smoothly down.

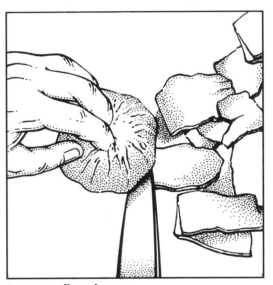

Remove all peel.

3. **The aroma of the fruit should be fresh and pleasing, with no off odors. For this reason do not store them close to onions, truffles or other items that emit strong odors.**

4. **Avoid fruits with excessively thick skins, or skins which are bruised or broken in any manner.**

HANDLING & STORAGE

As a culinarian, it is important that you remember that fruit is a living organism even after it is picked. This means that it continues to breathe and age. The higher the respiration level of the fruit, the faster it ages. The higher the storage temperature, the higher the respiration rate. For this reason it is best to store the majority of fruits under refrigeration.

Although fruits should be stored under refrigeration, caution must be exercised to prevent freezing. Fruits which have been allowed to freeze even partially will wilt rapidly when they thaw. They develop very soft flesh and can possibly discolor. It is difficult to state one overall temperature for the storage of fruits, because, as with vegetables, each differs. For oranges, 32°F with 90 percent humidity is best; for lemons 58-60°F with 90 percent humidity, and for grapefruit 50°F with 85 percent humidity is considered best. Apples on the other hand are best stored at 85 to 90 percent humidity and 30 to 32°F.

CONCLUSION

The handling and preparation of fruits and vegetables is, in many ways, simple. Yet the results are extremely rewarding. These versatile food items bring color and variety to any meal. When properly handled they contribute greatly to the health of the consumer. As a culinarian, strive to protect this valuable resource.

REVIEW QUESTIONS

1. Define the term *fruit*.
2. Discuss the flavor characteristics of fruit.
3. Discuss the texture characteristics of fruit.
4. Discuss the preparation of soft fruits.
5. List three fruits susceptible to enzymatic browning and how to avoid it.
6. Should fruits be seeded before service to the guest?
7. List four guidelines for peeling and paring fruit.
8. Discuss the cooking of fresh fruit.
9. List four guides for the selection of fruit.
10. Discuss the nutritive value of fruit.

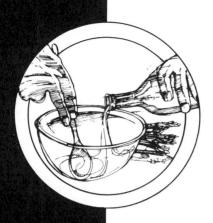

Chapter 11

CHAPTER OBJECTIVES

- **To introduce vegetables as an ingredient.**

- **To introduce the various groups of vegetables used in the kitchen.**

- **To discuss factors affecting the preparation of vegetables.**

- **To discuss the handling of vegetables.**

- **To discuss methods for cooking vegetables.**

- **To explain the balance between classical preparation and nutritional preparation.**

Vegetables

The term *vegetable* refers to all plants or parts of plants which can be eaten raw, cooked or preserved in some form. The general nature of the term requires that we narrow it in some manner to make it a manageable subject. We will do this in two ways. First, we divide the vegetables into two large groupings for purposes of discussion. This chapter will deal with vegetables other than those considered TUBER or ROOT VEGETABLES. These will be discussed at length in Chapter 12. In this chapter, vegetables will be broken down into related sub-groups to allow us to begin to identity the various kinds.

As a food stuff, vegetables play an important role in the human diet. They provide vitamins and minerals as well as flavor not available in meats, cereals, dairy products and fruit. There are two goals the culinarian should work toward for using vegetables to produce well balanced, nutritional, flavorful meals.

1. **BE FAMILIAR WITH THE VARIOUS TYPES OF VEGETABLES AVAILABLE AND WORK TO DEVELOP AN UNDERSTANDING OF THEIR NUTRITIONAL, TEXTURAL, COLOR AND FLAVOR VALUE IN COOKING.**
2. **LEARN THE METHODS OF PREPARATION WHICH WILL PROTECT THE NUTRITIONAL, TEXTURAL, COLOR AND FLAVOR VALUE OF VEGETABLES WHEN COOKED.**

There is far more to using vegetables as a food stuff than just cleaning and cooking them. You must strive to make the best use of them as part of the overall meal and diet. These two goals seem very simple, but are not.

There is no single book which can tell you everything you need to know about the broad number of vegetables available. What we give you in this text is truly only an introduction. You will need to look, listen and read closely in the coming years to develop a sound knowledge in this area of food preparation.

TYPES & DESCRIPTIONS

CABBAGE FAMILY

The cabbage family is a group of crisp, pungent vegetables which come from different parts of the plant species known by the Latin name *brassica aleracea*. The varieties of this plant include cabbage, brussel sprouts, broccoli, cauliflower and kohlrabi.

CABBAGE

Head cabbage is formed by thick, overlapping leaves attached to a stem. The head ranges in color from a very light green, almost white, to dark green.

Also available is a red variety. Red cabbage is identical to the green/white variety except for color. Head cabbage should have well trimmed, solid, heavy heads when purchased. The heads should be fairly round and have no discolored veins.

This cabbage variety is good for boiling, steaming, frying, braising and sauteing. It is excellent stuffed, whether by the leaf or as a full head. Raw, it is often used for salads or in cole slaw. When pickled, cabbage is termed *sauerkraut*.

★ *NOTE: Cabbage should not be cooked for long periods of time. The longer it is exposed to heat the stronger its flavor becomes. To protect both its mild flavor and its crisp texture, use short cooking times.*

Chinese cabbage has long, loosely packed leaves. The color of the leaves is white, deepening to green at the stem. This is a mild flavored cabbage often used in oriental cooking and salads. To retain the vitamins and nutrients in the cabbage, cut or shredded cabbage should not be exposed to air for long periods of time. It should be cooked immediately.

Savoy cabbage has yellowish, crimped, wrinkled leaves. The size of the head is about the same as that of iceberg lettuce. Savoy has a mild flavor and the texture of the leaves make an interesting addition to cooked dishes and salads.

Cabbage stores well at 32°F and 90 percent relative humidity. Do not allow it to freeze, this will cause it to wilt. It should be kept in a well ventilated area in the refrigerator. Cabbage will wilt and loose quality quickly when held at room temperature.

BRUSSELS SPROUTS

Brussels sprouts are green in color and bright in appearance. They look like miniature heads of cabbage. Brussel sprouts were named for the Belgium city of Brussels, where they were first grown in the 13th century.

SELECTION & STORAGE

When purchased they should be firm and compact, not puffy. A soft, puffy sprout is usually poor in quality and flavor. Ones with wilted or yellowing leaves indicate aging. Available fresh or frozen, the majority of those sold in the United States are grown in California, New York, and Oregon. Fresh brussels sprouts should be held at 32°F with 90 percent relative humidity, and used as soon as possible.

PREPARATION

1) Peel off any wilted or yellowing leaves and trim the stem end as close to the sprout as possible without detaching any leaves.

2) Cut a shallow cross in the bottom of the stem to allow the stem end to cook as quickly as the tender leaves. If this is not done the leaves will lose their bright green color and slightly crisp texture before the stem is tender.

3) To protect the nutritional value of this vegetable, use short cooking times whenever possible and as little water as possible.

4) Sprouts can be boiled, baked or steamed.

5) Steamed sprouts are often finished with rendered bacon, sauteed mushrooms, toasted sliced almonds or poppy seeds.

CAULIFLOWER

The term *cauliflower* comes from a Latin term meaning cabbage flower or stalk flower, a cultivated descendant of the common cabbage. It has only become an important crop in the United States since 1920.

SELECTION & STORAGE

A quality cauliflower will have curd (flowers) creamy white in color, with only small amounts of spotting or speckling. The head should be compact, with no sign of growth of the smaller flowers in the head.

When buying fresh cauliflower watch for the following:

1) Yellowish curds are an indication of poor growing conditions or poor handling and aging.

2) The texture of the curd should not be rice-like in appearance.

3) Loose open flowers indicate overmaturity.

Cauliflower can be purchased fresh or frozen. The annual supply is fairly constant with the heaviest being in September, October, and November.

PREPARATION

When preparing fresh cauliflower:

1) The head can be cooked whole once the leaves and middle core are removed.

2) The head can also be broken into florets and cooked.

3) When the stem end of the head or florets yields to the touch of a fork, the cauliflower is done.

4) Cauliflower can be served boiled with butte; steamed; deep-fried; pureed with hollandaise sauce; raw in salads; au gratin, or as an addition to soups.

☆ NOTE: Soak the head in cold salt water for one hour. This freshens it and will remove any small insects which may be hidden in the flowers.

Cauliflower has certain characteristics which require that you remember the following:

1) Avoid over cooking Cauliflower. When overcooked it will break apart and become mushy.

2) If you are cooking with water high in alkali (hard water), add one teaspoon of fresh lemon juice for each quart of water. High alkali water will turn the flowers yellow and soft.

3) For this same reason never use soda in cooking cauliflower.

4) Adding milk to the cooking water heightens the white color of the cauliflower and adds a slight sweetness to the flavor.

KOHLRABI

Kohlrabi is light green to white in color, round or globular in shape and averages 3-6 inches in diameter. Its leaves are similar to a turnip's leaves. The term *kohlrabi* is of German origin and means "cabbage turnip." It should be stored at 32°F with 95-98 percent relative humidity.

Kohlrabi can be cooked like spinach. It is best when steamed, then peeled and cut julienne. It can be served hot with butter or marinated in French dressing. Cold, it can be served as a salad or as an accompaniment to cold meat. The first version of cole slaw was made with kohlrabi. That is where the "cole" comes from, it is a nickname for kohlrabi.

BROCCOLI

Broccoli has a deep green color in the leaves, and stems with deep green or purplish green, compact buds in the head. Yellow flowers in the buds indicate old, tough broccoli. The more yellow seen in a bunch, the lower the quality. Broccoli should be stored for as short a period of time as possible, at 32°F and 95 percent relative humidity.

Although fresh broccoli is available year-round, frozen broccoli is often used. It has a softer texture and less flavor than fresh. Fresh is in shortest supply in July and August.

PREPARATION

This versatile vegetable can be used in a similar manner to cauliflower. To protect the nutrients, very little water and short cooking times should be used in preparation. It can be steamed, pureed, baked in casseroles, used raw in salads, served topped with hollandaise or mornay sauce, polonaise or amandine. This is only a partial list of the possibilities.

The difficulty in properly cooking broccoli is protecting the color and texture of the blossom end. When even slightly overcooked it turns an unappetizing brownish-green color and the buds become mushy. Since the thick stocks take longer to cook than the tender buds, cook with the stem end covered in water and the blossom end uncovered. This allows the stems to cook in the boiling water while the buds cook in the steam rising off the water. The result is a stem of broccoli with a tender yet crisp stem and flower, both with a bright green color.

When properly prepared the deep green color of broccoli will become brighter and deeper with exposure to heat; however, extended cooking will ruin the color. A few guides or pointers for preparing broccoli follow.

1) Split the stems of whole broccoli before cooking. This exposes more surface area and promotes faster cooking.

2) When cooking broccoli pieces, cook stems first, and add the florets briefly before the stems are done.

3) When preparing frozen broccoli, remember that it has been blanched in processing. Shorter cooking times are needed.

4) Defrost frozen broccoli before cooking, this will expose the outer surface of the broccoli to the shortest possible cooking time.

5) A good method for preparing large quantities without overcooking is to shock the par-cooked broccoli in ice water and then heat as needed for service.

STALK VEGETABLES

Stalk vegetables are plant stems that are high in cellulose fibers. These fibers are the strings that hold the stalks erect under the weight of the leaves and buds. As the plant ages, the fibers toughen. For use in eating, stalk vegetables should be young. Tough fibers will not soften with cooking and should be trimmed away before being used. Stalk vegetables include asparagus, celery and bok choy.

ASPARAGUS

There are two types of asparagus, white and green. There is a vast difference in the taste or texture of the two. White asparagus is more expensive, because it must be shielded from the sun to keep it white. White asparagus cannot be eaten raw, it is too tough. It should be partially peeled before cooking.

SELECTION & STORAGE

Fresh asparagus should have straight stalks and compact, pointed tips. There should only be approximately an inch of tough woody base. Spears with open or seedy tips that are flat or ridged are old and will be of poor eating quality. A soft tip is an indication that the asparagus is not of acceptable quality.

Asparagus is available fresh, frozen or canned. Peak season is from April to June. Fresh product should be stored at 41°F. The bottom of the stalks should be kept damp with wet paper towels. Fresh asparagus is highly perishable and should be used as soon as possible.

PREPARATION

To prepare fresh asparagus:

1) Hold the stalk near the bottom and bend. The stalk will break where the base becomes tough and inedible.

2) The outside flesh of the stalk is like your skin, very tough. Removing it will give the guest a much more enjoyable product; however, nutritionally, this is a waste of fiber. Although peeling is necessary for white asparagus, it is not necessarily recommended for young green asparagus.

3) Cleaned asparagus should be gathered in bunches of similar size stalks and tied together.

4) Cook by placing stem end down in boiling water. This is done to protect the buds from being overcooked and knocked off the stem by the action of the water.

5) Asparagus will brighten in color when first exposed to the hot water. Cook it just until tender. If overcooked, it will become soft and develop a brownish, green color.

Asparagus is used in a number of ways. It is complemented by butter, hollandaise sauce and vinaigrette dressings of all types. Asparagus pieces can also be utilized in cold salads, soups or casseroles.

CELERY

Celery is a member of the parsley family *umbelliferal*. There are two types: Golden heart, which is very white in color, and pascal, which is dark or light green in color. Pascal, the most popular celery, is less stringy and has a distinct flavor.

SELECTION & STORAGE

A high quality, fresh celery should be light green in color, with a glossy appearance. The stalks should be of medium length and thickness. Stems should have a smooth interior surface. Leaves should be bright in color and fresh, with no sign of wilting.

The stalk of a good quality, fresh celery will break with a snap. Limp celery is old celery and should not be accepted. Celery with a watery, translucent appearance has been allowed to freeze. It is not suitable for service raw.

Fresh celery should be stored at 35°F with 90-95 percent relative humidity. It is available year-round, with the principal growers being California, Florida, Michigan and New York.

USAGE

Every part of the celery can be used in cooking. Trimmings and tender leaves are good for use in stocks. The outer ribs can be cooked as vegetables or as flavoring in various preparations. Celery can be eaten raw, diced and added to a variety of salads, where it adds texture, flavor and color. Celery can be braised, creamed or served au gratin. The celery seed is also used as a seasoning. In general, it is a valuable vegetable in food preparation.

SWISS CHARD

Swiss chard is a dark green vegetable, with crinkled leaves and a firm white stalk. Store swiss chard at 34°F with 90 percent relative humidity.

This is, in effect, two vegetables in one. The leaves may be cooked like greens, the white stem like celery. The white stems can be steamed, stir-fried or braised. The leaves should be cooked like spinach with only the liquid which adheres to them after washing. Cream of chard soup is a popular dish, which can also be made into a custard.

BOK CHOY

Bok choy resembles swiss chard and celery. The name means white vegetable. It is sometimes called *white mustard cabbage*. Bok choy is a large leafy green vegetable with long white stalks. Bok choy is excellent sauteed or steamed and is used extensively in oriental cooking.

LEAFY VEGETABLES

Leafy vegetables are plants grown specifically for their edible leaves. These vegetables include spinach, kale, collards and sorrel.

SPINACH

Spinach, when fresh, is a crisp, dark green leaf. The curly or flat leaves are best for cooking. Fresh spinach is available all year, with major supplies coming from California and Texas. It is best stored at 32°F, with 95-98 percent humidity. Spinach is also available frozen and canned.

PREPARATION

Preparing fresh spinach:

1) Begin by washing the spinach thoroughly in large quantities of cold water. This should be done two to three times.
2) Spinach cooks very quickly, so use short cooking times.
3) It usually needs only the liquid which clings to the leaves after washing.

Spinach is a versatile vegetable which can be served steamed with butter and garnished with chopped or sliced hard boiled egg, bacon or cheese. It is excellent sauteed without fat, with your choice of herbs, spices or other vegetables. Spinach blends well into many dishes, such as casseroles, mousse or creamed. It is popular, fresh, as a salad.

KALE

Kale has hardy, curly leaves, which are deep green in color. High quality bunches should have large leaves, be free of bruises, clean and with little discoloration. It should be stored at 40°F, with high humidity.

Kale can be used as a steamed vegetable or served raw as a garnish. It is desirable becaause of its ability to hold its shape longer at room temperature. When preparing kale for cooking, cut off and discard the root ends, tough stems and any discolored leaves. The tough, middle ribs of the leaves should also be removed and discarded. Wash it well in plenty of lightly salted water to remove dirt, sand and any tiny insects.

COLLARDS

Collards are a leafy vegetable with a bright green color and crisp leaves. Select collards that are free of blemishes or wilting. This vegetable is available fresh, frozen or canned. The largest supplies come from Virginia and Georgia, with the largest amounts available January through April. They should be stored at 32°F with 90 percent relative humidity.

Proper washing is essential in the preparation of collards. The leaves retain sand and dirt which cannot be removed by a cursory rinsing. As with spinach, they should be washed in cold water, two to three times before being used.

Collards tend to be a favorite vegetable in the southern United States. There they are boiled with salt pork or hog jowls. Another method of preparing collards is to render bacon or salt pork then add coarsely shredded collards to them. (Other oils, such as olive oil can be substitued for the pork fats if desired.) The mixture is covered and allowed to sweat until tender. It is served with lemon slices or vinegar.

SORREL

Sorrel has narrow, pointed leaves in the shape of an arrowhead. They are a dull light green color. Sorrel is high in oxalic acid, giving it a slightly sour taste. It is a spring vegetable similar to spinach and can be prepared as a vegetable or added to soups.

SALAD GREENS

This grouping is what are termed the LETTUCES. They are members of the daisy family. Salad greens include endive and lettuce of all types.

ENDIVE

Curly endive grows in a head. It is a grouping of narrow, ragged edged leaves which curl at the ends. The center of the head is yellowish-white and has a milder taste than the bitter outside green leaves. It is used primarily as an ingredient in green salads or as a garnish. However, it can be simmered gently until tender or added to a combination of other greens for cooking.

Willoof chicory (belgium endive) is a tightly folded plant that grows upright in thin elongated stalks. It is usually very white in color. When purchased fresh, it should be crisp, with tender leaves. Avoid heads with brown or yellow discoloration. This endive is most often served raw as a salad green. However, it is good braised or charcoal broiled.

LETTUCE

Lettuce, one of the earliest known vegetables, was served at the table of Persian kings 25 centuries ago. It is believed to be a native plant of the Mediterranean and Near East. Lettuce is grown in many parts of the world today.

Crisphead (iceberg) lettuce grows as a compact, overlaying, set of green to greenish white leaves. Fresh heads should be firm but not hard. Lighter, springier heads of lettuce will have a sweeter taste. They are also easier to separate for use in salads or sandwiches. The head of lettuce should have a fresh appearance, free from burned or rusty looking areas. 85 percent of the iceberg lettuce in the United States comes from Arizona or California.

Butterhead (Boston bibb) lettuce grows in a head of loosely overlapping leaves. The outer leaves are light green color, the inner leaves light yellow. This lettuce has soft, pliable leaves which have a delicate, buttery flavor.

Romaine (cos), a long, loaf-shaped head of lettuce has long, narrow, smooth edged leaves. The outer leaves are dark green, the inner leaves golden yellow. While the leaves appear coarse, they are really sweet, tender and crisp.

Leaf lettuce grows as a bunch of leaves which loosely branch from a center stalk. The leaf is curly and can vary in color from dark green, to light green to red tipped, depending on the variety. The leaves are crisp in texture, but more delicate than iceberg.

Most lettuces can be stored two to three weeks at 32°F. They are used in a wide variety of salads, sandwiches and garnishes.

SEEDS, EDIBLE PODS, & YOUNG SHOOTS

This is a broad category of vegetables. It includes peas, snow peas, beans of all types, bean sprouts, corn and others.

PEAS

The pea comes from a vine cultivated for the rounded, smooth or wrinkled, edible protein rich seed. When purchasing fresh peas, select fairly large, bright green, angular pods. They should be well filled and snap readily. A yellowish pod indicates aging and will be tough. Mildewed, swollen or speckled pods should be avoided. Fresh peas lose part of their natural sugar content rapidly after picking. To retain quality they should be stored immediately at 32°F. They will store better in the pod than shelled. High quality peas are available fresh, frozen, canned or dried.

This nutritious vegetable should be cooked in as little water as possible. It should be cooked al dente. Peas can be served with butter, creamed, in salads, soups or stews.

SNOW PEAS

This type of pea is picked in the very early stages of development, when the pea within the pod is very small. The entire pod is tender and edible. Flat Chinese-type snow peas should be three to four inches long; one inch wide, and very bright green in color.

Snow peas are in plentiful supply May through September. They are available, but more expensive, the rest of the year. Frozen snow peas are available; however, the quality is only fair.

USAGE

This pea is used extensively in Oriental cooking. It can be sauteed or mixed with other vegetables. They are excellent in salads and stuffed with soft cheese as appetizers. The mild crisp flavor and bright color of the fresh snow pea is becoming more popular in all types of cooking.

BEAN SPROUTS

Bean sprouts can be the sprouts of any germinated bean, but most commonly are sprouts of mung or soy beans. They normally are golden, cream or white colored, with a tendril-like appearance. When purchased fresh, they should be crisp and have moist tips. Bean sprouts are also available canned. The shorter the sprout, the more tender it is. Old sprouts develop a strong, musty, earthy flavor. Young sprouts are preferred for their fresh, delicate flavor. Used often in Oriental cooking, they also add a different texture and flavor to all types of salads and sandwiches.

BEANS

Bean is the name given to edible seeds. Historically three types, soy, kidney and broad beans, have been important food sources.

Soybean is native to China. It has been cultivated there for 4,000 years. Today, the United States is the largest producer of soybean, where it is used in oil, food production and as animal feed.

Haricot (kidney bean) is of American origin. It was first cultivated by the Aztec Indians of South America. The name *haricot* is derived from the Aztec word "ayacote." Other varieties of this group of beans are black bean, lima bean, pigeon pea, black-eyed pea and pinto bean.

Fava bean, also called the broad bean, was named for its broad, plump shape. It was cultivated in the Stone Age and served as a staple food of ancient Egypt, Greece and Rome. The Fava bean is long, round and feels velvety on the outside of the pod.

String beans grow as long, straight pods. They are crisp enough to snap easily when bent. String beans are either green or waxy yellow in color. Green and wax beans are available fresh, frozen or canned.

PREPARATION

When cooking fresh string beans:

1) The tough ends are clipped and the fibrous strip on the pod is removed and discarded.

2) They should be cooked quickly in boiling liquid just until al dente.

3) Frozen green and wax beans will not require as much cooking time as a fresh string bean.

4) Canned vegetables are cooked in the canning process and do not need further cooking. It is only necessary to heat canned green or wax beans to 150°F internal.

5) These beans, when cooked, can also be marinated and used in salads.

Lima beans are flat and kidney shaped. When fresh, the pod should be well filled and of a dark green color. The fresh bean should be plump, with a tender skin of green to greenish-white color. They should be stored for short periods of time only, at 45-50°F and 85 percent humidity. Lima beans are available fresh, frozen, canned or dried. To prepare fresh lima beans, boil until tender, then saute in butter. A popular dish in the Southern United States is called succotash. This is a combination of corn kernels and lima beans, served as a side dish.

CORN

There are over 200 varieties of corn grown in the United States. The type used as a vegetable in the kitchen is the kernel of what is termed *sweet corn*. It is picked while the kernels are still soft and milky. The kernels may be either white or yellow in color. This variety and others are used to produce a number of by-products, such as starch, syrup and meal.

SELECTION & STORAGE

When purchasing fresh corn, the husk should be a fresh green color. Kernels need to be tender, milky, and with no large spaces between the rows. Well developed corn has an even number of rows of kernels, generally 12 or 14. Kernels that do not puncture rather easily when pressed are old. They will be dry and tough. Corn is available fresh, frozen or canned. While fresh corn is available year-round, the best supply and best quality is from May to September.

USAGE

Corn cooked on the cob should be boiled in lightly salted water (milk is also good in the cooking water) until the kernels are tender. Do not overcook, or the kernels will become dry and tough. Corn kernels, fresh, frozen, or canned, can be simmered, steamed or sauteed.

VEGETABLE FRUITS

Botanically, vegetable fruits are considered fruits; however, they are used in the kitchen as vegetables. Tomatoes, egglplant, peppers and various types of squash are prime examples of this group.

CUCUMBERS

Cucumbers, botanically, are considered a berry. One of the oldest known cultivated plants, its origin has been traced to 9750 B.C. in the area of Thailand. Today there are over 20 different species of cucumber. These include green, white, yellow, long, short, thin, stubby, smooth skinned, rough skinned, early maturing, late maturing and others. The newest on the market are European or English cucumbers. These are seedless, lighter green in color and 2 to 2 1/4 inches in diameter. These are grown exclusively in hot houses.

SELECTION & STORAGE

Cucumbers are normally purchased fresh or pickled. When choosing fresh cucumbers, select those that are fresh, firm and brilliant green in color. Older cucumbers tend to be dull green. Their flesh becomes soft and spongy.

Although available year round from Florida, California, South Carolina, and North Carolina, the heaviest supply is May through August. Store fresh cucumbers at moderately cold temperatures, 45-50°F, with 85 percent relative humidity.

USAGE

Cucumbers can be eaten raw, cooked or pickled. Raw and pickled, they are normally used in salads, sandwich fillings, or as a garnish. As a cooked vegetable they are best braised or lightly sauteed. The meat of the cucumber softens quickly when heated, so use short cooking times.

In preparation remember that the skin is the storehouse of valuable nutrients and the meat of the cucumber is mostly water.

OKRA

This is a tender, furry pod, light green in color. It originated in Africa, with the name "guingumbo" or "kingumbo".

SELECTION & STORAGE

When fresh, the pod will snap easily or puncture when light pressure is applied. Okra is best when two to four inches in length. The larger pods are tough and dry. Okra is available fresh or frozen. Store fresh okra at 50°F, with 85-95 percent relative humidity. It should be stored fresh no longer than two weeks.

USAGE

Okra is a popular ingredient in Creole-style cooking. It exudes a polysaccharide gum which acts as a natural thickening agent in Gumbo. Okra is good in soups and stews. It combines well with other vegetables, especially tomatoes. Rapid cooking preserves the flavor and texture of okra. It will not become sticky if it is not subjected to long cooking times. Okra should not be cooked in copper, iron, brass or tin pots because it will turn dark in color.

EGGPLANT

Eggplant is a large, heavy vegetable, usually pear shaped and dark purple in color. They are believed to have originated in India and are best known in Oriental, Middle Eastern and Balkan cooking. The shape and color of the plants can vary widely. Eggplants range from round to cucumber shaped. In color they can be purple, purple-black, yellowish, white, red, or striped.

SELECTION & STORAGE

Large, heavier plants have more seeds. Young, smaller plants have less seeds and a bitter flavor. Eggplants are heaviest in supply August to September and lightest in February. Normally, they are only purchased fresh.

USAGE

When preparing eggplant:

1) It is not eaten raw, but can be eaten marinated.

2) If it has a bitter flavor, soak it briefly in salt water before cooking.

3) Eggplant is best known as a basic ingredient in ratatouille and eggplant parmesan.

4) Eggplant can be fried, sauteed, or combined with other vegetables in many types of casseroles.

TOMATOES

Tomatoes are native to Peru. They were brought to North America and Europe by the Spanish Conquistadors. By definition, tomatoes are a berry. They are pulpy, contain one or more seeds and no stones. They can vary in shape from somewhat spherical to plum shaped or an elongated pear shape. Tomatoes are usually red, but can be yellow.

Tomatoes were once referred to as the *love apple* and were thought to be poisonous. It was believed they were the biblical forbidden fruit. This myth arose from the fact that the tomato is a member of the nightshade family. Some species of this family are poisonous, such as belladonna, deadly nightshade and black henbane. Because of this, the tomato was cultivated solely as an ornamental plant when first introduced from South America.

SELECTION & STORAGE

Tomatoes are available fresh, canned or dried. Fresh tomatoes are available year-round. They should be held at 50°F if not fully ripened. At this temperature they will slowly continue to ripen and can normally be held for several weeks. When fully ripened, they should be stored at colder temperatures, but not frozen. Tomatoes can be purchased ethylene gas ripened or vine ripened. Although the vine ripened may have a fuller flavor, they are softer and deteriorate more quickly.

USAGE

Tomatoes are an extremely versatile vegetable-fruit. They are eaten raw in salads, fried, made into soups and sauces. They are a cornerstone of many southern Italian, Mexican, and Caribbean dishes.

PEPPERS

Garden peppers are classified in two categories. The mild/sweet peppers include the popular bell pepper. The hot/pungent group includes the chili, pimento and cayenne. Peppers are available fresh, canned or pickled (hot/pungent varieties).

The most widely used pepper in the United States is the mild/sweet bell pepper. These can be purchased green or red in color, according to the peppers maturity. The bell pepper is also available in shades of brown, deep purple, orange and yellow. These brightly colored peppers normally have sweeter flavor than the green pepper, though they are all bell peppers.

SELECTION & STORAGE

The best quality fresh peppers are well shaped, thick walled, firm with a glossy color. Fresh peppers should not be stored below 45°F, the ideal temperature being 46-48°F, with 85 percent relative humidity. They will hold well for 12-15 days.

Peppers are in constant supply year-round, with the heaviest supply being spring and summer. In the summer they come from the southern, midwestern and eastern United States, in winter from California, Texas and Florida.

USAGE

Peppers are delicious stuffed, sliced and sauteed. They add flavor, color, and texture to soups, stews, and sauces. Peppers can be marinated and served in salads, or used raw as an addition to other salad mixtures.

SQUASH

Squash are gourds that are eaten for their meat, and sometimes seeds. The rind may be eaten, depending on the type of squash. Most squashes are in greatest supply during late summer and early fall. However, those termed summer squash are in reasonable supply year-round. There are several types of squash available. Each is valued for its own distinctive flavor and texture.

Summer squash includes yellow crookneck and zucchini. These types of squash are very popular and are 98 percent edible. Both the skin and seeds of this squash are eaten. They have a tender, either yellow or green skin. When fresh they should be semi-soft.

Winter squash includes acorn and butternut squash. The skin and seeds of these are inedible. Acorn squash is dark green in color with tinges of orange in the skin. It is called acorn because of its similarity in shape to the nut. The flesh of acorn squash is a pale, creamy yellow, with a fine grained, dense texture.

Butternut squash is nearly cylindrical with a bulbous end. The skin is smooth, hard and light creamy brown or dark yellow in color. The flesh of butternut squash is dark yellow to orange, with a fine grain and dense texture.

Winter squash are best baked and glazed. Summer squash can be boiled, sauteed or baked. It is good mixed with other vegetables in saute dishes. Winter and summer squash are good additions to soups and stews. The pulp of these squash can be used in pies, baked goods, muffins, quick breads and custards.

Winter squash should be stored at 50-60°F with 70-75 percent relative humidity. It keeps well for three to six months. Summer squash is best stored at 32-34°F with 85-90 percent relative humidity. Winter and summer squashes are available fresh or frozen; however, the quality of the fresh is preferred. Other types of these squash include pattypan, cymling, chayote and hubbard.

Pumpkin is a bright orange squash, normally available fresh in late October. The pureed pulp of the pumpkin is available canned, year-round. It is a popular ingredient in pies and custards. Pumpkin is also good in soups, breads, cookies and stuffings. The seeds of the pumpkin are good roasted.

To prepare fresh pumpkin:

1) Cut in 1/2 or 1/4 and remove the seeds and stringy portion.

2) Remove the rind and cut into smaller pieces.

3) Cook covered in a small amount of lightly salted water until tender.

4) When tender, allow to drain thirty minutes to remove the excess moisture.

Pumpkin can also be baked. One five-pound pumpkin yields 4 1/2 cups of mashed, cooked pumpkin.

Spaghetti squash, also known as cucuzzi, calabash or suzza melon, is an edible growth, often classified as squash. It is round and somewhat cylindrical in shape, with a tough skin and bright yellow in color. When raw, the flesh is dense and tight. After cooking the flesh will string like spaghetti.

To prepare spaghetti squash:

1) Bake it whole or in pieces.
   a) If baking it whole, the skin should be poked generously with a fork to allow steam to escape.

b) If cooking the squash in pieces, remove the seeds.

2) Bake it in a 325°F oven until tender.

3) When done, remove the seeds and scoop out the center flesh.

4) This will pull way in long thread-like strands.

5) Saute the pulp in butter or other fat or oil, and/or serve with an appropriate sauce.

BULBS

Bulbs are stems holding a food reserve in the fleshy, overlapping leaves which give shape to the vegetable. Common examples of this group are onion, shallot and garlic.

ONIONS

The onion is a common garden vegetable, an edible bulb, with a pungent flavor and aroma. Most onions are of the single bulb variety. They range in color from silvery white through yellow to red. Onions vary in shape, including round, oval and pear-shaped. They are grown in all parts of the world and are the most widely used flavoring agent.

SELECTION & STORAGE

Onions, except green onions and leeks, are sold only after a drying period. The flavor is usually pungent, but can be bland or sweet depending on the variety. The warmer the climate, the sweeter the onion.

Select fresh onions which are well shaped, bright, hard bulbs. Onion are also available dried, pre-chopped in oil, or as juice. Fresh onions should be stored in a dry area, with no more than a 70-75 percent relative humidity. Higher humidity will cause root growth and decay will occur.

USAGE

Onions are an excellent flavoring agent. They can be used raw or cooked. Onions are good boiled, baked, sauteed, fried, creamed, steamed, roasted and pickled. Use them in soups, stews, sauces or salads.

SCALLION

The term *scallion* does not refer to one singular type of bulb. It can be any shoot from the white onion variety, pulled before the bulb has formed. This includes green onions and shallots. According to Webster it also includes leeks.

GREEN ONIONS

These are onions which are harvested young. The tender green tops can be eaten along with the immature white bottom bulb. These are used extensively in the kitchen, both raw and cooked.

SHALLOTS

These are bulbs which grow in clusters. They are tiny, spherical and a bit elongated. Shallots have a dry, papery skin. The flesh varies in color from white to tinged with purple. Shallots have a subtle flavor of both onion and garlic. They are excellent in all types of cooked dishes.

LEEKS

Leeks look like overgrown scallions. They have flat green leaves and a long white stalk. They are 1 to 1-1/2 inches in diameter and 6 to 8 inches in length. Their flavor is more subtle than that of the onion and is used to flavor stocks and sauces. They can also be baked or braised. Caution should be used in cleaning leeks to be sure all sand and grit is removed from between each inside layer.

CHIVES

These are tiny onions, whose roots and tops are used for flavoring. The greens are pencil thin and can be purchased fresh, freeze-dried, frozen or canned.

GARLIC

Garlic is a bulbous, rooted plant. It is a compound bulb consisting of several smaller sections of cloves. A garlic bulb is sometimes referred to as a bunch, fist or head. The smaller attached pieces are called cloves.

STORAGE

It has a distinctive odor from the organic sulphur compounds it contains. Garlic must be stored away from all other foods to prevent the odor from permeating them. It is available in a variety of forms. The supply of fresh garlic is heaviest July to September. Fresh, it should be stored in a cool, dry place, away from direct sunlight.

USAGE

Over the centuries many claims have been made concerning the medicinal value of this plant. One thing cannot be disputed; however, it is a great flavoring agent. It can be roasted whole, minced, chopped, pureed or sliced to add flavor to hundreds of dishes.

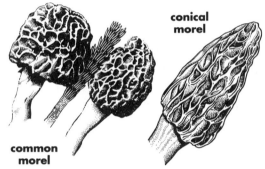

conical morel

common morel

EDIBLE FUNGI MUSHROOMS

Mushrooms are not actually a vegetable. They are an edible fungus. Mushrooms have been cultivated as a food in Europe since the 17th century. We include them here because of the manner in which they are used in food preparation, basically as a vegetable.

There are over 38,000 kinds of mushrooms. Three-quarters of these are edible. The ones more commonly used in the American kitchen are champignon de Paris, chantrelles, enokis, morels, and cepes.

SELECTION & STORAGE

Most are cultivated indoors and sold fresh. They are in greatest supply in November and December. However, they are available year-round. When purchasing, pick ones which have smooth unblemished skin, and caps that are

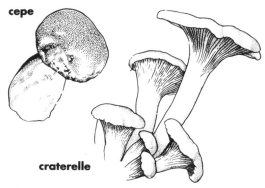

cepe

craterelle

closed around the stem. A mushroom with a cap which is opening, exposing the gills, is old and will be tough.

Mushrooms are very moist and continue to absorb moisture readily when stored. They should be stored refrigerated, unwashed, and loosely covered so that they can breathe.

USAGE

Prepare mushrooms by trimming the very bottom of the stem. Wipe off all dirt with a damp towel. Do not soak them in water, they will get soggy. Mushrooms contain protein and will become tough if overcooked. Use short cooking times.

Mushrooms are a very versatile food item. They can add flavor and texture to meat, poultry, seafood, cheese, and egg dishes. The mushroom is also popular prepared as a side dish, sauteed or fried. They are excellent, raw, in salads or stuffed as an appetizer.

Champignon de Paris

This is the type of mushroom most often cultivated in the United States. They are off-white or tan in color. They range in size from 3/4 to 3 inches. This mushroom has a flavor which is subtle and slightly earthy.

Chantrelle (Trumpet)

This is a trumpet-shaped, edible mushroom. Most common is the girolle or golden chantrelle. It has a cap which is crumpled and pleated with a yellow color. They are one to three inches across and about the same in height. Grown around the world in temperate climates, such as Japan, India and the United States, they keep well refrigerated. They are good in egg dishes, sauces or stewed meats.

Enoki

This type is relatively new on the market in the United States. They have a very delicate white, three to four-inch stem, with a tiny white cap. Similar in appearance to a bean sprout with a cap, they are pale ivory in color. They are pretty as a garnish, but must be handled delicately. Enokis do not hold well, and must be used immediately.

Morel

Also known as sponge mushrooms, the cap of this type has a sponge like appearance. They are yellow-brown in color and two to five inches high. The interior of the cap and stem are hollow. Morels are found in wooded clearings and orchards during the spring.

They are considered one of the most desirable mushrooms and are very expensive. They can be purchased dried or fresh. Use them with meat, fish or poultry for their robust flavor. They can be sauted or added to egg dishes such as omelettes.

★ *NOTE There is a mushroom called a false morel which has a separation from the cap to the stem. A true morel has a cap that is actually part of the stem. When cut in half the hollow of the stem extends unimpeded into the cap. Sometimes, if you do not inspect your mushrooms carefully, you will get a mixed batch, even in the dried varieties.*

The false morel contains antibuse, which causes a violent reaction when consumed with alcohol. The true morel contains a very small amount of this and, for this reason, both should be served cooked as opposed to raw.

Cepe

These are sometimes called king bolete, cepe, steeinpilz and poicino. These are large mushrooms with a cap shaped like a hamburger bun. They have a thick, club shaped stem which is often bulb-like at the base. Cepe are usually three to six inches across the cap and four to seven inches in height. Their color ranges from brown to iced brown on the cap and white or pale brown on the stem. The flesh of a cepe is solid and white. They do not have gills under the cap, but a spongy layer peppered with hundreds of tiny holes.

This variety, which grows wild under pine or evergreen trees, is native to central and northern Europe, and certain areas of the Pacific Northwest of America. They preserve well after cooking by canning, pickling or freezing. They are also available dry.

These mushrooms are best sauteed. They have a sweet, nutty flavor, plus an interesting crunchy texture.

TRUFFLES

These are the tuber of varieties of edible fungi native to many parts of the world. They grow near the roots of oak and beech trees. The truffle is not visible from above the ground. When they are gathered in autumn, special dogs and pigs are used to find them. They sniff them out, following their scent. They are then dug out of the ground by hand.

The two most prized types of truffles are: Perigord, which is black and from France, and the piedmontese, which is white and from Alba or Italy. Black truffles are 1/2 to 3 inches wide, dark brown to black in color. They are irregularly shaped, with a pebbly texture on the outside.

Truffles are very expensive and can be purchased fresh or canned. When canned, you can buy either whole truffles or peelings. Truffles are used in soups, sauces, salads, and meat dishes. They are a favorite for garnishment of cold and hot dishes.

SPECIALTY VEGETABLES

There are vegetables which do not fit in any other category.

ARTICHOKE

This vegetable resembles a thistle, with thick overlapping leaves, tipped with thorns. They are usually dark green, but can also be bluish, violet, brown or red, depending on the variety. Heads vary in size from three to five inches in diameter.

Inside the covering of leaves is the heart, which is surrounded by a fine hair-like growth called the choke. If permitted to mature, the choke would become a flower. This choke is not edible. The base of each leaf and the heart are edible.

STORAGE

Artichokes can be purchased fresh, with a constant supply from California. When fresh, they can be stored briefly at 32°F, with 95 percent relative humidity. Artichokes can also be purchased canned.

USAGE

Cooked artichokes are eaten by stripping the cooked leaves and eating the bottom of them dipped in an appropriate sauce, such as hollandaise or vinaigrette. When the heart is exposed, it can be removed and eaten. When cooking, add a little lemon juice to help retain color. Artichokes can also be stuffed with seafood or meat mixtures.

RHUBARB

A field-grown rhubarb is a rich, dark red color, with coarse foliage, very large green leaves resembling elephant ears. It has a very tart flavor. Hothouse rhubarb is light pink, with smaller leaves and a much milder flavor.

SELECTION & STORAGE

A good quality rhubarb is fresh, firm, crisp and tender. It can be stored two to four weeks at 32°F. It wilts rapidly at room temperature. The major suppliers of this vegetable are Washington, Michigan and California.

USAGE

The use of this plant for medicinal and cooking purposes dates back to 2700 B.C. in China and Mongolia. Only the stalk is edible. The leaves are bitter from oxalic acid and can be fatal if eaten in quantity. Rhubarb is popular in puddings, pies, tarts, jams and jellies. It is normally cooked with sugar.

METHODS OF PREPARATION

The preparation of vegetables is far more than just the application of heat. Your goal should be to preserve and enhance their fresh flavor, texture, color and nutritional content. To do this you must keep several factors in mind.

TEXTURE

Vegetable fiber, such as CELLULOSE and PECTIN, give vegetables shape and firmness. These are changed during cooking. The amount of fiber present varies from plant to plant. For example, spinach has less fiber than a turnip. There are sometimes variations in the amount of fiber from one part of a plant to another, such as the stem of the broccoli and the buds. The maturity of a vegetable may create a change in its fiber content. Consider a young baby carrot, which is tender, and an old carrot, which is tough and hard.

The fiber in the plant is affected by many things in the cooking process. Some make the fiber tougher, others make it softer. Fibers are toughened by acids, such as lemon juice, vinegar and tomato products. Sugars strengthen cellulose. If your goal is to make a vegetable softer you will need to be careful with the addition of acids and sugars.

Alkali and heat soften vegetable fibers. Alkalis such as baking soda or hard water destroy vegetable fibers making them soft and mushy. Heat is the foremost enemy of vegetable fibers. Cooking vegetables for long periods of time softens them. If you want to serve crisp, fresh tasting vegetables, you must control these factors.

DEGREE OF DONENESS

Vegetables are said to be done when they have reached the desired degree of doneness. This not only varies from veg-

---

GUIDELINES FOR PROPER DONENESS OF VEGETABLES

1. DO NOT OVERCOOK VEGETABLES.
2. COOK VEGETABLES AS CLOSE TO SERVICE AS POSSIBLE. REMEMBER THAT THEY CONTINUE TO COOK WHEN HELD IN A HOT TABLE.
3. IF YOU DO HAVE TO COOK AHEAD, UNDERCOOK THE VEGETABLES SLIGHTLY. THIS WILL ALLOW FOR SOME HOLDING TIME OR REHEATING.
4. WHEN PRE-COOKING FOR REHEATING, SHOCK THE VEGETABLES IN ICE WATER TO STOP THE COOKING PROCESS.
5. ALWAYS CUT UNIFORM-SIZE PIECES TO ENSURE EVEN COOKING THROUGHOUT A BATCH OF VEGETABLES.
6. VEGETABLES WITH TOUGH AND TENDER PARTS NEED SPECIAL ATTENTION.
   A. PEEL THE STEMS OF ASPARAGUS.
   B. PEEL AND SPLIT THE STEMS OF BROCCOLI.
   C. SCORE THE BASE OR STEM END OF BRUSSEL SPROUTS.
   D. TAKE SPECIAL CARE TO PROTECT THE BUDS OF BROCCOLI AND ASPARAGUS FROM EXTENDED HEAT.
7. DO NOT MIX BATCHES OF COOKED VEGETABLES. EACH BATCH IS COOKED TO A SLIGHTLY DIFFERENT DONENESS AND, IF MIXED, A VARIATION OF COLOR AND TEXTURE CAN OCCUR.
8. REMEMBER, YOUR GOAL IS TO ENHANCE THE FRESH, CRISP, FLAVOR OF THE VEGETABLE, NOT DIMINISH IT.

Figure 1

etable to vegetable, but from one region of the country and world to another. As a rule of thumb, keep vegetables slightly firm to the bite, *al dente*. Listed in Figure One are guidelines for gaining proper doneness in your vegetables.

FLAVOR

Changes in mild flavored vegetables occur in the cooking process. They are extracted by the moisture present when being cooked. The moisture then evaporates and flavor is lost. To prevent this, cook vegetables in the least amount of water possible. Use just enough water to cover the vegetables and, whenever possible, steam the vegetables.

To cook vegetables quickly and reduce flavor loss, start them in boiling water. This reduces the length of time they are in the liquid. Salt added to the cooking liquid also helps reduce flavor loss by increasing the water temperature and enhancing the flavor of the vegetable.

Strong flavored vegetables, such as onions, cabbage, garlic, leeks, brussel sprouts, cauliflower, broccoli, turnips and rutabagas, may need some reduction in their strong flavors. It is best to cook them uncovered, in a larger quantity of water to allow some of the harsh flavor to dissipate.

COLOR

It is not unusual for vegetables to be accepted or rejected by the guest solely on the basis of their color when presented. Preserving as much of the natural color as possible is important. A high level of visual quality is a must.

The color of a vegetable is determined by the pigment it contains. Pigment is the coloring matter within the cells and tissue of the plant. The various types of pigments are effected differently by heat, acid, alkali and other elements involved in cooking. To maintain as much color as possible in your cooked vegetables, you need to know what these pigments are and how they are affected.

Flavones is the pigment in white vegetables. It is present in potato, onion, cauliflower, white cabbage, cucumber, zucchini and the white of celery. This pigment stays white in an acid medium and turns yellow in an alkaline medium. Overcooking will also turn vegetables containing this pigment yellow or gray. This reaction is not reversible. Adding acid to yellowed white vegetables will not return them to their original white color.

To retain the white color of the flavones pigment:

1. COOK THEM UNCOVERED. THIS ALLOWS THE ACIDS RELEASED BY THE VEGETABLE DURING COOKING TO ESCAPE.
2. USE SHORT COOKING TIMES.
3. ADD A SMALL AMOUNT OF LEMON JUICE, CREAM OF TARTAR OR VINEGAR TO THE COOKING LIQUID TO CREATE A SLIGHTLY ACID MEDIUM.

Anthocyanin pigment gives some red vegetables their color. It is present in very few vegetables, primarily red cabbage, purple peppers, purple tomatillos, purple potatoes, radishes and eggplant skins. Anthocyanin is the pigment present in most berries and flowers. It is strongly affected by acid and alkali mediums. An alkali medium will turn them blue or blue-green in color. An acid medium will give them a brighter red color. This red pigment is easily dissolved in water. Excessive amounts of water when cooking will leach the color out of the vegetable.

To retain the red color given by the anthocyanin pigment:

1. COOK RED CABBAGE WITH A SMALL AMOUNT OF ACID, LEMON JUICE, CREAM OF TARTAR OR VINEGAR OR SPRINKLE WITH A FOOD ACID AT THE END OF THE COOKING PROCESS. AN EXAMPLE OF THIS TYPE OF PREPARATION IS BRAISED RED CABBAGE WITH THE ADDITION OF A TART COOKING ACID.
2. USE ONLY AS MUCH WATER AS NECESSARY.

Chlorophyll Pigment provides green vegetables with their color. Present in all green plants, its enemies are heat and acid.

To retain as much of the natural green color as possible:

1. COOK THEM UNCOVERED TO ALLOW THE VEGETABLES' VOLATILE ACIDS TO ESCAPE. WHEN THE VEGETABLES ARE COOKED WITH A COVER, THE PLANTS' NATURAL ACID IS LEECHED INTO THE COOKING LIQUID AND IS TRAPPED THERE CREATING AN ACIDIC COOKING MEDIUM. THIS, COMBINED WITH THE HEAT PRESENT, DESTROYS THE PIGMENT.
2. COOK THEM QUICKLY, UNTIL JUST AL DENTE. EXTENDED EXPOSURE TO HEAT WILL DESTROY THE COLOR AND LEACH OUT NUTRIENTS.
3. COOK THE VEGETABLES IN SMALL BATCHES. THIS REDUCES THE COOKING AND HOLDING TIME.
4. DO NOT HOLD FOR LONG PERIODS OF TIME. IF IT IS NECESSARY TO PRE-COOK, SHOCK AND THEN REHEAT THEM AS NEEDED.
5. STEAM GREEN VEGETABLES WHENEVER POSSIBLE. THIS SHORTENS THE COOKING TIME, ALLOWS FAR LESS ACID BUILDUP, AND RETAINS MORE COLOR.

Carotene Pigments give color to yellow and orange vegetables. These include carrots, corn, winter squash, rutabagas, sweet potatoes, tomato and red peppers. This is the most stable of the color pigments. It is only slightly affected by acids or alkalis: However, long cooking can dull the color. As with most vegetables short cooking times help retain flavor and vitamins. This pigment is fat soluble and will leach out into the fat used to cook the item. This is where the red grease comes from that floats to the surface of stews and meat soups which contain tomato or carrot.

NUTRIENTS

One of the major challenges of cooking vegetables is the preservation of the nutrients they contain. Most vegetables are sources of vitamin A and C, as well as rich in other vitamins and minerals. Many of these nutrients are destroyed when the vegetable is cooked.

There are six major causes of nutrient loss.

1. HIGH COOKING TEMPERATURES.
2. LONG EXPOSURE OF NUTRIENTS TO EVEN, LOW HEAT, EVEN SUNLIGHT.
3. LEACHING, BEING DISSOLVED IN WATER DURING COOKING.
4. ALKALI.
5. PLANT ENZYMES WHICH ARE ACTIVE IN WARM TEMPERATURES, BUT KILLED BY HIGH HEAT.
6. EXPOSURE TO OXYGEN.

As can be seen by a quick glance at this list, the real enemy here is the cooking process. Although it improves flavor, with the exception of stopping the natural enzymes in the vegetable which cause decay, cooking in no way helps vitamins or minerals. Yet, we cook vegetables. WHY? For the flavor and texture changes we create in controlled circumstances.

Our goal is to bring about the changes we want with as little nutrient loss as possible. This can be done by:

1) COOKING WITH STEAM WHENEVER POSSIBLE TO REDUCE THE LEACHING WHICH RESULTS IN BOILING AND SIMMERING.
2) USING SHORT COOKING TIMES.
3) AVOIDING THE USE OF BAKING SODA, OR OTHER FORMS OF ALKALI IN COOKED VEGETABLES. TRUE, BAKING SODA WILL TURN BROCCOLI BRIGHT GREEN, BUT IT WILL ALSO LESSEN ITS NUTRITIONAL FOOD VALUE.
4) STORING FRESH VEGETABLES OUT OF DIRECT SUNLIGHT AND IN CLOSED CONTAINERS TO MINIMIZE VITAMIN LOSES.
5) NOT DISCARDING THE LIQUOR IN THE CAN WHEN USING CANNED VEGETABLES. SERVE IT WITH THE VEGETABLES.

It is possible to serve good tasting, attractive, nutritious cooked vegetables. To do this you must constantly be aware

3 Peeling Techniques

Remove thin skins (1/8" thick) with a vegetable peeler.

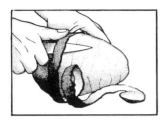
Remove thick skins (3/8" thick) with a small sharp knife.

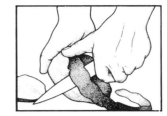
Peel celeriac with a medium-sized knife to remove bark-like skin.

of the effect your preparation techniques have on the end product.

HANDLING FRESH, FROZEN AND CANNED VEGETABLES

FRESH VEGETABLES
Cleaning

All fresh vegetables should be washed thoroughly before being used. For root vegetables, such as carrots, scrub them with a brush, if they are not going to be peeled. When cleaned they should be drained well. Use a colander or perforated pan so the moisture can drain away from the vegetables.

Most fresh vegetables should not be soaked for long periods. Soaking leaches the flavor and nutrients from the vegetables. An exception would be cabbage, broccoli, brussel sprouts and cauliflower. These may be soaked briefly in cold, salted water to drive out possible insects. Limp vegetables, such as spinach, can be soaked briefly in cold water to restore crispness.

Peeling and Cutting

All vegetables should be peeled as thinly as possible. A thick peeling discards valuable nutrients located under the skin. Cut your vegetables to a uniform thickness. This will allow for even cooking.

Peeling and cutting should be done as close to service as possible to prevent excessive drying and vitamin loss due to oxidation. Always save any edible trimmings and peelings for use in appropriate soups, stocks and vegetable purees.

Storage

In general, store potatoes, onions and winter squash in a cool, dry, dark place. The ideal temperature range is 50-65°F. Other vegetables should be refrigerated.

Do not wash vegetables before storing. Many have a natural or manmade coating on them to prevent moisture and nutrient loss. Wrap them to prevent drying or keep the relative humidity high in the cooler.

Purchase vegetables as close to when they will be used as possible. Although some vegetables have a good shelf life, many have a very short holding life. Always keep storage areas clean and rotate stock, using the oldest produce first.

FROZEN VEGETABLES

Frozen vegetables have been blanched before freezing. Blanching is

---

STANDARDS OF QUALITY FOR COOKED VEGETABLES

1. BRIGHT NATURAL COLORS.
2. CUT NEATLY AND UNIFORMLY.
3. ATTRACTIVELY ARRANGED ON PLATE OR PLATTER.
4. IMAGINATIVE AND APPROPRIATE COMBINATIONS.
5. COOKED TO THE PROPER DEGREE OF DONENESS.
6. SERVED WITH THE CORRECT AMOUNT OF COOKING LIQUID OR COMPLEMENTARY SAUCE.
7. HAVE A FULL BODIED, NATURAL FLAVOR.
8. LIGHTLY AND APPROPRIATELY SEASONED.

the placement of a food in boiling water or steam for a brief time. This kills the natural plant enzymes which would otherwise continue to age the vegetable even when frozen. This also means that they are partially cooked, so much shorter cooking times are needed. Normally, they should be cooked from the frozen state. The exception is corn on the cob or vegetables which freeze into a solid block, such as spinach. These vegetables would first be thawed under refrigeration.

CANNED VEGETABLES

Never accept, or open, puffed, swollen, leaking, rusted or badly dented cans. The product may be tainted and can be poisonous. Always wipe the top of the can before opening to prevent accumulated dust from being transferred to the contents of the can.

Remember that canned vegetables are already fully cooked. It is only necessary to heat them to the correct serving temperature. The best way to do this is to drain the vegetable's liquor into a pan. Bring the liquid to a boil and reduce by one half to two thirds. Add seasonings and the vegetable, then return to serving temperature. This method reduces cooking time; conserves flavor and nutrients, and prevents as much color loss as possible.

It is important that canned vegetables not be overcooked. They already have a soft texture, and this can quickly become mush or, in the case of corn, very dry. They should be heated as close to serving time as possible. Do not hold them for long periods on a steam table.

Store canned vegetables in a cool, dry, dark place. They should be up off the floor. Discard any cans which show signs of damage, such as those mentioned earlier.

COOKING VEGETABLES

BOILING/STEAMING

Nearly all vegetables can be boiled or steamed. These cooking methods are the most often used. Both are easy, economical and can be adapted to many forms of preparations. Often, vegetables are partially cooked (blanched) by these methods, then finished in another manner. Figures Two and Three state how to boil or steam vegetables.

SAUTEING AND PAN-FRYING

The primary differences between saute and pan-fry are the amount of oil used and cooking time. For saute, you cook the item quickly in a small amount of fat. In pan-frying, the item is cooked partially submerged in fat, at a lower temperature and for a longer time. Both methods may be used to finish cooking pre-cooked or blanched vegetables. They may also be used to cook them from a raw state. Figures Four and Five give procedures for these preparation methods.

BRAISING

This slow, moist heat cooking method is used with a number of vegetables. It is an especially good process for those vegetables which might have tough fibers, such as carrots or celery. There are many variations and no hard and fast rules for braised vegetables. The basic characteristics are given in figure Six.

BAKING VEGETABLES

Baking is utilized in the preparation of starchy vegetables, such as winter squash, yams and potatoes, and some moist vegetables, such as tomatoes and onions. Starchy vegetables are baked because the dry heat produces a desirable texture in the final product. The slow, surrounding heat cooks the product undisturbed. This allows it to make the best use of its own moisture and starch content in cooking.

Baking of most vegetables is simply a matter of cleaning them, placing them in a preheated oven, and allowing them to cook to the desired degree of doneness. This works well for self-contained vegetables such as baked acorn squash, and baked potatoes. (Note: These vegetables should be pierced first to prevent them from exploding during cooking.) However, there are vegetables which are suitable to be combined with a particu-

lar sauce and baked. Examples of these are corn pudding and baked beans.

DEEP-FRYING VEGETABLES

Deep-frying is cooking an item completely submerged in hot fat or oil. Although potatoes and onion rings are the most popular vegetables for this type of preparation, others can be deep-fried. Vegetables cooked in this manner are divided into five categories.

1. BATTER DIPPED AND FRIED.
2. BREADED AND FRIED.
3. WITHOUT COATING AND FRIED.
4. VEGETABLE FRITTERS.
5. VEGETABLE CROQUETTES.

The method by which each of these is prepared prior to frying will depend on the item being fried and the final prod-

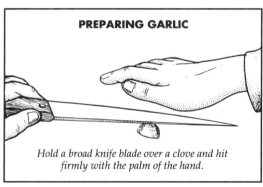

PREPARING GARLIC

Hold a broad knife blade over a clove and hit firmly with the palm of the hand.

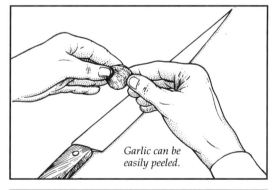

Garlic can be easily peeled.

Chop garlic finely.

For paste, sprinkle chopped garlic with salt and mash with broad side of knife blade.

DEEP-FRYING VEGETABLES

1. ASSEMBLE ALL EQUIPMENT AND PREPARE VEGETABLES.
2. PREHEAT FRYER TO 325-350°F.
3. BREAD, DIP, ETC., IF REQUIRED.
4. PLACE FOOD IN FRYER, BEING CAREFUL NOT TO OVERCROWD.
5. FRY TO DESIRED DONENESS. THE PRODUCT SHOULD BE COOKED THROUGH AND GOLDEN BROWN.
6. REMOVE AND ALLOW TO DRAIN.
7. SEASON AWAY FROM HOT FAT AND SERVE IMMEDIATELY.
8. IF IT IS NECESSARY TO HOLD THE ITEM BRIEFLY, DO NOT COVER OR THE PRODUCT WILL BECOME SOGGY.

NOTE: GOOD VEGETABLES FOR FRYING INCLUDE: EGGPLANT, MUSHROOMS, ONION RINGS, ZUCCHINI, POTATOES AND CAULIFLOWER.

Figure 7

---

uct desired. Figure nine gives the basic procedures for deep- frying vegetables.

NUTRITION TIPS

The methods for cooking vegetables covered in this chapter are heavily based on classical preparation. From a nutritional standpoint this, at times, puts the methods at odds with contemporary nutritional cooking guidelines. This is not an insurmountable problem for the culinarian.

What is required to bring balance between the two is the application of your knowledge. One of the primary concerns nutritionally is the addition of fat to the vegetable preparation. With the exception of deep-frying and pan-frying, this does not present a major problem. The use of herbs and seasonings as a replacement for fat-based sauces is an excellent place to start. Expand your use of vegetable purees as sauces and heighten the flavor of items with acidulates (lemon, lime, balsamic vinegar). Possibly try replacing heavy cream sauces with sauces based on non-fat yogurt. Keep the amount of oil and fat used in saute to a bare minimum and use vegetable oil or olive oil in place of butter or margarine.

Making these types of changes in conjunction with your efforts to protect the nutritional value of the vegetables will quickly bring about a balance between classical preparation and nutritional guidelines. Remember, the culinarian's goal is always to produce good tasting, attractive and nutritious food.

CONCLUSION

The preparation of vegetables is a cornerstone of cooking. It requires a concern for the nutritional value, texture, flavor, and color of the item. To achieve a balance of these four factors requires a knowledge of the affect of heat, acid, and other physical actions on the vegetable. When the factors and what affects them are understood, the results can and should be excellent.

REVIEW QUESTIONS

1. Define the term *vegetables*.
2. State the two goals of the culinarian in regard to vegetable preparation.
3. List and define the major vegetable groupings.
4. List and discuss the four factors considered in vegetable preparation.
5. List the eight standards of quality for cooked vegetables.
6. Discuss the handling of fresh, frozen and canned vegetables.
7. List the steps for broiling, sauteing and braising vegetables.
8. Discuss the balance between classical preparation of vegetables and contemporary nutritional guidelines.

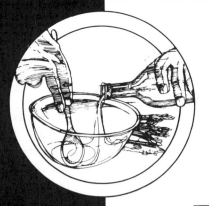

Chapter 12

Potatoes

& other Tubers

CHAPTER OBJECTIVES

• To introduce tubers as an ingredient.

• To introduce the various types of tubers used in the kitchen.

• To discuss factors affecting the preparation of tubers.

• To discuss methods for cooking potatoes.

• To introduce the potato as a distinctive type of tuber.

• To introduce the various types of potatoes.

• To discuss factors affecting the preparation of potatoes.

• To discuss methods for cooking potatoes.

There is often confusion when the term TUBER is used. Tubers are generally considered to be vegetables such as potatoes and jeruselum artichokes. These are formed from underground stems which extend from the root of the plant. Tuber also includes, by definition, root plants, such as carrots, radishes or parsnips, which are the thickened roots of plants. However, they are normally separated from other tubers. Vegetables such as kohlrabi and turnip are combinations of the thickened root and stem of the plant.

As confusing as this may seem, it simply means that there are many types of vegetables in the category of tubers. Some of these vegetables are not thought of by the cook as being related, yet they are. Most tubers have a compact, tight structure. However, there is a large difference in the starch content of the various types.

To make this large group of vegetables more manageable, they are divided into two parts in this chapter. We discuss those termed *potatoes* separately due to their wide variety of types and versatility. The other vegetables categorized as tubers are grouped under the heading of general tubers.

GENERAL TUBERS

General tubers include a wide variety of vegetables which cannot be readily included in broad descriptions for preparation and use. It is also not practical to cover all tubers that could be included in this group in this text. Those discussed here are the more common ones used in the kitchen.

Jerusalem Artichokes are irregularly shaped, fairly large, white or purplish in color and have a thick skin. In appearance it is similar to a knobby potato. Jerusalem artichokes have a nutty flavor and can be used in a variety of ways. They can be prepared in the same manner that you would prepare potatoes. However, remember that they are sweeter.

Prior to cooking they should be thoroughly cleaned. If old, this artichoke should be peeled thinly. The younger tubers can be cooked without peeling. Jerusalem artichokes can be eaten raw in salads, sauteed, boiled, steamed, baked, deep-fried, pureed or marinated. When boiling or pureeing, it is best to par-cook the tuber. Jerusalem artichokes are an excellent accompaniment for meat dishes.

NOTE: Avoid using aluminum pots for boiling. They can cause the tuber to discolor.

Japanese/Chinese Artichokes are white tubers which have no skin and are small, oblong and ring-like in shape. To prepare this tuber, wash and scrub it well. It can be used raw in salads, or boiled for a short time and then baked or fried.

Garden Beets (Table Beets) are the thickened lower part of the stem and upper part of the root of a biennial plant. They vary from flat to round to long in size. The most widely used variety of beet is the red beet. However, there are also varieties with white, yellow or reddish-white ringed flesh.

Beets can be used raw or cooked. The preferred method for cooking cleaned raw beets is boiling. Cooked beets can be sliced, diced or cut in strips and used in salads or pickled.

Carrots are a vegetable almost taken for granted. We use them so often that they lose their separate identity as a vegetable. They are a basic ingredient in a variety of preparations in the kitchen.

There are two types of carrots. EARLY SUMMER CARROTS are sold with or without their leaves. This long, cylindrical, slender root has firm leaves and a vivid orange color. The shape of the carrot may vary some with the variety. WINTER CARROTS are a large fleshy root with a reddish-orange color and lighter core. The color of root varies with the type and where it is grown. Carrots grow best in cool, wet summers. A good red color in the carrot usually means a high carotene pigment content.

Carrots are used in as many ways, if not more, than potatoes. The only place where this does not apply is in industrial processing. In this case the volume and applications are not quite as extensive as the potato.

How carrots are used in the kitchen is determined, primarily, by their age. Baby carrots only need to be well rinsed before using. Fairly young carrots should be scrubbed with a vegetable brush. Older carrots need to be peeled before use. It is preferable to use a peeler, not a knife. Using a knife wastes too much flesh. Older woody

Celeriac

Underutilized but with potential for many uses, celeriac is superb hot or cold due to its mild, subtle flavor.

carrots, unless used for stock, should have their cores removed before using. Cut the carrot in quarters, lengthwise, and pry the core out with the tip of a small knife.

Carrots of all types can be eaten raw, cut into strips or grated in salads. Miniature and young baby carrots can be quickly cooked without water, steamed, blanched or sauteed. Young carrots can be cut in various shapes and sizes. They can be served mixed with other colorful vegetables, such as peas, celery or turnips. They are good glazed, creamed or used in salads. Mature, older carrots make good flavoring for stocks and sauces. These carrots are good added to stew, roasts or soups. They can also be braised, pureed or used in desserts.

Celeriac is a variety of celery, also known as celery root, celery knob or turnip root celery. The leaves are dark green and strongly aromatic. The bulb-type root is light brown. The smaller the root, the more tender and less woody it will be.

Celeriac should be peeled before cooking. Normally it is cut into strips, slices or chunks. It can be marinated and served as a salad. It is primarily used in soups or stews, but can be braised, boiled, baked or stewed. Cut and grated celeraic rapidly turns brown. This can be prevented by immersing it in water with a little lemon juice.

Fennel is a leafy bulb with a pure white to greenish white bulbous base, green upper stalks, and grass green, fern-like shoots. The tuber varies in shape from flat to spherical.

There are two types of fennel: BOLOGNESE has a short, tender leaf and stem which can be eaten raw, FLORENTINE has longer leaves and stem which must be cooked.

The distinctly anise (licorice) taste of fennel is popular in Middle Eastern and Indian cooking. The stem and tuber are also used in the manufacture of liqueurs, such as Anisette and Chartreuse.

All parts of this plant are used in food production. Fennel leaves are utilized only as flavoring for various dishes. The seeds are often used in breads and Italian sausage. The bulb and stem can be eaten raw, shredded for use in salads. As a cooked vegetable, it is particularly good braised, but can be boiled, baked or stewed.

Kohlrabi in German, the word means "cabbage turnip." This tuber's flavor is similar to the turnip. Kohlrabi is a flat to oval shaped tuber. It shows above the ground due to the thickening of the stem. The tuber is either pale green in color, or bluish-violet if anthocyanin pigment is present. Both the tuber and leaf of the young plant can be eaten. The tuber is most widely used stewed, added to soups or chopped raw in salads.

Water Chestnuts are flattish-round tuberous root stocks. They have a brown to dark brown skin, with a yellowish-white flesh. Their flavor is crisp and sweet. They are primarily purchased canned. Water chestnuts are often peeled and used in Oriental recipes, soups and other dishes. They can also be boiled unpeeled, the skin removed and then eaten either as is or baked with other seasonings.

Parsnips look like white carrots. They are a fleshy, thickened, creamy white taproot (the main root of the plant that grows straight down in the ground) with a rather aromatic flavor. The sweet flavor of this root makes it a very good eating vegetable. To prepare parsnips, wash and peel the tuber. Then, if needed, dice, slice or cut it in strips. Parsnips can be used in soup and stew or baked or mashed as a separate vegetable.

Radish is an herb-type plant which forms a thickened tap root. The best known type of radish in the United States is the round, red, bulbous

Early Summer Carrot

variety. There are a variety of other radishes including those which are bi-colored or white and have longish, blunt or pointed roots.

Radishes can be sliced or grated. They are most often eaten raw in salads or used as a garnish. However, they are sometimes eaten on bread.

Rutabaga is a large tuber that has an inverted pear-shaped root vegetable. It grows to be considerably larger than the potato or turnip. It is an angular, round, turnip-type plant of medium height, with yellow or white flesh.

The yellow fleshed varieties are good for eating fresh. When preparing fresh, yellow fleshed swedes, peel them. They can then be cut into chips and boiled, mashed or prepared with a sauce. They can also be grated and used in soups or uncooked dishes.

The white fleshed swedes are usually diced in blocks during processing and dried. They are used by manufacturers in dried and canned soups.

Salsify is a straight, white, fleshy root, about 20 inches long, with brown-black skin. It resembles a thin parsnip. It is also called the OYSTER PLANT or VEGETABLE OYSTER for its subtle, faintly oyster flavor.

Salsify has a distant black-skinned European relative, longer and more slender, called SCORZONERA. This vegetable's flavor is similar to salsify, but with a hint of coconut. The two are used interchangeably.

To prepare these tubers, peel and cut the roots into 1-1/2 to 2-inch chunks. Salsify discolors and turns brown, when exposed to air. To prevent this, it should be soaked in water which has a slight amount of acid added (lemon juice or vinegar).

Salsify and scorzonera are blanched and then finished in various ways. Both can be cooked whole, after the skin is scrubbed. Peel the root, after cooking, by slipping the skins off under cold running water. When peeled, blanch, steam, saute, puree, cream or glaze them. They are excellent with grilled meats, when lightly sauteed in butter and sprinkled with herbs.

Garden Turnips are flat, semi-long to long, white-fleshed tubers, which sometimes have colored heads. The young tubers have a mild flavor. Usually, turnips are eaten cooked, because raw turnips sometimes have a strong, bitter taste. To prepare, wash and peel the tuber, then cut into strips, slices or chunks and stew.

Sweet Potatoes and Yams, botan-ically, are two distinct plants. Although these are tubers, like potatoes and frequently are cooked in the same manner, they belong to different families. Sweet potatoes belong to the Ipomoa (morning glory) family. Yams are from a vine-type plant, charac-terized by a larger root with woody outer skin.

Yams grow only in the tropics. Sweet potatoes are grown all over the United States. African slaves who ate sweet potatoes in America called them *nyam*, using the name of the tropical tuber they had known in Africa. From this name developed the word "yam."

The potato is not related to the sweet potato or yam. The major difference being that a sweet potato is a swollen root. The potato is a rhizome, a tuberous swelling at the tip of the root.

There are two basic types of sweet potatoes. One has a pale yellow skin and flesh. The other is sweeter and more moist, with a darker orange skin and flesh. It is the darker orange sweet potato which is mistakenly called a yam in the southern United States.

The fleshy thickened root often forms wild shapes, from round, to oval, to oblong. The color varies from white or light yellow to reddish-violet. They grow in length up to 10 inches, and up to 4-3/4 inches in diameter.

All sweet potatoes do not taste the same. The most popular variety is the darker orange variety. It has a sweeter taste and is more moist, with a less mealy texture. Select medium to small tubers for cooking. The mature, larger sweet potatoes are too fibrous for good eating.

The paler skin and flesh variety is best for baking whole. For boiling or mashing, the coral-orange fleshed sweet potato is preferable.

To prepare sweet potatoes, peel and cut into chunks or slices. Wash and then boil, bake or fry in batter. They are good steamed, pureed or shaped into balls with flour and then baked or fried in oil. Sweet potatoes are also excellent in casseroles or baked whole.

Sweet potatoes, particularly the Malayan pink variety, are made into jam. They can be preserved in syrup and are similar to glazed chestnuts. The leaves of the young sweet potato can be eaten like spinach. Sweet potatoes are also made into pies, cakes and souffles. New uses have been developed for this tuber, such as sweet potato chips, similar to potato chips, but higher in vitamins and carbohydrates. There are also sweet potato flakes, similar to corn flakes, which are used as a cereal and in pie filling and casseroles.

POTATOES

Native to the Andes Mountains of South America, potatoes have been cultivated by the native Americans since 3,000 B.C. The first Europeans introduced to potatoes were Pizarro's men, Spanish Conquistadors, in about 1553. The potatoes grown by the Indians were the size of peanuts, or at best plums, and the Spaniards first thought that they were truffles.

Potatoes were called *papas* by the Indians. This word is still in use in Spanish Latin America. The Spaniards called them *patatas*, which is close to their word for sweet potato, *batata*.

The potato was brought to Spain by the Conquistadors and is believed to have been under cultivation in Galicia by the end of the 16th century. Sir Francis Drake brought the potato to England in the 1580's. In those days the word potato, unmodified, meant sweet potato.

In the 18th century, first botanists, and then statesmen began to appreciate the advantages of the potato. It had a much higher yield per acre than cereal crops. The tuber was less vulnerable to damage from weather and the warfare of the time because it grew underground. The potato began to be grown as a staple in Germany, France, England and especially, Ireland, where it staved off famine in 1740.

A century later, the Irish were so dependent on the potato that, when a blight caused crop failure, the great "Potato Famine" occurred. The result was a large emigration of Irish to America. Despite some lack of enthusiasm in certain circles, potatoes continued to grow in popularity in the latter half of the 19th century and on into the 20th century. It is a staple food in many parts of the world today.

TYPES

The potato is the edible, starchy tuber of the common plant, SOLANUM TUBEROSUM, a perennial of the nightshade family. Being related to the deadly nightshade does not make the potato harmful, but it does mean that all green parts of the plant are toxic. Other edible members of this family are the tomato, eggplant and tomatillo.

These tubers are neither the fruit nor the root of the potato plant. They are a portion of the underground stem, which grows slightly above the roots. Each plant may yield a half dozen or more tubers. Potatoes do not grow from seeds, but from sprouting tubers. These are called seed potatoes.

Potatoes may be round, oval, irregular, oblong or even kidney shaped. They vary in weight up to one pound. Depending on the variety, they range in color from whitish brown through purple. The interior color ranges from white to light yellow.

There is a wide variety of types of potatoes. Each potato growing country has its own regional varieties. These varieties are usually divided in three groups: Early, mid-early and mid-late to late. Today, more than 5,000 strains of potatoes exist in research laboratories. There are about 2,000 varieties grown around the world.

Only a few of the known species are grown commercially in each region. Varieties of potatoes have been developed for various growing climates and the cuisine of various regions of the world. In the United States, approximately 160 varieties are grown.

Although each area of the country produces many varieties, only four of these are normally available in the stores.

Each of the four commonly sold varieties has its own cooking qualities. The species may not always be called by the same name, but the characteristics are easily recognized. According to the United States Department of Agriculture the four basic types are RUSSETS, ROUND REDS, LONG WHITES and ROUND WHITES.

Russet/Idaho potatoes are long, flat and oblong, with rounded ends. Russets have a rough, dry, fairly thick and netted, brown skin. The flesh is whitish, with a dry, mealy texture. This potato is high in starch and low in moisture content. Russet/Idaho potatoes are used in many ways, but are considered best for baking, deep-frying, mashing, soups, barbecues, scones, cakes and breads.

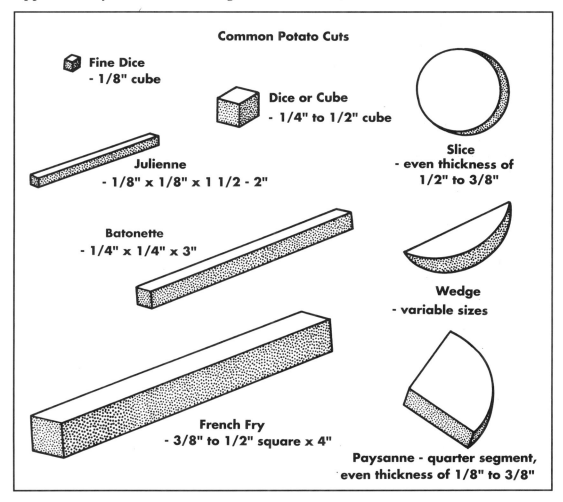

Common Potato Cuts

Fine Dice
- 1/8" cube

Dice or Cube
- 1/4" to 1/2" cube

Slice
- even thickness of 1/2" to 3/8"

Julienne
- 1/8" x 1/8" x 1 1/2 - 2"

Batonette
- 1/4" x 1/4" x 3"

Wedge
- variable sizes

French Fry
- 3/8" to 1/2" square x 4"

Paysanne - quarter segment, even thickness of 1/8" to 3/8"

Red Rounds, also called RED PONTIAC and NORLAND, are small, round potatoes with deep eyes. The skin of this potato is thin, smooth and red-purple in color. They have a creamy, white, moist flesh, with a firm and waxy texture. This potato is high in moisture and low in starch content. They are best for boiling, steaming and in salads.

Large White Ovals are also called CALIFORNIA LONG WHITES, RUSSET BURBANK and NORGOLD RUSSET. These potatoes are long and oval shaped, with pointed ends. Their skin is thin, smooth and has a pale yellowish color and the flesh is waxy and firm. They have few eyes.

The large white ovals are very versatile. They are ideally suited for boiling, baking, pan-frying, deep-frying, mashing, shredding and grating. These potatoes are good in soups, stews and casseroles.

Round Whites are smallish and round, with a smooth, beige skin. Their flesh is creamy in color, moist, waxy and firm in texture. The moisture content is high and the starch content low in this potato. This type of russet includes SUPERIOR and KATAHDIN from Maine and Long Island, and TRIUMPHS from Nebraska. They are best for boiling, braising, stewing and salads.

New Potatoes are not a special type of potato. They are young tubers, gathered before the crop is mature. At this stage, the enzymes have not yet converted the sugars into starch.

New potatoes are small, with delicate, almost translucent skin. They have a high moisture content, resulting in a waxy texture. These potatoes will only keep about a week. Fresh new potatoes are only available for a few weeks each year. Depending on the climate, there are usually three potato crops each year. Each crop produces a limited number of new potatoes. Two of the best varieties are grown in France. These are the DUTCH YELLOW LONG and the DUTCH RED LONG.

Early or new crop, main crop and late crop new potatoes, are especially good for simple preparations, such as boiling for use in salads, either hot or cold. New potatoes, after scrubbing, can be placed directly in boiling water. They are an exception to the rule that root vegetables should be started

---

MARKET FORMS OF POTATOES

1. FRESH, UNPROCESSED.

2. FRESH, PEELED, TREATED TO PREVENT OXIDATION. THESE WILL KEEP FOR 5-7 DAYS AT 40°F. (THESE SHOULD BE RINSED BEFORE USE TO REMOVE ANY SULFITES. SULFITES CAN CAUSE ALLERGIC REACTIONS IN SOME PEOPLE.)

3. CANNED: AVAILABLE WHOLE, SLICED, DICED, PLAIN, AND WITH OTHER IN-GREDIENTS, SUCH AS SALAD OR CREAM SAUCE.

4. FRENCH FRIES: BLANCHED AND FROZEN. AVAILABLE IN A WIDE VARIETY OF SIZES AND CUTS. BEST IF COOKED FROM THE FROZEN STATE. REFRIGERATED AND OVEN OR MICROWAVE FRENCH FRIES ARE BECOMING AVAILABLE.

5. OTHER FROZEN, PREPARED PRODUCTS ARE AVAILABLE, INCLUDING: HASH BROWNS, PUFFS, STUFFED, BAKED, CROQUETTES, CASSEROLES WITH A VARIETY OF SAUCES.

6. DEHYDRATED: AVAILABLE IN GRANULES OR FLAKES FOR PREPARING MASHED PO-TATOES. DEHYDRATED SLICED ARE AVAILABLE IN VARIOUS THICKNESSES FOR OTHER USES. THESE REQUIRE RECONSTITUTION WITH HOT WATER OR MILK AND OTHER FLAVORINGS.

Figure 1

cooking in cold water, and those vegetables grown above ground should be started cooking in boiling water.

AVAILABLE FORMS

The demands of time and labor have made processed potato products very popular. The result of this demand is a wide variety of processed potato products. Many of these are very good, and great time savers. However, for the best quality, there is no substitute for well prepared fresh potatoes. Figure One lists the more common of the available forms of potatoes.

UTILIZATION

Potatoes have numerous uses in the kitchen, but some varieties are better suited for certain types of preparation. The matching of potato and preparation method is based on starch content.

In general, old potatoes (mature potatoes held in storage from the previous year's crop) have more starch. They have lost moisture and will absorb other flavors easily. They are best used in making potato pancakes, stews, scalloped dishes and potato salads.

Low starch potatoes have a more moist, crisper flesh. It holds its shape better in boiling and salad making. To determine the starch content of a potato, rub two cut halves together. If they stick together the starch content is high.

Starch content also varies with the variety of potato. HIGH STARCH varieties are russet burbank and Idaho. They have a dry mealy quality that keeps them light and fluffy when baked. These varieties also make good mashed and french fried potatoes. The mealy texture causes them to fall apart when boiled.

MEDIUM STARCH varieties are round white, Maine potatoes and katahdins. Sometimes marketed as Eastern or all-purpose potatoes, they are a little waxier than russets. They can be used for boiling, mashing and roasting. These can be baked, but will be more watery than the russets.

LOW STARCH includes red rounds and new potatoes. When well cleaned they are ideally suited to be steamed or boiled with the skins on. They can also be sliced for salads. These potatoes do not easily fall apart.

An additional factor in using potatoes is texture. The texture of a potato is termed MEALY or WAXY. MEALY POTATOES are drier and generally contain more starch. Their cells tend to separate when cooked. They are best for mashing and baking. WAXY POTATOES have cells which are more cohesive. They are best for cutting in slices for casserole dishes or chunks in salad.

The method to tell the difference between a mealy potato and a waxy potato is to place a potato in a brine of one part salt to eleven parts water. A waxy potato will float. A mealy potato will sink because of their denser flesh.

PREPARATION

Some potato recipes are very simple, but many are complex, using a combination of cooking methods. For example, to make potato croquettes you first boil or steam the potatoes. Then you puree them, combining the puree with other ingredients. The mixture is then shaped, breaded and finally deep-fried. Cooking methods for potatoes are essentially the same as those used for other vegetables, with only a few adjustments for the product.

Potatoes can be eaten with or without their skins. When possible, they should be prepared with the skin on. Many of the potato's vitamins and minerals are in the skin or just below it. In older, mature potatoes this is not as much of a problem, but in young potatoes they should be cooked with the skin on.

MOIST METHODS
BOILING & STEAMING

Boiled or steamed potatoes are served as is and are also the basis for other preparations. They can be cooked peeled or unpeeled. There are three guides to cooking potatoes in this manner.

1. BOILED POTATOES ARE GENERALLY STARTED IN COLD WATER. THIS ALLOWS GRADUAL HEAT PENETRATION AND UNIFORM COOKING.

2. POTATOES ARE NOT NORMALLY COOLED IN COLD WATER, AS SOME VEGETABLES ARE. THIS WOULD MAKE THEM SOGGY AND STICKY, DUE TO THE STARCH THEY EXUDE. IF THEY NEED TO BE COOLED BEFORE THEY ARE USED THEY SHOULD BE RAPIDLY COOLED. THIS IS ESPECIALLY IMPORTANT WHEN THEY ARE COOKED AFTER BEING PEELED.

3. MANY NUTRIENTS ARE WATER SOLUBLE. FOR THIS REASON ALL VEGETABLES SHOULD BE COOKED IN AS LITTLE WATER AS POSSIBLE TO PREVENT LOSS OF THESE NUTRIENTS.

PARBOILED/BLANCHING

Parboiled or blanched potatoes are never served without further cooking in some form. This is a preliminary step to further preparation. It speeds their final cooking and saves time at service. Potatoes are usually shaped before parboiling, such as rissolee, parisienne, fondante or savoyarde.

STEWING/BRAISING

Potatoes are often stewed or braised with other ingredients. This is done in a covered pan either on top of the stove or in the oven. Examples are scalloped, gratin, Hungarian, boulangere, bouillon potatoes and potatoes baked *en casserole*.

FAT METHODS

Cooking potatoes in or with some type of fat gives them a crisp, rich flavor. Potatoes cooked in fat, such as butter, lard or oil, also lose fewer vitamins. The negative side effects are the addition of calories and fat to the menu item.

ROASTING, GRILLING/BROILING

Oven/pan-roasted potatoes are usually peeled and shaped or cut in halves, possibly thirds. They are arranged in a shallow baking pan and coated with oil, fat and/or roast drippings.

Often they are cooked in the pan with the roast, adding the flavor of the pan juices to the potato. They should be added to the pan during the last hour or so of cooking, depending on their size. Cooked with meat or separately, turn the potatoes occasionally to allow even browning.

Grilling is done under or over a close source of intense heat. Potatoes are cut in wedges or slices; brushed with oil or other fat, and placed on the grid. They should be basted often during the cooking process.

SHALLOW FRYING

The procedures for pan-frying and sauteing potatoes are the same as for other vegetables. This type of preparation has many variations, some made with pre-cooked or blanched potatoes and some with raw potatoes. Many of these preparations are excellent ways to use leftover cooked potatoes.

This type of preparation can be divided into two categories based on the production method.

POTATOES MIXED OR TOSSED WHILE COOKING - The potatoes are cut into pieces or small shapes, then cooked in a small amount of fat. They are turned and tossed in the pan to allow the pieces to brown on all sides. This type includes rissolee, parisienne, hash browns, lyonnaise, chateau and home-fried potatoes.

POTATOES COOKED AND SERVED IN

COMPACT CAKES - These types of potatoes are not mixed while cooking, but are made into cakes. The cakes are browned on both sides. This category includes potato pancakes and Macaire potatoes.

DEEP FRYING

The rules which apply to deep-frying other foods apply to potatoes. There are two major types of deep-fried potato preparations.

POTATOES FRIED RAW - These are raw, scrubbed potatoes, cut into various shapes, normally small sizes, and deep-fried until golden brown and crisp. These include french fries and potato chips.

French fries are made in a variety of types. These include: straw, gaufrette, matchsticks, julienne, pont-neuf and bataille for example. The main difference is either how they are cut or how they are seasoned after cooking.

French fries are one of the most popular and important items in American food service. It is important to know how to prepare them correctly. Although there are many blanched and frozen french fries available, it is helpful to know how to prepare them using fresh potatoes.

It is best to cook french fries in two stages. Although, it is possible to cook them in one stage, this is impractical in large volume operations. The long cooking time required slows down service. The most common practice is to blanch the prepared potatoes at a lower temperature. This allows the potatoes to be cooked through without browning. They are then drained and refrigerated until needed for service. Individual portions can be quickly browned, at a higher temperature, as orders are needed.

OVEN BAKED FRIES - These are an alternative to deep-frying. This technique is often used for larger cuts or wedges in dishes such as pont-neuf or country fries. This type of preparation is a good idea when dealing with guests who are counting calories.

To make oven baked fries, brush the prepared large cuts or wedges of potatoes with oil or an oil and butter mixture. Place them on a greased baking sheet. The wedges should not be touching. Bake them in a pre-heated 400^0F oven for 45 minutes to 1 hour. Turn the wedges several times to allow browning on all sides.

DRY METHOD

The best cooking method to preserve the potatoes' maximum mineral elements and taste, is baking. Baked in its skin, in the ashes of the hearth, as in the days before modern ovens and ranges, or now in an oven, when done correctly, the taste is excellent. It makes it possible to eat potatoes without salt, if needed.

BAKING & MICROWAVING

The "baked potato" has become another American standard menu item. Although, very simple to prepare, for some reason, the procedure seems to be misunderstood or needlessly complicated. Poorly baked potatoes with grey flesh and soggy skin are all too commonly served. Properly baked potatoes have flesh which is white, fluffy, mealy and steamy, with a crisp skin. Baked potatoes of this kind are not served often enough.

Potatoes bake best if simply scrubbed clean and pricked a few times with a fork to allow steam to escape. Bake them on a low rack in the oven for a crisper skin. The longer the potato bakes, the more crisp the skin becomes. The potatoes should be turned over halfway through the cooking time. Test the doneness of the potato by pressing the potato between your thumb and fingers. It should feel soft and mealy.

If you like your potatoes with a

crisp skin, never wrap them in foil for baking. A potato wrapped in foil does not bake. It steams in its own moisture. The texture of a steamed potato is different from that of a baked potato.

Microwaving potatoes is principally the same as baking them. Scrub them clean, prick with a fork and zap away. Follow the manufacturer's suggestion for the correct cooking time until you determine the best time. The one difference in a microwaved potato and a baked potato is the skin. A microwaved potato will not usually develop a crisp skin.

NUTRITIONAL INFORMATION

Potatoes and other tubers have particular value in maintaining a balanced diet. While some members of this group are lower in calories (turnips, carrots and celeriac) and others have a more substantial caloric value (sweet potatoes, potatoes and parsnips), they all are very low in fat content.

In addition, most tubers and root vegetables have amounts of various minerals (potassium in most all, calcium in beets and potatoes), and vitamins (sweet potatoes and potatoes are high in vitamins B and C, carrots in Vitamin A). The fact that tubers and root vegetables are filling yet provide many essential nutrients make them a valuable part of our diet.

There is a general misconception that when trying to lose weight or avoid fatty foods one should skip potatoes. It is only when potatoes are fried with large amounts of fat (french fries, home fries), or have fatty items added to them (sour cream, bacon bits, butter, with baked potato), that they carry unnecessary calories and fat.

The dangers in green potatoes can be mentioned here. This is not a matter of nutrition, but does relate to whether or not potatoes are healthy. The danger lies in the alkaloids present in the potato. Most known alkaloids are poisonous at high levels. At low levels, most disrupt animal metabolism. Only the potato seriously threatens humans with alkaloid poisoning.

The production of this complex in the potato tuber, especially the small or immature ones, is stimulated by exposure to light and very cold or fairly warm storage temperatures. Harmless amounts of the alkaloids solanine and chaconine are normally present in the potato, and contribute to its characteristic flavor. However, higher levels, resulting from mishandling should be avoided.

Fortunately there are warning signals, which tell us when there is a high level of alkaloids present. Potatoes also produce chlorophyll when exposed to light, so green potatoes are automatically suspect. A burning, pepper-like taste on the tongue also indicates high levels.

These substances are not destroyed by heating; they must be physically removed. Most alkaloids are concentrated within 1/16-inch of the surface. Peeling a slightly green potato deeply will make it safe to eat. Potato sprouts are rich in alkaloids. They should be thoroughly removed before the potato is cooked.

STORAGE

Potatoes, purchased fresh, should be stored in a cool, dark place. Ideally, store them at 45-50^{0}F in a ventilated, but not drafty area. Idaho or russet potatoes can be kept for 1-2 weeks under these conditions. Purchase new potatoes for quick usage. They do not store well.

Do not refrigerate potatoes. The cold environment of the refrigerator encourages excessive conversion of the potatoes' starches to sugar. This chemical process makes the potato unnaturally sweet. As the man said, "IF YOU WANT A SWEET POTATO BUY A SWEET POTATO!"

Potatoes and onions each give off a gas which negatively affects the other. They should be stored away from each other. Open and inspect potatoes bought prepackaged as soon as possible, removing any spoiled tubers. One bad potato can spread its affliction quickly to others.

CONCLUSION

The tubers used in the kitchen bring variety of flavor, texture and color to a meal. They also provide important nutrients. As we have discussed in this chapter, potatoes are the most popular tuber, but hardly the only one. When you are planning a meal, consider the use of other tubers for an enjoyable change.

REVIEW QUESTIONS

1. Define *tuber* and *root plant.*
2. List and define four types of general tubers.
3. Discuss the difference between a sweet potato, yam, and potato.
4. Discuss the two basic types of sweet potatoes and their preparation.
5. Define the term *potato.*
6. List the four basic types of potatoes.
7. Define the term *new potato.*
8. Discuss the best uses for both low and high starch content potatoes.
9. Define the terms *mealy* and *waxy* in relation to potatoes and their preparation.
10. List the three basic guides for boiling and steaming potatoes.
11. Discuss the methods of potato preparation using fat.
12. Discuss the preparation of a baked potato.
13. Discuss the value of potatoes and tubers in a balanced diet.

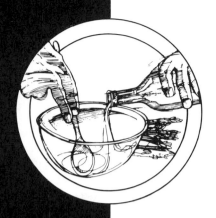

Chapter 13

CHAPTER OBJECTIVES

- Introduce farinaceous foods as a group of ingredients and products.
- Discuss the composition and structure of rice.
- Discuss methods of preparing rice.
- Introduce wild rice as an ingredient.
- Discuss the composition of the different cereal/grains.
- Discuss the preparation of cereal/grains.
- Discuss pasta and its preparation.
- Discuss noodles and their preparation.
- Discuss specialty items incorporated in farinaceous cookery.

Farinaceous
Cookery

Farinaceous cookery involves preparation of the staples in the diet. Webster defines farinaceous as containing or being made of meal or flour. It is also defined as containing or being rich in starch. These are the starchy foods so important to the diet. Farina is the Italian word for flour. All variations of this word derive from the Latin word *far* which means "spelt." Spelt was a staple grain of the ancient Phoenicians. It is from this heritage that the English term *farina* came to mean a "flour" or "meal." The flour or meal may be from any of a number of products, including cereal grains, potatoes, nuts, beans and others.

In the United States the term *farina* is applied to the white granular cereal made from the white inner portion of the wheat kernels. This inner portion of the wheat kernel is termed the endosperm. In this context farina is a cereal product generally prepared as a breakfast cereal. Farina is also another name for semolina or wheat middlings. These are the hard wheat left in the milling machine after the finer flour has sifted out. Semolina is used to produce the majority of pasta.

You can see that the term *farina* has more than one interpretation, depending upon the context in which it is used. In this chapter the term *farina* is defined as starchy foods. Under this heading we will consider all pasta, rice and cereal grains. These items compose the bulk of many meals. Since farina encompasses a wide variety of products used in the kitchen, we divide these products into three areas of concentration: rice, pasta and cereal grains.

RICE

Rice is an important food crop. It provides over one half of the world's population with a low cost, palatable and nutritious food source. Over 90 percent of the world's rice crop is produced and consumed in Asia and on adjacent islands. Despite this enormous production, the United States exports rice to that area of the world. The United States is one of the few countries which does not use all of the rice which it produces.

The major rice-producing states in the United States are: Arkansas, California, Louisiana, Mississippi and Texas. It is in these areas that the soil, temperatures and water for irrigation are best for growing rice.

The rice varieties grown in the United States include long grain, medium grain and short grain types. Rice is classified by the length of the grain. The term *long* refers to a rice grain that is four to five times as long as it is wide. Medium and short grain rice are shorter in relation to the width of the grain.

The length of the rice grain affects the character of the cooked product. Long grain rice, when cooked, separates and looks light and fluffy. These are preferred characteristics for pilaf and side dishes eaten with curries, chicken meat dishes or stew. Short grain rice, when cooked, is plumper and generally tender, moist and sticky. This is the preferred rice for the steamed rice eaten with Japanese and Chinese food. It is valued in western cuisine for preparation of risotto, croquettes, puddings and molds, because its starchy consistency acts as a good binder. Medium grain rice has characteristics which fall between the other two. It may be considered a good all-purpose rice.

COMPOSITION AND STRUCTURE

The rice most commonly consumed in the United States is WHITE

The structure of various grains:
A – Bran
B – Endospem
C – Germ

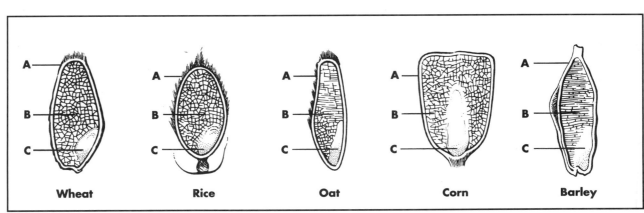

| Wheat | Rice | Oat | Corn | Barley |

or POLISHED RICE. This is grains of rice, of any length, from which the germ has been removed. The resulting rice has a far superior shelf life. The germ of the rice is the part most likely to become rancid or to be infested with insects.

In the 1840's when this type of processing was first developed, it was seen as a great innovation. There was a massive reduction in the amount of each year's crops which were lost due to spoilage. However, as early as 1886, it was suspected that this was not a perfect system. Research conducted by the Dutch East India Company in Asia led to the discovery in 1901 of the importance of the germ in both rice and flour. It was this research which eventually led to the discovery of vitamins. However, that is another story completely. What is important to the culinarian is the relation of the processing to the nutritional value of the rice.

The polished rice consumed most widely in the United States has been through four stages of processing. First the rice is thrashed, separating the rice grain from the stalk. This results in what is called Paddy Rice. The Paddy Rice is then milled the first time. This milling removes only the tough outer husk and produces what is called Whole or Brown Rice. In the second stage the bran and embryo/germ are removed from the rice grain by milling. The result is termed White Rice. The germ (which has been removed) contains a large percentage of the protein, fat, minerals and vitamins. The rice is then washed, cleaned and polished. The final step is coating the rice grain with a layer of corn syrup and talc to give it a pearly luster.

As can be seen, rice which goes beyond the first stage of milling loses many of its nutritional elements. Because of this, several processing methods have been devised to reduce the loss or to replace what is lost. The vitamins of primary concern are the B vitamins. While not the only ones lost, they are of great importance for a balanced diet.

The first method widely considered to reduce loss of nutritional value is to undermill or underpolish the rice. Rice processed in this manner does not have the customary white luster of polished rice. This type is also still prone to insect infestation and flavor deterioration.

A second method is that of increasing vitamin retention by parboiling the rough rice prior to milling. Commercially this type is called Converted Rice. This process allows some of the B vitamins and minerals in the germ to permeate the endosperm. The resulting milled product is enhanced nutritionally.

A third method is probably the most widely used in the United States. This is artificial enrichment of the milled rice grain. A pre-mix has been developed in which the rice is wetted with a solution of thiamine and niacin. The grains are then dried and covered with a protective coating. A second coating of Iron Pyrophosphate is then distributed over the rice. When dry, it is covered with another protective coating. This Enriched Rice provides nutritional value similar to brown rice.

An additional processing method for rice is that of Quick-Cooking. The purpose here is not nutrition. It is convenience. The rice is cooked to gelatinize the starch and then dried. This processed rice has a porous structure that will permit rapid rehydration, usually within five minutes. Quick-Cooking rice does not produce long, separate grains, and has a tendency to congeal.

METHOD OF PREPARATION

Because rice is cleaned before packaging, it is neither necessary nor desirable to wash it before cooking. Washing rice prior to cooking tends to increase the loss of soluble nutrients. In Far Eastern rice markets, rice is often washed or sprinkled to keep the starch dust at a minimum. This process also washes away valuable nutrients.

A common abuse of the nutritional components of rice in the kitchen is pre-rinsing. For example recipes for Spanish rice may include the procedure for soaking and washing rice in water several times. The purpose is. to remove excess starch. This will result in a product with completely separate rice grains; however, the same result can be achieved by sauteing the grains of rice briefly in hot fat or oil to seal in the starch. This is the method used for Rice Pilaf.

The use of excess water for cooking rice should also be avoided. Nutrients are discarded with the excess cooking water when the cooked rice is drained. The accepted method today is to cook rice in only the amount of water or other liquid needed to achieve the correct degree of tenderness.

Many of the old recipes for rice call for a sufficient amount of water to allow the rice to whirl like snowflakes within the cooking water to produce a boiled rice. In view of the loss of nutrients when the excess water is removed, we recommend the following proportion of water to rice. For each seven ounces of polished long grain white rice use 16 to 20 ounces of water. The aspiring culinarian must remember that the cooking quality of a rice is related to its type and processing. For this reason it may be necessary to experiment to find that perfect combination of rice and water (liquid) which will result in the perfect rice.

There are a number of factors which affect the cooking of rice. To begin with, each variety of rice has

---

BOILED RICE

INGREDIENT	AMOUNT
WHITE LONG GRAIN RICE	14 OZ
WATER	36 OZ
SALT	1/2 OZ
BUTTER	1 OZ

METHOD

1. MEASURE INGREDIENTS AS REQUIRED.
2. IN A HEAVY BOTTOMED POT, BRING WATER AND SALT TO A RAPID BOIL.
3. ADD RICE TO BOILING WATER.
4. RETURN WATER TO A BOIL AND REDUCE TO A SIMMER. COVER AND LET SIMMER, UNDISTURBED FOR 15 MINUTES.
5. CHECK, IF ALL WATER HAS NOT BEEN ABSORBED CONTINUE ON VERY LOW HEAT UNTIL ABSORPTION IS COMPLETE.
6. GENTLY BLEND BUTTER INTO COOKED RICE AND REMOVE TO SERVICE PAN TO BE HELD FOR SERVICE.

(OPTIONAL METHOD — BRING WATER TO RAPID BOIL AND ADD RICE. RETURN TO BOIL AND THEN COVER AND TURN OFF HEAT. LET PAN SIT COVERED AND UNDISTURBED FOR EIGHTEEN MINUTES. THE TIME MAY NEED TO BE LENGTHENED SLIGHTLY FOR SHORTER, HARDER GRAINS OF RICE. HOWEVER, THIS METHOD, WHEN MATCHED TO THE RICE, PRODUCES A SUPERBLY COOKED RICE WITHOUT THE POSSIBILITY OF SCORCHING.)

Figure 1

certain specific processing and cooking characteristics. Most long grain rice has a tendency to cook dry and fluffy. The cooked grains remain intact and do not stick together. Short grains, on the other hand, cook more firmly and tend to be more sticky. Medium grain rice is somewhere in the middle. The cooking method you choose must match the type of rice and the type of rice must match the end product desired. One common factor is that rice which yields a clear, translucent grain is preferred to those which have an opaque or chalky center.

The amount of cooked rice that a cup of uncooked rice yields is determined by its type and processing. The amounts we list here are averages. They can act as a guide for your production needs.

RICE YIELD

1 CUP UNCOOKED REGULAR WHITE MILLED RICE YIELDS 3 CUPS COOKED.

1 CUP UNCOOKED PARBOILED RICE YIELDS 4 CUPS COOKED.

1 CUP UNCOOKED BROWN RICE YIELDS 4 CUPS COOKED.

1 CUP PRE-COOKED RICE YIELDS 2-3 CUPS COOKED RICE.

The yield and quality of the rice can easily be affected by excess evaporation of water before the rice is added, or mishandling of the rice during cooking. The major cause of reduced yield and lower quality cooked rice is overstirring the rice. This causes breakage of the grains, which compacts the rice and mars its eye appeal.

The basic preparation methods for rice are BOILED and PILAF. An example recipe for boiled rice is given in Figure One.

Rice Pilaf is a method of preparing rice which is well known in the Orient, Turkey and Greece. The word in other writings may be seen as Pilaff, Pilaw, Pilav or Pilau, yet all refer to the same form of preparation. Here the rice is cooked with other ingredients, such as meat or vegetables. The classical cuisine is concerned with the rice only, except for specialty pilaf. The better the rice quality, the better the resulting pilaf.

The method for preparing Pilaf is first to saute finely diced onions (other vegetables and herbs can be added as desired) in hot fat or oil in a heavy bottomed sauce pot and then to add the rice. The rice should be sauteed until it takes on a slightly golden color. Depending on the quality and type of rice used, 1 1/2 to 2 times the quantity of water or other liquid is added (1 cup rice to 1 1/2 cups liquid is the normal ratio). The mixture is then covered, brought to a boil and placed in a moderate oven to cook undisturbed. The cooking time for a pilaf is twenty to twenty-four minutes. It is important to leave the mixture sealed, particularly in the early cooking stage, to allow steam to accumulate in the pan. This will produce a light fluffy rice. Measurement of the liquid exactly is very important to have a properly textured pilaf. There is no opportunity to add additional liquid. Too little liquid will produce a hard crunchy grain, while too much liquid will result in a soft mushy grain. Carefully read the recipe being used and experiment to find the best balance for the rice being used.

Pilaf is used in making molds or ring forms. Single molds or *timbales* may be used for plain pilaf as a side dish or garnish. Ring forms or borders are very practical for serving pilaf specialties, since meat or seafood may be easily served within the border of rice. To make the rice stick together, a little grated cheese and hot broth mixed into the rice before molding will bind it. However, the forms must be dipped in water before filling to prevent sticking.

OVEN BAKED RICE

INGREDIENTS	AMOUNT
RICE (REGULAR WHITE)	7 OZ
WATER OR OTHER LIQUID	16 OZ
SALT	1/4 TSP

METHOD
1. MEASURE INGREDIENTS AS REQUIRED.
2. PLACE RICE IN BAKING PAN WHICH HAS A TIGHT FITTING LID. BRING WATER AND SALT TO A BOIL AND POUR OVER RICE.
4. COVER AND PLACE IN 350°F OVEN. BAKE FOR APPROXIMATELY 25 MINUTES, OR UNTIL RICE IS TENDER AND ALL LIQUID IS ABSORBED.
5. FINISH FOR SERVICE AS DESIRED.
(FOR BROWN OR PARBOILED RICE USE 20 OZ WATER AND BAKE 45 TO 50 MINUTES.)

Figure 2

The word *pilaf* is an expression which can also mean a complete entree of rice with other ingredients in it. Typical specialties of this type are: arroz con pollo, Egyptian-, Algerian- or Greek-style lamb pilaf. The most common use of pilaf is with the meat or seafood cooked separately and served with the pilaf rice and the connecting sauce.

Another common method of rice preparation is termed OVEN BAKED. This method is similar to that of pilaf, but the rice is not sauteed prior to cooking. An example recipe is shown in Figure Two.

RISOTTO is a typical Italian rice specialty. We mention it here as an example of a preparation for rice which has only been through the first milling stage. This type of rice retains a degree of starch which makes the liquid in which the rice cooks soupy. There are two major methods for making risotto. The first is the way the Italian household prepares it and the other is the way the restaurant prepares it. The goal of both methods is the production of a dish which is neither a soup nor pudding. It should be a thick, but fluid, rice dish, in which the liquid has been made saucy with fresh pats of butter, freshly grated cheese and broth added little by little to achieve the correct consistency.

The ingredients for risotto are oil, onions, whole or brown rice, salt, bay leaf, beef or chicken broth, butter and freshly grated parmesan cheese. The oil is placed in a heavy bottomed sauce pot to a thickness just covering the bottom of the pan. When the oil is hot, the onions are added and cooked until glassy. The rice is added and cooked until it changes color, but not browned. At this point the broth is added to the rice mixture to equal 2 parts broth to 1 part rice and the seasoning is added. The sauce pot is covered tightly and cooked on top of the stove or in the oven (not on a direct fire) slowly for twenty minutes. At this time the cook creates the liquid which is the magic of a true risotto. By adding butter, grated cheese and additional broth the sauce of the rice is developed. This can be done on top of the stove, allowing gradual cooking and adjustment to achieve the risotto thickness. The risotto is then poured into a bordered dish or casserole and a little cheese is sprinkled on top. This is considered to be plain risotto.

For restaurant preparation of this

type of risotto, where large quantities and varying serving times are required, it is necessary to alter the process slightly. The risotto for the restaurant should be made in two stages. The first would be the preparation of a regular pilaf, only using brown or whole rice. This can then be held until needed. As portions of risotto are called for, the cook will use the pilaf as a base to which will be added the butter, grated cheese and additional broth to create the risotto sauce.

Often a different flavored risotto is served. Besides the broth, other ingredients, such as saffron for the yellow Milanese-type, tomato paste for the tomato risotto or curry powder for curried risotto, are cooked with the rice and broth. The finished risotto can also be used as a base for service of meat or seafood dishes, such as with scallopini, piccatas, spezattini, clams, oysters or even with fresh mushroom toppings.

Rice has a versatility which is valuable to meal preparation and is a food stuff which is readily available. While not as popular in the United States as the potato, it is increasing in popularity every day. Nutritionally it is a smart choice because it is low in fat and it is a complex carbohydrate. In most forms, rice is extremely digestible, nourishing and palatable.

WILD RICE

Wild rice is not actually a rice. It is the grain of one of the most beautiful, single stemmed aquatic plants in America, a wild grass. The plant is tall, round stemmed and has flat pointed leaves. The stem is round and hollow with a hooked root which anchors it firmly to the bottom of lakes and rivers. The plant grows four to ten feet tall. The heads of the grain are a pale green with flecks of yellow. As they mature they shade to a soft purple. The wild rice kernel is about three-quarters of an inch long, slender, dark in color and quite hard when dry.

Wild rice is one of the few crops in the United States which is still harvested by hand. Attempts to machine harvest the grain have proven to be too efficient, resulting in the disappearance of the grass from the area harvested. It appears that the methods used by the Native American Indians, who are still the primary harvester of this grain, leave behind sufficient grain for the grass to continue to grow.

The value of this grain lies in its unique nutty flavor and its nutritional value. Being easily digestible, it is used in hospitals for patients with digestive disorders. It is a high cost luxury food by virtue of its limited availability. Wild rice is extremely susceptible to all types of natural enemies. It is the favored food of many species of birds and is particularly susceptible to drought and wind storms.

Humankind's eager search for new commercial foods, however, may lead to experimentation with and cultivation of this valued grain. Currently an organization has been formed in Minnesota whose purpose is to make a large business of wild rice. Their goal is to control harvesting and sale of the annual crop. Efforts to build machinery to husk, dry and grade the grain have been reported.

When properly prepared, wild rice is considered one of the finest accompaniments for wild game, such as duck, geese or venison. It should always be washed before cooking. This product is best when gently simmered in three pints of water for each pint of grain, for approximately 45 minutes. The grains burst open when fully cooked to release a wonderful aroma which prepares the diner for the pleasures in flavor to follow.

DIFFERENT CEREALS/ GRAINS

The items covered by the term Farina are numerous, so we discuss in this final grouping only the more common of the cereals and grains used in the kitchen. Wheat, rye, oats, barley, corn, rice and buckwheat are the principal cereals used in the United States. The form in which they are used varies with the kind of cereal. Some, especially wheat and rye, are ground into flour for use in making baked products. A variety of cereals are used for breakfast foods.

CORN

Next to wheat, corn is the grain most used in the United States. Called *Indian corn, maize* and *sweet corn*; in the culinary sense, corn means the cereal grain *Zea May*s which is native to the Americas. This is what we will discuss here. However, it should be remembered that in England the term means wheat or, in a larger sense, any or all grains.

Corn, a grass of the *gramineae* family, is believed to be descended from the *teosinte*. This is a plant which grows wild in the Mexican highlands. Corn is cultivated all over the world today. It is one of the largest and most luxuriant of grain grasses. Dent corn, a common variety in the United States, easily reaches heights of 9 to 10 feet. The corn kernels grow in rows on large ears, which measure up to 15 inches.

In the United States, Dent or Field corn is the most common, however, this variety is used mostly for livestock feed and food processing. It is the Sweet or Green varieties of Flint corn which are most important in culinary preparation. These are used for canned, frozen or cob corn. The ear of corn is picked just short of ripeness. At this stage the kernels are plump and well filled, but still soft and milky. When allowed to stay on the stalk too long, the kernels become tough and dry.

Within the varieties of corn there are strains of both yellow and white color. Although preference for white or yellow corn or cornmeal is primarily a

regional matter, there is a nutritional advantage to yellow corn. Yellow corn contains more vitamin A, in the form of carotene. Both colors are rich in the B vitamins, particularly riboflavin, vitamin C and small amounts of minerals, including phosphorous and iron.

The kernel of the corn consists of three parts. The center is the starchy core called the endosperm. Next is the embryo/germ, which is composed of up to 50 percent oil. The outside of the kernel is the hull or bran. White and yellow corn grains are both ground into meal. CORNMEAL, yellow and white, is made by grinding the kernels of corn to a coarse mixture. It can be produced from the entire corn kernel or from a refined product.

Cornmeal can be prepared by grinding whole grain. This type is called STONE GROUND. It avoids heating the grain and uses the whole kernel. Many think its flavor is richer because the germ oil is retained. However, the fat content of the germ portion of the whole grain makes storage difficult. As with wheat and rice, it is very vulnerable to insect infestation and rancidity. It is excellent for simple forms of cornbread, but does not blend that easily with wheat flour.

The more commonly used process is called GRANULATED. This process involves grinding the corn on steel rollers after it has been kiln dried. The rollers break and remove the husk and germ almost entirely. This gives the meal a dry and granular feel. It contains only a small amount of fat, usually less than 15 percent. This product also contains more starch than whole ground cornmeal.

Cornmeal is used to make breads, cakes and pastries. In Europe, coarse cornmeal is used to make a mush which has several national variations: Rumania's *mamaliga*, Italy's *polenta*, and France's *armotte*. Mealy porridge, a type of cornmeal mush, is a staple food in Africa.

Early settlers of North America learned to make cornmeal from the Native Americans. They used it to make a mush called *samp*. The name was taken from the Narragansett Indian word *nasaump*. The early attempts to make bread from the meal failed. Cornmeal has very little gluten, without which the bread could not develop a structure to rise. From the Indians the settlers learned to make simple breads, such as corn pone and ash cakes. Later as wheat became more available, the innovative settlers discovered that by mixing cornmeal and wheat flour about half and half they produced breads which had the rich flavor and texture of the corn, yet the lighter fluffier texture of wheat breads. Cornbread, cornbread muffins and Boston brown bread are examples of these types of bread which are still popular today.

In Mexico, the Indians bypassed the process of making cornmeal. Instead they boiled the kernels and mashed them into a paste called *masa*. This paste was used as a dough to make tortillas, a thin, flat, unleavened bread. These have also become popular in the United States.

CORNSTARCH is a highly refined and pulverized starch, made from corn. In refining, the raw starch from the corn is broken up, washed, siphoned and repeatedly strained. The straining removes particles and fiber. Having been pulverized it is then dried to reduce the moisture content to about 10 percent.

Cornstarch is chiefly used to thicken liquids. As a thickener it is first mixed with a little cold liquid, then added to the mixture (soup, sauce, pudding, etc.). The mixture is then brought to a boil. The mixture must be stirred constantly to prevent lumping. Cornstarch is valued for the translucent appearance that it gives to the thickened liquid. This is far preferred in fruit cookery and Chinese cuisine, instead of the opaque appearance of liquids thickened with flour. Cornstarch is also used to lighten cakes and pastries at a ratio of one part cornstarch to four parts flour.

WHEAT

Wheat is a grass of the genus *Triticum*. It is an annual or biennial, according to the variety, and is the major cereal grain of the world's temperate regions. Worldwide, it leads rice in the amount produced and the acreage sown with it.

Wheat contains large amounts of gluten. Gluten is the elastic, sticky, tough substance formed from the insoluble proteins of wheat flour during dough development. It is the gluten which allows expansion of air cells within the dough as it warms. This is essential to a leavened product. Consequently, wheat makes better bread than other grains. The only other grain which contains appreciable amounts of gluten is rye.

Wheat varieties are grouped in categories according to the texture of their kernels. The basic categories are termed *hard* and *soft*.

HARD wheat, as a group, contains more protein/gluten. They are the preferred flours for bread making. *Durum*, the hardest wheat, is used mainly in Macaroni and Pasta production. English wheat and the red winter and spring wheat of the West, North and Central regions of the United States are used for bread making.

SOFT wheat are less hardy plants. As a group they contain less protein/gluten and yield a whiter flour. They are preferred for cake, pastry, quick bread and breakfast food preparation. In these types of items the tougher, chewier texture provided by the gluten is undesirable.

The processing of wheat is the same as that of corn. However, one additional process included in the production of wheat flour is bleaching.

This is done to gain the fine white color which the American consumer prefers. The culinarian should be aware that some individuals have an aversion to bleached flour. Unbleached flour is becoming more and more readily available and may need to be considered for use in the future.

A grain of wheat has at its center the endosperm or kernel. This comprises the majority of the weight of the grain. It is a floury mass of starch and gluten encased in a layer of aleurone. This is rich in proteins and mineral salts, such as phosphate of calcium, magnesium and potassium. The aleurone is part of the bran layer. This is mainly cellulose. At one end of the grain and encased in the bran layer is the embryo/germ. This is a living part of the grain. It contains a high proportion of fat, proteins and vitamins. In the production of white flour the germ and bran are removed. When the germ and bran are left intact, the product is termed either *whole-wheat flour* or *graham flour*, depending on the processing. These are considered far more nutritious, yet as with corn and rice, spoil far more rapidly. Whole-wheat flour also produces a heavier, denser bread. The fine textured, light and spongy bread which the American consumer has come to know is a product of the finely refined wheat flour.

The wheat germ, a byproduct of the milling process, is sold as a separate product. It has a pleasant, nutty flavor and may be added to white flour for bread making. It is used as a topping for soups, stews, salads and as a breakfast cereal. Wheat germ can be purchased toasted and vacuum packaged, or raw. Due to its oil content, once it is opened, it should be stored under refrigeration.

PRINCIPLES OF COOKING CEREALS/GRAINS

In cooking grains, the essential action is gelatinization of the cereal starch. Water driven into the starch granule by the force of heat unravels the starch molecule. The temperature at which this happens will vary from one type of starch to another (the norm is 160-180°F), but when it occurs it is termed *pasting*. Once the starch molecules have unfolded, the heat in the cooking process causes these molecules to form a cross-linked network that traps liquid inside the links. This is called gelation (thickening). As the item cools the gel stiffens. Enough water and heat is needed to create a soft starch gel.

Cooking also brings about a change of flavor. This change is due to the conversion of some complex starch into more simple sugars, such as glucose, maltose and others. The amount of water necessary to achieve the gel and flavor change of the cereal will vary with the type of grain and method by which it was processed. Caution must be used in preparing all farina. Gelatinization of starch granules takes place very quickly when the temperature is sufficiently high. This means that continued exposure to high heat can easily result in the cereal forming lumps or sticking to the pan and scorching.

Your goal is to prepare a mixture that forms a soft (not sticky) gel, free of lumps of starch and having a pleasant flavor. Finely ground cereals tend to lump easily when they are cooked. To prevent this, the cereal should be combined with enough cold liquid to form a paste before it is added to the remainder of the liquid, which has been brought to the boiling point.

Another way to cook cereal free of lumps is to sprinkle it slowly into rapidly boiling water. Add one to two teaspoons of salt for each quart of water. For the first few minutes, the cereal is cooked directly over the heat. Then it is removed and held over hot water. If the cereal is held for an extended period of time, it may be necessary to adjust its thickness by adding more liquid. The grains continue to exude starch while the cereal is warm, causing it to continue to thicken.

Cereals must be cooked long enough to cook the starch, to form a paste and to change the flavor. Because of modern methods of cereal processing, long, slow cooking is no longer necessary. Studies have shown that the starch may be completely gelatinized when the cereal is boiled over a direct flame for one to two minutes, and then cooked over hot water for 10 to 15 minutes.

The amount of water used to cook the cereal should be only what is needed to achieve the correct thickness. Draining cereals after cooking removes soluble nutrients, especially thiamine.

NUTRITION TIPS

All cereals are excellent sources of energy. This stems from the high starch and fat content, even though as a whole, cereals are considered to be low in fat. Starch is the main polysaccharide present in cereals. However, small amounts of dextrin are found after grinding. Fats are found mainly in the germ, consisting of the fatty acids, oleic and linoleic.

All cereal grains contain good amounts of minerals. However, these minerals may not be available for use by the human body due to chemical binding which naturally occurs. Calcium, phosphorous and iron are the minerals present in the largest amounts.

Cereal grains also have good amounts of the B vitamins and thiamine. Yet, with the exception of yellow corn, they contain no vitamin A. Cereal grains also contain no ascorbic acid (vitamin C).

Cereal grains are an incomplete protein group, lacking in either lysine, threonine and tryptophan, the essential amino acids. To form a complete protein they must be paired with other incomplete proteins, such as beans or meat. When paired in this manner, cereal grains are extremely valuable as a protein source.

The major problem with cereal grain as a nutritional source is the processing and heat of cooking. As discussed earlier, the milling process removes the germ which is the warehouse for many of the nutrients of the grain. The heat of cooking destroys many vitamins. It is necessary for the cook to protect the nutrients available in the cereal and for the manufacturer to find ways to either retain or replace nutrients in processing.

PASTA, NOODLES, & OTHER

In its simplest form pasta is a combination of durum wheat, water and often eggs or possibly oil. It is shaped in a wide variety of ways and can be flavored with the addition of vegetables during processing. Pasta is antiquity itself. Its origins are not well known, but, according to food writer Elizabeth David, macaroni was made from *spelta* (small brown wheat). It first made its appearance in the reign of Prince Teodoric in Ravenna. Popular belief is that the explorer Marco Polo introduced pasta into Italy from China. In fact, the first known reference to pasta can be traced to Sicily. During the Middle Ages, when Sicily was under Arab domination, pasta is first mentioned in historical accounts. It was Catherine De Medici who introduced pasta to France. It came to be used by the French chefs in the preparation of timbales, gratins, desserts and as a garnish for soups. It has been during this century that pasta has become popular as an entree like it is often used in Italy.

Basic pasta can be categorized in two ways: Ingredients and preparation method or intended end usage. The category of ingredients and preparation method includes two major types: FRESH PASTA (Homemade Pasta, *pasta vatta in casa*) and FACTORY MASS-PRODUCED PASTA.

FACTORY MASS-PRODUCED

Factory mass-produced pasta is made from a dough of semolina and water. Seldom is egg added to the dough. The factory produced pasta is either flat or cylindrical, depending on how it was processed. Flat pasta is made by running the dough between rollers to form thin sheets. These are then cut into whatever shape is needed by a punch or stamp. Cylindrical pasta is made by forcing the dough through a pierced plate (die). The size and shape of the holes in the die determine the final shape of the pasta. It may be solid, such as spaghetti, or hollow such as penna. The drying process is important in this type of production. Care must be taken to ensure that the pasta will mature and keep well.

COMPOSITION AND STRUCTURE

Factory produced pasta includes a group referred to as MACARONI PRODUCTS. This group is sometimes called ALIMENTARY PASTES. It includes such products as macaroni, spaghetti, vermicelli and egg noodles. The main ingredient in the macaroni group is a special durum flour with high gluten content. This flour is well suited to the manufacture of these products. The standard of identity established by the United States Food and Drug Administration for macaroni products allows the use of only certain basic raw ingredients in macaroni products. These ingredients are semolina, durum flour, farina, flour or any combination of two or more of these and water. The standard does allow egg white solids, disodium phosphate, onions, celery, garlic, bay leaf, salt and other seasonings as optional ingredients.

FLOUR

Macaroni products produced from durum have a characteristic yellow color. This color is considered a sign of good quality. It is a result of the carotenoid pigments in the durum wheat. This type of wheat also gives the quality macaroni product its hard and translucent finish. This is highly valued by the manufacturer and user. It is a macaroni which is dry; resistant to breakage, and has a clear, more uniform color. Macaroni made from the harder durum also takes less time to cook.

A macaroni which is manufactured from a blend, such as durum and semolina produces a softer dough which can be fed through a plate with less pressure. It is more resistant to overcooking and thereby causes less cloudiness in the cooking water. Products made with a granular-type durum have properties that lie between those of the flour products and the semolina products.

EGG

Any macaroni product which has the word *egg* added must contain egg solids. These solids can be fresh, frozen or dried. They can be egg yolks or whole eggs. Egg yolks are most commonly used in the production of egg macaroni products. The use of egg white reduces the coloring achieved with the egg yolk.

DISODIUM PHOSPHATE

Disodium phosphate increases the alkalinity of the macaroni product. This allows the starch grains to gelatinize faster. Put simply, it allows the product to cook slightly faster.

Good quality dried pasta has a dry, smooth, even appearance. The color should be a translucent ivory, verging on yellow. It should break cleanly. Good quality pasta quadruples in volume when cooked.

FRESH PASTA

In the past, fresh pasta was only made by small businesses or in the home. This type of pasta is now produced in larger quantities and shipped and held longer due to improved packaging methods. It is far more readily available for use in operations of all sizes. It can be made with flour instead of semolina and always contains eggs. Fresh pasta must be used before it dries to gain the most benefit from the eggs.

COMPOSITION AND STRUCTURE

The composition and structure of fresh pasta, compared to factory mass-produced pasta, yields an overriding difference in texture and taste. This difference is a result of the type of ingredients used and the manner in which they are handled.

FLOUR

Fresh pasta is often made from what is referred to simply as flour. This may or may not be the durum-type flour used in the factory pro-

duced pasta. The result is a flour which has a softer texture and lower gluten content. This type of flour develops into a softer looser dough.

EGG

Egg is always included in fresh pasta. This creates a product which has a richer, fuller flavor. It also reduces the stability of the product and shortens its shelf life.

OIL

This is not a required ingredient in fresh pasta. However, when used, it shortens the strands of gluten in the dough, allowing the leavening power of the eggs to raise the pasta. This results in a softer product than does the durum and water-based pasta.

Fresh pasta is normally rolled and cut, whereas the factory produced

MAKING PASTA DOUGH

Make well in center of flour.

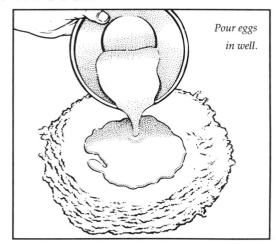
Pour eggs in well.

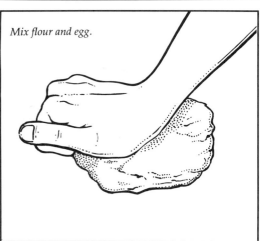
Mix flour and egg.

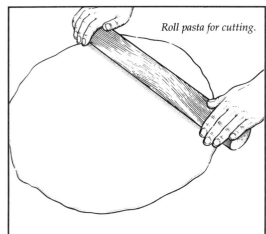
Roll pasta for cutting.

pasta is often extruded. The primary factors in handling fresh pasta are its shorter shelf life; shorter cooking time, and softer texture. The rich flavor of the pasta is something which is valued in many dishes.

TYPES OF FRESH AND FACTORY MASS-PRODUCED PASTA

The overall grouping of Pasta can be further divided by intended usage. The four basic categories are: Pasta for soup; pasta for boiling; pasta for baking, and filled pasta.

Pasta for Soup is very small and made in various shapes. This group includes vermicelli, linguini (small grains), pennette (small quills), stelline (little stars), risoni (rice grains), conchigilette (little shells) and anellini (little rings, sometimes serrated). These pastas are used in soups to provide texture, flavor and slight thickening.

Pasta for Boiling is the largest grouping. This group includes macaroni, rigatoni, penne, pasta shells (conchiglie), nests (pappardelle), butterflies (farfelle), spirals (eliche), spaghetti or fediline. The list is growing daily as pasta lovers on both sides of the Atlantic experiment with new shapes and forms for a very old food form. These pastas are used as entree replacements or as filler in casserole dishes and side dishes. They are used as the main ingredient in salads and many other dishes.

Pasta for Baking must first be cooked in water or other liquid. It provides flavor, texture and stability to the dish. The types used include tortiglioni, bucatini, conchiglie, cravatine and lasagna (smooth or wavy edge).

Filled Pasta are used to encase a stuffing. These pastas are stuffed with cheese, vegetable, meat or a sweet filling for a dessert. The pasta may come prefilled or ready to stuff, depending on the type. The most common types include cannelloni, ravioli and manicotti. Types which are

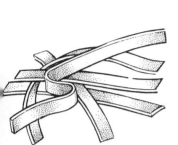

Fettucine

BASIC PASTA FORMULA
YIELD: 1 LB OR 4-6 SERVINGS

INGREDIENTS	AMOUNT
FLOUR (ALL PURPOSE)	7 OZ
EGGS (LARGE)	3 EA
SALT	1/4 TSP
OLIVE OIL	1/2 OZ
WATER (LUKEWARM)	1/2 OZ

METHOD
1. MEASURE ALL INGREDIENTS ACCORDING TO QUANTITY NEEDED.
2. BREAK EGGS INTO A BOWL, ADD SALT, OLIVE OIL AND WATER, THEN MIX WELL.
3. PLACE FLOUR IN A LARGER BOWL AND FORM A WELL IN ITS CENTER.
4. POUR THE EGG MIXTURE INTO THE WELL AND GRADUALLY INCORPORATE THE FLOUR INTO THE EGG MIXTURE UNTIL ALL LIQUID IS ABSORBED.
5. SCRAPE WALLS OF BOWL AND INCORPORATE WELL.
6. LIGHTLY DUST YOUR HAND AND A FLAT SURFACE WITH FLOUR. PLACE DOUGH ON FLOURED SURFACE AND KNEAD WITH THE HEEL OF YOUR HAND FOR 8-9 MINUTES OR UNTIL SMOOTH AND SATINY.
7. COVER BOWL WITH A DAMP TOWEL AND LET REST AT LEAST 15 MINUTES.
8. ROLL OUT DOUGH EITHER BY HAND OR WITH A PASTA MACHINE AND CUT AS DESIRED.

Figure 3

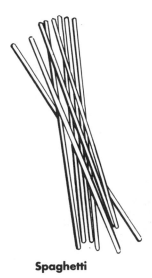

Spaghetti

Lasagne

becoming more popular as the popularity of pasta grows are tortellini and tortelloni, agnoloti (small slippers), capelleti (little hats) and lumache (large shells).

The decision of whether to use fresh or factory pasta will depend on the end product desired, type of operation and time requirements. There is a difference in taste due largely to the egg content in the fresh and the drying (aging) of the factory pasta. There is also a great difference in cooking time required. Normally it will take factory produced pasta as much as fifteen minutes to cook, while a fresh pasta will take five minutes or less.

PREPARATION METHODS

MAKING PASTA

It is not difficult to make fresh pasta. This is a product for which you simply have to develop a feel. The biggest problem with making pasta is that flours differ, as do eggs. Flour varies in its ability to absorb liquids. Eggs vary in size and thereby liquid content. Since fresh pasta is a combination of flour and eggs, it is difficult to be totally exact in the amounts of each ingredient needed for the perfect pasta. The basic rule is that for every egg, use three ounces of flour (all-purpose or bread). The addition of water and oil to a fresh pasta is at the discretion of the person making it. We suggest (see recipe, Figure One) a combination of eggs, all-purpose flour, salt, olive oil and lukewarm water. This combination works best with American flours.

COOKING PASTA

All pasta, fresh or dried, should be cooked in salted boiling water or liquid. The pasta must be added after the water is boiling to prevent the pieces sticking together. The quantity of water used should be sufficient to allow the pasta to swell and swim freely. (The normal ratio is one gallon water, two tablespoons salt, and one pound of pasta.) It is by sealing pasta in fast boiling water in this way that it is possible to obtain the degree of cooking known as *al dente*.

Small pasta should be sprinkled into briskly boiling salted water. For long pasta, such as dried spaghetti, gradually push it into the boiling water. By allowing the long strands to soften and bend, then stirring gently to prevent sticking together, it is possible to cook the spaghetti, linguini or other types without breaking them into pieces.

The cooking time will vary with the quality and type of the pasta and the hardness of the water. Even if a set cooking time is indicated on the instructions, it is best to test the doneness early to avoid overcooking. Figure Four shows example cooking times for dry pasta. In each case the cooking time begins when the water comes back to a boil after the addition of the pasta.

The handling of pasta after cooking will vary with the intended use. If the pasta is to be served in a salad it should be drained; rinsed under cold water, and immediately mixed with a small amount of oil to prevent sticking. Rinsing with cold water will remove excess starch,

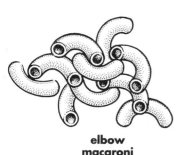

**elbow
macaroni**

ravioli

manicotti

reducing sticking. This also lowers the temperature of the pasta, stopping the cooking process. When pasta is to be refrigerated prior to service, it is important to shock it with cold water. This prevents carry-over cooking after removal from the heat source.

Pasta which is to be served hot should be drained. (If it is to be used immediately, it is not necessary to rinse or oil it.) The boiling hot sauce can then be poured on it. Stir the mixture quickly and serve it immediately with appropriate accompaniments. If the pasta is to be held and reheated at time of service, it should be rinsed; lightly oiled, and held under refrigeration until needed. The pasta may then be reheated at service by a short immersion in boiling hot water.

The range of sauces for pasta is growing as rapidly as the forms and shapes. The traditional thick sauces (bolognaise and milanaise) based on tomato and often containing ham, minced/ground meat, seafood, cheese, anchovies and other items are losing ground to newer, lighter sauces. The intermingling of cuisines has opened a new era in the adaptability of highly prized pasta. When reading and experimenting with the sauce chapter, be creative in the possibility of applications to pasta. This outstanding, versatile starch will have many faces in the future.

Note: All pasta, served hot or cold, must be well drained. The water which clings to pasta can destroy the texture, appearance and flavor of the sauce it is served with.

NOODLES

Noodles are an ancient food which can be traced to both ancient Rome and China. They have remained a strong culinary tradition down through the centuries. The Italian tradition spread throughout the western world. The Chinese tradition spread throughout Asia, including Japan, Southwest Asia, and westward through Burma, India and the Middle East.

Noodles are a product made from a dough consisting of flour, eggs and water. The addition of other flavorings, such as vegetable or seafood purees, is becoming more common. Also, the addition of herbs is fairly common. As with pasta the egg may be deleted if desired. The word *noodle* derives from the German word *nudel*. While the western noodle is primarily produced from wheat flour, the Chinese or Asian noodle may also be produced from rice, soy, mung bean, potato or seaweed.

Although noodles are actually a type of pasta, we address them separately because of the difference in types of flour and meal used to produce them. For example, while Italian pasta is a popular and complex type of western noodle, the German noodle is prepared from ordinary wheat flour, not semolina.

TYPES

The standard of identification for commercially produced, western style noodles requires a minimum five percent egg solids content. Commercial noodles are sold fresh and dried. They are flat in shape, with width varying from 1/16" up to 1/2".

Chinese egg noodles come in both narrow and wide cuts. They are sold both fresh and dried. The wheat noodles are usually flat. Some of the more common Asian noodles are:

BEAN THREAD NOODLE: Made from the mung bean, these are thin translucent noodles. Generally these are simmered in soups or soaked in hot dishes. They are also added to Chinese hot-pot dishes and Japanese Mizutaki. The Japanese term for this noodle is *Shirataki*.

SHRIMP NOODLES: Made from a puree of shrimp (shrimp paste)

blended with wheat flour. This Southeast Asian specialty is an example of the flavored noodles which are used to complement particular dishes.

SOBA: Made from buckwheat flour and has a slightly greenish color. This is a favorite of the Japanese. It is a major seller in the fast growing fast-food operations in Japan.

SOMEN: This is a Japanese wheat vermicelli-type noodle. It is used in soups and cold dishes.

UDON: This is the thickest of the Japanese wheat noodles. It is used in both hot and cold dishes.

The variety of Chinese and Asian noodles is enormous. The limits of their usage lies only in the mind of the cook.

COOKING NOODLES

The preparation of western style noodles is the same as that of cooking pasta. Refer to the methods of preparation for pasta. The same care should be used to prevent the noodles sticking together or being over-cooked. Certain types of Chinese and Asian noodles are fried. This is a specialized type of preparation which requires close attention to the manufacturer's directions.

As with pasta, noodles are used as garnish, starch or entree replacement. They provide filler, flavor, texture and color to casseroles, salads and a broad range of other dishes. The Chinese and Asian noodles are becoming very popular. They are playing, and will probably continue to play, a big role in the intermingling of cuisines to create new flavors and textures.

POLENTA

This is a Northern Italian porridge or mush, usually made from cornmeal (maize). However, it can be made from barley meal and, in certain areas, from chestnut meal. The polenta is closely related to the Greek *poltos*, which are various cereal porridges.

This product does not fit well into the major categories of farinaceous cookery. However, it is a farina product in the broad sense of being a starchy food. It is prepared by boiling cornmeal in salted water. Traditionally it is then finished by mixing in butter or olive oil and then pouring the mixture into a round, wooden tray to cool. The cooled polenta is cut into squares or lozenges (diamond shapes). It is served pan-fried, baked or gratin, as an accompaniment served much the same as pasta or rice would be.

A polenta made with milk is often used for dessert preparation. The polenta may also be flavored with stock or white wine in accordance with the dish it accompanies. In Italy the large grained bergamo and verona varieties of maize are preferred for making polenta. These varieties require longer cooking times, yet deliver a superior texture and flavor.

Although polenta is not a common item in the United States, it is worthy of study by the aspiring culinarian. Whether served in the more traditional manner or fried, it is an extremely versatile starch. It can be used as croquettes, fritters, gratins, croutes or timbales, or it can be served plain with butter and cheese. When served with a sauce or flavored with vegetables, ham or white truffle, it can truly be a fine addition to a meal.

GNOCCHI

Gnocchi are small dumplings made of flour, semolina, potato and/or choux paste. The gnocchi mixture usually includes eggs, either whole or only yolks, which provide the structure for the flour. Additional liquid may be water, milk or cream. Milk or cream are the preferred choices because of the richness and body they provide to the mixture. Butter or some other type of shortening is added to allow the gluten in the mixture to stretch and rise, achieving a more tender product. As with polenta, this is a product which does not fit easily into the broader farinaceous categories. The item is Italian in origin, however, it is also found in Austro-Hungarian and Alsatian cookery where it may be referred to as *knodel, noques, knepfle* or *quenelles*. All of these are quite similar and may be considered a gnocchi, since the word means "lumps."

Traditionally the gnocchi is first poached and then cooked *au gratin* in the oven and served as a hot entree. The basic ingredients are varied with the incorporation of cooked vegetables such as spinach, pumpkin, green vegetables or beet root, which give the gnocchi color. Additional flavors and textures are achieved by adding different types of cheeses (emmenthaler, parmesan, ricotta). Chicken liver, brains, herbs and condiments can also be included. The type of flour or meal chosen will also determine the flavor and texture of the gnocchi. The addition of choux paste creates a much lighter product. The use of cornmeal creates a far more dense one. Your choice of ingredients should be based on the overall components of the meal. Some examples of various types of gnocchi are given in Figure Five.

Spaetzle

The word *spaetzle* means "little sparrow." In Alsace, it is also spelled *spatzele* or *spetzli*. Spaetzle is a mixture of flour, eggs and cream which is formed into small dumplings which are poached in boiling water. This is a specialty of Alsace and Southern Germany. Another product which does not fit well into other categories, spaetzle is used to garnish sauces and meat dishes, especially game. It can be served as an entree, au gratin, with cream or noisette butter or with small croutons. In Wurttemberg, spaetzle

---

GNOCCHI VARIATIONS

GNOCCHI ROMAINE: PREPARED WITH SEMOLINA COOKED IN MILK AND BUTTER. IT IS SEASONED WITH SALT, PEPPER AND NUTMEG. RAW EGG YOLKS ARE BLENDED INTO THE MIXTURE, WHICH IS THEN POURED INTO BUTTERED BAKING PANS TO COOL. THE GNOCCHI CAN THEN BE CUT INTO PREFERRED SHAPES.

GNOCCHI VENITIENNE: PREPARED WITH TWO THIRDS MASHED POTATOES AND ONE THIRD FINELY CHOPPED, COOKED CHICKEN. THESE ARE WELL BLENDED WITH BUTTER, CREAM, RAW EGGS AND GRATED CHEESE. THE MIXTURE IS THEN SEASONED WITH SALT AND PEPPER, FORMED INTO SMALL DUMPLINGS, AND POACHED.

GNOCCHI PARISIENNE: PREPARED WITH A BASIC PASTE OF POTATO, MILK, BUTTER, RAW WHOLE EGGS AND SALT. THIS IS THE SAME BASIC PASTE USED FOR DUCHESS POTATO MIXTURE. FOR GNOCCHI PARISIENNE ADD 2 TO 3 OUNCES OF GRATED PARMESAN CHEESE TO EACH POUND OF PASTE. THE PASTE IS THEN PLACED IN A PASTRY BAG WITH A ROUND TUBE. THE MIXTURE IS PRESSED FROM THE BAG INTO BOILING SALTED WATER. IT IS CUT INTO 1 INCH PIECES AS IT IS PRESSED. WHEN THE GNOCCHI IS FULLY COOKED IT RISES TO THE TOP. IT IS DRAINED AND PLACED IN A BAKING DISH LINED WITH A SAUCE MORNAY, COVERED WITH MORE SAUCE AND SPRINKLED WITH GRATED PARMESAN CHEESE. THE DISH IS THEN DOTTED WITH RAW BUTTER AND BROWNED IN A SLOW OVEN.

Figure 5

SPAETZLE

INGREDIENTS	AMOUNT
FLOUR (SIFTED)	1 LB
EGGS (LARGE)	5 EA
NUTMEG	PINCH
SALT & PEPPER	TO TASTE
WATER	2 TO 2-1/2 OZ

METHOD
1. BEAT EGGS WITH 1-1/2 OZ WATER.
2. SIFT DRY INGREDIENTS TOGETHER.
3. MAKE WELL IN DRY INGREDIENTS AND ADD EGG MIXTURE.
4. BLEND INTO SMOOTH PASTE, ADDING ADDITIONAL WATER IF NEEDED TO MAKE A MEDIUM PASTE.
5. PLACE ON WOODEN BOARD AND CUT WITH SPATULA INTO DESIRED PIECES.
6. DROP PIECES INDIVIDUALLY INTO BOILING SALTED WATER.
7. WHEN COOKED, DRY SPAETZLE ON A CLOTH AND TOSS WITH BUTTER IN A FRYING PAN.
8. SERVE IN DEEP DISH WITH NOISETTE BUTTER.

Figure 6

dumplings are similar to small quenelles, made with liver puree or cheese.

Although spaetzle is usually made with milk or cream, it can be made with water. The resulting product will not have the richness of flavor, nor the same texture, unless the fat content and sugars of the milk and cream are replaced in some other way. (The culinarian must always remember that milk and cream bring more than just moisture to a mixture.) As with the pasta and noodles, it is possible to vary the flavor, color and texture of the spaetzle by adding fresh herbs or pureed vegetables before cooking.

Spaetzle is always cooked in boiling salted water. However, the handling of the spaetzle before placing it in the water will depend on the moisture content of the mixture. A thicker spaetzle paste is placed on a board and cut into the size pieces desired before being placed in the boiling water. A thinner paste is forced through a colander or spaetzle maker, directly into the boiling water. See Figure Six for an example recipe for spaetzle.

CONCLUSION

The items and preparation methods presented in this chapter comprise an important rung on the ladder to mastery of culinary expertise. Often regarded as merely secondary items in meal preparation, farinaceous food items are in actuality some of the most important. They are truly the staples of the human diet. These products also represent a very desirable part of the meal. They should be selected and prepared with care. The items involved in farinaceous cookery reinforce the fact that no item in a meal is unimportant. Farinaceous products provide important nutritional value, as well as color, flavor and texture in the dining experience of your guest.

REVIEW QUESTIONS

1. Define the term *farinaceous*.
2. Discuss the various grain lengths of rice and their importance in preparation.
3. Define the term *polished rice*.
4. Discuss the preparation of rice, including the normal proportions of water to polished rice.
5. Define *rice pilaf*.
6. Discuss wild rice.
7. Discuss corn as a cereal/grain.
8. Discuss the difference between hard and soft wheat.
9. What is in the bran layer of wheat?
10. Discuss the cooking of cereal/grains.
11. Discuss the difference between factory and fresh pasta.
12. List four categories of pasta based on the intended end use.
13. Discuss cooking pasta and noodles.
14. What is the difference between pasta and noodles?
15. Define and discuss *polenta, gnocchi* and *spaetzle*.

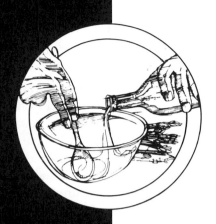

Chapter 14

CHAPTER OBJECTIVES

- **To introduce stock/ fond as a culinary preparation and ingredient.**
- **To discuss the elements of a stock.**
- **To discuss the basic types of stocks.**
- **To introduce principles of preparing stocks.**
- **To discuss the basic preparations from stock.**
- **To discuss court bouillon.**

Stock

Stock is a supportive framework or structure, according to the dictionary. This is its primary definition. Stock is also defined as the original source from which something is derived. For the culinarian, it means "a liquid in which meat, fish or vegetables are simmered." It is the basis for soup, sauce, gravy or stew. Although specified and stated differently, stock in the kitchen serves the same purpose as in the first two definitions.

According to Larousse, stock, also termed FOND, is a "liquid base for making a sauce, stew or braised dish." Escoffier perceived stocks as one of the principal culinary preparations, because they form the base for many other preparations. If not properly made, whatever is made from it will be of poor quality. Stocks definitely act as the supporting structure and framework for what comes after.

This chapter will discuss stocks and the other preparations closely associated with them. These include essences, glazes, court bouillons and savory aspic jellies. We will begin with stock, which is the base for all of the others with the exception of court bouillon.

STOCK/FOND

The word fond comes from the word foundation. Just as a foundation is the base for a house, fond is the base for much of cooking. Almost every culinary preparation requires a fond. For all practical purposes stock and fond have the same meaning.

Fond is the result of the extraction and concentration of taste and nutrients. This is done using liquid as a base with a variety of foodstuffs. The four elements of a fond are shown in Figure One.

TYPES

There are three basic kinds of stock/fond: White stock (Fond Blanc), brown stock (Fond Brun) and vegetable or neutral stock (Fond Maigre). The classifications refer, in general, to contents and preparation method of the stock, not necessarily to color. A white stock made with beef and beef bones will be slightly brown in color but it is a white stock nontheless due to the method of preparation.

WHITE STOCK is made with white meat or beef, veal bones, chicken carcasses and aromatic vegetables. The bones, or meat, are put in cold liquid and slowly brought to a boil. The mirepoix (flavoring base of diced vegetables and occasionally pork fat) is sweated in suitable fat and then added to the liquid before it develops any color. The mixture is reduced to a simmer to finish cooking. This stock is used for white sauce, blanquettes, fricassee and poached dishes.

BROWN STOCK is made with beef, veal and poultry meat and bones. The bones are roasted till golden in color, not burnt. The mirepoix is added when the bones are three-quarters roasted. Tomato product may also be added at this time. When the bones and mirepoix are golden in color, cold liquid is added and the mixture is slowly brought to a boil, then reduced to a simmer to finish cooking. This stock is used for brown sauces and gravies; braised dishes, and meat glazes.

VEGETABLE STOCK is basically a neutral stock composed of vegetables and aromatic herbs sauteed gently in butter and then cooked in liquid. This is a relatively new type of stock which is gaining popularity. Its use has been limited to vegetarian cooking and making veloutés. The trend is toward more utilization of this subtle and flavorful stock.

Figure Two shows a recipe for white stock. This gives the basic method for stock preparation. Brown stock would be prepared in the same manner, except the bones and mirepoix would be browned. Brown stock is shown in Figure Three.

FISH STOCK (Fume de Poisson) is categorized separately from the other basic stocks because of its limited usage. The

---

FOUR ELEMENTS OF A FOND

1. NOURISHING ELEMENTS, INCLUDING MEAT, BONE, FISH HEAD, FISH TRIMMINGS AND VEGETABLES OF ACCEPTABLE QUALITY.
2. AROMATICS AND SPICES FROM THE MIREPOIX, BOUQUET GARNI, HERBS AND ROOTS.
3. LIQUID, SUCH AS WATER, WINE, REMOUILLAGE (2ND BOUILLON) OR CONSOMME.
4. SEASONING, THIS IS SALT ONLY. NORMALLY SALT SHOULD NOT BE USED IN STOCK. ONE OUNCE PER GALLON OF REDUCED STOCK WILL ENHANCE ITS FLAVOR. (IN SMALL AMOUNTS SALT CAN SERVE TO EXTRACT PROTEINS FROM FISH AND MEAT, GIVING THE FINAL SAUCE SHINE AND FLAVOR.) IF THE STOCK IS TO BE MADE INTO A GLAZE (GLACE) THE SALT MUST BE OMITTED OR THE CONCENTRATION WILL BE TOO SALTY.

Figure 1

WHITE STOCK
(CHICKEN, VEAL, BEEF)
YIELD: 15 GAL

INGREDIENTS	QUANTITY
BONES, CUT SMALL	60 LB
COLD WATER	18 GAL
MIREPOIX (DICED):	
ONION	3 LB
CARROT OR PARSNIP	3 LB
CELERY	3 LB
LEEK	2 LB
BUTTER	1 LB
THYME	1 TBSP
BOUQUET GARNI	1 LARGE
BAY LEAF	10-15 EA

METHOD OF PREPARATION
1. PLACE BONES IN STOCK POT AND COVER WITH THE COLD WATER.
2. BRING SLOWLY TO A BOIL AND SKIM THE SCUM.
3. SAUTE MIREPOIX IN BUTTER UNTIL GOLDEN.
4. ADD SAUTEED MIREPOIX AND AROMATICS TO STOCK.
5. SIMMER: 5-6 HOURS FOR CHICKEN. 8-10 HOURS FOR VEAL.
6. PASS THROUGH A FINE STRAINER, LABEL, COOL AND REFRIGERATE.

Figure 2

---

basis of fish preparation is the fumet or fond. It has been said that all fish produce a fumet, but not all fumet are equal. Some fish produce better quality stock than others. The result from some fish are stocks which are too gelatinous and fishy tasting. Fish which are oily yield stock that has a bitter taste or that is milky.

Classical preparation calls for the bones of specific fish for fumet. Dover sole, turbot, brill and whiting are recommended for their superior flavor. However, the important thing is that the fish is fresh and that its flesh is white. A few guidelines are listed below.

1. Do not use trimmings from oily fish, such as salmon, mackerel, bluefish, etc.

2. Flounder or lemon sole will work for sole fumet. Halibut for turbot and striped bass for brill.

3. The freshest local whitefish by any name is what you want.

4. Sometimes the complementary juices of oyster, mussel or clam are added to fish fumet. This liquid should not be reduced. It is used as an additive only.

An example recipe for fish stock is given in Figure Four. Note the shorter cooking time for this stock. The fragile, soft bones of fish do not require the longer cooking times of meat and poultry. Too long a cooking time can also cause harsh flavors to develop in fish stock.

PREPARATION OF STOCK

Stocks appear to be a simple item to prepare. Do not be misled. Although the ingredients are simple and the method

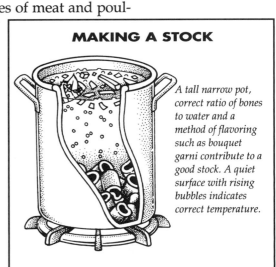

MAKING A STOCK

A tall narrow pot, correct ratio of bones to water and a method of flavoring such as bouquet garni contribute to a good stock. A quiet surface with rising bubbles indicates correct temperature.

BROWN STOCK

(BEEF OR VEAL)

YIELD: 15 GAL

INGREDIENTS	QUANTITY
BONES, CUT SMALL	60 LB
MIREPOIX (DICED):	
ONION	3 LB
CARROT OR PARSNIP	3 LB
CELERY	3 LB
LEEK	2 LB
COLD WATER OR REMOUILLAGE	18 GAL
TOMATO PRODUCT	(OPTIONAL)
THYME	1 TBSP
BAY LEAF	10-15 EA

METHOD OF PREPARATION

1. PLACE BONES IN A ROASTING PAN AND BROWN IN A 350°F OVEN.
2. WHEN BONES ARE 3/4 DONE, PLACE MIREPOIX OVER THE BONES AND FINISH BROWNING.
3. WHEN BROWNED, REMOVE BONES AND MIREPOIX AND PLACE IN STOCK POT WITH AROMATICS.
4. REMOVE THE FAT FROM THE ROASTING PAN. DEGLAZE ROASTING PAN WITH WATER OR REMOUILLAGE AND ADD TO THE STOCK POT.
5. ADD THE REMAINING COLD WATER OR REMOUILLAGE TO COVER THE BONES.
6. BRING TO A BOIL; REDUCE TO A SIMMER, AND SKIM.
7. SIMMER FOR 8-10 HOURS.
8. PASS THROUGH A FINE STRAINER, LABEL, COOL AND REFRIGERATE.

Figure 3

simplistic, you must use great care. This is a base from which you will create a wide variety of other dishes, so the stock must be right. As with any other preparation, you must start with quality ingredients.

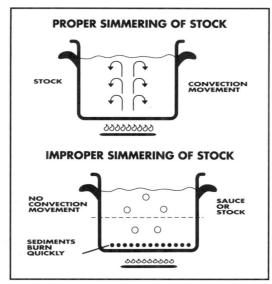

The four principle steps in producing a quality stock are:

1. Start with cold liquid.
2. Allow natural clarification to occur.
3. Skim carefully.
4. Simmer, do not boil.

COLD LIQUID TO START

Beginning with a cold liquid prevents the sealing of the items. This makes it possible to release the flavors of the food, enhancing the liquid. This is a form of cooking by interchange. The flavors of the meat, bones, poultry, etc. are transferred to the liquid surrounding them.

This interchange occurs whether the bones and vegetables are browned or not. However, when they are browned an additional flavor is added. This is caused by the caramelization of the natural sugars which occurs during brown-

FISH STOCK
(FUMET DE POISSON)
YIELD: 3 GAL

INGREDIENTS	AMOUNT
FISH BONES WITH HEADS	12 LB
COLD WATER	3 1/2 GAL
MIREPOIX (DICED):	
ONION	8 OZ
CELERY	4 OZ
LEEK	4 OZ
BUTTER	2 OZ
WHITE WINE (CHABLIS)	1 QT
BAY LEAF	2 EA
PARSLEY	AS NEEDED
THYME	1 GOOD PINCH

METHOD OF PREPARATION

1. CLEAN BONES AND HEADS IN COLD RUNNING WATER. BREAK THE LARGE BONES. REMOVE ANY BLACK SKIN, BLOOD CLOTS AND GILLS.
2. SAUTE MIREPOIX AND AROMATICS IN BUTTER. COVER AND LET SWEAT IN THEIR OWN JUICES.
3. ADD FISH BONES, COVER AND LET SWEAT FOR A FEW MINUTES.
4. ADD WHITE WINE AND COVER WITH COLD WATER.
5. BRING TO A SLOW BOIL AND SIMMER UNCOVERED FOR UP TO 45 MINUTES.
6. PASS THROUGH A FINE STRAINER, LABEL, COOL AND REFRIGERATE.

Figure 4

ing. It adds a richness of flavor and color, not achieved otherwise.

NATURAL CLARIFICATION

A high quality stock has a clear, clean appearance. This requires that it be clarified. Pouring the cooked stock through a fine sieve is not the kind of clarification that we mean here. It is the removal of the many minute particles which form in the cooking process.

Albumin is a protein complex found in muscles, blood, milk, egg white and many vegetable tissues, such as leeks. It is soluble only in cold water. Albumin is valued for its property of clarification by coagulation (forming a mass) when exposed to heat. The slower the application of heat, the better the removal of cloudiness from liquid.

Bringing stock slowly to a boil gives the albumin time to pass into the solution. As its proteins coagulate, they attract particles in the liquid. The action is similar to that of a magnet. However, as with the magnet, when disturbed they will drop the particles.

Do not wash your bones and meat prior to cooking stock. Fresh meat and bones do not need to be washed. Also, do not bring the stock to a boil and then throw away the first boil. All the clarifying elements and light aromatics are then wasted. This reduces the flavor and increases your chances of producing a cloudy stock.

Cloudiness normally is the result of stock being boiled too long and fast over high heat. This extended boiling breaks down the texture of the bone fibers. When this happens, the particles become blended and suspended in the liquid. This makes it difficult, if not impossible, to clarify.

A slight amount of cloudiness is normal in stock. The lack of blood in the

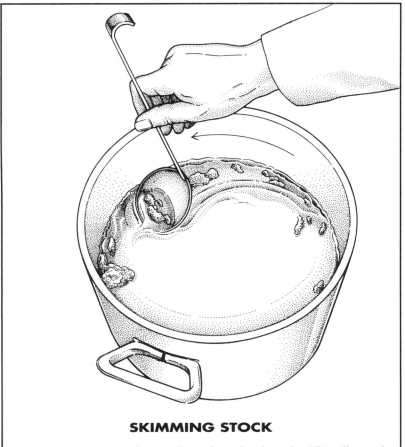

SKIMMING STOCK

Use the underside of the ladle to rapidly stir the stock at the surface. This will cause the gray particles to move toward the pot sides. Tip the ladle toward the side of the pot and run the lip of the ladle under the scum as shown, while taking as little stock as possible.

bones used in stock creates a lack of albumin. There is not sufficient protein to attract all the particles. How you boost the protein level and increase clarity will be discussed in detail in the chapter on soups, where consomme is discussed. However, because of the lack of albumin, you must give what is there a chance to do its job.

SKIMMING

As the stock cooks and the albumin coagulates, fat and scum will rise to the top of the pot. It is important to remove all of it. This removal is called skimming, carefully lifting fat and scum from the surface.

The mirepoix of vegetables is finely cut for the best flavor extraction. This and the aromatics float on the top of the pot. This can make it difficult to skim properly. To make it easier to skim, add the mirepoix and aromatics after about 1/4 of the cooking time has lapsed. The largest accumulation of fat and scum will occur in the early cooking of the stock. Once the mirepoix and aromatics are added, do not skim unless necessary. Let the stock cook undisturbed.

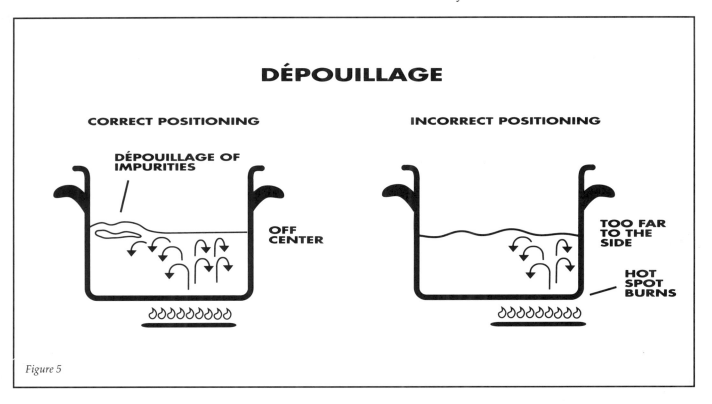

Figure 5

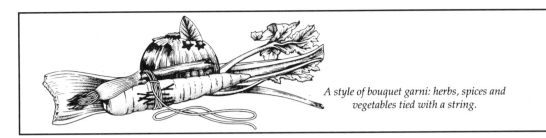

A style of bouquet garni: herbs, spices and vegetables tied with a string.

SIMMERING

This very simple operation is often misunderstood. Improper application of it generates most of the burned stocks and sauces. Simmering is when liquid is hot enough to form small bubbles that rise from the bottom of the pan. The bubbles break just below the top surface of the liquid. As they rise and break a slight turbulence occurs. When the temperature is too high, this turbulence is too great. If the temperature is too low, there is little or no movement in the liquid. Simmering, when correct, creates a slight roll in the liquid.

Simmering is important in the cooking of stocks and sauces. When the slight roll of the simmer is not present, the coarser particles and sediments will settle on the bottom of the pan. This creates an insulating layer between the heat and the stock, which will burn. When it burns, it imparts an unwanted burnt flavor to the stock.

FISH ESSENCE
YIELD: 1 QT

INGREDIENTS	AMOUNT
CLEANED HEAD, BONE AND TRIMMINGS FROM SOLE OR WHITING	4.5 LB
BUTTER	3.5 OZ
SLICED ONION	4.5 OZ
MUSHROOM TRIMMINGS	11 OZ
PARSLEY STALKS	2 OZ
DRY WHITE WINE	8 OZ
CLEAR FISH STOCK	3 PT
LEMON	JUICE OF ONE
SALT	PINCH

METHOD OF PREPARATION

1. MELT BUTTER; ADD ONIONS, MUSHROOM TRIMMINGS AND PARSLEY STALKS, AND SWEAT WITHOUT COLORING.
2. ADD THE FISH BONES AND TRIMMINGS. COVER AND ALLOW TO STEW GENTLY FOR 15 MINUTES, TURNING THE INGREDIENTS OCCASIONALLY.
3. ADD THE WINE AND REDUCE BY HALF, UNCOVERED.
4. ADD FISH STOCK, LEMON JUICE AND SALT.
5. BRING TO A BOIL; SKIM CAREFULLY, AND ALLOW TO SIMMER GENTLY FOR 15 MINUTES.
6. STRAIN THROUGH A FINE STRAINER AND COOL AS REQUIRED.

NOTE: THIS ESSENCE IS USED FOR THE SHALLOW POACHING OF FILLETS OF SOLE, TURBOT AND BRILL. AFTER BEING COOKED, THE REMAINING COOKING LIQUOR IS REDUCED AND ADDED TO THE SAUCE ACCOMPANYING THE FILLETS.

Figure 6

Too much action in the liquid can harm stock. The heavy rolling action of a high boil will break up the scum and fat. This makes it difficult to skim the stock. The fast rolling action also does not allow the albumin to gather the fine particles.

Improper placement of the pot on the fire can limit the simmering action and make it difficult to skim the stock. Figure Five illustrates the best placement of the pot on the fire.

OTHER FACTORS

REMOUILLAGE means "second wetting." After draining away the first stock, more water is added and the mixture is simmered again. This extracts additional flavor from the elements. This yields a weak stock, but it is richer than water. The remouillage is often used as the liquid for making a new stock, thereby yielding a richer stock.

EXCESSIVE PIGMENTATION is removed from stock by active carbon. The production of clear aspic from a brown stock may require this. The stock is filtered over active carbon. Active carbon is either charcoal, burnt pea pods or animal black (crushed burnt bones). This will remove part of the color of the stock. However, this process also removes part of the flavor as well. This is rarely done in today's kitchens.

BURNT BONES AND MIREPOIX will damage the stock's flavor and color. They impart a burnt, bitter taste to the stock and act as active carbon in the stock. The result is a stock with a lighter color and flavor. When browning bones and mirepoix for brown stock, brown them, do not burn them.

PREPARATIONS FROM STOCK

ESSENCES

Essences are stocks made in a reduced form. This creates a concentrated flavor. As shown in Figure Six, essence is made in the same manner as stock, but with less liquid.

Essence is used to boost the flavor of a stock, soup or sauce. The addition of this concentrated flavor is meant to enhance the already good flavor of the item. The best essences are made from highly flavored items, such as celery, truffles, mushrooms, morel, etc.

Essences are not meant as saviors of preparations made from stock poor in flavor and quality. It is much easier to prepare a rich, succulent, high quality stock, than to try to save a poor stock with essence. Using a good stock at the start is far better and more efficient.

Normally, it is better to add the product to the stock during preparation, rather than to prepare a special essence. Many chefs believe the use of essences is meaningless if the basic stocks themselves have high quality strength and flavor.

GLAZE/GLACE

Glazes unite, in a reduced form, the principal strength and flavor of the ingredients in the stock. They have been reduced to the consistency of syrup. (See example recipe in Figure Seven) This distinguishes them from the essences, which are only the extraction of the flavor of the product being used. The various glazes of meat, poultry, game and fish are widely used in modern cooking.

Glazes serve four basic purposes in cooking. In most cases, there are advantages to be gained from using a glaze instead of an essence.

1. GLAZES GIVE A BRILLIANT SHINE AND MOIST COATING TO A FINISHED DISH.

2. THEY REINFORCE THE QUALITY AND TONE OF SAUCES.

3. GLAZES STRENGTHEN THE FLAVOR AND BODY OF A PREPARATION MADE FROM A WEAK STOCK.

4. GLAZES CAN ACT AS SAUCES WHEN PROPERLY BUTTERED OR CREAMED TO MATCH THE DISH THEY ARE TO BE USED WITH.

Many chefs of the "old school" do not allow the use of glazes. They justify this opposition by suggesting each culinary preparation should be prepared from its proper basic ingredients. It is their opinion that, if this is done, then the product will produce its own glaze.

Certainly the theory of these chefs is correct. However, the theory is based on the cook not being limited by time or expense. This is rarely a situation which exists in the modern kitchen. If glazes are made well, and used judiciously without abuse, they can be valuable in the kitchen. It is possible to gain excellent results when they are used properly.

SAVORY & ASPIC JELLIES

This chapter discusses aspic jelly only as it relates to stocks. Complete discussion of the various types of aspic can be found in Chapter 24. Jellies are highly clarified and concentrated forms of stock. Through reduction it is possible for the cook to concentrate the natural gelatin content of the stock, creating a jelly. These are used to coat cold foods, providing moisture, protection and flavor for the product.

These jellies gain their savor and quality from the flavor of the stock used. It is the quality of the stock which ultimately determines the quality of the jelly.

Development of the high amount of gelatin needed for a jelly calls for some special ingredients. Calves feet and pork rind are both used. They are high in natural gelatin. The goal is to make a

---

MEAT GLAZE
YIELD: 1 QT

INGREDIENTS	AMOUNT
BROWN STOCK (THIS SHOULD BE GOOD RICH STOCK.)	1 GAL

METHOD
1. PLACE BROWN STOCK IN A HEAVY BOTTOMED STOCK POT. COOK OVER MODERATE HEAT, ALLOWING IT TO REDUCE.
2. AFTER A SUITABLE AMOUNT OF REDUCTION HAS OCCURRED, STRAIN THE STOCK INTO A SMALLER POT. CONTINUE THIS PROCESS AS THE REDUCTION PROGRESSES.
3. SKIM THE STOCK CAREFULLY THROUGHOUT THE PROCESS. THIS WILL DETERMINE THE QUALITY OF THE GLAZE.
4. AS THE STOCK REDUCES, GRADUALLY REDUCE THE HEAT. WHEN THE REDUCTION IS NEARLY COMPLETE, IT MUST BE OVER A VERY MODERATE HEAT TO PREVENT SCORCHING.
5. THE GLAZE IS READY WHEN IT ADHERES TO THE BACK OF A SPOON. IT SHOULD BE A GLOSSY, TRANSLUCENT, SYRUPY COATING. THIS STAGE IS NORMALLY REACHED AFTER A REDUCTION OF $^2/_3$ - $^3/_4$ OF THE ORIGINAL QUANTITY.

NOTE:
FOR A LIGHTER COLORED, CLEAR GLAZE, WHITE STOCK SHOULD BE USED INSTEAD OF BROWN STOCK. CHICKEN GLAZE IS MADE IN THE SAME WAY AS MEAT GLAZE USING CHICKEN STOCK. GAME GLAZE IS MADE THE SAME AS MEAT GLAZE USING GAME STOCK. TO PRODUCE A GLAZE WITH A SPECIFIC GAME FLAVOR, USE GAME STOCK OF THE TYPE NEEDED. FISH GLAZE IS NOT USED AS MUCH AS MEAT AND CHICKEN GLAZE. HOWEVER, IT IS MADE IN THE SAME MANNER, USING FISH STOCK. THE FISH ESSENCE USED FOR POACHING WILL HAVE A MORE DELICATE FLAVOR THAN FISH GLAZE. MOST CHEFS PREFER TO REDUCE IT AND ADD IT TO A SAUCE INSTEAD OF FISH GLAZE.

Figure 7

jelly which will set without the use of added gelatin. These also yield a jelly which sets with a soft consistency.

When possible, jellies should be made without added gelatin. However, this is not always possible. During the summer months, it is important that you test the consistency of the stock. This is done before clarifying by placing a little stock on ice. If the stock does not set well, add a few leaves of gelatin.

Artificial coloring is not recommended in aspic jelly. Normally, a quality stock will develop enough color naturally. If a deep amber color is desired for a savory, add some madeira. This will also heighten the flavor.

Make stock jellies a day ahead of time. When they have finished cooking, skim and strain the jelly. Then allow it to cool overnight. While cooling, the stock congeals. The small amount of fat which was held in suspension during cooking is released to the surface. It accumulates and solidifies on top of the stock for easy removal. Sediment in the stock will settle to the bottom of the pan. Careful removal of the jelly from the pan will leave this sediment in the pan. The result is a crystal clear jelly. A standard recipe for aspic jelly is in Chapter 24.

COURT BOUILLON

Court bouillon is not actually a stock preparation. However, it is used in a similar manner. It is a flavorful poaching liquid used for fish and shellfish and some other items, such as sweetbreads.

A court bouillon is made up of three elements: Aromatics and spices; salt, and liquid. (Refer to Figure Eight for recipe.) The mixture is not complete in nutritional elements. The flavor of the bouillon is created when fish are poached in it. It is then reduced and added to the sauce or possibly kept for future poaching. Basic guides for using court bouillon are given below.

1. COURT BOUILLON IS ALWAYS PREPARED IN ADVANCE FOR ALL FISH EXCEPT TURBOT. THE TIME FOR POACHING IS NORMALLY LESS THAN HALF AN HOUR.

2. WHOLE FISH SHOULD BE IMMERSED IN COLD COURT BOUILLON AND THEN BROUGHT TO POACHING TEMPERATURE.

3. SLICED FISH SHOULD BE PLACED IN BOILING COURT BOUILLON AND REDUCED TO A SIMMER. THE EXCEPTIONS ARE SMALL TROUT, CARP OR PIKE PREPARED AU BLEU (FRESHLY GUTTED AND WITH THE SCALES ON), AND SHELLFISH.

PLAIN COURT BOUILLON

The quantity of court bouillon is determined by the amount and size of the fish being cooked. It is composed of salted water, one quart of milk per quart of water and some thin slices of peeled lemon. This is used for turbot and sole.

OTHER TYPES OF COURT BOUILLON:

1. Just salted water. (For sea bass.)

2. Salted water, carrots, parsley, bay leaves, thyme and vinegar.
   (For large salmon-trout.)

3. Water, wine and aromatics. (For salmon, trout, eel or pike.)

4. A matelotes preparation uses red wine instead of white wine.

Figure 8

4. When poaching in a small amount of liquid, the mirepoix is placed under the strainer in the pan with enough liquid to cover one-third of the piece of fish. Fish cooked in this manner should be frequently basted to prevent drying.

5. Court bouillon for lobster should always be at a full boil when the lobster is immersed. This is also true for small or medium fish au bleu.

6. Fish which is to be served cold is cooled in the court bouillon. This improves flavor; however, the cooking time should be reduced to allow for carry-over cooking.

7. Shellfish are always cooled in the court bouillon, again be careful of overcooking.

CONVENIENCE BASES AND GLAZES

White and brown stocks, the base for all great classic sauces, take time to prepare. It is necessary to have the bones and trimmings, the essential elements for making stock. In the classical kitchen this presented little problem. Butchering of all types of meat, poultry, game and fish was done routinely. This made the elements for stock readily available. In addition, there was normally a large staff, many of whom could spend the time needed to prepare stocks properly.

In today's kitchens, meat, poultry and fish items are often bought ready-to-cook. The elements for stock are then not as available. The staff is also smaller in today's kitchens, particularly in restaurants. These factors make the production of fresh stock difficult for some operations.

This situation has created a market for what are called bases. These are concentrated stocks which are normally granular or paste in form. When diluted with water (follow manufacturers' directions), they are used as fresh stock would be. Properly used, they will provide an acceptable product. However, there is a wide variance of qualities of this product on the market. Many contain high levels of salt and monosodium glutamate, which can yield a very salty, unsatisfactory stock. They must be used with discretion.

Although there is no substitute for fresh stock, if you must use a base, choose carefully. Glazes, which are true reductions, without sodium additives are becoming more readily available. Study and keep abreast of the new items being developed. Your goal is to have the best stock possible in your kitchen.

CONCLUSION

A simple stock is one the most important elements in the production of high quality dishes. It is really the foundation upon which your culinary creation stands. Be sure that it is a strong foundation, one which is clear, pure and flavorful.

REVIEW QUESTIONS

1. Define the terms *stock* and *fond*.
2. List and discuss the four elements of a fond.
3. List the three basic types of fond and discuss how they are different from each other.
4. Discuss why fish stock is categorized separately from the other stocks.
5. List and discuss the four basic steps to produce a quality stock.
6. Define *essence, glaze,* and *aspic.*
7. Discuss the preparation of court bouillon.
8. Discuss the use of convenience bases.

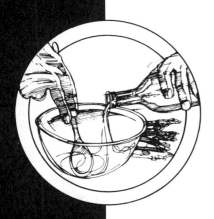

Chapter 15

CHAPTER OBJECTIVES

- **To define the term soup.**
- **To introduce the classifications of soups.**
- **To discuss clear soups.**
- **To discuss the preparation of clear soups.**
- **To discuss thick soups.**
- **To discuss the preparation of thick soups.**
- **To discuss specialty soups.**
- **To discuss the garnishment of soups.**
- **To discuss the service of soups.**

Soups

Where did soup begin? Scholars do not agree on a time or place. *Soupe*, the French word, was once used to describe various ingredients put into a bouillon or broth made of meat or fish. By the Middle Ages the word had become a part of every European language. Webster's *New World Dictionary* traces the English word *soup* back to the medieval, old English root words *soupen* and *supan*. Both words meant "to sup or drink." The word *suppa*, meaning "to eat the evening meal," developed into the term *supper*. There are some scholars who feel the word *soup* is derived from two sanskrit words, *su* ("good") and *po* ("to nourish").

Soups have held an important place in the cuisine of every culture since the dawn of humanity. Its ingredients and preparation are a reflection of the customs and economics of the times. Archaeology shows that primitive people made fireproof vessels. In these they cooked meats, grains and vegetables in liquid.

Apicius, in the first century A.D., included in his cookbook recipes for barley soup. Also included was the recipe for a sweet liquid mixture made of apricots, honey, wine vinegar, peppermint and liquamen, a substance made from salted fish entrails. This fruit soup was available commercially in trademarked pots as early as 400 B.C.

By the 14th century, soup became more refined. In 1375, Guillaume Tirel, known as Taillevent, included in his book *Le Viandier* recipes for simple, clear soups of ginger and garlic. Also included were recipes for *Garbure*, a rich vegetable soup thickened with bread, and *German broth* made of wine, bacon, onions, almonds, cinnamon, ginger, cloves and saffron.

WHAT IS SOUP TODAY?

It took almost a century to bring soups to the perfection of today. Modern cooking has replaced the sturdy dishes of the past with simple, savory preparations. Ones which are veritable wonders of delicacy and taste.

George Auguste Escoffier, the master of world cuisine in the late 19th and early 20th centuries, believed that soups, and the stocks they were based upon, were of utmost importance in modern cuisine. In his famous *Le Guide Culinaire,* Escoffier states:

"Stock is everything in cooking. Without it, nothing can be done. If one's stock is good, what remains of the work is easy..."

The role of soup has remained unchanged for 10,000 years. Good soup is still the ultimate food for stimulating our appetites; nourishing our bodies, and sustaining our spirits. Soup is now what Grimmond De La Reyniere described so well:

"It is to a dinner what a portico or a peristyle is to a building; that is to say, it is not only the first part of it, but it must be devised in such a manner as to set the tone of the whole banquet, in the same way as the overture of an opera announces the subject of the work."

The soup must be in harmony with the whole menu. Among all the items making up the menu of a gourmet dinner, soups require the strictest attention. They should have a most delicate perfection. The good or bad impression that they make on the guest, affects the success of the entire meal that follows.

The preparation of soup is a cooking accomplishment of the highest order and is considered by some to be the ultimate achievement. Yet, from the cook's point of view it is almost effortless. The greatest part of the work is done unattended in the simmering pot.

TYPES & DEFINITIONS

Soups of the old classical kitchen were complete dishes in themselves, containing, apart from the liquid and vegetable garnish, a wide variety of meat, poultry, game and fish. It is only the liquid part of these classical dishes which retains the name *soup* today. Their preparation is much more simplified, taking almost a hundred years to arrive at the state of perfection they have reached today.

In creating a soup which is light and savory, consistent with today's concept of taste and nutrition, there has been a failure to maintain a system of classification for the new soups. For example, thick soups include bisque, purees, coulis, veloutés and creams. Each of these should logically designate a separate preparation, different for each type.

In this text we will try, not without difficulty, to lessen the confusion that exists. We will categorize each type, giving the reason for the classification of

CLASSIFICATION OF SOUPS

CLEAR	THICK	SPECIALTY
BROTHS	PUREE/COULIS/BISQUE	NATIONAL & REGIONAL TYPES
CONSOMMES	VEGETABLE SOUPS	COLD SOUPS
ESSENCES	CREAM SOUPS	
JELLIED SOUPS	VELOUTÉ SOUPS	

Figure 1

the various forms. The beginning of this process is the dividing of soups into three large groups: Clear soups, thick soups and special soups. Figure One shows what types of soups are included in each of these groups.

CLEAR SOUPS

Clear soups are all prepared in the same manner, whether made from meat, poultry, game, fish, shellfish, turtle or vegetables. Consommes are one of the subcategories of clear soups. Always clarified, sometimes thickened with a little tapioca, they normally include a light garnish in keeping with the character of the consomme. Broth is another subcategory. They should not be clarified in the same manner as the consommes. Their clearness comes from very careful cooking. The last two subcategories of clear soups include all essences and chilled jellied soups.

Thin, clear soups are a good first course. They stimulate the appetite in a subtle manner. These soups may be more time consuming, especially the ones requiring a clarification process. They are not difficult to make, but do require attention and time.

BROTH

The terms *broth* and *bouillon* can be used interchangeably; however, in French cookery, the term bouillon applies mainly to the liquid part of a *pot-au-feu*, "boiled beef dinner." Broths are among the simplest soups to prepare. Normally, their flavor comes from long simmering of a variety of ingredients together in one pot. An assortment of separately cooked foods may be added at various times during cooking, depending on the cooking requirements of the individual items. All the ingredients should finish cooking at the same time. The plain, unclarified broth from boiling meat, fish or vegetables is used instead of water or white stock for cooking certain dishes, and for the preparation of soups and sauces.

The French *poule au pot* ("chicken in the pot"), Italian *zuppa pavese* ("soup with eggs"), and Austrian *leberknodeln* ("liver dumpling") are all examples of broths with garnishes. Jewish chicken soup with matzoh balls or dumplings is just as basic. Chinese egg drop soup is simply broth with eggs. Many other Asian broth soups are enlivened by the addition of such spices as chili pepper or the more exotic lemon grass.

Common additions for broths include: Sherry or Madeira, lemon, hot pepper sauce, red wine for beef and white wine for veal. Pasta and rice can also be used but may cloud the broth and should be cooked separately, then added.

Broths can be accompanied by baked, toasted or fried bread croutes, which are bread crusts, sometimes rubbed with garlic, grated parmesan or swiss cheese. The selection of what is rubbed on it would depend on the nature of the broth. Common garnishes for broths are chopped or finely minced fresh herbs. These include chervil, chives, parsley, scallions and others.

Broth, itself, can become a one dish meal if the amount and variety of ingredients are increased. They are then served with the meats and vegetables from the pot in which they are cooked. As with the poultry based *poule au pot*, soups such as *bouillabaisse* and *Scotch broth* often make up a two-course meal. The broth is the first course and the fish or meat is the main course.

Modern households no longer have

BEEF BROTH

Ordinary meat stock made in a big stock pot is called BEEF BROTH OR BOUILLON. This serves as a basis for most clear soups. If it is prepared with all of the usual nutritive and aromatic ingredients it should be very savory.

YIELD: 1-1/2 GAL

INGREDIENTS	AMOUNT
NOURISHING	
1. LEAN BEEF, NECK, SHANK, SHOULDERS	4 1/2 LB
2. BEEF KNUCKLE WITH BONE	3 1/4 LB
AROMATIC	
3. WHITE TURNIPS	2-3 EA
4. PARSNIPS	1 EA
5. LEEKS TIED IN A BUNDLE	3-4 EA
6. CELERY	2 STALKS
7. ONION, MEDIUM	1 EA
8. CLOVES, WHOLE	2 EA
9. GARLIC CLOVE	1 EA
10. THYME	1 SPRIG (SMALL PINCH IF DRIED)
11. BAY LEAF	1/2 EA
LIQUID	
12. WATER, COLD	1 GAL, 3 QT, 1 PT

METHOD
1. TIE THE MEAT WITH A STRING AND PLACE IN LARGE STOCK POT. (NOTE: TO EXTRACT THE MAXIMUM AMOUNT OF FLAVOR FROM THE BONES, BREAK THEM INTO PIECES.)
2. ADD WATER, BRING GENTLY TO A BOIL AND REDUCE TO A SIMMER. (NOTE: IT IS BETTER TO ADJUST SEASONING AT THE END, THAN TO ADD TOO MUCH AT THE BEGINNING.)
3. WHEN BOILING IS ESTABLISHED, A LAYER OF SLIGHTLY COAGULATED ALBUMEN (SCUM) FORMS ON THE SURFACE. REMOVE THIS CAREFULLY.
4. CONTINUE TO SKIM THE POT CLEAN, UNTIL NO MORE COAGULATION RISES TO THE SURFACE.
5. SEASON WITH 2 TBS COARSE SALT
6. SPIKE ONION WITH THE CLOVES.
7. PLACE ALL VEGETABLES INTO THE STOCK POT, SIMMER VERY SLOWLY FOR 5 HOURS. (NOTE: THE BOILING ACTION SHOULD ONLY BE BARELY PERCEPTIBLE.)
8. REMOVE SURPLUS FAT CAREFULLY.
9. STRAIN STOCK THROUGH CHEESECLOTH, MUSLIN OR VERY FINE SIEVE.
10. COOL, COVER AND REFRIGERATE IF NOT TO BE USED IMMEDIATELY.

Figure 2

QUICK BEEF BROTH
Yield: 1 gal

INGREDIENTS	AMOUNT
1. BEEF, COARSELY CHOPPED	16-20 OZ
2. CARROT, SMALL	4 EA
3. WHITE LEEK	4 EA
4. CELERY, SMALL STALK	4 EA
5. ONION, MEDIUM	4 EA
6. CLOVE, WHOLE	4 EA
7. WATER	1 GAL, 1 QT, 1C

METHOD

1. PLACE ALL INGREDIENTS IN POT WITH WATER, BRING TO A BOIL, REDUCE HEAT AND SIMMER GENTLY FOR 20 MINUTES.
2. STRAIN.

NOTE: A) QUICK VEAL BROTH: PREPARE USING THE SAME METHOD, BUT WITH LEAN VEAL (HAUNCH OR SHOULDER) INSTEAD OF BEEF.

B) QUICK CHICKEN BROTH: PREPARE USING THE SAME METHOD, BUT WITH 14-18 OZ. CHICKEN WINGS INSTEAD OF THE BEEF.

Depending on the purpose of these broths, a little thyme or parsley and salt and pepper may be added.

Figure 3

stock pots bubbling away permanently on a corner of the stove. The same is true of many smaller, more limited, commercial kitchens; however, broth is still the basis of many recipes. Figures Three through Five give a few simple and quick recipes for broths and bouillons. The two vegetable broths are included because of their potential application as an alternative for modern preparations which are not meat based. The use of a pressure cooker can greatly speed up the cooking time of stocks. (Consult the manufacturer's recommended cooking times.) These can be kept in the refrigerator for three days, or longer, if brought to a boil and quickly cooled before refrigerating.

VEGETABLE BOUILLON

1. Use the mirepoix that is generally included in a stock pot. Nearly any other vegetable can be added to the pot, taking into consideration those vegetables which might give a bitter or "off" taste, i.e. celery leaves.
2. Clean, then dice the mirepoix.
3. Sweat gently in butter or fat.
4. Pour boiling water over them to cover.
5. Add a bouquet garni, salt and pepper (optional).
6. Simmer until the vegetables are cooked.
7. Strain and serve.

NOTE: An alternate method is simply to add all of the ingredients to boiling water and simmer until cooked.

Figure 4

CONSOMME

Consomme is a concentrated, thin, clear soup made from meat, poultry or fish. The word has the same origin as consummate, meaning to bring to completion or to perfection. A consomme is cooked long enough for most of the nutritive properties of the ingredients to be extracted into the liquid. In the most general sense, consomme is a meat, poultry or fish stock which has gone through a special clarification process, served hot or cold, and normally at the beginning of the dinner meal.

Consomme is the most sophisticated of all stock based soups. It is made by reducing veal, beef, chicken, and today more frequently than in the past, game or fish stock. The liquid is then clarified, enriching it with nutritive and aromatic substances, producing a transparent, sparkling liquid. Its clarity is deceptive since good consomme has "punch." It has a heady aroma and strong flavor that is neither bland nor salty, thin nor heavy. This soup may be garnished in many different ways depending on the base from which it is made.

PREPARATION OF CONSOMME

Figures Six through Nine give preparation methods for basic consommes. The purpose of the procedures are discussed here.

THE STOCK

Beef and chicken are the most common types; however, fish and game are gaining in popularity. While the ordinary stock pot is filled mostly with bones, the consomme stock or broth is made stronger and richer. A piece of boiling beef, chicken or fish, depending on the type being prepared, is added to the pot. The preparation at this point is the same as that for a good quality stock. The preparation is almost identical to making a beef broth. Refer to Figure Two.

CLARIFICATION

The term *consomme double* describes the process whereby the meat or fish flavor is extracted twice; first when making the stock, second when clarifying the consomme. It is the clarification which makes it a true consomme. Not exactly a speedy or inexpensive process, it is the best way to produce a rich and flavorful broth.

The clarification process is simple. Well flavored, fat-free stock is brought slowly to a boil while a clarification mixture is whisked in. As the albumin in the egg whites and the the ground meat in the clarification mixture cooks, it expands and rises to the top of the stock. It forms a gray froth of coagulated proteins which form a filter. This is called the RAFT. The consomme is left to simmer for approximately an hour. (The mixture is not allowed to boil once the raft has formed. The strong rolling action would break the raft apart.) This allows the impurities to percolate through the filter, leaving the liquid consomme crystal clear and sparkling.

FLAVOR AND COLOR

While the egg whites clarify the liquid, they also absorb flavor. Ground or finely chopped vegetables are added to the stock. They provide flavor to the consomme and body to the raft. As well, ground meats which are in character with the consomme are added. The blood in the meats add flavor and act as a clarifying agent.

Madeira or sherry can be added just before serving, or possibly during clarification. Such flavorings should be merely an embellishment.

Consomme should have a clear tint. Meat consomme should be darker than that of chicken or fish.

THICKENING CONSOMME

Consommes are thickened naturally by their gelatin content. The gelatin content of consomme gives it a smooth texture when hot, and sets it, when chilled, to a shivering jelly. Ideally, the original stock should be made with enough bones to provide the gelatin to set the consomme. Gelatin, however, can be added during the last part of the clarification process to ensure that the consomme sets properly.

Consommes may also be thickened with egg yolks, fresh cream, tapioca or arrowroot. The use of these thickeners would depend on the type of consomme being prepared.

GARNISH

Consomme garnish is added just before serving, so that it does not cloud the soup. No ingredients should be larger than the size of a pea, and all cut garnishes must fit within the well of a bouillon spoon. Chopped herbs, small quenelles, pasta, brunoise of vegetables and royales are appropriate garnishes. One tablespoon per serving is sufficient.

Good accompaniments for consommes are cheese straws, wafers, small puffs or pate a choux. The accompaniment should not compete with the consomme.

BASIC CLARIFICATION PROCESS FOR CONSOMME

(The clarification process in this recipe is applicable to all consommes. The only change required would be the use of appropriate corresponding ingredients.)

YIELD: APPROX 1 GAL FINISHED PRODUCT

INGREDIENTS	AMOUNT
1. EGG WHITES	3 TO 4 EA
2. LEAN GROUND MEAT, NECK OR SHANK	1 LB
3. MIREPOIX, FINELY DICED, INCLUDING WHITE OF LEEKS AND PARSLEY STEMS	1 LB
4. SMALL ONION, CARAMELIZED AND SPIKED WITH CLOVES	1/2 EA
5. CRUSHED TOMATOES	8 OZ
6. DEFATTED, COLD, JELLIED WHITE STOCK	1 GAL, 1 QT
7. SALT & PEPPER	TO TASTE

METHOD

1. IN A STAINLESS STEEL BOWL, WHIP EGG WHITES UNTIL FROTHY.

2. ADD GROUND MEAT, MIREPOIX, ONION AND TOMATOES TO EGG WHITES AND LET MARINATE 2 HOURS.

3. STIR THE CLARIFICATION MIXTURE INTO THE COLD STOCK, IN A STOCK POT. NOTE: IT IS BEST TO USE A STOCK POT WITH A DRAIN SPIGOT. THIS ALLOWS THE DRAINING OF THE CONSOMME FOR STRAINING, WITHOUT DISTURBING THE RAFT.

4. PLACE STOCK POT ON A MODERATE FIRE, IN A WAY THAT IT WILL NOT BOIL TOO QUICKLY.

5. WITH A SPATULA, STIR THE MIXTURE FROM TIME TO TIME, TO PREVENT IT FROM STICKING TO THE BOTTOM.

NOTE: UNDER THE INFLUENCE OF HEAT THE ALBUMEN FROM THE MEAT AND EGG WHITES, DISSOLVED IN COLD STOCK, WILL COAGULATE AND EXPAND IN VOLUME, RISING AND ACCUMULATING ON THE SURFACE OF THE STOCK IN THE FORM OF A RAFT.

6. WHEN THE STOCK COMES TO THE FIRST GENTLE BOIL, LOWER THE HEAT AND, WITH A LADLE, MAKE A VENT/HOLE IN THE SOLID CLARIFICATION FILTER OR RAFT.
NOTE: THIS LETS THE CONSOMME BUBBLE WITHOUT BREAKING THE FILTER INTO PIECES.

7. SIMMER THE CONSOMME FOR 40 TO 60 MINUTES TO EXTRACT ALL FLAVORS FULLY.

8. TO STRAIN, PLACE A DAMP CHEESECLOTH OVER A FINE MESH STRAINER AND LADLE THE CONSOMME INTO IT.
(THIS IS DONE WHEN USING A POT WITHOUT A DRAIN SPIGOT.)
NOTE: LET ALL THE LIQUID DRAIN THROUGH SLOWLY.

9. ONCE STRAINED, IF NOT USED IMMEDIATELY, RAPID COOLING IS NEEDED TO PREVENT FERMENTATION.

11. WHEN COOL, COVER, LABEL AND REFRIGERATE.

Figure 6

CHICKEN CONSOMME

For the stock proceed as for beef broth (Figure Two), but replace the lean beef with a small chicken and 3 or 4 giblets which have all been browned in the oven. Replace the shin of beef with 12-3/4 lb veal knuckle. For clarification, proceed as in Figure Six using 4 or 5 chopped chicken giblets instead of chopped beef. The cooked chicken may then be used for croquettes, patties or other items.

Figure 7

GAME CONSOMME

(THE PROPORTIONS OF THE VARIOUS TYPES OF GAME CAN BE ADJUSTED ACCORDING TO AVAILABILITY.)

YIELD: APPROX 5 QT

INGREDIENTS	AMOUNT
1. VENISON, NECK OR SHOULDER	4 1/2 LB
2. HARE OR RABBIT, FOREQUARTER	2 1/4 LB
3. PHEASANT, OLD	1 EA
4. PARTRIDGE	1 EA
5. CARROT	11 OZ
6. LEEKS	11 OZ
7. ONIONS	11 OZ
8. CELERY	5 OZ
9. PARSLEY SPRIGS	2 OZ
10. GARLIC CLOVE	2 EA
11. THYME SPRIGS	2 EA
12. BAY LEAF	1 EA
13. JUNIPER BERRIES	2 OZ
14. CLOVES, WHOLE	3 EA
15. SALT	1 1/2 OZ
16. WATER, COLD	1 GAL , 2 QT

METHOD

1. CLEAN GAME.
2. BROWN GAME IN LIGHTLY GREASED PAN IN A 475°F OVEN.
3. PLACE GAME AND ITS JUICES INTO A SUITABLE STOCK POT, ADD WATER AND BRING TO A BOIL.
4. PREPARE AND CHOP VEGETABLES, AND BROWN IN A PAN.
5. TIE JUNIPER BERRIES AND CLOVES IN A CHEESECLOTH BAG.
6. WHEN THE STOCK HAS COME TO A BOIL, ADD THE VEGETABLES AND HERBS. RETURN TO A BOIL.
7. SIMMER GENTLY FOR 3-1/2 HOURS.
8. REMOVE SURPLUS FAT AND STRAIN THE STOCK.
9. SERVE AS SOUP OR CLARIFY IN THE SAME MANNER AS WHITE STOCK (FIGURE SIX.) NOTE: THE GAME USED IN THIS CONSOMME CAN BE BONED AND THE COOKED MEATS MADE INTO CROQUETTES, PUREE OR SALPICON, AND USED FOR VARIOUS GARNISHES OR SALADS.

Figure 8

FISH CONSOMME

YIELD: APPROX. 5 QT

INGREDIENTS	AMOUNT
STOCK	
1. SOLE, PIKE OR SIMILAR WHITE FISH	3 LB
2. FISH BONES OF FLAT FISH	1 1/4 LB
3. FISH HEADS OF WHITE FISH	2 1/4 LB
4. ONIONS	11 OZ
5. LEEKS	7 OZ
6. PARSLEY SPRIGS	3 OZ
7. CELERY	1 OZ
8. THYME SPRIG & BAY LEAF	1 EA
9. SALT	1 1/2 OZ
10. WHITE WINE	1 PT
CLARIFYING MIXTURE	
11. WHITE FLESHED FISH, UNCOOKED, GROUND	3 LB
12. LEEKS	5 OZ
13. PARSLEY SPRIGS	2 OZ
14. EGG WHITES	4 EA

METHOD

1. PROCEED AS FOR BEEF BROTH, BUT CHOP THE ONIONS AND LEEKS FINELY AND BOIL SLOWLY FOR 45 MINUTES ONLY.
2. USING THE CLARIFYING MIXTURE, PROCEED AS IN FIGURE SIX, BUT COOK VERY SLOWLY AND ONLY FOR ABOUT 30 MINUTES.
3. STRAIN CONSOMME, SERVE IMMEDIATELY OR STORE UNDER REFRIGERATION.

Figure 9

ESSENCES

Essences are a derivation of the mentioned consommes with special flavors. The flavors come from extracts of aromatics and flavorful herbs, plants, vegetables or fungus. The most common are essence of celery, essence of tarragon, essence of truffles and essence of tomatoes. Essences or extracts from game birds are also used, but are usually reserved for special gastronomic dinners. The game most used in this manner are wild duck, partridge, quail and pheasant.

There are also special consommes flavored with wines, usually fortified wines. These wines are added at the last minute, just before serving. The ratio of about one pint of wine per gallon of consomme, using Madeira, port, sherry or Marsala, will add a fine, distinct flavor.

These special consommes are made in the same manner as the others. The exception is that they may need an increased quantity of meat for clarification. It may also be necessary to increase the amount of aromatics to maintain the characteristic flavor of the consomme.

PREPARATION OF SPECIAL CONSOMMES WITH ESSENCES

CONSOMME WITH CELERY ESSENCE - Finely chop the inner stalks of a head of celery. Add these to the other ingredients when clarifying the consomme.

CONSOMME WITH WINE - Strain the consomme, and when nearly cold, add 2/3 cup of Madeira, Marsala, port or sherry.

CONSOMME WITH ESSENCE OF TARRAGON - Add 3/4 oz fresh tarragon leaves to the consomme after it has been clarified and before straining. Let the mixture set for the flavor to infuse.

JELLIED SOUPS

The idea of chilled soups may seem somewhat strange, and that of jellied soups possibly grotesque. However, during warm seasons or in warm regions, they are definitely appropriate. A jellied consomme is a pleasant addition to a meal.

Many soups do not have to be prepared originally to be served chilled. It is more of an adaption of a normal preparation. In the same way, most clear soups may be jellied with the addition of a little unflavored gelatin.

PREPARATION OF CHILLED AND JELLIED CONSOMMES

JELLIED CONSOMMES (CONSOMME EN GELEE) undergo the same preparation as regular consomme. The strength of the consomme's natural gel is tested. (Refer to Chapter 24 for a complete discussion of gelatin.) If it is not strong enough, natural gelatin is carefully added. The gel should be just past the point of liquid, but never rubbery. Seasoning in jellied consomme must be spicier than in regular consomme.

CONSOMME MADRILENE is prepared by adding tomatoes or tomato trimmings and a little red pepper to the clarification mixture of the consomme. The flavor of tomatoes should be prominent in the consomme. It should have a lightly reddish, natural color.

CONSOMME PORTUGUESE is finished with tomato puree and tomato juice during cooking of this consomme. Once the puree and juice are added the consomme is cooked for another half hour without boiling. This infuses the flavor and color. The consomme is then strained through a mousseline and finished as for other cold consommes with the addition of a small amount of cayenne pepper.

CONSOMME NEAPOLITAN is prepared in the same manner as Portuguese but with the addition of port wine or Marsala wine.

To close the book on the subject of clear soups, here are some guidelines for the the production of a superior product.

NOTES AND TIPS ON CLEAR SOUPS

1. CLEAR SOUPS ARE MADE BY ONE METHOD ONLY, WHETHER BASED ON MEAT, POULTRY, GAME, FISH, SHELLFISH OR TURTLE. THEY ARE ALWAYS CLEAR SOUPS, WHETHER SIMPLE (BROTH) OR COMPLEX (CONSOMME), TO WHICH IS ADDED A SUITABLE LIGHT GARNISH.

2. WHITE STOCK (MEAT, POULTRY, GAME, FISH OR SHELLFISH) IS GENERALLY USED IN THE PREPARATION OF CLARIFIED CONSOMMES. BROWN STOCK CAN BE USED WITH SUCCESS.

3. FOR CLARIFIED CONSOMMES, MORE THAN FOR BROTH, USE THE MEAT OF OLD ANIMALS. THE CONSOMME WILL BE STRONGER, MORE MELLOW AND MORE FLAVORFUL. THE FLESH OF THE YOUNG ANIMAL DOES NOT HAVE THE RICHNESS OF FLAVOR.

4. THE PROCESS FOR MAKING BROTH AND CONSOMME IS A CONSTANT, ONLY THE INGREDIENTS CHANGE.

5. FISH CONSOMMES WERE RARELY USED, MOSTLY DURING LENT, IN THE PAST. HOWEVER, THEY ARE BECOMING MORE POPULAR WITH THEIR LIGHTER AND MORE SUBTLE FLAVORS. THE USUAL GARNITURE IS LITTLE QUENELLES OF THE FISH WHICH IS USED TO GIVE THE CONSOMME ITS NATURE.

6. LAST MINUTE ADDITIONS CAN IMPROVE THE CHARACTER OF A SOUP, ADD THEM JUST BEFORE SERVING, OTHERWISE THEY WILL SEPARATE FROM THE SOUP.

   A) STRONG FLAVORINGS, SUCH AS HERBS, WINES AND SPICES, ARE STIRRED INTO THE SOUP ITSELF.

   B) WHISK WHOLE EGG; MIX CHOPPED HERBS INTO IT, AND STIR INTO SIMMERING SOUP FROM A HEIGHT THAT WILL FORM A "STRING."

7. SOUPS SHOULD BE SERVED PIPING HOT, IF HOT, AND WELL CHILLED, IF COLD. THIS IS

PARTICULARLY IMPORTANT FOR CON-
SOMMES.

8. STAY AWAY FROM USING TOO MANY EGG
WHITES IN THE CLARIFICATION PROCESS
FOR CONSOMME. IT IS BETTER TO
INCREASE THE QUANTITY OF MEAT USED.
A STANDARD RATIO IS THREE EGG WHITES
PER GALLON OF CONSOMME.

THICK SOUPS

Thick soups is a term used for soups served as a substantial first course of a meal or as the main dish. They are not necessarily thickened. They may be made with meat stock, poultry stock, fish stock, shellfish stock or vegetable stock. To the stock are added various ingredients, giving them their particular taste and usually heavy consistency.

There are several kinds of thick soups. The soup *liaison*, "binding or thickening," may be from a variety of sources. It can result naturally from the major ingredients of the soup. The dissolving of farinaceous ingredients (such as roux, cooked rice, bread boiled to a pulp, puree of a starchy vegetable or others, in the soup can thicken it. Many thick soups are bound with a liaison of egg yolks and cream, just before serving.

We will divide thick soups into four subsections for our discussion.

A) Purees, Coulis and Bisques
B) Velouté Soups
C) Cream Soups
D) Vegetable Soups

PUREES, COULIS AND BISQUES

PUREES are either purees of starchy vegetables or leguminous plants. The liaison is achieved naturally by the starch content of the vegetable. The purees using edible seeds, pulses (such as beans and lentils) and those using starchy vegetables as the main ingredient need no additional thickening agent. The vegetables already contain the necessary thickening quality. Succulent vegetables, such as carrots, broccoli, pumpkin, celery and various herbs, must have added thickening agents.

The puree itself will not hold together and bind.

COULIS is the term best used for purees of poultry, game, fish and shellfish. Today it is sometimes used for purees of fruits and non-farinaceous vegetables.

BISQUE, in relation to what we have already mentioned, describes a specific type of preparation involving a puree. From the origin of the bisque to the end of the 18th century, the term referred to soups based on poultry and pigeon. While this is no longer the case, it is still a specialized preparation.

PUREES AND COULIS

Purees of starchy vegetables or leguminous plants are made of vegetables rich in starch. These include white or red dried beans, kidney beans, lentils, split peas and others. These vegetables contain enough starch naturally so that they do not need added elements to bind.

Purees of fresh vegetables, less rich in starch, do need added binders. Often those added are cooked rice or a puree of some vegetable richer in starch content.

The secret of a good pureed soup is thorough cooking. The cooking insures that the starchy ingredients, which give it body, are well blended in the puree. The consistency of a pureed soup will vary with the ingredients used and the way in which they are processed. A food mill produces a more coarsely textured puree than does a food processor. The finest consistency is achieved by straining the pureed soup through a fine sieve prior to service.

Among the classic pureed soups are VICHYSSOISE, leek with potato; POTAGE CRECY, carrots thickened with rice, and POTAGE SAINT GERMAINE, split pea flavored with ham. In Provence, fish soups may be pureed, and in Italy some cooks work their minestrone through a food mill. At one time, poultry, meat and game purees were popular soups in Europe. The most familiar of this type today is POTAGE A LA REINE, a rich puree based on chicken stock. As was stated earlier, those types of purees are termed coulis. Figure Eleven gives a recipe for such a soup.

There is also a group of half pureed soups, which are often based on root vegetables or corn. In these the solid ingredients are pureed to thicken the broth, with the other ingredients left in pieces for texture.

A recipe for possibly the best known pureed soup in the United States, split pea, is given in Figure Ten. The method of preparation in this recipe can be adjusted for most other pureed type soups.

PUREE OF SPLIT PEA SOUP
YIELD: APPROX 1 GAL
20, 6 OZ SERVINGS

INGREDIENTS	AMOUNT
1. SALT PORK, GROUND OR FINELY DICED	4 OZ
MIREPOIX	
2. ONION, FINELY DICED	8 OZ
3. CELERY, FINELY DICED	4 OZ
4. CARROTS, FINELY DICED	4 OZ
5. GARLIC CLOVE, FINELY MINCED	1 EA
6. WHITE STOCK, VEAL OR CHICKEN	4 QT
7. HAM BONE OR SMOKED HAM HOCK (OPTIONAL)	1 EA
8. GREEN SPLIT PEAS, RINSED AND DRAINED	2 LB
9. BOUQUET GARNI (THYME, BAY LEAF, PARSLEY STEMS)	1 EA
10. SALT & PEPPER	TO TASTE

METHOD
1. IN A HOT RONDEAU OR HEAVY SAUCE POT, RENDER SALT PORK.
2. ADD THE MIREPOIX AND SWEAT GENTLY OVER MODERATE HEAT, UNTIL SOFT AND TRANSLUCENT.
   NOTE: DO NOT CARAMELIZE THE MIREPOIX. THIS WILL GIVE A DARK COLOR AND BROWNED FLAVOR TO THE PUREE.
3. ADD HAM BONE OR HOCK, AND STOCK, BRING TO A BOIL.
4. ADD RINSED AND DRAINED SPLIT PEAS AND BOUQUET GARNI.
5. BRING TO BOIL, LOWER HEAT AND SIMMER GENTLY FOR APPROXIMATELY 1 HOUR.
6. REMOVE HAM HOCK, BONE AND BOUQUET GARNI.
7. PUREE REMAINDER THROUGH FOOD MILL, FOOD PROCESSOR OR BLENDER.
8. RETURN TO SUITABLE POT AND RETURN TO HEAT. BRING TO A BOIL.
9. ADJUST CONSISTENCY BY ADDING ADDITIONAL THICKENER, IF TOO THIN, OR STOCK, IF TOO THICK. THEN STRAIN THROUGH A FINE SIEVE.
10. ADJUST SEASONING.
11. TRIM MEAT OFF THE HAM HOCK, DICE AND ADD TO SOUP AS GARNISH.
12. SERVE WITH FRIED OR TOASTED CRISP CROUTONS.

VARIATIONS:
PUREE OF WHITE BEAN SOUP
PUREE OF BLACK BEAN
PUREE OF YELLOW SPLIT PEA
PUREE OF CARROT

Figure 10

COULIS OF GAME
YIELD: 15 SERVINGS

INGREDIENTS	AMOUNTS
1. GAME MEAT, PREFERABLY VENISON	1 LB
2. LENTILS	14 OZ
3. GAME STOCK	3 QTS
4. ONION SPIKED WITH CLOVES AND BAY LEAF	1 EA
5. BRANDY	2 OZ
6. CREAM	6 OZ
7. SALT, PEPPER	TO TASTE
8. GAME MEAT, COOKED, CUBED	6 OZ

METHOD
1. BOIL THE GAME AND LENTILS IN THE STOCK WITH THE SPIKED ONION.
2. COOK UNTIL THE MEAT IS TENDER.
3. GRIND THE ENTIRE MIXTURE.
4. FLAMBE THE MIXTURE WITH BRANDY.
5. ADD THE CREAM. SEASON TO TASTE.
6. GARNISH WITH THE CUBED GAME MEAT.

Figure 11

BISQUES

A bisque is a creamy puree that concentrates the essence of a single ingredient into a rich perfumed soup. The thickening ingredient is rice or crust of bread fried in butter. Traditionally the base for bisque has been shellfish. This is cooked with mirepoix.

The name bisque is sometimes loosely applied to cream soups of shellfish or vegetables, such as crab or tomato. Generally these do not follow the classic cooking procedure of using rice or crust of bread as the binder. Be careful in your use of the term. These are not bisques. It is the procedure which makes it a bisque. Most popular are shellfish bisques, but game, poultry and full flavored vegetables, such as tomato, are also suitable, though less traditional.

Shellfish bisque follows a classical preparation. It is a complicated process designed to bring out the maximum flavor. The steps are listed below.

1. THE PRINCIPAL INGREDIENTS ARE OFTEN SAUTEED AND FLAMBÉD. THIS IS ESPECIALLY TRUE IF LIVE SHELLFISH ARE USED.
2. FISH STOCK AND AROMATICS ARE ADDED, ALONG WITH RICE FOR THICKENING.
3. WHEN ALL THE INGREDIENTS ARE COOKED THE BISQUE IS PUREED. THIS USED TO BE DONE WITH A MORTAR AND PESTLE, BUT TODAY IT IS DONE IN A FOOD PROCESSOR OR BLENDER.
4. THE BISQUE IS THEN SIEVED BEFORE RETURNING TO THE HEAT TO SIMMER. THIS SECOND HEATING MARRIES THE FLAVORS.
5. SCRUPULOUS COOKS THEN SIEVE IT AGAIN. THIS TIME THROUGH THE FINEST OF CONICAL SIEVES OR MUSLIN CLOTH.
6. IT IS FINALLY ENRICHED WITH CREAM, GIVING IT THAT CHARACTERISTIC VELVETY TEXTURE WHICH IS TRULY A BISQUE.

The seasoning of bisque is critical. Often a hint of cayenne is added as a foil to the rich texture and flavor. Some recipes call for a final enrichment of shellfish butter. Figure Twelve gives a recipe for a basic bisque.

Bisques are best garnished with items which represent the base. For example, for shellfish bisque use small shellfish, like shrimp or possibly sliced crab or lobster meat, or claw meat. Creme fraiche or tiny quenelles can also be used. The bisque is normally accompanied by fried croutons.

BASIC SHRIMP BISQUE

YIELD: 1 GAL

20, 6 OZ SERVINGS

INGREDIENTS	AMOUNT
1. OLIVE OIL	2 OZ
2. BUTTER	2 OZ
3. BROKEN SHRIMPS, PIECES & HEADS	1 1/2 LB
4. WHITE MIREPOIX (ONION, LEEK, CELERY) FINELY DICED	1 1/2 LB
5. GARLIC AND SHALLOTS	2 CLOVES OF EA
6. BRANDY	4 OZ
7. WHITE WINE	8 OZ
8. TOMATO PUREE/CONCASSE	8 OZ
9. AROMATICS (THYME, TARRAGON, FENNEL, SAFFRON)	1 PINCH EA
10. FISH STOCK	1 GAL
11. RAW RICE	1 C
11. HEAVY CREAM	1 PT
12. SALT & PEPPER	TO TASTE
13. SMALL, COOKED PINK SHRIMPS (AS GARNISH)	8 OZ
14. FINELY CHOPPED FRESH HERBS FOR GARNISH	AS NEEDED

NOTE: THE BEST SHRIMP TO USE FOR BISQUE ARE THE SMALL GRAY OR PINK. HOWEVER, ANY SHRIMP CAN BE SUBSTITUTED, PREFERABLY WITH THEIR HEADS ON.

METHOD

1. IN A HOT RONDEAU, ADD OIL AND BUTTER.

2. ADD SHRIMPS, SHELLS, HEADS AND MIREPOIX. CARAMELIZE WELL TO EXTRACT THE FLAVOR AND COLOR.

3. FLAMBÉ WITH BRANDY, DEGLAZE WITH WHITE WINE.

4. ADD TOMATO PRODUCT AND AROMATICS.

5. ADD BOILING STOCK AND BRING TO A BOIL.

6. ADD RICE AND REDUCE TO A SIMMER.

7. WHILE SIMMERING, BRING HEAVY CREAM TO A BOIL IN A SEPARATE POT.

8. WHEN RICE IS COOKED AND ITS STARCH RELEASED, STRAIN SOLIDS AND PUREE THEM IN A FOOD PROCESSOR OR BLENDER.

9. RETURN PUREED SOLIDS TO THE LIQUID AND BRING TO A BOIL.

10. STRAIN THROUGH LARGE SIZE CHINOIS, PRESSING WELL TO EXTRACT ALL LIQUID AND FLAVOR.

11. RETURN TO SUITABLE POT AND BRING BACK TO A BOIL.

12. ADD HEAVY CREAM AND ADJUST SEASONINGS AS NEEDED.

13. STRAIN THROUGH CHEESECLOTH/MUSLIN, USING THE MILKING METHOD.

14. PLACE IN SUITABLE POT AND RETURN TO A BOIL.

15. ADD SAUTEED SHRIMP GARNISH TO BISQUE AND A SPRINKLE OF FRESH FINE HERBS AT SERVICE.

Figure 12

CREAM AND VELOUTÉ SOUPS

We have combined the cream and velouté soups for discussion, because of their similarities. In general, these soups are flavored versions of two types of sauces, prepared thin. The sauces are velouté and bechamel. The primary difference between the two being that cream soups are based on bechamel sauce and velouté soups are based on velouté sauce. In recent times, the lines between cream and veloute soups have become blurred primarily due to "short cuts" which have been used in kitchen production. Parts of each method have been married resulting in one type of soup, which is always called a cream. To preserve the integrity of the subject, both methods of preparation are presented.

The standards of quality are the same for both soups, and are based on three factors.

1. THICKNESS - SHOULD BE ABOUT THE CONSISTENCY OF A CREAM OR SYRUP. THE SOUP IS NOT THICK, BUT WILL COAT THE BACK OF A SPOON.

PREPARATION OF CREAM & VELOUTÉ SOUPS

(The following methods apply to most cream and veloute soups. Remember that individual ingredients may require some variation.)

1. PREPARE A LIGHT VELOUTE OR BECHAMEL SAUCE USING A SUITABLE ROUX. NOTE: BINDING OF THE SAUCE CAN BE DONE WITH CORN STARCH, WAXY MAIZE OR OTHER STARCH. THIS WILL GIVE THE SOUP GREATER RESISTANCE TO BREAKING WHEN EXPOSED TO HEAT, HOWEVER THESE TYPES OF THICKENERS WILL NOT GIVE THE SOUP THE RICHNESS OF BODY AND FLAVOR THAT IS ACHIEVED WITH A BUTTER ROUX.

2. PREPARE THE MAIN FLAVORING INGREDIENTS:
   A) CUT VEGETABLES INTO THIN SLICES OR SMALL DICES.
   B) SWEAT THEM IN BUTTER.
   NOTE: A) THIS DOES THREE THINGS: 1) REMOVES MOST OF THE ACIDITY FROM THE VEGETABLES. 2) SATURATES THEM WITH BUTTER. 3) DEVELOPS FLAVOR.
   B) DO NOT BROWN THE VEGETABLES. THE BROWNING WILL COLOR THE SOUPS AND BRING A DISTINCTLY BROWN, CARAMELIZED FLAVOR WHICH IS NOT NEEDED OR WANTED IN THESE SOUPS. C) GREEN LEAFY VEGETABLES SHOULD BE BLANCHED BEFORE BEING SWEATED IN BUTTER.

3. ADD THE BECHAMEL OR VELOUTE TO THE FLAVORING INGREDIENTS FROM STEP 2 AND SIMMER UNTIL TENDER. NOTE: ONCE THE SAUCE IS ADDED, SCORCHING CAN EASILY OCCUR, BECAUSE OF THE STARCH CONTENT. BE CAREFUL TO USE MODERATE FIRES AND TO STIR OCCASIONALLY.

4. SKIM ANY FAT OR SCUM CAREFULLY FROM THE SURFACE OF THE SOUP.

5. PUREE THE SOUP BY PASSING THROUGH A FOOD MILL, FOOD PROCESSOR OR BLENDER.
   NOTE: IT IS POSSIBLE TO EXTRACT AN ACCEPTABLE AMOUNT OF FLAVOR FROM THE SOLID ITEMS BY PASSING THE SOUP THROUGH A FINE CHINA CAP. IF THIS IS THE METHOD USED, PRESS DOWN HARD ON THE SOLIDS TO EXTRACT THE FLAVORFUL LIQUIDS.

6. ADD HOT BROTH TO THE FLAVORED VELOUTÉ TO GAIN THE DESIRED CONSISTENCY, BOILED CREAM TO THE FLAVORED BECHAMEL.

7. ADJUST SEASONING AS NEEDED.

8. AT SERVICE TIME, FINISH WITH THE APPROPRIATE LIAISON OR HEAVY CREAM.

9. ADD GARNISH AND SERVE IMMEDIATELY.

Figure 13

---

2. **TEXTURE** - SHOULD BE SMOOTH, CREAMY AND VELVETY WITH NO LUMPS OR GRAININESS. THE SOUP MUST DISAPPEAR COMPLETELY ON THE PALATE.

3. **TASTE** - SHOULD HAVE A DISTINCT, DELICATE FLAVOR OF THE MAIN INGREDIENTS. FOR EXAMPLE, CREAM PRINCESS SHOULD HAVE THE FLAVOR OF ASPARAGUS AND CHICKEN.

VELOUTÉ

Practically speaking, the preparation of creams and veloutés are basically the same. However, the veloutés differ from the creams in that the foundation is always a VELOUTÉ SAUCE, one whose preparation is in harmony with the nature of the ingredients of the soup being prepared. This means using either meat, vegetable, poultry, game, fish or shellfish stock in the preparation. In addition, the final liaison in velouté soups is five to six egg yolks per cup of heavy cream for each quart of velouté soup. This differs from the cream soups where strictly heavy cream is used. Figure Thirteen gives the method of preparation for most cream and velouté soups.

VELOUTÉ SOUPS ARE ALWAYS COMPOSED OF 4 MAIN ITEMS:

1. A PUREE OF THE MAIN FLAVOR/INGREDIENT.

2. AN ORDINARY MEAT, POULTRY, GAME, VEGETABLE OR FISH VELOUTÉ. THIS SHOULD BE PREPARED A LITTLE THINNER THAN USUAL.

3. A LIAISON COMPOSED OF EGG YOLK AND CREAM.

4. A GARNISH IN KEEPING WITH THE NATURE OF THE SOUP.

CREAM SOUPS

Cream soups use many of the same ingredients as pureed soups, however they are richer, smoother and more refined in texture. Nearly any vegetable makes an excellent cream soup, especially those which are lighter, more delicately flavored. Examples are cream of asparagus, cream of cauliflower, cream of spinach, cream of watercress and two of the most popular soups in America, cream of tomato and cream of mushroom.

The preparation of cream soups, although almost identical to velouté preparation does have the following differences.

1. In all cases, whatever the nature of the soup, light bechamel is substituted for velouté.

2. The correct consistency of the soup is obtained by adding boiled milk or light cream instead of broth.

3. Creams do not require egg yolk liaison.

4. Creams are not buttered, but are finished with heavy cream.

5. The same garnishing as velouté applies to cream soups.

SPECIAL FACTORS FOR MAKING CREAM SOUPS

Because cream soups contain milk and cream, curdling is a common occurrence. The heat of cooking, combined with the natural acidity of many other ingredients are usually the cause of curdling. Cream soups are thickened, normally, with some type of starch, which helps to prevent curdling. However, they are thin sauces, meaning their starch content is somewhat low and they are by no means curdleproof.

There are three guides to avoiding curdling. They are not foolproof, but they do help to produce smooth, creamy textured soups.

1. **THICKEN THE MILK BEFORE ADDING IT TO THE SOUP. THIS PRODUCES A THIN BECHAMEL WHICH IS RELATIVELY STABLE.**

2. **WHENEVER POSSIBLE, SWEAT THE VEGETABLES IN BUTTER. THIS REMOVES THE NATURAL ACIDITY AND NEUTRALIZES THE ENZYMES OF THE VEGETABLES. IF IT IS NOT POSSIBLE TO SWEAT THE VEGETABLES, BLANCH THEM IN SALTED BOILING WATER. THE LATTER MAY BE NECESSARY FOR SOME FAT RESTRICTED PREPARATIONS.**

CREAM OF BROCCOLI

YIELD: 1 GAL

20, 6 OZ SERVINGS

INGREDIENTS	AMOUNT
1. CLARIFIED BUTTER	4 OZ
2. MEDIUM ONION, FINELY DICED	1 EA
3. CHOPPED FRESH BROCCOLI (REMOVE TOUGH, COARSE STEMS)	2 LB
4. LIGHT BECHAMEL (10-13 OZ OF ROUX PER GAL OF MILK)	3 QT
5. BOILED MILK, HOT	8 OZ, AS NEEDED
6. SALT & PEPPER	TO TASTE
7. HEAVY CREAM	2 C
8. SMALL BROCCOLI FLORETS, BLANCHED, DRAINED & NOT CHOPPED (KEEP GARNISHES SMALL, WHOLE AND WITH FULL IDENTITY.)	6 OZ

METHOD

1. HEAT BUTTER IN A HEAVY SAUCE POT.
2. ADD ONION AND SWEAT TILL TRANSLUCENT.
3. ADD CHOPPED BROCCOLI AND SWEAT TILL SOFT.
4. ADD LIGHT BECHAMEL AND BRING TO A BOIL.
5. LOWER HEAT AND SIMMER GENTLY 8 TO 10 MINUTES, UNTIL BROCCOLI IS FULLY TENDER.
6. STRAIN THE SOLIDS AND PUREE FINELY IN FOOD MILL, FOOD PROCESSOR OR BLENDER.
7. RETURN THE PUREED SOLIDS TO THE LIQUID AND BRING TO BOIL.
8. ADJUST THE CONSISTENCY WITH BOILED MILK, AS NEEDED.
9. ADJUST THE SEASONINGS AS NEEDED.
10. STRAIN THROUGH A VERY FINE SIEVE (CHINOIS) OR CHEESECLOTH, USING THE MILKING METHOD.
11. RETURN THE SOUP TO A BOIL, COMPLETE THE LIAISON FINALE WITH BOILED HEAVY CREAM.
12. ADD FLORET GARNISH JUST BEFORE SERVICE.

Figure 14

3. **ALWAYS BOIL THE MILK OR CREAM <u>BEFORE</u> ADDING TO THE HOT SOUPS, NEVER <u>AFTER</u>.**

An example recipe for a cream soup is given in Figure Fourteen. Preparation of other types of velouté and cream soups would follow the same method, with the exceptions discussed above.

Both cream soups and veloutés can be garnished in the same manner as other thickened soups. This would include pasta products, rice, barley, julienne, chiffonade, or brunoise of vegetables, quenelles and buds or florets of vegetables.

VEGETABLE SOUPS

Any soup containing one or more vegetables, cut in dice, brunoise, julienne, chiffonade or paysanne and eaten with the liquid they have flavored, is classified as vegetable soup or potage. Some recipes may call for flour thickening. However, vegetable soup is usually made of clear broth in which potatoes and other ingredients, such as tomatoes, give the broth a certain thickness.

Vegetable soups, of which paysanne (peasant type) is the typical example, do not demand great precision in the amount of vegetables used. They do need care and attention to produce a quality product. The preparation of a basic vegetable soup would be as follows:

1. INGREDIENTS ARE CUT INTO SIMILAR SHAPES, SIZES.
2. BRAISE THE VEGETABLES WELL IN BUTTER. THIS EXPELS THEIR MOISTURE AND ACIDITY WHILE SATURATING THEM WITH BUTTER.
3. ADD LIQUID AND SIMMER UNTIL SOLID INGREDIENTS ARE TENDER AND THE BROTH WELL FLAVORED. NOTE: AT TIMES THE BASIC LIQUID IS COLD WATER, SINCE THE LONG COOKING TIME ALLOWS THE INGREDIENTS TO CONTRIBUTE THEIR FLAVOR TO THE LIQUID.

This preparation is very simple, yet vegetable soups are often the pride of a kitchen. This may be attributed to the more complex and sophisticated variations. In these, ingredients are added according to their individual cooking times. The goal is to have each ingredient finish cooking at the same time. This allows each vegetable to have the correct texture within the soup. This is especially important when delicate, quick cooking ingredients, such as green beans, go into the pot with slow cooking vegetables, such as dried beans.

You must remember that vegetables with a strong flavor must be used in smaller quantities than others. If they are not, their flavor will over shadow the flavor of all others.

TYPES

SIMPLE VEGETABLE SOUP is a basic example to follow for other soups included in this group. From this process other soups are derived by adding or subtracting vegetables. In some variations a certain type of meat will be added while cooking. These modifications may change the name of the soup and its classification.

To make simple vegetable soup:

1. SELECT THE MOST COMMON VEGETABLES: CARROTS, LEEKS, CELERY AND ONIONS. (ONION SHOULD EQUAL 1/4 THE WEIGHT OF THE FIRST THREE.)
2. ADD GREEN PEPPERS AND TURNIPS.
3. CUT THE VEGETABLES IN THE SIZE AND SHAPES DESIRED. THESE MAY BE BRUNOISE, MEDIUM DICE, PAYSANNE OR JULIENNE
4. BRAISE THE VEGETABLES IN BUTTER.
5. ADD A BOUQUET GARNI AND BROTH.
6. SEASON WITH SALT & PEPPER.
7. COOK SLOWLY FOR APPROXIMATELY 1 HOUR.

POTAGE A LA FERMIERE

INGREDIENTS	AMOUNT
1. BUTTER	2 OZ
2. CARROT, TURNIP, WHITE OF LEEK, ONION (CUT EACH PAYSANNE), WHITE HEART OF CABBAGE (SHREDDED)	4 1/2 OZ OF EA
3. BROTH	1 1/2 QT
4. SMALL BOUQUET GARNI	1 EA
5. SALT & PEPPER	TO TASTE

METHOD

1. IN LARGE, HEAVY SAUCE POT HEAT BUTTER.
2. ADD VEGETABLES AND STEW GENTLY, UNTIL SOFT AND TRANSLUCENT.
3. ADD BOUQUET GARNI AND BROTH.
4. BRING TO BOIL AND SIMMER GENTLY UNTIL VEGETABLES ARE TENDER.
5. ADJUST SEASONING AS NEEDED.
6. SERVE WITH THIN SLICES OF TOASTED FRENCH BREAD IN THE SOUP.

Figure 15

FARMSTYLE VEGETABLE SOUP
YIELD: 20 SERVINGS

INGREDIENTS	AMOUNTS
1. CARROTS, CUT IN 2 IN LENGTHS	1 1/2 LBS
2. ONIONS, MEDIUM, SLICED	6 EA
3. LEEKS, SLICED	4 EA
4. CELERY, SLICED	6 OZ
5. GREEN BEANS, CUT	6 OZ
6. GREEN AND RED PEPPER, CUT IN STRIPS	6 OZ
7. CORN, STRIPPED FROM TWO LARGE EARS	6 OZ
8. LIMA BEANS, FRESHLY SHELLED	6 OZ
9. PEAS, FRESHLY SHELLED	6 OZ
10. ZUCCHINI, SLICED	6 OZ
11. TURNIP, CUBED	6 OZ
12. TOMATOES, PEELED AND SLICED	8 EA
13. GARLIC, CRUSHED	3 CLOVES
14. SALT AND PEPPER	TO TASTE
15. BEEF BROTH	2 GAL
16. PARSLEY, CHOPPED	1 C
17. BASIL	2 TSP
18. OREGANO	2 TSP

METHOD
1. POUR THE BROTH INTO A POT LARGE ENOUGH TO HOLD 5 GALLONS.
2. SEASON THE BROTH WITH SALT AND PEPPER.
3. ADD ALL OF THE VEGETABLES AND HERBS.
4. STIR GENTLY TO MIX.
5. BRING TO THE BOILING POINT, THEN REDUCE THE HEAT AND COVER.
6. SIMMER WITHOUT STIRRING FOR ABOUT ONE HOUR (UNTIL ALL VEGETABLES ARE TENDER.)
7. SEASON TO TASTE.

Figure 16

8. ADD FINELY SHREDDED CABBAGE AND SIMMER TEN MINUTES.
9. CORRECT SEASONING AND ADD PARSLEY, CHIVES OR CHERVIL AT SERVICE .

There are a wide variety of classic variations on this type of soup. These include potage cultivateur, potage paysanne and potage bonne femme. Figure Fifteen gives an example recipe for potage a la fermiere.

Some of the best vegetable soups are those which are happenstance, "kitchen sink" type soups made from various leftovers and assorted ingredients that are added according to the creativity and caprice of the cook. This type of soup is in all likelihood the derivative of the very first soups prepared. In the United States, vegetable beef is an extremely popular variation. An example of this type of "homestyle" soup follows in Figure Sixteen.

SPECIALTY SOUPS

This category includes soups of a specific national or regional origin which do not necessarily fit easily into the other classifications. A good example of this are the American chowders. Almost every country can boast of at least one national soup, many have several. When making these types of soups, you must imitate as closely as possible the original product. Usually the soups have a specific flavoring which comes from certain spices or ingredients. These normally have a pungent flavor not found in any other area. Making these soups calls for the highest level of cooking skill and talent to arrive at an authentic result.

As you gain experience in making soups and as you change jobs from one area of the country to another, you will find soups changing. The change may only be that one spice is left out or another added. Remember, sometimes the recipes of the house do not always agree with one's training. However, if it is popular with the customers, it is right for that particular area. Your own innovations can improve many things as you gain knowledge and understanding of the wants of the people in each area where you work.

International cook books, in particular, will furnish the culinarian with authentic recipes. This text can only suggest the major ingredients to create interest. Here we mention, as examples, a few national soups from various countries.

NATIONAL AND REGIONAL TYPES
AMERICA

America is known for its chowders, gumbos, oyster stew, she crab soup and Philadelphia pepper pot, to name a few.

Chowders

Chowders, some of the premier American soups, are chunky, hearty

---

BASIC FISH CHOWDER
NEW ENGLAND STYLE
YIELD: 2 1/2 GAL
50, 6 OZ SERVINGS

INGREDIENTS	AMOUNT
1. SALT PORK, FINELY MINCED INTO A PASTE	12 OZ
2. ONIONS, PAYSANNE	1 1/2 LB
3. LEEKS, MOSTLY WHITE PART, PAYSANNE CUT	1 1/2 LB
4. FLOUR, ALL-PURPOSE	8 OZ
5. POTATOES, PAYSANNE	3 LB
6. FISH STOCK	2 GAL
7. BOUQUET GARNI	1 LARGE
8. DAIRY PRODUCTS (MILK, 1/2 & 1/2, OR CREAM)	2 QT
9. ASSORTED FISH, TRIMMED AND DICED 1/2" x 1/2" x 1/2"	3 TO 5 LB
10. SALT & PEPPER	TO TASTE
11. FRESH HERBS, FINELY CHOPPED	2 C

METHOD
1. HEAT RONDEAU, ADD SALT PORK AND RENDER.
2. ADD ONIONS AND LEEKS. SWEAT UNTIL TRANSLUCENT.
3. ADD FLOUR AND COOK A FEW MINUTES TO BLEND WELL.
4. ADD DICED POTATOES, STIRRING & BLENDING WELL.
5. GRADUALLY ADD BOILING STOCK ALLOWING IT TO DISSOLVE WELL.
6. ADD BOUQUET GARNI, BRING TO BOIL AND SIMMER 30 MINUTES.
7. SEPARATELY, BRING DAIRY PRODUCT TO A BOIL.
8. ADD DICED FISH TO SOUP AND RETURN TO BOIL, STIRRING GENTLY.
9. ADD BOILED DAIRY PRODUCT TO SOUP AND ADJUST SEASONING.
10. SPRINKLE WITH FINE HERBS JUST BEFORE SERVING.

Figure 17

soups. They are sometimes so full of good things that they are more like stews than soups. Like other specialty, regional soups, chowders resist being categorized. However, most are based on fish, shellfish or vegetables, and contain potatoes, salt pork and milk or cream.

The most famous are the New England fish and clam chowders, and the hundreds, possibly, thousands of variations. All are based on the same principles. Figure Seventeen gives an example recipe for fish chowder.

New England clam chowder would contain chopped clams and clam broth in place of the fish and fish stock in the above recipe. Traditional New England chowders would not have been thickened by flour, but by the natural thickening occuring as the potatoes cook, and by the addition of broken up crackers during service. Manhattan clam chowder differs from New England style in that it contains no dairy product and it does contain tomatoes. Both styles of chowder are commonly seasoned with thyme. Two other favorites are corn chowder and potato chowder.

Gumbo

GUMBO is the pride of the state of Louisiana. It takes its name from an African word for *okra*, the ingredient

---

SEAFOOD GUMBO
YIELD: 2 1/2 GAL

INGREDIENTS	AMOUNT
1. BACON, FINELY MINCED	8 SLICES
2. COOKED HAM, FINELY MINCED	8 OZ
3. ONION, CELERY, LEEKS, GREEN & RED PEPPERS, ALL PAYSANNE CUT	1 LB OF EACH
4. GARLIC CLOVES, CRUSHED	2 EA
5. FISH STOCK, FLAVORFUL	2 GAL
6. FLOUR, ROASTED, SIFTED	8 OZ
7. BOUQUET GARNI, LARGE	1 EA
8. CAROLINA RICE, RAW	1 C
9. TOMATOES, LARGE, PEELED, SEEDED, CONCASSE	8 EA
10. OLIVE OIL	4 OZ
11. OKRA, SLICED	2 1/2 LB
12. BAY/PINK SHRIMP, SMALL, COOKED, FOR GARNISH	2 LB
13. FILE POWDER	2 TBS
14. SALT, PEPPER & CAYENNE	TO TASTE

METHOD
1. IN HOT RONDEAU, RENDER BACON ADD HAM.
2. ADD ONION, CELERY, GREEN PEPPER, LEEK, GARLIC AND SWEAT UNTIL TRANSLUCENT.
3. ADD ROASTED FLOUR AND COOK INTO A BROWN ROUX.
4. DILUTE WITH STOCK, AND BRING TO BOIL.
5. ADD RICE AND BOUQUET GARNI, AND SIMMER.
6. WHEN RICE IS COOKED, ABOUT 25-30 MINUTES, ADD DICED TOMATOES.
7. IN OLIVE OIL, SAUTE SLICED OKRA AND ADD TO GUMBO ALONG WITH THE SHRIMP.
8. ADJUST SEASONINGS AS NEEDED.
9. DILUTE FILE POWDER WITH SOME COLD STOCK AND STIR INTO GUMBO.
   NOTE: DO NOT BOIL ANY LONGER AFTER ADDING THE FILE POWDER.
   THE RICE CAN BE COOKED SEPARATELY AND SERVED WITH THE GUMBO.

Figure 18

that gives this soup its characteristic gelatinous texture.

Many gumbos are roux based, but the term *roux* takes on new meaning in Louisiana's Creole and Cajun communities. The flour and fat are cooked much longer and at a higher temperature, so the roux is very close to being burnt.

Gumbos are as much stew as they are soup. Their emphasis is on fully developed layers of flavor. Chicken may be paired with ham, green pepper and oysters; shrimp with oysters, okra, garlic and onion; duck with andouille sausage. A variety called GREEN GUMBO is made with spinach, beet tops, turnips, mustard greens and collard greens. Plain boiled or steamed rice is the usual accompaniment for gumbo. An sample gumbo recipe is given Figure Eighteen.

AUSTRIA

KOHL SUPPE (CABBAGE SOUP)

1. SHRED (CHISELER) ONE CABBAGE AND BRAISE IN LARD.
2. BLEND FLOUR TO OBTAIN A ROUX, AND COOK UNTIL BLOND.
3. POUR INTO BOILING STOCK, STIRRING VIGOROUSLY,
4. SEASON WITH SALT, PEPPER AND CARAWAY SEED, THEN SIMMER ABOUT 1-1/2 HOURS.
5. BEFORE SERVING, ADD SLICES OF SMOKED SAUSAGE.

FRANCE

One of the most famous of all soups in the modern restaurant kitchen is FRENCH ONION SOUP GRATINEE. Its popularity is based on its simplicity in flavor and texture and even more so because,

---

FRENCH ONION SOUP GRATINEE
YIELD: 24 PORTIONS

INGREDIENTS	AMOUNTS
1. BUTTER	4 OZ
2. ONIONS, SLICED THIN	5 LBS
3. BEEF STOCK	3 1/2 QTS
4. CHICKEN STOCK	3 QTS
5. BAY LEAF	2 EA
6. THYME	2 TSP
7. SALT AND PEPPER	TO TASTE
8. SHERRY (OPTIONAL)	5 OZ
9. FRENCH BREAD	
10. SWISS CHEESE, COARSELY GRATED	1 1/2 LB

METHOD

1. HEAT THE BUTTER UNTIL MELTED.
2. ADD ONIONS, COOK UNTIL GOLDEN BROWN.
3. ADD STOCKS AND HERBS AND BRING TO A BOIL.
4. SIMMER UNTIL THE ONIONS ARE TENDER, ABOUT 25 MINUTES.
5. ADJUST SEASONINGS. ADD SHERRY IF DESIRED.
6. KEEP THE SOUP HOT FOR SERVICE.
7. CUT THE FRENCH BREAD INTO 1/2 THICK SLICES.
8. TOAST THE SLICES UNDER THE BROILER OR IN THE OVEN.
9. FOR SERVICE, FILL A SOUP CROCK WITH HOT SOUP. PLACE ENOUGH SLICES OF BREAD ON TOP OF THE SOUP TO COVER. COVER TOP WITH CHEESE. PLACE UNDER BROILER UNTIL THE CHEESE IS BUBBLING AND LIGHTLY BROWNED. SERVE IMMEDIATELY.

Figure 19

---

perhaps, it falls into the realm of "comfort foods." It is one of the simplest soups to prepare, and one of the most appreciated.

BOUILLABAISSE MARSEILLAISE is a specialty dear to the southeastern part of France, and is a meal in itself. It is claimed that "No one can make a bouillabaisse like in Marseille." Since it depends greatly on the fish it is made from for its flavor, the following fish are required for making bouillabaisse:

Racasse	Merland de Palangre
Chapon	Fielas
Saint-Pierre	Boudrevil
Rouquiers	Langoustes
Congre	Dorade
	Rougets

These are not all available in the United States, but the following excellent substitutes are available.

Lobster	Whiting
Haddock	Eel
Sea Bass	Turbot
Crab	Red Snapper
	Sole

TO PREPARE:
1. CUT THE LARGE FISH IN PIECES, 2" IN LENGTH AND LEAVE THE SMALL FISH WHOLE.
2. PLACE DICED ONIONS, LEEKS, TOMATOES, CRUSHED GARLIC, CHOPPED PARSLEY, SAFFRON, BAY LEAVES, THYME AND FENNEL IN THE BOTTOM OF A SAUCEPAN WITH OIL.
3. ARRANGE THE CHUNKS OF FISH WITH FIRM FLESH ON TOP OF THE VEGETABLES, RESERVING THE OTHER, SOFT FLESH FISH FOR LATER.
4. ADD SUFFICIENT WATER TO COVER THE FISH, SEASON WITH SALT & PEPPER.
5. BRING TO A BOIL AND SIMMER FOR 15 TO 20 MINUTES.
6. THEN ADD THE REMAINING FISH AND CONTINUE TO COOK FOR 5 TO 10 MINUTES.
7. REMOVE FROM THE FIRE, STRAIN THE LIQUID INTO SOUP PLATES ON TOP OF SLICED FRENCH BREAD.
8. ARRANGE THE FISH ON A PLATTER, SPRINKLE WITH CHOPPED PARSLEY, AND SERVE WITH BROTH.

This particular soup requires a fast boiling process to make it possible for the oil and water to blend together. Do not overcook or the fish will break and lose its appearance and flavor.

GREECE
AVGOLEMONO is a soup made of rice cooked in meat broth. It is finished with well beaten eggs and fresh lemon juice.

HUNGARY
GULYA'S LEVES (GOULASH SOUP)
TO GIVE THIS SOUP ITS TRUE TASTE, USE HUNGARIAN PAPRIKA. IT HAS ITS OWN DISTINCTIVE FLAVOR.
1. COOK 1 LB. OF SLICED ONION IN LARD UNTIL BROWN.
2. ADD 2 LBS. OF BEEF BRISKET CUT IN STRIPS 1" LONG; 2 FRESH TOMATOES, PEELED, SEEDED AND CHOPPED; 2 PIMENTOES, SLICED.
3. SEASON WITH PAPRIKA, SALT AND PEPPER, THEN SIMMER FOR 30 MINUTES.
4. ADD 1 GALLON LIGHT STOCK AND COOK UNTIL MEAT IS DONE.
5. ADD 2 OR 3 MEDIUM SIZED POTATOES, RAW AND DICED, AND COOK UNTIL POTATOES ARE TENDER.
6. SERVE WITH SLICED SMOKED SAUSAGES AND TOP WITH CHOPPED PARSLEY.

INDIA
MULLIGATAWNY is a cream of curry soup which is considered to be a classic example of a national soup.
TO PREPARE IT:
1. DICE ONIONS AND APPLES, THEN BRAISE LIGHTLY IN BUTTER.
2. ADD CURRY POWDER AND STIR.
3. MAKE A ROUX AND ADD CHICKEN BROTH TO IT. ADD THIS AND A BOUQUET GARNI TO THE ONION AND APPLE MIXTURE.
4. SEASON WITH SALT AND PEPPER, AND BRING TO A BOIL. SIMMER FOR 1 1/2 TO 2 HOURS.
5. SKIM WHILE COOKING, STRAIN THROUGH SIEVE WHEN COOKED.
6. FINISH WITH CREAM.
7. GARNISH WITH SMALL DICED CHICKEN.
8. SERVE WITH *RICE INDIA STYLE* (CURRIED) AS AN ACCOMPANIMENT.

ITALY

MINESTRONE is a thick soup made of any vegetables available at the market.
FOR EXAMPLE:

1. BRAISE PAYSANNE CUT CARROTS, ONIONS, LEEKS, CELERY, CABBAGE, TURNIPS AND STRING BEANS IN BUTTER OR OLIVE OIL.
2. ADD BROTH AND HAM BONE AND BRING TO A BOIL.
3. ADD WHITE BEANS AND SEASON WITH SALT, PEPPER AND HERBS. COOK UNTIL ALL VEGETABLES ARE TENDER.
4. FINISH WITH COOKED SPAGHETTI CUT 1/2" LONG, COOKED RICE, CHOPPED TOMATOES, FRESH PARSLEY AND CRUSHED GARLIC.
5. SERVE WITH PARMESAN CHEESE.

THIS SOUP MUST BE THICK.

MILLE-FANTI

1. PLACE IN A MIXING BOWL 4 OZ. FRESH BREAD CRUMBS, AND 2 OZ PARMESAN CHEESE.
2. ADD SLOWLY 3 EGGS, BEATEN.
3. SEASON WITH SALT & PEPPER, AND NUTMEG.
4. POUR IN BOILING CONSOMME.
5. SET ASIDE, OFF THE FIRE, FOR A FEW MINUTES.
6. BREAK THE COOKED MIXTURE WITH A WHIP BEFORE SERVING.

RUSSIA

BORSCHT

1. CUT JULIENNE, 1/2 LB OF FRESH BEETS, 2 LEEKS, 1 ONION, AND 1 SMALL HEAD OF CABBAGE.
2. BRAISE VEGETABLES IN BUTTER, THEN ADD 2 GALLONS OF STOCK.
3. ADD A BOUQUET GARNI WITH MARJORAM AND FENNEL, THE JUICE OF 4 FRESHLY GRATED BEETS, 1 LB OF BLANCHED BEEF BRISKET, AND 1 SMALL, HALF ROASTED, DUCK.
4. COOK SLOWLY UNTIL TENDER.
5. REMOVE ALL MEAT AND DICE FOR GARNITURE, THEN ADD BACK TO POTAGE.
6. ADD SLICED SMOKED SAUSAGE, AND CHOPPED PARSLEY BEFORE SERVING.
7. GARNISH WITH SOUR CREAM, BOILED POTATOES, OR CUCUMBER SLICES.

SCOTLAND

SCOTCH MUTTON BROTH

1. BRAISE BRUNOISE CUT CARROTS, LEEKS, TURNIPS, CELERY AND ONION IN BUTTER.
2. ADD MUTTON BROTH, LAMB SHOULDER. SEASON WITH SALT AND PEPPER, AND COOK FOR 1 HOUR.
3. ADD BARLEY AND THE MEAT SAVED FROM THE BROTH, CUT IN LARGE DICE.
4. CONTINUE TO COOK UNTIL BARLEY IS TENDER.
5. SERVE WITH CHOPPED PARSLEY

From this brief sampling one can see the multitudes and varieties of national and regional types. A few more examples follow.

AMERICA: WISCONSIN BEER CHEESE SOUP, TURTLE SOUP
BELGIUM: HOCHEPOT FLAMANDE
CARIBBEAN: SNAPPER CHOWDER, CONCH CHOWDER, CUBAN BLACK BEAN
CHINA: WONTON, EGG DROP AND HOT AND SOUR SOUPS
ENGLAND: OXTAIL SOUP
FRANCE: PETITE MARMITE
GERMANY: LIVER DUMPLING SOUP
SCOTLAND: COCK-A-LEEKIE, SHEEPSHEAD SOUP

COLD SOUPS

This is a special category because this grouping of soups is served differently from any other: Well chilled, in chilled cups or bowls. The popularity of the cold soup has increased in the United States in recent years, as the American dining public has become more willing to experiment with new trends; and, as the population has moved to a hotter climate.

Many soups that are prepared to be a hot soup can be changed into a cold soup by simply chilling them well and making minor alterations to the structure and flavor. For instance, many purees can be served chilled if they are made with little or no butter, and thinned with cream after chilling. JELLIED CONSOMME was addressed in the section on clear soups because the method of preparation is so closely tied in to the preparation of the hot consomme. Some examples of hot soups that can be served cold are cream of watercress, lobster bisque and borscht.

CHILLED VICHYSSOISE

This famous cold soup is easy to make. Chilled vichyssoise is a combination of leeks and potatoes, and is an example of improving on nature's work. It is the creation of Chef Louis Diat, for many years executive chef of the Ritz-Carlton Hotel in New York City, and author of many cook books. His creation tastes best if made the day before it is to be served.

TO PREPARE:

1. CUT LEEKS AND ONIONS ROUGHLY, THEN BRAISE LIGHTLY IN BUTTER.

2. ADD BOUQUET GARNI, PAYSANNE CUT POTATOES, AND COVER WITH CHICKEN BROTH.

3. SEASON WITH SALT AND PEPPER AND COOK TO PUREE.

4. STRAIN THROUGH A SIEVE, COOL AND CHILL.

5. THIN THE PUREE WITH CREAM AND ADJUST THE SEASONING, ADDING CAYENNE PEPPER.

6. SERVE ICED AND TOPPED WITH FRESHLY SNIPPED CHIVES.

GASZPACHO
YIELD: 20 SERVINGS

INGREDIENTS	AMOUNTS
1. GARLIC CLOVES	6 EA
2. BREAD CUBES, SOFT, CRUSTS REMOVED	3 CUPS
3. WINE VINEGAR	6 OZ
4. TOMATOES, MEDIUM -SIZED, PEELED AND CHOPPED	12 EA
5. CUCUMBER, PEELED, SEEDED AND CHOPPED	3 EA
6. GREEN PEPPER, LARGE, SEEDED, DICED	2 EA
7. RED PEPPER, LARGE, SEEDED, DICED	1 EA
8. OLIVE OIL	6 OZ
9. COLD WATER	1 QT, 1 PT
10. TOMATO JUICE	1 QT, 1 PT
11. SALT, PEPPER, CUMIN	TO TASTE
12. SCALLIONS, CHOPPED	1-1/2 CUPS
13. CROUTONS (OPTIONAL)	

METHOD
1. CHOP THE GARLIC, ADDING A LITTLE SALT AS YOU GO.
2. MIX GARLIC WITH THE BREAD CRUMBS AND VINEGAR IN A BOWL, AND WORK THIS MIXTURE INTO A PASTE.
3. ADD NINE OF THE TOMATOES AND HALF OF THE CUCUMBER. MASH FINE OR WHIRL IN A BLENDER.
4. MIX THIS PUREEE WITH THE REST OF THE TOMATOES AND CUCMBERS AND THE DICED PEPPERS.
5. CHILL.
6. BEFORE SERVING, STIR IN THE OIL, WATER AND TOMATO JUICE. ADD MORE VINEGAR TO TASTE.
7. SEASON TO TASTE WITH SALT, PEPPER AND CUMIN.
8. GARNISH EACH PORTION WITH SCALLIONS AND CROUTONS, IF DESIRED AND, IF AVAILABLE, A LITTLE SAFFRON.

Figure 20

GAZPACHO

GAZPACHO is a specialty Spanish soup. A recipe for gazpacho is given in Figure Twenty.

FRUIT SOUPS

Fruit soups are popular in Scandinavian and Slavic countries in Europe. They are also a favorite breakfast item in Japan. However, they are rarities, or at least curiosities, to the majority of soup eaters in this part of the world.

Whether hot or cold, they offer new tastes and textures, as well as delicate flavors. Fruit soups may even be served successfully as desserts. The recipe in Figure Twenty One is excellent served with ice cream.

GARNISHES FOR SOUPS

The dining public, as a rule, is not partial to additives or foreign objects (often unidentified), swimming about in their soup. If the dish is well made, it should be allowed to speak for itself. To give soup visual appeal, nothing is more successful than a sprinkling of fresh, finely chopped parsley. Despite this prejudice against many garnishes, there are occasions, and soups, which are enhanced by them.

GARNISH IN THE SOUP

The garniture of a soup may take many forms. Major ingredients, such as the vegetables in clear soup are often considered garnishes. Meats, poultry, seafood, pasta products, grains, barley and rice can all be used as garnish for soups. When these items are used they are treated as part of the preparation and not as something added.

Consommes, like consomme celestine or consomme brunoise, are often named after their garnish. Vegetable cream soups and veloutés are usually garnished with carefully cut pieces of the vegetable from which they are made. Sometimes leftovers, such as sausages and other meat items, can be

---

SCANDINAVIAN FRUIT SOUP

INGREDIENTS	AMOUNT
1. WATER	1 QT, 1 PT
2. CORNSTARCH	1/4 C
3. SALT	1 TSP
4. LEMON JUICE	3 TBSP
5. CINNAMON	1/2 STICK
6. PRUNES, DRIED	4 OZ
7. RAISINS, SEEDLESS	8 OZ
8. APPLES, TART, DICED	1/2 C
9. SUGAR	1/4 C
10. CHERRY OR GRAPE JUICE	1 C
11. RED WINE, SWEET	1/4 C

METHOD

1. MIX WATER, CORNSTARCH & SALT IN SAUCEPAN AND BRING TO A BOIL, STIRRING OCCASIONALLY.
2. ADD INGREDIENTS 4-10 AND SIMMER FOR 30-45 MINUTES.
3. COOL THE MIXTURE, THEN CHILL OVERNIGHT IN REFRIGERATOR.
4. STRAIN THROUGH A MOUSSELINE. (IF A CHUNKY TEXTURE IS DESIRED, THE SOUP WOULD NOT NEED TO BE STRAINED.)
5. ADD WINE AND ADJUST SEASONING WITH SALT AND LEMON JUICE AS NEEDED.
6. SERVE ICED WITH CHOPPED FRESH MINT FOR GARNISH.

Figure 21

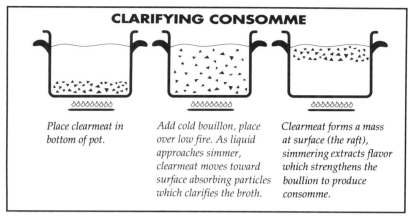

CLARIFYING CONSOMME

Place clearmeat in bottom of pot.

Add cold bouillon, place over low fire. As liquid approaches simmer, clearmeat moves toward surface absorbing particles which clarifies the broth.

Clearmeat forms a mass at surface (the raft), simmering extracts flavor which strengthens the bouillion to produce consomme.

used as a garnish. This helps keep your food costs down.

Soups are often finished with some type of garnish. What type depends on the nature of the soup and the recipe. Whatever is chosen as garnish, every effort should be made to have it act as a meaningful part of the soup, not just an added fluff. The garnishes discussed here are those which are most commonly used. Figure 22 lists the most common types of garnish for various types of soups.

CROUTES & CROUTONS

These two items are often confused as the same item. There is a difference between them. CROUTES are made from *flute* or *baguette*, a long, thin, french bread. The crust of bread only is cut in pieces about 1-1/2 inches long, then buttered, and dried in the oven.

CROUTONS are prepared in two ways. The most popular is the crouton for French onion soup, which is made using a thin slice of french bread. The slice is sprinkled with clarified butter, topped with grated cheese, then dried and toasted in the oven. The crouton commonly used for pureed soups is made from a loaf of white bread. The loaf is diced small and then fried in clarified butter or buttered then dried and browned in the oven.

EGGS/ROYALE

EGGS can be whisked through a china cap into boiling soup for an attractive garnish.

ROYALE is a more complex egg preparation used in soup garniture, usually for broth or consomme. For a plain royale one egg and three egg yolks are beat and one cup of consomme or milk is added. The mixture is then strained through cheesecloth or a fine sieve into a buttered deep dish. It is then poached in a baine marie like a custard. Royales must be cut after being completely chilled in the refrigerator. They are cut using very small cutters, specially designed for this purpose.

Different colored royales are made by mixing a puree of vegetables with the egg and egg yolk. This provides a natural color and flavor which can make a good addition to a soup. Food coloring should not be used to replace the vegetable puree since it provides no flavor. The most common vegetables used for royales are carrots, celery, asparagus and peas. Cook and reduce the vegetable almost completely, then puree. Blend the puree with a spoon of cream sauce; season lightly, and blend with egg and egg yolk. Cook this mixture as you would the plain royale.

OTHER GARNISHES

PASTA is a popular garnish for soups. Vermicelli, fine Italian noodles, alphabet pasta and small ravioli are commonly used.

PROFITEROLLES are an interesting item. They are balls the size of a peanut, made of pate a choux. They may be filled with a meat or vegetable puree or served plain like a crouton.

QUENELLES are an excellent garnish for soups of various types, this item is discussed fully in Chapter 23, Forcemeat and Mousse.

VEGETABLES cut in different shapes or forms are the most commonly used garnishes. They are cut brunoise, julienne, printaniere or some other form and then cooked in salt water. The vegetable is quick chilled after cooking and held for use with consommes and cream soups.

These garnishes are fairly standard; require a minimum of preparation, and generally are made from regular stock items.

THICK SOUPS	LEGUME SOUPS	HOT OR CHILLED CREAM SOUPS
CRISP DICED BACON	CRISP DICED BACON	CRISP DICED BACON
GRATED CHEESE	CROUTONS	GRATED CHEESE
CROUTONS	FRANKFURTERS (1/4" ROUND CUT)	CROUTONS
FINELY CHOPPED FRESH HERBS	FINELY CHOPPED FRESH HERBS	FINELY CHOPPED FRESH HERBS
	PAPER THIN LEMON SLICES	GRATED LEMON RIND
	FINELY CHOPPED ONION	CHOPPED NUTS
		PAPRIKA

HOT CLEAR SOUPS	CHILLED THIN SOUPS	JELLIED SOUPS
AVOCADO SLICES	AVOCADO SLICES	CAVIAR (BLACK LUMPFISH ROE
DUMPLINGS	THIN SLICED CUCUMBER	OR RED SALMON ROE)
FINELY CHOPPED FRESH HERBS	FINELY CHOPPED FRESH HERBS	FINELY CHOPPED FRESH HERBS
PAPER THIN SLICES OF LEMON,	PAPER THIN SLICES OF LEMON,	PAPER THIN SLICES OR WEDGES
LIME OR ORANGE	LIME OR ORANGE	OF LEMON, LIME OR ORANGE
JULIENNE OF COOKED MEATS	JULIENNE OF COOKED MEATS	
OR VEGETABLES	OR VEGETABLES	
COOKED THIN PASTA	THIN SLICED TOMATO	

SUGGESTED HERBS FOR GARNISH - BASIL, CHIVES, MARJORAM, PARSLEY, SUMMER SAVORY, TARRAGON, WATERCRESS

Figure 22

TOPPINGS

The use of toppings for soups must be done with care. They should be placed on the soup just at service, so they will not sink or lose their fresh appearance. Their flavor must be complementary to the soup. The food used as a topping should be attractive in itself, but not overdone. It is to complement the soup, not hide it. Less is definitely better for toppings.

Clear soups are generally served without toppings. This allows the attractiveness of the sparkling clear broths and carefully cut vegetable garnishes to show. The occasional exception is a sprinkle of chervil, finely sliced chives or chopped fine herbs or parsley.

Thick soups, especially those that are all one color, are often decorated with a topping. Suggested toppings for these are:

FRESH HERBS, USUALLY FINELY CHOPPED
TOASTED SLICED ALMONDS OR HAZELNUTS
TOASTED SHREDDED COCONUT
SIEVED EGG YOLK OR SLICED EGG WHITE
GRATED PARMESAN
TOASTED CROUTONS
CRUMBLED BACON BITS
SOUR OR WHIPPED CREAM AND CREAM
    FRAICHE.

Whatever topping is used, it must add both to the appearance and flavor of the soup.

SERVICE OF SOUPS

The standard portion size for soup is six ounces in a soup or bouillon cup as part of a meal. As a main course the portion should be about ten ounces in a deep soup plate or soup tureen.

As with all foods, the temperature must be correct for the product to be good. Serve **COLD SOUPS COLD**, in chilled bowls or iced. Serve **HOT SOUPS HOT**, in hot cups or bowls. A rule of thumb is that the thinner the soup, such as consomme, the hotter it should be.

The easiest service of soups is for banquets or large numbers of people all at once. The soup is brought to the highest possible temperature at the last moment. It is then served in the shortest possible time, fresh and piping hot.

The situation is more challenging for service which is spread over a period of several hours. In the past, soup was placed in the baine-marie in the steam table at the beginning of service and held until the end of service. This is no longer accepted as the best method. Today, soups for a la carte and menu service can be made in large batches, cooled and then refrigerated. Small batches can then be re-heated on a frequent basis. However, the best method is the use of the new marvel of the age, the microwave. Individual portions can be re-heated as needed. They are piping hot in only a few minutes, normally without loss or deterioration of quality.

REVIEW QUESTIONS

1. Define the term *soup*.
2. How are soups classified?
3. What is the difference between a broth and a consomme?
4. What is a double consomme?
5. Discuss the five steps in consomme preparation.
6. How does a consomme clarify?
8. How is a jellied consomme prepared?
9. Define the term *essence* as it relates to soups.
10. List the seven tips on preparation of clear soups.
11. List the four subgroupings of thick soups.
12. Define *puree*, *bisque* and *coulis*.
13. What are the differences between a cream and velouté soup?
14. Discuss the preparation of simple vegetable soup.
15. What are the primary examples of American national soups? Discuss each.
16. Discuss the proper garnishing of a soup.
17. How do croutes and croutons differ?
18. What is egg royale?
19. Discuss the service of soups.

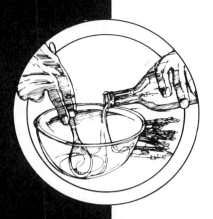

Chapter 16

CHAPTER OBJECTIVES

- **To introduce sauces as a cornerstone of culinary preparation.**
- **To introduce the essentials of a good sauce.**
- **To discuss the function of a sauce.**
- **To identify the components of a sauce.**
- **To discuss thickening agents and their function in the sauce.**
- **To discuss the preparation of roux.**
- **To discuss starches used as thickening agents.**
- **To discuss liaison.**
- **To introduce the five physical properties of a sauce.**
- **To discuss the cleaning of a sauce.**
- **To identify the mother sauces and discuss their preparation.**
- **To discuss compound and reduction sauces.**
- **To introduce hot emulsion sauces and discuss their preparation.**
- **To discuss various other sauce preparations.**

Hot Sauces

According to the *New Larousse Gastronomique*, sauces are a hot or cold seasoned liquid, either served with or used in the cooking of a dish. *Webster's Ninth New Collegiate Dictionary* defines sauce as a fluid dressing or topping which adds zest or piquancy. These describe a term which has broad application. It is a term which includes everything from the classic French sauces to salad dressings, fruit toppings, gravies and others.

Due to the broad nature of this category, we have divided sauces in this text into two major groupings: Hot sauces and cold sauces. This chapter will deal with the hot sauces. The cold sauces will be discussed in Chapter 22.

By way of introduction let us first clarify one point. HOT OR COLD, THE FUNCTION OF A SAUCE IS TO ADD FLAVOR THAT IS COMPATIBLE WITH THE INGREDIENTS OF THE DISH.

It was Talleyrand who claimed that England had three sauces and 360 religions, while France had three religions and 360 sauces. There is no question that, in most instances, sauces comprise the honor and glory of classical French cuisine. They have contributed to its dominance of the culinary world and their importance is disputed by no one. Sauces *are* the orchestration and accompaniment of a fine meal. They allow good chefs and cooks to demonstrate their talents.

Sauces have evolved, as has civilization. Medieval sauces, which relied on ancient condiments like garum and spikenard, were either very spicy, sweet and/or sour. This was, at the time, a result of necessity. They were designed to mask the harsh flavors of poorly prepared, slightly spoiled foods. They consisted mainly of spicy stocks based on wine, verjuice (the juice of unripe fruit) and cooking juices sometimes blended with toasted bread crumbs.

It was not until the 17th and 18th centuries that more refined and aromatic preparations, bechamel, soubise and mayonnaise began to appear, and mirepoix began to be used. It was Careme who began to classify sauces. The hot sauces, which are far more numerous, where subdivided into brown and white sauces. Cold sauces are usually based on mayonnaise or vinaigrette and their variations.

The classical list was gradually increased with sauces brought by chefs who had worked in other countries. The diversity of the French countryside also added to the list a variety of recipes based on regional ingredients. Items such as fresh cream for sauce normande, garlic for sauce aioli and mustard for dijon sauce helped to expand the repertoire.

The evolution of sauces continued under Escoffier and continues today. Currently, there are many classical sauces still used; however, there is a move toward lighter sauces. This shift to lighter sauces has been taking place for a number of years, but has become more intense with the increased interest of the guest in healthier meals.

Experience, which plays such a major role in culinary work, is nowhere so important as in the preparation of sauces. They must not only flatter the palate, but also vary in savor, consistency and viscosity to suit the dish they accompany. In a well ordered dinner, each dish differs from the preceding ones and from those that follow, and this includes the sauces.

Sauces must, through the perfection of their preparation, be served and combined in a manner allowing easy digestion by the frequently disordered stomachs of the guest. Any sauce should be smooth; light but not liquid; glossy to the eye, and distinctive in taste. When these conditions are fulfilled, the sauce is always easy to digest, even for tired stomachs.

An essential point in the making of a sauce is the seasoning. The seasonings should be only sufficient to act as a complementary factor, not to form a recognizable part of the sauce or dish. If seasonings are excessive, they modify or even destroy the flavor of the dish with which they are used. Too often the poor flavor of a badly made sauce is corrected by excessive seasoning. This is an absolutely deplorable practice.

Each sauce possesses its own well defined, special flavor. This flavor is the result of the combined flavors of all its ingredients. When used with or in a another dish, the sauce becomes a complement to the dish, not a distinct addition to it.

The renown of French cuisine is the result of its sauces. The saucier is a magician dealing in chemistry. His craft is a culinary slight of hand from which well-made stocks emerge, becoming the roots from which, like plants, sauces grow. Their liaisons, full and appealing in form, are the catalysts of the sauces' ultimate being. The strength of the process is such that the final results, the great sauces of France, must be described as the cornerstone of cuisine.

The last, but most crucial, point in this introduction to sauces is that they cannot be rushed. It takes many hours to bring to perfection a demi-glace. Do not rush into anything. Take the time! Time and care will result in the making of a great sauce. Plan ahead: What comes first? What follows? What takes longer? Review the whole operation in your head, move by move. Do not rush. Give your ingredients and elements a chance to do their work. Step by step is how you are going to make the sauce right.

To begin the study of sauce making review Chapter 14. That chapter discusses the making of fonds, glazes and essences. These are indispensible to the making of sauces. If they are not made correctly, then the quality of the sauce will be lacking.

ESSENTIALS OF A GOOD SAUCE

A sauce may be thick or thin, strained or contain visible ingredients. Thick or thin, light or dark, hot or cold and irrespective of its origins, a well-made sauce should have the following characteristics:

1. IT MUST HAVE A DISTINCTIVE TEXTURE (UNCTUOUS FOR MAYONNAISE, FROTHY FOR SABAYON, GLOSSY FOR DEMI-GLACE, AND SO ON).
2. IT MUST HAVE BODY WITH THE FLAVORS CONCENTRATED TO JUST THE RIGHT DEGREE, MILD OR PUNGENT, TO COMPLEMENT THE REST OF THE DISH.
3. THE COLOR OF THE SAUCE MUST ACCENT THE DISH IT IS BEING SERVED WITH, SUCH AS PAIRING A LIGHT WHITE BUTTER SAUCE WITH A SALMON MOUSSELINE OR A YELLOW MUSTARD SAUCE WITH KIDNEYS.
4. IT MUST HAVE THE RIGHT CONSISTENCY. VELOUTÉ SAUCES AND WHITE BUTTER SAUCES SHOULD FORM A SEMI-TRANSPARENT VEIL OVER THE FOOD, WHILE BROWN SAUCES SHOULD BE TRANSLUCENT, GIVING A LIGHT GLAZE TO THE MEATS BENEATH.

☆ **NOTE:** ONLY WHITE SAUCES, HOLLANDAISE AND BEARNAISE (EMULSION SAUCES), SOME PASTA SAUCES, AND SOME SWEET SAUCES ARE THICK ENOUGH TO COAT THE INGREDIENTS OF A DISH. EVEN THEN THE SHAPE AND COLOR OF THE FOOD BENEATH SHOULD BE DISCERNIBLE. A SAUCE SHOULD NEVER BE GLUTINOUS, EVEN WHEN DESIGNED TO BIND SOUFFLES OR TO ENRICH GRATINS OF VEGETABLES THAT HAVE A HIGH WATER CONTENT. ORDINARILY SAUCES THAT ARE TO BE SERVED COLD NEED TO BE THICKER THAN THOSE TO BE SERVED HOT.

If the sauce you make has the characteristics of a good sauce, there are certain qualities it will add to the foods it is part of or accompanies. A sauce contributes to the food it is served with in five ways:

1. MOISTNESS.
2. FLAVOR.
3. RICHNESS.
4. APPEARANCE - COLOR AND SHINE.
5. INTEREST AND APPETITE APPEAL.

COMPONENTS OF A SAUCE

The major sauces are made basically of three components:

1. A LIQUID, THE BODY OF THE SAUCE.
2. A THICKENING AGENT.
3. THE FLAVORING AND SEASONING INGREDIENTS.

To understand the sauce making process, you must first learn to prepare these components. You need an understanding of how to combine and assemble them into finished sauces.

LIQUID

A liquid ingredient provides the body or base of most sauces. There are four liquids which are the base for a group of sauces termed Mother sauces, foundation sauces, base sauces or grande sauces:

WHITE STOCK (chicken, veal, fish, vegetable) is used for VELOUTÉ SAUCES.

BROWN STOCK is used for ESPAGNOLE (DEMI-GLACE).

Combining roux and liquid

a. When using *hot* roux, combining it with liquid is a two-step process. In Step 1 add part of the *cold* liquid to the hot roux, blending it in with a whip. In Step 2, blend in the rest of the liquid, *hot*.

b. When using *cold* roux, it can be combined with a *hot* liquid, over heat, by blending it in with a whip a little at a time. Do not try to combine hot roux with a hot liquid or cold with cold.

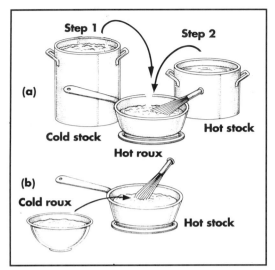

MILK is used for BECHAMEL.
TOMATO SAUCE AND STOCK is used for TOMATO SAUCE.

The making of the various stocks is discussed at length in Chapter 14. You should review it carefully before continuing to study sauces.

THICKENING AGENTS

A sauce must be thick enough to cling lightly to the food. If it is not, it will simply run off the food and form a puddle on the plate. However, this does not mean that the sauce has to be heavy or pasty.

Although starches are the most commonly used thickening agents in the kitchen, there are others. In order to prepare high quality sauces you must be able to handle thickening agents of many types properly.

ROUX

Roux represents the primary thickening compound of the mother sauces. Its preparation appears to be extremely simple, but in reality is crucial to the making of a good sauce.

COMPOSITION OF A ROUX

A ROUX IS A COOKED MIXTURE OF ABOUT 50 PERCENT SIFTED BREAD OR ALL-PURPOSE FLOUR AND 50 PERCENT CLARIFIED FAT, USUALLY BUTTER.

Fat in the roux acts as the bridge between the liquid of the sauce and the thickening agent, in this case the flour. To add the flour directly to the liquid would result in lumping. The fat makes the thickening agent easily soluble in the liquid. Clarified butter is preferred for roux because:

1. The power of absorption is greater in clarified butter.
2. The water and casein in butter make it more difficult to get a smooth, even blend of butter and flour.

Butter in roux gives only a slight savoring note to the sauce and is eliminated by depouillage (cleaning the sauce).

A combination of clarified butter and clarified chicken fat works well and is less expensive. However, when chicken fat is used, the amount of flour will need to be increased by three ounces per pound of roux, because the flour will not as readily absorb the chicken fat.

Bread flour or all-purpose flour are recommended because of their higher gluten content. The increased gluten content gives the flour greater binding ability. Sifting of the flour is recommended to remove lumps and possible foreign matter. It also loosens the flour particles, making them easier to combine with the clarified fat.

TYPES OF ROUX

There are three types of roux: WHITE ROUX, BLOND ROUX and BROWN ROUX. The rouxs each contain the same ingredients, but differ in coloration during cooking. Your choice of roux for your sauce will affect the flavor of the finished sauce.

WHITE ROUX IS USED FOR ALL CREAM SAUCES.

BLOND ROUX IS USED FOR ALL VELOUTÉ SAUCES.

BROWN ROUX IS USED FOR ALL BROWN SAUCES.

The white and blond rouxs require less cooking time and can be made as needed. Brown roux requires a longer cooking time and is normally cooked in advance, in large batches.

COOKING THE ROUX

The time allowed for cooking a roux cannot be precisely stated. It depends on the degree of heat. The more intense the heat, the quicker the roux will cook. However, as a rule, the longer and slower the roux is cooked, the better.

Every roux should be cooked slowly for a relatively long period of time, until the taste, humidity and acidity of the raw flour has disappeared. Among the various elements that make up flour, starch alone has the ability to bind. The starch granules, when toasted slowly, begin to unwind a bit. When heat and water are both present the granules unwind even more and can form a gel (thickener). If you try to unwind them too quickly with the addition of too much water, too fast, lumps will result. The toasting of the starch granules in fat allows complete separation of the granules, thereby effecting maximum exposure for maximum absorption. What is created is a mass capable of absorbing six times its own weight of liquid when cooked.

When cooking of the roux is started with very high heat, the starch gets burnt which destroys the chemical groups responsible for the thickening of the sauce, as well as resulting in flavor changes. Swelling is limited to only those parts of the starch which are least burnt. The binding power of the roux is reduced greatly. Double or triple the amount of burnt roux is needed to gain the same sauce thickness that would result from a roux which was made properly.

The excess amount of roux used in the sauce will "choke it up" without binding it. This prevents it from clearing. This will be explained further in the part of this chapter dealing with *depouillage*. At the same time, the cellulose and burnt starch give a bitter taste to the sauce. No treatment can remove this off flavor.

The problem of burnt roux is particularly important when making brown roux. This roux is to be brown, not burnt. Brown roux is considered cooked when it has a fine, light brown color and gives off an aroma of hazelnuts, characteristic of baked flour.

The balance between brown and burnt can be a delicate one. An improvement can be made in the brown roux by spreading the flour on a baking sheet or roasting pan and letting it brown slowly and lightly in the oven. When combined with the pre-browned flour, the butter will not have to cook as long for the roux to achieve its color and flavor.

ROUX AND ALUMINUM POTS

An additional problem in the preparation of rouxs is the type of pan used. We are not talking about the shape or size of the pan but about the metal from which it is made. When cooking a roux, you have to stir it often to provide even heat distribution and to avoid burned spots. If you are using a pot or pan made of aluminum this can cause some problems. If you use a utensil which will scratch the aluminum, aluminum needles and powders will be produced. These can turn your roux, and thereby your sauce, grayish-green.

Stainless steel pots and pans should be used for the preparation of sauces when possible. If using an aluminum pot, it is recommended that you always use a utensil which will not scratch. However, the utensil that scratches the least is a wooden spoon and they are, theoretically, not permitted by health regulations for use in commercial kitchens. Stainless steel whisks are not good with aluminum pans, because they are heavier than aluminum and will scratch it.

There is no absolute solution to this dilemma. You will have no choice, on many occasions, but to use utensils which do scrape the pan. If it is necessary to use aluminum pots and pans, then you should make every effort to scrape the pan as little as possible with the whisk or spoon used.

USING THE ROUX

The amount of roux needed to thicken a sauce to the correct consistency will vary slightly depending on the situation. FOR GENERAL USE, 10-12 OUNCES OF ROUX PER GALLON FOR SOUPS AND 12-15 OUNCES PER GALLON FOR SAUCES. HEAVIER VISCOSITY, GREATER THICKNESS, IS REACHED BY REDUCTION, NOT BY ADDING MORE ROUX. Remember that excessive roux will choke the sauce and mar the flavor.

The questions of hot to cold or cold to hot, and stock to roux or roux to stock, are often discussed. There is one cardinal rule when it comes to bringing the liquid and roux together. NEVER COMBINE ROUX AND STOCK AT THE SAME TEMPERATURE. To do so will give poor results.

Beyond this, any of the above combinations are workable and give similar results. However, when the novice culinarian is making large quantities of sauce, the following method gives the best results.

1. Slowly add hot stock to cold roux. Measure the quantities; roux is a formula.
2. Make a solid paste with stock and roux, then a liquid paste, by whisking.
3. Continue to add the remainder of the measured stock, stirring constantly.
4. Bring sauce to a boil, stirring often.

ALL SAUCES HAVE TO BE BROUGHT TO A BOIL AFTER THE ROUX IS ADDED. There are two reasons for this:

1. To allow the thickening agent to develop its full potential.
2. To sterilize the sauce. This destroys the bacteria present in the sauce, reducing the risk of it turning sour in the holding table during service.

OTHER STARCHES

As we have discussed, starches are the main thickening agent in cooking. It is starch that gives a sauce its viscosity and consistency. Thickening by starch is effected by the formation of a stable paste through heat. Although it is the starch in flour that is the most often used, there are a variety of starches available for use in sauces. Now we are mainly concerned with the use of starch in its pure form, refined carbohydrates. These are used in the sauce kitchen for work with the sauce, *fond de veau lie*, or as the final liaison for demi-glace.

Types of starches which are available include:

CORNSTARCH - An excellent, all-purpose starch. It is easy to work with and is inexpensive; however, it has poor holding quality; gives sauces an opalescent tinge, and a slight taste of corn.

ARROWROOT - This is the best starch for shine and transparency in a sauce, but is difficult to work with. It gives too much elasticity to sauces. Arrowroot is expensive and has good holding qualities.

TAPIOCA STARCH - This is very similar in use to arrowroot, but much cheaper. It is easier to work with and does not give excessive elasticity to the sauce. It is the best to use in the kitchen.

The majority of these starches are added to the liquid of the sauce in the form of a slurry or whitewash. This is kitchen slang for a mixture of a starch, such as cornstarch and a cold liquid: Water, stock, fruit juice, wine. Just enough liquid is added to liquefy the starch. The adding of the starch directly to a hot liquid will result in lumping.

FINAL LIAISON

Liaison is the French term for any mixture used for thickening or binding sauces, soups and other culinary preparations. This includes roux and other starch thickeners. However, in today's commercial kitchen, the term is usually used to refer specifically to a mixture of egg and cream used to finish sauces and soups. Liaison is also used to describe the process of the thickening itself.

A liaison can be similar to an emulsion. They can be made with thickening agents or emulsifiers, like the butter in *monter une sauce au beurre.* Liaison can also be composed of blood, such as in dishes like *civets* or *canard a la rouennaise.*

The objective of the saucier is to bind and enrich a light stock or liquid to make a thickened sauce. The last part of this process is the *liaison finale* (final liaison), "the last touch before serving." It is classified as an uncooked liaison because it is critical that the sauce should not boil once the liaison has been added. They are made with starch, beurre manie, egg yolk, blood, fats (butter, cream, foie gras) or vegetable purees. We will discuss a variety of these types.

LIAISON FINALE WITH STARCH - When a sauce seems too thin, it can be bound with a mixture of potato starch or other starch dissolved in a little cold water or white wine. The mixture is gradually poured into the boiling sauce, while whisking rapidly with a wire whip.

This process can be used in the completion of demi-glace, using potato or other starch. It adds luster to the sauce and saves some preparation time. If the amount used is small, you are still making a true demi-glace. However, if the amount is increased, the result becomes too similar to a *jus de veau lie* and you defeat your purpose.

LIAISON FINALE WITH BEURRE MANIE - Again for a sauce that seems too thin, this butter and flour mixture may be used. The mixture is one part flour to two parts butter. Whisk the beurre manie into the simmering sauce bit by bit with a wire whip until you achieve the desired consistency. The sauce will start to thicken almost immediately. A sauce thickened with beurre manie should not be allowed to come to a boil. When boiled, the sauce will develop an unpleasant taste of raw flour. If this happens, then the flour taste must be fully cooked out, which requires a great deal of time.

LIAISON FINALE WITH EGG YOLK - For this liaison, the egg yolks are first whisked with a wire whip, and cream is added if desired. A cupful of hot liquid is gradually whisked into the yolks to temper them. This mixture is then stirred into the sauce. Whipping of the sauce continues while it is heating; however, it is not returned to a boil. If the temperature goes above 160°F, the yolk cells will begin to harden and the sauce will curdle.

LIAISON FINALE WITH BLOOD - This is done with the blood of poultry or game, or the coral and tomalley of lobster. The principle is the same as with the standard egg yolk liaison. This liaison can be mixed with heavy cream taking the place of the egg yolk. The sauce is not allowed to boil once the liaison is added. Traditional uses for this liaison include *coq au vin*, *civet of game* and *lobster a l'Americaine.*

LIAISON FINALE WITH VEGETABLE PUREE - This is a valuable procedure used in modern cuisine. The liaison is made with a precise amount of finely pureed, cooked vegetable(s). The puree is easily made in a food processor or blender.

Depending on the recipe, the vegetables may be cooked with the meat or fish for which they will later bind the sauce. They may also be cooked separately. These liaisons are composed of very new aromatic harmonies of subtle and flavorful vegetable mixtures

LIAISON FINALE WITH FAT - These liaisons are normally based on butter, cream or foie gras.

<u>Butter</u> - The expression *monter une sauce au beurre* means "to lift a sauce with butter." The purpose of this liaison is not only to thicken, but especially to enrich the sauce. The process is done over a very low heat. Small pieces of paste butter (they can be a compound butter) are added to the hot sauce while gently rotating the bottom of the pan on the heat. This is one way to improve any sauce without changing the basic taste.

<u>Cream</u> - To thicken a sauce with cream, usually a sauce started with pan juice or the deglaze of a sautoir, simply

add heavy cream to the sauce and bring to a boil. Lower to a simmer and reduce the sauce to the desired consistency. This liaison is used for dishes such as *steak au poivre* or *veal chop a la creme*.

Foie Gras - This is similar to a liaison with butter. In a blender, puree together a mixture of two parts foie gras to one part heavy cream. Off the heat, whisk the foie gras mixture into the hot sauce with a wire whip. This is used for sauces containing truffles, such as Perigourdine.

USING A BASIC LIAISON

1. Whisk together the egg yolks and cream in a bowl. The normal proportions are six egg yolks per cup of heavy cream.
2. Very slowly add a little of the hot sauce to the liaison, whisking constantly. This is called tempering.
3. Remove sauce pot from the heat and gradually stir in the tempered liaison, stirring well.
4. Return the sauce to low heat to warm it gently. Be careful not to go over 180°F or it will curdle. It should never come to a boil.
5. Hold for service at 140-180°F .

SEASONINGS AND FLAVORING AGENTS

The seasoning and flavoring agents used in sauces are virtually unlimited. However, there are some ingredients which are associated with particular sauces. These will be discussed later in this chapter under the heading of **Classification of Sauces**.

The cardinal rule of flavoring and seasoning, no matter what the sauce, is that it should be well balanced. A well balanced sauce aims for a subtle equilibrium of many ingredients, with no single flavor dominating.

The food it is to accompany must be taken into consideration to insure that the sauce complements, not overwhelms, the dish. The very origin of the word *sauce*, from the Latin *salso* mean-

ing "salty," emphasizes its role in highlighting the flavor of a dish.

A sauce should always taste too strong by itself. Its flavor should be too concentrated to be palatable in quantity. If a sauce is to be reduced, it should be lightly seasoned only, since it will become too concentrated as the liquid reduces.

Whether or not a sauce is to be given a final enrichment of liaison, cream, butter or garnishes, it must be checked carefully for seasonings before serving. The final and most important touch in perfecting a sauce is to adjust the seasoning.

As for specific instructions for seasoning, these are difficult to give. Carefully follow recipes, measure ingredients, and *taste, taste, taste* and *taste again*! Experience is a good teacher in this matter.

WINES IN SAUCES

The wine is in the sauce for a specific purpose, to add suble flavor and richness. If the cook drinks the wine, they won't have much to show for their ability, no matter how good a saucier they are. There is nothing wrong with testing, and it is strongly advised that you do so. Whether you like wine or not, taste it, recognize the taste you are adding to your sauces. How will you ever know that the Madeira sauce, that started out from a near perfect demi-glace, did not flourish because the Madeira used was of poor quality? Taste it, find out through your own experience.

The guidelines for using wines in sauces are:

1. Reduce wines by boiling. This will reduce the volume, concentrate the flavor and evaporate some of their alcohol content.
2. Reduction lessens the acidity of white wine. Acidity can cause other ingredients, such as cream, to curdle.
3. Red wine reduction makes its perfume stronger. This is also true of brandies.

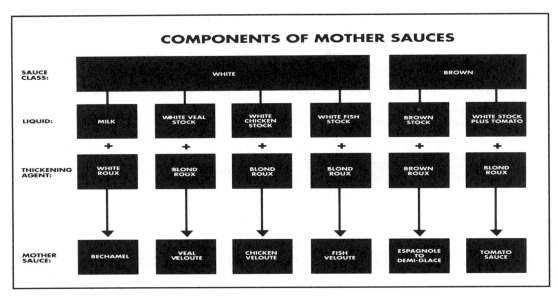

COMPONENTS OF MOTHER SAUCES

SAUCE CLASS:	WHITE				BROWN	
LIQUID:	MILK	WHITE VEAL STOCK	WHITE CHICKEN STOCK	WHITE FISH STOCK	BROWN STOCK	WHITE STOCK PLUS TOMATO
	+	+	+	+	+	+
THICKENING AGENT:	WHITE ROUX	BLOND ROUX	BLOND ROUX	BLOND ROUX	BROWN ROUX	BLOND ROUX
MOTHER SAUCE:	BECHAMEL	VEAL VELOUTE	CHICKEN VELOUTE	FISH VELOUTE	ESPAGNOLE TO DEMI-GLACE	TOMATO SAUCE

4. Fortified wines, such as port or Madeira, have delicate perfumes, which are easily destroyed. They work best unheated and added at the last minute.

MILK AND CREAM IN SAUCES

Milk and cream are not simple liquids, but emulsions of fat globules in water. The emulsifying agent is casein. Like all emulsions, they are not stable and are subject to flocculation (curdling).

If milk or cream are not fresh, they may look and taste good, but when heated the bacteria will grow and they will curdle. This wastes the soup or sauce. To prevent this: BOIL MILK AND CREAM BEFORE USING THEM.

If the milk or cream curdles, you will know it is bad and not waste the other ingredients. There is one way to catch back a sauce in which the cream has curdled. Try to *remonte*, rebuild, the sauce with cold, heavy cream. This does not work every time.

REDUCTION OF SAUCES

Reduction is placed under neither the category of thickeners nor flavoring agent, because it is integral to both. The key to many sauces is *reduction*, cooking over high heat to evaporate the liquid, concentrate the flavor and, at the same time, achieve the right consistency.

Reduction is essential for many classic French sauces, particularly those, such as velouté, which are based on stock and roux. As a general rule, the longer a sauce is simmered, the more subtle and mellow its taste. Leaving the pan uncovered during reduction speeds evaporation and concentration of the liquid.

The normal reduction of a sauce requires gentle simmering. A hard boil may cause the sauce to become cloudy. The reduction may take anywhere from a few minutes to an hour or more. The amount of time required will depend on the ingredients used.

MAKING MOTHER SAUCES

The making of a sauce, in this case a mother sauce, can be broken down into a series of steps. As we discussed in the introduction to this chapter, sauces are produced step by step with each step building upon the other.

1. PRODUCE THE TYPE OF STOCK NEEDED. DEGREASE, FILTER AND REDUCE UNTIL PROPER TASTE AND CONCENTRATION IS ACHIEVED. (SEE CHAPTER 14, STOCKS)

2. PRODUCE THE TYPE OF ROUX NEEDED. (SEE THICKENING AGENTS IN THIS CHAPTER.)

3. CREATE THE LIAISON BETWEEN THE ROUX AND STOCK. THIS INVOLVES THE BINDING OF THE SAUCE WITH THE CORRECT PER-

CENT OF ROUX. CLEAN THE SAUCE BY DEPOUILLAGE.

4. DEVELOP THE FIVE PHYSICAL PROPERTIES OF THE SAUCE:

A. VISCOSITY: THIS IS THE RESISTANCE OF THE SAUCE TO MOVEMENT. CONSISTENCY IS GIVEN BY THE THICKENING AGENT AND REDUCTION. IN GENERAL, IT IS BEST TO THICKEN A SAUCE PARTIALLY WITH A ROUX AND THEN TO BRING IT TO THE PROPER VISCOSITY BY SIMMERING FOR A LONG PERIOD. THIS WILL ASSIST IN THE OPERATION OF DEPOUILLAGE.

B. TEXTURE: PROPER DISTRIBUTION IN THE SIZE OF PARTICLES IN THE SAUCE IS GIVEN BY THE PERFECT COMBINING AND HOMOGENIZING OF THE ROUX AND STOCK. THIS PERFECTION IS ACHIEVED BY THOROUGH SIMMERING AND DEPOUILLEMENT OF ALL IMPURITIES FROM THE ROUX AND STOCK. THE SAUCE IS GIVEN A FINAL FINISH TO ITS TEXTURE BY STRAINING IT THROUGH A CHINOIS MOUSSELINE.

C. COLOR: THE PROPER COLOR OF A SAUCE IS THE RESULT OF ITS COMPONENTS. THE STOCK, ROUX AND VARIOUS SEASONINGS AND FLAVORINGS ALL ADD COLOR TO THE SAUCE. THE COLOR OF EACH SAUCE IS PART OF ITS OVERALL CHARACTER.

D. LUSTER: THIS IS THE DEGREE TO WHICH THE SAUCE REFLECTS LIGHT. THIS SHINE COMES FROM THE STARCHES USED AND THE PROCESS OF DEPOUILLEMENT, WHICH MAKES DEMI-GLACE SHINE LIKE A MIRROR.

E. OPACITY: THIS IS THE DEGREE OF TRANSPARENCY IN A SAUCE. IT IS THE RESULT OF GLUTEN IN THE ROUX, EGG YOLKS, BLOOD AND MILK PRODUCTS, SUCH AS CREAM AND BUTTER. THERE ARE THREE DEGREES OF TRANSPARENCY OF A SAUCE:

1. OPAQUE - LIGHT DOES NOT PASS THROUGH.

2. TRANSLUCENT - LIGHT IS DIFFUSED.

3. TRANSPARENT - LIGHT PASSES THROUGH.

NOTE: IF YOU WANT TO PRODUCE A TRANSPARENT SAUCE, USE STARCH AND NONE OF THE ELEMENTS THAT GIVE OPACITY. IF YOU WISH TO MAKE A SAUCE THAT IS TRANSLUCENT, USE A COMBINATION OF STARCH AND THE ELEMENTS WHICH CAUSE OPACITY.

Within the steps given above we have mentioned two processes which have not yet been discussed: Depouillage and straining.

DEPOUILLAGE/CLEANING OF A SAUCE

This is the most important process in building a sauce. Without it you have only a gross, raw product, full of impurities and fat. Any sauce using a roux must be depouilled. This process complements the liaison of the roux and stock. Depouillage, as applied to sauces, is the removal of all the fat and impurities from the flour and stock in the sauce. The key factor in being able to depouille a sauce successfully is the use of only 10-13 percent roux per weight of the sauce you are producing. This ratio will allow enough stock to make the roux a liquid, thereby allowing the impurities to rise during reduction.

The process is really quite simple.

1. AFTER THE ROUX AND STOCK ARE BLENDED TOGETHER, BRING THE SAUCE TO A BOIL.

2. REDUCE THE HEAT AND LET THE SAUCE SIMMER AT A SLIGHTLY ROLLING BOIL OFF CENTER. THIS WILL CAUSE THE IMPURITIES AND FATS TO ACCUMULATE ON ONE SIDE OF THE RUSSE OR RONDEAU.

3. CAREFULLY SKIM OFF THE ACCUMULATION.

It is impossible to have a decent, fully finished sauce without this operation, **UNLESS YOU WORK WITHOUT A ROUX**. This process gives veloutés their texture and demi-glace its shine and translucency. It takes at least one hour to properly depouille a velouté, and up to eight hours for demi-glace, the ultimate stage of refinement for an Espagnole sauce.

★**NOTE:** There would be a great advantage to preparing roux either from a pure form of starch, refined carbohydrates, or from substances with similar properties, such as farinaceous foods, arrowroot, cornstarch or others. It is only habit that causes flour to still be used as the binding element of roux. The time is not too distant when the advantage of using pure starches will be recognized.

They will be used because the volume of starch and butter needed will be half that of the old method. Using pure starch forms and strong, rich brown stock, a demi-glace can be made in half the time. The sauce will be clearer and more brilliant.

STRAINING OF SAUCES

By mastering the appropriate making and utilization of a roux, you should be able to make a smooth, lump-free sauce. However, to bring a sauce's texture to perfection, to create the velvety smoothness that is so important to a good sauce, straining is most important. Remember, even a slight graininess that cannot be seen, can be felt on the tongue.

Straining the sauce improves the smoothness and increases the luster. Solid ingredients are removed and the blending of the liquid ingredients is improved by straining. The finer the mesh size, the smoother and more glossy the sauce will be. The preferred utensil for straining a sauce is a conical mesh sieve. These are available in various mesh sizes.

★ **NOTE:** Straining of sauces is always done before the final garnish is added. It would make little sense to add a garnish and immediately strain it back out.

CLASSIFICATION OF SAUCES

You now have the basic information needed to make a perfect sauce. The question now becomes: **WHAT KIND?** As we stated earlier in this chapter, there is a large variety of sauces. It is difficult to find a system for the classication of sauces which is perfect. As a basis we use the system of sauce classification first established by Escoffier. The Escoffier system is based on MOTHER SAUCES, COMPOUND SAUCES and a broad grouping of OTHER SAUCES.

THE FOUR MOTHER SAUCES

The family of sauces called *mother sauces* derives its name from its primary place in the hierarchy of culinary art. The four mother sauces form a foundation for many culinary preparations. The name *mother sauce* is especially appropriate because this group spawns the *compound sauces*, the majority of the sauces of the classical kitchen.

The four mother sauces: BECHAMEL, VELOUTÉ, ESPAGNOLE (DEMI-GLACE), and TOMATO SAUCE are always served hot. There is a derivative which is an exception, *chaud-froid*, where the sauce is prepared hot and used cold. This is explained fully in Chapter 24.

Mother sauces have a great value because of their use and resiliency. When prepared properly, they have a relatively long shelf life in the refrigerator. Preparation of a mother sauce is a time consuming task. Therefore, mother sauces are normally prepared in bulk and refrigerated. The saucier uses them as a base for the compound sauces needed each day. Following are five points that are similar to all mother sauces:

CHARACTERISTICS OF A MOTHER SAUCE

1. SPAWNS MULTIPLE COMPOUND SAUCES.

2. FOUNDATION FOR MANY OTHER CULINARY PREPARATIONS INCLUDING SOUPS, CASSEROLES, LIQUIDS FOR BRAISING, ETC.

3. STABLE STRUCTURE MEANS REHEATING WITHOUT BREAKING DOWN.

4. THICKENED LIQUID BASE.

5. SHELF LIFE ALLOWS FOR FLEXIBILITY AND CREATIVITY OF USE.

Listed below is a sampling of the sauces which are produced from the mother sauces.

THE MOTHER SAUCES

BROWN --- TOMATO, ESPAGNOLE (DEMI-GLACE)

WHITE --- BECHAMEL, VELOUTÉS

THE COMPOUND SAUCES

FROM TOMATO
PROVENCALE, PORTUGUESE

FROM DEMI-GLACE
MUSHROOM, BORDELAISE, MADEIRA, CHASSEUR, POIVRADE, ROBERT, DIABLE, PERIGUEX, BRIGADE

FROM BECHAMEL
CREAM, MORNAY, SOUBISE

FROM VEAL VELOUTÉ
ALLEMANDE, SMITANE, POULETTE

FROM POULTRY VELOUTÉ
ALBUFERA, IVOIRE, SUPREME

FROM FISH VELOUTÉ
BERCY BLANCHE, NORMANDE

THE SHELLFISH SAUCES
NEWBURG, AMERICAINE

OTHER SAUCES

In this category are the sauces which are not directly based on mother sauces. The subdivisions we use here

---

TOMATO SAUCE
YIELD: 1 GAL

INGREDIENTS	AMOUNT
1. SALT PORK, DICED OR HAM SHANK, CUT UP	6 OZ
2. MIREPOIX, FINELY DICED	1 LB
3. GARLIC, MINCED	2 CLOVES
4. THYME	2 PINCHES
5. BAY LEAVES	2 MEDIUM
6. PARSLEY STEMS	1 BUNCH
7. SUGAR	1 OZ
8. ROUX, BLOND	8 OZ
9. TOMATOES, FRESH, RIPE, PEELED AND CHOPPED (OPTIONAL SUBSTITUTE - TOMATOES, CANNED, CRUSHED)	8 LB (2, NO. 2 1/2 CANS)
10. TOMATO PUREE, CANNED	1, NO. 2 1/2 CAN
11. WHITE STOCK, VEAL OR CHICKEN	2 QT
12. SEASONING (SALT, PEPPER, WORCESTERSHIRE)	AS NEEDED

METHOD
1. MELT PORK IN RONDEAU AND COOK TO BLOND COLOR.
2. SWEAT MIREPOIX, GARLIC AND AROMATICS IN RENDERED PORK FAT. NOTE: OLIVE OIL CAN BE USED TO REPLACE THE RENDERED PORK FAT.
3. ADD BLOND ROUX AND DILUTE WITH FOND BLANC.
4. ADD TOMATOES, TOMATO PUREE AND SUGAR.
5. BRING TO A BOIL, STIRRING OFTEN.
6. COVER AND SIMMER IN MODERATE, 300°F, OVEN FOR ABOUT 2 HOURS.
7. DEGREASE, AND ADJUST SEASONING.
8. PASS THROUGH FINE FOOD MILL, THEN THROUGH CHINOIS TO ACHIEVE SMOOTH TEXTURE.
9. BUTTER TOP TO AVOID CRUST FORMING, PLACE IN COOLING BATH. WHEN COOL, LABEL AND REFRIGERATE.

Figure 1

are the most common and could be divided even further.

THE HOT EMULSION SAUCES
BEURRE BLANC
HOLLANDAISE: MALTAISE, MOUSSELINE, MOUTARDE, NOISETTE
BEARNAISE: CHORON, FOYAT, PALOISE, TYROLIENNE

BUTTER SAUCES
CLARIFIED, MEUNIERE, BEURRE NOISETTE, BEURRE NOIR

COMPOUND BUTTERS
SHALLOT, MAITRE D'HOTEL, MARCHAND DE VIN, BERCY, CHATEAUBRIAND, COLBERT, PIMIENTO, RED AND GREEN BUTTER, SHRIMP, LOBSTER, CRAYFISH

MISCELLANEOUS SAUCES
GRAVIES, A LA MINUTE REDUCTIONS, BARBECUE, NUT SAUCES, SWEET AND SOUR SAUCE

It is not possible to learn all of the compound and other sauces here. It is advised that for future reference you use reliable, respected books. For a listing of these, refer to the bibliography in this text.

PREPARING MOTHER SAUCES

The preparation of mother sauces is critical to the quality of the compound sauces prepared from them. As already stated, a poor stock will yield a poor sauce. The same is true of mother sauces. If the mother sauce is of poor quality the compound sauce will also be poor. The recommendations and recipes given here are intended to help you master the production of perfect sauces.

BROWN SAUCES

TOMATO SAUCE

We begin in Figure One with a recipe for a basic tomato sauce. This sauce is used either on its own or as an addition to other sauces. This sauce is thickened with roux but frequently it is made without roux in today's commercial kitchen.

It bears mentioning that a variation of this sauce is the tomato sauce that is widely used for Italian cooking throughout the United States, specifically, in pastas, pizzas and casseroles. In general, the differences between these sauces and the sauce listed in Figure One are that they would not contain roux, stock and the pork product, and, in all likelihood, would contain a canned tomato product such as puree or paste, and may contain the herbs oregano and basil.

The procedure for these popular sauces is basic.

1. Saute chopped vegetables in oil. Always onion and garlic, often celery, mushrooms and green pepper, sometimes carrots and other vegetables.

2. Add tomato product, fresh or canned. Any number of types may be utlized including: Paste, puree, tomato sauce, chopped tomatoes, whole tomatoes, tomato juice. The thing to remember here is combining these products to bring the right consistency in thickness after reduction.

3. Add herbs, spices and other flavoring agents. Oregano, parsley and basil above all; chervil, lemon grass, bay leaf, cumin are among many possibilities. Sometimes wine is added, especially red wine.

4. This melange is slowly simmered, babied, coddled and mothered until the consistency is perfect and the aroma begins to make you swoon.

ESPAGNOLE (DEMI-GLACE)

The reason why espagnole and demi-glace are linked is not because they are the same sauce. It is because these two preparations are bound so closely together in any discussion of the mother sauces. Demi-glace can not be made without making espagnole first, yet to make the compound sauces that follow this alignment you must first make demi-glace.

ESPAGNOLE SAUCE

Espagnole, the original brown sauce, has been the glory of the French kitchen. The name dates from the 18th century, when the finest ham, an essential ingredient of espagnole, was said to come from Spain. Two or three days were required to make the sauce. First, the roux was slowly browned to develop flavor. Then a rich, brown stock (the preparation of this alone was a day's work) was added together with pieces of veal, ham, a stewing fowl or a game bird. A recipe for espagnole sauce is given in Figure Two.

PREPARATION OF DEMI-GLACE

Espagnole is the halfway point in the production of traditional demi-glace. By the combining of an equivalent amount of espagnole and brown stock, with appropriate mirepoix and then continued reduction and depouillage, the perfection of traditional demi-glace is achieved. This method of preparing a demi-glace is in keeping with Escoffier, who advocated it in his *Le Guide Culinaire*. A recipe for a traditional demi-glace is given in Figure Three.

ESPAGNOLE SAUCE
YIELD: 1 GAL

INGREDIENTS		AMOUNT
1. BROWN STOCK (VEAL, BEEF)		6 QT
2. BROWN ROUX		13 OZ
3. SLAB BACON, DICE & BLANCHED		8 OZ
4. MIREPOIX (CARROT, ONION, CELERY) DICE		2 LB
5. BOUQUET GARNI, LARGE		1 EA
CONSISTING OF:		
THYME	2 PINCHES	
BAY LEAVES	2 MEDIUM	
PARSLEY STEMS	1 BUNCH	
6. TOMATO PUREE		1 QT
7. SEASONING		AS NEEDED
8. BUTTER		AS NEEDED

METHOD

1. IN A BOWL, DISSOLVE COLD ROUX WITH HOT STOCK, MAKING A SOLID PASTE. THEN LIQUEFY THE PASTE BY ADDING MORE LIQUID.
2. STIR TEMPERED ROUX INTO BOILING BROWN STOCK WITH SPATULA OR WHISK AND BRING TO BOIL.
4. ADD TOMATO PUREE AND BOUQUET GARNI TO BOILING SAUCE.
3. RENDER THE BACON IN SAUTOIR, ADD MIREPOIX AND SAUTE UNTIL GOLDEN. ADD TO BOILING SAUCE.
5. MOVE POT OFF CENTER AND ADJUST FIRE TO SLOW BOIL, ALLOWING SCUM TO ACCUMULATE TO ONE SIDE. THEN SKIM IMPURITIES FROM SURFACE. (REVIEW DEPOUILLAGE.)
   NOTE: THE TIME REQUIRED FOR DEPOUILLAGE WILL VARY ACCORDING TO THE QUALITY OF THE STOCK AND ROUX. A MINIMUM OF AT LEAST TWO HOURS SHOULD BE CONSIDERED FOR APPROPRIATE DEPOUILLAGE AND REDUCTION.
6. WHEN REDUCED TO 1 GAL, ADJUST SEASONING.
7. STRAIN THROUGH FINE CHINOIS.
8. BUTTER TOP TO AVOID FORMATION OF SKIN. LABEL, COOL AND REFRIGERATE.

Figure 2

```
                          DEMI-GLACE
                         YIELD: 1 GAL
  INGREDIENTS                                    AMOUNT
  1.  BROWN VEAL STOCK                           1 GAL
  2.  ESPAGNOLE                                  1 GAL
  3.  BOUQUET GARNI WITH TARRAGON                1 EA
  4.  MADEIRA WINE                               8 OZ
  5.  SEASONING                                  AS NEEDED

  METHOD
  1.  ADD BROWN VEAL STOCK TO ESPAGNOLE, BRING TO A ROLLING BOIL, STIRRING
      OFTEN.
  2.  ADD BOUQUET GARNI. PLACE POT OFF CENTER.
  3.  SIMMER (LIGHT ROLLING BOIL) AND REDUCE VOLUME BY HALF.
  4.  DEPOUILLE FREQUENTLY, UP TO 8 HOURS, UNTIL THE SAUCE IS VERY SHINY
      AND TRANSLUCENT, HAVING REMOVED ALL OF ITS IMPURITIES.
  5.  ADJUST SEASONING, STRAIN THROUGH CHINOIS MOUSSELINE AND ADD
      MADEIRA WINE.
  6.  IF NOT USED IMMEDIATELY, COOL, STIRRING FREQUENTLY. THIS IS CALLED
      "VANNER." THIS WILL PREVENT THE FORMATION OF A THICK SKIN, AND
      CONSEQUENTLY LUMPS.
  7.  WHEN COMPLETELY COOLED, BUTTER TOP, LABEL, COVER AND REFRIGERATE.

  NOTE:  A) A SAUTEED MIREPOIX WITH DICED VEAL SHANKS MAY BE ADDED IF THE
  BROWN VEAL STOCK IS NOT SUFFICIENTLY RICH. IN THIS CASE, THE DEMI-GLACE
  IN PROCESS WILL HAVE TO BE STRAINED HALFWAY THROUGH, TO ALLOW A GOOD
  DEPOUILLAGE IN THE SECOND HALF OF THE PROCESS.

  B) MUSHROOM PEELINGS AND TRIMMINGS CAN BE ADDED TO THE SAUCE IF DESIRED.

  C) THE MADEIRA WINE CAN BE REPLACED BY A GOOD, DRY SHERRY. THIS IS STRICTLY
  A MATTER OF PERSONAL TASTE.

  Figure 3
```

There is no shortcut for demi-glace that contains roux, or, for that matter, for any sauce containing roux. You have to depouille for 1 1/2 hours for velouté or espagnole and 8 hours for demi-glace to achieve the right amount of shine and transparency. Any attempt to simplify the process will result in an inferior product.

JUS DE VEAU LIE / QUICK DEMI-GLACE

Today, because of concerns for lighter sauces and labor factors, many chefs prepare demi-glace from strong brown veal stock which is reduced by half with mirepoix and aromatics, then thickened lightly with a modified starch.

In other words, a demi-glace may be considered to be a well flavored brown veal stock, reduced by half. This is the meaning of DEMI. It is lightly thickened by a "clean" starch and bound by its own gelatin content. As we stated earlier in our discussion of starches, it is only habit that causes chefs to continue to use flour roux as the thickening agent for demi-glace. It is the strength and reduction of the sauce which gives demi-glace its characteristic shine and flavor, not the roux.

This is why *jus de veau lie* was brought back into fashion. It is quicker and easier, being simply a good brown veal stock reduced by half and thickened with arrowroot or tapioca starch, and well flavored. It replaces and looks like a demi-glace, but is not full-bodied like a demi-glace. It is closer to an essence, however, it is a good substitute for demi-glace and has its own merits if put in proper perspective. A recipe for this sauce is given in Figure Four.

JUS DE VEAU LIE/QUICK DEMI-GLACE
(A quick & contemporary method of production)
YIELD: 1 1/2 GAL

INGREDIENTS	AMOUNT
1. FAT, IN ANY COMBINATION (EX. - 2 OZ OLIVE OIL, 2 OZ BUTTER, 2 OZ BACON FAT)	6 OZ
2. MIREPOIX (CARROTS, ONIONS, CELERY, MUSHROOM STEMS & TRIM), DICED	1 1/2 LB EA, 6 LB TOTAL
3. SHALLOTS, COARSELY CHOPPED	4 OZ
4. GARLIC, COARSELY CHOPPED	1 OZ
5. PARSLEY STEMS, COARSELY CHOPPED	1 OZ
6. TOMATO PUREE, PREVIOUSLY BROWNED IN OVEN	3 LB 2 OZ
7. RED BURGUNDY WINE	1 QT
8. REDUCED, STRONG BROWN VEAL STOCK	8 QT
9. BAY LEAVES	3 EA
10. DRY TARRAGON LEAVES, DRY THYME LEAVES, SALT, CRACKED BLACK PEPPER	1 TBSP OF EA
11. WORCESTERSHIRE SAUCE	2 TBSP
12. CLEAR GEL, ARROWROOT OR CORNSTARCH	4 OZ
13. SHERRY OR MADEIRA WINE	8 OZ

METHOD
1. IN A LARGE RONDEAU, HEAT FAT.
2. ADD MIREPOIX AND CARAMELIZE WELL OVER HIGH HEAT, STIRRING OFTEN.
3. WHEN UNIFORMLY CARAMELIZED, NOT BURNED, ADD SHALLOTS, GARLIC, PARSLEY STEMS AND BROWNED TOMATO PUREE.
4. CONTINUE TO BROWN OVER MEDIUM HEAT, STIRRING OFTEN. BE CAREFUL NOT TO BURN OR SCORCH.
5. WHEN MIXTURE IS A UNIFORM LIGHT BROWN COLOR, DEGLAZE WITH RED WINE AND SIMMER, REDUCING VOLUME BY HALF.
6. STIR IN THE SEASONINGS AND STRONG VEAL STOCK. BRING TO A BOIL.
7. REDUCE HEAT, SIMMERING GENTLY UNTIL VOLUME IS REDUCED BY 1/3. SKIM FAT AND SCUM FROM SAUCE OCCASIONALLY.
8. STRAIN FIRST THROUGH A COARSE CHINOIS, PRESSING WELL TO EXTRACT ALL MOISTURE AND FLAVOR.
9. RETURN TO HEAT, BRING TO A BOIL.
10. DILUTE STARCH WITH SHERRY OR MADEIRA AND STIR INTO BOILING SAUCE.
11. BRING BACK TO BOILING, CHECK SEASONING AND ADJUST AS NEEDED.
12. STRAIN THROUGH CHEESECLOTH, USING MILKING METHOD.
13. USE AS YOU WOULD TRADITIONAL DEMI-GLACE.
NOTE: THERE ARE TWO CRUCIAL FACTORS IN THIS PREPARATION:
A) A PERFECT VEAL STOCK, REDUCED BY HALF IS NEEDED TO HAVE THE FULL BODY AND FLAVOR.
B) THE PROPER AND FULL CARAMELIZATION OF THE MIREPOIX AND TOMATO PUREE IS NEEDED TO GIVE THE FINE FLAVOR AND COLOR OF A LONG SIMMERED AND REDUCED, TRADITIONAL DEMI-GLACE.

Figure 4

THE VELOUTÉS
(Rich – Lean)

I
ORDINARY VELOUTE
(Rich)
YIELD: 1 GAL

INGREDIENTS	AMOUNT
1. WHITE VEAL STOCK	1 GAL
2. BLOND ROUX	15 OZ
3. OPTIONAL: MUSHROOMS, TRIMMINGS (MUST BE WHITE)	5 OZ
4. SALT & PEPPER	TO TASTE

II
ALL POULTRY VELOUTÉS
(Rich)
YIELD: 1 GAL

INGREDIENTS	AMOUNT
1. WHITE CHICKEN STOCK	1 GAL
2. BLOND ROUX	15 OZ
3. SALT & PEPPER	TO TASTE

III
FISH OR VEGETABLE VELOUTÉ
(Lean)
YIELD: 1 GAL

INGREDIENTS	AMOUNT
1. WHITE FISH STOCK OR VEGETABLE STOCK	1 GAL
2. BLOND ROUX	15 OZ
3. SALT & PEPPER	TO TASTE

METHOD OF PREPARATION FOR ALL VELOUTÉS

1. IN A BOWL, SLOWLY ADD A LITTLE HOT STOCK TO COLD ROUX, MAKING A SOLID PASTE. THEN ADD MORE HOT LIQUID TO MAKE A LIQUID PASTE.

2. WHIP THE LIQUID PASTE INTO BOILING STOCK, STIRRING CONSTANTLY. (THE CONSTANT STIRRING PREVENTS THE ROUX FROM SETTLING TO THE BOTTOM.)

3. BRING TO A BOIL, THEN ADJUST HEAT SOURCE AND MOVE PAN OFF CENTER FOR DEPOUILLAGE.

4. REDUCE TO PROPER CONSISTENCY AND DEPOUILLE OCCASIONALLY, ESTABLISHING THE FIVE PHYSICAL PROPERTIES OF THE SAUCE.

5. ADJUST SEASONING.

6. STRAIN THROUGH CHINOIS MOUSSELINE.

7. BUTTER TOP TO PREVENT FORMATION OF SKIN, COOL RAPIDLY, LABEL & REFRIGERATE.

Figure 5

GRAND JUS LIE / THICKENED VEAL JUICES

Currently this sauce is very much in favor in the commercial kitchen. Although sometimes used incorrectly and to excess, it does deserve consideration. It has a good level of taste and shine, but is not really an appropriate replacement for demi-glace. This is regular strength brown veal stock, lightly flavored and thickened with modified starches, arrowroot, cornstarch, clear gel or others. It is not designed as a base for compound sauces. It is, however, ideal for reduction sauces which will be discussed later in this chapter.

WHITE SAUCES

The preparation of white sauces does not require as much labor as that for brown sauces. However, the fact remains that short cuts lead to a pasty, wobbly sauce which nobody likes to eat. To avoid a pasty consistency and grey, grisly look, all white sauces must be cooked long enough to produce a silky, creamy-white finish.

The white and blond rouxs are used in these sauces. Remember, roux which is not cooked properly will not produce a fine white sauce. Review the discussion of roux in this chapter.

It is good culinary practice to strain the white sauces before finishing or adding garnish. Straining is done through a muslin cloth or fine china cap. The finished sauce is then placed in a baine marie, with a few flakes of fresh butter on top to avoid the formation of a skin.

Two groups of white sauces are considered here. Those made with milk, such as bechamel, and the various veloutés made with concentrated stocks instead of milk.

VELOUTÉS

The veloutés are the finer grade of white sauces. This is based on the fact that they are made from strong flavorful liquids, such as chicken broth or fish broth, not milk. The veloutés are not in themselves a finished sauce. They are an intermediate product on the way to making a basic velouté sauce or a compound sauce. Both a basic velouté sauce and the compound sauce derivatives require the addition of a final liaison such as cream, chips of butter or the egg and cream mixture before they have the correct thickness, consistency and flavor. Once sauces have had the final liaison added they do not keep very well and they do not have as much use or resiliency.

No matter what kind of velouté (which stock has been used) the sauce receives the classical name. The best classical white sauce is the SUPREME SAUCE, made with chicken stock. Next is the ALLEMANDE SAUCE, made with strong veal stock. The important white fish sauce is prepared with fish stock and is called the WHITE WINE SAUCE or BERCY, with the addition of white wine. Recipes for basic veloute variations are given in Figure Five.

BECHAMEL SAUCE

The base of this sauce is milk. It may be flavored in a wide variety of ways and is an ingredient in many dishes. Recipes for bechamel are given in Figure Six.

COMPOUND SAUCES FROM MOTHER SAUCES

Compound sauces are derivatives of mother sauces. They have accessory elements added to modify or give the dominant taste. Compound sauces should have the same physical properties (VISCOSITY, TEXTURE, COLOR, LUSTER, OPACITY) as the mother sauces.

CLASSIFICATION OF COMPOUND SAUCES

There are many compound sauces that are prepared from mother sauces. These are divided into two categories: Small brown sauces and small white sauces.

BECHAMEL
(Lean – Rich)

I
BECHAMEL (Lean)
YIELD: 1 GAL

INGREDIENTS	AMOUNT
1. MILK (OPTIONAL: LOW FAT MILK)	1 GAL
2. WHITE ROUX (SEE NOTE)	15 OZ
3. SALT	TO TASTE
4. NUTMEG	PINCH OR SCRATCH
5. ONION CLOUTE	1 EA

(SPIKE I SMALL ONION WITH 2 CLOVES AND 1 BAY LEAF.)

II
BECHAMEL (Rich)
YIELD: 1 GAL

INGREDIENTS	AMOUNT
1. MILK	1 GAL
2. WHITE ROUX (SEE NOTE)	15 OZ
3. SALT	TO TASTE
4. WHITE PEPPER	TO TASTE
5. NUTMEG	PINCH OR SCRATCH
6. ONION CLOUTE (SPIKED ONION)	1 EA
7. VEAL, LEAN, DICED, BLANCHED	12 OZ
8. ONION, DICED, SAUTEED TRANSLUCENT	4 OZ

NOTE: BECAUSE IT IS DIFFICULT TO DEPOUILLE A BECHAMEL (THE CASEIN IN THE MILK EMULSIFIES THE FAT), THE WHITE ROUX USED SHOULD BE PREPARED WITH CLARIFIED BUTTER. THIS WILL HELP AVOID ANY TASTE BEING GIVEN TO THE SAUCE BY THE TYPE OF FAT USED.

METHOD FOR BECHAMEL LEAN & RICH
1. BOIL MILK.
2. IN A BOWL, SLOWLY ADD A LITTLE HOT MILK TO COLD ROUX, MAKING A SOLID PASTE. THEN ADD MORE MILK TO MAKE A LIQUID PASTE.
2. WHIP THE LIQUID PASTE INTO THE BOILED MILK. STIR CONSTANTLY TO PREVENT THE ROUX FROM SETTLING TO THE BOTTOM AND BURNING.
3. BRING TO A ROLLING BOIL AND ADD ONION CLOUTE.

NOTE: FOR RICH BECHAMEL FOUR STEPS ARE ADDED AT THIS POINT.
(1) BLANCH VEAL, REFRESH AND DRAIN.
(2) SAUTE DICED ONION IN A LITTLE BUTTER TILL TRANSLUCENT.
(3) ADD VEAL AND STEW LIGHTLY TO A BLOND COLOR.
(4) ADD PREPARED ONION AND VEAL TO SAUCE.

4. COVER AND COOK IN MODERATE OVEN, 300°F, FOR 30 TO 45 MINUTES, STIRRING OCCASIONALLY.
5. WHEN COOKED, REMOVE FROM OVEN, DEGREASE, ADJUST SEASONING, INCLUDING A "SCRATCH" OF NUTMEG.
6. STRAIN THROUGH A CHINOIS MOUSSELINE. BUTTER TOP TO PREVENT FORMATION OF A SKIN. COOL RAPIDLY, LABEL, COVER & REFRIGERATE.

NOTE: BECHAMEL RICH = BECHAMEL LEAN + VEAL & ONION.

Figure 6

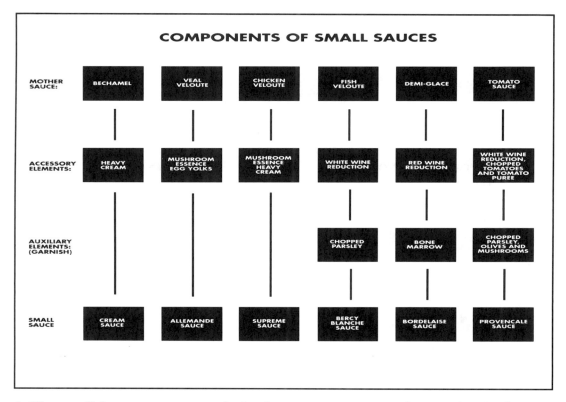

COMPONENTS OF SMALL SAUCES

MOTHER SAUCE:	BECHAMEL	VEAL VELOUTE	CHICKEN VELOUTE	FISH VELOUTE	DEMI-GLACE	TOMATO SAUCE
ACCESSORY ELEMENTS:	HEAVY CREAM	MUSHROOM ESSENCE EGG YOLKS	MUSHROOM ESSENCE HEAVY CREAM	WHITE WINE REDUCTION	RED WINE REDUCTION	WHITE WINE REDUCTION, CHOPPED TOMATOES AND TOMATO PUREE
AUXILIARY ELEMENTS: (GARNISH)				CHOPPED PARSLEY	BONE MARROW	CHOPPED PARSLEY, OLIVES AND MUSHROOMS
SMALL SAUCE	CREAM SAUCE	ALLEMANDE SAUCE	SUPREME SAUCE	BERCY BLANCHE SAUCE	BORDELAISE SAUCE	PROVENCALE SAUCE

1. The small brown sauces are derived from demi-glace. These are usually reduction sauces.

2. The small white sauces are derived from bechamel or the veloutés.

There are many compound sauces and good sauciers will continue to learn new variations throughout their lives.

BUILDING A COMPOUND SAUCE

As with any sauce, compound sauces are made in a series of steps, each building on the other, working toward balance and perfection. The steps in building a compound sauce are:

1. Add accessory elements to the mother sauce and let simmer. Reduce the volume to gain the five physical properties of the sauce.

   NOTE: If the elements added are liquid, you will have to work hard to achieve the five physical properties. You do not want the addition to dilute the sauce but to become a flavor booster and additive. Concentrating sauces is a culinary process of concentrating flavors. In this process you must work to maintain the correct balance of all flavors.

2. Add basic seasoning.

3. Strain through a chinois mousseline to improve texture and remove coarse elements.

4. Finish sauce with a *liaison finale* or *monter au beurre*. This is done just before service.

5. Add auxiliary elements, garnish.

ACCESSORY ELEMENTS

Accessory elements are the different ingredients added to the mother sauce, to modify or give the dominant flavor of the resulting compound sauce. These may include mushroom, ham, onion, horseradish, bone marrow, wine and an unlimited list of others.

These elements are added to the sauce and the sauce is then cooked to extract the flavor from them. They are rarely served in the sauce. An example would be SAUCE CHAMPIGNON, which actually has no mushrooms in it. It is made either with mushroom essence and demi-glace, or mushrooms simmered in demi-glace. After simmering for two hours, the mushrooms are not suitable to be served. The sauce with the mushrooms is pressed through a chinois mousseline to extract all their juices and flavor. The solids are then discarded.

A garnish of tourned or sliced mushrooms that have been sauteed is then added. However this garnish of mushrooms is optional. It is not this garnish of mushrooms that makes the sauce a champignon. It is the flavor extracted from the discarded mushrooms, or from the essence.

GARNISH/AUXILIARY ELEMENTS

Many times, cooks do not understand the difference between a sauce and a garnish. For example, they will speak of a SAUCE MILANAISE when, really, there is no such sauce. There is a GARNITURE MILANAISE: Tongue, ham, mushrooms and truffles. This garniture is usually added to tomato sauce, but cannot be called sauce milanaise!

A garnish is any element added to a sauce after its completion, any element too coarse to pass through a chinois mousseline. Garnishes are generally used as a reminder of the origin of the dish. A lobster sauce served on sole would be served with a garnish of diced lobster.

★ NOTE: Demi-glace is an espagnole sauce at the height of its perfection, through reduction and depouillage.

BORDELAISE SAUCE
(Compound Sauce Using Demi-Glace)
YIELD: 1 QT

INGREDIENTS	AMOUNT
1. BUTTER	2 OZ
2. SHALLOTS, FINELY CHOPPED	3 OZ
3. RED BORDEAUX OR DRY RED WINE	8 OZ
4. BAY LEAF, OR BOUQUET GARNI	1 EA
5. THYME	1 PINCH
6. MIGNONETTE PEPPER	1 PINCH
7. DEMI-GLACE	1 1/2 QT
8. JUICE OF LEMON	1/2 LEMON
9. BEEF MARROW, POACHED & DICED	6 OZ
10. SALT & PEPPER	TO TASTE

METHOD
1. SAUTE SHALLOTS WITH BUTTER IN RUSSE UNTIL TRANSLUCENT, WITHOUT COLORING.
2. ADD RED WINE, SPICES AND REDUCE BY HALF.
3. ADD DEMI-GLACE, GENTLY SIMMER FOR 25-30 MINUTES.
4. DEPOUILLE WELL AND STRAIN THROUGH CHINOIS MOUSSELINE.
5. ADD A FEW DROPS OF LEMON JUICE AND SEASON TO TASTE.
6. ADD BEEF MARROW JUST BEFORE SERVING.

NOTE: A LIAISON FINALE (MONTER UNE SAUCE AU BEURRE) USING 6 OZ OF MARCHAND DE VIN BUTTER WILL MAKE THIS SAUCE SMOOTHER, BUT LESS CLEAR. IT IS ESPECIALLY SUITABLE FOR GRILLED MEAT.

VARIATIONS: SAUCE BONNEFOY IS THE SAME AS BORDELAISE, USING WHITE BORDEAUX WINE. IN THIS CASE THE LIAISON FINALE SHOULD BE DONE WITH BERCY BUTTER.

Figure 7

CREAM SAUCE
(Compound Sauce Using Bechamel)
YIELD: 1 QT

INGREDIENTS	AMOUNT
1. BECHAMEL SAUCE (RICH OR LEAN)	1 QT
2. HEAVY CREAM	10 OZ
3. BUTTER, SOFTENED	2 OZ
4. LEMON JUICE, FRESH	FROM 1 LEMON
5. SEASONING	TO TASTE

METHOD
1. IN A NON-ALUMINUM RUSSE, BRING BECHAMEL AND 5 OZ. OF CREAM TO A BOIL. NOTE: HEAVY CREAM SHOULD BE BOILED PRIOR TO BEING ADDED TO THE SAUCE.
2. SIMMER, REDUCING TO PROPER VISCOSITY, STIRRING OFTEN.
3. REMOVE FROM HEAT, AND STIR IN REMAINDER OF HEAVY CREAM, BUTTER AND LEMON JUICE.
4. ADJUST SEASONING, THEN STRAIN THROUGH A CHINOIS MOUSSELINE.
5. LIGHTLY BUTTER TOP TO PREVENT SKIN FROM FORMING. LABEL AND COVER.

Figure 8

SAUCE ALLEMANDE
(Compound Sauce Using Veal Veloute)
YIELD: 1 QT

INGREDIENTS	AMOUNT
1. MUSHROOM ESSENCE	8 OZ
2. VEAL WHITE STOCK	16 OZ
3. VEAL VELOUTE	1 QT
4. EGG YOLKS	5 EA
5. LEMON JUICE, FRESH	FROM 1/2 LEMON
6. SEASONING (SALT, PEPPER, & NUTMEG)	TO TASTE
7. BUTTER, FRESH, IN PASTE	3 OZ, APPRX.

METHOD
1. IN A NON-ALUMINUM RUSSE, COMBINE INGREDIENTS 1-5.
2. SLOWLY BRING TO A BOIL, THEN SIMMER, REDUCING BY 1/3. STIR OFTEN TO PREVENT BURNING OR SCORCHING ON THE BOTTOM OF THE PAN.
3. ADJUST SEASONING, THEN PASS THROUGH A CHINOIS MOUSSELINE.
4. FINISH LIAISON FINALE WITH SOFTENED BUTTER.
5. LIGHTLY BUTTER TO PREVENT SKIN FROM FORMING. LABEL AND COVER.

NOTE: ALLEMANDE IS THICKENED WITH EGG YOLKS; HOWEVER, IT CAN BE BOILED AFTER THE EGG YOLKS ARE ADDED. THEY WILL NOT SCRAMBLE. IT IS ESSENTIAL, HOWEVER, THAT ALL INGREDIENTS BE COLD WHEN YOU START, SINCE GRADUAL HEATING OF THE YOLKS IS ALSO CRUCIAL TO THE TEXTURE OF THE SAUCE.

Figure 9

SAUCE SUPREME
(Compound Sauce Using Chicken Velouté)
YIELD: 1 QT

INGREDIENTS	AMOUNT
1. CHICKEN VELOUTE	1 QT
2. WHITE STOCK, CHICKEN OR VEAL	1 PT
3. MUSHROOM ESSENCE	6 OZ
4. HEAVY CREAM	8 OZ
5. BUTTER, IN PASTE	3 OZ

METHOD

1. IN A NON-ALUMINUM RUSSE, STIR TOGETHER VELOUTÉ, STOCK, ESSENCE AND HALF OF THE CREAM (4 OZ).
2. BRING TO A BOIL, THEN SIMMER, REDUCING BY 1/3. STIR CONSTANTLY.
3. ADJUST SEASONING, THEN STRAIN THROUGH A CHINOIS MOUSSELINE.
4. MIX TOGETHER THE REMAINING HEAVY CREAM AND BUTTER.
5. REMOVE FROM HEAT AND FINISH LIAISON FINALE WITH THE CREAM AND BUTTER MIXTURE.
6. LIGHTLY BUTTER TOP TO PREVENT SKIN FROM FORMING. LABEL AND COVER.

NOTE: IT IS FROM THIS SAUCE THAT ALL THE OTHER CHICKEN VELOUTE COMPOUND SAUCES ARE DERIVED. IT IS A CHICKEN VELOUTÉ CARRIED TO THE HIGHEST POINT OF PERFECTION.

Figure 10

Therefore, theoretically, espagnole cannot be used interchangeably with or instead of demi-glace in the production of brown compound sauces.

There are very few compound sauces made from tomato sauce. The main use of tomato sauce is as an additive to other sauces or alone.

PREPARING COMPOUND SAUCES

The variety of compound sauces from mother sauce is virtually unlimited. However, there are certain compound sauces that are considered basic to good culinary preparation. The purpose of this text is not to give recipes, but methods, principles and knowledge. In this process Figures Seven, Eight, Nine, Ten and Eleven have example recipes for compound sauces.

COMPOUND SAUCES FROM REDUCTION

These are a specific type of compound sauce. They require a careful reduction of liquid before the addition of the mother sauce in order to build a unique flavor component. Two examples are bordelaise and bercy blanche, shown in Figures Seven and Eleven.

The technique for this type of reduction is simple.

SHALLOTS OR ONIONS + LIQUID + SPICES + WELL DEPOUILLED MOTHER SAUCE + LIAISON FINALE

Shallots are usually preferred instead of onions, except in a few recipes, such as smitane. The flavor of the shallot is more subtle. However, onions and scallions are sometimes a good substitute when food cost prohibits the use of shallots.

The technique of production for a reduction sauce is as follows:
1. Saute the shallots or onions until translucent, without coloring. If they take the slightest coloration, your sauce will taste like onion soup.
2. Add the liquid, generally this is wine, but vinegar or marinade may also be used.

BERCY BLANCHE
(Compound Sauce Using Fish Velouté)
YIELD: 1 QT

INGREDIENTS	AMOUNT
1. SHALLOTS	6 OZ (1 C)
2. CLARIFIED BUTTER	AS NEEDED
3. DRY WHITE WINE	12 OZ
4. FISH FUMET	12 OZ
5. FISH VELOUTE	1 QT
6. BOUQUET GARNI	1 SMALL
7. BERCY OR MAITRE D'HOTEL BUTTER	6 OZ
8. HEAVY CREAM	6 OZ
9. SEASONING	TO TASTE
10. LEMON JUICE	AS NEEDED
11. PARSLEY, FINELY CHOPPED	4 OZ (1 C)

METHOD

1. IN A NON-ALUMINUM RUSSE, SAUTE SHALLOTS IN CLARIFIED BUTTER WITHOUT COLORING.
2. ADD WHITE WINE AND FISH FUMET, THEN REDUCE BY 1/2.
3. ADD BOUQUET GARNI AND FISH VELOUTE. BRING TO A BOIL AND SIMMER 10-15 MINUTES.
4. DEPOUILLE WELL AND STRAIN THROUGH A CHINOIS MOUSSELINE.
5. BLEND THE BERCY BUTTER AND CREAM FOR LIAISON FINALE.
6. FINISH SAUCE BY ADDING THE LIAISON FINALE OF BERCY BUTTER AND CREAM.
7. ADJUST SEASONING WITH FRESHLY GROUND WHITE PEPPER AND ADD A FEW DROPS OF LEMON JUICE TO SPARKLE THE TASTE IF NEEDED.
8. LIGHTLY BUTTER TO PREVENT SKIN FROM FORMING. LABEL AND COVER.
9. JUST BEFORE SERVING, ADD FRESHLY CHOPPED PARSLEY.

Figure 11

3. Spices, generally including thyme, bay leaf and mignonette pepper, but is not limited to this. NOTE: Do not let the pepper reduce more than 10 minutes or a bitter taste will develop.
4. Reduce until almost dry, but not burned.
5. Add the mother sauce and let simmer for 20-30 minutes.
6. Pass through a chinois mousseline and finish with butter if needed. Add garnish as needed.

SHELLFISH SAUCES

Shellfish sauces are the most delicate in taste and represent the highest level of technique in sauce preparation. They are produced primarily from fish veloute and/or bechamel sauce, so they are a compound sauce derivative of the mother sauce.

★NOTE: The use of fish velouté and cream is the same as the use of bechamel and fish stock, if the proportions are equal.

All shellfish sauces have three elements in common.:

1. CAYENNE PEPPER IS USED TO SPARKLE THE TASTE AND MAKE THE SAUCE SLIGHTLY SPICY.
2. A COMPOUND BUTTER MADE FROM A CRUSTACEAN OFTEN IS USED AS A LIAISON FINALE.
3. THESE SAUCES ARE CHARACTERIZED BY THEIR COLOR, WHICH IS DERIVED FROM THE SHELL OF THE CRUSTACEAN. AN

IMPROVEMENT CAN EE MADE IN THE COLOR BY ADDING A TCUCH OF TOMATO, OR A DASH OF PAPRIKA, BUT SHOULD NOT BE OVERUSED.

The majority of the shellfish taste is contained in the head and shell of the crustacean, not so much in the body. For this reason, any process involving cooking shellfish or making a shellfish sauce, must involve extraction of flavor from the shell.

To extract the flavor, the shell must be exposed to heat. This develops the flavor along with red color. Salt is also used to extract flavor. Sauteing shellfish in hot fat and coarse salt will bring out their flavor.

The most common procedure used for handling shellfish for sauce is to saute the crustacean in fat, normally a combination of olive oil and butter. The use of a blender is ideally suited to puree or paste the shellfish to extract the full flavor. Once pureed, it is added to the veloute and cooked. The sauce is then strained, leaving the full flavor extracted from the shells.

The meat from the shellfish can be removed before the shells are pureed. The meat is then either pureed, diced or chopped and added to the finished sauce as a garnish. It can also be served as a dish, such as Lobster a la Americaine, or as a garnish in a soup. Figure Twelve gives an example recipe for a shellfish sauce.

OTHER SAUCES

EMULSIFIED SAUCES

Emulsified sauces are preparations which bring together elements which do not readily mix. Due to the importance of understanding emulsions and their preparation, Chapter 4 of this text discusses the subject in detail. Review this chapter before preparing the hot

---

NEWBURG SAUCE
(Shellfish Sauce)
YIELD: 1 QT

INGREDIENTS		AMOUNT
1.	SHRIMP, HEADS, SHELLS & PIECES, CHOPPED	1 LB
2.	CLARIFIED BUTTER	AS NEEDED
3.	MIREPOIX, FINELY DICED	1 LB
4.	CAYENNE PEPPER	2 PINCHES
4.	PAPRIKA	1 TSP
5.	SHERRY OR MADEIRA WINE	1 C
6.	FISH VELOUTE	1 QT
7.	HEAVY CREAM	1 C
8.	SEASONING	AS NEEDED

METHOD
1. IN A HEAVY RUSSE, SAUTE SHRIMP PIECES IN VERY HOT, CLARIFIED BUTTER.
2. ADD MIREPOIX AND CAYENNE PEPPER AFTER RED COLOR HAS DEVELOPED IN SHELLS. SAUTE MIREPOIX UNTIL TRANSLUCENT.
3. ADD PAPRIKA AND WINE, THEN REDUCE BY 1/2.
4. ADD FISH VELOUTE, BRING TO A BOIL AND SIMMER 15-20 MINUTES.
5. STRAIN THROUGH A CHINOIS MOUSSELINE, THEN ADJUST SEASONING.
6. PRESSING WELL TO EXTRACT ALL FLAVORS.
7. LIAISON FINALE WITH HEAVY CREAM AND/OR CRUSTACEAN BUTTER.
8. LIGHTLY BUTTER TOP. LABEL & COVER.

Figure 12

emulsified sauces presented here. Chief among the hot emulsified sauces are two based on egg yolks: HOLLANDAISE, flavored with lemon juice, and BEARNAISE, flavored with vinegar, shallot and tarragon. The third basic butter sauce is WHITE BUTTER SAUCE, (BEURRE BLANC SAUCE) which is not stabilized by the addition of egg yolk. Beurre blanc sauce is thinner and separates more easily.

The quality of all these sauces depends on the use of the best, fresh, unsalted butter.

Emulsified sauces are notorious for their tendency to separate. The key to making them is to create, and then maintain the emulsion/suspension. At the start, the butter should be added very slowly until the sauce thickens, showing that the emulsion has begun.

If an emulsified sauce is subjected to too high a temperature, or allowed to stand for too long, it will separate. When making an emulsified sauce with egg yolk, the base of the pan should never be more than hand hot. If it is hotter, the eggs will start to solidify and the sauce will curdle.

Hollandaise and bearnaise sauce are both served warm. Hollandaise may be served by itself or blended with a small quantity of bechamel or veloute and used as a coating for light meats or fish. White butter sauce should be scarcely more than tepid when it is served. There are also emulsion sauces which are served cold, such as mayonnaise. These will be discussed in Chapter 22.

PRODUCTION OF EMULSIFIED SAUCES

The production of an emulsified sauce over heat requires constant adjustment of the heat. The heat is adjusted to prevent the sauce from curdling or separating, because of being too hot or cold.

The basic guidelines for producing an emulsion sauce are:

1. THE YOLKS SHOULD BE COOKED SLOWLY, OVER MODERATE HEAT. FROM TIME-TO-TIME, REMOVE THEM FROM THE HEAT SOURCE TO LOWER THE TEMPERATURE.
2. THE BUTTER SHOULD BE IN THE SAME TEMPERATURE RANGE AS THE YOLK MIXTURE, AND WORKED IN A WARM PLACE.
3. WHEN THE BUTTER HAS BECOME ABSORBED, THE SAUCE SHOULD BE THICK AND FIRM.
4. WHEN THICK AND FIRM, THE SAUCE IS BROUGHT TO THE CORRECT CONSISTENCY BY ADDING A LITTLE WATER TO LIGHTEN IT SLIGHTLY.
5. EMULSION SAUCES ARE USUALLY COMPLETED BY ADDING A FEW DROPS OF LEMON JUICE AND ARE THEN PASSED THROUGH A FINE SIEVE OR MUSLIN CLOTH.

REMONTAGE OF A BROKEN EMULSION

Before discussing the various types of emulsion sauces, we should talk about a few ways to repair broken sauces. Emulsion sauces are easily broken, even by the most experienced chef saucier. When this happens:

1. IF THE EGG YOLKS BECOME TOO THICK, THE HEAT IS TOO HIGH. LOWER THE HEAT AND ADD A FEW DROPS OF COLD WATER TO THE MIXTURE.
2. IF THE EGG YOLKS FOAM, BUT DO NOT THICKEN, THE HEAT IS TOO LOW. CORRECT BY INCREASING THE HEAT SLIGHTLY.
3. IF THE SAUCE CURDLES AT THE END OF THE PROCESS IT HAS COOLED TOO MUCH OR HAS GOTTEN TOO HOT.

A) IF IT IS TOO COLD, PUT A LITTLE HOT WATER IN A BOWL AND GRADUALLY WHISK THE SAUCE INTO IT.

B) IF IT IS TOO HOT, DO THE SAME THING WITH A LITTLE COLD WATER IN THE BOWL.
NOTE: BOTH OF THESE METHODS WILL SAVE THE SAUCE; HOWEVER, IT WILL NOT REGAIN THE LIGHTNESS IT SHOULD HAVE HAD.

TYPES OF EMULSIFIED SAUCES

WHITE BUTTER SAUCE/BEURRE BLANC

This sauce is originally from the Loire Valley in France. It was made with the excellent local butter and white muscadet wine. It has become a sauce used worldwide and has developed an astonishing versatility.

The four basic ingredients are white wine, vinegar, shallots and butter. The first three ingredients are reduced to a glaze and mounted with the butter. Vigorous whisking is vital, particularly when the first batch of butter is added. At no stage during the whisking should the pan's temperature be more than warm.

The butter should be pre-softened to a paste, so that it forms an emulsion rather than melting to an oil. The whisking process takes only two to three minutes, so the sauce can be made at the last moment. Keeping it warm, even for a few minutes, can cause it to separate.

The emulsion in a white butter sauce is based on the whey/milk solids in the butter. Therefore, the old trick of adding a tablespoon of cream, the equivalent of more milk solids, to the glaze before mounting with the butter makes the sauce less likely to separate. However, the addition of cream detracts slightly from the butter flavor.

As a further precaution against the sauce breaking after the butter is added, the finished white butter sauce can be heated rapidly to just below the boiling point as it is whisked hard. NOTE: The emulsion must be complete before placing the sauce over high heat.

A few formal variations of white butter sauce exist, such as that made with red wine. The sauce is an inspiration for many contemporary variations. Most of these are made from cooking juices, whether meat, fish or poultry. The juices are reduced to a glaze and mounted with butter. Wine may or may not be included in the reduction, and the glaze may be enriched with cream before the butter is added.

White butter sauce is usually served with poached fish, or hot fish and vegetable terrines. An example recipe for white butter sauce is given in Figure Thirteen.

BEARNAISE

Bearnaise is not a hollandaise prepared with a reduction of tarragon. It is

---

BASIC BEURRE BLANC
(White Butter Sauce)
YIELD: 1 C

INGREDIENTS	AMOUNT
1. SWEET BUTTER	1/2 C
2. STRONGLY REDUCED FISH FUMET	2 TBSP
3. DRY WHITE WINE	2 TBSP
4. HERB VINEGAR	2 TBSP
5. FINELY SLICED SHALLOTS	2 TBSP

METHOD
1. CUT THE BUTTER INTO SMALL PIECES AND LEAVE AT ROOM TEMPERATURE TO SOFTEN.
2. PLACE SHALLOTS, FISH STOCK, WHITE WINE, AND VINEGAR IN A 2-QT, HEAVY STAINLESS STEEL SAUCEPAN AND BOIL ON A HIGH HEAT UNTIL LIQUID IS REDUCED TO 2 TBSP. (AT THIS POINT WATCH THE REDUCTION CAREFULLY, IT CAN EASILY BURN.)
3. TURN HEAT DOWN TO VERY LOW AND SLOWLY WHISK IN THE BUTTER, 1 OZ AT A TIME.
4. CONTINUE TO STIR OVER HEAT UNTIL 170°F, THEN STRAIN THROUGH A SIEVE.
5. THE SAUCE SHOULD BE SERVED IMMEDIATELY.

Figure 13

a sauce on its own. Bearnaise is thicker and has a more pungent flavor than hollandaise. The essential point in making bearnaise is the whisking, which equalizes the temperature of the egg yolks as they coagulate, and also whisks air into the sauce to lighten it. Egg yolks are whisked with a reduction of tarragon, vinegar, white wine, peppercorns and shallots. The result is a thick, close textured mousse. Clarified butter is then whisked in, as you would for a hollandaise.

This sauce may be served as is, or it may be strained through a fine mesh strainer. If strained, a little more finely chopped tarragon and chervil is added. Bearnaise should not be served very hot, as it is really a mayonnaise with butter. It only needs to be warm, it will curdle if overheated.

Bearnaise sauce is best served with hearty foods, such as broiled steak, lamb and salmon. For reheating and storage, see hollandaise. The handling principles are the same for both sauces. An example recipe for bearnaise is given in Figure Fourteen.

BEARNAISE
YIELD: 1 QT

INGREDIENTS	AMOUNT
1. WINE VINEGAR	4 OZ
2. WHITE WINE	4 OZ
3. SHALLOTS, FINELY CHOPPED	6 MEDIUM
4. FRESH TARRAGON, FINELY CHOPPED	3 TBSP
(IF DRY TARRAGON IS USED)	(1 TBSP)
5. FRESH CHERVIL, FINELY CHOPPED	3 TSP
(IF DRY CHERVIL IS USED)	(1 TSP)
6. MIGNONETTE PEPPER, FINELY CRUSHED	1 TSP
7. EGG YOLKS	6 EA
8. UNSALTED BUTTER, MELTED	1 PT
9. SEASONING	TO TASTE
10. TARRAGON LEAVES IN VINEGAR, FINELY CHOPPED	1 TSP

METHOD

1. IN A HEAVY NON-ALUMINUM RUSSE, COMBINE INGREDIENTS 1-6 AND BRING TO BOIL, THEN REDUCE BY 2/3. REMOVE FROM HEAT AND LET COOL.
2. SEPARATE EGG YOLKS FROM WHITES, PLACING YOLKS IN A STAINLESS STEEL BOWL OF SUITABLE SIZE.
3. ADD COOLED REDUCTION AND A PINCH OF SALT, WHIPPING SLIGHTLY, UNTIL THEY CHANGE IN COLOR.
4. ADD A LITTLE WATER AND WHIP TO A FROTH.
5. PROGRESSIVELY COOK OVER A DOUBLE BOILER OR SOURCE OF LOW HEAT, WHIPPING CONSTANTLY UNTIL CONSISTENCY REACHES A HEAVY PEAK.
6. REMOVE FROM HEAT, SLOWLY ADD MELTED BUTTER WHICH IS AT SAME TEMPERATURE AS THE EGG MIXTURE.
7. ADJUST SEASONING AND STRAIN THROUGH A FINE SIEVE.
8. ADD GARNISH OF TARRAGON LEAVES IN VINEGAR, FINELY CHOPPED. LABEL AND KEEP WARM.

NOTE: IF YOU NOTICE THE SAUCE GETTING TOO THICK AND SOLID WHILE YOU ARE WHIPPING THE SAUCE, FROM TIME TO TIME, ADD A FEW DROPS OF TEPID WATER. THIS IS PREFERABLE TO SUDDENLY ADDING EXTRA LIQUID TO LIGHTEN THE SAUCE WHEN FINISHED.

Figure 14

HOLLANDAISE

A hollandaise is merely a bearnaise in which the vinegar/shallot/tarragon reduction is replaced by a reduction of salt, mignonette pepper, white wine vinegar and equal amounts of water. Otherwise the procedure is identical.

The most reliable method for making hollandaise is to produce a "mousse" by whisking egg yolks with water, one tablespoon per yolk, over heat or in a double boiler. The process should take at least three minutes, by which time, the mousse should be light, but close textured. The mousse acts as the stabilizer, allowing the melted butter to be added without the sauce separating. An example recipe for hollandaise is given in Figure Fifteen.

Formerly hollandaise was seasoned with a reduction of vinegar, but today, lemon juice is more common. Hollandaise may be served plain or with flavorings. It is a good accompaniment for poached fish, eggs and vegetables.

Both hollandaise and bearnaise have several derivatives. A few flavorful ingredients can be added to either sauce then forming a new sauce which by way of the altering of the flavor is a better accompaniment for certain foods. Following is a list of several examples.

FROM HOLLANDAISE:

SAUCE MALTAISE: TO 1 QT OF HOLLANDAISE,

HOLLANDAISE
YIELD: 1 QT

INGREDIENTS	AMOUNT
1. EGG YOLKS	5 EA
2. COLD WATER	2-3 OZ
3. WHITE WINE VINEGAR	1 TBSP
4. UNSALTED BUTTER, MELTED	1 PT
5. FRESH LEMON JUICE	FROM 1 LEMON
6. CAYENNE PEPPER, SALT	AS NEEDED

METHOD

1. SEPARATE EGG YOLKS FROM WHITES. PLACE YOLKS IN SUITABLE STAINLESS STEEL BOWL.
2. ADD A PINCH OF SALT AND WHIP LIGHTLY.
3. AS SOON AS YOU NOTICE A CHANGE IN COLOR FROM LIGHTER YELLOW TO DARKER YELLOW, ADD WATER AND VINEGAR, AND WHIP TO A FROTH, AT LEAST UNTIL DOUBLE IN VOLUME.
4. COOK OVER DOUBLE BOILER OR SOURCE OF LOW HEAT, WHIPPING CONSTANTLY, UNTIL CONSISTENCY REACHES A SOFT PEAK.
5. REMOVE FROM HEAT, SLOWLY ADD MELTED BUTTER WHICH IS THE SAME TEMPERATURE AS EGG MIX. FROM TIME TO TIME LIGHTEN THE SAUCE BY ADDING A FEW DROPS OF HOT OR COLD WATER OR LEMON JUICE AND SALT IF NEEDED.
6. ADJUST SEASONING WITH A DASH OF CAYENNE AND LEMON JUICE.
7. STRAIN THROUGH A FINE MOUSSELINE OR MUSLIN CLOTH, LABEL AND KEEP WARM.

NOTE: HOLLANDAISE IS CHARACTERIZED BY ITS TEXTURE, WHICH IS THAT OF AN AERATED FOAM CREATED BY THE WATER AND EGG YOLKS BEING WHIPPED TO A FROTH BEFORE COOKING. THE MORE WATER, THE MORE VOLUME AND LIGHTER THE HOLLANDAISE.

Figure 15

ADD 3 TO 4 OZ OF THE JUICE FROM A BLOOD-ORANGE AND 2 TSP OF GRATED ORANGE RIND. ESPECIALLY GOOD WITH ASPARAGUS. SAUCE MOUSSELINE: TO 1 QT OF HOLLANDAISE, FOLD IN 1 PT OF STIFFLY-WHIPPED HEAVY CREAM. ESPECIALLY GOOD WITH SHELLFISH DISHES.

FROM BEARNAISE:
SAUCE CHORON: TO 1 QT OF BEARNAISE, ADD 2 OZ TOMATO PASTE. ESPECIALLY GOOD WITH GRILLED POULTRY, VEAL OR PORK.
SAUCE FOYOT: TO 1 QT OF BEARNAISE, ADD 2 OZ GLACE DE VIANDE. ESPECIALLY GOOD WITH GRILLED BEEF.

★ **NOTE:** The consistency of sauces, which are made by the same method as hollandaise, may be varied at will. For instance, the number of egg yolks may be increased if a very thick sauce is desired. Or the number may be decreased if a thinner sauce is needed. As a rule, if a thick sauce is required, the yolks should be well cooked, but the sauce kept almost cold in the making.

Experience alone, the fruit of long practice, can teach the various devices which enable the skilled chef to obtain different results from the same kind and quality of material. However, it all begins with remembering that the absorbing power of one egg yolk is approximately three ounces of butter. This equals five to six yolks per pound of butter used.

BUTTER SAUCES

Professional cuisine classifies those sauces made primarily of butters, such as PLAIN DRAWN FRESH BUTTER, FRESH BUTTER or CLARIFIED BUTTER. These are butters from which the milk and other residues have been removed.

FRESH CHURNED BUTTER, unsalted, may be drawn and served immediately with food.

SALTED BUTTER, and not so fresh butter, must be clarified before being served. To clarify butter, it is cooked over slow heat until the milk and other residues in the butter have attached themselves to the bottom of the pan. The oils of the butter can then be easily removed by pouring it through a cheesecloth or muslin. The butter must be golden clear and is served hot in sauce bowls.

BEURRE NOISETTE is butter heated gently to a light brown color and so that it gives a nutty aroma. In principle, fish is cooked *a la meuniere* in this butter. However, it is also used as an accompaniment for fish, sweetbreads, eggs and certain vegetables.

BEURRE MEUNIERE occurs when the butter reaches the point of beurre noisette, the cooking is finished with a dash of lemon juice and a pinch of chopped, fresh parsley, just before covering pieces of fish or vegetables.

BEURRE NOIR is a misnomer for black butter. *Noir* means "black," but the butter is not actually black. The butter is cooked the same as beurre noisette, only it should be a little darker. This butter can also be an accompaniment as in beurre noisette. When the smoking point is reached, the cooking is topped by the addition of capers or vinegar. The vinegar, or any acid, has the effect of thickening the butter. This allows you to coat your pieces with it. This butter has a strong flavor and must be used in a manner to heighten flavor of the item it is accompanying rather than overpowering it.

COMPOUND BUTTERS

The term *compound butter* applies to a variety of preparations.
A) Butter cooked to various degrees.
B) Simple compound butter, which is generally butter with one or more substances added, usually chopped or pureed.
C) More complex butter, such as crustacean butter, used as a medium to extract the taste from various shellfish, thus yielding a large group of sauces, the shellfish sauces.
D) Hot compound butters used as sauces, such as beurre blanc or lemon butter.

E) The modern technique of producing butter sauces by using the properties of cream in order to serve beurre blanc and lemon butter at a higher temperature than the normal melting point of butter. This is the use of cream as an emulsifier, as in liaison finale.

With the exception of the shellfish butters, compound butters are not greatly used in kitchens. They are used, in some cases, to accentuate the savor of another sauce. In this they are very useful. Because of this, they are recommended since they enable you to give a flavor to the derivatives of a bechamel or veloute that could not be achieved by other means.

The more commonly used compound butters are:

BERCY BUTTER   MAITRE D'HOTEL BUTTER
CHATEAUBRIAND BUTTER
COLBERT BUTTER   PIMIENTO BUTTER
MARCHAND DE VIN BUTTER
ESCARGOT BUTTER   SHALLOT BUTTER
TARRAGON BUTTER   GREEN BUTTER
SHELLFISH BUTTER: RED BUTTER, SHRIMP
BUTTER, CRAYFISH BUTTER, LOBSTER BUTTER

SHELLFISH BUTTERS, such as lobster, crayfish, shrimp and others, have a finer color and are freer of shell particles, when prepared with heat. As much of an advantage as heat can be, it can also create problems. If used to excess, it can remove the delicacy of the crustacean's flavor and create a disagreeable taste.

Example recipes for compound butters are given in Figures Sixteen, Seventeen and Eighteen.

BERCY BUTTER
(Compound Butter)

INGREDIENTS		AMOUNT
1.	WHITE WINE	1 PT
2.	SHALLOTS, FINELY CHOPPED	2 OZ
3.	PARSLEY, CHOPPED	1 TSP
4.	BEEF MARROW, CUT INTO CUBES AND POACHED IN SALT WATER.	2 OZ
5.	LEMON JUICE, FRESH	FEW DROPS
6.	GROUND PEPPER	TO TASTE
7.	BUTTER, SOFTENED INTO A CREAM	8 OZ

METHOD
1. PLACE WINE AND SHALLOTS IN SMALL SAUCE PAN AND BRING TO A BOIL, THEN REDUCE TO A SIMMER.
2. REDUCE LIQUID BY 1/2.
3. REMOVE REDUCTION FROM HEAT AND ADD REMAINDER OF INGREDIENTS, CREAMING THE MIXTURE TOGETHER.

NOTE: THIS BUTTER MUST NOT BE COMPLETELY MELTED AND IS SERVED PRIMARILY WITH GRILLED MEATS.

Figure 16

MAITRE D'HOTEL BUTTER
(Compound Butter)

THIS IS BUTTER SOFTENED INTO A CREAM. IT IS THEN MIXED WITH CHOPPED PARSLEY, SALT, BLACK PEPPER AND LEMON JUICE. IT IS PRIMARILY USED WITH GRILLED MEATS.

Figure 17

MISCELLANEOUS SAUCES

GRAVY

Gravy is made from meat juices which congeal and caramelize in the bottom of a roasting pan or heavy frying pan. For red meats, gravy should be dark brown and for lighter meats or poultry, it should be a golden color.

To add extra flavor to gravy made from roasts, cook a quartered onion and carrot, together with any bones, in the pan with the meat. If the juices begin to burn on the bottom of the pan as the roast cooks, add a little stock or water. When the juices are not dark enough at the end of cooking, reduce them beyond a glaze, until caramelized. This adds color and flavor to the gravy.

Gravy can be thick or thin, flavored or plain. For unthickened gravy:
1. All the fat is removed from the pan. NOTE: If butter was used for roasting, some cooks like to keep the flavored fat for use in other preparations.
2. Add stock, wine, water or a mixture of these to the pan and boil. Stir the mixture to deglaze the caramelized juices.
3. Reduce the gravy until concentrated, strain and season to taste.

For a thickened gravy:
1. Leave one to two tablespoons of fat in the pan, and stir in one to two tablespoons of flour.
2. Cook the roux thoroughly. Browning is the key to a good thickened gravy.
3. Add the stock, wine or water, and reduce until the gravy thickens.

Consistency is a matter of taste when making gravy; however, the taste of the flour should be fully cooked. No gravy, regardless of the thickness or color, should be pasty or gooey. The gravy may be too thin to coat a spoon, or it can be thick and rich. Milk, cream or sour cream may be added, or even coffee, as used in America with ham or in Sweden with roast lamb.

A LA MINUTE REDUCTIONS

This is a special preparation which has become more common. These sauces are made in concert with a dish as it is being prepared, or *a la minute*. Mostly these sauces are made when meat, fish or poultry is sauteed. It is the simple reduction of the pan juices of the item sauteed after deglazing them in a suitable liquid. In other words, they are simple essences.

Liquids such as stock, wine, fortified wine, meat glaze, cream, fruit juice and flavored vinegars are typical. After the liquid has been reduced it may be thickened with a liaison finale, seasoned and have accesory elemements added.

These reduction sauces have a special place in today's kitchen because they save greatly in the area of labor and food cost. Something is lost in terms of the subtlety of flavor that can only be developed through preparing sauces using classical methods, but these types of sauces provide a very useful alternative.

BARBECUE SAUCES

Barbecue sauces so often come from a bottle that the term has become identified in most people's minds with the commercial, highly spiced, tomato based sauces. When made from scratch they are far more versatile. A soy sauce-based mixture with a touch of sugar goes well with ham and pork, while olive oil and lemon complement fish.

A barbecue sauce is intended primarily for brushing meats, poultry and fish, flavoring and giving moisture to them during cooking. Pronounced flavors, such as mustard, chili and lemon are appropriate ingredients for barbecue sauce. Sweet/sour mixtures are also popular, the sugar helping to form a crust on the item. Most importantly, a barbecue sauce should be thick enough to cling to food which helps to prevent it from dripping onto the coals.

NUT SAUCES

There are two ways nuts can be used in sauces: As thickeners, or infused as nut milk.

The effect of nuts as thickeners in a sauce varies, according to the way they are treated. No matter how finely chopped, nuts will always add a coarse, slightly crunchy texture. For a smooth consistency they must be pounded with a mortar and pestle, normally with other ingredients, or pureed in a blender or food processor.

Recipes for nut sauces are characteristic of particular regions of the world. Almond sauces are popular in parts of India and the Mediterranean. Coconut sauces are typical of Asia and the Caribbean, while walnut sauces are popular in Southeast Asia, some parts of Africa and the southern United States.

SAVORY AND SWEET FRUIT SAUCES

SAVORY FRUIT SAUCES are more a condiment than a sauce. Most fruit sauces consist of little more than fruit pulp with sweetener. It is the fruits themselves that lend character to the sauce. For example, apple sauce made with Golden Delicious apples is quite different from that made with the Granny Smith variety. A savory fruit sauce is usually quite thick and is often served cold.

SWEET FRUIT SAUCES are not just sweeter versions of the fruit sauces that accompany meat (SAVORY FRUIT SAUCES.) They are generally thinner, and designed to fulfill the role of coating, as well as accompanying desserts. Many are based on jelly or jam, while others are made from a simple fruit puree, strained and sometimes sweetened. They may also be enhanced with a fruit liqueur and lemon juice, which prevents discoloration of the fruit. Soft fruits, such as berries, kiwi, persimmon and cooked rhubarb, make particularly good sauces. Some fruits, such as peach, discolor quickly, so the sauce should be served immediately.

SAVORY SABAYON

This sauce is made in a similar manner as hollandaise, by whisking egg yolks and well reduced fish or veal stock over the heat to form a mousse. The sauce is occasionally mounted with butter.

CUSTARDS

Standard proportions for custard sauce are five egg yolks per two cups of milk. However, more yolks can be added for richness. Classically, no starch is used, although the addition of cornstarch is an economical way to get a thicker sauce.

With the starch, fewer eggs are needed and the custard is less likely to curdle. There are variations of this sauce, but remember that an acid ingredient, such as orange juice, will curdle the milk.

After the initial whisking to thicken the egg yolks and sugar slightly, the sauce should be stirred over the heat with a wooden spoon or spatula. It should cook to a creamy, not frothy, consistency. Gentle cooking is vital and some cooks prefer to use a double boiler.

If the sauce curdles, strain it into a cold bowl. Working the sauce in a blender helps to re-emulsify, but cannot save an overworked sauce. This sauce can be stored under refrigeration for up to two days.

CONCLUSION

This discussion of sauces is by no means comprehensive. We have touched on the basic principles of what constitutes a sauce and methods for preparing sauces of various types. Left for your future study are the innovations occurring in the area of thickeners and flavor combinations.

The use of modified starches in the preparation of a quick demi-glace, as mentioned in this chapter, is an example of the manner in which sauces can be prepared with less fat content and yet be full-bodied and flavorful. Utilization of pureed vegetables and fruits to thicken sauces is an area that has barely begun to be explored in full. You will find that by using the traditional preparation methods as guides and not laws written in stone, that the possibilities for creating interesting, flavorful and healthy sauces are unlimited.

The function of the sauce is to add compatible flavor to an item. This basic rule allows for a great deal of latitude in the development of sauces. Put to work the basic information provided here and begin to create your own sauces, always remembering that the sauce's purpose is to enhance, not mask, the flavor of the item.

REVIEW QUESTIONS

1. Discuss the function of a sauce.
2. List the four essentials of a good sauce.
3. List the three components of a sauce.
4. What type of liquids are used in sauces?
5. Define *roux* and discuss the various types.
6. Discuss the cooking of a roux.
7. Discuss how a roux is used.
8. List and discuss other starches used in sauce preparation.
9. Define *liaison finale* and list three types with definitions of each.
10. Discuss the use of seasonings in sauces.
11. What is the importance of reduction in the preparation of sauces?
12. List and discuss the five physical properties of a sauce.
13. What is *depouillage*?
14. List the four mother sauces and discuss each.
15. What is *jus de veau lie*?
16. What is the difference between a rich and lean velouté? Bechamel sauce?
17. Define *grand jus lie*.
18. Define *compound sauce*.
19. What is a reduction sauce? Discuss the different types.
20. List three types of emulsion sauces and discuss the preparation of each.
21. Define and discuss compound butter, shellfish sauce and gravy.

Chapter 17

CHAPTER OBJECTIVES

• **Discuss the history of meats.**

• **Discuss the physical and chemical composition of meat.**

• **Introduce the factors considered in meat selection.**

• **Discuss the basic cuts of beef, veal, pork and lamb.**

• **Introduce guidelines for the storage of fresh and frozen meats.**

• **Discuss methods of tenderizing meat.**

• **Discuss cooking meat.**

• **Discuss carving meat.**

Meats
Beef, Veal, Lamb & Pork

This chapter is concerned with those meats which are from livestock, these being farm animals kept for use and profit. These meats are derived from three species of animals: Bovine (ox or cow), ovine (sheep) and porcine (swine).

These animals are all inherently different in shape, size and, ultimately, taste. However, they do share a wide variety of common characteristics. We will discuss both the differences and similarities of the various animals as we progress in this chapter. First we will begin with a short history of each as a food source.

For lamb, pork and beef (as well as veal), ease of domestication was a major factor in their development as a primary food source. The fact that these animals could be readily caught, confined, and bred for use as a food made them a ready source of supply.

HISTORY OF MEATS

BEEF

The beef consumed in the United States today comes from domesticated cattle which have developed over thousands of years. Their ancestors were wild aurochs, Bos Primigenius. These were first domesticated in Anatolia and Greece in about 6,000 B.C. Cattle were introduced to the West Indies when Columbus brought them with him on his second voyage to the new world. Soon after they were also brought to the region of Florida by the Spanish.

From the earliest times, the preparation of beef called for the use of the finest spices and aromatics. The Greeks and Romans prepared beef dishes with an abundance of pepper and other spices. This was not because the meat was less than fresh or lacked flavor. The elaborate preparation was because the valuable beef was felt to warrant the use of the equally costly and precious spices. These fine ingredients were used for special occasions and were a sign of the wealth of the household.

In Europe, beef has always been available in less quantity than other meats. During the middle ages, the fare of the common man was salt pork and mutton. Beef was a food of the very wealthy. Farmers in Britain maintained herds of cattle, as well as sheep; yet, the only slaughtering took place at the beginning of winter, when grazing ended. The meat, both beef and mutton, was eaten fresh. Meat which could not be eaten at slaughtering time was salted for use in the following months.

"Turnip Townsend" was partially responsible for beef becoming more readily available in England and, later, in Europe. Lord Townsend conducted a unique experiment which showed that livestock could be kept alive during the winter by being fed turnips. These efforts later inspired Robert Bakewell to become England's first commercial stockbreeder. Bakewell saw the need for a hardier, heavier breed of cattle, which would be more productive.

This interest in the raising and breeding of livestock, along with the English people's natural liking of beef, gained for them a reputation as a nation of beefeaters by the 18th century. It was in London that a truly revolutionary culinary turn was taken. The cooking of massive roasts on spits before an open fire was challenged by a new idea, the refinement of butchering beef by the cutting of steaks.

"Beefsteak" became so popular that clubs were formed to "study beef under the most favorable circumstances." The "SUBLIME SOCIETY OF BEEFSTEAKS" was established in Covent Garden in 1735. Their motto was "BEEF AND LIBERTY" and their symbol a gridiron upon which steaks were broiled.

In France, the "bifteck" was noted by the epicure Brillat-Savarin. Steaks were implemented in grand cuisine during the "belle epoque" at the end of the 19th century. A chef de cuisine dedicated a recipe for strips of filet to Count Stroganoff. Rossini, the composer, was honored by the Cafe Anglais with tournedos Rossini, filet mignon served with a truffle and sauce Madeira.

The popularity of beef has continued to grow in England and Europe. It is in America, however, that it has gained the greatest stature. America, where the hearty breeds brought by the Spanish Conquistadors to Texas and Florida readily adapted to the buffalo grass and expanse of grazing land. These earlier cattle, later to become known as the Texas longhorn, were eventually bred to the more refined herefords brought from England, forming the basis of the infant American cattle industry.

By the middle of the 19th century, Americans were already becoming beefeaters. The steak was quickly accepted as a preferred presentation. One cut was named for the establishments where it was commonly served, the coach stops known as "Porterhouses."

Many beef dishes served in America are descendents of much earlier preparations. The method for preparing corned beef developed in England and was brought to the Americas by early settlers. Meat pies of the English settlers made good use of leftover roasts and were easily baked in large outdoor ovens. Pot roast was named for the vessel in which it was cooked, the Dutch oven of the early New Englanders, or the estouffade of the French immigrants. Even that all-American favorite, the hamburger, is a 20th century update of the minced beef eaten by the colonists.

VEAL

Veal is the meat of dairy calves, usually slaughtered at three months of age. It is a meat of great delicacy, light pink in color, soft in texture, and mild of flavor as a result of being fed only milk. Veal has always been a sought after meat in France and Italy. In these countries, as in the United States today, calves were raised strictly on milk for the sole purpose of producing veal.

Norman invaders of England brought with them a love of veal. The Norman chefs prepared "blancmange," veal cooked with milk and almonds, and taught the English to prepare "veal bukkenade," veal cooked with eggs, milk and spices, a medieval version of "veal blanquette."

The popularity of veal in medieval France can be attributed to the influence of the Italian chefs brought by Catherine de Medici to the court of King Henry II of France when they were married. The scallop cut of veal was first introduced to Italy in the city of Milan. During the 16th century the city was part of the Spanish Empire and the Spanish conquerors brought their love for this cut of veal with them. It is thought that "scallopini Milanese" was named for the scallop shell, which was the emblem of Spain's patron saint, St. James. It was a tribute to the scallop bearers, the troops of Charles V.

The scallopini later was given another name, again as a result of a military conquest. When Milan was captured by the Austrian soldiers of Marshal Radetsky, he brought the scallopini back to Austria with him. It was introduced to the Imperial kitchens of Emperor Franz Joseph in Vienna where it became the famed "weiner schnitzel."

LAMB

The ancestry of domesticated sheep and goats goes back farther than that of cattle and pigs. The earliest evidence of domesticating animals is placed at around 9,000 B.C. in Northern Iraq. The long-haired mouflon sheep, Ovis Orientalis, were kept for their fleece and meat. At about this same time the bezoar goat, Capra Hircus Aegarus, whose remains have been found at Jericho, was also being domesticated. The bezoar still can be found in southwest Asia, and a small number of mouflon sheep remain in Corsica and Sardinia.

The merino and drente of Holland, and Britain's Norfolk blackface are direct descendents of these ancient breeds. The long hair of the original breeds has been replaced in modern sheep and goats through selective breeding. Today the animals have woolly fleece. Modern breeders are concentrating on a nearly naked, but very virile breed, the Wiltshire horn ram. This animal is fat and meaty. It is used on a broad basis for crossbreeding.

Sheep are valued for far more than just their meat. Like cattle, they yield both meat and milk. Although the milk of the sheep and goat is not very popular in the United States, it is the primary milk source in many parts of the world. Of as great or greater importance than the meat of the sheep is its wool. However, those animals raised for their wool are not normally raised for slaughter. They will be eventually, but that is not their primary purpose.

The preferred meat from the sheep is termed *lamb*. This must come from sheep under one year old, which are termed *lambs*. The animal over a year old is is termed *mutton*. The lamb carcass yields smaller, more tender cuts of meat. Mutton is a fatter, stronger tasting meat. The large majority of Americans who eat the meat of sheep prefer the milder, more tender flavor of lamb over mutton.

Domestic lamb is best when it is five to seven months old. This type is often called spring, summer or early lamb. In the past, mutton was more popular than lamb because of the larger size roasts. For centuries, all over Europe, people had been used to large cuts of meat roasting before an open fire. At the time, many courses were served together and a large roast was less likely to cool quickly on the table. Lamb was a seasonal luxury. Over the decades mutton came to be associated with poverty. It was considered to be the food of the poor. This was a foolish association, since the poor could not even afford meat on a regular basis and ate mostly bread, cheese, root vegetables, turnips and potatoes, with broth, salt pork or bacon being a luxury.

In America, lamb and mutton never became widely popular. Possibly this was because of its association with the poor, but more likely it was because of the readily available supplies of beef and pork. The consumption of lamb in the United States for many decades was limited to dishes such as Irish stew, crown roast, lamb chops with mint jelly and the traditional leg of spring lamb at Easter time.

Times are changing and so is the American taste. The use of lamb in the American kitchen is growing. Foreign influences, such as the recent popularity of kabobs and Shaslik from the middle east, are part of the reason. The primary reason is the refinement of the breeds of sheep and of the processing methods. The lamb available in America today is said by some to have less flavor because of the efforts made at improving productivity. The fact remains that the flesh is of superior eating quality when compared to the previous lambs processed. Lamb is also becoming a more affordable meat as production increases and, with the influx of large quantities of lamb from New Zealand, competition increases. It is a type of meat which the culinarian will need to continue learning about as it evolves in the future.

PORK

Pork was probably first roasted and eaten by the Chinese. Excavation of Neolithic sites in China have unearthed evidence that pigs were the only domesticated animal and were used for food. It was from Asia that Sus Scrofa Vittatus, a more easily handled and cross-bred type of pig, was introduced to Europe and America in the 18th century. It is from this breed of pigs that most of the modern breeds originated.

Controversy is ever present when pork is discussed as a food source. This is a result of its religious significance. In certain religions pork is taboo as food. The reason for this is widely argued and no single answer has been formulated. One theory suggests that pork has similarities to human flesh, cannibals having sometimes referred to man as "long pig." Another theory is that because the pig is subject to some of the same diseases as man, it may be perceived as an unclean animal. Possibly the taboo developed in religious observations for reasons of sanitation and health. Whatever the reason, the taboos still exist today and will affect your culinary preparations according to the guests you serve.

The taboo against pork is by no means universal. It is considered by many nations and peoples to be a prime, tender meat. Its history has long been one of providing food for both the rich and poor. For centuries the European peasantry depended on a limited supply of fresh pigs and a slightly larger supply of salt or pickled pork for their meat. The navies of the world rationed salt pork to their seamen. The rich often viewed pork as food for the poor, particular the salted and pickled versions. Salt pork was a staple of the settlers moving west across America in wagon trains.

The hearty, resilient, adaptable pig was part of every homestead in the settling of America. They readily adapted to the various climates and vegetation. The hearty pig was a primary meat in the American diet long before the beef cattle had really been developed. This hearty animal was turned loose in the woods to forage for itself and then, when slaughtered, was used to the last ounce, including the head, entrails and feet.

The pork eaten in America today does not have the same flavor or texture as that of the early settlers. The pig will eat almost anything; however, today the diet of this omnivorous and greedy animal is controlled by the farmer. They are fed specially developed feeds designed to give the animal the right balance of fatty tissue, muscle and bone. Their diet includes grasses and various cereals which provide the necessary balance of protein, minerals and vitamins. Though lacking some in natural flavor, the flesh of the pig today is more tender and less fatty. Its history and the improvements in breeding and feeds have made pork the second most popular meat in the United States.

COMPOSITION

The composition of meat, whether from beef, veal, calf, sheep, lamb or swine, has both physical and chemical characteristics. The physical characteristics are: Muscle tissue and fibrous connective tissue; adipose tissue (commonly termed *fat*), and bone (skeletal) tissue. The chemical characteristics consist of water, protein, fats, carbohydrates, minerals and vitamins.

PHYSICAL COMPOSITION

The physical make-up of the meat is composed of items which can be physically separated when the carcass is cut.

Yet each of these plays a role in the flavor and texture of the cooked meat.

MUSCLE

The muscle of the animal is divided into three types: Skeletal, cardiac and smooth (also termed visceral muscle). Of these types, it is the skeletal muscle which makes up the majority of muscle weight on the carcass. Skeletal muscle is muscle tissue which is attached directly or indirectly to bone. It gives support to the skeleton and assists in movement.

The cardiac muscle, as its name implies, is what forms the animal's heart. This muscle differs in composition from skeletal muscle. The smooth muscle is found in the stomach, reproductive organs and circulatory system of the animal.

Since it is the skeletal muscle which is the major type, it is of the greatest concern to the culinarian. The muscles are intertwined with fibrous connective tissue (this is referred to as the muscle sheath) and fat. How these bundles of muscle and tissue are used by the animal will determine how tender they are when prepared.

Coarse, long muscle fibers yield a less tender meat. The thinner, smaller muscle fibers are more tender. Muscles located along the shoulders and legs, which are used for movement, will have more connective tissues and are less tender. The muscles in the back are for support and move less. They will yield a more tender meat.

ADIPOSE TISSUE

Adipose is commonly termed *fat*. It is known that as the animal ages the concentration of the fat increases if the animal is well fed. The amount of fat in the carcass is affected by the feeding and handling of the animal and by genetics.

When the animal first begins to gain fat it is deposited internally around the organs of the body and in the pelvic area. As the animal continues to age, fat is deposited externally, just under the skin. This is often called FINISH. Additional fat begins to be deposited between the muscles (seam fat) and within the muscle (marbling). The marbling of the carcass in the ribeye is used as one of the factors in grading beef.

Marbling, the fat contained within the muscle, is a factor in the preparation of meat. It has a large effect on the JUICINESS, FLAVOR and, to a lesser extent, TENDERNESS of prepared meats. This type of fat lies between the muscle fibers. Well marbled beef generally tastes better and is usually more tender than beef with little marbling.

The juiciness of the meat may also be affected by the SURFACE FAT on a particular cut of meat. Surface fat protects large roasts and other cuts from drying out, particularly during roasting. Barding and larding are two methods of providing the additional fat needed to prevent excessive drying in lean pieces of meat; however these can add significantly to the calories in a serving of meat. These are discussed later in this chapter.

It should be noted that the types of fats contained in meat are a topic of great discussion. The focus of many of these discussions are the nutritional aspects of the fats. As a culinarian you need to realize that all types of meat, in moderation, can certainly be a portion of a healthy diet. Selection of meats according to fat content may be a method of attracting customers concerned about their fat intake. The lower the grade of meat, the more skill needed for satisfactory preparation since fat content influences juiciness, tenderness and flavor; however, less fat also translates into fewer calories in the final product.

BONE AND SKELETAL TISSUE

Skeletal tissue consists of the ligaments, tendons, cartilage and bone of the animal. The skeletal tissue of the animal which forms bones is termed as being *ossified*. This means it has become bone. The cartilage within the animal

also ossifies as the animal matures. It is this process of bone formation which is used as another factor in grading veal, calf, beef, lamb and mutton carcasses.

It should be remembered that, although ossified (changed into bone), the bone is still living tissue. It is the tissue of the bone which yields many of the nutrients and minerals of the carcass, but are less often consumed, unless extracted in stock. Ligaments, tendons and cartilage yield little or no food energy, (calories). The bone of the animal can supply certain minerals (especially calcium and phosphorous) if extracted correctly, as in stock. The bones used to make stock yield food energy from the fat contained in the bone marrow.

CHEMICAL COMPOSITION

WATER

Water content of the muscle tissue of the animal affects flavor, color and texture of the meat. There is a wide variance between the amount contained in animals of different ages. The muscle of veal may contain as much as 72 percent, while that of mature beef contains as little as 45 percent. How the meat is handled can affect the amount of water it retains. Grinding, chopping, cutting and exposure to heat, salt or acidity can all change the moisture content of the meat.

PROTEIN

The proteins contained in the meat have a major effect on the final product prepared from the meat. These proteins are generally grouped into three classes: Myofibrillar, stromal and sarcoplasmic. Each of these groups performs a different function within the meat.

MYOFIBRILLAR PROTEINS make up the majority of the actual muscle fibers and affect the muscles' ability to relax and contract. The handling of the meat during and after slaughter will affect the action of this group of proteins. If the muscles are contracted when the meat is prepared, it will be less tender.

STROMAL PROTEINS make up the connective tissue in the muscle of the animal. There are three types within meat: Collagen, elastin and reticulin. Of these, the reticulin is of the least concern to the culinarian in preparation. This type of stromal protein is present in much smaller amounts and is most commonly found in younger animals. It is thought that reticulin may be a precursor to either collagen or elastin.

Collagen is the protein found in greatest quantity in the animal, composing up to 20 to 25 percent of the animal's total protein. The primary function of collagen in the animal is to provide strength and support. It helps to form the skin of the animal. Collagen plays a part in the tenderness of the meat. It is readily broken down in cooking with moist heat. This white, thin, semitransparent protein contracts and softens into a mass during cooking. This provides the cooked meat with a plump appearance. The tough collagen is converted to tender gelatin when processed at the proper temperature.

Elastin, the stromal protein found in the circulatory system and connective tissue of the animal, provides elasticity. This protein does not break down when exposed to moist heat. Often referred to as the "yellow" connective tissue, elastin must be removed in the cutting of the meat. This protein also increases in the carcass as the age of the animal increases.

SARCOPLASMIC PROTEINS provide the pigmentation (color) for the flesh of the animal, primarily in the form of MYO-GLOBIN. It is the amount of myoglobin present and the amount of exposure to oxygen that induces the bright red color of the meat when butchered.

Sarcoplasmic proteins also include specific ENZYMES present in the muscle. These are naturally occurring enzymes which continue to function after the animal is slaughtered. During the aging process it is proteolytic proteins (enzymes) which degrade the myofib-rillar protein. Remember that this is the protein which contracts in post-mortem rigor mortis, toughening the meat. The longer the meat is held at the proper temperature for the enzymes to do their work, the more tender the meat will become.

NITROGENOUS EXTRACTIVES are related to the proteins in the meat, but are not true proteins. These substances are water-soluble and some increase the flow of gastric juices when a cooked meat is eaten. Found in greater amounts in the muscle of older animals, and those muscles which are more active, these substances are the major source of flavor and aroma .

Overall, proteins from animal sources are utilized the most efficiently by the human body. Protein from meat is digested 80 to 90 percent. Plant protein (such as beans and rice, or lentils and corn combinations) is only digested at a rate of 50 to 60 percent. All essential amino acids necessary for the growth and maintenance of the human body are contained in the correct combination in all animal proteins.

FAT

Fat contributes to the flavor of prepared meat. For example, in smoked meat, it is the fat which absorbs much of the smoked flavor. There are also many fat-soluble flavor compounds which add to our enjoyment of eating meat, such as garlic. The cooking method used to prepare meat, as well as the mouth feel and tenderness of the prepared meat are all affected by the fat content of the meat.

The fats in the animal's body vary from soft to solid. This variation is related to the species of the animal and to the placement of the fat in the body of the animal. The fat located closer to the skin will normally be soft and more unsaturated. The fat in the more external parts of the body must act as an insulator. This is better accomplished by the softer fat. Those fats surrounding the vital organs

Figure 1

in the body are harder and more saturated. Fat deposited within the muscles (marbling) is less saturated.

Although location of the fat in the carcass is important in the type of fat, species plays an even greater role. The fat of the lamb is generally more saturated and more solid. The fat of the pig is generally softer and more unsaturated. The firmness of beef fat falls between lamb and pork. Both saturated and unsaturated fats yield nine calories per one gram of fat, while protein and carbohydrates yield four calories per one gram.

CARBOHYDRATES, MINERALS AND VITAMINS

Meats are not normally considered as a source of carbohydrates. However, carbohydrates are present in the live animal. These are in the form of glycogen (a storage form of carbohydrates) in the liver and muscles, as well as glucose in the muscles and blood. The primary importance of these carbohydrates is their effect on the meat during the aging process. Through a very complex series of changes the carbohydrates lower the pH of the muscles, a result of increased muscle acidity. The color, texture, tenderness and water-holding capacity of the muscle is affected by the acidity level of the muscle.

The vigorous stress or exercise of the animal before slaughter can lower the glycogen level. This makes less carbohydrates available for lowering the pH and results in dark, firm, dry muscle. When the drop in pH occurs too rapidly after slaughter, the meat may be pale and soft. The effect of reactions on muscle color can affect the grading process for the carcass.

Minerals and vitamins in the meat, not just protein and fat, are significant to the human diet. Iron and zinc, plus the majority of the vitamin B-complex are present in meat.

Besides supplying essential protein and calories from fat and protein, meat supplies a nutrient-rich source of zinc, iron, calcium (all essential minerals) and B vitamins, including B_{12}. Vitamin B_{12} can only be obtained from animal sources or vitamin supplements. Obtaining nutrients from the diet is always more desirable.

SELECTION

The variety of factors that must be considered when selecting cattle on the hoof, after slaughter or after butchering can be confusing. The culinarian is not usually an expert on the characteristics of cattle, veal, lamb or pigs. However, you do need to understand how the quality of the animal is determined. It is this information that will allow you to make an intelligent decision when buying.

It is true that the breeding, feeding and raising of domestic animals has greatly improved in just the last twenty years. However, even with all the improvements, all animals are not created equal. For this reason, the United States Department of Agriculture (USDA), by authority of the Meat Inspection Act of 1906, Poultry Product Inspection Act of 1957 and other new and revised acts, has developed a broad array of regulations and guidelines relating to the processing of meat. These fall into two categories, the first being inspection and the second grading. The aging and packing of the meat are also important factors for consideration in the selection process.

INSPECTION

Inspection of animals and carcasses by the USDA is often confused with grading. The two are not the same. Inspection guarantees the wholesomeness and accurate labeling of products. This does not determine the quality or yield rating of the carcass.

Wholesomeness is a term often used in discussion of food, both fresh and processed. The basic definition of this word from a legal standpoint, is the

Figure 1

determination of whether or not a food item is fit for human consumption. This does not mean that it is of high or low quality, just that it can be consumed by a human being without making them ill (assuming proper handling and preparation prior to consumption).

Federal regulation requires the inspection of all meats. The inspection of the meat is indicated on the carcass by a round stamp. The stamp is shown in Figure One. Some states also have Federally sanctioned state meat inspection programs with requirements equal to the USDA standards. You should never accept meat into your facility without evidence (usually the inspection stamp on the box) that the meat has been inspected.

GRADING

Grading of meat is divided into two types: Quality and yield. Quality of the carcass indicates the eating characteristics of the meat from the carcass. Yield grading is the determination of the quantity of usable meat that the carcass will yield. It is possible to have a meat carcass which has very high yield (very lean) yet is of low quality or one that is high quality but low yield (very fat).

QUALITY GRADING
BEEF

Quality grading is based on a variety of factors. The texture, firmness and color of the lean meat on the carcass are judged. Also the maturity (age of the animal from which the carcass comes) and marbling are considered. Grading is not required by law. There are packers who use private grading systems. These packers often give their own brand names to different grades. An example of this is "Certified Angus."

The grades of beef are PRIME, CHOICE, SELECT, STANDARD, COMMERCIAL, UTILITY, CUTTER and CANNER. Cattle on the hoof are graded based on the conformation (shape) of the body.

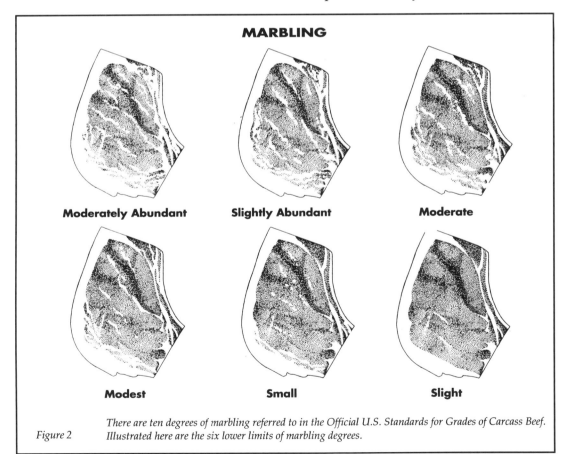

MARBLING

Moderately Abundant	**Slightly Abundant**	**Moderate**
Modest	**Small**	**Slight**

Figure 2   *There are ten degrees of marbling referred to in the Official U.S. Standards for Grades of Carcass Beef. Illustrated here are the six lower limits of marbling degrees.*

Marbling is very important in the quality grading of beef. There are ten degrees of marbling used in the grading process, but six are the most common. Figure Two shows the degree of marbling termed moderately abundant, slightly abundant, moderate, modest, small and slight. Remembering the effect that marbling has on the juiciness, tenderness and flavor of the cooked meat, you can see the difference in the quality of these cuts of meat.

VEAL

Veal carcasses are quality graded, with the grades being: PRIME, CHOICE, GOOD, STANDARD, UTILITY and CULL. The quality of lean veal is not based on marbling as it is for beef. The grade is determined by the quantity of feathering and flank streaking. This is the fat interspersed in the lean meat between the ribs of the carcass and in the flank area. The amount of fat present within and inside of the flank is a factor. The color of the meat is also a factor. These factors combined with the overall conformation of the animal on the hoof determine the grade.

PORK

Pork uses a grading system based on yield only. The four grades are U.S. Nos. 1 through 4. They are graded based on cutability while the quality of the meat is evaluated separately.

LAMB

Lamb has quality grades of PRIME, CHOICE, GOOD, UTILITY and CULL. The major factor in the quality grading of lamb and mutton carcasses is maturity (age). There are three maturity categories, LAMB, YEARLING MUTTON and MUTTON. Each type of carcass is evaluated for color, texture and flank streaking. Increased fat deposits and a bright pink color to the meat are indicators of high quality lamb. Mutton has a coarser texture and is dark red.

YIELD GRADING

Yield grading is the determination by the grader of the difference in the cutability of the carcass. Cutability is the quantity of saleable meat the carcass will yield as either boneless or semi-boneless retail cuts. This grade is based on external and internal fat and the size of the ribeye area (REA) in comparison to the carcass weight.

The yield grades are USDA 1 through 5 with USDA 1 having the most saleable meat. Veal is not graded for yield. Pork is graded for yield only. Beef and lamb are both yield graded on the scale of one to five.

Fatness of the carcass (that which must be trimmed in the preparation of retail cuts) has the greatest affect on yield grades. A high yield grade (5 or 4) carcass will yield a greater quantity of fat and a lower quantity of lean meat. The REA of the beef carcass, which is measured at the 12th rib, is considered an indicator of the overall muscularity of the carcass. A carcass with a higher ratio of muscle to bone and fat in the REA will receive a lower yield grade number (1 or 2).

Yield grades are extremely important when purchasing sides of beef or primal cuts. The purchase of other food service cuts will not normally require the buyer to consider yield grade; however, all consumers indirectly pay for cutting loses resulting from poor carcass yield.

AGING

The aging of the beef carcass is necessary for the development of tenderness. Very soon after the animal is slaughtered rigor mortis, a stiffening of muscle tissue, occurs. This condition normally disappears gradually within a period of seven to ten days in larger beef carcasses.

Enzymes within the muscles work on the connective tissue in the muscles even after slaughter. It is the action of these enzymes which reduce the stiffness caused by rigor mortis. In the process of tenderizing the meat, the enzymes also develop the flavor of the meat.

The dry aging process is possible for beef only when the carcass has a fat cover. This cover protects the carcass from drying and buildups of high levels of bacteria during the aging period. Since veal is young at slaughter it is not aged. Pork also does not require aging.

The aging process has developed over the centuries as understanding has developed of the process. The two types of aging currently in use are DRY AGING and VACUUM-PACK AGING.

Dry aging is based on the control of the flow of air around the carcasses and the temperature and humidity of the environment. This type of aging is done in specially designed aging coolers where these factors can be strictly controlled. These controls prevent excessive, unacceptable levels of bacteria growth on the carcass. They also minimize moisture loss from the meat. Dry aging is an expensive process due to storage costs and weight loss due to drying and extra trimming. However, the flavor developed in this process is thought by some to be superior.

Vacuum-pack aging is an accepted method of aging beef. The meat is sealed in a vacuum in air and moisture proof plastic bags. This process removes the air from the meat's package protecting it from air and bacteria. This process not only extends the shelf life of the cut meat, but prevents weight loss due to moisture loss. Vacuum-pack aged meats often have a musty odor when first opened, but this quickly disappears as they are exposed to air. This process does not develop the flavor that dry aging does; however, it is less expensive, and is a good compromise for most food service operations.

Although the enzymes in the meat degrade the protein during aging, when the environment and time period for aging are properly controlled, the meat is not spoiled. IF MEAT SMELLS OR TASTES SPOILED, IT IS. PROPERLY AGED MEAT DOES NOT HAVE AN OFF-TASTE, JUST AN INCREASE IN TENDERNESS AND FLAVOR.

BASIC CUTS OF MEAT

The meat processors who supply food service establishments generally follow the exact cutting specifications and labeling called for by the INSTITUTIONAL MEAT PURCHASERS SPECIFICATIONS (IMPS). These specifications state the manner of the cut and its name, and also assign the cut a number. The IMPS number greatly simplifies the purchasing process. When used, it tells the meat purveyor exactly what you expect to receive. The National Association of Meat Purveyors also uses the same specifications, and assigns NAMP numbers in the "Meat Buyers Guide." These standards are based on a consideration of the bone and muscle configuration of the carcass in relation to the best utilization and preparation methods for each cut. IMPS and NAMP have helped to standardize meat cutting for the food service industry in the United States.

Meats are available in a variety of different forms. These include: WHOLE CARCASSES, PARTIAL CARCASSES, PRIMALS, SUB-PRIMALS and FABRICATED CUTS. Beef, lamb, veal and pork may be purchased in some or all of these forms.

WHOLE CARCASS

A whole carcass, with the exception of that of a hog, is the whole animal, without entrails, head, feet and hide. The carcass of a hog has only the entrails, hair and head removed. A whole carcass is difficult to handle, requiring special skill and equipment, as well as labor. In light of the handling problems and the fact that there are few operations which can utilize the whole carcass fully, few food service operations purchase whole carcasses.

PARTIAL CARCASS

This form of meat is more commonly referred to as SIDES, QUARTERS, FORESADDLES and HINDSADDLES. These designations represent the first step in breaking down a carcass. Although these larger cuts are no longer frequently used in food service, there are still establishments that do cut their own meat from these partial carcasses.

SIDES AND QUARTERS - BEEF IS SPLIT THROUGH THE BACKBONE INTO SIDES. THE SIDES ARE THEN DIVIDED BETWEEN THE 12TH AND 13TH RIBS INTO A FOREQUARTER AND HINDQUARTER.

FORESADDLE AND HINDSADDLE - VEAL AND LAMB ARE NOT SPLIT INTO SIDES, BUT ARE DIVIDED BETWEEN THE 12TH AND 13TH RIBS INTO THE FORESADDLE AND HINDSADDLE.

It should be noted, pork carcasses are not divided in this manner. They are cut directly into primal cuts.

PRIMAL or WHOLESALE CUTS

Primal cuts break the carcass into pieces of a more manageable size. They are small enough to be used in most food service kitchens, yet large enough to be cut into a variety of cuts for different uses. The primal cuts are better suited for total utilization in the food service kitchen. The starting point for small cuts is always the primal cut. You need to be able to identify each primal cut and the most important cuts that come from it. The cuts discussed in this chapter are designated by NAMP name and number.

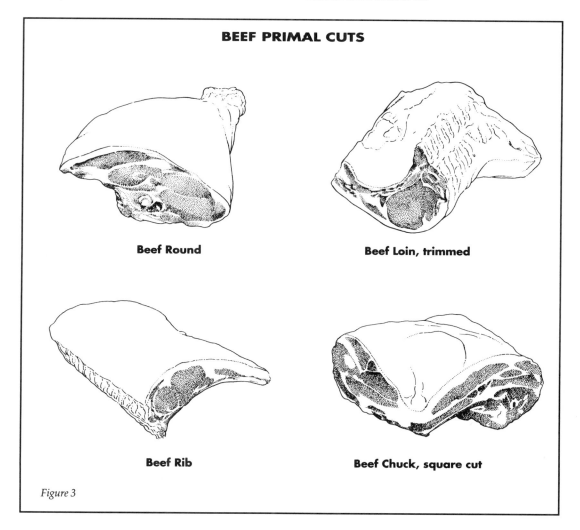

BEEF PRIMAL CUTS

Beef Round

Beef Loin, trimmed

Beef Rib

Beef Chuck, square cut

Figure 3

BEEF CUTS

The most versatile of all meats, beef, offers the greatest variety and challenge to the chef. More than any other meat, the quality varies with age, breed and feed. Most of the beef we use comes from steers, the young castrated males that have been fattened for the table. Steers are slaughtered at about 18 months of age. The carcass weight is 500 to 600 pounds at this age.

The breed of cattle affects both the size of the carcass and the meat itself, in fatness or leanness, and coarseness or fine grain. The one constant is that no matter what the feed or breed of the steer, the least expensive cuts are those which are tougher.

With all animals, the tougher cuts are those from the parts of the animal which moved the most. These include the lower leg (shanks), shoulder, flanks, neck and tail. The most expensive cuts of the steer will come from the parts which moved the least. These most tender and best parts are from the hindquarter and the ribs in the forequarter.

A beef carcass is split into four quarters, with a side of beef being the matched fore and hind quarter of the carcass. The primal cuts from the beef carcass are shown in Figure Three. The primal cuts of beef can be broken into a variety of food service cuts.

PRIMAL BEEF ROUND

The PRIMAL BEEF ROUND (#158) has the rump and shank on. This is the hind leg of the steer, an excellent source of lean meat. It contains little bone and connective tissue. The round is cut from the hindquarter. It is separated from the untrimmed loin and flank on a straight line starting at a point on the backbone, which is the junction of the last sacral vertebra and the first caudal vertebra,

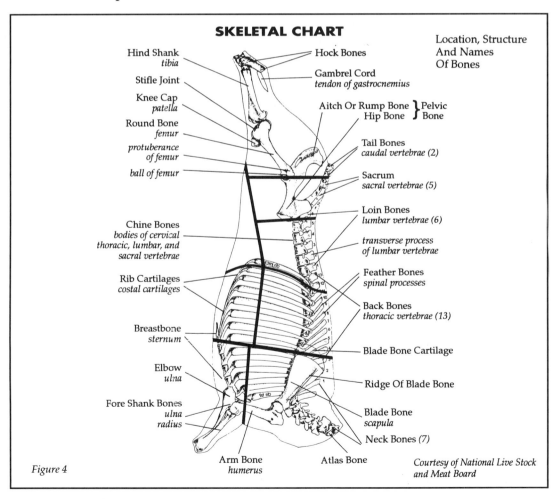

SKELETAL CHART

Location, Structure And Names Of Bones

Hind Shank
tibia

Hock Bones

Gambrel Cord
tendon of gastrocnemius

Stifle Joint

Knee Cap
patella

Aitch Or Rump Bone } Pelvic
Hip Bone } Bone

Round Bone
femur

protuberance of femur

Tail Bones
caudal vertebrae (2)

ball of femur

Sacrum
sacral vertebrae (5)

Loin Bones
lumbar vertebrae (6)

Chine Bones
bodies of cervical thoracic, lumbar, and sacral vertebrae

transverse process of lumbar vertebrae

Feather Bones
spinal processes

Rib Cartilages
costal cartilages

Back Bones
thoracic vertebrae (13)

Breastbone
sternum

Blade Bone Cartilage

Elbow
ulna

Ridge Of Blade Bone

Fore Shank Bones
ulna
radius

Blade Bone
scapula

Neck Bones (7)

Figure 4

Arm Bone
humerus

Atlas Bone

Courtesy of National Live Stock and Meat Board

247

passing through a second point, which is immediately anterior to the protuberance of the femur bone. This exposes the ball of the femur bone. The cut then continues along the same straight line across the leg. This will become clearer when you refer to the skeletal chart in Figure Four. The BEEF ROUND with the rump and shank off (#164) is often roasted and then carved for large parties.

The primal round can be divided into other food service cuts. The smaller cuts from the round can be roasted at higher temperatures, or marinated, possibly scored, and broiled as steaks. The other primary cuts are the TOP ROUND (#168 and #169), BOTTOM ROUND (#170 and #171) and KNUCKLE (#167).

TOP ROUND is the inside portion of the round. Because of its location, it is more tender than other parts of the round. This is the most expensive single cut from the round.

KNUCKLE is that portion of the round which is ventral to the round bone. The kneecap and the surrounding heavy connective tissue should be trimmed to achieve no less than 75 percent lean.

BOTTOM ROUND is comprised of the outside muscle, heel attached, of the round and the boneless rump intact in one piece. It must be trimmed reasonably free of heavy connective tissue and large exposed ligaments.

TRIMMED BEEF LOIN

A trimmed BEEF LOIN (#172) contains the short loin and sirloin (loin end) in one piece. This primal cut is divided into three major parts.

The SIRLOIN (#181) is the portion of sirloin on the loin end which remains after the removal of all bones and the butt end of the tenderloin. This cut yields the sirloin butt from which the top and bottom sirloin butt are prepared.

The SHORT LOIN (#173) is the anterior portion of the loin remaining after the removal of the sirloin on the loin end. This cut yields the STRIP LOIN (#175). It is from the short loin that PORTERHOUSE

(#1173), T-BONE (#1174) and STRIP LOIN STEAK (#1179) are prepared.

The FULL TENDERLOIN (#189) is removed from the full loin in one piece. It has to be trimmed so that the fat does not exceed 3/4 inch in thickness at the butt end and up to the point where the large lymph gland is exposed. It must be trimmed free of all ragged and thin edges.

PRIMAL BEEF RIB

PRIMAL BEEF RIB (#103) is the part of the forequarter remaining after the crosscut chuck and short plate are removed. This primal includes portions seven ribs, the sixth to twelfth, the section of the backbone attached to the ribs and the posterior tip of the blade bone. This primal is purchased in a variety of cuts including: Oven prepared regular rib; special roast ready rib, and ribeye roll.

The OVEN-PREPARED REGULAR RIB (#104) is that portion of a seven-rib bone which is made by a straight cut across the ribs starting at a fixed point determined by measuring off not more than four inches from the outer tip of the rib-eye muscle, at the twelfth rib and counting in a straight line through a fixed point determined by measuring off not more than eight inches from the outer tip of the rib-eye muscle at the sixth rib. The chine bone must be entirely removed and the blade bone and cartilage must be removed.

The SPECIAL ROAST READY RIB, TIED (#109A) may be roasted with or without bones. If boned, it has to be tied to retain its shape. The chine bone must be completely removed. Additionally the exterior fat layer is lifted, and the lean muscle with the blade bone is removed. When these parts have been removed, the fat covering must be returned to its natural position and held in place by loops of strong twine.

The RIB-EYE ROLL (#112) is the eye muscle of the rib. All other muscles and all bones, backstrap, the blade bone, related cartilage and outside fat covering must be removed and excluded. The rib-eye roast may be tied with twine or cut into rib-eye steaks. This cut is considered a juicy, but less expensive, steak because of its partially grainy structure.

SQUARE CUT CHUCK

SQUARE CUT CHUCK (#113) is the top shoulder of the forequarter. It is suitable for any kitchen, because it yields juicy, medium lean meat. The meat is suitable for stew meat, ground beef or pot roast.

SHOULDER CLOD (#114) is cut from the square cut chuck. It is the large outside muscle system posterior to the elbow joint. The shoulder clod includes, at the thicker end, all muscles which overlay the natural seam and, at the thinner end, all muscles above the posterior portion of the blade bone.

The BONELESS SQUARE CUT CHUCK (#115) may or may not include the clod. If it is to be used for stew meat, the clod is included. For use as pot roast, the clod is removed.

OTHER BEEF CUTS

SHANK is usually removed from the forequareter with the brisket and then separated from the brisket on its natural seam. Shank, boned, makes the best meat for consomme preparation. Some specialties, such as Hungarian goulash, are best prepared from the shank.

BRISKET (#118) is a partial flat piece, square in shape, usually removed from the forequarter with the shank. Inside fat from the heart must be excluded from the brisket. Additionally, the bones should be removed for any preparation.

SHORT PLATE (#121) is from the forequarter. It is the bottom of the rib cage from the sixth to the twelfth rib. Short ribs and skirt steak come from this cut.

FLANK STEAK (#193) is the flat, oval-shaped muscle embedded in the inside

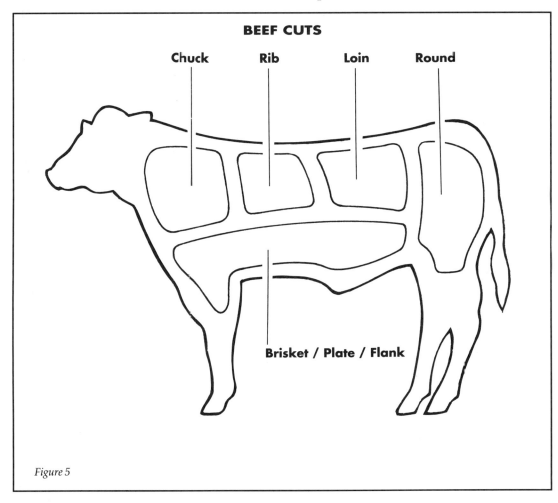

BEEF CUTS

Chuck   Rib   Loin   Round

Brisket / Plate / Flank

Figure 5

of the flank. It should be practically free of fat and membranous tissue.

These basic cuts are the beginning of your familiarity with beef. Space does not allow a complete listing here of all the available cuts. Figure Five shows some of the most common food service cuts. Some we have discussed, some we have not. You must continue to work to gain a full appreciation and understanding of this versatile meat.

VEAL CUTS

The quality of veal is judged, to a large extent, by its color. The lighter color of the meat, the greater the proportion of the calf's diet was milk and the more tender it will be. More mature veal is pink or rosey pink, with a creamy, white fat. Veal, having little internal fat, has a tendency to be dry. For this reason it is often braised, larded or cut thinly and sauteed.

Calf meat has gained recent popularity. This type of meat has a more reddish color as a result of the grass in its diet. The tenderness and delicate flavor of veal are sacrificed in this type of meat.

A veal carcass is divided into two portions, the FORESADDLE and HINDSADDLE. Veal carcasses range in weight from 60 to 175 pounds. They are divided into three weight ranges: 60-100 pounds, 101-140 pounds and 141-175 pounds. The 141-175 range veal is preferred, but often runs into problems by not being milk fed.

FORESADDLE

The foresaddle yields the SHOULDER (chuck); HOTEL RACK (rib), and BREAST/FORESHANK, primal cuts.

Shoulder

The shoulder portion of the foresaddle is designated the four-rib veal chuck after the removal of the hotel rack and breast. This cut is used to prepare the SQUARE CUT CHUCK (#309) by removing the foreshanks and brisket. In general, the shoulder cuts are not

very tender and should normally be cooked with moist heat.

The veal chuck yields the SHOULDER CLOD (#310), the large outside muscle lying above the rear edge of the shoulder blade. Dry heat cooking is possible for this cut, but larding or other added fat may be necessary. The majority of these pieces may be cut into roasts, chops, steaks and shoulder cutlets.

Rack

The SEVEN-RIB HOTEL RACK (#306) is usually cut into chops or scallops for sauteing or braising, but may be roasted whole as a crown roast. A Bracelet is also called a double rack. It is separated from the foresaddle by cutting between the fifth and sixth ribs so the sixth through 12th ribs remain in the hotel-rack.

A Hotel Rack is a trimmed double rack remaining after the breast portions have been removed. The breast must be removed from the racks on a straight line from the sixth rib to the twelfth rib, not more than four inches from the extreme outer tip of the ribeye. Split lengthwise, the hotel rack renders ribcutlets or a veal rack ribeye.

Breast/Foreshank

VEAL BREAST (#313) is the plate and skirt portion of the forequarter remaining in one piece after removing the foreshank. This portion yields riblets, stew meat and rolled breast. Braising and roasting are the best methods for cooking these veal cuts.

The FORESHANK is the foreleg portion of the chuck. It must be separated from the brisket by a cut following the natural seam. Shanks are best braised or cooked in liquid.

HINDSADDLE

The hindsaddle yields the VEAL LEG (#334) and VEAL LOIN (#331) primal cuts. This part of the veal carcass provides the majority of the better cuts.

Veal leg is that portion of the hindsaddle remaining after the removal of

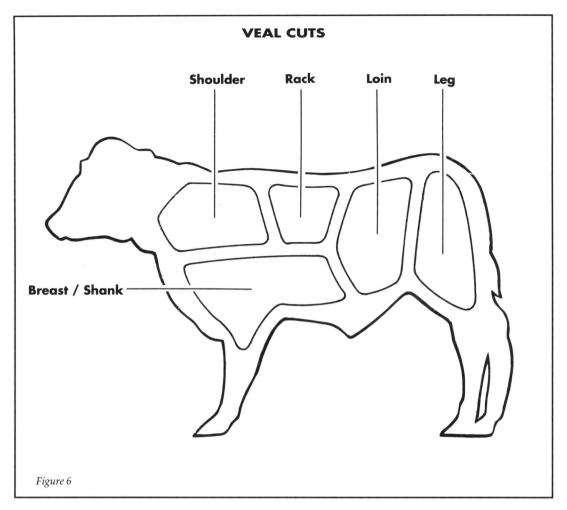

VEAL CUTS

Shoulder   Rack   Loin   Leg

Breast / Shank

Figure 6

the loin. The veal loin may be split. The legs, double, are split lengthwise, centrally through the spine. The next step is removal of the pelvic bone, back bones and tail bones. Then remove the shank and shankbone. The round bone, femur, is extracted by cutting between the inside and outside muscles in a straight line through the natural seam. This leaves the boneless leg intact in one piece. This is sold as BONELESS ROAST READY VEAL LEG (#335), or as TBS VEAL LEG (#348) which includes the top round, bottom round, knuckle and sirloin. The hindshank also comes from the leg. The boneless leg can be netted or tied and roasted whole.

The leg is usually divided into roasts with or without bone. The boned leg may be separated at the seams and joints to obtain: Top round; bottom round; knuckle; sirloin, and hindshank. These portions may also be roasted. The

leg may be processed further to prepare other items. To make veal cutlets, the individual pieces from the leg are used. For especially tender veal cutlet and scallopini, the tenderloin, top round or back muscle of the loins is preferred. These cuts are suitable for saute. Braising is the best cooking method for the hindshank and any of its smaller cuts.

VEAL LOIN (#331) (Double), is both loins remaining all in one piece as a pair after separating them from the hindsaddle. The cut is made at the anterior end of the hip bone, leaving all the hip bone in the leg. The tenderloin and kidney knob should remain in it.

TRIMMED VEAL LOIN (#332) is that portion of the loin left after the flank portions have been removed. Whether the kidney knob remains in the loin depends on the specifications of the buyer.

The loin yields the expensive chops that are used for braising or sauteing. It is also sold with the bone as a roast. The flank meat is usually cubed or ground. The trimmed loin can be split to cut loin chops.

PORK CUTS

The majority of the pork sold to the food service industry comes from very young hogs, usually between five and seven months of age. Meat from older animals tends to be less tender due to changes in the connective tissue which occur as an animal ages.

Quality pork has soft gray-pink colored meat with white fat. The grades of pork mentioned earlier are based on yield, the amount of usable loin meat, not on quality. A U.S. No. 1 carcass yields more than 53 percent of carcass weight in cuts of fresh leg, loin, picnic and shoulder. The majority of pork sold today is No. 1. Pork producers have worked to breed leaner hogs. Pork car-

casses may weigh in the range of 120 to 164 pounds and 165 to 209 pounds. From these carcasses, wholesale and fabricated cuts are produced.

FRESH HAM

FRESH HAM (#401) ranges in weight from 14 to 17 pounds, 17 to 20 pounds, 20 to 26 pounds or 26 or more pounds per piece. This is the largest single piece from the pork carcass. Fresh ham must be closely trimmed and well rounded at the cushion and butt end. The maximum thickness of fat may range from one inch on a 14 to 17 pound hams to two inches on 26 or more pound hams. When the shank is removed from the #401 fresh ham it is a SHORT SHANK FRESH HAM (#401A). Fresh hams can also be specified skinned or boneless and tied.

PORK SHOULDER

PORK SHOULDER (#403) varies in

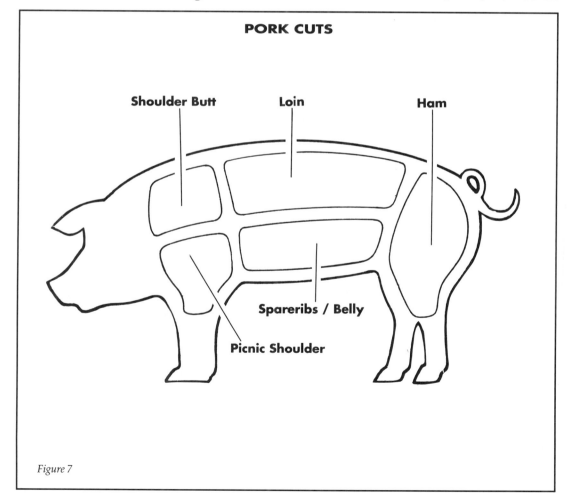

PORK CUTS

Shoulder Butt Loin Ham

Spareribs / Belly

Picnic Shoulder

Figure 7

weight from eight to 20 or more pounds. This cut is separated from the hog side by a cut made starting at a point in the armpit. The cut starts not more than one inch posterior to the elbow joint and continuing straight across the hog side perpendicular to the length of the side. The shoulder must be well faced without scoring the lean meat. The foot must be neatly sawed and cut off in or slightly above the upper joint of the knee. Fat thickness maximums for the pork shoulder range from 1 to 1 1/4 inches for the eight to 12 pound range to two inches for the 20 or more pound pieces.

This cut also yields other cuts, such as BOSTON BUTT or PICNIC SHOULDER. The picnic shoulder (#405) is a neatly cut piece, which leaves all the shoulder bones and not more than two inches of blade bone in the shoulder. The foot is cut off either long or short. The weight of a small shoulder picnic can range from four to six pounds to 12 or more pounds with fat thickness between 5/8 inches and 1 1/2 inches. This cut can be cooked fresh, but is often smoked.

The Boston butt (#406) is that portion of the pork shoulder remaining after the picnic shoulder is removed. It varies in weight from four to 10 pounds. It is suitable for roasting and smoking.

LOIN

PORK LOIN (#410) is cut from the hog side, after the removal of the shoulder, ham, belly and back fat. The loin is left with 11 or more ribs, seven lumbar vertebrae, and three sacral vertebrae. The loin is commonly available in sizes ranging from eight to 10 pounds to 14 to 16 pounds. The loin can be divided into several parts. Three of these are center-cut eight-rib loin, Canadian back and tenderloin.

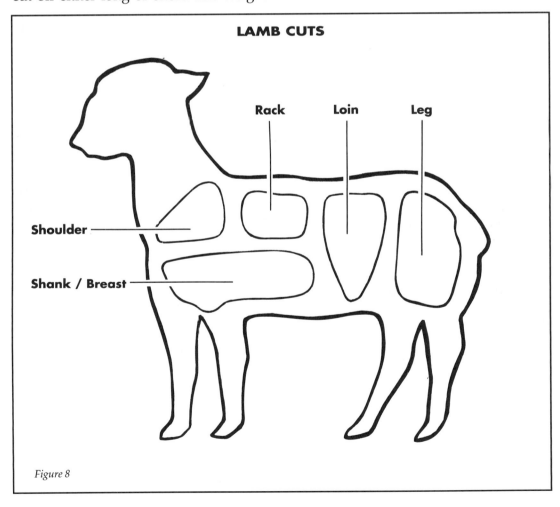

LAMB CUTS

Rack Loin Leg

Shoulder

Shank / Breast

Figure 8

CENTER-CUT EIGHT-RIB LOIN (#412) is cut immediately posterior to the blade bone with the loin end cut immediately anterior to the hip pelvic bone, which is excluded from the cut. The center-cut loin varies in weight from six to 14 pounds. A rib chop comes from the parts where the ribs are located. It is possible to buy a completely boneless loin.

The CANADIAN BACK (#414) is the major loin muscle of the loin. It is closely trimmed and cut fairly square at both ends.

PORK TENDERLOIN is contained within the loin. It may be boned out and treated as a separate cut, pork tenderloin (#415). It is the entire muscle, removed intact from the loin. It must be closely trimmed and practically free from lumbar, leaf and any other fat exceeding 1/8 inch thickness. Trimmed tenderloins are commonly available in 1/4 to 1/2 pound; 1/2 to 3/4 pound, and 3/4 to 1 pound weight ranges.

OTHER PORK CUTS

PORK SPARERIBS (#416) contain at least eleven ribs. They are the intact rib section, as removed by neatly "ribbing" the belly portion of the pork carcass midsection. The standard weight ranges for spareribs are three pounds or less, three to five pounds, and five pounds and up.

PORK BELLY (#408) is cut either with the skin on or skinless. It weighs between eight and 16 pounds. The belly must be separated from the FAT BACK on a straight line. The sides of the belly must be parallel and at right angles to the shoulder ends. The ham end of the belly may be cut on an angle so that the flank side is about one inch longer than the fat back side. The belly is cured and smoked and used for BACON.

LAMB CUTS

Quality lamb is well fed, finely grained and has a pinkish-red color. The weight of lambs, carcasses or fabricated cuts, varies greatly. There are four weight ranges for lamb.

Range 1: 30 to 41 pounds.
Range 2: 42 to 53 pounds.
Range 3: 54 to 65 pounds.
Range 4: 66 to 75 pounds.
Mutton weighs considerably more, from 55 to 130 pounds.

The lamb carcass is separated into four primal cuts: Square cut shoulder; hotel rack; double loin, and double legs. New lamb cuts, further processed from traditional cuts, offer convenient items. These include MEDALLIONS, DOUBLE BONE-LESS LOIN CHOPS, TENDERLOIN, BONELESS SIRLOIN, TOP ROUND, STEAMSHIP or 3/4 LEG, SHISH KEBABS, FAJITAS or STIR-FRY STRIPS, DENVER RIBS, FRENCHED RACKS and BENCH-READY LOINS.

The RACK (#204) is prepared from the bracelet after the breast is removed. The rack is available roast ready, split into single racks or frenched. The hotel rack also yields rib chops and frenched chops. All the cuts from this section make elegant food service entrees.

The chops, either rib or frenched, can be single or double cut. Frenched chops are rib chops with the tip of the rib bone exposed one to 1 1/2 inches. The rack and French rack, which has the exposed rib end, can be single with eight ribs for a rack of lamb for two, or cut into two single portion servings of four ribs each.

LAMB LOINS (#231) are prepared from the hindsaddle by removal of the legs. TRIMMED LOINS (#235) have the flank, hanging tenders, kidney knobs and lumbar and kidney fat removed. Loin, bone-in or boneless, is used for ROASTS, STEAKS, CHOPS, MEDALLIONS and NOISETTES.

LAMB LEGS (#233) are the posterior portion of the hindsaddle. Legs are available in a variety of forms: Shank removed; boneless and tied, or partially boneless. Leg of lamb is a tradition that has influenced cuisines worldwide. Usually done as a bone-in roast, the leg may be studded with garlic cloves and sprinkled with rosemary, thyme, oregano and marjoram. It also works great rolled, tied or netted, and may be barbecued.

Also from the leg comes the popular CENTER-CUT LEG STEAK. Start by removing the small rump portion. Save this for shish kebab cubes. Then cut slices one inch thick just above the stifle joint. The remainder of the leg leaves you with a TWO-PORTION DELUXE SHANK. This is perfect for tableside service. Shanks are ideal for commercial and institutional food service. Their low cost make them attractive for use on buffets. The lower shank can be cubed for stew or ground. The SIRLOIN (#245) yields sliced fillets, shish kebab cubes, smaller cubes for curry and thin slices for stroganoff or stir-fry.

STORAGE & HANDLING

The proper storage and handling of fresh meats requires close attention to detail. The basic guidelines are simple and brief. Yet when they are not adhered to, the rapid deterioration of the quality of the stored meat will result.

Guidelines for Storage of Fresh Meats

1. CHECK IN PURCHASES ON ARRIVAL. THIS IS TO ENSURE THAT PURCHASED MEAT IS OF GOOD QUALITY.
2. WRAP MEAT FOR STORAGE.
3. OPEN VACUUM-PACKAGED MEATS ONLY WHEN THEY ARE TO BE USED.
4. STORE FRESH MEATS AT 32°-36°F (0°-2°C). MEAT DOES NOT FREEZE UNTIL 28°F (-2°C).
5. KEEP MEATS SEPARATED FROM OTHER FOODS IN COOLER AND ON WORK TABLES TO PREVENT CROSS CONTAMINATION.
6. USE FRESH MEATS AS SOON AS POSSIBLE. THEY KEEP WELL FOR ONLY TWO TO FOUR DAYS. GROUND MEAT, BECAUSE OF MORE SURFACE AREA BEING EXPOSED TO BACTERIA AND OXYGEN, HAS AN EVEN SHORTER SHELF LIFE. CURED AND SMOKED PRODUCTS MAY KEEP UP TO A WEEK. HOWEVER, FOR ALL MEATS, FREQUENT DELIVERIES ARE BETTER THAN LONG STORAGE.
7. DO NOT TRY TO RESCUE MEATS THAT ARE GOING BAD BY FREEZING THEM. FREEZING WILL NOT IMPROVE THE QUALITY OF SPOILING MEAT.

8. KEEP COOLERS CLEAN AT ALL TIMES!

It is becoming more and more common for food service establishments to receive at least a portion of their meats frozen. Although this greatly improves the shelf life of the product, this is only true if the meat is properly handled before freezing; while frozen, and during thawing.

Guidelines for Storage of Frozen Meats

1. MEATS BEING FROZEN SHOULD BE WELL WRAPPED IN MOISTURE-VAPOR PROOF WRAPPING TO PREVENT FREEZER BURN.
2. STORE FROZEN MEATS AT -10°F OR COLDER.
3. ROTATE STOCK, FIRST IN/FIRST OUT. FROZEN MEATS DO NOT KEEP INDEFINITELY. RECOMMENDED SHELF LIFE AT -10°F IS 9 TO 12 MONTHS FOR BEEF; SIX MONTHS FOR VEAL AND LAMB; FOUR MONTHS FOR PORK, BECAUSE PORK FAT TURNS RANCID MORE READILY IN THE FREEZER.
4. THAW FROZEN MEAT CAREFULLY UNDER REFRIGERATION. DEFROSTING MEATS AT ROOM TEMPERATURE ENCOURAGES BACTERIAL GROWTH.
5. DO NOT REFREEZE THAWED MEATS, THIS INCREASES LOSS OF QUALITY AND MAY CAUSE INCREASED BACTERIAL GROWTH.
6. KEEP FREEZERS CLEAN AT ALL TIMES!

PREPARATION METHODS FOR MEATS

TENDERIZING MEATS

When needed, meat can be tenderized in a variety of ways. These include pounding, scoring or injecting the meat with enzymes, such as papaya juice. The last method is normally done commercially.

POUNDING is the breaking down of the connective tissue of the muscle by physically breaking it.

SCORING tenderizes by cutting the connective tissue of the muscle. This is often done for thin cuts of meat, such as flank steak or veal escalope before cooking.

INJECTION of enzymes into a cut of meat chemically denatures the connective tissue under the surface of the meat.

MARINATING is a method that tenderizes the surface of the meat, especially in thicker cuts. Marinating can also heighten the flavor of the meat. During long periods of marination, the juice is drawn from the product, so the marinade is often used in the cooking process.

Game and some cuts of beef require marination for two to three days in some cases. However, meats such as veal and variety meats should only be marinated for one to two hours, otherwise an excess of their natural juices will be lost. A complete discussion of the types and methods of marination is given in Chapter 4.

BARDING meat is done when there is a lack of natural fat. The fat, either natural or added, acts as a tenderizer and helps retain moisture when the meat is cooked. In medieval times the word *barde* referred to the armor used to protect horses during battle.

Barding uses thick slices of fat which are tied around the product. The fat melts during the cooking process, thus moistening the meat. Thin strips of bacon or pork fat may be used, with spices and herbs placed under them. Any barding fat remaining after the cooking process should be discarded before serving.

LARDING of meat is done for the same purpose as barding. Meat is larded by inserting strips of fat, called LARDONS, into lean meat. This enhances the flavor and retains the moisture of the meat. This method is usually used only in braising or stewing.

The fat may be soaked in brandy or spices prior to being used as lardons. This adds additional flavor to the meat. Pickled tongue is sometimes used for larding. When this product is sliced, an attractive pattern running through the meat is revealed. As the quality of meats improve through breeding, larding is becoming less used.

COOKING MEATS

BLANCHING

Blanching is usually used for soft variety meats, such as sweetbreads and brains. For the brains, blanching firms them. The sweetbreads are cleaned by the blanching.

Meats to be blanched should be place in an appropriate size stock pot and covered with cold water, then slowly brought to a boil. They are then simmered for five to ten minutes, depending on the size of the cut of meat. During the process, any scum that rises to the surface must be skimmed off. When the blanching process is complete, the meat is placed in a colander and rinsed with cold water. This will bring the cooking process to a stop.

STEWING

Stewing is a cooking method normally reserved for the tougher cuts of meats. The moist cooking will help to tenderize the meat. Meat stew or Ragout is similar in preparation to braising. In stewing, however, the meat is completely covered with the liquid.

The meat must be well trimmed of fat and sinew. It is then cut into pieces of uniform size. Beef or meat that requires lengthy cooking should be cut into larger pieces than the more tender meats such as veal, lamb or pork.

There are two different categories of stews, those which have browned meat and white stews in which the meat is not browned. Veal blanquette and fricassee of pork, both white stews, are made of meat simmered without browning, in white wine, veal stock or water. Various other ingredients are then added to the dish.

Stews are usually thickened at the beginning of the cooking process, when the meat is browned. However, beurre manie or arrowroot may be used at the end of the process too, along with egg yolks and cream for white stews. The increased interest in nutrition has encouraged the use of vegetable purees as thickening agents in stews.

Stewing meats is not only a method for tenderizing tough cuts of meat. When used properly, stewing allows exciting blends of flavor and texture to be created. It should be noted that cooking meats for long periods of time does breakdown fibers and creates a more tender product; however, it also reduces the amount of nutrients left at the completion of cooking.

POACHING

Poaching is used for fresh meats which are to be used as part of a salad or as a centerpiece for a cold entree. In addition poaching in unsalted water is often used for previously pickled, salted or cured meats, to soften them, yielding a more appetizing texture and taste. Poaching is advantageous because it adds no additional calories to the item and preserves many of the nutrients.

BOILED is a term which is used inaccurately in both the United States and Great Britain. The meat is not boiled, since this would break it apart. Meats termed *boiled* should actually be simmered. This allows the meat and other ingredients to cook without loosing their shape.

BROILING

Broiling is a dry heat cooking method which uses very high heat. When done correctly, the meat should cook quickly, forming a well-browned, flavorful crust on the outside and a juicy interior. This is another form of cooking which adds few calories to the meat.

The most tender cuts, with a good quantity of marbling, are the only ones suitable for this type of preparation. The tougher cuts require a greater quantity of moisture and longer, slower cooking to become tender. Even with the tender cuts, a layer of fat is desirable to help keep the meat moist. All connective tissue must be trimmed before cooking, or it will toughen when exposed to the high, dry heat.

The object of broiling is to cook the meat to the desired doneness and form the brown, flavorful crust. To achieve this the meat must be broiled at the right temperature. This temperature will be determined by the doneness desired by the customer and the thickness of the cut.

The thicker the cut and the greater the degree of doneness desired, the longer the cooking time and lower the temperature needed. The thinner the steak and the lower the degree of doneness desired, the shorter the cooking time and higher the temperature needed. Well done items often have to be finished in the oven to prevent excessive browning.

The doneness of the item can be checked either by checking internal temperature or by pressing with your finger. This is also true for pan broiled, grilled or sauteed meats. The standards of doneness for broiled meats are:

RARE means that the item has been seared on both sides. The meat offers no resistance when pressed. When cut, it is rare to almost blue in color, but should be warm all the way through.

MEDIUM RARE means that the meat has been placed on the hot surface and cooked until drops of blood rise to the upper surface, then turned and browned on the other side. When pressed, the meat should have a spongy feel. The color should be bright pink to red when cut.

MEDIUM means that the meat has been turned when drops of juice are visible on the surface. The other side is browned until the meat resists when pressed. When cut, the meat should be pink in the center.

WELL DONE means that the meat has been turned when drops of juice come to the surface and are clearly visible, then cooked until firm to the touch. The heat must fully penetrate to the center of the meat. When cut, there should be no trace of pink.

PANBROILING

Panbroiling is a method used for cooking thin strips of meat, such as minute steaks. Usually a heavy skillet is used, such as an iron skillet, to maintain an intensely high heat, allowing the meat to brown without overcooking. The skillet is well heated. The seasoned meat is placed in the heated skillet and when drops of juice are visible on the surface of the meat, it is turned. The other side of the meat is browned; removed from the skillet, and served immediately.

ROASTING

Roasting is one of the oldest methods of cooking meat. Originally it was done either on a spit or rod, turning slowly over an open fire. The most accepted manner today is in the oven. Usually only the finer cuts of meat are roasted.

To roast meats properly requires that a few basic guidelines be followed.

1. When roasting meats, they should be completely thawed. This insures even cooking.
2. Roasting is done in a roasting pan. The pan has low sides which allow moisture vapor to dissipate without collecting around the roast. (Remember, roasting is dry heat cooking. If the meat is covered, steam, and then condensation, will form around the roast. The meat is now being cooked in a moist environment, not a dry one. (COOK THE MEAT UNCOVERED WHEN ROASTING.)
3. Use a proper size pan. A pan which is too large will allow the drippings to spread too thinly in the bottom of the pan, and they will burn. This will ruin the flavor of the juices created for later use.
4. Baste the meat frequently with the natural juices. Even when the meat is barded or larded, it is important to keep it moist.

The length of time and cooking temperature for roasting will vary with the size and thickness of the cut of meat. The equipment used will also be a factor in selecting time and temperature. The novice culinarian will quickly notice that the thicker the meat, the lower the temperature required. The higher temperatures are only for the smaller cuts or pieces.

High temperature roasting causes fat to melt and much of the meat juices to evaporate. This results in both a reduction of weight and volume. This process can also result in the formation of a bitter, inedible crust on the meat. The overall effect of high temperature roasting is a reduction of the edible portion (EP) yield from the meat.

Searing method is the browning of the cut of meat on all sides. This is usually done using a little fat and high temperatures, 450°F or above. The meat is then roasted to the desired degree of doneness.

Those who favor this method, feel that it seals in the juices and develops a better flavor due to the more intense caramelization. The other side feels that with the exception of only the highest quality meats, the high heat may cause an excessive loss of juices and toughen-

---

INTERNAL MEAT TEMPERATURES

RARE	130°F	MEAT JUICES SHOULD RUN DARK RED.
MEDIUM RARE	140°F	MEAT JUICES SHOULD RUN RED.
MEDIUM	160°F	MEAT JUICES SHOULD RUN PINK.
WELL DONE	170°F	MEAT JUICES SHOULD RUN CLEAR.

ing of fibers. The meats most often cooked in this manner are those which do not have a fat cover.

Low heat method for roasts has become popular because of the increased yield. This method also requires less supervision, less clean up and often produces a more tender end product. The roast is placed, without searing, into a moderate oven. Depending on the size of the roast, it is cooked at 200°F to 300°F. The disadvantage of this method is less caramelization, therefore less flavor development. Additionally, there is concern that this method may be dangerous, if carried too far. Very low cooking temperatures can encourage bacteria growth.

Convection ovens are effective for roasting, when higher temperature roasting is desired. However, many chefs feel that the forced air in the oven has a drying effect on the meat and increases shrinkage.

Testing for doneness in a large cut of meat being roasted can be done in a variety of ways. However, the most reliable method is the use of a thermometer. This method is based on the principle that each stage of doneness is the result of reaching a specific internal temperature within the meat. The tip of the thermometer is heat sensitive and should be inserted to the center of the meat at its thickest point. The tip of the thermometer should not come in contact with the bone. The internal temperature and corresponding degree of doneness is listed below.

The needle method for checking doneness is where a long slender needle is inserted to the center of the meat and then withdrawn. The juices that flow from the hole, as well as the warmth of the needle when pressed to the lip, indicate the degree of doneness. The touch method is similar to that used in broiling; squeezing the product to detect its increased resistance as the meat cooks.

BRAISING/POT ROASTING

Braising/pot roasting is a method of preparation used for tougher cuts of meat. These have plenty of flavor, but little fat. This moist cooking method breaks down collagen, giving a higher gelatin content to the juices and making an ideal foundation for complex flavored sauces and dishes.

Whole pieces of meat are usually used in this preparation. The meat is cooked with lower heat, over a longer period of time so that the tough tissues are broken down. It is suggested that a heavy duty casserole, with a light fitting cover be used. This will increase the moisture and prevent the sauce from sticking.

If the meat is marinated before cooking, pat it dry, then brown slowly in a pan with a mirepoix. Slow caramelization penetrates deep into the surface of the meat, enhancing the drippings and ultimately the sauce.

When the meat is browned, add wine or marinade to the pan, then reduce uncovered at a temperature of 350°F. Next, add stock to one quarter of the meat's height; cover, and braise in the oven at 350°F. Baste and turn the meat frequently.

It is at this stage that flavorings ranging from aromatic herbs to tomato paste are added. In a true braise, all these ingredients will be strained out of the sauce three-quarters of the way through cooking, and the sauce reduced. The meat is then replaced and braised uncovered, basting regularly until tender.

STUFFING MEAT

Stuffing meat is a popular form of presentation. These stuffings are often a hearty mixture with a blend of contrasting flavors and full-bodied texture. The mixtures are usually meat based, using trimmings derived in the boning or preparation process.

Stuffings need plenty of flavor. This is normally derived from onion, garlic, pepper and aromatic herbs. Chopped vegetables provide color and texture.

Dried fruit and nuts complement the flavors of some meats, often combined with grains such as rice and bulgur wheat. Contrasting meats may also be used, such as seafood with beef in the classic carpetbag steak which is stuffed with oysters.

CARVING MEATS

There are two schools of thought for the carving of beef, ham, lamb and pork. One school believes that the meat should be cut down to the bone, against the grain. The other says that the meat should be cut with the grain in parallel slices until the bone is reached. Racks for either method can be purchased from kitchen supply houses.

A European-style ham machine holds the ham or leg of fresh pork firmly level while the knife is drawn towards the carver. In Scandinavia, where fresh pork roast is a popular national dish, guests prefer each slice to have an edge of crisp brown skin. Therefore the meat is carved to the bone, against the grain.

The source of the discussion about carving is the tenderness of the meat when served. Meat is supposed to be more tender when cut against the grain. Cutting against the grain does help the texture of stringy meat. However, if a joint is carved to the bone, each piece has a little of the rarer meat from the bone. This is particularly true in the case of lamb and beef. When meat is carved in this manner, those who prefer well done are sometimes unable to have the well done outside slices they desire.

RACKS OF LAMB, PORK, VEAL AND VENISON are always carved by dividing the chops for each portion and cutting against the grain. This is also the correct way of carving a crown roast, which is a rack or racks tied in a circle. To make carving easier, the butcher cuts the chops at the base, but does not separate them. The carver can then cut through the meat with ease after it is roasted.

Saddle of lamb is carved in thin slices with a thin carving knife. The cuts are made parallel to the backbone. Venison and hare are cut from the ribs in the same way, but the solid piece of meat is then sliced across the grain into thin slices.

Carving HAM, when not on a rack or in a ham machine, requires the placement of the ham, top facing up, on a platter. Hold it securely with a carving fork and cut a small triangular wedge down to the bone just above the shank end. Then, maintaining the same angle, slice down to the bone, cutting thin even slices. To prevent carving the center only, fan out the slicing to take in two sides. Turn the ham and carve in the same way. When the ham is half carved, turn again and alternate sides until only bone remains.

FRESH HAM is carved in a manner similar to smoked ham. Place it on a platter. Cut a wedge from the shank end. Then slice straight down to the bone.

LEG OF LAMB is carved by placing it on a carving board or platter, meat side up and bone side down. Hold securely with a carving fork and slice a small slice from the top. Slice across, with the grain, at a very slight downward angle. This should yield large, thin slices. The leg may also be carved down to the bone as with fresh ham.

SADDLE OF VEAL is carved by holding the saddle, meat side up, securely with a carving fork. Detach the meat from the center bone. Start at the top and run the knife down against the bone until the meat is only attached to the bone at the rib end. Cut into slices, as thick as chops, running against the grain. Several thin slices are sometimes preferable to thicker slices, because they are easier for the guest to cut and eat. Detach each slice from the rib.

ROAST BEEF is sliced in a variety of ways, depending on the cut of beef being served. RIB ROAST is carved in one of two ways. It can be laid on its face and slices made across into even slices, cutting free of the bone. Another method is to cut rib roast down to the bone from the top. The meat is always cut across the grain, whether standing or on its side. Either method may be used standing or in a boned rib roast.

FILET OF BEEF is sliced across the grain. Slices may be thin or up to 3/4 inch thick, running straight down. The meat is soft and has to be carved carefully with a very sharp knife. The center slices of the filet are the finest and are sometimes served first.

SIRLOIN ROAST is started by carving a section from the thick end. Then remove fat and gristle. Loosen the first few inches of meat from the bone. Cut the meat into thin slices at a slight angle to the bone. Loosen the meat from the bone as the slicing proceeds. Being a large heavy roast, it has to be held very firmly with a strong carving fork.

SUCKLING PIG is carved by cutting straight down the back. The skin is folded back and the fat lifted away, if possible. Next the ribs are cut into portions and served with the stuffing. There is so little meat on the ribs that each portion should also include second slices from the miniature hams. The shoulders and neck are the last to be served. The hams are the only large portions of meat on the suckling pig.

CONCLUSION

The proper preparation of meat is a process which begins before the meat is received in the kitchen. Meat must be carefully selected and specified, always considering the intended end use of the product. Selection and specification are the first steps in producing a quality final product while controlling food costs.

Knowledge of the composition of meat is a key to its proper utilization when it is received. Even the highest quality meat will become tough and tasteless when handled improperly. Cooking temperature, method and time must be suitable for the particular cut being prepared. When this basic principle is adhered to, the resulting product will be not only be good tasting, but nutritionally sound as well.

Meat preparation is often perceived as only a matter of exposing the raw product to any type of heat until it no longer bleeds. Meat preparation goes beyond just the haphazard and random application of heat. The culinarian has the opportunity to exhibit the fruits of careful and knowledgeable production of meat in a wide variety of forms.

REVIEW QUESTIONS

1. What are the four basic types of animals from which meat is derived?
2. Briefly discuss the history of any two of the following: Beef, veal, pork or lamb.
3. List the three types of muscle and discuss their characteristics.
4. Define and discuss *adipose tissue*.
5. Define and discuss *bone* and *skeletal tissue*.
6. Discuss the function of the various types of protein in meat.
7. Discuss fat as part of the chemical composition of meat.
8. Discuss the factors involved in selecting meats.
9. Define the three *types of aging*.
10. Define *IMPS* and *NAMPS*. Why are they so important?
11. List the primal beef cuts and the primary cuts that each primal yields.
12. List the two portions into which a veal carcass is divided and the cuts that each yields.
13. List the cuts that a hog carcass yields.
14. Discuss the breakdown of a lamb.
15. List the guidelines for the storage of fresh meat.
16. List and define four methods of tenderizing meat.
17. List and discuss two moist heat and two dry heat cooking methods used for meats.
18. Discuss how to test meat for doneness.
19. List the temperature range for rare, medium rare, medium and well done.
20. Discuss the carving of two types of meat.

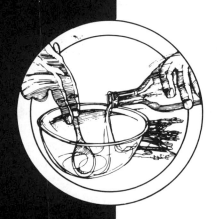

Chapter 18

CHAPTER OBJECTIVES

- **Defining poultry and the kinds of birds included in this grouping.**

- **Standards of quality and grading for poultry processing.**

- **Criteria for choosing poultry.**

- **Choosing the right preparation method for the bird.**

- **The importance of sanitary handling of poultry.**

- **Poultry as a nutritional meat choice.**

Poultry

All domestic birds prepared in today's kitchens are termed *poultry*. This includes chickens, turkeys, ducks, geese, guinea hens and domestic pigeons (squab). Chickens are descended from the jungle fowl *Gallus Bankiva* of the pheasant family *Phasianinae*. These birds were bred in the Indus Valley 4,000 years ago. Records show that the farmers of ancient Mesopotamia bred ducks. Geese were bred in Germany as early as 1,000 B.C. Geese raised today owe their ancestry to the Graylag (*Anser Feras*). The Muscovy duck originated in South America. All other varieties of ducks are traced by zoologists to the wild mallard.

The turkey bought today is not the wild turkey the pilgrims found in 1620. It is a descendant of *Meleagris Gallopov*. This turkey was domesticated by the Aztecs of Mexico. The Spanish conquistadors took it back to Spain. From Spain the turkey reached England.

Over the years, poultry farming has developed greatly. The demand for selective breeding for meat and eggs has led to automated production techniques. Today, poultry is more popular than the meat from any other animal or bird. In the past forty years, production in America has soared from 30 million broilers to over 300 million.

The composition, both physical (muscle, adipose tissue and bone) and chemical (water, protein and fat) of poultry is similar to that of meats, which was discussed in Chapter 17. There are two primary differences worthy of mention. Poultry normally has little pigmentation and the effects of rigor mortis pass within four hours after slaughter.

CRITERIA FOR SELECTION

Selecting the right type of poultry for preparation is a matter of considering the product you are producing and the types and quality of poultry available. A good reference for determining the type of poultry to be used will be the chart presented in Figure Two of this chapter. This chart lists the more commonly purchased poultry and is designed to act as a quick reference, not as your final source for all poultry.

The quality of the bird will be the next determination, after the type is chosen. In America the processing of poultry is closely supervised by the U.S. Department of Agriculture (USDA). The USDA requires inspection of all poultry processing plants and the birds being processed. This inspection provides a guarantee of wholesomeness. Wholesomeness is defined as fit for human consumption. The commercial kitchen should purchase only USDA inspected poultry.

Another service offered by the USDA is grading. In addition to inspecting for wholesomeness, the USDA has also established standards of quality for poultry. Standards of quality are the various factors which determine the grade of the bird. The U.S. grades for poultry are A, B and C. Although the grading of poultry is not mandatory, it is normally used as a gauge for determining and specifying quality standards when purchasing for the commercial kitchen. There also are the U.S. Procurement Grades. These are used primarily for institutional processing. These grades, 1 & 2, place the emphasis on meat yield. This is similar to the yield grade used for beef.

Categories have been established to classify poultry beyond the inspection and grading process. There are four categories used to classify poultry.

KIND: This is the species, such as chicken, turkey or duck.

CLASS: The subdivision of kind, this will depend on age and sex, such as broiler or hen for chickens.

STYLE: This indicates the amount of cleaning and processing which the bird has received. This would include

---

QUALITY FACTORS

FAT COVERING	FLESHING
EXPOSED FLESH	DISCOLORATIONS
BROKEN BONES	MISSING PARTS
PINFEATHERS (PRESENT OR ABSENT)	

Figure 1

live birds (which are almost never purchased in foodservice); dressed birds which have been killed, bled and plucked (also rarely seen in foodservice), and ready-to-cook birds which are dressed and eviscerated with head and feet removed. This last type of bird may also be whole or cut into parts.

State of Refrigeration: Processed poultry currently comes either chilled or frozen. Chilled poultry may also be termed as fresh.

Though selection is based on the intended end use of the bird, there are some general rules for selection. Select fresh plump birds with compact bodies. The bird should have a pliable breast bone and broad breast. Look for skin free of blemishes. There should be enough fat under the skin to make the bird juicy. However, hard yellow fat in large amounts is not desirable. Each bird purchased should come with giblets: Gizzard, heart, liver and neck.

The names and weights of the birds usually suggest their uses. The poultry chart in Figure Two will serve as a guide for the selection and preparation of the most common poultry. The method of preparing the birds listed is not necessarily limited to what is listed. This is a listing of the most common usages. A broiler should be broiled based on its weight and name. However, it can also be broiled on a rotisserie; simmered in a strong chicken stock, or used for recipes where special tenderness and moistness are required. The fryer is for frying, but is the perfect size for casserole dishes and tender chicken salads.

The question of which is better for the table, a male or female bird, cannot be answered. There are differences of opinion regarding the eating quality of one sex of poultry over another. The French recommend a tender young hen. The central Europeans consider a young rooster a far greater delicacy. Americans eat young roosters as fryers, without being aware of it. The hen, which one would think would be the most tender, is not nearly as tender as a young rooster. The capon (castrated rooster) is plumper and juicier than either of them. Given a hen and a tom turkey raised under the same conditions the tom (male) will have better eating qualities. Baby turkeys have less meat and are less tender than the full grown bird. The selection of quality poultry which will result in the finest product requires knowledge and experience.

METHODS OF PREPARATION

The preparation of poultry calls for close attention to control of temperature. Overcooking removes too much moisture resulting in a dry product. Too little cooking will not raise the internal temperature of the meat high enough to destroy potentially harmful bacteria. Poultry should always be cooked well done (165°F.). The meat should separate easily from the bone and should be fork tender. There should be no redness visible in the joints or along the bone. An exception is the wild duck, which is traditionally served rare.

The cooking method for poultry should be suited to the age or class of the bird. The four basic methods of preparing young birds are broiled, fried (pan, deep or oven), sauteed and roasted. The three basic methods for preparing older birds are stewed or fricasseed; poached or boiled, and steamed.

Whatever cooking method is chosen, care must be taken by the culinarian not to pierce the breast of the bird. This will cause a loss of natural juices and a dry product. This is particularly important for whole roasted birds. When it is necessary to use a fork it should be stuck into the back or between the drumstick and the breast. Checking the internal temperature of a cooked bird with a thermometer is best done in the thigh. This not only protects the breast of the bird, but provides an accurate reading of a temperature representative of the whole bird.

POULTRY CHART

KIND/CLASS	DESCRIPTION	AGE	WEIGHT RANGE	PREPARATION	MARKET FORM
CHICKEN					
Rock Cornish Game Hen	Special breed of young chicken, very tender & delicate.	5-6 weeks	.75 - 2 #	Roast, Braise, Casserole.	Whole, Drawn, Fresh, Frozen.
Broiler or Fryer	Young chicken of either sex. Tender flesh & flexible cartilage. Smooth skin.	9 - 12 weeks	Broiler: 1.5 - 2.5#, Fryer: 2.5 - 3.5#	Broiled, Fried, Roasted, Braised, Casserole.	Whole, Drawn, Split, Quartered, Parts, Disjointed, Fresh, Frozen.
Roaster	Young chicken of either sex. Tender flesh, smooth skin. Less flexible cartilage.	3 - 5 months	3.5 - 5#	Roast, Braise, Stew, Boil.	Whole, Disjointed, Fresh, Frozen, Canned.
Capon	Castrated male chicken. Flesh very tender, well flavored, large breast, expensive.	under 8 months	5 - 8#	Roast.	Whole, Fresh, Frozen.
Hen Or Fowl	Mature female. Tough flesh, coarse skin, hardened breastbone cartilage.	over 10 months	3.5 - 6#	Boil, Stew, Fricassee.	Disjointed.
Cock or Rooster	Mature male. Coarse skin, tough dark meat.	over 10 months	4 - 6#	Boil, Stew, Fricassee.	Disjointed.
TURKEY					
Fryer/Roaster	Young bird of either sex. Tender flesh, smooth skin, flexible cartilage.	under 16 weeks	4 - 9#	Stew, Boil, Roast.	Whole.
Young Turkey (Hen or Tom)	Bird with tender flesh, firmer cartilage.	5 - 7 months	8 - 22#	Roasted.	Whole, Breast, Half turkey, Fresh, Frozen, Canned.
Yearling Turkey	Fully matured bird, still reasonably tender	under 15 months	10 - 30#	Roasted.	Whole, Breast, Half turkey, Fresh, Frozen, Canned.
Mature Turkey or Old Turkey (Hen or Tom)	Old bird, tough flesh, coarse skin.	over 15 months	10 - 30#	Roasted.	Whole, Breast, Half turkey, Fresh, Frozen, Canned, Processed.
DUCK					
Broiler or Fryer Duckling	Young tender bird, soft bill & windpipe.	under 8 weeks	2 - 4#	Roast, Spit, Broil.	Whole, Fresh, Frozen.
Roaster Duckling	Young tender bird with bill & windpipe just starting to harden.	16 weeks	4 - 6#	Roast, Spit, Broil.	Whole, Fresh, Frozen.
Mature Duck	Old bird, tough flesh, hard bill & windpipe.	over 16 weeks	4 - 10#	Roast, Stew.	Whole, Fresh, Frozen.

Figure 2

BROILING

Broiling means to cook by direct heat radiating from hot coals, a gas flame or electric element. This method is recommended for the small young chicken (1 1/2 to 2 1/2 pounds). The cooking time will be 15 to 35 minutes depending on the size. The breast and backbone of the broiler should be removed so it will lay flat. This will also make the chicken easier to eat and improve its appearance. To remove the backbone cut through the ribs along both sides of it. Remove the backbone and neck. Next open the carcass out. Split the thin skin covering the breastbone. Snap the breastbone out.

A broiler/fryer may be split in half lengthwise for cooking. It can also be quartered or cut into pieces. Before placing in broiler, bring wing tips onto cut side behind shoulder joints. The chicken is then placed skin side down in broiler pan or other shallow pan. Chicken should not be placed on broiler rack. It is important to place chicken only one layer deep. Do not crowd pan or leave any pan area exposed. Season the chicken as you wish. It is best to brush the product with butter or oil prior to broiling. Place pan in broiler seven to nine inches from the heat. Adjust the distance and the heat so that the surface of the chicken just begins to brown after 10 minutes cooking. After 10 minutes cooking, turn chicken skin side up. Brush with pan drippings or fat several times during broiling. A few of the various ways to broil a chicken are natural, barbecued and marinated.

ROASTING

Roasting was originally the cooking of large pieces of meat on a spit over an open fire. Today this method is called spit-roasting or barbecuing. The modern term *roasting* means cooked by dry heat in an oven. Little or no liquid is added when roasting. Seasoning of whole birds for roasting is best done by rubbing the inside of the body cavity or placing a bouquet garni in the cavity. Rubbing the skin of the bird does little for the flavor of the bird unless the skin is eaten, since there is little penetration of seasoning through the skin.

Larger birds (10 pounds+) cook best at lower temperatures (225-250°F); however, if a shorter cooking time is desired, the temperature still should not exceed 325°F and it will be necessary to baste the bird occasionally to prevent excessive drying. (Caution: Do not baste the bird with stock. This will dry the bird.) For birds less than 10 pounds but more than three pounds, slower cooking temperatures are still best; however, searing is recommended to gain proper browning. Small birds (less than three pounds), such as cornish game hen and broiler, are best roasted at higher temperatures. These birds are small enough that excessive drying does not occur at these temperatures.

A plump young chicken weighing two to three pounds is best for roasting. If the bird is not stuffed, the cavity may be rubbed with salt and trussed (tied). The bird is placed in a shallow pan with the breast side up. Brush the skin with butter or oil. Place the chicken in a preheated standard oven at 375° to 400°F. When the bird is 120° to 130° F. internal (2/3's done) cut the trussing. At this time the chicken is turned breast side down and brushed with pan drippings. The bird is done when the juices run clear (show no sign of blood). The drumsticks will feel soft to the touch and move easily. If the bird is to be carved it should stand for 10 minutes after being removed from the oven.

POACHING

Poaching is an excellent preparation method for chicken. It allows for the development of a high degree of flavor without the addition of calories. There are a number of classical poached chicken preparations such as Veronique (with grapes) and Princess (with asparagus). The delicate flavor of poached chicken is suitable for a wide variety of secondary preparations and is used in a number of Oriental dishes.

To poach a whole chicken, blanch the dressed and trussed bird to remove excess blood and foreign matter. The bird is then placed in a pot and covered with broth or a mixture of water and white wine. A bouquet garni and an onion with bay leaf attached with three cloves is added. The chicken pot is brought to a boil and reduced to a very low simmer (160° to 175°F.) This can be done with or without a cover on the pot. Poaching is also a popular method of preparation for the boneless breast of the chicken.

Poached poultry must be skinned before being served. Proper service of the whole bird calls for the legs to be broken away from the body and the breast meat peeled from the body, leaving the bone structure intact. A strong broth is usually the result of this preparation method. This broth is used for preparing sauces. It also is used as a holding liquid for the poached bird.

SAUTEING

Sauteing is best suited for boneless chicken breast, thin slices of turkey and similar quick cooking cuts of poultry. Larger pieces may be sauteed until brown, then finished by other methods like baking and braising. In classical cuisine there are preparations for chicken called "sautes." These are really braising methods which use the saute to brown the chicken. This browning develops richer, deeper flavor through caramelization. The full flavor of the chicken is gained when the item finishes cooking in sauce made by deglazing the saute pan.

Since saute is cooking food quickly in a small amount of fat, the food must be sized. Sizing means cutting the poultry into pieces which will form a coating quickly to prevent the juices from escaping. The correct temperature and sizing are the secrets to sauteing. A medium to high heat (325° to 475°F.) must be used.

STIR-FRY

Stir-fry is a quick cooking method similar to sauteing. Poultry, and chicken in particular, is well suited for this method of preparation. Peanut oil is the preferred oil because it does not spatter like other oils. The chicken must be completely deboned for best results in stir-frying. It is important that all ingredients, whether diced or sliced, be the same size. This will insure proper and uniform cooking and assist in maintaining juices.

GRILLING

Grilling works best with younger, more tender poultry, such as broilers/fryers. Use a lower grilling temperature than with other meats. The outside can easily burn before the inside is done. Poultry is started with the skin side towards the heat. This helps to prevent loss of juices. The item should be brushed with butter or fat before and during grilling. Season the chicken before grilling. Marinades can be used to enhance the flavor of the item.

CUTTING A CHICKEN FOR FRYING, STEWING, FRICASSEEING

Properly cutting the chicken or other poultry for cooking is important. The cooking quality, eating quality and appearance quality are all affected by the cutting of the chicken. Always use a sharp knife. REMEMBER, SAFETY FIRST. Cut the skin between the legs and the body. Bend legs back far enough to snap the hip joints. Cut through the tendons to the hip joints. Take off the second joint and drumstick from each side in one piece. Separate thigh and leg at the joint. Break the wing joints and cut off the wing. Make a cut from the breastbone, following the ribs to the wing joints. Holding the breastbone firmly with one hand and backbone with the other, tear them apart. Start with the knife at a right angle to the upper part of the breastbone. Make a cut as far back as the wing joint. Split the breast into two halves if desired. Cut the back into two halves.

BONING A BIRD

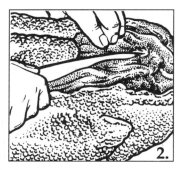 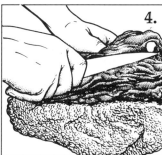 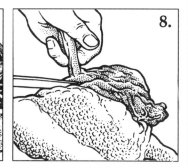

1. Use a boning knife to cut off the wing tip and middle section. Leave the largest wing bone. Slit skin along backbone from neck to tail. Cut out the wishbone.
2. Carefully remove skin and flesh from carcass by cutting with short, sharp knife strokes. Ease the flesh and skin away from carcass after each cut.
3. Cut the flesh from the saber-shaped bone near the wing. Remove the bone.
4. Sever the ball and socket joints that connect the wing and thigh
bones to the carcass. They should be separate from the carcass, but still attached to the skin.
5. Continue cutting until you reach the ridge of the breast bone, where the skin and bones meet. Turn the bird around and repeat steps 2, 3 and 4. When finished, the meat will be detached from bones except along ridge of breast bone.
6. Pull carefully to separate breast bone and carcass from flesh. The partially boned bird can be stuffed at this point.
7. To complete bone, hold the outside of the wing bone, cut through the tendons and scrape the meat from the bone. Pull out the bone.
8. Cut through the tendons attaching the flesh to the leg bone. Use the knife to scrape the meat from the bone, pushing it away as if sharpening a pencil. Cut the bone free of the skin.
9. Repeat on the other side, then push the leg and wing skin side out. Most of the skin will have meat attached to it.

PAN-FRY

Pan-fry is a common method for preparing broiler/fryer chickens. There are two methods of pan-frying.

1) COOK THE PIECES OF CHICKEN 15 TO 25 MINUTES, TURNING ONLY ONCE.
2) WHEN THE PIECES OF CHICKEN ARE LIGHTLY BROWNED (10 TO 15 MINUTES), LOWER HEAT AND COVER PAN TIGHTLY. COOK SLOWLY UNTIL DONE (APPROXIMATELY 10 MINUTES).

Whichever method is used, the chicken is cut into pieces. It is then moistened with liquid (water, milk, egg or a combination) and coated with a seasoned flour mixture. The chicken is cooked in a heavy skillet with a 1/4-inch layer of fat in it. The larger pieces of chicken are started first, placing smaller pieces in between as the chicken browns. The side which is to be face up on the plate is browned first for best appearance. The flour left after coating the pieces is used to make gravy with the pan drippings.

DEEP-FRIED

Fried chicken, whether pan-fried or deep-fried, is a very popular chicken preparation. Although often considered to be a relatively simple dish to prepare, it can be easily ruined if the basic rules of good frying are not observed. Like other fried food, the outside must be dried and protected by some kind of breading or batter. This may consist of a flour, breadcrumb or cornmeal mixture. The liquid used to form a good coating may be milk, buttermilk, chicken broth or water. It may contain egg, egg yolk or egg white. The mixture will be decided by the flavor and texture desired. The seasoning used is limited only by the likes and dislikes of the customer or cook.

Deep-fried chicken is best when a broiler/fryer is used. Larger birds will require precooking prior to deep frying. The breaded chicken is cooked in deep fat at 325° to 350°F. Overloading the fryer will cause the temperature to drop too low and will result in an oil soaked, soft crusted product. For the best product with a crisp crust, load your fryer so that the pieces lay one layer deep in the fat without crowding. It will take 18 to 22 minutes for the pieces to cook. Cooking time will vary with the size of the pieces. The common rule of thumb for determining the doneness of a fried food is that when it floats it is done. However, it is best to check the internal temperature of two to three representative pieces before deciding if the chicken is done.

Additional methods for making fried chicken include the combination of steaming, deep-frying and baking; the combination of pan-frying and baking, and oven-fried. These cannot be called deep-fried in the purest sense; however, they are commonly used in quantity production. The cook must remember that there will be a change in flavor and texture of the finished product.

FRY/STEAM/BAKE: Deep-fry the coated pieces for 5 to 8 minutes. Remove from fryer and place on a sheet pan. Place in pressure steamer for 5 minutes. Remove from steamer and place in 425°F standard oven for 5 to 8 minutes or until crisp.

PAN-FRY/BAKE: Follow pan-fry method except after the chicken is lightly browned, place one layer deep in a shallow baking pan. Sprinkle with clarified butter and chicken broth. Bake at 350°F for 30 to 40 minutes or until done. Do not allow the product to become too dry. Turn once, adding liquid if needed.

OVEN-FRIED: Coat chicken pieces with seasoned flour. Sprinkle with clarified butter and bake at 350°F for 30 to 40 minutes. Turn the pieces once.

STEWING

Stewing is best for birds over one year old. Birds of this kind are less tender, calling for moist heat to give them a better eating quality. Stewing means to cook by simmering in a small amount of liquid. The meat of the chicken cooked this way is used for creaming, a la king or newburg; for pie, salads, sandwiches, shortcakes, souffles, timbales and of course, stews.

FRICASSEEING

Fricasseeing calls for placing the whole or cut up chicken into a pot large enough to cover the meat with 1-1/2 inches of cold water. The water is brought to a boil and then reduced to a simmer. The chicken is simmered for approximately 40 minutes. At this point a mirepoix, bay leaf and desired seasonings are added. The mixture is simmered for another 20 to 40 minutes, or until tender, then the chicken is removed. It is then skinned and deboned. The chicken stock is added to a medium textured roux of chicken fat and flour. This mixture is brought to a boil and reduced to simmer for 5 to 8 minutes. The chicken meat is added to the sauce and then finished with half and half or heavy cream. The vegetables of the mirepoix may be used as garnish. The final mixture should be seasoned to taste.

STEAMING

Steaming reduces cooking time. The advantage of steaming for any meat is the reduced loss of nutrients. The item is not covered in liquid, so the nutrients are not washed away. However, there is also a lack of flavor development with steaming. This is a good preparation method when the cooked meat is to be used in a casserole, creamed dishes or salad preparations.

USE OF POULTRY GIBLETS

The gizzard, heart, and liver are commonly called giblets. The giblets and neck are normally cooked separately from the bird. This is because of their strong, distinctive flavor. To cook, rinse the giblets and drain. Refrigerate the liver. Place gizzard, heart and neck into a sauce pan and cover with cold water. Season to taste and cover with bouquet vegetables. Bring to a boil and reduce to a simmer. Simmer until done. (For chicken, one hour, and for turkey, two hours.) Use the meat and stock for sauces, gravies, stuffings, soups and other dishes. The chicken liver is used for hot and cold dishes. These include omelettes, pate, spreads, or main dishes, salads and hors d'oeuvres. The cooking method for livers will vary with the dish being prepared.

Poultry is rich and delicate. It is adaptable to almost all cooking methods. Breast of turkey may be baked en papillote (in special oiled paper). The uncooked white meat of poultry can be made into quenelles and mousselines or into sausages (see Chapter 28). The methods listed here are only the beginning.

A number of flavor enhancers can be used with poultry. For under the broiler: Rosemary, savory, marjoram, cayenne, sesame seeds and chervil work well. On top of the range: Paprika, sage, thyme, ginger, marjoram, basil, sesame seeds and tarragon do a good job. In the oven: Saffron, sage, poultry seasoning, savory, rosemary, thyme, dill, ginger, allspice, parsley, mace, nutmeg and oregano are the high performers. For more complete information on herbs and spices see Chapter 5.

HANDLING & STORAGE

Proper handling and storage are critical to the quality of the dish prepared with poultry. It is best to thaw poultry before cooking, except for stews or fricassee. Place the frozen bird in the refrigerator, keeping it in its original freezer wrapper. Allow two hours per pound to defrost the bird under refrigeration. Pre-planning is the key to proper thawing of any food item. Remember, it can take as many as three days in the refrigerator to thaw a large turkey. Thawing of food at room temperature is always a risky business. Slow defrosting under refrigeration is always the best method. (See Chapter 2 for sanitary food handling.)

Fresh poultry should be stored in the coldest part of the refrigerator. It should be used within two days. Always remove chicken from the market wrapping. Remove the giblets from the cavity of the bird. Re-wrap the bird loosely before refrigerating. Giblets should be washed and stored separately. As with all food items, poultry needs the air circulation in the refrigerator. Do not overcrowd the cooler.

Leftover poultry stored in a large container can sour quickly. Cooked chicken should be stored in small quantities in separate containers. Poultry is perishable and its flavor deteriorates rapidly. Normal shelf life for the cooked meat is two to three days under refrigeration. When storing it, wrap it tightly in foil or plastic wrap. Warm casserole dishes or other dishes containing chicken must be chilled quickly to prevent spoilage. If needed, use an ice bath before refrigerating.

Frozen poultry should be wrapped tightly in freezer paper. Be careful to prevent tearing. Exposed flesh will be subject to freezer burn. If a bird is split, a layer of paper should be placed between the two halves before wrapping. All frozen foods should be stored at -10°F to keep the best quality.

NUTRITIONAL TIPS

Poultry is highly prized for its nutritional value. Its fat content is lower than that of meats. Chicken, light meat (raw) without skin contains 1.7 grams of fat per 100 grams of edible flesh. Turkey (raw) with skin contains 4.3 grams of fat per 100 grams of edible flesh. These levels of fat compare very favorably to beef (chuck, raw) which has 23.6 grams of fat per 100 grams of edible flesh. It is not total fat content, but, as we mentioned in the chapter on meats, the type of fatty acids contained in the muscle that is important. Chicken contains 0.4 grams of saturated and 0.8 grams of unsaturated fatty acids per 100 grams of edi-

CALORIE CONTENT OF CHICKEN

LIGHT MEAT WITHOUT SKIN, RAW, 100GM = 117 CALORIES
LIGHT MEAT WITHOUT SKIN, COOKED, ROASTED, 100GM = 181 CALORIES
DARK MEAT WITHOUT SKIN, RAW, 100 GM = 130 CALORIES
DARK MEAT WITHOUT SKIN, COOKED, ROASTED, 100 GM = 184 CALORIES

ble flesh compared to beef which contains 10.0 grams of saturated and 11.7 grams of unsaturated fatty acids per 100 grams of edible flesh. When a fat is a concern to your guest, chicken is an excellent product to consider.

Chicken and other poultry are not only lower in fat, they are excellent sources of high quality protein. Poultry, in general, is a very good to excellent source of niacin and a fair source of iron. The light meat of chicken has lower fat content and is roughly twice as high in niacin content than dark meat. The dark meat of the chicken is higher in iron. In addition, poultry is a source of calcium, phosphorous and iron minerals. Important vitamins present in poultry are riboflavin, thiamine and niacin.

CONCLUSION

The future of poultry is very promising. It is an inexpensive, high quality protein supply. Naturally low in fat and calories, it has a secure place as a choice of the nutrition-conscious eater. Turkey has perhaps the brightest future. Production techniques continue to improve, providing a year-round source of protein. Ham, hot dogs and pastrami made from turkey are only a few of the products becoming widely accepted by the public. The improved breeding of ducks are creating a duck which has less fat and more breast meat. Improved handling and processing is resulting in more tender, moist duck with improved flavor. There will be a much wider selection of poultry to choose from in the future with a greater degree of customer acceptance.

REVIEW QUESTIONS

1. Define *poultry* and state the types of birds included in this grouping.
2. List four factors which are used to determine quality and grade of poultry.
3. What is a Procurement grade?
4. State and define each of the four classifications of poultry.
5. Name two types of chicken and state the cooking methods and market forms for each.
6. Name two types of turkey and state the cooking method and market form for each.
7. Name two types of duck and state the cooking method and market form for each.
8. Discuss roasting as a preparation method for poultry.
9. Discuss poaching as a preparation method for poultry.
10. Discuss pan-frying and deep-frying as preparation methods for poultry.
11. Why is control of temperature important in handling poultry?
12. Why is poultry considered a good choice as a nutritional meat?
13. Define *giblets* and discuss their preparation.

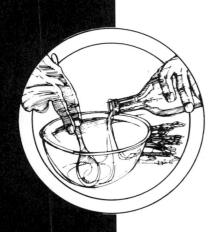

Chapter 19

CHAPTER OBJECTIVES

- **Introduce and define the term game.**
- **Discuss hanging game.**
- **Discuss the various types of game.**
- **Discuss the preparation of game.**
- **Discuss the storage and handling of game.**

Game

Humankind became meat eaters by first killing and eating smaller animals and birds. We eventually devised ways to kill those bigger than ourselves. Finally we advanced to the point of domesticating certain types of animals and birds. These were raised in a more controlled manner, closer to humans. By doing this we created a food source which could be gathered without having to roam large areas and with less danger to ourselves. Through this advancement we changed to a degree the type and character of meat which we eat. Although today we value highly the meat of domesticated animals and birds, the desire remains to enjoy the flavor of what is termed *game*.

The word GAME, for culinary purposes, means birds and animals hunted for food. Many of these, such as pheasants, partridges, quails and rabbits, are now reared domestically, yet are still classified as game. Game was prized at the ancient banquets. At a banquet given by King Richard II of England in 1387, three tons of thirst provoking, salted venison were served along with 400 rabbits, 12 boars, 50 swans and 150 pheasants, curlews and cranes.

The game used in the American kitchen today is divided into two types: FEATHERED or FURRED. Whether feathered or furred, game differs from domesticated animals because of the taste and texture of its meat. The meat of game is generally darker, stronger tasting and often tougher. These characteristics increase with the age of game. It is also more pronounced in some game than in others.

In this chapter we will discuss the characteristics of game and how these influence preparation. The types of game most commonly used today will be discussed.

HANGING GAME

Preservation methods in the days before refrigeration were questionable at best. Although hanging is traditional, it is a mistake to think that game must be mature. (*Mature* being game which has been aged for a period of time before eating.) History suggests that game was not always eaten when well matured. Apicius, the Roman, wrote during the reign of Tiberius that birds should be boiled with their feathers on to prevent them from going bad. The Egyptians preserved their game birds by salting them, a practice also observed in 14th century England.

Although hanging game may not have been as traditional as once thought, there is still sound basis for it. Wild animals have denser flesh and less connective tissue than domestic animals. Further, they store more glycogen in their muscle (a form of starch and the only sugar that animals store for immediate use). Domestic animals are not required to work as hard and do not store high levels of glycogen, storing fat instead. The wild animal requires the glycogen to sustain the short bursts of high energy needed for escaping predators, in most instances the domestic animal does not.

The amount of glycogen in the animal is important to the hanging process. As with aging in domestic animals (this is discussed fully in Chapter 17), the glycogen is needed for the production of acid, which assists in relaxing the muscles as the animal goes through rigor mortis. In other words, hanging allows the meat to go through a natural tenderization process. The bottom line is that wild animals exercise more and are therefore tougher, plus they have more glycogen. However, if the animal is killed after being chased, the glycogen levels will be reduced greatly and the meat will have a different taste and texture. It is the acids developed from the glycogen which contributes to the flavor of game.

While it is true that game can be eaten at a more advanced stage of decay than many domesticated meats, care must be taken when hanging it. Wild animals that are hung are not immune to contamination by microbes (bacteria). However, the acids produced from the glycogen present do inhibit their growth. An additional natural safeguard in microbial contamination is the skin or feathers of the carcass. If you are going to hang meat for several days at room temperature, you will get microbes. Leaving the skin and feathers on helps to protect the animal from these bacteria.

Game should be hung in a cool, dry, airy place, which is protected from insects and rodents. As a general rule you should hang a carcass until you detect the first whiff of tainting. In birds this occurs around the crop or vent.

(Although birds are hung, there is no need to, if you object to the taste.) It is important to remove all surfaces exposed to air before cooking and serving the meat. (It is recommended that you review the discussion of composition and aging in Chapter 17 for a more complete understanding of the natural processes at work during the hanging of game.)

Whether the animal is hung head down or head up will often depend on the region. In Britain, birds are usually hung by their heads. Rabbits, and particularly hares, are hung head down. The blood of the hare is usually collected in a receptacle as it drains off and it is used to thicken the sauce in jugged hare.

✰NOTE: Game is not normally thoroughly bled. This is the reason it has a noticeably darker colored muscle tissue than that of slaughtered domestic animals.

Game purchased from an inspected source is normally prepared and hung correctly. You can specify in advance your exact requirements for the type of game needed. Commercial food service operations should always purchase from inspected sources. Remember that we are responsible for the wholesomeness of every product we serve to the consumer. Approximate hanging times for commonly used, freshly killed game are shown in Figure One.

SELECTION

Age is the major consideration when selecting game because it determines the method of cooking. While indications of age are by no means infallible, there are some general guidelines. Mature game birds have jaws which are set. If you can lift the bird by its lower jaw, without signs of breaking, it is an older bird.

When buying young birds look for clean, soft textured feet, pliable breastbones and round spurs. As birds age the breastbone becomes hard and brittle; breast meat becomes tougher and more solid, and spurs become longer and sharper. Also, young partridges have a pointed flight feather (the first large feather of the wing), while in older birds the feather is rounded. Spurs on cock pheasant are long and sharp for an old bird. Those on the young pheasant are blunt and pliable. The mature bird has a stiff breastbone.

When buying game animals, keep in mind that the ears of young hares (leverets) and rabbits split easily and are soft textured. Young rabbits and squirrels will be lighter in weight than older ones. Also their bodies will be more flexible, with soft pliable ears and hard sharp teeth.

In general, younger birds and animals have a better eating quality. The texture will be less tough and stringy. Meat of younger animals and birds is also more moist. As with humans, as

HANGING GAME	
GROUSE	3-4 DAYS
PHEASANT	6-14 DAYS
WOOD-PIGEON	7-8 DAYS
SNIPE & WOODCOCK	7-10 DAYS
HARE & RABBIT	2-3 DAYS
VENISON & BOAR	UP TO 3 WEEKS
QUAIL	DOES NOT NEED TO BE HUNG

Figure 1

they age game animals and birds become drier and tougher.

TYPES OF GAME AND PREPARATION METHODS

The game discussed here are those most common in the United States' kitchens today. Figure Two can be used as a quick reference for preparation of game birds. Game is divided here into two distinct categories: Feathered and furred. These classifications are a convenience rather than culinary principal.

FEATHERED GAME
GOOSE

There are two main classifications of geese: *Young goose* and *mature* or *old goose.* The young goose may be of either sex. Its meat is tender and it has a windpipe which is easily dented. A mature or old goose may be of either sex. It has tough flesh and a hardened windpipe.

Goose can be purchased year-round. It is available ready to cook, either fresh or frozen. It can also be purchased dressed. The meat of the goose is sweet, all dark,

---

GAME BIRD PREPARATION

NAME AND SERVINGS	APPROXIMATE AGE	DRESSED WEIGHT IN LBS.	PREPARATION	MARKET FORM
GOOSE (1 lb. (raw) per serving)	9-10 MONTHS	4-14	ROAST	WHOLE
PIGEON, REGULAR (1 serves 1)	28 DAYS	8-15 OZ 12 OZ	ROAST	WHOLE
PIGEON, JUMBO (1 jumbo serves 1-2)		14-16 OZ		
PHEASANT, BABY (1 serves 1)	8-10 WEEKS	1-1.25	ROAST, BRAISE	WHOLE
BROILER (1 serves 2)	10 WEEKS	1.5	"	"
MATURE COCK (1 serves 4)	20-22 WEEKS	3-3.5	"	"
MATURE HEN (1 serves 3-4)	20-22 WEEKS	1.75-2	"	"
PARTRIDGE, CHUKAR (1 serves 1)	18 WEEKS	1	ROAST, BRAISE, CASSEROLE	WHOLE
WILD DUCK, MALLARD (1 serves 2)	6 MONTHS	2	ROAST, BROIL, BRAISE	WHOLE (SERVE BREAST ONLY)
CANVASBACK (1 serves 2)	6 MONTHS	2-2.5	"	"
TEAL (1 serves 1)	6 MONTHS	1.5-2	"	"
WILD TURKEY, MATURE HEN (1 serves 6)	6 MONTHS	6	ROAST, SMOKE	WHOLE
MATURE GOBBLER (1 serves 12)	12 MONTHS	12	"	"
QUAIL (1-2 per serving)	12-14 WEEKS	4-5 OZ	ROAST, BRAISE, SAUTE, BROIL	WHOLE

Figure 2

---

tender and juicy. The popular sizes vary from four to fourteen pounds of ready-to-cook weight. About one pound of ready-to-cook weight per serving is a good allowance in choosing a size.

PREPARATION OF GOOSE

To prepare the goose for cooking, remove the giblets and neck, if included, from the cavity. Remove any large layers of fat. The bird is now ready to be stuffed and trussed. The use of stuffing in the goose is optional.

To truss the bird, begin by bringing the neck skin onto the back and fasten with a skewer. Either bring the wing tips onto the back and let them rest atop the neck skin or simply let them rest against the side of the breast. The choice of handling the wings will depend on the appearance desired after cooking the bird. Try it each way and see which you prefer.

To finish trussing the bird, place four to five skewers horizontally across the abdominal opening. Lace cord

around these skewers as you would lace your shoes, starting with the middle of the cord across the top skewer. The excess cord should be looped around the ends of the drumsticks and drawn taut. Finish by tying the remaining cord around a skewer placed above the tail of the goose on its back. If the drumstick ends do not reach to the tail, tighten the cord between them and tie securely.

ROASTING

Place the trussed goose, breast down, in a shallow uncovered pan. Do not add water or fat to the pan. Roast the prepared goose in a 325°F standard oven. During roasting, the fat should be removed from the pan periodically. This will keep the fat color light, not too brown. Save the fat for making sauce or gravy. When the goose is almost 2/3's done, turn it breast up. Prick the breast with a fork to allow the excess fat to escape during the remaining roasting time. To test for doneness, move the drumstick up and down. The joints

---

TRUSSING A BIRD

To prepare: draw the bird. If already drawn, remove the giblets. Remove any piece of fat around tail cavity. Remove the wishbone. With breast up, push legs back and down to allow the ends to sit straight up. Trussing keeps in the stuffing and holds the bird together so that legs or wings don't overcook. It also keeps the bird manageable for carving.

To Truss by hand: 1. Pass the string under the tail end and cross above the legs. 2. Pass the crossed ends of string between the legs. Put the chicken on its left side and draw the string over the left wing. 3. Cover the neck with breast skin and then attach the string between the neck end and shoulders. 4. Knot both ends of the string on the right hand side.

To Truss with a needle: 1. Push needle through wing, breast and into neck skin. Continue under backbone, pushing the needle through the other wing (2). 3. The needle passes through the end of the leg and through the breast. 4. Needle comes out the other leg. 5. Tie up the two ends.

should yield readily or twist out. Also, the drumstick meat should feel very soft.

The first step in preparing a goose, if it is frozen, is to thaw it under refrigeration. Then proceed as you would with a fresh goose.

DUCK

The most famous variety of duck is *mallard*. It is from this species that all other domestic varieties of ducks are descended. Other types, which are hunted as game, include *teal, widgeon, shoveler, pochard* and *scaup*. These are not meaty birds. They are, however, considered to be good eating. Wild duck is best prepared by roasting.

To roast a wild duck such as mallard or teal (approximately 4 pounds), it is best to salt and season the bird's cavity and under the breast skin two hours or more prior to cooking. (Use your choice of herbs such as sage, marjoram, thyme or basil for this.) This will allow the flavors to begin to penetrate the bird. (Remember to be careful not to bruise the breast in handling, this will darken it and make it drier when cooked.) Prepare a base in the bottom of an appropriate roasting pan using the giblets and excess fat from the duck along with a standard mirepoix. Add a quantity of vegetable or chicken stock to the pan sufficient to cover the base and prevent it from browning excessively.

Lightly oil the duck with olive oil and place it breast down on the base in the roasting pan. Cover and bake in a 450°F oven for 25 minutes. This allows the seasonings to be steamed into the bird and helps to moisturize the meat. Remove the cover from the pan and allow the bird to cook at 400°F for another 30 minutes. At this point, carefully turn the bird breast side up in the pan and continue to cook for approximately 30 minutes, until nicely browned. Any excess fat can be removed from the pan and the remaining juices used to make an appropriate sauce to accompany the roast duck.

GROUSE

British red grouse, considered the king of the game birds, has not been successfully raised domestically. Other members of the grouse family in Europe include: *Ptarmigan, capercaillie, hazel hen* and *blackcock*. These varieties are considered inferior for preparation. In North America the grouse family includes *sage grouse, spruce grouse, sierra grouse, ruffed grouse* and *prairie chicken.* Grouse can be roasted, broiled or grilled if young. Older birds should be served braised or in casserole.

PARTRIDGE

Related to the pheasant, the *partridge* is a smaller bird. It is usually considered to have superior eating quality. The name partridge is often applied to quail or ruffed grouse in the United States. There are a variety of species, including the *French* or *red legged partridge* and the *rock partridge*. In France, partridge is cooked with cabbage and other vegetables and made into a decorative mold called a "chartreuse". Otherwise, young birds are best roasted and older birds braised or served in casserole.

PHEASANT

The *pheasant* is a pleasing table bird which has a mild flavor. There a number of varieties of pheasant throughout the world. The type found in the United States was imported from Shanghai as a game bird in the late 19th century. Perhaps the most popular of the game birds, pheasant responds well to hanging. Farm-reared birds are sold oven-ready, fresh or frozen. One bird will usually serve two people. Pheasant is most often roasted.

PIGEON

Pigeon is classified as either raised or wild. *Raised pigeon* has rich, dark meat that lends itself well to roasting. It is best in preparations where the breast is served rare and thinly sliced on the plate with sauce.

Wild pigeon or dove is often tough and strongly flavored. These birds are best suited to casserole, pie, stewing or braising. There are many excellent dishes based on pigeon, such as the North African recipes which features it in a delicate pie made of fine pastry, sugar and nuts, called a "Bastilla".

QUAIL

Quail is a tasty, less expensive alternative to pigeon. Like partridge, quail is related to the pheasant. (In America there is some confusion over the names for quail and partridge. The American quail, or bobwhite, is also known as partridge or Massena quail.) There are several varieties of quail in the United States and Europe. The *California quail* and *European quail* are reared on farms and sold as gourmet items in restaurants. Quail can be roasted, sauteed or broiled. It is often featured in haute cuisine dishes, particularly served in aspic.

SNIPE

Snipe is related to the woodcock. It is best roasted and, like the woodcock, is often cooked with its entrails.

WOODCOCK

Woodcock, according to Larousse, is considered to be the best winged game bird. Common in France and the United States, it is recommended that it not hang too long. It is best roasted or braised. Woodcock is often cooked with its entrails, which are considered by many to be a delicacy.

EXOTIC GAME BIRDS

Songbirds, such as *larks, thrushes* and *warblers,* are considered gourmet delicacies in Southern Europe (Italy, Spain, and the south of France). The *garden bunting* is a particular prize. It once nested in the thousands, but now is increasingly rare. Such small birds are usually barbed with fat and vine leaves and roasted. Often they are cooked with their entrails to add flavor. They may be roasted on a spit; boned and stuffed with mushrooms or foie gras, or combined with forcemeat for use in terrines.

REMOVING SINEW FROM BIRDS

Turkey, goose, mature duck, chicken and game birds have large sinews that must be removed from the leg before drawing. To do this, locate the sinews lying along the bone and pull them out with a pliers. Additionally, slit the leg skin with a knife and locate the sinews. Then insert a sharpening steel underneath the sinews and twist it around to break them. Continue turning until the sinews are pulled completely from the leg meat. Then trim the leg for cooking.

PREPARATION TIPS FOR GAME BIRDS

Game birds are often served with fried straw potatoes or fried potato pancakes. In England they are served with fried bread crumbs and bread sauce. The French like the birds on a crouton with a thin layer of liver pate. The juices or gravy from game birds may be made into a sauce. This may be sweetened with fruit. A fruit compote of berries may be served separately.

The roasting temperatures given here for game birds are only a general guideline. The exact temperature you use will depend on your oven and the bird you are cooking.

ROASTING TEMPERATURES

SMALL GAME BIRDS
450°F
15 to 30 MIN.

DUCK & MEDIUM GAME BIRDS
400°F
RARE   15 MIN PER LB
WELL DONE   20 MIN PER LB

LARGE GAME BIRDS
425°F
RARE   12 MIN PER LB
WELL DONE   15 MIN PER LB

FURRED GAME

BEAR

The *European bear* and the *American bear* are occasionally enjoyed for their steaks, but bear paws are considered to be the prime part. Bear meat has a musty taste and should be marinated for a long period of time. It is most popular in German and Russian cooking. However, bear paw is also a delicacy of northern China. After marinating, bear can be roasted, braised or sauteed.

BOAR

The *European wild boar*, although plentiful on the continent, and in some parts of America, is still best known for its medieval associations. During this time in history it was a common table item. Today, however, it is only served on rare occasions in select restaurants.

Only the meat of the young boar is really tender. The meat of older animals needs to be hung for two to three days before being used. The flesh should be marinated before cooking to tenderize the meat and reduce the strong, gamey flavor. Boar can be roasted, sauteed or barbecued. It is most popular in German and Russian cooking.

DEER

Today, the meat of any animal from the *deer* or *Cervidae* family is called VENISON. The word is from the Latin term *Venari*, meaning "to hunt." At one time all game was called venison, the prize of the hunt. Venison is one of the most popular game meats. However, unless the animal is very young, it needs to be hung and marinated. The best meat is taken from the buck in its second year. The haunch is the most popular cut, although the loin and fillets also make good eating.

Deer, in general, are eaten for their meat and liver; however, smoked elk tongue is considered a delicacy. Young, tender venison may be broiled; grilled, or larded with pork fat and roasted. Some cooks prefer to pour sour cream over the roast before cooking, adding not only fat to the venison, but acid which helps to tenderize.

Nutritionally, venison is a well kept secret. Beef has almost 30 percent intramuscular fat. Intramuscular fat is the distribution of fat in streaks through the meat, called marbling. Although this improves tenderness and contributes to flavor, it is also a potential health hazard. Venison has almost no marbling, less than three percent. It is a very lean yet nutritious food. In addition, venison has approximately one-third the calories per ounce as beef, and the cholesterol level is much lower.

AXIS DEER

The *axis deer* provides the highest quality, best tasting venison. Tests at Texas A&M University have proven axis venison is more tender, moist and milder tasting than *red deer* or other venison. Axis deer has the flavor and texture that appeals to the American taste. It has less than two percent fat and it also has one-third the calories of beef. It is ideal for the weight conscious diner.

BLACKBUCK ANTELOPE

Blackbuck antelope is originally native to India and surrounding countries. It is now raised domestically in the United States. Evolving near the equator, the blackbuck develops almost no body fat, yet retains the highest percentage of moisture of any wild game meat harvested. Blackbuck meat has less than one-third the calories of beef. The meat is extremely fine-grained, with a mild flavor. It can be prepared similar to deer.

BUFFALO

For centuries *buffalo* was a staple meat for the Plains Indians. It has now become a rare delicacy. While becoming more widely available, it is expensive. The flavor of buffalo is similar to beef, yet slightly stronger. The better cuts, such as the loin, can be roasted, grilled or braised. The remainder of the buffalo is best suited for braising, or some other method which will cook it slowly with exposure to high levels of moisture. Buffalo has a tendency to be tough, stringy and dry; however, it does deliver a somewhat unique flavor, which is quite good when barbecued.

BEEFALO

Pawnee Bill was one of the first, of many to try to breed the hardy buffalo with the tender, but seemingly fragile, beef cow, creating *beefalo*. The effort is still being pursued today. It is now considered an alternative for beef. Nutritionally it is much lower in fat. In this contest between the genes of the beef and the buffalo, normally the buffalo wins. The meat of the crossbred beefalo is more similar to the buffalo than the beef cow. For this reason it should be handled much the same as buffalo.

NORTH AMERICAN BIGHORN SHEEP

The *North American bighorn sheep* has a taste similar to mutton. In preparation it is handled the same as mutton. The preparation of lamb and mutton is discussed in Chapter 17.

HASENPFEFFER
YIELD: 10 SERVINGS

INGREDIENTS	AMOUNTS
1. HARE, CUT IN PIECES	4 LBS
2. MARINADE:	
RED WINE	1 QT
WINE VINEGAR	3/4 CUP
MIREPOIX	1/2 LB
JUNIPER BERRIES	4
BAY LEAVES	2
PEPPERCORNS	8
GARLIC, CLOVE	1
3. OIL	4 OZ
4. FLOUR	3 OZ
5. SALT	2 TSP
6. BROWN STOCK	1 QT
7. BACON, DICED, BROWNED	1/2 LB
8. ONIONS, SMALL	1/2 LB
9. MUSHROOMS, SAUTEED	10 OZ
10. CROUTONS, HEART SHAPED	10

METHOD

1. MARINATE HARE, UNDER REFRIGERATION, FOR 4 DAYS. DRAIN. SEPARATE THE MEAT FROM THE MIREPOIX.
2. SEAR THE HARE IN HOT OIL, BROWNING, ADD THE MIREPOIX AND SAUTE.
3. SPRINKLE FLOUR OVER ENTIRETY AND SAUTE FURTHER UNTIL THE FLOUR IS BROWNED.
4. HEAT MARINADE UNTIL BOILING. STRAIN. WITH THE STOCK, POUR OVER THE MEAT.
5. SEASON TO TASTE AND COOK UNTIL THE MEAT IS TENDER.
6. REMOVE THE MEAT FROM THE SAUCE.
7. STRAIN SAUCE. POUR BACK OVER THE MEAT.
8. GARNISH WITH BACON, MUSHROOMS, GLAZED ONIONS AND THE CROUTONS.

Figure 3

OTHER LARGE GAME

There are other large game which are rarely seen in the United State's kitchens, yet when they do appear, they are treated the same as venison. These include: *Arctic reindeer, American elk, caribou, antelope* and *gazelle*.

HARE

Hare, though belonging to the same family as rabbits, are gamier. They are also larger. Their flesh is darker and has a stronger flavor. The hare cannot be raised in captivity. The *European hare* and the *blue mountain hare* are particularly popular in northern Europe. Young hares do not need to be hung and can be roasted. The older animals, two years or older, should be hung and the meat made into casseroles, stews and pates.

Like other game, wild rabbits are lean and must be kept moist during cooking. It may be marinated and simmered in a rich sauce, or cooked in a terrine. The finest section for preparation is the saddle cut, roasted on the bone or cut into fillets. Some dishes with hare are the German casserole with red wine called *Hasenpfeffer*, and the French dish *Lievre a la Royale*. The method for preparing hasenpfeffer is Figure Three.

RABBIT

The meat of *rabbits* is generally tender, light and delicate. It closely resembles chicken in flavor and texture. Rabbit does not need to be hung. Curiously it has never become a haute cuisine ingredient, but has always been a countryman's dish. Countless recipes for rabbit pie and stew testify to this trend. It may also be sauteed, or cut into pieces and baked with herbs.

EXOTIC SMALL GAME

There are a wide variety of small game animals which are not often found on the restaurant menu, yet are hunted and eaten in different parts of the United States. Some of these are regional specialties. Rodents, including the *gray squirrel*, are traditional ingredients in Brunswick stew, along with okra, tomato, corn, lima beans and bell peppers.

The *muskrat* and *South American guinea pig* are raised for food and barbecued or fricasseed. *Woodchucks* or *groundhogs* can weigh up to 25 pounds and have rich red meat. They can be stewed or roasted. The *badger* is rarely eaten today and is protected in many European countries. The *raccoon* may be stuffed with herbs, onions, dried fruit and nuts. *Opossum*, eaten in the southern United States, is sometimes stuffed and roasted.

Armadillo, known as the "poor man's pig" during the Depression, may be baked in its shell (armor) with herb stuffing. It can also be made into spicy sausage or used in chili. This is practiced from Texas to South America. Spined animals, such as the *hedge hog* or *porcupine*, are prepared by rolling the animal in clay and baking. When the clay cools, the quills peel with the clay.

EXOTIC REPTILES

For the more adventurous eater there are available a number of unusual meats. Farm-raised reptiles, such as *alligator, crocodile* and *snakes* are becoming more popular. As the farming techniques are refined, the supply is becoming greater and the quality of the meat appears to be better. Farm-raised alligator is sometimes compared to lobster and is usually braised or sliced and deep-fried. The French eat *grass snake* prepared in the same manner as eel.

PREPARATION TIPS FOR ALL GAME

Game meat, as a rule, responds best to roasting. Young game birds, in particular, should be roasted, and traditionally are left unstuffed. In practice, however, large birds, such as pheasant and ptarmigan, may be stuffed with seasoned ground beef. This will help keep the flesh moist. Older, tougher game should be cooked in a casserole, braised or made into pies, pates and terrines. Marinating game meat in a mixture of oil, vinegar, wine or beer, with herbs and spices will help make tough meat tender and enhance its flavor. (For a complete discussion of marinating see Chapter 5.) Additional tips for game preparation are given in Figure Four.

STORAGE AND HANDLING

Game meat should be refrigerated, like other meats. If it is uncooked, cover or wrap tightly. For the best flavor, use the meat within three to four days. Before storing venison, in particular, the fat should be trimmed. The characteristic venison flavor seems concentrated in the fat, for this reason it should be completely trimmed to reduce strong flavor. (Venison fat also turns rancid more quickly than fat on domestic animals.)

Deer and birds must be hung before freezing. No amount of hanging after they have been frozen will help. You should freeze only high quality meat. Remember that the maximum storage time for game is less than that for meat from domesticated animals. For best eating, game should be used within four months.

Game, such as venison, is best frozen in small packages. These will freeze and thaw faster. Label all packages with name of product, date frozen and its

---

PREPARATION OF WILD GAME VARIETY MEATS

1. BRAINS SHOULD BE CLEANED AND WASHED IN COLD WATER BEFORE PREPARATION. THEY CAN BE FRIED OR BOILED SLOWLY FOR HALF AN HOUR.

2. WHEN PREPARING HEART, REMOVE THE VALVES AND TOUGH FIBROUS TISSUES. IT THEN CAN BE BRAISED OR CUT INTO SMALL CHUNKS AND USED IN SOUPS OR STEWS.

3. KIDNEYS ARE BEST FRIED. HALVE THEM AND THEN SLIT EACH HALF TWICE ON THE INSIDE, BUT DO NOT CUT CLEAR THROUGH. BE SURE TO LEAVE THE FAT ON THE KIDNEY, THIS IMPROVES FLAVOR AND TEXTURE. THE KIDNEY SHOULD BE FRIED UNTIL ALL BLUENESS HAS DISAPPEARED.

4. THE LIVER SHOULD BE PARBOILED, BEING CAREFUL TO SKIM OFF THE SCUM WHICH RISES TO THE TOP OF THE COOKING POT. NEXT, SOAK THE LIVER IN COLD SALT WATER, RINSE IN WARM WATER, WIPE DRY. THEN EITHER FRY THE WHOLE LIVER IN BACON GREASE OR SLICE IT THINLY AND DIP EACH SLICE IN SEASONED FLOUR AND FRY.

5. TO PREPARE TONGUE, SOAK IT FOR ONE HOUR, THEN RINSE IN COLD CLEAN WATER. PLACE THE TONGUE IN A POT OF COLD WATER; BRING TO A BOIL, AND SIMMER FOR TWO HOURS, OR UNTIL TENDER, ADDING WHATEVER SPICES YOU DESIRE.

6. SAUSAGE MADE FROM GAME MEAT UTILIZES THE TOUGHER PARTS OF THE GAME. MINCE THE RAW MEAT WITH HALF AS MUCH SALT PORK. SEASON WITH PEPPER AND SAGE. IT CAN THEN BE MADE INTO PATTIES AND FRIED.

Figure 4

weight. You should cook frozen and thawed game as you would fresh game.

CONCLUSION

Although game is not something served in every establishment or cooked in every kitchen, it is an important part of a future chef's learning experience. As health consciousness increases in the U.S., the popularity of certain game may very well increase. You need to be able to react to this when the time comes. A word of caution, however, check local laws and health codes before serving game. Service of game in a public dining room is prohibited in some areas of the United States. In addition, be careful in the selection of your source for game. It should be an inspected, approved source. Without this, you have no assurance of either quality or, most importantly, wholesomeness.

REVIEW QUESTIONS

1. Define the term *game*.
2. Discuss the hanging of game.
3. How does game differ from domestic animals?
4. What is the primary factor in the selection of game?
5. Discuss the preparation of duck and goose.
6. How do you truss a bird for roasting?
7. Discuss the preparation of two types of game birds other than the duck and goose.
8. At what temperature and for how long should game birds be cooked?
9. Define the term *venison*.
10. Discuss venison in comparison to beef.
11. What type of deer is best suited to the American market and why?
12. Discuss the preparation of two types of furred game, other than venison.
13. What type of animals are considered to be exotic small game?
14. List tips for preparing game variety meats.
15. Discuss the storage and handling of game.

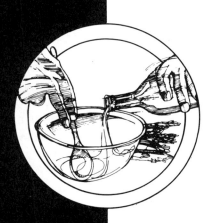

Chapter 20

CHAPTER OBJECTIVES

- **To discuss the composition and structure of fish and seafood as a group.**

- **To introduce the various categories of fish.**

- **To discuss the sixteen major groups of fish.**

- **To introduce the categories of shellfish.**

- **To discuss the categories of shellfish.**

- **To discuss general preparation techniques for fish and seafood.**

- **To discuss specialized preparation methods for specific items.**

- **To discuss the available forms of fish.**

Seafood
and Freshwater Fish

There are more than 20,000 species of fish in the waters of the world, yet we utilize only a fraction of this resource's annual harvest potential. Although 50 percent of the fish (primarily the small multicolored coral fish and species which favor deep water) are unacceptable for commercial use, only about a dozen different species appear regularly in American and European markets. (The Portuguese and Japanese are exceptional in that over 60 species appear in their markets.) The European catch consists mainly of cod, hake, herring, mackerel, pilchard and anchovy. This is out of about 160 species available in the Mediterranean Sea. The American demand is for salmon, flounder, cod, halibut, trout, perch and bass.

The introduction of refrigerated air transport for flowers in the 1960's precipitated a revolutionary change in the fish industry. In 1969 the LD3 container was used for the transport of fresh fish by air. This made fresh fish available anywhere a jet could fly. Another revolutionary change in the fish industry is aqua-culture. Although this has been practiced in limited forms for centuries, it has expanded widely in the last few years. Literally, it is the cultivation of the natural produce of water. Currently there is expasion of aquaculture in all areas. This is an exciting development in view of the needs of a hungry world. One cubic acre of ocean can produce 3,000 pounds of edible product. This far exceeds the capabilities of an acre of tillable soil.

Trout, salmon, shrimp and some other shellfish, catfish and other species are being farmed successfully. Consistency of flavor and texture is a benefit of the farmed fish. Wild fish can vary enormously in this area. However, the farm-raised fish rarely attains the excellence of the finest wild species. It seems that a slight reduction of flavor will be accepted as a reasonable trade for a more consistent supply at a more stable price.

The large number of species and the number of these available at any given point in time can make the selection and preparation of fish and seafood both exciting and confusing. It is important that the chef have an understanding of the differences in taste, texture and bone structure of the various kinds of fish. Oily, rich-fleshed fish, such as mackerel and herring, are different from the white-fleshed fish such as hake. The texture of the cod, which is coarse, differs from that of the sole, which is fine and delicate. Firmness of the flesh varies from the very firm shark to the soft whiting. Our goal in this chapter is to start you on the road to acquiring the knowledge you need to master the preparation of fish.

COMPOSITION AND STRUCTURE

The edible flesh of fish and seafood, like that of meat and poultry, consists of water, proteins, fats, as well as small amounts of minerals, vitamins and trace elements. The differences between fish and meat or poultry are more important than the similarities.

The most important difference is that fish have very little connective tissue. It is this lack of connective tissue that makes the following statements true.

1. FISH COOKS VERY QUICKLY, EVEN AT LOW HEAT, SINCE ALL THAT IS REQUIRED IS SUFFICIENT HEAT TO COAGULATE THE PROTEINS.
2. FISH IS NATURALLY TENDER AND, IF IT BECOMES TOUGH IN COOKING, IT IS NOT DUE TO CONNECTIVE TISSUE, BUT TO THE EXTENDED EXPOSURE OF THE PROTEINS TO HEAT.
3. COOKED FISH MUST BE HANDLED CAREFULLY OR IT WILL FALL APART.
4. UNLIKE IN THE PREPARATION OF MEAT AND POULTRY, MOIST HEAT COOKING IS USED NOT TO CREATE TENDERNESS, BUT TO PRESERVE MOISTURE AND PROVIDE VARIETY.

TYPES & DEFINITIONS

Fish and seafood may be grouped into categories by both their structure and the preparation techniques and methods used for cooking them. Shark, for example, has a cartilaginous structure (a skeleton largely composed of cartilage) and no transverse bone (the fine bones which extend horizontally from the spine of the fish). It requires a different preparation method than shad, which must be carefully dissected to avoid a product full of bones.

Flat fish, such as sole, and fish with compressed bones are more suited to filleting than cutting into steaks, like the shark. Small fish, such as herring and trout are often cooked whole, with the bone in.

FISH

FAT & LEAN

The fat content of fish ranges from 0.1 percent for haddock to 20 percent for eel. This single characteristic has a great effect upon the cooking method chosen for a fish. Lean fish are those that are low in fat, such as flounder, sole, cod, red snapper, bass, perch, halibut and pike. Fat fish are those which are high in fat, such as salmon, tuna, trout, butterfish and mackerel. Lean fish, having almost no fat content, can easily become dry, particularly when overcooked. Fat fish contain enough fat to enable them to tolerate more heat without becoming dry.

ADDITIONAL CATEGORIES

While fat and lean are important characteristics in fish, they are not the only ones. Texture; moisture; grain of the meat, and density of the flesh are also important in choosing the best preparation method. Fish can be further broken down based on these other traits. When categorized in this manner there are currently sixteen major groupings:

1. SMALL FLATFISH.
2. LARGE FLATFISH.
3. RAY AND SKATE.
4. CAVIARS AND OTHER ROES (THE EGGS OF FISH ARE DISCUSSED FULLY IN CHAPTER 27.).
5. SHARK & STURGEON.
6. MEATY FISH.
7. MONKFISH.
8. FIRM WHITE FISH.
9. FLAKY WHITE FISH.
10. THE COD FAMILY.
11. THIN BODIED FISH.
12. BONY FISH.
13. SALMON AND TROUT.
14. FRESH WATER SPECIES.
15. RICH OILY FISH.
16. LONG BODIED FISH.

Each of these groupings has its own characteristics which are important to the culinarian. We will discuss each group.

SMALL FLATFISH

When born, flatfish swim upright like many other fish. As the fish matures, it turns sideways and one eye moves to the other side. Depending on the species, the eye may move right or left. This category includes sole (Dover, gray, Pacific petrale and lemon) and flounder (winter and Pacific). Dover sole is considered to have the greatest versatility and taste in this category; however, true Dover sole is not found in the coastal waters of the United States.

★NOTE: Pacific flounder and lemon sole are often marketed in the U.S. as Dover sole.

These fish are firm fleshed with a nutty, sweet flavor. Dover sole has inspired many classic dishes and is most often served poached with a velouté or butter sauce. Sole or flounder may also be dredged in flour then sauteed. These fish are good for broiling, steaming or baking (en papillote), and served with a butter sauce. Sole is also one of the best fish for use in fish terrines.

LARGE FLATFISH

The flavor of these fish is succulent, with a firm white flesh. When cooked they are tender and moist. Turbot, brill, halibut and John Dory are in this class. The Pacific halibut are considered to have the best flavor, being both milder and drier in flavor than the turbot. Greenland and California halibut have a softer texture and less flavor. They are considered to be inferior to the Atlantic and Pacific varieties. The John Dory is not a flatfish in the true sense, but has a compressed body. It is handled and cooked in the same manner as the other fish in this grouping.

All of the fish in this group are high in gelatin with prominent bones. They make excellent stock. The large turbot, brill and halibut are usually cut into steaks. Large halibut and John Dory may be cut into four fillets that are called loins. A 3-5 pound rectangular loin section is called a "fletch". The fillets are cooked like steaks.

RAY AND SKATE

Rays and skates are cartilaginous fish. For both of these fish the wings are the parts which are eaten. The wings are composed of semitransparent bars of cartilage which are surrounded by long, narrow strips of close-textured, gelatinous flesh.

The wings are often poached in vinegar or court bouillon to counteract the glutinous texture. After poaching, the skin can easily be removed from the wings. Rays and skates can also be floured and sauteed or fricasseed.

SHARK AND STURGEON

Shark and sturgeon are also cartilaginous fish. The meat is often pink, but may also vary from white to beige. Deep red color in shark flesh can be due to bruising; to the variety of the fish, or to the cut originating from an oily region of the shark. Whatever the cause, red meat is considered inferior because it will retain a strong flavor.

Shark meat may have an ammonia-type odor. In the water, urea is excreted through the skin. Enzymatic action turns this into ammonia after the shark is slaughtered. The strong odor and flavor can be reduced by soaking the flesh in milk or in a mixture of vinegar and water prior to cooking. The meat can be braised, stewed, fried or cut into steaks and broiled.

Sturgeon is a prehistoric, armor-scaled fish known as a source for caviar. Its firm white meat resembles that of shark. The sturgeon lives half of its life in fresh water and half in salt water. There are 30 known species which are distributed throughout the Northern Hemisphere. It may be poached, smoked, pan-fried or broiled. It is considered a delicacy when smoked.

MEATY FISH

This grouping includes tuna, swordfish and marlin. They are most commonly marketed in restaurants in steak form. The flesh of these fish varies in color from dark red to light. They are suitable for broiling as steaks or kebabs; barbecued; steamed; braised with vegetables, or cut raw and used in sashimi and sushi.

Tuna is found in warm seas around the world and six species of varying size are marketed in the U.S. Varieties of tuna include bluefish, skipjack, bonito, albacore, big-eye and yellow-fin. Albacore, often called the chicken of the sea, is the only white-fleshed tuna and the preferred variety for canning. Big-eye tuna also has a lighter meat and is the preferred tuna of the Japanese. In the United States, yellow-fin (Hawaiian ahi) is considered the finest and most versatile for eating.

Like other oily fish, tuna should be eaten as fresh as possible. The quality of the meat of the tuna can vary widely from tuna to tuna and even within the fish itself due to its large size. Handling of the tuna at sea is very important to the resulting quality of the meat. Excessive struggling during capture causes the body temperature to rise and "burn the meat." This affects the appearance, texture and flavor of the flesh. The various parts of the tuna may be prized in certain regions for particular uses. For example, the belly (the part containing the greatest amount of oil) of the bluefin is prized by the Japanese for a type of sashimi called Toro.

Named for its long sword-like nose, the swordfish is found throughout the world. There are, however, variations in the size of the fish due to the condition of its habitat. This popular fish is often cut into steaks and broiled. However, it is subject to naturally high levels of mercury (a toxic substance) and is monitored in several countries, such as Italy, Japan and the United States. The swordfish is also susceptible to a parasitic worm, which is harmless when cooked, but results in meat which is unattractive.

Marlin, also called spearfish, has a short spike nose. It is similar in appearance to swordfish, although plumper and more muscular. There are four species of marlin, of which the white and blue are native to the Atlantic. The striped and black marlin are particularly valued by the Japanese and are native to the Pacific.

More rare than the marlin is the sailfish which is named for its high dorsal fin. It is not as good as the marlin for eating but can be smoked with great success.

The meaty fish are sometimes compared in flavor and texture to veal, however they may have a very strong taste. This is especially true of the dark-fleshed varieties. This strong flavor can be reduced by soaking in salted water or marinating prior to cooking.

MONKFISH

The monkfish is also called the anglerfish. It has a unique texture and flavor. The slightly chewy texture and mild flavor with a slight sweetness has made it very popular and earned it the nickname "poor man's lobster." It is native to the Mediterranean and both sides of the Atlantic and averages 10 pounds in weight. The tail section of this fish is the most important part, yielding two fillets/loins, one on each side of a cartilaginous structure. As the nickname implies, this meat may be substituted in dishes where lobster is usually required.

FIRM WHITE FISH

Snapper, grouper, orange roughy and mahi mahi are all part of this grouping. They offer juicy, firm flesh with an excellent flavor. The size of these fish varies greatly, but all have large heads and may be cooked whole if small. The larger fish may be filleted or cut into steaks.

Snapper is a warmer water fish, which gets its name from the energetic way it shuts its mouth, and is highly sought after. Red snapper, in particular, is at the top of the popularity list. Due to its expense, other fish are often passed off for red snapper, such as the red drum or redfish, and various Pacific rockfish. These fish are often sold as skinned fillets. For this reason, it is suggested that you always purchase red snapper with its skin still on.

Red snapper and silk snapper are acknowledged as being the best eating of this species. Silks have yellow eyes and a black edged tail. Reds have red eyes and are all red. Both have the same texture and flavor. Other good snappers, such as the gray or mangrove, yellow-tail muttonfish, and the small, red lane snapper are also used with excellent results.

Grouper are also found in warmer waters, and many range in size from two to four pounds. There are some varieties, such as the jew fish found in the Gulf of Mexico or South America, which can weigh as much as 700 pounds. The larger grouper have a coarser texture, so most of the commercial catch are 50 pounds and smaller.

Common grouper, such as the Nassau, black and red grouper are the most popular. The red grouper is the most sought after. The flesh of the grouper closely resembles that of the snapper. The flesh of the snapper and grouper are good for all types of preparations from steaming to barbecuing, which attests to their popularity.

Orange roughy is a deep-sea New Zealand fish. It was once passed off as snapper, having a similar taste and texture. It is a full-bodied fish with a slightly yellow flesh and bright orange skin. It has become popular in its own right and is marketed under its own name.

Dolphin fish or mahi mahi, as the Hawaiians call it, is found in warm water in both the Atlantic and Pacific. The fish has vibrant colors which fade immediately after being caught. Ranging in weight from 5 to 40 pounds, those 15 pounds or more have a better taste.

The flesh of the mahi mahi has a pinkish quality which fades when cooked. This meats cooks quite rapidly, which often causes dryness. The flesh becomes flaky and has a mild, almost sweet flavor after cooking.

★NOTE: This fish is <u>not</u> related to the dolphin (a mammal) or in any way to the porpoise family.

FLAKY WHITE FISH

Bass, mullet, drum and croaker are all included in this grouping. Bass is a general term which has been applied to many fresh- and salt-water fish which are actually unrelated as far as species goes. The one thing they all have in common however, is their fine-grained, firm flesh.

Sea bass are a migratory fish. They live much of the year close to shore or just off-shore and move to deep, warmer waters during the winter. These fish range in color from blue-gray to black. In America, the striped east coast sea bass is held in high regard. The common sea bass is popular in Europe.

Mullet resemble trout with a color closer to that of bass, and range from gray to spotted or striped. Though having a reputation of being bony, the flesh of this fish is fine-textured, mild and slightly oily. Red mullet, usually found in the Mediterranean, is brilliant red and related to the American goatfish. This small fish is usually cooked whole, skin on, with its entrails, giving it a desired gamey flavor.

Drum and croaker are found along the Atlantic coast. Their names come from the resonating sound made by the muscles attached to their air bladders. Drum are a small fish (up to 10 pounds) that have a mild flavor, sometimes described as tasteless. They have a coarse texture and careful handling is important for this species.

One notable drum is the red drum, commonly known as the redfish. It achieved fame by its use in Cajun cooking as Blackened Redfish. In fact this type became so popular that shortages have occurred and in many states the red drum/redfish is now protected. Black drum or weakfish (sea trout) are now used in its place and are becoming popular in their own right.

★NOTE: Do not use drum in ceviche or sashimi; they are prone to parasites.

This family also includes the Pacific white sea bass and Atlantic spotted, speckled or gray sea trout. Although confusing, these are not truly related to true bass or trout. The kingfish is another species of drum, as is the silver perch.

The croaker also belongs to the drum family and is found in the western Atlantic. This fish is not extensively used or desired due to its soft flesh and bland taste. Because the flesh has such softness, it must be cooked with the bone on and is usually pan-fried.

COD FAMILY

An abundant fish, this family includes cod, haddock, hake and pollack. This somewhat flaky, mild flavored, firm-fleshed, cold water fish has been a staple in kitchens since medieval times. The abundance of this fish off the coast of New England was one reason for the rapid colonization of that area during the early part of United States history.

This family forms almost one-half of the world commercial catch of fish each year. In most markets, the sandy-brown Atlantic cod and the Pacific cod are indistinguishable. However, the Atlantic is preferred in the United States and Europe while the Pacific is exported to Japan and Russia.

Atlantic Cod weighing 100 pounds have been caught in the past. Continued large-scale harvesting has dwindled supplies to the point of scarcity. Anything currently caught over 25 pounds is classed as jumbo and left in the sea. Scrod is a term that often appears on menus. This is not a fish, but a size classification of the cod family, ranging from 1.5 to 2.5 pounds.

Salted dried cod was for years a staple in the diet of many coastal cultures. However, with improved technology it has lost some of its popularity. Fresh and frozen cod are more readily available now. The cod is used in a variety of ways. Cod oil is an important source of vitamins, cod roe is eaten fresh, smoked or salted. The cheeks of cod are sweet and sold separately, as is the tongue. Cod flesh is good for all types of preparation; however, it is already a very moist fish so poaching sometimes makes it soggy.

The haddock is a close relative of the cod, but less abundant. It is easily identified by the black mark resembling a thumb print behind the gills. Also a cold water fish, its flesh is slightly softer than that of the cod and it is smaller in size.

Hake and whiting are inferior to the cod, having a much softer flesh. They are often poached, steamed or pureed into quenelles or mousselines for this reason. Hake is generally larger than whiting and can reach 25 pounds. Whiting is sold under one pound in weight.

Atlantic pollack is similar in flavor to the hake, but has a coarser texture. Its gray flesh whitens when cooked. This fish is currently a popular source of surimi, a seafood analog such as artificial crab meat. Pollack is found in both the Atlantic and Pacific.

THIN-BODIED FISH

Jacks, including pompano and sea bream, are fish which have oval bodies and a characteristic "Y" tail. These fish are found in tropical waters around the world. The meat of pompano and sea bream is firm, with a white to pink color, and full flavor; however, bream has a lighter fragrance and taste.

Horse mackerel or scrad, despite the name, is also a jack. However, it resembles the mackerel and has less flavor. The yellow tail and amberjack are also used by restaurants. The yellow tail

may be used for sashimi, but the amberjack is very susceptible to parasites and should never be eaten raw.

Sea bream are sold under many names. Striped sheepshead, pomfret, or Ray's bream are familiar to most chefs. They are normally cooked whole on the bone, due to their compressed body structure.

BONY FISH

The gurnard (seardion), scorpion fish and rockfish offer little in the way of meat. They have large heads and a prominent bone structure. They are valued for making stocks, soups and sauces. Gurnard is prominent in this grouping. The red gurnard or sea robin is the most desired of the gurnard family. It is sometimes passed for the red mullet, though the flesh is drier and not of the same quality.

Scorpion fish is a sought-after fish, called by the French the red racasse. It has firm, white flesh which is used in Bouillabaisse and also bakes well. This fish is found on both coasts. The weaver and specter are related fish which are used in Bouillabaisse. Both have poisonous spines and are found in the Eastern Atlantic and Mediterranean.

Rockfish are a large family of fish whose flesh varies from firm to soft. It is sometimes passed off as snapper, but the flesh is inferior and sometimes hard to handle. The Pacific ocean perch and yellowtail rockfish are in this family.

All fish in this grouping must be gutted and washed thoroughly before cooking. They require a great deal of help from herbs and vegetables to add flavor. However, for the most part, they do come into their own in soups and stocks.

SALMON AND TROUT

Salmon and trout have a different appearance from the outside, yet when filleting them you will find they are similar in flesh texture and bone structure. Similar preparation techniques are used for both. Members of both the trout and salmon family are being farmed successfully and are very popular.

Salmon are divided into two groups: Pacific and Atlantic. The six varieties of Pacific salmon are kin (chinook); sockeye (red salmon); coho (silver salmon), which has a light colored flesh with a delicate flavor; pink salmon; chum (dog salmon), and cherry salmon (found only on the Asian side of the Pacific). The Atlantic salmon has a lighter flesh and is slightly fattier than Pacific salmon. All salmon are similar in appearance. They have small heads, silvery skin with different markings and can weigh up to 100 pounds. The farmed salmon is becoming popular due to its consistency and availability, but its flavor has not approached that of wild salmon.

Trout can live in both fresh or salt water. The most sought-after trout is the fresh-water rainbow trout. On the Pacific coast of the United States the rainbow trout travels the water ways to the Pacific where it thrives in the salt water, becoming the steelhead trout. These trout can grow to 50 pounds with a pink, tasty flesh. It is often smoked or served fresh, and has a caviar with a fine reputation. Other trouts include the brook trout, pink spotted Dolly Varden trout and speckled trout. The lake trout or gray trout, native to Canada and North America, is fattier than most.

The habitat and food supply effect the taste, texture and color of the meat of both fish. The pink tone of the farm-raised fish is due to their controlled diet. In the wild this color comes from the crustaceans found in the waters where these fish are found.

Poaching and steaming are good preparation methods for this group of fish, serving them with broth-based sauces. Sauteing, broiling, poaching and baking are also used often. Salmon is one fish which can hold up to braising. Pate, terrines and mousselines are great ways to use up scraps or by-products and are popular on menus.

FRESHWATER FISH

These fish are usually mild and delicate in flavor. Supplies of freshwater fish have dwindled in recent years due to pollution of the waters. The possibility of contamination from polluted waters is greater in freshwater fish. The toxins tend to collect in the skin and in a thin layer just below the skin of the fish. It is always best to skin and remove the fat from fish before cooking.

★NOTE: In general, the more oily parts of a fish should be avoided unless it is a deep water fish.

Carp is a coarse-textured fish which sometimes has a sweet flavor, depending on its habitat. If the carp has been living in the mud, for example, it will have a poor flavor. This is one reason why the carp is farmed. In clean water it is often better than the wild. Baking on the bone and braising are two popular preparation techniques. The mild flavor of carp is highlighted by sauces with a hint of sweetness.

The North American pike, grass pickerel and muskellunge all belong to the same family. They have long bodies and sharp teeth. The pike is a predator and has a sweet, fine-textured quality. It is one of the most sought-after fresh-water fish. A problem with the pike family are its hair-line bones. These are almost impossible to remove by hand, especially in the smaller fish. Because of this, pike is often pureed and run through a sieve, then used in quenelles or mousselines.

Catfish is enjoying increased popularity across the country. It has become the number one farm-raised fish in the United States. The firm white flesh of the catfish has excellent qualities for any preparation method, but deep fat frying is still the most popular.

Whitefish is a varied family of fish with saltwater relatives. It is the largest fresh-water catch coming from the rivers and lakes of Canada. They have a rich, slightly flaky, pleasant taste. The lake herring in Europe is a dark-fleshed relative of this fish. The most famous of the family is the lake whitefish that comes from the Great Lakes. This fish smokes well; may be poached whole, and the fillets may be lightly sauteed.

Perch, a name used for some saltwater fish, is also a widely used name for various freshwater fish. The freshwater yellow perch found in the Great Lakes and all its tributaries, as well as the European perch are small fish. Usually sold whole, butterflied or filleted, they are good for pan-frying.

RICH, OILY, DARK-FLESHED FISH

This grouping includes herring, sardine, shad, mackerel and bluefish. Though the texture of these fish varies from the relative firmness of one or two species of mackerel to the unmistakably soft texture of the herring, most seem to lean towards the softer side.

The most common of these fish is the herring. It is used extensively in Norway and Denmark. This fish is eaten pickled, cured and, rarely, fresh. Herring roe is also popular sauteed. Anchovy is an oily fish which is often sold salted, but is quite good fresh when fried or baked.

Shad, with its characteristic gold color, is known for its roe. It also has a delicate fine-textured flesh. An extremely bony fish, it requires careful preparation.

Mackerel is found in a dozen species. As a group, mackerels are identified by their iridescent skin, with blue-green to gold shades and mottled lateral lines. The flesh is usually very rich and fine textured. Atlantic mackerel weigh under five pounds and the European Spanish mackerel is a small fatty fish. The American Spanish mackerel is larger and leaner than the European, usually weighing three to four pounds. Cero mackerel has a lighter flesh than most mackerel. Frigate mackerel has very dark flesh, almost the color of tuna. The king mackerel is the largest, weighing as much as 100 pounds.

Usually very bony, the fish in this category need careful handling. They become very strong in taste rapidly due to the high fat content. They must be cut and chilled immediately after being caught to avoid oxidation and an acid taste. There are also certain oily fish which produce histamines in their flesh which can cause allergic reactions if not handled properly.

In general, fish from this group hold their shape well when cooked. This allows for the use of a variety of cooking methods, such as broiling, sauteing, frying, pan-frying, steaming and poaching.

LONG-BODIED FISH

The primary fish in this group is the eel. Those caught commercially are caught in two stages: The elvers, or small immature eel, and the fully grown eel, which are caught when the eels return to the sea to spawn. They are sold live and are best eaten when mature enough to be fatty.

The common eel grows to a length of about one yard and its meat is very firm, slightly oily and has a subtle flavor. The conger eel, sold mostly in Europe, is larger than the common eel. The meat is considerably less palatable. The moray and sand eel often have a muddy taste. Lampreys look like eels, but are cartilaginous.

Eels are a gelatinous fish. When pounded and allowed to cool they will cut to a savory jelly. All these fish may be boned, and the long meaty fillets are often broiled. The gar in this family has a lighter meat and may be poached or sauteed. Steaks from the eels are also used in soups and stews.

SHELLFISH

Shellfish may be divided into three distinct classifications.

CRUSTACEANS - THESE ARE ANIMALS WITH A BONY, OUTER JOINTED SKELETON OR SHELL. THIS GROUP INCLUDES LOBSTER, CRAYFISH, CRAB, SHRIMP AND PRAWN,

AMONG OTHERS. THIS CLASS SHEDS ITS SHELL PERIODICALLY AS IT GROWS LARGER.

MOLLUSKS - THESE ARE ANIMALS WHICH ARE UNIVALVED (ONE SHELL) OR BIVALVED (TWO SHELL). THE SHELLS EXPAND AS THE ANIMAL GROWS. SNAILS, CONCH AND ABALONE ARE UNIVALVED. CLAMS, OYSTERS AND MUSSELS ARE BIVALVED.

CEPHALOPODS - THOUGH TECHNICALLY CLASSED AS MOLLUSKS, THESE ANIMALS HAVE A REDUCED INTERNAL SHELL CALLED A PEN OR CUTTLEBONE, AS IN THE CASE OF THE CUTTLEFISH. THIS CLASS INCLUDES SQUID, OCTOPUS AND CUTTLEFISH. THESE FISH SHARE MANY OF THE PREPARATION TECHNIQUES OF THE PREVIOUS TWO CLASSES.

CRUSTACEANS

Crustaceans lend themselves well to all preparation techniques. The shells themselves can be simmered for shellfish butter. The meat can be taken from the shell and deep fat fried, sauteed, baked, broiled, poached, steamed or reformed into patties and pan fried.

CRAB

Crabs have been used as food for many centuries throughout the world. The important American crab industry got its start when the first soft-shell crabs were shipped from Crisfield, Maryland, in 1873. There are six main varieties of crabs which are used in the kitchen: Blue, dungeness, spider (queen), oyster, rock and king. Crabs may be featured on the menu boiled, fried, grilled, baked, steamed, roasted, as cakes, casserole, newburg, croustades, curry, salad, cocktail, mousse, aspic, bisque, chowder, croquettes, pies and the list goes on.

CRAYFISH

Crayfish (or crawfish) are small, freshwater crustaceans which are found in lakes and waters of the U.S. from the Atlantic to the Pacific. Although found in abundance in the slower, brackish waters of the Mississippi valley, wherever they are found they are used as food for humans. They are similar to the lobster, averaging in length from two to eight inches. Some have been known to attain a weight of six pounds. They are prepared and cooked in the same manner as shrimp. They are delicious in cocktails and various seafood casseroles.

LOBSTER

Accepted universally as the king of shellfish, the clawed lobster has many close relatives which are always in high demand. The North Atlantic lobster stands out from its cousins because of its larger, fleshier claws and wider tail.

The Mediterranean lobster or spiny lobster is often called rock lobster, crawfish or langoustine with its brownish-pink color. The locust or flat lobster with its broad, flat body has less meat than the spiny lobster. Found in the Mediterranean and along the Atlantic coast of America and Europe, they are related to the Australian flathead locust lobster, which is also know as the Moretown Bay bug. The North Atlantic clawed lobster tends to have a sweeter taste than that of the spiny lobster.

All lobsters must be alive when cooked. When facilities are not available to keep lobsters alive, it is best to buy those that are already cooked, either fresh or frozen.

SHRIMP, PRAWN AND SCAMPI

Shrimp, prawns and scampi are the most popular type of shellfish. They differ very little, except in size. The small shrimp, normally little more than an inch in length, are the most well known worldwide. Bay shrimp is the term used for these in North America, but the tiny gray shrimp found in Great Britain are sought after for their pungent, almost spicy taste. The effort involved in catching and properly cleaning these small tasty shrimp adds to their expense. They are very good for salads, canapes, on buttered bread or in soups.

Medium-sized shrimp are called prawns in some areas of the world, but in North America are known as shrimp. This size includes a variety of species and colors worldwide. All, however, have a distinctive firm flesh. These shrimp are less fragile than the tiny bay shrimp, but still require careful handling. They can easily deteriorate and spoil. Their delicate flavor can quickly be overwhelmed by seasonings. These shrimp are the most versatile, lending themselves well to frying, sauteing, casseroles, kebabs or shrimp cocktail.

Jumbo shrimp or prawns are of a size that often yields less than 10 per pound with their heads on. At this size the prawn develops special characteristics in both taste and texture. The huge tiger shrimp and Spanish gambas are found in this class.

Scampi, which is often confused with the prawn, is really a part of the lobster family. This is evidenced by its long narrow claws. The scampi is known in France as langoustines, in Norway as the Norway lobster, and is also called the Dublin Bay prawn. Though similar in size to the prawn, they are more fragile and have a more subtle flavor.

MOLLUSKS

This class has three distinct categories: Univalves, bivalves and cephalopods. Whether eaten raw or cooked, mollusks with shells must be alive when received and used. Univalves, like snails, should retreat into their shells when poked. Bivalves, like clams, should be tightly closed; however, scallops and soft-shell clams never close completely even when alive.

Mollusks are very susceptible to pollution and can carry a variety of diseases such as hepatitis. Because of this they are strictly controlled by the government as to where and when they are caught. You should not purchase or gather mollusks in the wild if you are in doubt of the safety of the water. Purging or soaking will not eliminate the disease from the mollusks.

UNIVALVES

The two largest univalves are the conch and abalone found in the Mediterranean, South Pacific and along both coasts of North and South America. These are some of the few univalves which do not require cooking before being removed from the shell. Both can be eaten raw, but tend to be tough. This natural toughness is best reduced by thin slicing or pounding before cooking.

Snails, the best known of the univalves, are actually land animals. Today they are fattened on cabbage, wheat and oats before being harvested. The Burgundian or Roman snail, the African achatina, and the small petit gris are the most common of the cultivated snails. The achatina is the largest.

The small winkles and periwinkles, the limpet and the welk are also members of this family, but are found in the ocean.

BIVALVES

More than 12 species make up this versatile class. Scallops, oysters and mussels are perhaps the most notable. They are adaptable to a wide variety of cooking methods, ranging from marinated ceviche-style scallops to raw or deep-fried oysters.

Oysters are the most prized member of the mollusk family. Their taste depends less on the species and more on where they are grown. There are a number of types, but the Portuguese oyster is longer than the common oyster and the lower shell is deeper, forming a cup for the oyster. This type, available year-round, is considered best for cooking.

★NOTE: Old superstitions die hard. This is true with the oyster. Although the old superstition that oysters could only be eaten in months with an "r" has been proven to be a complete myth, there are still those who believe it. This belief came from the fact that certain oysters spawn during the summer months. It was believed that they were not suitable for eating during the spawning season. This is not true. Oysters of first class quality are available the year round.

Americans eat only the "eye" muscle of the scallop, both bay and deep sea. Europeans eat all of the scallop, just as we eat the whole clam and oyster. Scallops can be cooked in any manner that other shellfish can be cooked.

Clams are very popular in the United States and offer a wide variety of preparation alternatives. There are two primary categories of clams: Soft-shell or hard-shell. The soft-shell clam is also called longneck steamer or sand gaper. This clam has a protruding neck and the shell never is able to shut tightly.

Clams with hard shells come in a variety of shapes and sizes from stubby round to long razor shapes. Though the shells may be white to purple, the flesh is usually beige to cream in color, with a red coral speckle occasionally. Smaller hard-shell clams are eaten raw and larger ones, due to their tough nature, are cut or chopped and used in chowders, fritters and sauces.

In the Eastern United States, the hard-shell quahog is graded according to its size. Chowder is a medium to large clam, cherrystone a small, and littleneck a very small clam. The soft-shell clams are graded as large and steamers (medium).

Mussels have a cream to orange meat and usually have blue to black pointed shells. They are susceptible to pollution, so gathering them in the wild is no longer recommended. For this reason, farming of mussels is becoming more and more popular. Though some species may be eaten raw, generally mussels are steamed, made into soups, stuffed, baked or broiled.

CEPHALOPODS

Squid, the most popular of this class, octopus and cuttlefish are used in many ethnic dishes. Cephalopods are very meaty, but within each is a cartilage or cellophane-like skeleton. The squid is the sweeter of the meats, but all must be either quickly cooked in high heat, or for long periods of time under slow heat, since they become tough very easily.

AVAILABLE FORMS OF FISH

Fish are available in a variety of forms. The form in which it is purchased will depend on its intended use and the skill of the staff. The forms include:

Round (whole) fish are fish as they come from the water.

Drawn fish are whole fish which have been dressed. They have been cleaned, the gills and intestines removed. This is termed *gutted*.

Roast is a large chunk or tail section of a large, firm fish.

Steak is a crosscut section of a large fish cut three-quarters of an inch to one and one-half inch. Depending on the size of the fish, it may be whole, including the backbone or cut in half or quarters with the backbone removed.

Loin, as discussed earlier, is a longitudinal cut from the fish, such as tuna or swordfish.

Fillet is a side of the fish removed from the central vertebrae (backbone). Fillets may come with or without skin.

Butterfly Fillet is two fillets held together by the belly or back skin of the fish.

Escallops are diagonal slices 3/8" thick, cut from a large fillet.

While it is true that the majority of commercial food operations purchase fish processed in some form, there are those which still buy round or drawn fish. There are four reasons for this:
1. The operation finds it is less expensive to train their personnel than to pay the purveyor for cutting the fish.
2. The location of the operation may be in an area where the fish can be picked up from the boats daily.
3. The operation needs the fish bones for stock.

CUTTING FISH

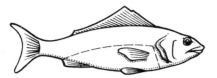

A. Drawn: viscera removed.

B. Dressed: viscera, scales, head, tail and fins removed.

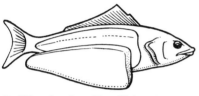

C. Fillets: boneless sides of fish with skin on or off.

D. Steaks: cross-section slices, each with a section of backbone.

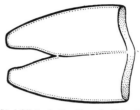

E. Butterflied fillets: both sides of a fish still joined, but with bones removed.

F. Sticks: cross section slices of fillets.

Figure 1

4. The operation serves the fish in a manner which requires whole fish or special presentations.

Of course, volume and availability often dictate what forms are used, but all the benefits and determinants should be weighed carefully. The major forms are diagrammed in Figure One.

PREPARATION METHODS

The preparation of fish and seafood may be intricate or very simple. The determining factors will be the intended end use and the product itself. The preparation of many of these items is very similar; however, there are those which require special handling, either in the form of pre-preparation or in the actual cooking. For this reason this section is broken into generalized discussion of cooking methods and specialized discussion of cooking. The amount of fish needed for one person, depending upon the cut, is shown in Figure Two.

AMOUNT OF FISH TO PURCHASE

ONE POUND OF WHOLE OR ROUND FISH SERVES ONE PERSON

ONE POUND OF DRAWN FISH SERVES ONE PERSON

ONE-HALF POUND OF DRESSED FISH SERVES ONE PERSON

ONE-THIRD TO ONE-HALF POUND OF FISH STEAKS SERVES ONE PERSON

ONE-THIRD TO ONE-HALF POUND OF FISH FILLETS SERVES ONE PERSON

Figure 2

GENERAL PREPARATION TECHNIQUES

SAUTEING AND PAN-FRYING

Almost any fish is good sauteed, whether left whole (if small) or in the form of steaks or fillets. Firm-fleshed fish, such as salmon, monkfish and sole

1. Set fillet skin side down on cutting board. With a thin bladed boning knife, make a small cut between the skin and meat of the fillet.

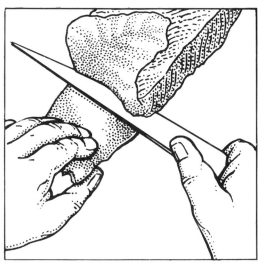

2. Hold the skin down with one hand. Move the knife away from you with a gentle sawing motion while you pull the skin with your free hand.

are most suitable for this cooking method.

The use of a pan with a non-stick surface is best for this preparation. It minimizes the amount of oil required, helping to preserve the nutritional benefits of the natural, low-fat content of the fish.

To prepare a pan-fried fish, the fish may be coated first with seasoned flour, cornmeal (southern-style), oatmeal (Scottish-style) or other suitable ingredient. This will seal the fish and achieve the proper crusting needed.

The coated fish is then fried in fat. The fat used also has an effect on the end product in both flavor and browning. Clarified butter is excellent for flavor and browning, but only when a medium temperature saute can be used. A mixture of oil and clarified butter will give some of the same properties of flavor and browning, yet allow a higher frying temperature. Many ethnic cuisines require the use of specific oils in their recipes, such as olive oil or lard.

A variation of pan frying is the use of a heavy ridged pan. The fish cooks on the ridges, above the fat and acquires a brown, grilled lattice pattern.

One classic method for sauteing fish is called *a la meuniere*. In this preparation the product is dredged in flour and sauteed in clarified butter. It is then plated and sprinkled with lemon juice and chopped parsley. Freshly prepared hot brown butter is immediately poured over it. When the hot butter contacts the lemon juice it creates a froth. The fish is then served immediately.

POACHING

Most types of fish are well suited to poaching, a gentle method of cooking that adds flavor and keeps the fish moist. As you know, poaching is cooking in liquid at a very low heat. Fillets and other small portions are sometimes cooked in a small amount of fish fumet or wine. They are then served in a sauce made of the poaching liquid.

For whole fish, a court bouillon is used. The head and bones of the whole fish contribute to the flavor of the poaching liquid. The acid in the court bouillon helps firm the flesh of the fish. Flavorings, such as anise and fennel, may be used to add complementary flavors to the fish and bouillon.

Although court bouillon is the most common poaching liquid, fish may be poached in milk. Poaching in milk removes strong flavors from salted or smoked varieties.

Fish which are to be poached are best gutted through the gills. This prevents the stomach vent from curling open during cooking. If the stomach has been split, the fish may be wrapped with cheesecloth to prevent curling.

The vessel chosen for poaching will depend upon the fish being cooked. Small fish may be shallow-poached in any appropriately sized, heat proof dish. However, with larger fish a special fish poacher should be used.

The best results are gained when fish are started in cold liquid. Starting the fish to poach in hot liquid can cause the skin to shrink and crack.

Fish can be poached either on top of the stove or in the oven. Either way, proper timing of the item is important. For smaller fish, the cooking time begins as soon as the heat is turned on. The timing begins, for larger fish, as soon as the poaching liquid begins to bubble. After poaching, the fish should either be drained to avoid weeping on the plate, or served in an appropriate container to utilize the stock in presentation.

Poached fish may be served hot or cold. Cold poached fish is often the basis for today's vinaigrette seafood salads. Fish salads with mayonnaise bases are also popular.

STEAMING

This is a popular cooking style for many fish varieties. When surrounded by moisture, the flesh of the fish remains juicy. Steaming displays the individual characteristics of the fish clearly. This makes it possible to present several contrasting types and textures of fish on the same plate, offering an interesting combination to the guest.

Steaming in its purest form is often combined with other methods to produce the needed results. There are two things common to most steamed items:

1. The item cooks in its own juices plus a small amount of liquid which is usually added.
2. The item is served with its cooking liquid.

In some cases, barely enough liquid is added to cover the fish. In other cases a little liquid may be added and then the item is allowed to cook in the steam trapped by the lid of the vessel. The term often used in Cajun cooking *etouffee* (ay-too-vay) and the French term *etuver* (ay-too-vay) are both used for this procedure. The terms are usually translated as "stew," but more precisely mean stewed with little or no liquid.

There are four variations of steam cooking you should consider.

1. THE PRODUCT IS COOKED FOR A FEW MINUTES IN FAT OVER LOW HEAT, ALONG WITH FLAVORINGS SUCH AS CELERY AND ONIONS, AND THEN A LITTLE LIQUID IS ADDED. THE VESSEL IS COVERED AND COOKING CONTINUES. EXAMPLE: FISH STEW.

2. THE FISH IS PLACED IN A POT WITH LIQUIDS AND FLAVORING INGREDIENTS. THE POT IS COVERED AND THE ITEM STEAMS IN ITS OWN JUICES. EXAMPLE: MUSSELS MARINIERE.

3. COMPARTMENT STEAMING IS PLACEMENT OF THE FISH ON A GRATE OR IN A BASKET OVER LIQUID AND GENTLY STEAMING IT. THIS CAN BE DONE WITH WATER; HOWEVER, THE USE OF AROMATIC VEGETABLE BROTH, WINE OR CITRUS JUICE WILL PRODUCE SUBTLE FLAVORS IN THE FINAL PRODUCT. EXAMPLE: CHINESE STYLE, BAMBOO STEAMED FISH.
NOTE: CARE SHOULD BE TAKEN IN THIS METHOD NOT TO PRESSURE STEAM, AND HIGH TEMPERATURES SHOULD BE AVOIDED SO AS NOT TO MAKE THE FISH TOUGH.

4. THE PRODUCT MAY BE SAUTEED OVER HEAT, THEN OTHER INGREDIENTS AND LIQUIDS ARE ADDED. THE ITEM IS THEN COVERED AND COOKED OVER A LOW HEAT. EXAMPLE: LOBSTER AMERICAN.
NOTE: A VARIATION OF THE ABOVE METHODS IS "EN PAPILLOTE." THE FISH IS WRAPPED IN PAPER SO THE STEAM CANNOT ESCAPE. THE FISH IS THEN PLACED IN THE OVEN AND COOKED. THE PAPER ACTS AS THE CONTAINER, ALLOWING THE FISH TO STEAM IN ITS OWN JUICES, AS WELL AS WHATEVER FLAVORINGS WERE ADDED.

BROILING - BARBECUING

Broiling, a dry-heat cooking method, is best suited for fat fish since they will not tend to dry out as much. However, all fish, fat or lean, may be marinated or coated with a small amount of oil to reduce this drying process.

Whole fish, up to five pounds, may be broiled with some success. Their bones will help keep them moist and their skin will protect them from the intense heat. Small slices, however, are better for broiling. When broiling fillets with the skin on, the cut side should be cooked first and presented upwards on the plate. Leaving the skin on the fillet will help hold them together. Thin fillets may be broiled or cooked only on the cut side. Thick fillets require turning when being cooked or broiled.

★NOTE: Special fish racks may be used for barbecuing. These help prevent the whole fish from breaking up.

Fish may be dredged with flour and dipped in melted butter then broiled. This forms a protective crust which will help to maintain the moisture. The fish may also be coated with fat and cornmeal or breadcrumbs to provide protection against excessive drying.

★NOTE: Broiling of fish can be one of the healthier methods of preparation. Care should be taken to use as little fat as possible, yet not produce a dry product.

BAKING

When baking whole fish, it is placed in a pan which has been oiled, buttered or sprayed with a non-stick pan coating, then seasoned. Moisture may be supplied by sprinkling the fish with butter, lemon, wine, cider or stock. The head, if left on helps to keep the fish moist because of the water it releases during baking. The fish should be scored to prevent curling. Most recipes call for whole fish to be baked uncovered. This allows the development of a light brown crust during baking.

Variation may be created by stuffing the abdominal cavity of the fish with an appropriate stuffing. Layers of vegetables and flavorings may be put beneath the fish to form the base for sauces at the conclusion of the cooking process.

If fish fillets or steaks are being baked, an appropriate stuffing may be placed on top to protect the flesh of the fish during baking. Basting may also be done during baking to prevent drying.

An advantage to baking fish is that it may help to counteract the strong flavor of oily fish, but also suits the delicate fish that flake easily. However, very firm fish, like monkfish, have a tendency to become tough if not basted often with plenty of liquid.

DEEP-FRYING

This has been the most popular method of preparing fish in the past and remains popular today, although it is losing some ground. Deep-frying requires good quality frying fat, a batter or breading to protect the fish from the hot fat and protect the hot fat from the fish. A proper frying temperature must be used to ensure a crisp, brown crust.

The best fish for frying is lean fish. This can include small or whole fish like shellfish or smelt, or whole fish cut into smaller portions. Fried fish must be served immediately because its quality rapidly deteriorates after it is removed from the fat.

PROCEDURE FOR BAKING FISH

1. **Prepare and season fish (whole, steaks, fillets) as directed in the recipe.**

2. **Place fish on oiled or buttered baking sheets and brush tops well with oil or butter.**

   An alternative method is to dip the fish in oil or melted butter to coat both sides and place on ungreased baking sheet.

3. **Apply toppings, if desired, such as seasoned bread crumbs; lemon slices; mushrooms or other vegetable garnish, or sauce.**

4. **Bake the fish at 350°F until done. If the fish is lean and doesn't have a moist topping, baste with oil or butter during baking.**

Figure 4

TESTS FOR DONENESS IN FISH

1. The fish just separates into flakes; that is, it is beginning to flake but does not fall apart easily.

2. If bone is present, the flesh separates from the bone, and the bone is no longer pink.

3. The flesh has turned from translucent to opaque (usually white, depending on the kind of fish).

Figure 5

RECOMMENDATIONS FOR COOKING LEAN & FAT FISH

LEAN FISH:

Since lean fish has almost no fat, it can easily become very dry, especially if overcooked. It is often served with sauces to enhance the moistness and give it richness.

1. Dry Heat Method - If it is broiled or baked, it should be basted generously with butter or oil. Take special care not to overcook.

2. Dry Heat Method with Fat - These fish are good for frying and sauteing, they gain palatability from the added fat.

3. Moist Heat Method - These fish are especially well suited for poaching or cooking en papillote, which preserves their moisture. Both are excellent methods of cooking without adding fat.

FAT FISH

The fat in these fish enables them to tolerate more heat without becoming dry.

1. Dry Heat Method - These fish are well suited to this method. The dry heat helps to eliminate some of the excess oiliness.

2. Dry Heat Method with Fat - Large fat fish like salmon, or stronger flavored fish like bluefish or mackerel are rarely cooked in fat. Smaller ones like trout are often pan-fried. Take care to avoid excessive greasiness. Drain the fish well before serving.

3. Moist Heat Method - These fish, like lean fish, can be cooked by moist heat. Poached salmon and trout are very popular.

Figure 6

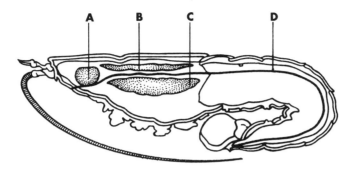

LOBSTER

A. Stomach – discard
B. Coral – delicacy added to sauces.

C. Tomalley – eaten plain or removed and used in sauce.
D. Intestinal vein – discard.

RAW FISH DISHES

For all raw fish dishes the freshest fish and marinades must be used. Thin slices are usually used, such as for Latin American Ceviche. However, whole fish marinated with coarse salt and dill, such as salmon Gravlax, are also popular.

The designation "marinated raw fish" is actually somewhat misleading. The acid used in the marinating "cooks" the fish by acting on the albumen. The result is that the flesh is whitened and stiffened, while retaining a fresh, clean flavor. Lemon or lime juice are the most commonly used acids, but fruit vinegars may also be used. Oil, herbs and spices are used in the marinade to add desired flavors.

Sashimi, a raw fish dish, and *sushi*, a vinegared rice wrapped in seaweed which may or may not contain raw or cooked fish, are dishes from Japan. For these dishes, the raw fish must come from impeccable sources to ensure quality. Freshwater fish and fish that spend part of their lives in fresh water are not used since they often harbor parasites. The highest sanitation and handling procedures must be followed. The potential risk of food-borne illness is great.

DONENESS AND FLAKING

When fish is cooked, the flesh breaks apart into its natural separations. This is called *flaking*. Most books, somewhat misleadingly, state that fish is done when it flakes easily. Unfortunately, some cooks interpret this as meaning "nearly falling apart." Fish, like most foods, is subject to carry-over cooking. Because of this, when cooked until it is falling apart, or even close to it, it will be very dried out when served to the customer. Remember, fish is very delicate and easily overcooked. Figure Five shows the basic guidelines for doneness in fish.

SPECIALIZED PREPARATION TECHNIQUES

LOBSTER

As we previously stated, all lobsters must be alive when cooked. The manner in which a live lobster is cooked is relatively simple. Place the lobster in boiling water. Boil for 14-22 minutes, depending on size, until it turns red. As soon as it changes colors, lift it carefully out (you do not want to break off the claws) and lay it on a flat surface to drain.

The next step is to open the boiled

TO CLEAN THE CRAB

1. Break off the tail or "apron" that is folded under the body at the rear.

2. Hold the crab with one hand with the back toward you, grab the top shell with your other hand and pull the shell away from the body. Use firm pressure, but be careful not to break the shell, you will probably wish to save it for Crab Diable or some other dish.

3. Remove the gills.

4. After removing the gills, hold the crab under running water and remove the digestive tract.

5. Hold the body in both hands and bend back until it breaks in two, or split the crab along the middle crease with a quick chop of a knife.

Figure 7

lobster. This is done by:

1. Starting at the mouth, split the lobster open from end to end.

2. Remove the dark vein that runs from the head to the tail.

3. Remove the stomach, this is the small sac in the back of the head and the tamale (the liver). Note: The tamale is a gathering point for any pollution-based toxins in the lobster. Although considered a delicacy, at the present time it is not recommended that it be served to the guest.

4. Do not remove the coral (the roe or eggs).

5. Carefully draw out the body meat with a fork.

6. Twist off the claws, then the legs.

7. Carefully crack the claws with a wooden mallet and extract the meat. You need to try to get it in one piece.

8. Either use the meat immediately or store in the refrigerator until ready to use.

CRACKED CRAB

Follow the procedure for cleaning the crab in Figure Seven, then proceed:

1. With a sharp knife, cut the body sections about halfway through.

2. Remove the legs by cutting at the joints next to the body.

3. With a wooden mallet, crack the leg sections carefully, but enough so that the customer can easily pick the leg meat from the shell.

4. If served hot, arrange them on a hot platter and serve with lemon and mayonnaise, or some other savory sauce.

5. If served cold, arrange the bodies on a bed of crisp lettuce with the legs draped over the top of the bodies and covered with shaved ice. Garnish with lemon and tomato. Send a nutcracker and nut pick with the waiter for the customer's use.

Figure 8

Another lobster preparation is broiled live lobster. To broil lobster:

1. Kill the lobster by cutting the spinal cord by inserting a sharp knife between the body and tail segments.
2. Split the lobster open from head to tail.
3. Remove the black vein that runs from head to tail.
4. Remove the stomach from the back of the head and the tamale.
5. Crack the claws with a wooden mallet.
6. The lobster is now ready to broil.
7. Brush the lobster with melted butter, sprinkle with salt and pepper.
8. Broil slowly for 15 to 20 minutes, depending on the size of the lobster.
9. Serve immediately on a hot platter with melted butter. Garnish with lemon and parsley.

CRAB

The soft-shell crab, a specialty of the East Coast of the U.S. is a blue crab (shore crab) caught when shedding its shell. The new-forming shell is soft and translucent. The crab is trimmed of its gills and eyes. It is then eaten whole, usually fried crisp or sauteed in ample amounts of butter.

When cooking crabs the number one rule is that the crabs must be kept alive and lively until the moment of cooking. Crabs may be either steamed or boiled. Boiling is the preferred method because the crabs can be observed during cooking. This helps, since the minute the crabs turn red they are done.

To boil crabs, the water must be boiling before putting the crabs into the pot. Use lightly salted water. In fact, sea water is preferred. Boil the crabs for 20 minutes, or until they turn red. Immediately plunge them into cold water just long enough to keep them from cooking longer.

If you are planning to serve the crabs as a cold dish in the shell, ice them immediately and place in the refrigerator until very cold. Then follow the procedures given in Figure Eight for cracked crab. For best results, clean the crab after it is completely chilled.

Hot crab in the shell is a delicious treat. If you are planning to serve the crab in this manner, it should be cleaned while still hot. Again refer to the procedures in Figure Seven. Once cracked it should be served immediately.

If you are planning to pick the meat for salads or casserole dishes, clean and pick the crab after it is chilled. In this

CLEANING OF SNAILS

1. Remove the protective covering at the openings.

2. Wash the snails in cold water several times.

3. Make a mixture of salted cold water, vinegar and a little flour, the thickness of heavy cream.

4. Soak them in this mixture for a couple of hours so that the snails can absorb the mixture.

5. Wash the snails in more clean cold water and keep washing until the snails are free of any stickiness.

6. Boil the snails for five minutes in water.

7. Drain the snails and remove the meat from the shells.

8. Cover the snails completely with salted water or a mixture of half white wine and water. Add some shallots, carrots, onions, celery and a sprig of parsley. Add one teaspoon salt per quart of liquid.

9. Simmer over a low fire until they are cooked, a minimum of three hours.

10. Let them cool in their own liquid.

11. Boil the shells separately in salted water, with lemon added, to cleanse them.

12. When cool, place the meat and shells in tight containers in the refrigerator.

Figure 10

case follow the procedures for picked legs and meat given in Figure Nine.

SHRIMP

Raw shrimp may be cooked in a simple saltwater mixture or in a court bouillon. Lemon or white wine may be used as flavoring agents. Exactly what is used, both as the cooking medium and the flavoring agent will depend on the intended end use of the product and the preferences of the chef.

There are two basic rules for the cooking of shrimp.

1. The sand vein, the black streak down the back of the shrimp, must be removed from all shrimp before serving.

2. Shrimp should only be simmered long enough to turn pink.

CRAYFISH

Proper pre-preparation of crayfish starts with proper cleaning. The cleaning of the crayfish is important, although with farmed crayfish it is often unnecessary since they are purged before being sold. If the crayfish you are using have not been purged there two methods of cleaning them.

Wild crayfish are cleaned by removing the bitter tasting intestine from the tail. This can be done while the crayfish is still alive. Wearing a glove as protection from the sharp claws, hold the body of the crayfish firmly in one hand. With the other hand, grasp the central flange at one end of the tail and twist, pulling gently. The dark intestine can then be carefully drawn out.

Live crayfish may also be purged by placing them in salt water prior to cook-

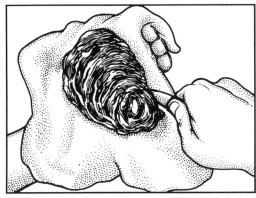

A. Hold the oyster in your hand with a towel. Holding the oyster knife near the tip, insert blade between the shells near the hinge.

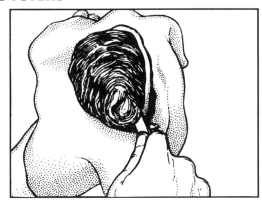

B. Twist the knife to break the hinge.

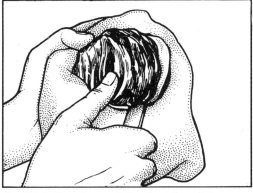

*C. Slide knife under top shell and cut through the **adductor** muscle (which closes the shell.) Take care not to cut the flesh or it will lose plumpness.*

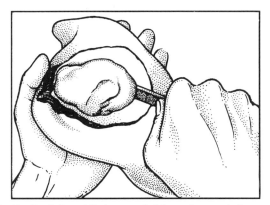

D. Carefully cut the lower end of the oyster muscle from the bottom shell. Remove any shell particles before serving.

ing. This causes them to purge their intestines of any bitter material.

WILD SNAILS

Wild snails must be cleaned or purged of poisonous herbs or pesticides. To accomplish this they should be placed in a moist box for a week and fed lettuce leaves, flour or cornmeal.

The snails are then cooked in water to draw them out of their shells. Any that do not move should be discarded. The remaining shells should be tossed with coarse salt and allowed to sit for 10-15 minutes so they froth. This draws out the slime. They are then rinsed in cold water and drained.

The largest percentage of snails consumed in America are imported "canned" from France; however, Figure Ten gives the procedure for clean-

ing snails. Many Americans look upon the snail with disdain, yet those who are learning to accept the snail as a delicacy are discovering an unusually wonderful treat.

BIVALVES

The first step in the preparation of any bivalve is to prepare it properly for opening. The bivalve should be scrubbed in cold water with a brush, then rinsed thoroughly. This is necessary to remove the dirt and mud from the outside of the shell. If this is not done, when the bivalve is opened, the meat will be contaminated.

Once the outside of the bivalve is cleaned, it is opened. Bivalves may be prepared in a variety of ways including: broiling and deep-frying. To broil them, the shell may be opened and the meat

CLEANING CEPHALOPODS

TO CLEAN A SQUID

1. Pull the head and tentacles apart.
2. Empty the body of the squid by squeezing it with your fingers.
3. Pull out the cartilage and dispose of it.
4. Peel off the outer veiling of the body. It peels off easily.
5. Remove the eyes from the tentacles.
6. Dip the tentacles in and out of boiling water for a minute, then peel off the veiling (the skin) and the cups.
7. Rinse the bodies and tentacles in cold running water.
8. The squid is now ready to cook.

TO CLEAN AN OCTOPUS

Octopus comes fresh, dried or canned.

1. Canned octopus needs only to be washed thoroughly and drained. It is then ready for cooking.
2. Fresh octopus:
   a. Wash and rinse the octopus several times in cold water.
   b. Then, because of its toughness, it must be pounded until the tissues have been broken down.
   c. The eye, mouth and middle are discarded.
   d. Cut the octopus into uniform pieces and cut the tentacles into chunks. It is now ready to cook.

TO CLEAN CUTTLEFISH

Cuttlefish is cleaned by using the same method as for squid, except that it must be vigorously pounded.

NOTE: Squid, octopus and cuttlefish can all be cooked in the same manner. Recipes that apply to one, apply to all. They may be stewed, sauteed or french fried, and they add flavor to soups and chowders.

Figure 11

removed. After the shells are washed, and the meat placed back in a half of the shell with a topping, they are broiled. Tender mollusks such as scallops and some clams may be shucked, drained and sauteed in butter or deep-fried in very hot oil and served with condiments. Bivalves are also very good in soups such as chowders; steamed; cooked with rich mixtures such as Paella, or even served raw.

OYSTERS

Opening an oyster is possibly one of the largest challenges in their preparation. To open them, insert the point of an oyster knife between the shells just next to the hinge. Cut through the muscle that holds the shells together. Separate the shells and partially loosen the meat, but do not cut the meat completely loose. Remove any pieces of broken shell and rinse in ice cold water. If the oyster is being served raw, serve ice cold with appropriate condiments.

SCALLOPS

Scallops are easily cleaned by placing the fresh closed scallops in a pan in a hot oven just long enough for the shells to open wide. Cut the shells apart and remove the meat. Soak the shells in some water and bicarbonate of soda for approximately one half hour. This bleaches the shells for use in cooking of casseroles later. The meat of the scallop is excellent sauteed with tomatoes and garlic; deep fat fried, or prepared in the classical fashion of *coquille st. jacques.*

CLAMS AND MUSSELS

Cleaned clams are ready to be steamed or shucked. Clams that are to be shucked for frying or stewing are placed into boiling water for three to four minutes. They are removed from the boiling water and placed into ice water until chilled. When chilled, insert a slim knife between the shells and pry the shells apart. Remove the meat and reserve any liquid for future use.

If your clams are to be shucked for service raw on the half shell; in cocktails, or chilled on ice, they are not placed in boiling water. Simply insert a thin sharp knife between the shells of the cleaned clam and cut around the entire clam while twisting the knife to pry the shell open. Carefully cut the clam away from the shell and rinse in salted water. The clam is now ready to use. Do not cut the clam free of the shell if it is to be used for clams on the half shell. (If you are lucky to obtain some live mussels, clean them as you would clams.)

CEPHALOPODS

The meat of these mollusks can be cooked in most of the ways other fish are. However, they do require some specialized cleaning. Figure Eleven gives the cleaning procedures for squid, octopus and cuttlefish.

CONCLUSION

Preparing fish and seafood requires a working knowledge of the characteristics of the types available. This is an ongoing, never ending endeavor, since, as the common varieties becoming scarcer, new varieties are brought to market to replace them. This presents great challenges for the culinarian. The new varieties require experimentation to determine the most suitable cooking method for each. Farm raised products often have flavors and textures somewhat different from their wild counterparts, again requiring consideration in selection of preparation method. Nutritional concerns increasingly direct culinarians toward innovative preparation techniques and rethinking of traditional cooking methods. This chapter has provided you with sound principles to face the challenges and opportunities that lay ahead.

REVIEW QUESTIONS

1. Define *aquaculture*.
2. What is the major difference between fish and meat or poultry?
3. Discuss the difference between fat and lean fish.
4. List the sixteen major categories of fish and state a major characteristic of each.
5. List the three classifications of shellfish and define each.
6. Discuss the difference in handling bivalves and univalves.
7. List and define eight forms in which fish may be purchased.
8. Select two cooking methods and discuss their application to fish and seafood preparation.
9. Discuss the preparation of fat and lean fish.
10. List three methods of determining the doneness of fish.
11. List the steps for cooking and opening a boiled lobster.
12. List the steps for cleaning a crab.
13. State the basic rules for cooking shrimp.
14. Describe how to open an oyster.
15. What is the first step in preparing both bivalves and univalves?
16. Discuss how a squid is cleaned.

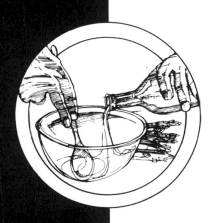

Chapter 21

CHAPTER OBJECTIVES

- **To define break-fast cookery.**
- **To discuss the importance of mise en place in break-fast cookery.**
- **To discuss egg cookery.**
- **To discuss break-fast cereals.**
- **To discuss prepa-ration of breakfast meats.**
- **To discuss prepa-ration of breakfast potatoes.**
- **To discuss pan-cakes and waffles.**
- **To discuss break-fast breads.**
- **To discuss fruits and fruit juices used at breakfast.**

Breakfast

Breakfast cookery is not the preparation of one particular type of food, such as meats. It is, rather, the production of a variety of food types associated with the day's first meal. The foods prepared for this meal vary from one country and region to another. In this chapter we will discuss those types of dishes preferred in the United States. Although there is variation even within the U.S., there is still a great deal of commonality.

Preparation of breakfast draws upon knowledge and skills from all areas of the kitchen. Pancakes and waffles require a certain amount of expertise from the bake shop. Preparation of eggs, meat and cereals calls on the skills of the hot kitchen; fresh juices, fruits and other accompaniments demand a familiarity with the cold kitchen. In light of this, this chapter will deal with the major components of breakfast in the U.S., with frequent reference to other chapters within this text.

MISE EN PLACE & BREAKFAST PREPARATION

All food preparation requires thorough mise en place to insure quality food and expeditious production. However, when foods are to be prepared to order (as ordered by the customer in the dining room) with only minimal precooking of items, mise en place is of paramount importance. This is the case with breakfast, which is often prepared to the order.

Many of the items associated with breakfast do not readily lend themselves to being cooked and held for even short periods of time. For example, pancakes and waffles become dry and brittle when held under dry heat lamps, or tough and limp when held in moist heat, such as a steam table. An egg cooked over easy will become a hard cooked egg when held too long in any type of heat.

To overcome possible problems associated with cooking food as it is ordered, it is necessary to have all of the mixes and individual ingredients ready to be cooked when the order is placed by the customer. When your mise en place is properly done it is possible to prepare a wide variety of items quickly and serve them at their best to the guest.

EGG COOKERY

The mainstay of breakfast in the U.S. is the glorious egg. This versatile wonder of nature was discussed in Chapter 9. (You would do well to review it before continuing with this chapter.) Based on what you learned in Chapter 9, you are ready to discuss specific methods of preparation. A basic rule for eggs used in breakfast cookery is freshness. You should use only the freshest egg. Remember, as an egg ages, the white begins to thin and the yolk begins to flatten. Neither of these characteristics is desirable in an egg prepared for breakfast, particularly one which is fried or poached.

There are six methods of egg preparation which are most commonly used in breakfast cookery.

1) **BOILED IN SHELL.**
   A. **HARD-BOILED**
   B. **SOFT-BOILED**
2) **FRIED EGGS.**
3) **SCRAMBLED EGGS.**
4) **OMELET.**
5) **POACHED EGGS.**
6) **SHIRRED EGGS.**

BOILED EGGS

Boiled eggs are one of the most widely used types of cooked eggs. This use, however, is not always at the breakfast meal. The hard-boiled egg is used as an ingredient in many dishes and as a garnish for many dishes. Both soft-boiled and hard-boiled eggs are popular breakfast items. The hard- and soft-boiled egg are prepared in the same manner but with a difference in the cooking time.

★NOTE: Eggs are not actually boiled. Although termed hard- or soft-boiled, they are hard- or soft-cooked in simmering water. The rapid agitation of boiling water will cause unnecessary cracking of the egg.

To prepare boiled eggs:

1) Select only those eggs which are free of cracks. Eggs which have cracks will seep during the cooking process and will not be suitable for service.

2) Bring a quantity of water sufficient to cover the eggs completely, to a rapid boil.

3) Carefully lower the eggs into the water and reduce to a simmer (180°-185°F).

4) Cook for 3-8 minutes for soft-boiled eggs and 10 minutes for hard-boiled eggs.

It should be noted that if the hard-cooked egg is to be used cold or at a later time, it should be cooled immediately. The surface of the hard-boiled egg's yolk may sometimes develop a grayish-green layer. This is a result of the formation of ferrous sulfide, a problem that is talked about with scrambled eggs. This is a reaction between the iron in the yolk and the sulphur in the white or yolk of the egg. The best way to prevent this is to cook eggs just long enough for them to be hard-cooked and then to cool them as quickly as possible.

FRIED EGGS

Most American chefs will admit that the fried egg probably tops the list of breakfast orders. There are four types of fried eggs: Over easy, hard fried, basted and sunny-side up. The preparation of each of the four types begins in the same manner, but the steps for finishing them are different.

To prepare an egg over easy, hard fried, basted or sunny-side up follow the guidelines listed below.

1) Heat a saute or frying pan and then add the fat, clarified butter, bacon fat, shortening, oil or margarine.

2) When the fat bubbles, slip the eggs into the pan. It is best if the eggs are cracked open into a dish before being placed in the pan.

3) A. For over-easy:
   1) Cook the egg until the white is set.
   2) Flip the egg by pushing the pan forward and then pulling back sharply. The curvature of the egg pan should allow the egg to flip over.
   3) Continue to cook until the white is firmly set but the yolk is still soft.

   B. For hard fried:
   1) Cook the egg until the white is set.
   2) Puncture the yolk of the egg, then flip in the same manner as that for over-easy.
   3) Continue to cook until both the white and yolk are firmly set.

A. Cook eggs on one side until white is set.

B. Lift the pan and tilt it away from you. Eggs will slide to far rim of pan.

C. Flip your wrist upward, and pull the pan toward you, and the eggs will turn over. Take care not to flip too hard or yolks will break.

C. For basted:
  1) (Do not flip.) Baste the yolk of the egg with hot fat or cover the pan and allow the egg to steam slightly. In either case the egg yolk is slightly whitened. The egg is cooked until the white is firmly set and the egg yolk is thoroughly heated but soft.
D. For sunny-side up:
  1. Cook the egg, without flipping or basting, until the white is set firmly and the yolk is thoroughly heated but soft.

★NOTE: The preparation of any type of fried egg requires close attention to the amount of heat used. Too high a heat cooks the egg too quickly, toughening the bottom and leaving the yolk cold. This is particularly a problem with basted and sunny-side up eggs. The temperature should be sufficient to allow the egg to cook to the desired degree of doneness without being toughened, yet heating the white and yolk thoroughly.

The traditional fried egg can also be prepared on the griddle. The steps remain the same with the exception being that the eggs will be turned with a spatula. Eggs are often cooked on the griddle using an egg ring to insure a perfectly round shape for the final product.

There is an additional method of preparing a fried egg which is not often used. This is the deep-frying of an egg. French cuisine, on rare occasions calls for this type of egg. The raw egg is slid into a skillet half-filled with hot fat. The eggs rapidly expand and frizzle. Using two wooden spatulas, the expanded egg white is pushed toward the egg yolk center and re-formed into the shape of an egg.

The fried egg is removed after one to two minutes in the hot fat, otherwise excessive browning will occur. The cooking should be rapid enough that the yolk remains liquid. The cooked egg is served on a slice of toast, a grilled tomato with bacon or in other ways. It may also be used to garnish some meat dishes, such as *veal marengo.*

SCRAMBLED EGGS

Scrambled eggs are another popular breakfast item. They can be prepared with or without the addition of milk, depending on the preference of the chef and the guest. To prepare scrambled eggs:

1) Beat the desired number of eggs until well blended. If milk is used, the normal proportion is 1/2 cup to 6 eggs, and it is added when the eggs are beaten.

2) Heat a saute or frying pan and add fat.

3) When the fat bubbles, pour your beaten egg into the pan. The fat should be hot, but not excessively so or the eggs will frizzle.

4) Shake the pan while stirring the eggs. There should be no egg whites showing, and the eggs should be cooked to a creamy consistency. The longer you cook the scrambled egg, the tougher it becomes. It is best to remove it from the heat slightly undercooked, allowing the carry-over heat to finish setting the egg.

Scrambled eggs may be served in many ways: On anchovy toast, with cooked diced sweetbreads, with boiled calf brains, with diced cooked ham, bacon, minced onion, chopped olives or sliced mushrooms, to name a few. Scrambled eggs Grand Mere have small dices of bread fried in clarified butter added to them and are then sprinkled with chopped parsley.

Scrambled eggs are a common item on breakfast and brunch buffets. However, ferrous sulfide is a problem, as discussed with boiled eggs, when cooked eggs are held warm for long periods. In

MAKING AN OMELET

1. Mix eggs.

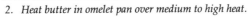

2. Heat butter in omelet pan over medium to high heat.

3. Add eggs to hot pan, shake the pan back and forth and stir the eggs in a circular motion to draw uncooked eggs to pan surface.

4. Use the spatula to check for proper doneness.

5. Add filling. Fold one side over onto other side.

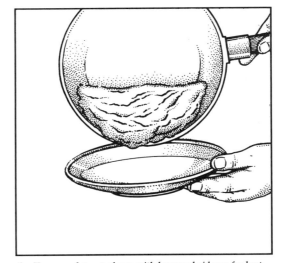

6. Turn omelet out of pan with browned side up for best appearance.

the case of scrambled eggs, the exposure to heat over an extended period can turn them an unappetizing green color. This can be minimized by blending cream or cream sauce into the eggs while they are still slightly undercooked.

OMELETS

Omelets have been and continue to be a popular breakfast item and are also often seen on menus at other times of the day. It is the versatility of this dish which makes it a highly desirable menu item. In reality the basic omelet is nothing more than scrambled eggs enclosed in a coating of coagulated egg. It can be served plain or embellished with countless garnitures, some of which are culinary classics.

There are a variety of types of omelets: Rolled, folded in half, thirds, left flat or puffed. The type prepared will be determined by the preferences of the chef and the guest. Additionally there is disagreement as to whether water, milk or cream should be added to the beaten egg. There are chefs who claim that the incorporation of milk or cream enriches an omelet. Other chefs proclaim the virtue of water, stating that it makes the omelet lighter; they feel that the milk or cream toughens the omelet. Standing clear of this dispute are those chefs who declare the self-sufficiency of the egg. They see no need to add anything to something which is already perfect.

Whichever side you choose in this discussion, the basic method for preparation remains the same. To prepare a basic omelet:

1) Begin as you would for scrambled eggs, but as the eggs set up, stop stirring and shake the pan. It is necessary to let the eggs set, but not stick to the pan.
2) When the eggs are just at the soft, runny stage, add your filler.
3) At this point the omelet may be rolled, folded in half or thirds depending on the technique used.

Omelets may be filled with a wide variety of items, such as chicken livers, cheese, mushrooms, spinach, seafood, herbs, asparagus and many others. A few of the classical omelet finishes are *omelet fermiere*, which has very lean diced cooked ham added to the beaten egg. This type of omelet is not folded. It is served pancake style (open face) and may need to be finished under the salamander to prevent the bottom from becoming too brown.

The *omelet parmentier* is served American-style, folded. Sauteed, diced potato and chopped parsley are added just at the point of the egg setting and then the omelet is folded and served hot.

An additional type of omelet is the *souffle omelet*. For this dish the white and yolk of the egg are separated. The whites are whipped separately to the consistency of whipped cream. The egg yolks are then beaten and the whites are folded into them. The mixture is poured into a pan which is hot and lubricated. The omelet is cooked on top of the range until the bottom is set and, depending on your philosophy, slightly brown. The egg pan is then placed in either the oven or the salamander to finish.

The result is a puffy, souffle-like omelet. It can be filled by slitting, adding filler, then folding. However, it is also possible to add the filler just after the bottom of the omelet has set and allow it to cook in the omelet. This type of omelet is well suited for use as a dessert when filled with a fruit filling or topped with a sweet sauce.

SPECIAL CONSIDERATIONS IN OMELET MAKING

This extremely simple preparation is complicated when a few basic things are allowed to get out of hand. Temperature is extremely important. If the temperature of the fat and pan is too low the egg will not set properly and is likely to stick to the pan. If the temperature is too high the outside of the omelet will brown excessively before the egg is set.

While there may be disagreement among chefs as to whether or not omelets should be browned or not, there is agreement that they should not be frizzled or burned.

The condition of the omelet pan itself is of major importance. The rolling and folding of the omelet is done with the assistance of the shape of the pan, more so than spatulas. For this to take place the eggs must be able to slip across the surface of the pan. The use of fat assists in this; however, the goal is to use as little fat as possible. The surface of the pan itself must be well seasoned. A folded omelet can, and often is, prepared on the griddle; however, as with the pan, the griddle must be well seasoned to allow the use of as little fat as possible.

The pans used for omelets, scrambled eggs or fried egg preparations are normally either fry pans or saute pans. Whichever type of pan is used, unless it has a surface that has a non-stick coating, it must be properly prepared. This is termed seasoning the pan. First, clean the pan well with soap, water and a scouring pad. Then rinse and dry it. Next, heat the pan until the bottom is just barely too hot to touch with your hand. Remove it from the heat and rub with cooking oil, then let it stand overnight. Just before making your first omelet, rub the pan with a little salt and a paper towel. If the pan is used only for omelets, simply rub it with salt and put it away. If it is necessary to wash it with soap and water, then repeat the process.

POACHED EGGS

Poached eggs are used in a variety of ways in breakfast service. One difficulty of this preparation method is keeping the form of the egg in the cooking process. This is much easier when only the freshest eggs are used. The whites will remain more closely gathered around the yolk and not spread out in thin wisps. The yolk in the cooked egg should remain soft and tender. To prepare poached eggs:

1) Put sufficient water in a pan of suitable size. Add a small amount of salt and vinegar or lemon juice to the water. These help to hold the white around the egg yolk.

2) Bring the water to a boil and reduce to a simmer.

3) Crack your eggs into dishes and then slide into the simmering water. Then cook the eggs until the desired degree of doneness is reached.

4) Carefully remove from the water with a slotted spoon.

★NOTE: The result should be a semiliquid egg yolk enclosed in the cooked white of the egg. If the egg is not to be served immediately, place it in an ice water bath to stop the cooking process. It can then be easily re-heated for service later by placing in simmering water for 30 or more seconds.

Poached eggs are often served on toast or with a corned beef or roast beef hash. They are also used in the preparation of *eggs benedict*, a classical brunch dish. To prepare eggs benedict, toast an english muffin half and butter lightly, then place a lightly grilled slice of canadian bacon on the muffin, then an egg poached in the method given earlier. Finally top the preparation with hollandaise sauce and serve immediately.

SHIRRED EGGS

Shirred eggs are prepared in a special kind of dish. The shirred egg dish can be chinaware, or metal skillets in a variety of sizes. The prepared egg is served in the dish.

The dish is buttered and then placed on a hot stove top. Crack your eggs into a dish and slide into the shirred dish when the butter just begins to brown. Finish the egg in a hot oven, but just long enough to set the white. The yolk should still be liquid.

Shirred eggs should be assembled

with the garnishes placed to one side in the dish. The purpose of this is to keep them from touching the yolk of the egg. The finished dish should contain the cooked, but liquid yolk to one side and the garnish to the other, with the solid cooked egg white over all.

There are many variations of the basic shirred egg. The most common is that of the country-style eggs with bacon or ham. Cooked bacon or grilled ham slices are placed to one side, in the bottom of the buttered dish. The eggs are then placed on top, with the yolk placed opposite the garnish. The dish is then finished in the oven and served immediately. Other variations included *eggs hunter-style* garnished with chicken livers and a spoon of brown sauce; *eggs meyerbeer*, prepared with grilled lamb kidney; *eggs a la Reine*, made with sweet breads and *eggs princesse*, which include white asparagus tips and hollandaise sauce.

In addition to these six methods there are a wide variety of others which are used for special preparation. One is *eggs en croute* which is egg cooked in a crepe. A crepe is placed in the buttered compartment of a muffin pan and the excess crepe is trimmed off. One egg is slid into each crepe and then dotted with butter and seasoned with salt and pepper. The muffin pan is then placed in an oven and cooked until the egg white is almost set and the yolk is glossy. It is best to remove the dish from the oven when the egg is slightly under done. It will continue to cook on the steam table if it is being held before service. This dish can be topped with bacon, sausage, cheese, mushrooms or a suitable sauce.

Eggs en cocotte are served in a small silver, earthenware or porcelain saucepan which has a small handle. The cocotte is warmed and garnished, and the eggs are slid into it. The cocotte is then carefully placed in a warm water bath that is within 1/2 inch of the brim of the cocotte. It is partially covered, to allow steam to escape, and is placed in an oven for approximately 8 to 10 minutes. The dish is cooked until the whites are almost set and the yolk is glossy.

BREAKFAST CEREALS

Cereals of various types are a common breakfast item. These include the cold cereals which can be offered in a pleasing display on a buffet for the guests to serve themselves, or served at the table. They are served with milk or cream and sugar at the very least. An assortment of fresh fruits, such as bananas, blueberries, strawberries, apples and raisins may also be offered with them.

Oatmeal, cream of wheat, muesli and hominy grits are all examples of hot cereals often served at breakfast. The preparation of hot cereals is discussed in Chapter 13 (Farinaceous Cookery). The majority of these cereals are served with the same accompaniments as cold cereals. However, in the case of hominy grits, they may be used as a replacement for potatoes on the breakfast menu. In this case they are not served with sugar or cream.

BREAKFAST MEATS

The most popular breakfast meats are bacon, country sausage and ham. (These items are discussed more fully in Chapter 28 of this text. It is recommended that you preview this chapter for a fuller understanding of meats used in breakfast cookery.) The pre-cooking of the bacon and sausage is an important part of the mise en place for the breakfast cook. Country sausage, either patties or links may be placed on sheet pans and baked in the oven at 350-375°F. Be careful not to overcook the sausage, it dries out easily. Sausage links may also be pre-prepped by blanching them in water. They can then be drained and held for service. When needed, the sausages can quickly be lightly browned on the griddle or in a heavy fry pan. This method keeps the links moist yet they can be rapidly finished.

LYONNAISE POTATOES

YIELD: 25, 4-1/2 OZ PORTIONS

INGREDIENTS	AMOUNT
POTATOES, WASHED	8 LB
ONIONS, YELLOW, THIN SLICED	1 LB 5 OZ.
VEGETABLE OIL	4 OZ
CLARIFIED BUTTER	4 OZ
SALT & PEPPER	TO TASTE

METHOD

1. PLACE POTATOES IN A PERFORATED HOTEL PAN AND COOK IN A STEAMER FOR APPROXIMATELY 20 MINUTES OR UNTIL THEY CAN BE EASILY PIERCED WITH A FORK. REMOVE FROM THE STEAMER AND PLACE THEM IN THE REFRIGERATOR TO COOL.
2. PEEL THE POTATOES AND SLICE THEM 1/4 INCH THICK.
3. HEAT A LARGE SAUTE PAN AND PLACE HALF OF THE OIL AND HALF OF THE BUTTER IN IT.
4. WHEN THE OIL AND BUTTER MIXTURE IS HOT, ADD THE ONIONS. SAUTE THEM UNTIL GLASSY AND SLIGHTLY BROWNED, THEN REMOVE AND HOLD THEM WARM.
5. ADD THE REMAINING OIL AND BUTTER TO THE PAN AND HEAT. WHEN HOT, ADD THE POTATOES AND COOK OVER HIGH HEAT, TOSSING THEM IN THE PAN BY SHAKING AND ROTATING IT, YET ALLOWING THEM TO BROWN.
6. WHEN THE POTATOES ARE BROWNED, ADD THE COOKED ONIONS AND CONTINUE TO COOK JUST UNTIL THE ONIONS AND POTATOES ARE WELL BLENDED BY TOSSING AND FLAVORS ARE COMBINED.
7. SEASON THE MIXTURE TO TASTE WITH SALT AND PEPPER. THEN SERVE IMMEDIATELY OR REMOVE THEM TO A HOT HOLDING UNIT FOR SERVICE LATER.

NOTE: BE CAREFUL IN COOKING THE POTATOES NOT TO BREAK THEM INTO SMALL PIECES. THE DISH SHOULD HAVE AN ABUNDANCE OF WHOLE POTATO SLICES THAT ARE WELL BROWNED.

Figure 1

The sausages often utilized for the breakfast meal, country style and link, are raw sausages, generally made of fresh ground pork. These must be thoroughly cooked to protect against bacterial contamination. This does not mean, however, that they must be cooked until they are dried out.

Country style, patty and link sausages can be cooked to order. This reduces waste from overproduction, as well as giving the guest the freshest possible product. When cooking them to order, use either the griddle or a heavy fry pan. Cooking them at 325-350°F will allow the sausages to cook through without excessive browning or drying.

Bacon may also be pre-cooked by being placed in individual slices (if time allows, give each slice a single twist to reduce shrinkage) on sheet pans and baked off in an oven at 350-375°F. for 10-12 minutes. A word of caution in cooking bacon is needed. Generally bacon is thinly sliced. Once it begins to cook, it does so rapidly. It should be monitored closely to prevent it becoming too done. It is also best to place the

PANCAKES
(GRIDDLE CAKES)
YIELD: 85, 3 OZ PANCAKES

INGREDIENTS	AMOUNT
EGGS, LARGE	13 EA
SALT	1.25 OZ
SUGAR	5 OZ
MILK	1 GAL
FLOUR, ALL-PURPOSE	5 LB
BAKING POWDER	5 OZ
MELTED BUTTER OR MARGARINE	10 OZ
VANILLA	1 TBS

METHOD

1. WHISK EGGS WELL, ADD SUGAR AND CONTINUE TO WHISK UNTIL LIGHT, THEN ADD MILK AND VANILLA.
2. BLEND ALL DRY INGREDIENTS THOROUGHLY.
3. ADD LIQUID INGREDIENTS TO DRY INGREDIENTS AND MIX JUST ENOUGH TO INCORPORATE. NOTE: IF THE MIXTURE IS STILL SLIGHTLY LUMPY, IT IS NOT A PROBLEM.
4. LADLE 3 OZ OF BATTER ONTO A HOT (350-375°F) GRIDDLE, SWIRLING TO MAKE IT ROUND AND SPREADING IT INTO AN EVEN, THIN CIRCLE SHAPE. NOTE: IT IS IMPORTANT TO KEEP THE PANCAKES THE SAME SIZE AND SHAPE.
5. COOK UNTIL THE CAKE BUBBLES AND FORMS PITS ON TOP, THEN TURN AND COOK THE UNCOOKED SIDE UNTIL SLIGHTLY BROWNED.
6. SERVE IMMEDIATELY ON A HOT PLATE WITH BUTTER AND SYRUP OR OTHER ACCOMPANIMENTS.

NOTE: THIS BATTER MAY BE MADE AND REFRIGERATED OVERNIGHT, HOWEVER IT MAY BE NECESSARY TO INCREASE THE QUANTITY OF BAKING POWDER SLIGHTLY.

Figure 2

bacon slices on a rack in the sheet pan when possible. This is also true for sausages. This will allow the fats to accumulate away from the meat as it cooks, resulting in a less greasy finished product. Here again it is important that it not be overcooked.

As with sausages, bacon can be cooked by the order. This can be done in a heavy fry pan; however, it is best done on a griddle. When cooking bacon on the griddle, 350°F. is the preferred temperature. This temperature allows the bacon to cook and brown evenly, without excessive shrinkage or burnt edges. Bacon cooks best on the griddle when some type of weight is used to prevent it from curling, which does not affect flavor but does mar the appearance of the finished product.

Ham is a breakfast meat that is best not pre-cooked. It may be pre-sliced and portioned, however it is not necessary to pre-cook it. When placed on a hot griddle, in a heavy hot fry pan or in a hot broiler, it will cook very quickly. Pre-cooking will only make ham dry and unappetizing.

The portioning and, if desired for sausage and bacon, panning of these meats may be done the day before they are to be used. When pre-prepping

WAFFLES

YIELD: 92, 3 OZ WAFFLES

INGREDIENTS	AMOUNT
EGGS, LARGE	15 EA
SALT	1.25 OZ
SUGAR	10 OZ
MILK	7-8 PT
FLOUR, ALL-PURPOSE	5 LB
BAKING POWDER	5 OZ
MELTED BUTTER OR MARGARINE	20 OZ
VANILLA	1 TBS

METHOD

1. SEPARATE EGGS, RESERVING EGG WHITES FOR LATER.
2. WHISK EGG YOLKS WELL. ADD SUGAR AND CONTINUE TO WHISK UNTIL LIGHT, THEN ADD THE MILK AND VANILLA.
3. BLEND ALL THE DRY INGREDIENTS THOROUGHLY.
4. ADD THE LIQUID INGREDIENTS, EXCEPT EGG WHITES, TO THE DRY INGREDIENTS AND MIX JUST ENOUGH TO INCORPORATE. NOTE: IF THE MIXTURE IS STILL SLIGHTLY LUMPY, IT IS NOT A PROBLEM.
5. WHIP THE EGG WHITES TO A SOFT PEAK AND FOLD INTO THE BATTER.
6. LADLE 3 OZ OF BATTER ONTO A HOT WAFFLE IRON (350-375°F). (MOST WAFFLE IRONS HAVE A PRESET TEMPERATURE.) COOK FOR APPROXIMATELY 2 MINUTES, OR UNTIL STEAM IS NO LONGER COMING FROM THE IRON. (MANY WAFFLE IRONS HAVE PRESET TIMERS.)
6. SERVE IMMEDIATELY ON HOT PLATE WITH BUTTER AND SYRUP OR OTHER ACCOMPANIMENTS.

NOTE: WAFFLE BATTER CAN BE PREPARED THE DAY BEFORE USE AND REFRIGERATED. HOWEVER, THE EGG WHITES MUST BE HELD SEPARATELY AND WHIPPED AND FOLDED INTO THE MIXTURE JUST PRIOR TO SERVICE.

NOTE: Pancakes or waffles may have blueberries, nuts or other fruits added to them when being cooked. After pouring the batter on the griddle or in the waffle iron, place a few blueberries or nuts on it for a tasty variation.

Figure 3

meats in this manner they must be tightly wrapped and properly refrigerated until used. As with all hot foods, they must be served hot.

BREAKFAST POTATOES

Hash browns, home fries and cottage fries are all examples of the types of potatoes served at breakfast. The pre-prepping of the potatoes is just as important a part of your mise en place as the pre-portioning of breakfast meats. The potatoes from which the items are to be prepared are normally cooked and processed the day before. The whole potatoes are thoroughly scrubbed, then steamed or boiled until they can be pierced with a fork using slight pressure. They are then peeled and shredded for hash browns; peeled and sliced thin for home fries, or peeled and sliced one-quarter inch thick for cottage fries. The potatoes are then refrigerated and held till needed. At

WHITE HOUSE MUFFINS
(ADAPTED FROM THE *WHITE HOUSE COOKBOOK*, PUBLISHED IN 1892)
YIELD: 24, 3 OZ MUFFINS

INGREDIENTS	AMOUNT
FLOUR, ALL-PURPOSE	1.5 LB
EGGS, LARGE	6 EA
SUGAR, GRANULATED	1.5 OZ
BAKING POWDER	1.5 OZ
BUTTER, MELTED	1.5 OZ
SALT	.25 OZ
WHIPPING CREAM, LIGHT	1 QT, 1/2 C

METHOD

1. SEPARATE EGGS AND RESERVE THE WHITES FOR LATER USE.
2. WHISK EGG YOLKS, ADD THE SUGAR AND CONTINUE TO WHISK UNTIL LIGHT. ADD THE CREAM AND WHISK TILL MIXTURE IS WELL BLENDED.
3. BLEND THE FLOUR, SALT AND BAKING POWDER THOROUGHLY.
4. LIGHTLY BLEND HALF OF THE FLOUR MIXTURE WITH THE LIQUID MIXTURE, THEN ADD THE MELTED BUTTER AND BLEND.
5. ADD THE REMAINING FLOUR MIXTURE AND BLEND TILL ALL THE FLOUR IS WETTED.
6. WHIP THE EGG WHITES TO SOFT PEAKS AND FOLD INTO THE MIXTURE.
7. PLACE 3 OZ OF THE BATTER INTO EACH WELL GREASED MUFFIN CUP.
8. BAKE IMMEDIATELY AT 375°F FOR 18-20 MINUTES OR UNTIL LIGHTLY BROWNED AND SET.
9. SERVE WARM WITH BUTTER AND JAMS.

BISCUITS
YIELD: 200, 1.5 OZ BISCUITS

INGREDIENTS	AMOUNT
FLOUR, ALL-PURPOSE	8.5 LB
BAKING POWDER	5.5 OZ
SALT	4 OZ
NON-FAT DRY MILK POWDER	12 OZ
VEGETABLE SHORTENING, EMULSIFIED	2.4 LB
COLD WATER	3 QT

METHOD

1. BLEND THE FLOUR, BAKING POWDER, SALT AND MILK POWDER IN THE MIXING BOWL OF A 30-QT MIXER, USING THE PADDLE, ON 1ST SPEED.
2. ADD THE SHORTENING TO THE MIXTURE AND CONTINUE TO BLEND ON 1ST SPEED UNTIL THE MIXTURE IS THE CONSISTENCY OF COARSE CORNMEAL.
3. ADD THE WATER AND MIX ONE MINUTE ON 1ST SPEED, DO NOT OVERMIX.
4. REMOVE THE DOUGH TO A FLOURED BENCH AND ROLL OUT TO A 1/2 INCH THICKNESS. CUT BISCUITS 2 1/2 INCHES IN DIAMETER AND PLACE ON LIGHTLY GREASED SHEET PANS.
5. BAKE IMMEDIATELY IN A 450°F OVEN FOR 10-15 MINUTES, OR UNTIL GOLDEN BROWN.
6. REMOVE FROM OVEN AND LIGHTLY BRUSH TOPS WITH MELTED BUTTER. SERVE HOT WITH BUTTER AND JAM.

Figure 4

service the amount of potatoes needed is sauteed in a fry pan or on a griddle in butter, margarine, oil, bacon fat or shortening and seasoned with salt and pepper. In this manner it is possible to serve the customer a freshly prepared potato in a short period of time.

An example recipe for *lyonnaise potatoes*, a common variation for breakfast service, is given in Figure One. Another interesting variation is preparation of the potatoes with the peel on. There is a great deal of nutritive value in the skin of the potato and it really is a shame to waste it. Simply prepare well washed potatoes as you would for home fries, cottage fries or lyonnaise, except slice the potato with the skin on. It makes for both a nutritious and good tasting dish.

PANCAKES & WAFFLES, ETC.

Two favorite breakfast items are pancakes and waffles. This seems to be true no matter what part of the United States you are in. Both are relatively simple to make and cook quickly; however, there is more difference between a pancake and a waffle than just the cooking surface (a pancake is cooked on a griddle and a waffle in a waffle iron). The mixtures are similar, but the waffle is normally a richer, lighter, crisper product.

The pancake and waffle contain virtually the same ingredients, as can be seen in Figures Two and Three; however, the amounts and handling of them differ. The waffle contains a higher quantity of fat, sugar and eggs. In addition, the eggs used in waffles are often separated. The yolks are blended with the other liquids and the whites are whipped separately. The whipped egg whites are then combined with the rest of the mixture just prior to cooking, giving it a lighter, crisper texture.

FRENCH TOAST

French toast is not as popular as waffles and pancakes, but has remained in solid demand at breakfast. This dish is bread (preferably slightly stale) dipped into egg or an egg, milk and sugar mixture. It is cooked either on a hot griddle or pan-fried in clarified butter. The most common method in the commercial kitchen is cooking it on the griddle. A standard batter would be 20 eggs, two cups sugar and one pint of milk, seasoned with vanilla and nutmeg. This can be prepared the day before and refrigerated until needed. Depending on the richness desired, cream can be used instead of milk. The bread is soaked briefly in the batter, allowing it to absorb part of the mixture, and then cooked on the griddle like a pancake. French toast is served sprinkled with powdered sugar and accompanied by butter and syrup.

BREAKFAST BREADS

A list of breads considered suitable for service at breakfast would be very long. The choice of the guest will change from one part of the country to another. The most common choices are toast, white, whole-wheat or other, and sweet rolls or doughnuts of various kinds. In many parts of the United States biscuits are considered a breakfast staple. In many places, muffins, english muffins or bagels are just as popular. Many of these items are discussed in Chapters 30-36 of this text dealing with baking.

Freshness is the primary consideration for breakfast breads. They should be served warm and fresh with suitable accompaniments. Fresh does not necessarily mean that the items must be baked the day they are served. It does mean that they have been handled and stored in a manner that has maintained their flavor and texture. There is a wide variety of prepared, frozen baked goods available, such as Danish rolls and biscuits, that are of high quality. When it is not possible for a kitchen to produce all of the baked goods needed, these are often used. Specialty items such as bagels may be purchased fresh from a high quality local source or frozen.

There are a variety of quick breads that can be prepared with little difficulty or equipment that will enhance the breakfast menu. In particular this includes muffins of all types and biscuits. Sample recipes for these are given in Figure Four.

FRESH FRUIT & JUICES

Breakfast is considered incomplete by many people if it does not include a glass of fruit juice or some fruit. The preparation and service of fresh fruit is discussed in Chapters 10 and 23. The types of fruit often served at breakfast include melons of all types, strawberries, raspberries, kiwis, grapefruit, oranges and bananas. The melons, oranges and grapefruit can be pre-prepped a day ahead, allowing for quick service. The other fruits should be prepared closer to service to prevent deterioration of their quality prior to service. (For a more complete discussion of the handling of these fruits see Chapter 10.) The fruits are often used as part of what is termed a continental breakfast which consists of an offering of breakfast pastries, fruits, fruit juices and cold cereals.

Fruit juices are still fresh squeezed in some kitchens; however, the more common practice is the purchase of bottled or canned juices. Commonly served juices include orange, grapefruit, apple, grape, tomato, cranberry and pineapple. Various juice blends, such as pineapple-orange and cranapple, are gaining popularity. Whichever type of juice is served and whether it is fresh squeezed or purchased, it should be served well chilled. If the juices are pre-poured or prepared from concentrate in advance of use, they must be protected from the odors and flavors of other foods because they are susceptible to strong odors and flavors.

CONCLUSION

The items we have discussed here as breakfast dishes are definitely applicable for the United States. However, as a culinarian, you must be aware that there is a great deal of difference between what individuals consider breakfast foods here and in other parts of the world. While bacon, fried eggs, hash browns, toast and coffee are regular fare here, in Japan the preference may be for some type of fish, fruit or a breakfast soup. In many parts of the world cheese, fruit and various rolls or breads are the standard breakfast fare. As you begin to expand your horizons, you will find that there is truly a world of difference between what is considered breakfast in the U.S. and in some other countries.

REVIEW QUESTIONS

1. Define *breakfast cookery.*
2. What is the importance of mise en place in breakfast cookery?
3. State how to prepare a boiled egg.
4. Why is a boiled egg not really boiled?
5. What are the four types of fried eggs?
6. Discuss the difference between the preparation of a basted and sunny-side up egg.
7. How does the deep-fried egg of French cuisine differ from the American fried egg?
8. State how to prepare scrambled eggs.
9. What causes the yolk of a hard-boiled egg to turn gray and scrambled eggs to turn green? How can this be avoided.?
10. State the basic preparation method for an omelet.
11. What does the phrase "seasoning a pan" mean?
12. State the method for poaching an egg.
13. How are poached eggs handled for quantity service?
14. Define *shirred eggs.*
15. Discuss the service of cereals at breakfast.
16. Discuss the pre-prep associated with bacon and sausage.
17. Discuss the preparation of hash browns, home fries and cottage fries.
18. How do pancakes and waffles differ?
19. How is french toast prepared?
20. What is the primary consideration for breakfast breads?
21. Discuss the service of fruits and fruits juices at breakfast.

Section IV
Garde Manger

Cold Sauces

Salads

Gelatin & Aspic Jelly

Forcemeat & Mousse

Pate, Terrines& other Garde Manger Products

Hors D'oeuvres & Appetizers

Charcuterie

Sandwiches

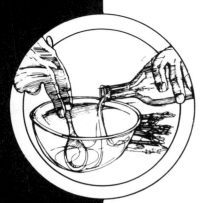

Chapter 22

Cold Sauces

CHAPTER OBJECTIVES

- **To define cold sauce.**
- **To introduce the basic groups of cold sauces.**
- **To discuss basic french dressing and its variations.**
- **To discuss mayonnaise and its variations.**
- **To discuss boiled dressing and its variations.**
- **To discuss other types of cold sauces.**
- **To discuss commercial versus scratch-made cold sauces.**
- **To discuss the storage and handling of cold sauces.**

According to the New Larousse Gastronomique, sauces are a "hot or cold seasoned liquid, either served with or used in the cooking of a dish." Webster's Ninth New Collegiate Dictionary defines sauce as a "fluid dressing or topping, which adds zest or piquancy." These definitions describe a term which has broad application. It is a term which includes everything from the classic French sauces to what are called salad dressings, fruit toppings, gravies and others.

The above paragraph should be familiar to you. It was used to open Chapter 16 which discussed hot sauces. It is repeated as a way to reinforce the relationship between hot and cold sauces. Commonly when sauces are mentioned or discussed those which are mentioned are the hot sauces. This would seem to indicate that the most important sauces are the ones which are served hot, and this is not true. Sauces both hot and cold are cornerstones of culinary preparation. As we stated in Chapter 16, "By way of introduction let us first clarify one point. Hot or cold, the function of a sauce is to add flavor to a dish that is compatible with the ingredients in the dish." It is sauces which broaden the possible variations of dishes into infinity.

It is possible that cold sauces are sometimes given less attention than hot sauces because they are perceived as salad dressings. While it is true that many cold sauces are what we term salad dressings, this does not change the fact that they are sauces. One definition given by Webster's Ninth New Collegiate Dictionary for dressing is "a sauce for adding to a dish (as a salad)." Salad dressings are, in fact, very popular sauces. They are so popular that many people think of them in the same context as condiments such as ketchup. In reality, one of the most commonly used condiments is the base of a great many cold sauces (salad dressings). This condiment is mayonnaise, or is it a condiment? Mayonnaise is a cold sauce. How can it be a condiment? The same dictionary defines condiment as "something used to enhance the flavor of food." Is that not basically what we said about sauces in general?

If you are confused, do not be. The simple fact is that sauce is a broad category incorporating many combinations of ingredients. Many cold sauces have become so commonly available to the average consumer in a ready-to-use form that it is often forgotten that in reality they are sauces. The bottled blue cheese dressing, the bottled mayonnaise and salad dressing (actually boiled dressing), even the infamous bottled ketchup, are all sauces which have become condiments by virtue of the consumer's everyday use of them. The one commonality that each of these cold sauces has is that they are primarily created to be served either cold or at room temperature.

Cold sauces are placed in the section of this text dealing with garde manger because they are most often associated with the salads, sandwiches and hors d'oeuvres which are produced by the garde manger department of the kitchen. The sauces discussed in this chapter are those used primarily in this manner. They are either used as dressing for a salad, spread for a sandwich or as a marinade for salad items.

The purpose of a dressing is to enhance the flavor of the other ingredients in the salad. The mixture which accomplishes this best will normally be slightly acid and tangy in flavor. These same dressings may also be used as a marinade for the ingredients of the salad. When this is done, the item is allowed to steep/soak in the flavored liquid, flavoring, tenderizing and preserving the ingredients. The amount of time the ingredients are left in the marinade will depend on their size and texture. For a complete discussion of marination and flavoring agents see Chapter 5.

TYPES

The variety of cold sauces is as broad as the hot sauces, which is virtually endless. This field of possibilities can be categorized into four groups:

1. Those based on *basic French* dressing.
2. Those based on *mayonnaise*.
3. Those based on *boiled dressing*.
4. Specialty sauces which do not relate to the other three.

It is evident that, as with the hot sauces, the ability to prepare certain basic sauces makes it possible to create an extensive number of other cold sauces by simply adding various ingredients to the basic sauce.

A primary difference between the three primary cold sauces is that basic french and mayonnaise are emulsion sauces, while boiled dressing is not. It is recommended that prior to reading the remainder of this chapter, you review Chapter 4 which discusses emulsions and their preparation in detail.

BASIC FRENCH

This is the simplest of the three primary cold sauces. The basis of this sauce is nothing more than vinegar, oil, salt and pepper. What is created is a very temporary emulsion. Although the acid in the vinegar does assist in creating the emulsion, it is not sufficient for it to remain stable. The result is a dressing which will quickly separate once mixing is stopped. A recipe for basic French is shown in Figure One.

The proportion of oil to vinegar/acid for basic French is normally three parts oil to one part vinegar; however, the proportions can change, depending on what items the sauce is to be used with and in what manner. The goal of the culinarian is to achieve a balance of oil and vinegar which will enhance the flavor of the salad, not overpower it. For example, the marinade for a three-bean salad has more vinegar than oil because sugar is added. The sweetness of the sugar counteracts the acidity of the vinegar.

An additional consideration in the proportion of oil to vinegar is the type of oil and vinegar or other acid used. Olive oil has a stronger taste than a peanut or soybean oil, so less would need to be used. A vinegar is more acidic than lemon or lime juice. It may be necessary to increase the amount of acid in relation to the oil if lemon or lime juice is used instead of vinegar.

Basic French is traditionally made using salad oil and vinegar. However, the principal behind the sauce can be adapted to a wide variety of oils and acids. While these may not be consid-ered a true basic French, their preparation and use is the same. An example would be to use raspberry vinegar and walnut oil. With the addition of fresh basil and oregano the result is a variation of basic French which will bring a different flavor to a salad. The principle used is the same: Oil to give texture (and in the case of walnut oil, flavor) and acidity to improve flavor. The selection of herbs and spices which may be added to basic french to create different flavors is as extensive as the lists of herbs and spices given in Chapter 5.

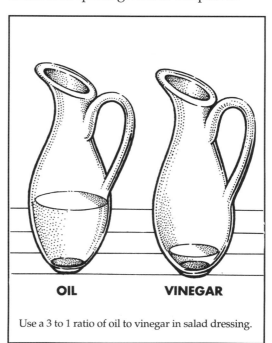

Use a 3 to 1 ratio of oil to vinegar in salad dressing.

LEMON-LIME FRENCH
YIELD: 3 CUPS

INGREDIENT	AMOUNT
LEMON JUICE, FRESH	4 OZ
LIME JUICE, FRESH	4 OZ
SUGAR	1 1/2 TSP
SALT	1 TBSP
SALAD OIL	16 OZ

METHOD
1. PLACE MEASURED FRUIT JUICES IN STAINLESS STEEL MIXING BOWL OF APPROPRIATE SIZE.
2. ADD SALT AND SUGAR, WHISKING TO DISSOLVE THEM.
3. ADD THE OIL, WHISKING RAPIDLY.
4. RE-WHISK JUST PRIOR TO SERVICE.

Figure 2

Flavor enhancers may be added to the sauce to create new and different flavors. Commonly used ones include sugar, soy sauce, honey and all types of flavored vinegars or wines. An excellent flavor enhancer for basic French is fruit juice. Replacement of all or part of the vinegar with a citrus juice such as

---

EMULSIFIED FRENCH
YIELD: 1 QT

INGREDIENT	AMOUNT
EGGS, WHOLE	2 EA
DRY MUSTARD	1 TBSP
PAPRIKA	1 TBSP
WHITE PEPPER	1 1/2 TSP
SALT	1 TBSP
SALAD OIL	24 OZ
VINEGAR, CIDER OR WINE	9 OZ

METHOD
1. PLACE EGGS IN A STAINLESS STEEL MIXING BOWL OF APPROPRIATE SIZE AND BEAT WELL WITH A WHISK.
2. BLEND MUSTARD, PAPRIKA, SALT, AND WHITE PEPPER TOGETHER, THEN ADD TO EGGS, WHISKING TILL WELL BLENDED.
3. WHISKING VERY RAPIDLY, BEGIN TO ADD THE OIL IN A VERY THIN STREAM, INCREASING THE THICKNESS OF THE STREAM SLIGHTLY ONCE THE EMULSION BEGINS TO FORM.
4. AS THE SAUCE THICKENS, ADD THE VINEGAR IN SMALL AMOUNTS TO THIN IT OUT.
5. ALTERNATE THE ADDITION OF VINEGAR AND OIL UNTIL ALL ARE USED.
   NOTE: EMULSIFIED FRENCH DRESSING SHOULD BE OF A POURABLE CONSISTENCY. WHEN FINISHED, IF THE SAUCE IS TOO THICK IT CAN BE THINNED WITH VINEGAR (IF IT DOES NOT ALREADY TASTE TOO TART) OR WATER (IF THE FLAVOR IS AS TART AS DESIRED).

Figure 3

---

orange, lemon, lime or grapefruit gives the sauce a different character which complements not only salad greens, but also fresh fruits. A recipe for a variation of this type is shown in Figure Two.

As we have stated, basic French is a very temporary emulsion. There are times when a more stable dressing, similar to basic French, is needed. This is accomplished by the addition of an emulsifier. This sauce is termed *emulsified French dressing*. There are two emulsifiers used in the recipe shown in Figure Three: egg and dry mustard. These ingredients help to stabilize the emulsion, improving its ability to distribute its flavors evenly through the salad and reducing the need to re-mix the sauce constantly. Although this improved stability has its advantages, it is gained at a price. The price is the different flavors which the emulsifiers introduce to the mixture and a change in texture and appearance.

Which sauce should be used, basic French or emulsified French? This is a question which can only be answered when its intended use is known and the preference of the guest is known. If the desired product is one which is light with only a slight enhancement of flavor, then basic French will probably be your choice. However, when it is preferable that the dressing stand out on the salad and the flavor be more prominent, then emulsified French will be your choice.

MAYONNAISE

Mayonnaise is an emulsion sauce, but, unlike basic French, it is stable. It is used both as a dressing for salads and as a spread for sandwiches. Many kitchens purchase commercially manufactured mayonnaise. The advantage of commercially prepared mayonnaise is that it saves time and labor and it is more stable than that prepared in the kitchen. The disadvantage is that its flavor is not as fresh and cannot be customized to the specifications of the chef.

The stability of mayonnaise is derived from its basic ingredients. Mayonnaise is a combination of egg yolk, oil, acid and seasoning. It is the lecithin in the egg yolk which acts as the primary emulsifier in the sauce. Any emulsion must be brought together

---

MAYONNAISE
YIELD: 1 QT

INGREDIENTS	AMOUNT
EGG YOLKS, (FROM FRESH, LARGE EGGS)	4 EA
SUGAR	1 TBSP
SALT	2 1/2 TSP
DRY MUSTARD	2 TSP
SALAD OIL	24 OZ
VINEGAR	2 1/2 OZ

METHOD
1. PLACE EGG YOLKS IN APPROPRIATE SIZE STAINLESS STEEL MIXING BOWL.
2. BLEND SUGAR, SALT AND DRY MUSTARD TOGETHER, THEN ADD TO EGG YOLKS.
3. BEAT WITH WHISK UNTIL WELL BLENDED.
4. WHISKING VERY RAPIDLY, BEGIN TO ADD THE OIL IN A VERY THIN STREAM, INCREASING THE THICKNESS OF THE STREAM SLIGHTLY ONCE THE EMULSION BEGINS TO FORM.
5. AS THE SAUCE THICKENS, ADD THE VINEGAR IN SMALL AMOUNTS TO THIN IT OUT.
6. ALTERNATE THE ADDITION OF VINEGAR AND OIL UNTIL ALL ARE USED.

Figure 4

BLUE CHEESE DRESSING
YIELD: 2 QT

INGREDIENT	AMOUNT
BLUE CHEESE	12 OZ
MAYONNAISE	1 QT
ONION, FINELY GRATED	2 TSP
WHITE PEPPER	1/2 TSP
SALT	TO TASTE
PINEAPPLE JUICE	3/4 CUP

METHOD
1. BLEND MAYONNAISE, GRATED ONION, PINEAPPLE JUICE AND THE WHITE PEPPER TOGETHER IN AN APPROPRIATE SIZE STAINLESS STEEL MIXING BOWL.
2. CRUMBLE THE BLUE CHEESE AND FOLD INTO THE MIXTURE.
3. CHECK FLAVOR AND ADD SALT AS NEEDED.
4. ALLOW DRESSING TO STAND FOR AT LEAST 3 HOURS (IN THE REFRIGERATOR) PRIOR TO SERVICE.

1000 ISLAND DRESSING
YIELD: 2 QT

INGREDIENT	AMOUNT
MAYONNAISE	1 QT
CHILI SAUCE	1 PT
SWEET PICKLE RELISH	1/2 C
GREEN OLIVES, CHOPPED	1/4 C
EGGS, HARD BOILED, CHOPPED	2 EA

METHOD
1. PLACE MEASURED MAYONNAISE AND CHILI SAUCE IN APPROPRIATE SIZE STAINLESS STEEL BOWL AND BLEND THOROUGHLY.
2. FOLD IN REMAINING INGREDIENTS.
3. ALLOW DRESSING TO STAND FOR AT LEAST 3 HOURS (IN THE REFRIGERATOR) PRIOR TO SERVICE.

Figure 5

carefully and mayonnaise is no exception. The balance between the egg yolk and the oil must be proper or separation will occur. Here again, review the discussion of emulsions and their formation in Chapter 4 before making mayonnaise. A basic recipe for mayonnaise is shown in Figure Four.

The proportion of oil to egg yolk in the recipe in Figure Four is standard. It is possible to make a richer mayonnaise by increasing the amount of oil; however, the possibility of separation is increased due to saturation. The preparation of an emulsion sauce always entails a risk of the sauce separating. Review the precautions given in Chapter 4 for making emulsions, as well as the methods by which they can be retrieved if separation does occur.

This recipe yields a mayonnaise which has a mild flavor and can be used in a variety of ways. When a specially flavored mayonnaise is needed, it is

TO MAKE FRUIT-FLAVORED VINEGAR:

1. BRING TO A SIMMER: 1 QUART OF WINE VINEGAR, 2 CUPS OF BERRIES.

2. POUR IN A CROCK OR JAR, COVER AND STEEP FOR TWO WEEKS. (REFRIGERATION IS NECESSARY)

3. STRAIN THROUGH CHEESE CLOTH INTO BOTTLES.

TO MAKE HERB-INFUSED OIL:

1. HALF FILL A BOTTLE (WINE BOTTLE IS EXCELLENT) WITH FRESH HERBS.

2. FILL THE BOTTLE FULL OF OLIVE OIL OR OTHER COMPLEMENTARY OIL.

3. STEEP FOR A MINIMUM WEEK'S TIME (PREFERABLY IN A SUNNY WINDOW.)

4. STRAIN, PRESS LEAVES FOR EXTRA FLAVOR.

5. STORE IN COVERED CONTAINER.

BOILED DRESSING
YIELD: 2 1/2 PINTS

INGREDIENT	AMOUNT
FLOUR, ALL-PURPOSE	1 1/2 OZ
SUGAR	1/4 OZ
DRY MUSTARD	1 TBSP
SALT	1 TBSP
WHITE PEPPER	1/3 TSP
PAPRIKA	1/2 TSP
EGG YOLKS, BEATEN	6 EA
MILK	1 QT
VINEGAR	4 OZ
LEMON JUICE	2 OZ
BUTTER	3 OZ

METHOD

1. BLEND TOGETHER FLOUR, SUGAR, DRY MUSTARD, SALT, WHITE PEPPER AND PAPRIKA.
2. PLACE BEATEN EGG YOLKS IN APPROPRIATE SIZE STAINLESS STEEL MIXING BOWL AND ADD DRY INGREDIENTS, WHISKING TILL SMOOTH.
3. ADD MILK AND MIX UNTIL WELL BLENDED.
4. SLOWLY ADD VINEGAR AND LEMON JUICE.
5. TRANSFER MIXTURE TO A DOUBLE BOILER AND COOK ON LOW HEAT, STIRRING CONSTANTLY, UNTIL THICK.
6. REMOVE FROM THE HEAT AND WHISK IN BUTTER.
7. TRANSFER TO A GLASS OR STAINLESS STEEL CONTAINER AND COOL.
   NOTE: THE DRESSING WILL THICKEN MORE AS IT COOLS.

Figure 6

TARTAR SAUCE

YIELD: **1 1/2** QT

INGREDIENT	AMOUNT
BOILED DRESSING	1 QT
PICKLE RELISH	1 C
CAPERS, DRAINED	1/2 C
ONION, FINELY CHOPPED	5 OZ

METHOD

1. PLACE ALL INGREDIENTS IN A STAINLESS STEEL MIXING BOWL OF APPROPRIATE SIZE AND BLEND WELL.
2. ALLOW TO STAND (UNDER REFRIGERATION) FOR ONE HOUR PRIOR TO SERVICE.

Figure 7

---

simply a matter of changing the character of the oil, acid and seasoning. This can be done in much the same manner as for basic French. Using oils with more flavor, such as olive oil, or special vinegars or acidic fruit juices, yields a mayonnaise which has a more pronounced flavor. The addition of herbs and spices, such as pureed garlic or onion, possibly fresh oregano, basil or cilantro, can give the mayonnaise a flavor that will spark a certain item it is to be used with. While changing the flavor of mayonnaise is not difficult, the balance of the oil to the egg must be maintained.

Mayonnaise is not used simply in a mild or flavored form. It is the base of many other cold sauces commonly used in the kitchen, such as blue cheese dressing, thousand island dressing, chantilly dressing and Russian dressing, to name only a few. Each of these sauces is prepared by adding ingredients to a standard mayonnaise. Recipes for 1000 island dressing and blue cheese dressing are shown in Figure Five.

BOILED DRESSING

Boiled dressing is an American innovation which has some similarity to mayonnaise, but contains less fat and is not an emulsion sauce. This is a starch-thickened sauce. Boiled dressing is not often prepared in the commercial kitchen. Normally it is purchased commercially manufactured. It is used both as a dressing for salads and a spread for sandwiches. A recipe for boiled dressing is shown in Figure Six.

Boiled dressing can be substituted in most recipes which are based on mayonnaise. The resulting sauce, however, will not have the same richness as when made with mayonnaise and may be slightly more tart in flavor. The boiled dressing contains far less fat, which is replaced by the starch and milk content. Which should be used, mayonnaise or boiled dressing, is a determination that will have to be made by the chef, based on a knowledge of the guest being served. Boiled dressing has gained a greater degree of acceptance over the years and it cannot be automatically assumed that all guests would prefer mayonnaise.

To prepare other sauces from boiled dressing, as already stated, use it as you would mayonnaise. The recipes for blue cheese and 1000 island dressing shown in Figure Six can be prepared with boiled dressing instead of mayonnaise. Figure Seven shows a recipe for tartar sauce, a cold sauce which is often served as accompaniment with fried or baked fish. This sauce can be made with either boiled dressing or mayonnaise. The recipe given is based on boiled dressing.

COCKTAIL SAUCE
YIELD: 2 QT

INGREDIENT	AMOUNT
CHILI SAUCE	1 QT
TOMATO KETCHUP	1 PT
WORCESTERSHIRE SAUCE	2 TBSP
LEMON JUICE	2 TBSP
TABASCO SAUCE	TO TASTE
HORSERADISH, GRATED	1 TBSP

METHOD
1. COMBINE ALL INGREDIENTS, BLENDING THOROUGHLY IN A STAINLESS STEEL MIXING BOWL.
2. ALLOW TO STAND FOR THREE HOURS (UNDER REFRIGERATION) PRIOR TO SERVICE.

Figure 8

OTHER COLD SAUCES

Cocktail sauce is one of the more commonly used cold sauces not based on those we have already discussed. A sauce which is both piquant and slightly acidic, containing both tomato product and horseradish, it is used extensively with seafood. A recipe for cocktail sauce is shown in Figure Eight.

There are a group of cold sauces referred to as the *cold English sauces*. Of these, cumberland, cold horseradish and mint sauce are the most commonly used. They are normally served with cold meats. Cumberland sauce is a cooked mixture of red currant jelly, port wine, shallots and orange and lemon zest, with a little dry mustard and cayenne. It is a slightly piquant sauce which goes very well with pork and venison.

Mint sauce is particularly associated with lamb, but goes well with pork and some game. This sauce is prepared with mint leaves, sugar and vinegar. When prepared properly, it is far different

SOUR CREAM DRESSING
YIELD: 1 QT

INGREDIENT	AMOUNT
SOUR CREAM	3 C
LEMON JUICE	1/2 C
ONION, GRATED	2 TSP
SALT	1 TSP
SUGAR	1/4 C
CAYENNE PEPPER	TO TASTE
TABASCO (OPTIONAL)	TO TASTE

METHOD
1. IN APPROPRIATE SIZE STAINLESS STEEL MIXING BOWL, BLEND ONION, LEMON JUICE, SALT, SUGAR AND CAYENNE.
2. INCORPORATE MIXTURE INTO SOUR CREAM GRADUALLY, THEN CONTINUE TO WHISK UNTIL THICK.

Figure 9

from the mint jelly which is sometimes substituted for it in the United States.

The cold horseradish sauce most often seen in the United States is a mayonnaise or boiled dressing based sauce. However, the English version is somewhat different. It is a combination of mustard, horseradish, sugar, salt, cream, vinegar and a stabilizer of either bread crumbs or flour.

Sour cream is another popular base for cold sauces. It meets the criteria of being slightly acidic and tangy in flavor, plus it is compatible with a wide variety of possible ingredients. The addition of pureed vegetables or fruit to sour cream with acid and flavoring agents yields a dressing which is rich and tangy. A recipe for a basic sour cream dressing is shown in Figure Nine.

Yogurt is another dairy product which is an excellent base for cold sauces. The use of low-fat or non-fat yogurt and pureed fruits or vegetables is an excellent way to produce a dressing for your fat- and cholesterol-conscious guest. The dressing is not as stable as those based on mayonnaise or boiled dressing; however, it can be prepared in such a quick manner that this is not a problem. It can be pre-pared almost as needed. Figure Ten shows a recipe for a yogurt-based fruit salad dressing.

NUTRITIONAL NOTE

Cold sauces are not exempt from the guest's concerns regarding eating and good health. Fat- and cholesterol-content are a major nutritional concern in the production of cold sauces. You should experiment with the use of less fats, oils and egg yolks. Use other ingredients, such as citrus juices or other acids, as flavor boosters instead of salt. Reduce the cholesterol content by substituting stocks lightly thickened with arrowroot instead of egg yolk as emulsifiers.

The development of nutritious, flavorful cold sauces is possible with the use of fruit and vegetable purees. Blend these with dairy products, such as low-fat or non-fat yogurt, mentioned earlier, or pureed low-fat cottage cheese.

With the increase in consumer awareness and concern for health and diet, a number of products labeled "light" or "no cholesterol" have begun to be marketed. The basic method of producing many of these items is the replacement of part of the oil in the

---

HONEY YOGURT DRESSING
YIELD: 1 QT

INGREDIENT	AMOUNT
YOGURT, NON-FAT PLAIN	3 C
HONEY	3/4 C
LEMON JUICE	1 TBSP
SALT	1/2 TSP
POPPY SEEDS	2 TBSP
EGG WHITE, BEATEN TO STIFF PEAK	1 EA

METHOD
1. COMBINE ALL INGREDIENTS EXCEPT THE EGG WHITE IN STAINLESS STEEL MIXING BOWL OF APPROPRIATE SIZE. BLEND THOROUGHLY.
2. FOLD IN BEATEN EGG WHITE.
3. HOLD NO LONGER THAN ONE HOUR BEFORE SERVICE.

Figure 10

product with water and replacement of natural emulsifiers, such as egg yolk which is high in cholesterol, with starch binders.

Although many of these products taste similar to the originals, they may react differently in preparations. For example, making a potato salad with a dressing that is thickened with cooked starches may require more moisture to achieve the same texture as a dressing prepared with egg yolk. It is always important to experiment with new products to see how they react in recipes. Normally it is only a matter of a few minor adjustments.

COMMERCIAL VERSUS SCRATCH

In the modern kitchen there are many important decisions to be made. Ones which involve products and ingredients, people and labor, and equally important, time and labor. All of these must be considered when deciding whether to make your cold sauces from scratch or to use a commercially produced product.

There is no question that the selection of pre-made dressings and other sauces is vast and growing almost daily. However, selection is not the only factor to be considered. There are three basic factors involved in the decision: Stability, application and convenience.

Stability - How important is it that you have a highly durable product? Will it be necessary, due to storage facilities or usage, to expose the sauce to high levels of heat or cold? Because of production demands, or staff limitations, do you need to hold large amounts of the item in storage? Commercial products are more durable. They are manufactured using emulsifiers and stabilizers not used in the everyday kitchen. True, there is nothing like the taste of a fresh-made mayonnaise, but if stability is what you desire, then commercially produced mayonnaise is what you need.

Application - You must determine where and how the product will be used. If the cold sauce is to be used primarily as a stabilizer and lubricant for a salad, then commercially prepared sauce may be fine. When you are serving it as an accompaniment to a dish, then the flavor of the product may be far more important. The control you have of the freshness and level of flavor you have when you make your own sauce may be needed.

Convenience - This is a very important factor, particularly in kitchens which are smaller and have less staff. The amount of labor you have available to produce a consistently high quality sauce is a major consideration. Also, will the product your staff produces have a consistent flavor. Often there is one staff member who has the ability to make the cold sauce. If you depend on one person, what happens when you run out on the person's day off? Will the product produced by other staff be consistent with that produced before? Everyone prefers to make their own cold sauces; however, it is important to look at the situation realistically.

STORAGE & HANDLING

The storage of cold sauces is affected by the acidity of the product. The low pH of these sauces can act as a preservative for other foods when they are tossed in them. The effect is similar to that of a brine or wet-curing.

Commercially produced cold sauces, which have not been opened, can be stored like any canned good, in a cool, dry, dark place. Once opened, they must be refrigerated in closed containers. All cold sauces should be stored in plastic or glass containers, not metal. The acidic nature of the sauces reacts with metal.

The ideal temperature for storage of cold sauces is 34-40°F. They do not freeze well. Emulsified dressings in particular will break when thawed.

CONCLUSION

The cold sauces produced in the kitchen add excitement and variety to the menu in the same fashion as the hot sauces. Their flavors often are more pronounced and they range from very rich to very light. Whether you make your own cold sauces or purchase them, their selection must be based on how well the sauce complements the item it is served with. A salad is not eaten for the dressing. It is eaten for the body of the salad, the greens, fruits or other ingredients. The sauce must enhance the flavor of these items, not mask it.

REVIEW QUESTIONS

1. Define the term *cold sauce.*
2. Discuss the term *condiment.*
3. List the four groups of cold sauces.
4. Discuss the preparation of basic french and how it can be varied.
5. What is emulsified french and how is it prepared?
6. Discuss the preparation of mayonnaise and how it can be flavored.
7. Discuss the role of mayonnaise as a base for other cold sauces.
8. Discuss the preparation of boiled dressing and how it's prepared.
9. Discuss the use of boiled dressing instead of mayonnaise.
10. Define *cocktail sauce, cumberland sauce, mint sauce* and *horseradish sauce.*
11. Discuss the three factors involved in the decision to purchase commercial cold sauces such as mayonnaise or boiled dressing.
12. What types of containers and temperatures should be used for storage of most cold sauces?
13. Nutritionally, what types of substitutions could be made in the preparation of cold sauces to reduce fat, cholesterol and salt content?
14. What is the purpose of a sauce?

Chapter 23

Salads

CHAPTER OBJECTIVES

• To define salad.

• To examine and discuss the preparation of salads as a general grouping.

• To discuss the preparation of vegetable salads.

• To discuss the preparation of pasta salads, rice salads and legume salads.

• To discuss the preparation of meat and poultry salads.

• To discuss the preparation of fruit salads.

Herba salata, the Latin equivalent of *salted greens*, is what the term *salad* derived from. This phrase suggests that the earliest salads were mixtures of pickled greens seasoned with salt. This culinary variation evolved by the time of Imperial Rome into mixtures of greens served with a fresh herb garnish and an oil-and-vinegar-based dressing.

The 17th and 18th centuries brought more additions to the humble culinary creation called salad. Lettuces of various types were used as a base with some type of meat, normally poultry, and mixed vegetables placed on top. Oil and vinegar were still used as the base of the dressing. Now a wide variety of items, such as grapes, beans, rice and flowers were used as garnish.

It was in the early 20th century that Escoffier created a salad of celery, partridge breast and truffles, with a dressing of virgin oil from Provence and mustard from Dijon. This was the *salades des fines gueules*. The phrase means "salads for those with fine palates." From this we have progressed to the variety of salads served today. The possibilities for salad combinations are limited only by the imagination of the chef. They may include leaf greens, raw and cooked vegetable salads, fruit, meat, legumes and rice-based salads to mention only a few.

The broad variety of salads, coupled with the sheer simplicity of many, make it difficult to classify them readily by types. We will begin by discussing salads as an overall grouping. Once the general characteristics and guidelines for salads have been discussed we will address smaller groupings based on the component which makes up the body of the salad. These include: Vegetables, pasta, rice, legumes, meat, poultry, seafood and fruit. The components of these types of salads are discussed in a variety of places in this text, vegetables in Chapters 11 and 12; pasta, rice and legumes in Chapter 13; meat in Chapters 17 and 18; seafood in Chapter 20, and fruits in Chapter 10. This is not to mention the discussion of fats and oils, dairy products and other items. It must be remembered that few preparations in the kitchen stand alone. What is required to produce high quality salads, as with any item in the kitchen, is a command of a broad range of knowledge.

SALADS: GENERAL

In many food service operations, salads are the course that is given the least consideration, both in planning and preparation. Chefs and managers often perceive it as a simple task that needs little or no training to perform. The result of this attitude is that many salads are of poor quality. We challenge you to consider the salad as an item of great importance. *What better way to impress your guests than by offering salads that are well thought out, nutritionally balanced, attractively displayed, refreshing and stimulating to the appetite.*

To accomplish this you must ensure that certain criteria are met in the preparation and service of the salad. These include, but are not limited to:

FRESH INGREDIENTS.

ATTRACTIVE PLATING.

PROPER TEXTURES.

EYE APPEAL.

WELL BALANCED FLAVOR.

The wide variety of salads makes it difficult to state exact rules for proper preparation of all salads. However, there are some rules of thumb that should be followed.

1. UTILIZE THE FRESHEST OF INGREDIENTS WHENEVER POSSIBLE, AND THOSE THAT ARE IN SEASON.
2. LIGHT VEGETABLES AND LEAF GREENS THAT ARE MILD IN FLAVOR SHOULD BE CRISP, BLEMISH FREE, AND TOSSED WITH A MARINADE OR TOPPED WITH A DRESSING JUST PRIOR TO SERVICE.
3. STRONGER TASTING VEGETABLES SUCH AS CARROTS AND CABBAGE COULD BE MARINATED OR DRESSED UP TO A DAY IN ADVANCE. THIS ALLOWS TIME FOR THE FLAVOR OF THE MARINADE OR DRESSING TO MARRY WITH THAT OF THE OTHER INGREDIENTS.
4. SERVE COLD SALAD IN A COLD DISH.
5. NEVER OVERCROWD THE PLATE. USE A PLATE LARGE ENOUGH TO ACCOMMODATE THE PRESENTATION YOU ARE MAKING AND STAY WITHIN THE WELL OF THE PLATE, NOT ON OR OVER THE EDGE.

The placement of salads within the menu, in general, is not limited to one specific area. Depending on composition, they can be used as an appetizer; entree; accompaniment or garnish; salad course before or after the entree, or as a dessert.

COMPOSITION OF A SALAD

There are four basic parts of a salad. Whether all four parts are used in the construction of a particular salad will be determined by the ingredients and presentation intended.

The *base* gives definition to the placement of the salad on the plate. An example would be a green lettuce leaf used as an underliner for a salad.

The *body* is the main ingredient of the salad. This should be the focal point and sits on top of the base. An example is the simple tossed salad or seafood salad that is placed on top of the underliner of leaf lettuce.

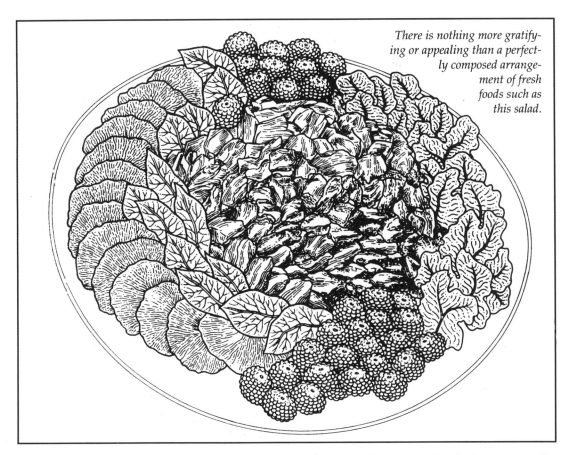

There is nothing more gratifying or appealing than a perfectly composed arrangement of fresh foods such as this salad.

Dressing is used to enhance and add flavor to the body of the salad. It makes the salad more palate pleasing. The dressing may be tossed with the body of the salad, such as in a simple salad or served as an accompaniment to be poured over the salad at the table.

The *garnish* adds form, color and texture to the salad. It should complement, not compete with the body of the salad. In most cases, when a salad is properly laid out no garnish is needed. The simple elegance of the salad mixture itself should provide ample eye appeal, taste and texture.

TYPES OF SALADS

There are three primary types of salad preparations: *Simple, mixed* and *combination.*

SIMPLE SALADS

A simple salad is a variety of one or more greens. A mild dressing, usually a light vinaigrette, is used so the delicate taste of the greens is not masked. This type of salad is normally used as a salad course before or after the entree. It both cleanses and stimulates the palate. Figure One shows a basic recipe for a simple salad.

MIXED SALADS

Mixed salads are composed of cooked or raw vegetables either marinated or served with a complementary dressing. A variety of marinades and dressings can be used; however, stronger marinades and long periods of marination should be reserved for hardier vegetables. These salads can be used as appetizers, accompaniment or garnish or as the salad course. Figure Two shows a representative recipe for a mixed salad.

COMBINATION SALADS

In a combination salad the ingredients are presented separately, but on the same plate. They can be served with a variety of dressings, and are usually served as an entree. Figure Three shows a recipe for a combination salad.

TOSSED SALAD
YIELD: 25 - 4 OZ PORTIONS

INGREDIENT	AMOUNT
ICEBERG LETTUCE	3 LB
ROMAINE LETTUCE	1 LB 8 OZ
BASIC FRENCH DRESSING	1 PT 1 C

METHOD
1. WASH AND BLOT DRY LETTUCES.
2. TEAR OR CUT LETTUCES INTO BITE-SIZE PIECES.
3. TOSS WITH DRESSING AT SERVICE.
4. PORTION ON CHILLED PLATES, GARNISH AS DESIRED.

NOTE: THE GREENS USED FOR THIS TYPE OF SALAD MAY INCLUDE BOSTON, BIBB OR LEAF LETTUCES, AS WELL AS ESCAROLE, ENDIVE, SPINACH, WATERCRESS AND OTHERS. THE PROPORTIONS OF ONE GREEN TO ANOTHER WILL VARY DEPENDING ON THE FLAVOR OF EACH GREEN. FOR EXAMPLE, A SLIGHTLY BITTER GREEN SUCH AS ESCAROLE SHOULD MAKE UP LESS OF THE TOTAL INGREDIENTS THAN A MILD LETTUCE SUCH AS BIBB.

Figure 1

MIXED VEGETABLE SALAD
YIELD: 10 - 4 OZ PORTIONS

INGREDIENTS	AMOUNT
BROCCOLI FLORETS (BLANCHED)	7 OZ
CARROTS, SLICED (STEAMED AL DENTE)	6 OZ
CAULIFLOWER FLORETS	7 OZ
ONIONS, SLICED THIN	4 OZ
GREEN BEANS, WHOLE, FRESH (STEAMED AL DENTE)	7 OZ
GREEN PEPPER, MEDIUM DICE	4 OZ
MARINADE	
CIDER VINEGAR	1/2 C
SUGAR	4 OZ
SOY SAUCE	4 TSP
CELERY SEED	1 TSP
WHITE PEPPER	TO TASTE
VEGETABLE OIL	2 TBSP

METHOD
1. COMBINE INGREDIENTS FOR MARINADE AND BLEND WELL.
2. COMBINE PREPARED VEGETABLES (ONIONS SEPARATED INTO RINGS) IN SUITABLE MIXING BOWL.
3. POUR MARINADE OVER VEGETABLES AND TOSS LIGHTLY, BEING CAREFUL NOT TO BREAK UP FLORETS OF BROCCOLI AND CAULIFLOWER.
4. PLACE IN REFRIGERATOR AND LET MARINATE FOR 6-12 HOURS.

Figure 2

CHEF SALAD

YIELD: 1 - 14 OZ PORTION

INGREDIENTS	AMOUNT
TOSSED SALAD	5 OZ
TURKEY BREAST, JULIENNE	2 OZ
HAM, JULIENNE	2 OZ
SWISS CHEESE, JULIENNE	2 OZ
HARD BOILED EGG, QUARTERED OR SLICED	1 EA
TOMATO WEDGE	3 EA

METHOD

1. PLACE TOSSED SALAD IN A SUITABLE CHILLED DISH.
2. ARRANGE JULIENNE ITEMS SEPARATELY ON TOP OF SALAD.
3. ARRANGE EGG AND TOMATO WEDGES IN AN ATTRACTIVE MANNER ON PLATE.
   NOTE: ALL ITEMS MUST BE WELL CHILLED TO INSURE CRISP TEXTURE.
3. SERVE WITH APPROPRIATE DRESSINGS.

Figure 3

SELECTION & PRESENTATION OF A SALAD

The variety of salads possible requires careful selection for presentation. It is important that the salad selected is appropriate to the overall menu. The ingredients of the salad itself must also be appropriate to each other.

The determination of a salad should take into consideration five primary factors to achieve balance within both the salad and the overall menu.

1. FLAVOR.
2. COLOR.
3. TEXTURE.
4. NUTRITION.
5. SIZE.

Flavor is the most important consideration in the preparation of all food. When planning a salad, flavor must be considered both from the standpoint of the balance of the salad's ingredients and the salad as an integral part of the overall meal being served. When selecting ingredients for a salad, your goal is to achieve a balance of the various ingredients that will yield a pleasant taste when combined, yet allow each to remain distinct. The flavor of the escarole in a tossed salad should not dominate the flavor of the bibb lettuce. It should enhance and complement it. In the same sense, the escarole should not be lost in a sea of bibb lettuce. The body of the salad should be distinct, yet enhanced by the garnish and dressing.

Selection of a salad as part of a meal requires a balance of tastes also. Remember that the meal is a total experience, yet is enjoyed in interrelated but separate parts. The flavor of the salad must allow for a smooth transition from the previous course to the one which will follow. On occasion the salad is actually used as an intermezzo, or palate cleanser, after a strongly flavored course.

The colors of the ingredients within the salad must combine to provide an appetizing, pleasing effect on the eye. This requires the use of color variation to prevent a bland appearance. This does not necessarily require the use of red vegetables in a simple green salad. It may, however, require the use of greens that have various shades of green. This creates a contrast that is both pleasing and interesting to the guest. The overall color of the salad must, at the same time, be in balance with the other foods presented. This is particularly true if the salad is presented

MILD FLAVORED GREENS

Oak Leaf Lettuce

Ruby Lettuce

TANGY FLAVORED GREENS

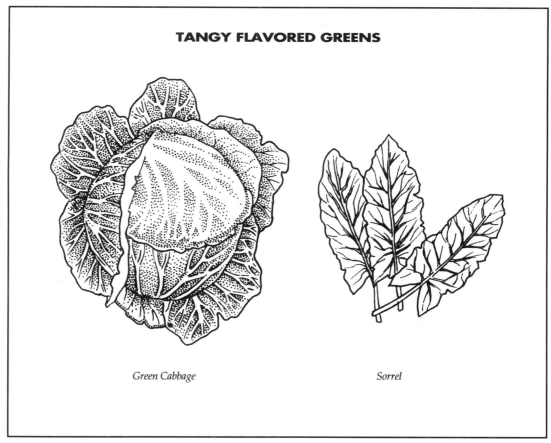

Green Cabbage

Sorrel

as an accompaniment to another dish or in a buffet setting.

The texture of the individual ingredients should create a pleasingly interesting mouth feel. The overall texture should add to, not detract from, the rest of the meal.

Nutritionally, the salad is a golden opportunity to increase the nutritional value of the overall meal, when it is served as an accompaniment. If the salad itself has been prepared in a manner that makes it a nutritionally sound dish, then it will add to the value of the meal. If the salad is used as the entree in the meal, then it should be carefully planned to replace other possible entrees not only in bulk, but nutritionally.

The size of the salad must be in balance with its position in the meal. If it is intended to be a substitute for the main course then it will be a generous portion. Yet, if it is to be a complementing item, then it should not exceed in size the other accompanying dishes.

LAYOUT

Layout of the salad requires concern for balance, as it does for all plated food items. The focal point, what the eye sees first, should be the main ingredient. The overall appearance of the salad should have a flow that is pleasing to the eye. It should not be overly busy or confused. In short, it should be elegantly simple.

The proper size plate or dish should be used. To crowd too much food of any kind onto too small a plate will make it not only unattractive, but also difficult for the guest to eat without having it fall off the plate onto the table. Remember to keep the food within the well of the plate, not up on the rim.

VEGETABLE SALADS

Vegetable salads may be simply defined as those prepared with vegetables. This broad grouping can be further divided into two categories: Greens with fresh vegetables and marinated vegetable salads (both fresh and cooked). Greens with fresh vegetables include tossed, Caesar and spinach salads to mention only a few. Marinated salads include cole slaw, carrot and raisin, three-bean and German potato salad.

METHOD OF PREPARATION

The preparation of vegetable salads begins with the proper receiving, storage and handling of the fresh vegetables, canned goods and pre-made salads. The product should be closely checked for quality when delivered and

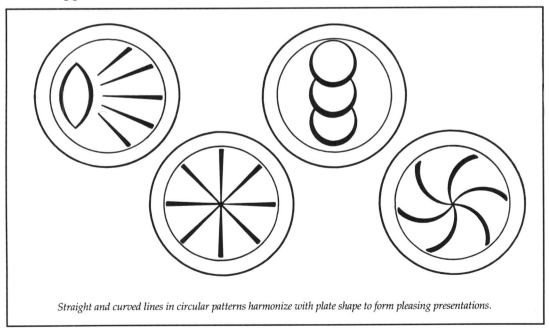

Straight and curved lines in circular patterns harmonize with plate shape to form pleasing presentations.

345

immediately stored at the proper temperatures. Greens and vegetables should be checked thoroughly for freshness and crispness. There should be no blemishes and the items must have a good color and taste. The characteristics of many vegetables and how they should be stored are discussed in Chapters 11 and 12 of this text.

Pre-made salads should be fresh and the packaging secure, with a tight seal. All pre-made salads should have an expiration date stamped on each container and this date should be carefully checked. Canned goods, when received, should be of the type ordered and in good condition.

Receiving fresh greens, other vegetables, canned goods and pre-made salads in good condition is just the beginning of the process to provide the customer with an attractive, tasty salad. Care should be taken in each step of preparation to ensure quality and sanitation control.

PROPER CLEANING AND DRYING

Before use, all vegetables should be washed thoroughly under cold running water, no matter how clean they appear coming out of the shipping case. Washing in this manner serves two purposes: Removal of dirt and insects and, in some cases, rejuvenation of the vegetable.

Fresh greens, in particular, often need to be revived after being being shipped and stored. Salad greens contain a high percentage of water and will bruise and wilt easily. A percentage of the greens' water content is normally lost during shipping. Washing in cold water helps to replenish that water, firming up the cell structure which in turn crisps up the vegetable.

Drying a vegetable properly after washing is also very important. Dressing will evenly coat greens only if they are clean and dry. For this reason, it is best to wash greens under cold running water in a colander. You may then shake the colander to remove excess water and let the greens air dry. An optional method is to salt the greens lightly to absorb any extra moisture; however, this can only be done when the greens are being served immediately. If the salted greens sit too long, the salt will draw water out of the cells and the result is a dry, wilted leaf.

Fresh greens may also be dried by spreading them out on sheet pans lined with absorbent paper towels after washing. They are then patted dry with additional paper towels. In operations that use very large quantities of leafy greens, mechanical spinning machines are sometimes used. These machines work in a manner similar to a washing machine spin cycle and use centrifugal force to remove water from the washed greens.

Mushrooms require special consideration in salad preparation. They are very porous, very much like a sponge. They should be washed under cold running water, in a colander and dried immediately. Mushrooms should not be allowed to stand in water because they will absorb it, becoming soft and discolored. Mushrooms may also be cleaned using a damp cloth. When slicing mushrooms, they should be quickly dipped into an acid (lemon juice or vinegar) and water solution; this will help to keep them white longer.

PROPER SIZE

Vegetables come in various sizes and shapes. They can be grated, chopped, or cut into any shape desired. The rule for vegetable salads is that they should be cut into bite size pieces unless they are being used for garnish. For example, a tossed green salad containing delicate bibb lettuce and romaine lettuce would not be complemented by cut carrots, even if the pieces are bite size. A grated or julienned carrot would be a more appropriate size and texture.

The proper method for sizing leafy greens is often discussed by chefs. There is disagreement as to whether the greens should be torn by hand or cut with a knife. Tearing lettuce leaves provides a more natural appearance, however cutting them with a knife is more suitable for speed and quantity production. Either way the size should stay consistent with bite size pieces.

USING COOKED VEGETABLES

Cooked vegetables are used in salads in a number of forms including canned, frozen, pickled or freshly cooked. Canned, pickled, and even frozen vegetables can be put to good use in mixed vegetable salad. You do need to remember that the canned vegetables have already been cooked. This can cause them to become overly soft if held too long in a marinade. These types of vegetables are also packed in a liquid; therefore, they should be drained before being marinated.

Pickled vegetables should be handled the same as canned, except that the flavor they have received in pickling must be considered when determining the dressing for the salad. Frozen vegetables have been blanched before freezing, which makes their texture softer. They cannot withstand long periods of marination; however, they can make an excellent last minute color addition or garnish for a mixed vegetable salad.

Preparation of your own cooked vegetables for salads normally requires that they be blanched. The vegetable is washed; peeled if needed, and sized. It is then blanched and immediately shocked in ice water. The vegetable is then dried before being dressed or placed in a marinade. Most usage of cooked vegetables is in premarinated mixed salads. The liquid should be drained from these salads just before service.

PROPER DRESSING AMOUNT

Soft vegetables and lettuce leaves are very thin and porous. Their taste is often faint and delicate, easily ruined by an excess of dressing. Remember that most dressings have a high content of salt and acids. These can break down cell structure and the crispness of the greens. Salt draws out moisture and then the leaf or vegetable absorbs the oil and vinegar of the dressing, causing the greens to become soggy and overpowered. Too much dressing or dressing added too far before service will result in the same soggy, wilted effect.

The proper amount of dressing should lightly coat the leaves and vegetables evenly. A good rule of thumb is one to two tablespoons of dressing is sufficient for a three- to four-ounce portion of salad.

PROPER TEMPERATURE

While not all salads are served cold, the majority are. Any salad which is to be served cold must be handled properly to protect the crisp, fresh flavor of its components. Some basic guidelines for preparing cold vegetable salads of any type are:

1. STORE FRESH VEGETABLES AT PROPER TEMPERATURES IMMEDIATELY UPON RECEIPT.

2. ALWAYS WASH VEGETABLES IN COLD RUNNING WATER BEFORE USE.

   NOTE: MOST VEGETABLES SHOULD NOT BE WASHED PRIOR TO BEING STORED, BECAUSE MANY HAVE PROTECTIVE COATINGS, SUCH AS CUCUMBERS, AND OTHERS CAN ABSORB TOO MUCH EXCESS MOISTURE. CLEANING OF THE VEGETABLES TAKES PLACE JUST PRIOR TO USE.

3. BRING OUT OF THE REFRIGERATOR ONLY THE AMOUNT OF VEGETABLES WHICH CAN BE WORKED WITHIN A SHORT PERIOD OF TIME.

4. KEEP FRESH VEGETABLES AT ROOM TEMPERATURE AS SHORT A TIME AS POSSIBLE WHEN PREPARING SALADS.

5. EVERYTHING USED IN THE PREPARATION OF THE SALAD SHOULD BE WELL CHILLED BEFORE BEING COMBINED WITH THE FRESH VEGETABLES.

6. **Set up cold salads only in well chilled dishes.**

The concern for temperature is two-fold. Naturally we are trying to ensure the texture and taste of the product. At the same time we are protecting the product from harmful bacteria and growth of bacteria. Remember to always work clean and maintain food at safe temperatures.

OTHER POINTS TO CONSIDER

The structure of salads as a group is in a continuous period of change. It is important to experiment, trying new vegetables and methods of presenting and preparing them. A few basic guides are needed in this experimentation.

1. **Salads using greens should have a light oil and acid (lemon juice or vinegar) type dressing.**

2. **It is always good to mix several types of greens together for a variety of color and texture.**

3. **When cheese, nuts or dried fruits are added to greens, they should be added in small amounts. Their purpose is to complement not dominate the delicate taste of the greens.**

4. **Using stronger tasting vegetables, such as carrots and cabbage, allows the use of a broader base of stronger dressings.**

5. **A combination of the crisp texture of fresh vegetables and greens with that of slightly wilting greens can be good. Examples are: Wilted greens as a salad base; braised endive and escarole; cooked radicchio and arugula; sauteed greens incorporated in salads, and watercress both raw and cooked blended together.**

SELECTION OF PRODUCT

Selection criteria for fresh produce and the various types of fresh produce are discussed in Chapters 11 and 12 in this text. There is, however, a broader spectrum of choice which will ultimately have an effect on the production of vegetable salads. There are a growing number of pre-cut vegetables available. These not only reduce waste, but also processing time.

An example is fresh broccoli. It is available in whole bunches, which can then be processed into florets. However, it is also available fresh, pre-cut into florets, with or without stems. Carrots are available whole, unpeeled; whole, peeled; pre-cut into sticks, coins; shredded; grated, etc. Onions are available fresh whole, fresh peeled, fresh chopped, diced or sliced. They are also available in dehydrated, freeze dried, powdered, frozen and canned form.

What form the vegetables are purchased in will be determined by the skill level of the staff, the equipment, the time available and the goals of the operation. The goal should always be to provide the guest with the best product for the price charged.

It is also possible to purchase a number of types of mixed salads pre-made. Three-bean salad, cole slaw and potato salad are only a few of the ones available. These products are often a good alternative to scratch production when time and staff are at a premium. They must be selected carefully, always keeping quality as the number one consideration.

HANDLING & STORAGE

Salad greens can be stored, after preparation, for only short periods of time. Ideally they should be stored in a plastic container with a tight fitting lid in order to maintain the proper humidity and to prevent them from drying out or absorbing odors. They are best stored at 35-40°F with high humidity.

Marinated salads should be stored in their marinade, under refrigeration. It improves raw vegetables for them to remain in the marinade for a period of time. This gives the acids in the marinade the opportunity to enter into the vegetable and enhance its flavor and texture.

Cooked vegetables can be stored in their marinade for only short periods of time, under refrigeration. Remember that cooking has already softened their cell structure, so extended storage in the marinade may cause excessive softening. The vegetables may become mushy and unappetizing.

Salads can be pre-plated on chilled plates and held in the refrigerator. Wrap them tightly with plastic wrap to prevent dehydration. A major problem with pre-plating is the dry appearance of the salad. It is best to plate the salads as close to service as possible.

PASTA SALADS

Pasta salads have grown in popularity as an appetizer, accompaniment to a main course, salad course and entree. Pasta salads can be divided into two basic types, according to the type of pasta used: Dried pasta and egg pasta.

Dried, extruded, pasta is made with semolina and water. These are the stronger, more durable pastas. These pastas are best paired with a robust, mayonnaise-based dressing. These pastas include spaghetti and macaroni.

Egg pastas, fresh and dried, are made with eggs and unbleached flour. These pastas are extremely porous and should be paired with a lighter oil and vinegar dressing. These pastas include fettucine and angel hair, among others.

Whichever type of pasta is used, the pasta itself deserves to be the main attraction and should not be upstaged by the dressing or other ingredients. The goal is to enhance the pasta, not overpower it.

METHOD OF PREPARATION

The use of pasta as the primary ingredient in a salad is similar to the manner in which lettuce is used. The delicate taste and texture of pasta, when cooked properly, allows it to mix well with a wide variety of other ingredients. Dressing, meats and vegetables nest very nicely in the folds and crevices of the various pasta shapes, preventing them from gathering at the bottom of the salad plate.

The basic guidelines for making a quality pasta salad are:

1. DRESSING IS VERY IMPORTANT IN PREPARING PASTA SALADS. THE PROPER AMOUNT IS JUST ENOUGH TO EVENLY COAT THE PASTA AND ALL OTHER INGREDIENTS. THERE SHOULD BE NO EXTRA DRESSING LEFT STANDING IN THE PLATE OR BOWL.

2. FOR MAXIMUM FLAVOR, PASTA SALADS SHOULD NOT BE SERVED RIGHT OUT OF THE REFRIGERATOR. WHEN VERY COLD THEIR FLAVOR IS SOMEWHAT SUBDUED AND THEIR TEXTURE IS STICKY. HOW MUCH THE SALAD CAN BE ALLOWED TO WARM WILL DEPEND ON THE OTHER INGREDIENTS USED IN THE SALAD AND THEIR VARIOUS SANITATION GUIDELINES.

3. IN ORDER TO CREATE AN ATTRACTIVE PASTA SALAD, CARE MUST BE TAKEN IN ITS PREPARATION.

   A. FRESH HERBS, SPICES AND OTHER FLAVOR ENHANCERS, SUCH AS GARLIC OR ONION, SHOULD BE MIXED DIRECTLY WITH THE FRESHLY COOKED PASTA OR WITH THE DRESSING. THIS ALLOWS FOR A MORE EVEN DISTRIBUTION OF FLAVORS AND BETTER BLENDING OF FLAVORS.

   B. MORE DURABLE FOODS, SUCH AS RAW VEGETABLES, MEATS AND SEAFOODS, SHOULD BE TOSSED WITH THE PASTA BEFORE ADDING DELICATE FOODS. THE DELICATE FOODS INCLUDE COOKED VEGETABLES WHICH COULD LOSE THEIR DISTINCTIVE SHAPES IF OVERLY TOSSED OR MIXED.

   C. SALAD DRESSINGS SHOULD BE TOSSED WITH THE PASTA SALAD EITHER BEFORE OR AFTER ADDING THE INGREDIENTS EXCEPT WITH DELICATE VEGETABLES. FOR EXAMPLE, TOMATOES WILL FALL APART IF

MANGO RICE SALAD

YIELD: 12 - 4 OZ SERVINGS

INGREDIENTS	AMOUNT
RICE, COOKED (LONG GRAIN POLISHED)	2 LB 2 OZ
RED PEPPERS, FRESH, CUT BRUNOISE	3 OZ
YELLOW PEPPER, FRESH, CUT BRUNOISE	3 OZ
MANGO, FRESH, MEDIUM DICE	6 OZ
HONEY	2 OZ
BASIC FRENCH DRESSING	6 OZ

METHOD

1. COMBINE DRESSING AND HONEY, BLENDING WELL.

2. PLACE COOKED RICE IN AN APPROPRIATELY SIZED STAINLESS STEEL MIXING BOWL; ADD DRESSING, AND TOSS WELL.

3. FOLD IN REMAINING INGREDIENTS AND ADJUST SEASONING IF NEEDED WITH A SMALL AMOUNT OF FRESH LEMON JUICE.

4. ALLOW SALAD TO MARINATE 4-6 HOURS UNDER REFRIGERATION BEFORE SERVICE.

Figure 4

TOSSED WITH THE PASTA, THEN TOSSED AGAIN WITH THE DRESSING. IT IS BEST WITH THICK DRESSINGS, TO COAT THE NOODLES FIRST THEN ADD THE VEGETABLES. IN ANY CASE , THE KEY IS TO HANDLE THE ADDED INGREDIENTS AS LITTLE AS POSSIBLE.

4. PASTA IS AVAILABLE IN A WIDE VARIETY OF SHAPES AND SIZES (THESE ARE DISCUSSED MORE FULLY IN CHAPTER 13 OF THIS TEXT.), BUT THE SMALLER SHAPES ARE BEST FOR BUFFETS WHERE THE GUESTS SERVE THEMSELVES.

5. THE PASTA IS THE BODY OF THE SALAD. THE OTHER INGREDIENTS ARE THE GARNISH AND THEIR AMOUNTS SHOULD REFLECT THIS.

SELECTION OF PRODUCT

The selection of a type of pasta for a salad will be based on the intended flavor and presentation of the salad. There are no hard and fast rules; however, pasta shapes are often associated with particular themes for meals. Shells are often used with seafood; wagon wheels for western menus, and orzo for cajun menus, because of its rice shape.

Linguini and other long strands of pasta are often used with vegetables such as broccoli or cauliflower, and with seafood like shrimp. The long strands of the pasta create a nest for these items to rest in, without slipping to the bottom of the service dish.

Selecting pasta as a salad ingredient is sound from a nutritional standpoint. Pastas, in general, are high in carbohydrates and low in fat. If combined with low fat, low calorie ingredients, they can be a great source of high energy food.

HANDLING AND STORAGE

The cooking and storage of pasta itself is discussed in Chapter 13 of this text. Pasta salads should be made ahead of time to allow the flavors to meld together. They should be stored at temperatures between 32-38°F, in plastic, airtight containers. When stored properly, they can be safely kept for two to three days.

Pasta salads which contain a number of ingredients that may be harmed by extended storage in the marinade or dressing can be stored in individual

CURRIED RICE SALAD
YIELD: 10 - 4 OZ SERVINGS

INGREDIENTS	AMOUNT
ONIONS, FINELY DICED	8 OZ
BUTTER	3 OZ
CURRY POWDER	4 TSP
WHITE WINE	3 OZ
WHITE WINE VINEGAR	2 OZ
RICE, LONG GRAIN POLISHED	7 OZ
CHICKEN STOCK	18 OZ
HAM, MEDIUM DICE	5 OZ
APPLES, DICED	2
BASIC FRENCH DRESSING	4 OZ

METHOD
1. SAUTÉ ONIONS IN BUTTER UNTIL GLASSY, ADD RICE AND CONTINUE TO SAUTE UNTIL RICE IS GOLDEN.
2. ADD CURRY POWDER, WINE AND VINEGAR AND REDUCE MIXTURE BY 1/2.
3. ADD HAM, APPLES AND STOCK; COVER PAN, AND PLACE IN 350°F OVEN FOR 25-30 MINUTES.
4. REMOVE MIXTURE FROM OVEN AND TRANSFER TO COOL, SHALLOW PAN, THEN PLACE IN REFRIGERATOR TO COOL.
5. GENTLY MIX DRESSING WITH COOLED PILAF, THEN PLATE AND GARNISH APPROPRIATELY.

Figure 5

parts. You can store the pasta, dressing and other ingredients separately, then combine them close to service time.

RICE

The basic guidelines given for pasta salads also apply to rice salads. Bearing these guides in mind, it should be noted that a key point in the preparation of rice salads is the preparation of the rice before it is made into a salad. The concern here is one of both taste and texture.

Texture is affected by the doneness of the rice. A rice which is sticky or mushy will result in a salad which has a congealed consistency when served. This cannot be overcome by the addition of oils. Review the discussion of the types of rice and methods for preparing rice in Chapter 13. Your goal is a rice which is al denté. Each grain should be plump and soft, but not sticky. This requires the correct ratio of water to rice and that the appropriate type of rice be used. The best rice for salads is long grain polished rice. This type of rice is normally prepared using seven ounces of rice to 16-20 ounces of water.

The flavor of the rice, and ultimately the salad, is affected by the manner in which it is prepared. *Cooked rice* (rice cooked in just slightly salted water) is best used when the rice is intended to act as the bulk of the salad, but the major flavor is to be derived from the garnishes. This type of rice is relatively bland allowing for the flavor of other items to standout easily. An example recipe for a rice salad of this type is given in Figure Four. In this dish, the red peppers and mangoes work with the dressing to give flavor to the mixture.

Rice may also be cooked in stocks with a variety of other flavor enhancers added, such as basic mirepoix or cooked in a pilaf manner. This type of preparation gives the rice a distinct flavor. Rice prepared in this manner will normally become more of the central focus of the salad's flavor, while still providing the bulk. Garnishes and dressing should be selected which will properly complement the flavor of the rice. Figure Five shows a recipe for this type of rice salad.

LEGUME SALADS

Legumes, beans and peas have long been used as the body of a variety of salads. The guidelines for preparing a quality legume salad are basically the same as those for the preparation of a pasta salad. As with the grain of rice used in salad preparation, the doneness of the bean or pea is very important. The eye appeal of the salad depends heavily on the shape and color of the beans. They need to be whole, not in pieces. This requires that they not be allowed to cook to the point of falling apart.

The texture of a legume salad also depends greatly on the doneness of the bean. Beans used in salads should be soft, not hard. This requires that the beans be cooked al denté. The balance in the cooking time must be such that the beans are whole, yet soft. A bean or pea which is mushy and falling apart will not do.

Beans and peas lend themselves to use with a variety of both mild and strong flavored ingredients. It is best, however, to use some flavor enhancer, such as onion, to spark their flavor. The texture of the bean is also complemented by items which are crisp and crunchy, such as celery or pickles.

Dressings used for legume salads may vary from the heavier mayonnaise-based to the lighter basic French-types. While it is true that the mayonnaise-based dressings bring to the salad a greater degree of fat (which is sometimes needed) and cling more readily to the beans and peas, a basic French is also good. Beans marinated in a basic French-type dressing readily meld flavors and produce a lighter salad.

Legumes of all types can be used to prepare salads, including the most commonly used ones such as kidney beans, navy beans, peas, red beans, wax beans and green beans. Each are good salad items; however, do not stop with them. Many other colorful, good tasting beans are available. Black beans make a very striking salad. The multicolored mixed beans, which are often available, can be used to create a very different salad item. Dried peas are commonly available in both green and yellow. These can also be combined for a very nice change of color. The versatile and usually economical legumes are an excellent salad item. Figure Six shows a recipe for a black bean salad.

MEAT AND POULTRY SALADS

Meat and poultry salads can be used as an appetizer, salad course or entree. Any type of meat can be used for preparation of a salad. Raw beef or lamb is used in the preparation of Carpaccio (A recipe for this dish is shown in Figure Seven.), where it is served raw or seared and very rare. Organ or varietal meats, such as tongue and sweetbreads, as well as various sausages, are a good choice for use in salads.

Poultry and meats used for salads may either be freshly cooked expressly for the salad or leftover from other preparations. In either case, they should always be wholesome, unspoiled meats. Remember that, while leftovers can be effectively used in the preparation of salads, it is not a method for saving poultry or meats, cooked or raw, which are already going bad. Examples of leftover meats which can be easily used are duck legs, chopped and mixed with rice and dressing or leftover beef roast, diced and added to a dressing or marinade.

METHOD OF PREPARATION

Preparation of salads with meat and poultry begins with the proper cooking and handling of the same. It requires proper cooking methods to ensure the correct flavor and texture for the meat. Additionally, if the meat used is a leftover it may require special handling to ensure that it retains the proper texture and flavor. Some basic guidelines include:

1. TOUGH CUTS OF MEAT, FRESHLY COOKED FOR SALADS MAY INCLUDE BRISKET, ROUND AND SHOULDER CLOD. THESE SHOULD BE SIMMERED OR BRAISED UNTIL TENDER, THEN SLICED OR DICED FOR THE SALAD.

2. FOR POULTRY, SUCH AS CHICKEN, OLDER BIRDS SHOULD BE SLOW SIMMERED UNTIL TENDER. YOUNG BIRDS ARE BEST WHEN THE BREAST, WHICH REQUIRES LESS COOKING TIME, IS COOKED SEPARATELY FROM THE LEGS AND THIGHS. BE CAREFUL NOT TO OVERCOOK POULTRY, IT DRIES OUT EASILY.

3. AS WITH ALL MEATS AND POULTRY, IF ROASTED, BRAISED OR POACHED, THE DEFATTED NATURAL DRIPPINGS MAKE

MEAT & POULTRY SALAD RECIPES

CARPACCIO
YIELD: 12 - 3.5 OZ PORTIONS

INGREDIENTS	AMOUNT
BEEF TENDERLOIN, PEELED & TRIMMED	1 LB 4 OZ
FRESH PARMESAN CHEESE (GRATED)	6 OZ
BLACK PEPPER, FRESHLY CRACKED	1 1/2 TSP
CAPERS	2 OZ
OLIVE OIL	1/2 C
CALAMATA OLIVES, PITTED, CHOPPED	24 EA

METHOD
1. THINLY SLICE THE BEEF TENDERLOIN. (PLACING THE TENDERLOIN IN THE FREEZER FOR 1 HOUR PRIOR TO SLICING WILL MAKE IT EASIER TO GET VERY THIN SLICES.)
2. ARRANGE 2 OZ OF THE SLICED TENDERLOIN IN A CIRCLE ON AN APPROPRIATELY SIZED PLATE.
3, SPRINKLE WITH PARMESAN CHEESE, CAPERS, PEPPER AND OLIVES ON TOP.
4. DRIZZLE WITH OLIVE OIL.
   NOTE: A SIMPLE MARINADE OF VEGETABLES WOULD ENHANCE THIS PLATE FOR ADDED COLOR AND FLAVOR.

CHICKEN SALAD WITH RASPBERRY VINAIGRETTE
YIELD: 4 - 5 OZ PORTIONS

INGREDIENTS	AMOUNT
BONELESS CHICKEN MEAT	1 LB
CHICKEN STOCK	3 TBSP
RASPBERRY VINEGAR	3 TBSP
RASPBERRY PUREE (FRESH OR FROZEN)	2 TBSP
SALT	1/4 TSP
BLACK PEPPER	1/8 TSP
SALAD OIL	1/4 C
SUGAR	1 TSP

METHOD
1. COOK AND DICE CHICKEN MEAT.
2. MIX REMAINDER OF INGREDIENTS IN APPROPRIATE SIZE STAINLESS STEEL MIXING BOWL, ADD CHICKEN AND MARINATE FOR 45 MINUTES.
3. DRAIN SALAD AND PLACE ON BIBB LETTUCE BASE.
4. GARNISH WITH FRESH RASPBERRIES AND MINT LEAF.
   NOTE: IF THE CHICKEN IS BAKED, YOU CAN DEGLAZE THE PAN WITH WATER OR WHITE WINE AND REDUCE TO 3 TBSP. THIS CAN THEN BE USED TO REPLACE THE CHICKEN STOCK IN THE RECIPE.

Figure 7

KIELBASA SALAD
YIELD: 5 - 4 OZ PORTIONS

INGREDIENTS	AMOUNT
KIELBASA SAUSAGE	16 OZ
ONION, THINLY SLICED	1 EA
VINEGAR	4 OZ
CHICKEN STOCK	3 OZ
SALT	1/4 TSP
SUGAR	1 TSP
OIL	1 1/2 OZ
COARSELY GROUND PEPPER	1 TSP

METHOD

1. SLICE SAUSAGE 1/2 INCH THICK, REMOVING OUTER SKIN/CASING IF TOUGH.
2. IN APPROPRIATELY SIZED BOWL MIX ONIONS WITH SLICED SAUSAGE.
3. IN SEPARATE BOWL MIX REMAINING INGREDIENTS UNTIL SUGAR AND SALT ARE DISSOLVED.
4. POUR DRESSING OVER SAUSAGE AND ONIONS, THEN MARINATE IN REFRIGERATOR FOR 2 HOURS.
5. DRAIN AND ARRANGE ON SPINACH LEAVES ON APPROPRIATE CHILLED PLATE.
6. GARNISH WITH FRESH DICED TOMATO CONCASSE AND CHOPPED FRESH CHIVES.

Figure 7

AN EXCELLENT ADDITION TO THE DRESSING. (SEE THE RECIPE GIVEN FOR CHICKEN SALAD IN FIGURE SEVEN.)

4. BRAINS SHOULD BE SOAKED IN VINEGAR AND WATER FOR APPROXIMATELY ONE HOUR TO LOOSEN THE MEMBRANE. THEY ARE THEN SLOWLY POACHED THEN COOLED BEFORE SLICING FOR SALAD.

5. TONGUE SHOULD BE SIMMERED UNTIL FORK TENDER AND THEN SLICED FOR PLATTER PRESENTATION OR DICED FOR A SALAD.

6. WHEN USING SAUSAGE IN SALADS, IT MAY BE BEST TO REMOVE THE OUTER CASING AND SLICE THE SAUSAGES. AN OIL AND VINEGAR DRESSING IS RECOMMENDED FOR SAUSAGE SALADS, BUT THE AMOUNT OF OIL USED SHOULD BE CUT BACK TO ALLOW FOR THE FAT FROM THE SAUSAGE ITSELF, WHICH WILL HELP CUT THE SHARPNESS OF THE VINEGAR. (SEE THE KIELBASA SALAD RECIPE GIVEN IN FIGURE SEVEN.)

7. LEFTOVERS SUCH AS BRAISED, SIMMERED OR ROASTED BEEF, LAMB, VEAL AND PORK, THAT WERE COOKED WELL-DONE, HAVE A TENDENCY TO LOSE FLAVOR AND BECOME DRY AFTER REFRIGERATION. TO REVIVE THE TEXTURE, ADD MOISTURE AND ENHANCE FLAVOR:

   A. CUT THE MEAT INTO THE DESIRED SHAPES FOR SALAD.

   B. MARINATE THE CUT MEAT IN VINAIGRETTE FOR 45-60 MINUTES.

   C. BLEND THE MARINATED MEAT WITH THE DESIRED DRESSING.

8. ROASTED AND BROILED MEATS THAT ARE COOKED MEDIUM TO RARE WILL STILL HAVE THEIR MOISTURE. PRE-MARINATING IS NOT NECESSARY AND A SEASONED OR PLAIN MAYONNAISE DRESSING CAN SIMPLY BE ADDED TO THEM AFTER THEY ARE CUT TO THE DESIRED SHAPE AND SIZE.

9. POACHED OR ROASTED CHICKEN, TURKEY OR DUCKLING, CAN YIELD NEAT, UNIFORM

SLICES FROM THE BREAST FOR SALAD AND DICED MEAT FROM THE LEG FLAVORED, CRISP VEGETABLES LIKE ONIONS, CELERY AND CUCUMBERS, OR FRUITS SUCH AS PINEAPPLE, GRAPES AND APPLES. ALL OF THESE WORK WELL IN MEAT SALADS. THESE NOT ONLY ENHANCE THE FLAVOR OF YOUR SALAD, BUT CAN ALSO EXTEND THE QUANTITY IF NEEDED.

Basic French dressing blended with a sufficient quantity of vegetable puree to color and flavor the dressing is an interesting way to dress a meat or poultry salad. The puree may be of broccoli, asparagus, tomatoes, bell peppers, etc. Let your imagination be your guide. Plain mayonnaise is great in these salads, but may be even better when flavored with herbs and spices to enhance the flavor. Another variation on the basic french is the addition of fruit purees, such as mango, raspberry or orange. This can be particularly good with poultry and game.

HANDLING & STORAGE

Meat and poultry salads are high protein foods and, as such, require constant refrigeration. Although the flavor of these salads will improve with slight warming fifteen to thirty minutes prior to service, the first consideration must be the wholesomeness of the food. From the standpoint of sanitation, you must consider how the meat and poultry were handled prior to their incorporation into the salad.

In general, meat salads should be stored at 32-38°F. They should be in airtight containers to prevent contamination and dehydration.

SEAFOOD SALADS

Fish and shellfish salads offer a unique and refreshing variation in a menu. The wide range of fish and shell fish currently available make the possible combinations almost endless. Bivalves, such as clams and oysters, can be purchased fresh, live in the

---

SEVICHE
YIELD: 12 - 4 OZ PORTIONS

INGREDIENTS	AMOUNT
FRESH REDFISH, THINLY SLICED	8 OZ
SEA SCALLOPS, THINLY SLICED	1 LB 8 OZ
SHRIMP, BOILED 3 MINUTES & PEELED	1 LB
LIME JUICE, FRESH SQUEEZED	1 CUP
RED ONION, FINE CHOP	4 OZ
PARSLEY, FRESH CHOPPED	1/3 OZ
OLIVE OIL, EXTRA VIRGIN	4 OZ
OREGANO, LEAF	1 TSP
SALT	1 TSP
BLACK PEPPER, GROUND	1/2 TSP

METHOD
1. CUT SHRIMP INTO THIRDS AND MIX WITH REDFISH AND SCALLOPS IN STAINLESS STEEL OR GLASS BOWL.
2. ADD LIME JUICE AND COVER, ALLOWING TO MARINATE FOR A MINIMUM OF 1 HOUR UNDER REFRIGERATION. NOTE: STIR AT LEAST ONCE TO ENSURE EVEN COATING OF THE ITEMS.
3. DRAIN THE SEAFOOD AND BLEND IN THE REMAINING INGREDIENTS.
4. MARINATE FOR AN ADDITIONAL HOUR AND SERVE.

Figure 8

MUSSEL SALAD WITH SAFFRON DRESSING

YIELD 8 PORTIONS

I. BODY:

INGREDIENTS	AMOUNT
MUSSELS, LIVE	32 EA
FISH STOCK	8 OZ
WHITE WINE, DRY	2 OZ
LEEK, WHITE PART ONLY, JULIENNE	2 OZ
SHALLOT, FINE CHOP	1.5 OZ
LEMON JUICE, FRESH	1 T

METHOD

1. COMBINE FISH STOCK, WINE, LEEKS AND SHALLOTS IN SAUCE PAN AND BRING TO A BOIL.
2. ADD MUSSELS AND COOK COVERED APPROXIMATELY 5-8 MINUTES UNTIL THEY OPEN.
3. REMOVE THE MUSSELS AND STRAIN THE LIQUID AND REDUCE BY 1/2, THEN RESERVE FOR LATER USE.

II. DRESSING:

INGREDIENTS	AMOUNT
SAFFRON, CRUMBLED	1 TSP
OLIVE OIL	1 TSP
SHALLOT, MINCED	1.5 OZ
BUTTERMILK	1/4 C
HEAVY CREAM	1 C
SOUR CREAM	1 C
SALT & PEPPER	TO TASTE

METHOD

1. HEAT OLIVE OIL AND SAUTE SHALLOTS UNTIL SOFT.
2. ADD REDUCTION FROM MUSSELS, BUTTERMILK, HEAVY CREAM AND CRUMBLED SAFFRON, THEN COOK TO DESIRED THICKNESS.
3. FOLD IN SOUR CREAM.
4. SEASON WITH SALT AND PEPPER.

III. GARNISH:

INGREDIENTS	AMOUNT
CELERY, JULIENNE	2 OZ
TOMATO CONCASSE, FRESH	3 OZ
TARRAGON, FRESH CHOPPED	1 TSP

METHOD

1. TOSS MUSSELS WITH DRESSING.
2. ARRANGE MUSSELS ON APPROPRIATE CHILLED PLATES AND GARNISH WITH REMAINING INGREDIENTS.

Figure 9

LOBSTER SALAD
YIELD: 8 - 4 OZ SERVINGS

INGREDIENTS	AMOUNT
LOBSTER MEAT, COOKED	1 LB
LARGE EGGS, HARD BOILED	2 EA
LEMON JUICE, FRESH	2 T
SHERRY	2 T
CELERY, SMALL DICE	.25 OZ
ONION, SMALL DICE	2 OZ
OLD BAY SEASONING	1 TSP
MAYONNAISE	2 OZ
WHIPPED CREAM	1/4 C
DIJON MUSTARD	2 OZ
PARSLEY, FRESH CHOPPED	1 T
LOBSTER CORAL	2 TSP
SALT & PEPPER	TO TASTE

METHOD
1. DICE LOBSTER MEAT AND MIX WITH EGGS, CELERY, AND ONION.
2. COMBINE MAYONNAISE, CREAM, LEMON JUICE, SHERRY, OLD BAY, DIJON, PARSLEY, AND CORAL.
3. FOLD MEAT AND EGGS INTO DRESSING AND SEASON.

Figure 10

SHRIMP REMOULADE
YIELD: 8 - 4 OZ PORTIONS

INGREDIENTS	AMOUNT
SHRIMP, 26-30 CT., COOKED AND PEELED	1 LB
OLIVE OIL	4 OZ
TARRAGON VINEGAR	4 OZ
DIJON MUSTARD	2 OZ
KETCHUP	4 OZ
GREEN ONIONS, FINE CHOPPED	3 OZ
GARLIC, MINCED	2 CLOVES
PAPRIKA	1 T
SALT	1 TSP
CAYENNE PEPPER	1/4 TSP

METHOD
1. CUT SHRIMP INTO MEDIUM DICE OR LEAVE WHOLE.
2. BLEND REMAINING INGREDIENTS AND COMBINE WITH SHRIMP.
3. PLACE ON BED OF LETTUCE ON APPROPRIATE SIZE CHILLED PLATE.
4. GARNISH APPROPRIATELY AND SERVE.

Figure 11

shell; shucked and canned, or smoked and canned.

Crustaceans, such as crab can be purchased live, canned, frozen whole, frozen meat or frozen culls. (A cull being a crab or lobster which has only one claw and can be purchased at a considerable reduction in price.) Shrimp is marketed fresh; frozen/cooked; frozen/uncooked, or canned. They range in size from three to 160 count per pound, providing for a wide selection of price ranges and types of dishes.

Fresh, frozen and canned seafoods are readily available. Here again the type used and preparation method chosen makes it possible to create an almost endless variety of salads. Review Chapter 20 for the particulars of the various types of fish and shellfish and the appropriate handling and preparation methods.

Salads are often prepared from small, whole or broken product, such as salad shrimp or pulled or shredded crab meat. This practice allows the production of high quality products at a lower cost. The cost savings are generated by the utilization of product which may not have suitable appearance for other types of presentation.

METHOD OF PREPARATION

Seafood which is to be used in salads may be prepared using either dry or moist heat cookery, depending on the end product desired. For example, Salad Nicoise is normally prepared using black nicoise olives, potatoes, green beans and anchovy fillets. However, an interesting variation is the use of a grilled or sauteed tuna or even canned tuna in place of the anchovy filets. Moist heat such as poaching, braising, steaming or boiling helps keep seafood firm and is the most commonly used method of cooking seafood for salads.

MARINATED/UNCOOKED SALADS

Tender seafoods like scallops and shrimp or firmly textured fish such as redfish may be marinated for several hours in a citrus juice, commonly lemon or lime juice. They are then served without being cooked, the dish being called Seviche. Contrary to popular opinion the seafood served in this manner is no longer raw. Marination of the product in the acid for approximately one hour causes the proteins in the fish and shellfish to firm up in a manner similar to exposure to heat. An example recipe for this dish is given in Figure Eight.

When serving fish or shellfish in this manner it must be remembered that safe handling is a must. Since the product is not heated, bacteria and their toxins are not destroyed. If the product is allowed to stand at temperatures in the danger zone, the possibility of contamination is very high.

BIVALVES/MOLLUSKS

Bivalves or mollusks like clams, oysters and mussels should be steamed in a pot or pressure cooker to allow more of the natural juices to be retained in the shell. It is possible, when they are steamed in a tightly closed pot or hotel pan in a steamer, to reduce the excess cooking liquid to be used as a flavor enhancer in the dressing.

Bivalves are complemented best by a vinaigrette dressing. They may also be marinated in a vinaigrette and then finished with a mayonnaise or mayonnaise-based dressing.

CRUSTACEANS

Crustaceans, such as lobster, crab and shrimp, should be cooked rapidly in boiling salted water or court bouillon. The timing for cooking these shellfish starts when the cooking liquid returns to a boil after they are added. Lobster should be cooked 10 minutes per pound and crab seven to eight minutes per pound.

Depending on the amount used for a salad, four to 12 ounces of raw weight should be allowed for each person to be

---

APPLE ORANGE SALAD

YIELD: **10** PORTIONS

INGREDIENTS	AMOUNT
ORANGE, LARGE	4
APPLES, WASHINGTON DELICIOUS, LARGE	4
HONEY YOGURT DRESSING	1 PT
BIBB LETTUCE	AS NEEDED

METHOD
1. PEEL AND SECTION ORANGE, THEN SEED THE SECTIONS.
2. SLICE EACH APPLE INTO 10 WEDGES, THEN DIP IN A LIGHT LEMON JUICE AND WATER SOLUTION.
3. PLACE AN UNDERLINER OF BIB LETTUCE ON AN APPROPRIATE SIZE CHILLED DISH, THEN PLACE 4 APPLE WEDGES AND 4-5 ORANGE SECTIONS ON EACH PLATE. THE DRESSING MAY BE SERVED SEPARATELY IN A SMALL DISH ON THE PLATE.

Figure 12

---

served. The juices extracted from crabs and lobster when cracking the shell can be used to flavor basic French, mayonnaise or chantilly-type dressings. These types of shellfish lend themselves to use with all types of dressings. Example recipes for shellfish are given in Figures Nine, Ten and Eleven.

FRESH FISH

Fresh fish such as salmon, tuna, flounder or haddock should be braised or poached. The court bouillon or cooking liquid should never reach higher than 175°F. This temperature is sufficient to cook the fish and kill bacteria, but low enough to cause mini-

---

WALDORF SALAD

YIELD: **8 - 3** OZ PORTIONS

INGREDIENTS	AMOUNT
APPLES, (ROME-TYPE) DICED, MEDIUM	1 LB 4 OZ
CELERY, DICED, MEDIUM	6 OZ
MAYONNAISE	2 OZ
SOUR CREAM	2 OZ
LEMON JUICE	2 TSP
WALNUTS, CHOPPED	1 OZ

METHOD
1. WASH, CORE AND DICE APPLES, THEN MARINATE BRIEFLY IN LIGHTLY SALTED WATER.
2. DRAIN APPLES AND COMBINE WITH CELERY AND WALNUTS IN APPROPRIATE SIZE STAINLESS STEEL BOWL, BEING CAREFUL NOT TO BRUISE APPLE DICES.
3. COMBINE MAYONNAISE, SOUR CREAM AND LEMON JUICE.
4. FOLD CELERY AND APPLES INTO DRESSING.
5. SERVE ON APPROPRIATE SIZE CHILLED PLATE WITH SUITABLE GARNISH.

Figure 13

---

mal problems with moisture loss or breaking the delicate flesh due to agitation of the liquid.

Fresh fish should cook no more than 10 minutes per inch of thickness. Braising and poaching, if done properly, yields a moist, flavorful fish for your salad. In addition, the court bouillon or stock which was added to cook the fish can be reduced and added to a dressing for flavor.

HANDLING & STORAGE

Seafood is considered to be a potentially hazardous food and should be handled accordingly. In the raw state it has a very short shelf life and must be refrigerated at every step throughout its handling. Seafood spoils rapidly and should be used as soon as possible after being received. Products from cooked seafood must be handled as other high protein foods. Store between 32-36°F in airtight containers.

FRUIT SALADS

Fruit salads are always a refreshing alternative to other types of salads. They range from the simple presentation of sliced fresh or formed fresh fruits with an appropriate dressing to mixed-type salads.

SIMPLE FRESH FRUIT SALADS

The primary concerns in the preparation of any fruit salad, whether simple or mixed, is the preservation of the natural color, flavor and texture of the fruit. Chapter 10 discusses in detail the preparation of fruit, including information regarding cleaning, peeling and selection. One item discussed that is extremely important in the presentation of fruit as simple salad is enzymatic browning.

The flesh of some fruits, such as bananas and apples, turns brown after being exposed to the air. This creates a problem in simple salad presentation. It is necessary to take steps to prevent this. The two most common methods are the dipping of the cut fruit in a light acid or salt solution. It is important that the fruit not be allowed to soak in these solutions or the fruit will taste like the solution.

Presentations of fresh fruit should be designed to take advantage of the color, texture and flavor of the fruits that are in season. An example would be combining the more acidic, tart flavored orange with apples and plums in late summer and early fall. Whatever fruits are used, they should be processed to make them as easy as possible for the guest to eat.

It is possible to cut fruits into a variety of shapes to add interest to a plate, such as melon balls and pineapple spears. However, all fruits lose texture rapidly once cut. It is best to cut as close to service as possible. They should always be refrigerated between being cut and being served.

A simple fruit salad will be dressed with a dressing that will complement the fruit. The yogurt dressing shown in Chapter 22 is a good example of a good dressing for a simple fruit salad. The dressing should be served separately from the fruit, allowing the guest to use it as desired. Figure Twelve shows a recipe for a simple fruit salad.

MIXED FRUIT SALAD

The preferred method for preparing mixed salad is to use fresh fruits that are in season; however, canned and dried fruits may also be used to good effect. The pieces of fruit, fresh, canned or dried, can be cut into bite-size pieces for the salad. The dressing should be used to enhance the flavor of the fruit.

If it is necessary to mix the fruit with the dressing in advance of service, fruits with a harder, crisper texture such as apples, peaches or pears should be used. Soft fruits, such as strawberries and raspberries, will quickly soften and become mushy when allowed to stand in a dressing or marinade.

A great deal of variety is possible in

fruit salads when nuts, such as almonds, walnuts or pecans, and crisp textured vegetables, such as celery, are also used. An example of this is the waldorf salad recipe given in Figure Thirteen.

All fruit salads should be stored under refrigeration in airtight containers.

CONCLUSION

Salads offer a variety of flavors, textures and colors which can highlight a meal. They can be used as an entree replacement. A properly prepared and presented simple fruit salad can even be used as a replacement for a dessert. It is this versatility in menu planning, combined with the possibilities for creative use of a broad range of food items, that continues to make these extremely popular dishes both for the chef and the guest. Nutritionally they present an opportunity to give the guest a good tasting, eye appealing alternative to other dishes. Give salads the attention, thought and care they deserve and they will serve you and your customer well.

REVIEW QUESTIONS

1. What is a salad?
2. What are the basic types of salads?
3. What are the parts of a salad?
4. Discuss the preparation of marinated vegetable salads.
5. Discuss the preparation and layout of salads.
7. What are the key points in the preparation of a fresh green salad?
8. Discuss the key points in the preparation of a pasta salad.
9. What are the important points in the production of a rice salad?
10. Define *legumes*.
11. Discuss the preparation of legume salads.
12. What are the two primary types of fruit salads?
13. Discuss the preparation of fruit salads.

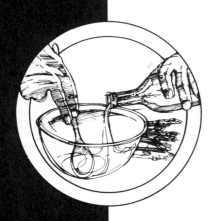

Chapter 24

CHAPTER OBJECTIVES

- **To introduce gelatin as a culinary ingredient.**
- **To discuss how gel forms.**
- **To discuss the preparation and use of gelatin.**
- **To define aspic jelly.**
- **To discuss the preparation of aspic jelly.**
- **To discuss the preparation and use of sauce chaud-froid.**
- **To discuss the preparation of dishes using aspic jelly.**
- **To discuss the use of aspic jelly for food decoration.**

Gelatin and Aspic Jelly

A thorough understanding of the properties of gelatin is a key to success with culinary preparations containing gelatin. Before discussing the various applications of gelatin in the kitchen, it is first necessary to discuss gelatin itself. The character of gelatin as a major ingredient is the same in all food preparations. It is for this reason that we will begin this chapter with a discussion of gelatin, then move on to aspic jelly, culinary applications and decorative techniques with aspic.

GELATIN

Gelatin is defined by the United States Pharmacopeia as "a product obtained by partial hydrolysis of collagen derived from skin, white connective tissue, and bones of animals." As a byproduct of animal processing, gelatin is a partial protein. When used in culinary preparations, it is always dissolved into some type of liquid.

WHAT IS IT?

Gelatin comes from a single strand of the protein collagen, which resembles a triple helix spiral. This is, of course, as it is seen through an electron microscope. As it is exposed to heat for an extended period, the bonds forming the three long chains holding the spiral together release. When this happens, the collagen is altered to produce three smaller strands of a protein called gelatin. Once the collagen is converted to gelatin it cannot be changed back.

When the gelatinous liquid cools, it forms a semi-soft gel. The gelatin has two phases known as *sol* and *gel*. Gelatin is the liquid sol when warm. It is the semi-solid gel when cool.

HOW DOES IT GEL?

As the temperature of a gelatin sol drops, the viscosity (thickness) of the liquid increases to the point where gel formation occurs. This happens at about 85°F. As the temperature of gel rises, the thickness decreases. A gelatinous solution can be converted from gel to liquid sol and back again, by heating or cooling.

Exactly how a gel is formed is not clearly understood. However, it is generally felt that during the cooling of the sol, the molecules of gelatin form strands and begin to link together. They create a three-way network, which traps the liquid inside.

As gel warms, the gelatin strands begin to release from each other. This frees the trapped liquid to flow again. An interesting fact is that, once a gel is formed, it can tolerate a higher temperature without melting, than it took to set it in the first place. In other words, the gel set at 85°F, but it will take more than that temperature to melt it.

A gel formed slowly by slow cooling will have a higher melting point than one which was set by quick cooling. The gel also becomes more rigid and stable with time. The greatest increase in firmness occurs during the first 24 hours.

TYPES & DEFINITIONS

The gelatin that we are specifiying here should not be confused with the flavored gelatins that are common in the household kitchen. This is about types of gelatin. According to the Pharmacopeia, there are type A and type B gelatins.

1. *Type A* gelatin is made from collagen-rich tissue and bone pre-treated with an acid. The acid increases the amount of collagen converted into gelatin. Commercially, pork skin is the raw material most often used to make type A gelatin.

2. *Type B* gelatin is made from collagen-rich tissue and bone pre-treated with an alkali. The alkali increases the amount of collagen converted to gelatin. Beef bone and calf skin are the raw materials most often used commercially for type B gelatin.

Gelatin is also categorized by strength and clarity. Both are based on what is termed *bloom number*. Gel strength is determined mechanically, by the manufacturer, using a *bloom gellometer*. This meter determines the amount of force needed to depress the surface of a given sample of gelatin a specified distance. The results are compared to the *bloom range*. This range is from 50 to 300. A bloom of 275 is most common. A few of the currently available gelatins rate as follow: Christie Gelatin, 250 bloom; Plymouth Rock Gelatin, 275 bloom; Kind & Know, 275 bloom;

Hormel, 300 & 275 bloom; Continental Seasonings, 300 bloom.

Bloom is also used to gauge the clarity of gelatin. A lower bloom normally has greater clarity. A higher bloom will have a lower quality of clarity.

HOW IS IT MANUFACTURED?

The main raw material used for gelatin manufacturer are cattle bones, scrap and piece cattle hides, and fresh or frozen pork skins. The minerals, fats and albuminoids are removed by chemical and physical treatment of the bones, hides and skins. This treatment is normally a diluted solution of hydrochloric acid.

The process produces a cold water, insoluble collagen. The collagen is thoroughly rinsed with cold water and the pH factor is adjusted. The rinsed collagen is heated with water in large extraction kettles, completing the conversion of collagen to soluble gelatin. This conversion is most rapid at temperatures approaching 212°F.

The resulting gelatin sol is allowed to gel in thin layers. These layers are dehydrated and packaged in dry forms. Each form, though identical in material content, requires a slightly different manner of reconstitution.

AVAILABLE FORMS

There are three forms of gelatin available. The types discussed here are *unflavored* or what is also called *natural gelatin*. *Sheet gelatin*, also known as *leaf gelatin*, is the original form all gelatin achieves in the drying process. All other forms are pulverized versions of this form. Sheets of gelatin are usually three inches by seven inches. Seven sheets equals one ounce in weight. Because of the larger unit size, sheet gelatin presents the least problem in reconstitution.

Granular gelatin has granules the size of fine sand. This is the type most commonly used in the professional kitchen. It is available in bulk or one pound boxes, depending on the manufacturer. Care must be taken in reconstitution of this product, because it lumps easily.

Powder gelatin is pulverized to a fine powder. It is the most commonly used type in the home kitchen. It is uniformly packaged in one tablespoon envelopes.

CULINARY APPLICATIONS

The culinary applications of gelatin are varied. Commercially it is used in the manufacture of gums, where it provides stability. It is used in marshmallows, for structure. In ice creams it inhibits crystal formation during freezing, improving texture, and provides stability, allowing the product to hold its form better in warmer temperatures. Gelatin desserts (prepared mixes of gelatin, sugar, acid, fruit flavorings and color) all use natural gelatin as a base. The list continues, but you are beginning to get some idea of this product's versatility in food production.

In the kitchen, professional and home, it is an ingredient in a variety of desserts, acting as a binder. Gelatin gives items form, such as the light, fluffy texture and body of chiffons, bavarian creams and charlottes, to name a few. In savory cold mousses, gelatin performs much the same function of binder, form giver and lightening agent.

In molded salads, any variety of cooked, cubed foods can be molded into a design of flavored gelatins. The gelatin not only binds and gives form, it also helps to carry flavor. Gelatin is used in many ways for cold food display. Decorative, edible work is possible with the correct and judicious use of gelatin.

HANDLING & STORAGE

Proper reconstitution of granulated gelatin calls for certain steps to be followed. These steps are shown in Figure One. Sheet gelatin, on the other hand, is somewhat easier to reconstitute. When sheet gelatin is rehydrated in cool water, the entire sheet can be lifted out of the water. It will look like a sheet of jelly. This rehydrated sheet can then be stirred directly into any warm liquid.

RECONSTITUTION OF GRANULATED DRY GELATIN

1. WEIGH GELATIN. THE WEIGHT WILL BE BASED ON THE DESIRED GELATIN-TO-LIQUID RATIO.
2. MEASURE LIQUID. THE LIQUID CAN BE ANY LIQUID SUITABLE FOR THE RECIPE, INCLUDING WATER, STOCK OR WINE. THE LIQUID MUST BE COOL.
3. REHYDRATE GELATIN: A) SPRINKLE DRY GRANULATED GELATIN EVENLY ONTO THE SURFACE OF A COOL LIQUID. NOTE: IN ORDER TO ELIMINATE LUMPING OF THE GELATIN, IT MUST BE CAREFULLY REHYDRATED BEFORE BEING DISSOLVED. B) ALLOW TIME, APPROXIMATELY 10 MINUTES, FOR THE GELATIN GRANULES TO ABSORB THE LIQUID. THIS STEP IS ALSO CALLED "BLOOMING." NOTE: AT THIS POINT, THE REHYDRATED GELATIN GRANULES WILL RESEMBLE APPLE SAUCE IN APPEARANCE.

NOTE: THE DRY GELATIN CAN BE REHYDRATED USING ALL OR PART OF THE LIQUID CALLED FOR IN THE RECIPE.

4 A. IF ONLY A PORTION OF THE LIQUID IS USED FOR RECONSTITUTION, STIR THE REHYDRATED GELATIN DIRECTLY INTO THE HEATED, REMAINING LIQUID.
   B. IF THE ENTIRE AMOUNT OF LIQUID IS USED FOR REHYDRATING, PLACE THE BLOOMED GELATIN AND LIQUID OVER HOT WATER UNTIL MELTED.

NOTE: THE BLOOMED GELATIN AND LIQUID, WHETHER IN THE MANNER OF 4A OR 4B, SHOULD BE HEATED SUFFICIENTLY FOR THE GELATIN GRANULES TO NO LONGER BE EVIDENT. YOU SHOULD HAVE, AT THIS STAGE, A CLEAR, UNIFIED LIQUID CALLED SOL.

Figure 1

HOW MUCH GELATIN SHOULD YOU USE?

One of the most difficult questions to answer in handling gelatin is, how much should you use? The old chef was right in saying "enough and not too much." The problem is, this still does not tell exactly how much. This is because there is no hard and fast rule. Figure Two is a chart of recommended concentrations of gelatin. However, before you turn to it and read it, please read the next few paragraphs first. They are an attempt to answer the question in as clear a manner as possible.

The concentration of gelatin in an aspic jelly determines the delicacy of the finished product. The greater the amount of gelatin in relation to the amount of water, hereafter called the ratio of gelatin to water, will result in a denser, more rubbery product. (We are back to those rubber balls they served in the school cafeteria.) To get a good balance you must understand the gelatin and how it functions. (Just what we have been talking about; yes, how those little chains form and break apart.) Plus you must learn the few basic principles we will now discuss.

The ratio of gelatin to liquid can best be expressed as ounces of gelatin per gallons of liquid. Remember, the liquid is the control. The chart in Figure Two is stated in this way.

Determining the ideal amount of gelatin needed in a preparation is a skill. One which requires practice, observation and evaluation to perfect. There are many times in cooking when the exact amount of gelatin needed, or naturally present, will not be known. The chart given here should serve as a starting point in developing your ability to recognize various unknown concentrations of gelatin. Compare the density of a gelled sample of known concentration, from the table, to one of unknown concentration.

EQUIVALENT GELATIN CONCENTRATIONS
(Based on 275 bloom in plain water.)

TYPE	RATIO	USAGE
DELICATE GEL	2 OZ/GAL	1) WHEN SLICING IS NOT REQUIRED. 2) INDIVIDUAL MOLDS OF DICED FOODS. 3) CUBED ASPIC TO ACCOMPANY GALANTINES, PATES OR TERRINES.
COATING GEL	4 OZ/GAL	1) EDIBLE GLAZES 2) EDIBLE CHAUD-FROID SAUCES
SLICEABLE GEL	8 OZ/GAL	MOLDING OF MULTI-PORTIONED ASPICS WHICH WILL REQUIRE SLICING.
HARD GEL	12 OZ/GAL	1) NON-EATING PURPOSES 2) POURED "ASPIC MIRRORS" FOR FOOD SHOW DISPLAYS. 3) GLAZING ITEMS FOR FOOD SHOW DISPLAY 4) CHAUD-FROIDS FOR DECORATION PURPOSES ONLY.

Figure 2

There are a variety of factors which affect the setting ability or strength of gelatin. Understanding the reactions in a mixture to be gelled when certain conditions exist, is a key to developing skill with gelatin. The following factors serve to weaken gel strength to varying degrees.

ACID – A LOWER pH (ACID) HAS A WEAKENING EFFECT ON GELATIN.

SUGAR – AN EXCESS OF SUGAR IN A RECIPE WILL WEAKEN GEL STRENGTH. HOWEVER, AN ADJUSTMENT IN RATIO IS NOT USUALLY NEEDED.

BROMELIN, FICIN, PAPAIN, ACTINIDIN – CERTAIN FRUITS, PARTICULARLY PINEAPPLES (BROMELIN), FIG (FICIN), PAPAYA (PAPAIN) AND KIWI (ACTINIDIN) IN THE RAW STATE CONTAIN AN ENZYME WHICH WILL DIGEST PROTEIN GELATIN, DESTROYING ITS ABILITY TO FORM A GEL. THESE FRUITS SHOULD BE COOKED BEFORE COMBINING WITH GELATIN.

TEMPERATURE – THE AMOUNT OF GELATIN IN PREPARATIONS INTENDED FOR SERVICE IN THE SUMMER, OR IN ANY WARM ROOM OR ENVIRONMENT, SHOULD BE INCREASED SLIGHTLY. THIS WILL ALLOW THE GEL TO HOLD ITS SHAPE, YET BE DELICATE WHEN EATEN.

There is no loss of gel strength by repeated melting and gelling. Boiling will not even weaken the strength of the gel. Extended boiling will, however, cause the development of off flavors and odors in the gelatin. Caution must also be used when applying heat to gelatin because it scorches easily. When scorched, it develops an unpleasant taste and unappetizing aroma.

There is a product on the market called *vegetable gelatin* or *agar-agar*. This product is unrelated to gelatin. Gelatin is a protein and agar-agar is a carbohydrate. However, it is used in some restricted diets. The vegetable gelatin will weaken with prolonged heating and boiling.

HOW SHOULD IT BE STORED?

Dry gelatin, if kept in airtight containers can be stored indefinitely. Its major enemies, when stored, are water and humidity. Gelatin is very hydrophilic, meaning it readily attracts and absorbs moisture. When this happens in storage, the gelatin will partially bloom and spoil.

Reconstituted gelatin must be stored under refrigeration. The gelled liquid has a refrigerated shelf life of about one week. After one week, molding can begin. Gelatins and products with a high content of gelatin do not freeze well. As a product freezes, ice crystals form. The crystals rupture the network of gelatin strands holding the liquid. When thawed the gelatin releases an excessive amount of water. Frozen gelatin also loses clarity when thawed.

ASPIC JELLY

There is a certain amount of confusion related to the term *aspic*. Aspic jelly and the term *aspic* are often used interchangeably, however they are different items. An *aspic jelly* or the French term *aspic gelee*, is a flavorful, gelatinous stock which has been carefully clarified. *Aspic* is a prepared dish in which slices or dices of poultry, meat, game, fish, seafood or fruit are molded in a clarified meat, fish or fruit jelly. To reduce the confusion, we will use these definitions.

As we stated, aspic jelly is a flavorful, gelatinous stock, which has been clarified. Any well-made stock, prepared with large amounts of bones, will gel when chilled; however, without the quality of being clarified, the jelly is not aspic jelly. At this point it is merely a savory jelly or fruit jelly, as the case may be. Although the savory and fruit jellies have uses in the kitchen, they cannot be used for preparations calling for aspic jelly.

In the broadest sense, it is color which classifies the *savory aspic jellies*. *Amber* is used with beef and game. *Light amber tone* is used with veal, poultry and pork. *White* (fish) has almost no amber tone and is used with fish and seafood.

PREPARATION

CLASSICAL METHOD

The classical method of preparing an aspic is making a stock with the addition of more collagen-rich products. In particular these include pork skin and calve's feet. Figures Four and Five give sample recipes for making various types of savory aspic jelly following the classical method. The classical method has two major stages in the production of aspic jelly. First comes preparation of the special stock, followed by clarification. This kind of aspic jelly depends solely on the gelatin present in the bones for gelling.

QUICK METHOD

The quick method for making savory aspic jelly is the adding of commercial gelatin to a prepared consomme. It is very practical for kitchens that use a limited amount of aspic jelly, but have consomme on hand on a regular basis. The flavor and clarity of this type of aspic jelly will depend on the qualities of the consomme used. Besides being quicker, there is also less chance of scorching when clarifying a consomme, compared to clarifying a jelly.

For a quick amber savory jelly:

1. Prepare a good quality brown stock, using bones of the type of meat with which the aspic jelly will be used.

2. Clarify as you would for consomme.

3. Chill a small portion of the clarified stock.

4. Distribute and rehydrate the desired amount of gelatin in the cooled portion of the stock.

5. Stir the bloomed gelatin into the remaining warm stock.

6. Chill a small sample in the refrigerator to evaluate the gel strength.

For a quick white aspic jelly follow the same procedure, except using fish consomme.

COMMERCIAL MIX

Commercial mixes are, without a doubt, the quickest method of producing aspic jelly. Commercially, savory aspic jelly is available in a dry, powder form from various manufacturers. They save time and effort on the part of the chef, but have a lower quality of flavor since little or no meat

AMBER SAVORY JELLY

STOCK

INGREDIENTS		AMOUNTS
1)	BONES: VEAL & CHICKEN	30 LB
2)	CALVES FEET, SPLIT	4 EA
3)	BEEF SHANKBONE	1 EA
4)	PORK SKIN	2 LB
5)	MIREPOIX	12 OZ
6)	SALT	2 TBS
7)	WATER, COLD	4 GAL

METHOD

1. COMBINE INGREDIENTS IN A HEAVY STOCK POT.
2. PREPARE AS YOU WOULD FOR A GOOD QUALITY STOCK (REFER TO CHAPTER 14), SIMMERING FOR 12 HOURS.
3. REDUCE OR CORRECT THE LIQUID CONTENT TO 3 GALLONS.
4. REFRIGERATE OVERNIGHT.
5. WHEN CHILLED, CAREFULLY LIFT OFF SURFACE FAT, RESERVE FOR OTHER USES.
6. REMOVE THE GELLED STOCK, BEING CAREFUL TO LEAVE THE SEDIMENT IN THE BOTTOM OF THE POT.
   NOTE: THIS CAN ALSO BE DONE BY CAREFULLY REHEATING THE JELLY AND THEN DECANTING, POURING THE LIQUID OFF CAREFULLY, WITHOUT DISTURBING THE SEDIMENT.

YOU NOW HAVE A PARTIALLY CLEAR, RICH, STRONG STOCK. WHEN CHILLED IT WILL GEL; HOWEVER, TO BE CONSIDERED ASPIC JELLY, IT MUST BE CLARIFIED FURTHER.

CLARIFICATION

INGREDIENTS		AMOUNT
1)	BEEF, FROM SHANK	6 LB
2)	MIREPOIX	12 OZ
3)	TOMATOES	2 EA
4)	THYME	1 TBS
5)	BAY LEAVES	2 EA
6)	PARSLEY STEMS	1 BUNCH
7)	BLACK PEPPERCORNS	1 TSP
8)	EGG WHITES	18 EA

METHOD

1. CLARIFY AS FOR CONSOMME (SEE CHAPTER 15) USING THE INGREDIENTS LISTED.
2. CAREFULLY STRAIN AND DEGREASE AS FOR CONSOMME.
3. CHILL TO GEL.

Figure 4

is used in the production of most commercial aspic jelly powders.

It is recommended that their flavor be fortified. Add a highly flavored clarification to the mix as part of the liquid for reconstitution. The clarity of the premium brands of these aspic jellies is normally very good. They are useful when small amounts of aspic jelly are needed periodically. These products should be reconstituted according to the manufacturers' directions.

WHITE ASPIC JELLY (FISH)

STOCK

INGREDIENTS	AMOUNT
1) WHITE FISH (NON-OILY)	3 LB 8 OZ
2) WHITE FISH BONES	3 LB 8 OZ
3) ONION	1 LB
4) PARSLEY STEMS	1 LB
5) MUSHROOM TRIMMINGS	8 OZ
6) WHITE FISH STOCK	3 GAL 2 QT

METHOD

1. PREPARE AS YOU WOULD FOR A GOOD QUALITY FISH STOCK, SIMMERING FOR 1 HOUR.
2. REFRIGERATE OVERNIGHT.
3. SKIM AND DECANT.

CLARIFICATION

INGREDIENTS	AMOUNT
1) EGG WHITES	21 EA
2) LEAN FISH, CHOPPED	6 LB
3) WHITE MIREPOIX	12 OZ

METHOD

1. CLARIFY AS YOU WOULD FOR CONSOMME, WITH THE LISTED INGREDIENTS.

NOTE: IN SPECIAL CIRCUMSTANCES FRESH OR PRESSED CAVIAR CAN BE USED IN THE CLARIFICATION OF FISH CONSOMME AT A RATIO OF 2 OZ. PER QUART OF STOCK.

Figure 5

THE ADDITION OF WINES

Wine may or may not be added to aspic jelly, depending on how it will be used. In all cases, the wine should be added when the jelly is very cool, yet still liquid. This will insure that the full aroma of the wine is preserved.

The recommended ratio of wines, such as madeira, sherry, and marsala is eight ounces per quart of jelly. For white wines the ratio is seven ounces per quart.

WHAT IS A GOOD ASPIC JELLY?

There are four characteristics of a good aspic jelly: Flavor, tooth, clarity and color. The *flavor* of an aspic jelly should be intense enough to make the mouth water. It should not be strong enough to mask the flavor of the main ingredients of a product. There are three parts to the flavor of aspic jelly. The first is depth of character. This comes from the proper preparation of the stock. The flavor should not be watery and weak. It should be full bodied and robust. Seasoning is another area. The aspic jelly needs to be sufficiently seasoned, we are primarily talking salt here, so that the flavors of the bound ingredients are not masked. Lastly, is the matter of acidity. Slightly elevating the level of acidity in the aspic jelly will serve to accent and enliven the flavors already present. This is done by adding wine, lemon juice or vinegar. However, it must be done with care. Remember that acid can alter the strength of the gel.

Tooth is the density or elasticity of the jelly. The jelly should be firm enough to hold the desired shape, yet once it is in the mouth it should melt immediately. The jelly should have no chewyness. There are two factors which determine the mouth feel of the aspic jelly. First, the ratio of gelatin in the jelly. This is addressed Figure Two. The other is the service temperature of the jelly.

There is a built-in problem when serving aspic jelly in a loaf form or other multi-portion size. The aspic jelly must be strong enough to allow clean slicing, yet delicate enough to offer good tooth. The best way to overcome this is to slice large aspics directly out of the refrigerator while they are still very cold, then let them warm up slightly, softening the gel, before service.

Aspic jelly should be absolutely crystal clear. Some dishes served *en gelee* do not need to be bound with a jelly which is absolutely clear. An example is "Daube de Boeuf en Gelee." This hearty dish is served with the naturally gelled broth from the cooking process. However, this gelled broth cannot be called an aspic jelly.

The range of color in an aspic jelly lies between the rich amber, almost brown, color of an aspic jelly for game, to a nearly colorless one for fish. Additional tones of red can be present depending on the choice of wine used in preparation.

Fruit aspic jellies can be colored to represent certain fruit flavors, such as green for lime and bright red for cherry. The jelly is colored using various food dyes. Although this is a common practice, it is not a good one for the professional chef. It should be confined to a narrow range of uses, such as children's desserts. A color derived naturally from fruit and vegetable juices or purees is preferable. It is not only more natural, but brings flavor and nutritional value with it.

HOW TO HANDLE AND STORE ASPIC JELLIES.

Aspic jelly is a *potentially hazardous food*, an ideal environment for the growth of bacteria. It is high in moisture content; high in protein, and comes from an animal source. To gain the longest possible shelf life and to insure wholesomeness, care must be taken in storing prepared aspic jelly.

Use only clean, sanitized containers for storage. Once jelly has set, handle it as little as possible. This will help to minimize the introduction of bacteria. For small quantities, pour it into a proper container and cool to 140°F before refrigerating. Once the jelly is placed in the refrigerator, allow it to set without stirring. When the gel sets as a single block, it seals itself. This exposes only the top surface of the aspic jelly to the air and possible contamination. As with any stored food, once set, the gel should be covered.

Large quantities of gel, after being strained into a suitable container, should be cooled down rapidly to about 90°F. Place the container of aspic jelly into a cold water bath, stirring the jelly until it reaches this temperature. The jelly can then be placed in the refrigerator to finish cooling and to set. Once set, cover the container.

RELATED CULINARY APPLICATIONS

SAUCE CHAUD-FROID

Chaud-froid translated means "hot-cold." The name refers to the fact that this sauce is applied hot and served cold. The high gelatin content of the sauce makes it possible to apply it to an item while still warm and flowing. As the cooling sauce gels, it adheres to the product. It gives a smooth, pristine surface, and seals the item from the air. There is a secondary usage of this term which will be discussed later under "prepared dishes."

Chaud-froid sauce is used for coating a variety of items, including galantines; terrines; cold timbales; whole or individual joints of poultry, meat, or game; whole or fillets of fish, and eggs. The reasons for using chaud-froid sauce are:

INGREDIENTS	AMOUNT
1) VELOUTÉ SAUCE (MEDIUM)	1 QT
2) MUSHROOM FUMET	1 C
3) ASPIC JELLY (COATING STRENGTH)	1 QT
4) CREAM	1 1/4 C

METHOD
1) COMBINE VELOUTE AND MUSHROOM FUMET, AND REDUCE TO 1 QT.
2) ADD MELTED JELLY AND STIR IN CREAM.
3) SIMMER 10 MINUTES.
4) ADJUST SEASONING, STRAIN THROUGH CHEESE CLOTH, AND COOL TO DESIRED THICKNESS.

Figure 6

1. Protection of an item from the air while sitting on a buffet.

2. The sauces act as a background or canvas on which to decorate. Plus the chaud-froid is an adornment in itself.

3. The sauce can complement the flavor of the coated item.

There are a wide variety of additions made to chaud-froid sauces, depending on the intended end use. The result is a broad range of colors and flavors, all called by the name chaud-froid.

TYPES

The most common method of categorizing chaud-froid sauces is color. What they all have in common is a high content of aspic jelly. The approach to chaud-froid sauces can vary, the two primary methods being the classical and contemporary.

CLASSICAL METHOD

Classical recipes call for a base of velouté or bechamel. This is reduced with stock suitable for the item with which it will be used. To this reduction a suitable aspic jelly and cream are added. This method is often used today. Figure Six shows a recipe for white chaud-froid sauce.

CONTEMPORARY METHOD

A modern variation of the sauce given in Figure Seven is prepared without a roux-based sauce. The result is chaud-froid sauce which has a less starchy mouth feel. The method is also faster. However, in all cases, attention must be given to developing the flavor of the sauce.

OTHER VARIATIONS

Chaud-froid sauce can be made in a variety of colors. As with any other preparation, there are certain ones considered to be basic. These basic colors are based on variations of the preparation method shown in Figure Eight. For *brown chaud-froid*, replace the cream with a reduced jus de veau. *Green chaud-froid* is made with the addition of the juice squeezed from one pound of pureed, fresh spinach. It will be necessary to strain this product well before using.

Red chaud-froid requires the adding of one teaspoon of good quality paprika, dissolved in a little water, plus one cup of tomato puree which has been lightly *pincered*, meaning sauteed or cooked. This sauce also needs to be strained before being applied. For *yellow chaud-froid* infuse a small amount of saf-

---

WHITE CHAUD-FROID SAUCE
CONTEMPORARY METHOD

INGREDIENTS	AMOUNT
1) CREAM	4 C
2) CORN STARCH	2 OZ
3) WHITE WINE, DRY	1 OZ
4) ASPIC JELLY (COATING STRENGTH)	1 1/2 QT
5) SALT	TO TASTE
6) WHITE PEPPER	TO TASTE

METHOD

1) REDUCE CREAM TO 2 CUPS.
2) DISSOLVE THE CORNSTARCH IN THE WINE, THIS SHOULD BE A SMOOTH SLUR.
3) ADD THE WINE AND CORNSTARCH SLUR TO THE HOT REDUCED CREAM AND ALLOW TO THICKEN.
4) GRADUALLY STIR IN THE HOT ASPIC JELLY.
5) SEASON TO TASTE AND STRAIN THROUGH CHEESECLOTH, COOL TO DESIRED THICKNESS.

Figure 7

---

fron into the cream used. Do not use too much saffron, inasmuch as the intense yellow color will be artificial and unappetizing in appearance.

APPLYING THE CHAUD-FROID SAUCE

PREPARING THE ITEM FOR COATING

Chaud-froid sauce is applied in a series of steps, beginning with the preparation of the item to be covered. It is assumed that it is already fully prepared and shaped; however, it must be properly prepped. As with painting a wall in your house, if the wall is dirty, broken or greasy it will affect the final appearance of the painted surface. It is the same with items to be coated with chaud-froid.

1. Items to be coated should be well chilled. The chill of the item adheres the sauce to the surface. Chaud-froid will run off the surface of a warm item before it can set.

2. The surface of the food to be coated should be smooth and trimmed of any rough edges. It is not possible to create a smooth, pristine covering when the undersurface is rough and jagged. For whole pieces or joints of poultry, the area to be coated normally has the skin removed.

3. Surface grease must be removed before the coating is applied. Neither aspic nor chaud-froid will stick to a greasy surface. The removal of the skin, as already mentioned, will also remove most of the surface grease.

4. The item to be covered should be blotted dry before coating. This will allow better adhesion of the sauce.

TEMPERING THE CHAUD-FROID

Chaud-froid sauce should be tempered before applying. Once the item has been properly prepped, the sauce may be tempered. This is a matter of bringing the temperature of the sauce, by either slightly heating or cooling, to a point which will allow the best, and easiest coating. Remember that gel takes place at approximately 85°F. Normally, the closer you can maintain the sauce to this temperature without it getting too thick, the more evenly it will coat. In the ideal situation, it should take only two to three coats of chaud-froid for a smooth, glistening finish.

Chaud-froid that is too warm (thin) when applied results in problems.

1. It tends to wash over the item, leaving only a very thin layer of sauce.

2. If extremely warm, it will melt away the layers already present, not apply a new layer.

3. This necessitates applying extra coats, increasing the probability of bubbles on the surface.

4. A thin, warm sauce takes more time than necessary to apply.

Chaud-froid which is too cool (thick) when applied creates its own set of problems.

1. The sauce will not coat the item smoothly because it sets too quickly, in runs.

2. The sauce will form lumps. These are then transferred to the surface of the item.

3. The layer of sauce will be too thick and uneven.

4. Cooler chaud-froid holds air bubbles better.

A sauce which is tempered to the right temperature will do the following:

1. The sauce will be easily controllable.

2. It will give a smooth, even coating.

3. It will make the application of the coating easier and more efficient.

LADLE METHOD OR DIPPING METHOD?

There are two ways to apply chaud-froid sauce. It can be either ladled on the item, or the item can be dipped into it. The *ladling method* is suitable for coating of large or small items.

Place the item(s) on a wire rack over a perfectly clean sheet pan. Line small items up in rank and file order, with at least one inch between them. When the items are on the screen, ladle the tempered sauce over small items using even strokes, *in one direction only.* Try to cover each item entirely with each pass. *Avoid dripping on previously coated items.*

Large items, which cannot be covered in a single pass, need a bit more care. Start with the lower areas first and finish with the higher areas. This allows sauce from the upper part of the piece to join that of the lower in a smooth even finish.

The use of a well cleaned sheet pan to catch the drippings of the sauce will reduce waste. The drippings that pass through the screen and solidify, can be re-melted in a water bath, strained and tempered for re-use.

The *dipping method* is ideal for smaller items such as timbales. It would be suitable for coating larger items, such as whole hams or turkeys, but the large amount of sauce needed to immerse such items make it impractical.

The coating of smaller items is much the same as coating petit fours. They are picked up on the end of an offset palette knife, or similarly bent tool. The offset of the tools makes it easier to dip the item. Once picked up the item is dipped into a deep, wide mouth bowl of tempered sauce. These items often float, so they must be gently steadied from the top with a fork or second palette knife.

After dipping, the item can be placed on a wire rack. However, with this method it is preferable to blot the item lightly on a moist towel to remove the excess sauce from the bottom. Then place the piece on a clean, flat tray. The blotting method is preferred because it saves time in trimming the item. A smooth edge is formed by the piece sitting directly on a flat tray.

When dipping items it is important to avoid splashing. This causes bubbles to form in the sauce. These are then transferred to the coating of the item.

Whichever method of coating is used, the items should be refrigerated between each coat and before the final trimming. Often, a second and possibly third coat are necessary to get a smooth, complete finish.

TRIMMING

Trimming is the final step in preparing the item for decoration. Carefully remove the item from the screen. Remember, you have created an artificial skin for the item. As the skin has set, it has stuck not only to the item, but also to the screen or pan upon which it rests. Carelessly ripping the items away from the screen or pan will pull off large sheets of the set skin. The items should be cut away from the screen or pan with the careful passing of a flexible palette or paring knife under them.

To create a smooth, even surface, trim the bottom with a sharp paring knife dipped in hot water. Carefully trim away any drips or rough edges. Line up the trimmed chaud-froids on a clean work tray. At this point they are no longer "items", they are chaud-froids. They only lack suitable decoration, if desired.

DECORATING THE CHAUD-FROIDS

The large or small chaud-froids can now be decorated with tasteful food items. You have many choices available at this point. A decorative technique traditionally used with chaud-froids involves aspic cutters. These are special cutters used to punch decorative shapes from various vegetables. These may then be arranged in any pleasing pattern, such as geometric, floral or abstract.

A more natural, pleasing effect comes from using small bits of food in their natural shapes and sizes. Capers, caviar, chives and olive halves are only a few examples. Whether using pieces punched from vegetables or small natural pieces of food, application is the same. Each component must be dipped into warm aspic jelly and applied to the surface of the chaud-froid. In the process of placing pieces, avoid dripping excess aspic on the surface. These beads of aspic are difficult to remove and can make the most beautiful designs look sloppy. More techniques of decoration will be discussed later in this chapter.

After the decorated chaud-froids have been chilled, they are glazed with a single coat of well-tempered aspic jelly. This will protect the chaud-froid sauce coating from the air. When the chaud-froid coating is left exposed to the air for more than a half-hour it becomes dull and dry looking. The final glaze of aspic keeps the chaud-froid looking fresh and sparkling.

QUALITY INDICATORS FOR CHAUD-FROID.

The quality of a chaud-froid coating has a major effect on the overall quality of the finished product. While it is true that chaud-froid cannot improve a poor quality item, it can lessen the quality of a well-made item. Chaud-froid is more than just a decorative or protective coating. It serves both of these functions, yet becomes part of the total piece. A grainy, poorly textured and flavorless timbale, once coated with chaud-froid will still be a grainy, poorly textured, flavorless timbale. Except now it has a coating. A flavorful, well textured timbale, coated with a starchy tasting, ragged, dull chaud-froid is reduced to a second rate product.

The quality of a chaud-froid is judged according to flavor, tooth, color and appearance.

1. Flavor -- The sauce should fully complement the dish with which it is served, whether the flavoring agent is wine or stock.

2. Tooth -- Chaud-froid should have a very delicate tooth. As it melts in the mouth, it should have a silky, smooth texture, similar to that of a well-made velouté or bechamel sauce.

3. Color -- Depending on the particular recipe and variations involved, chaud-froid can be many colors. However, the colors should originate from real food ingredients. The use of artificial coloring agents should be avoided. Most importantly, the colors must look natural and appetizing. Keep your colors pastel or with some earthtones. Very bright or "pure" colors tend to appear artificial and less appetizing.
4. Appearance -- The appearance of an item coated with chaud-froid sauce should be pristine, that is, neatly trimmed, perfectly smooth, shiny and free of bubbles. The thickness of the sauce coating, ideally, should be no more than 3/16-inch and the aspic glaze no more than 1/8-inch thick.

HANDLING & STORAGE

Chaud-froid sauces can be cooled and stored like aspic jelly. Reheat gelled chaud-froid over a hot water bath to prevent scorching.

COLLEES

Collees are chaud-froid sauces using mayonnaise, sour cream, heavy cream or a combination of these as their base. They are often used with fish and other light preparations. All the factors relating to the preparation, use and quality of chaud-froid sauces apply to collees.

Preparation of collee-type chaud-froid sauces is very simple. Combine three parts mayonnaise, sour cream or heavy cream with one part warm, strong aspic jelly. If using fresh mayonnaise, there is a possibility of the mixture separating when reheated. It is best to use the sauce before it has a chance to set. Commercially prepared mayonnaise has added stabilizers that eliminate this problem.

SOUPS

Some jellied consommes are similar in make-up to aspic jelly. The only differences are that they normally have less gelatin content and extra tomato product and celery for the clarification. *Consomme a la Madrilene* is an example of these types of consommes. Consommes are discussed more fully in Chapter 15.

PREPARED DISHES

ASPICS

This is the dish most commonly associated with aspic jelly, indeed the dish from which it derives its name. An aspic is a dish prepared with diced or sliced, fully cooked meat, poultry, game, fish, vegetables or fruit, molded in a savory aspic jelly. For a fruit aspic the mold would be flavored or sweet gelatin.

Most items labeled as aspics are bound with clarified aspic jelly. There are, however, some preparations bound with an unclarified gelatinous broth that are included in this category. An example would be the *Daube Boeuf en Gelee* we which discussed earlier in this chapter. It is more in character to serve this hearty preparation with its natural gelled broth, than with clarified jelly. Remember, however, this dish is included in the grouping of aspics, yet the unclarified gelled broth cannot be called aspic jelly. Figure Eight gives a sample recipe for an aspic of this type.

Menu language can often be confusing. This is the case with identifying aspics on the menu. Listed below are examples of terminology used for aspics on the menu.
   a) Aspic of fillets of sole.
   b) Aspic de volaille.
   c) Breast of chicken in aspic.
   d) Daube de boeuf en gelée.
   e) Poached shrimp in jelly.
   f) Daube de boeuf glacé.

CLASSICAL PREPARATION

In classical aspic preparation, the ratio of aspic jelly to meats or fish could be as high as 50/50. The jelly was emphasized as the main appeal of the dish. Steps for preparing a classical aspic are:

DAUBE de VEAU en GELÉE

INGREDIENTS	AMOUNT
1) SMOKED HAM HOCKS	3 EA
2) VEAL SHANK	1 EA
3) BEEF SHANK	1 LB
4) SACHET	1 EA
5) GARLIC	3 CLOVES
6) PARSLEY STEMS	1 BUNCH
7) WHITE WINE	1 C
8) TOMATO PUREE	1/4 C
9) ASPIC JELLY	1 QT
10) WATER	1 QT
11) WHITE MUSHROOMS, DICED	1 LB

METHOD

1) COMBINE ALL INGREDIENTS AND SIMMER UNTIL EACH PIECE OF MEAT IS VERY TENDER.
2) LIGHTLY OIL AND LINE A 2 LB. RECTANGULAR TERRINE MOLD WITH PLASTIC FILM, SMOOTHING OUT ANY WRINKLES.
3) REMOVE MEATS FROM BROTH AND COOL.
4) POACH MUSHROOMS IN THE BROTH.
5) REMOVE MUSHROOMS FROM BROTH AND ALLOW TO COOL.
6) REDUCE BROTH TO 1 PINT.
7) ADJUST THE SEASONING OF THE BROTH.
8) CHILL A SMALL AMOUNT OF BROTH AND CHECK STRENGTH OF GEL. ADJUST FOR A STIFFER GEL, IF NEEDED, BY ADDING MORE GELATIN OR FOR A SOFTER GEL BY ADDING MORE WATER.
9) COMBINE THE MEATS AND MUSHROOMS, GENTLY TOSSING IN A BOWL WITH 1 CUP OF THE WARM BROTH.
10) FILL PREPARED TERRINE WITH MEAT MIXTURE, UP TO THE SHOULDER OF THE MOLD. POUR ADDITIONAL BROTH OVER THE MEAT UNTIL THERE IS A SMOOTH LAYER OF BROTH AS THE TOP SURFACE.
11) CHILL THOROUGHLY.
12) THE ASPIC CAN NOW BE UNMOLDED AND DECORATED IF DESIRED. THE NATURAL APPEARANCE OF THE DICED MEATS IS NATURALLY APPEALING IF LEFT UNADORNED.

Figure 8

1. COAT THE INSIDE OF THE MOLD WITH A LAYER OF ASPIC JELLY.

NOTE: A) THE TYPE OF MOLD USUALLY USED FOR ASPIC IS ROUND WITH A FUNNEL IN THE CENTER.

B) SEE "LINING MOLDS" UNDER THE HEADING OF "DECORATION TECHNIQUES" IN THIS CHAPTER.

2. DECORATE THE LINED MOLD WITH ITEMS, SUCH AS THINLY SLICED VEGETABLES, SMOKED TONGUE, EGG WHITES, RADISHES AND SPRIGS OF HERBS. THE ITEMS ARE DIPPED IN ASPIC JELLY AND IMMEDIATELY SET IN PLACE IN THE MOLD.

3. FILL THE DECORATED MOLD WITH THE SLICED OR DICED MAIN ITEM(S).

NOTE: THIS CAN BE DONE IN A RANDOM FASHION OR THE ITEMS CAN BE LAYERED INTO THE MOLD WITH ALTERNATING LAYERS OF MELTED ASPIC JELLY.

4. POUR ASPIC JELLY OVER THE FILLED MOLD.

NOTE: THE ASPIC JELLY FILTERS DOWN

INTO THE INTERIOR OF THE MOLD, HELP-
ING TO SET THE INGREDIENTS IN PLACE.

5. THOROUGHLY CHILL THE MOLD, PREFER-
ABLY OVERNIGHT.

6. UNMOLD: DIP THE MOLD INTO WARM
WATER FOR A FEW SECONDS TO MELT
SLIGHTLY THE OUTER LAYER OF ASPIC
COATING THE MOLD. INVERT THE MOLD
AND INSERT A SMALL PALETTE KNIFE
BETWEEN THE MOLD AND THE ASPIC.
THIS WILL BREAK THE SUCTION HOLD-
ING THE ASPIC IN THE MOLD AND IT
WILL SLIDE OUT EASILY.

CONTEMPORARY PREPARATION

The contemporary approach differs
from the classical in three ways. First,
the item is usually decorated and coated
with aspic after being turned out. This
allows for more rapid production and
easier handling. Secondly, it can be
molded in terrines for easy portioning.
Lastly, more emphasis is placed on the
main item of the aspic, instead of the
aspic jelly. This is due to the current lack
of popularity of aspic jelly. The result is
a greater content of meats or fish, and
far less jelly than the classical style.

As with the classical style, the ingredients can either be layered into the
mold or tossed together and placed ran-
domly. Tossing would normally be done
with diced foods.

COLD MOUSSES & COLD MOUSSELINES

Cold mousses and cold mousselines
are closely associated with the use of
aspic jelly and gelatin. They are mentioned here simply to identify them as
such. They are discussed in full in
Chapter 25.

CHAUD-FROIDS

Having already discussed, earlier in
this chapter, the large and small poached
items which are coated with a chaud-
froid sauce, we now use the term differently. This usage of the term chaud-froid
refers to dishes prepared in the manner
of a fricassee or salmis. They are served
cold, in their natural sauce. The method
of preparation creates a sauce rich in
gelatin, which sets when cold.

USING ASPIC JELLY AS A GARNITURE

GALANTINES

The gelatinous stock used in the
poaching of galantines is often clarified; flavored with wine, and allowed
to set. It is then chopped or cut into

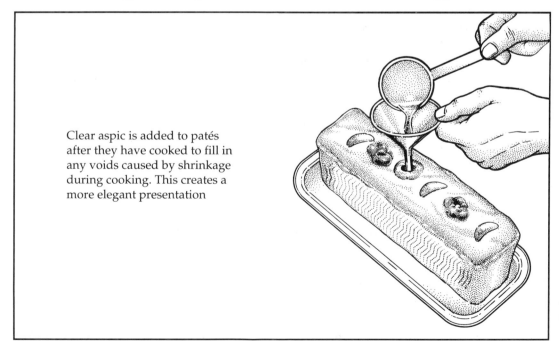

Clear aspic is added to patés
after they have cooked to fill in
any voids caused by shrinkage
during cooking. This creates a
more elegant presentation

small cubes and served as an accompaniment to the galantine. The jelly must be delicate and melt the instant it is in the mouth.

PATÉS

Jelly is not a by-product of the preparation of a paté, but does serve an important role in its preparation. The jelly not only fills the air spaces of the paté. It also adds flavor and texture. Aspic jelly used in paté must be a bit stronger to slice well. It should not, however, be rubbery.

TERRINES

Aspic is most commonly used in the preparation of a terrine to seal the mold after the terrine has been cooked and partially cooled. The aspic used should be of sliceable strength.

In a country-style terrine, a substantial amount of fat is rendered during cooking. The terrine is allowed to rest for about half an hour with the fat surrounding it to let it re-absorb some fat. After resting, the fat not absorbed is removed. This is replaced with aspic jelly, sealing the product away from the air. It also gives the terrine a more polished appearance when completely cold.

DECORATIVE TECHNIQUES INVOLVING ASPIC JELLY

TEMPERING

Tempering is vital to the success of any cold food decoration involving aspic jelly. The tempering of aspic jelly or gelatin is similar to tempering chocolate. It is the process of adjusting the viscosity, resistance to flow, of a gelatinous liquid. This is done by raising and lowering the temperature of the liquid. The method for tempering is discussed in Figure Nine.

TEMPERATURE RELATED FACTORS

Temperature will affect your work with gelatin and aspic jelly in many ways. In the preparation of molded sal-ads it can mean the difference between an attractive salad with a good tooth and one which is lumpy; has all the components in the bottom of the mold, and is grainy in texture. These factors and how they affect the quality of the salad are listed below.

When the gelatin is too warm, the viscosity is very thin. The following happens:

1. Solid items sink to the bottom of the mold.
2. Food is not evenly distributed within the mold.

When the gelatin is too cool, the viscosity is very thick. The following happens:

1. Solid items will be suspended.
2. Air pockets will form in stirring, resulting in a lumpy texture.

When the gelatin is at the ideal temperature, naturally the viscosity will be ideal also.

1. Solid items will evenly suspend in the liquid.
2. The mold will set with a consistent, smooth texture.

For coating with a gelatinous liquid, such as aspic jelly, chaud-froid sauce or others, temperature plays a major role in the quality of the finished piece. When the gelatin temperature is too warm, the viscosity is thin. The coating washes off the item being coated. When the gelatin is too cool with a thick viscosity, the coating is uneven and lumpy. The ideal temperature and viscosity of the gelatin will give an even glossy coating.

MASKING

Masking is the term applied to the technique of lining a mold with a layer of aspic jelly. A chaud-froid sauce or other gelatinous sauce can be used in the same manner as aspic jelly. The French term for masking is *chemiser*. For example, a mold can be lined with a thin chemise of aspic, bacon or fat back.

TEMPERING ASPIC JELLY OR GELATIN

EQUIPMENT NEEDED
1) POT CONTAINING HOT GELATIN SOL OR ASPIC JELLY.
2) BOWL #1 -MIXING BOWL TO HOLD ASPIC JELLY BEING TEMPERED, THIS BOWL SHOULD FIT EASILY INTO BOWL #2.
3) BOWL # 2 - LARGE BOWL OF COLD OR ICE WATER.

METHOD
1) CAREFULLY FILL BOWL #1 HALFWAY WITH WARM ASPIC FROM POT, AVOIDING SPLASHING AND CREATING AIR BUBBLES.
2) STABILIZE BOWL #2 BY PLACING IT ON A DAMP TOWEL, THIS WILL KEEP IT FROM SPINNING DURING THE TEMPERING PROCESS.
3) PLACE BOWL #1 INTO THE COLD WATER IN BOWL #2.
   NOTE: BOWL #1 SHOULD BARELY FLOAT OR AT LEAST SPIN EASILY, RIDING ON THE WATER IN BOWL #2.
4) WITH THE LEFT HAND, ROTATE BOWL #1 AGAINST THE ROUNDED BACK OF THE LADLE. AS THE BOWL IS ROTATED SEVERAL THINGS TAKE PLACE.
   A) AS THE BOWL ROTATES THE WARM ASPIC IS CONTINUALLY CIRCULATED OVER THE COOL WALLS OF THE MIXING BOWL.
   NOTE: AVOID EXCESSIVE TURBULENCE IN THE ASPIC. THIS WILL INCORPORATE TOO MUCH AIR INTO THE ASPIC JELLY, CREATING NUMEROUS TINY AIR BUBBLES.
   B) AS THE LIQUID COOLS, A CUSHION OF SETTING GEL WILL BEGIN TO FORM ON THE INNER SURFACE OF THE BOWL.
   C) DO NOT POSITION THE LADLE SO THAT THE LIP SCRAPES THE CUSHION OF GELATIN. THE CUSHION SHOULD SLIDE EASILY AGAINST THE ROUNDED BACK-SIDE OF THE LADLE.
5) AS THE CUSHION OF SETTING GEL BEGINS TO FORM, LIFT BOWL #1 OUT OF THE COLD WATER BATH.
6) CONTINUE TO SPIN THE BOWL AGAINST THE BACK OF THE LADLE. AS THE BOWL IS SPUN, THE REMAINING HEAT IN THE LIQUID ASPIC JELLY WILL BEGIN TO GRADUALLY MELT AWAY THE FORMED CUSHION.
   NOTE: IT IS THIS PROCESS THAT GRADUALLY COOLS THE ASPIC.
7) WHEN THE CUSHION IS COMPLETELY MELTED AWAY, RETURN BOWL #1 TO THE COLD WATER BATH AND ALLOW THE CUSHION TO FORM AGAIN.
   NOTE: WHEN THE CUSHION IS COMPLETELY MELTED AWAY, A SLIGHT "SCRAPING" OF THE LADLE WILL BE FELT THROUGH THE HANDLE OF THE LADLE.
8) REPEAT THE PROCESS UNTIL THE ASPIC IS OF THE DESIRED VISCOSITY.
   NOTE: A) THE CUSHION WILL FORM MORE SLOWLY WITH EACH COOLING.
   B) THE COOLER THE ASPIC JELLY IN THE BOWL BECOMES, THE MORE SLOWLY IT WILL MELT AWAY THE FORMED CUSHION WHEN THE BOWL IS REMOVED FROM THE COLD WATER.
   C) IF THE ASPIC BECOMES TOO COOL, IT WILL BEGIN TO SOLIDIFY AND CLUMP UP. TO REMEDY THIS, CAREFULLY LADLE IN HOT ASPIC JELLY. THIS WILL ASSIST IN THE "RE-MELTING" OF THE GELLED ASPIC.
   D) DO NOT PLACE THE BOWL INTO WARM WATER. THIS WILL RELEASE THE GELLED CUSHION FROM THE BOTTOM OF THE BOWL. WITH THIS LARGE PIECE OF ASPIC JELLY FLOATING FREELY IN THE BOWL, THERE WOULD BE NO CHOICE BUT TO START COMPLETELY OVER, BY RE-MELTING THE ENTIRE BOWL.
9) WHEN THE DESIRED VISCOSITY IS REACHED, IT IS ACCEPTABLE TO HAVE A CUSHION REMAINING ATTACHED TO THE BOTTOM OF THE BOWL, AS LONG AS THERE ARE NO FREE FLOATING LUMPS OF ASPIC JELLY IN THE TEMPERED PORTION.

Work carefully as the temperature of the aspic drops. There is a range of only a few degrees that separate a gelled liquid from a gelled solid.

Figure 9

LINING MOLDS

The traditional method, given in Figure Ten, can be used for both large and small molds. The contemporary method, given in Figure Eleven, can be used with long molds, such as rectangular terrines or tunnel molds, when a very even layer is needed.

DECORATING MASKED MOLDS

The decorating of these masked items with small bits of vegetables and other foods is done in one of two ways. In the case of a thin chemise of aspic jelly, the decorations can be dipped into cool aspic jelly and positioned on the chemise before the mold is filled. When the item is unmolded, this technique results in a very polished presentation with a glass-like finish. Using this method, care must be taken that the chemise is not too thick. A thick chemise will make it difficult to see the decorations.

Another method is to fill the mold and chill undecorated. When the item is turned out, it is then decorated. Decorations are dipped into tempered aspic jelly and carefully applied. The piece can then be glazed with aspic jelly.

A mold lined with chaud-froid sauce must be turned out and then decorated. The chaud-froid is opaque; any decoration applied under it will not show.

LINING PLATTERS & PLATES

When using silver platters for presentation of cold food, it is best to line them. Use a thin layer of tempered aspic jelly. This will inhibit any chemical reaction between the silver and the food.

This process is known as applying an *aspic mirror* to the platter. Where appropriate to the nature of the food being presented, a chaud-froid mirror can be applied instead. The steps for the procedure are:

1. PLACE A FLAT BOTTOMED PLATTER, WITH AT LEAST A 1/4-INCH LIP, IN THE REFRIGERATOR AND LEVEL IT.

2. TEMPER THE ASPIC JELLY OR CHAUD-FROID SAUCE AND PLACE IT IN A PITCHER OR OTHER SPOUTED CONTAINER. THE CONTAINER SHOULD BE LARGE ENOUGH TO HOLD ASPIC JELLY SUFFICIENT TO COVER THE PLATTER TO A THICKNESS OF A 1/8-INCH LAYER.

NOTE: BE SURE TO REMOVE ANY AIR BUBBLES FROM THE SURFACE OF THE ASPIC JELLY WHILE IT IS STILL IN THE PITCHER.

3. CAREFULLY POUR THE ASPIC JELLY ONTO THE PLATTER. START IN THE CENTER AND WORK OUT IN A CIRCULAR FASHION.

NOTE: A) IF BUBBLES FORM DURING THE POUR, POP THEM WITH THE TIP OF A HOT PARING KNIFE.

B) SHOULD THE ASPIC SPLASH UP OVER THE SIDE OF THE PLATTER LEAVING A "WASH MARK," DO NOT TRY TO WIPE IT OFF. ALLOW THE ASPIC TO SET, THEN CAREFULLY CUT AWAY THE EXCESS ASPIC JELLY WITH A PLASTIC KNIFE. NEVER SCRATCH THE SILVER IN THE PROCESS. IT IS NOT WORTH IT.

4. IF THE MIRROR IS OF CHAUD-FROID, WHEN SET, APPLY A SEAL OF CLEAR ASPIC JELLY IN THE SAME MANNER. THIS WILL KEEP THE CHAUD-FROID BRIGHT AND SHINY.

DECORATING ASPIC OR CHAUD-FROID MIRRORS

For an aspic mirror, a decorative overlay can be arranged directly on the platter before the mirror is poured. These are usually in the form of floral or geometric designs.

This is done by simply using some of the foods given as "foods for decorating" later in this chapter. Arrange the chosen inlay design on a damp plate first. The pieces of vegetable are easier to move around the plate if wet. Once the design is to your satisfaction, transfer it piece by piece to the tray. Secure each piece with a small spot of melted aspic jelly.

Give the design a chance to set, so it will not move when the other aspic jelly is applied. Apply the aspic jelly for the mirror in the manner already discussed. Caution, the likelihood of bubbles forming during the pour is greatest around the overlay.

When applying a design to an opaque mirror, such as chaud-froid, it must be placed on top of the mirror, but before the clear glaze is applied. From this point proceed as you would for an aspic mirror.

GLAZING

For a full discussion of the various glazing techniques, refer to the section of this chapter concerning "sauce chaud-froid." The techniques discussed there are applicable when glazing with aspic jelly.

Aspic jelly is used to glaze a wide variety of items. Large joints of meat may be decorated and glazed in the same manner as large chaud-froids. Slices of meats, vegetables and fruits may be glazed using the ladle or dipping method. Individually created garnishes for cold buffet platters can be glazed in the same manner as small chaud-froids.

CROUTONS

A very classical method of using aspic for decoration is the use of ASPIC CROUTONS. These are shapes, traditionally triangles, cut from aspic jelly poured in a sheet to a thickness of 1/4 -1/2 inch. These triangular croutons are called in French *dent de loup* meaning "wolf fangs." They are arranged in a border around the dish to be decorated. It should be noted that this method of decoration is seldom used in modern practice.

FOOD FOR DECORATING

Although any food item can be used as a decoration in some form, there are those which are more commonly used. We list here a few of these.

VEGETABLES
  LEEKS (GREEN)
  CHIVES
  EGGPLANT SKIN
  ZUCCHINI SKIN
  RED, YELLOW AND GREEN PEPPERS
  CARROTS
  PICKLED CUCUMBERS
  OLIVES
  TOMATOES
TRUFFLES
EGGS, HARD COOKED AND SLICED

CONCLUSION

This chapter includes discussions of knowledge and skills which are not often used in restaurants today, such as chaud-froid and aspic jelly. This does not lessen the importance of gelatins and naturally formed aspic jellies in the normal cooking process. An integral part of the production of a chocolate mousse or a strawberry chiffon is the proper preparation and use of the gelatin. The reduction of stocks and sauces to achieve body, luster and thickness is, in part, a concentration of the natural gelatin content of these items. While the more advanced techniques mentioned in this chapter may not be used everyday, a mastery of them reinforces a set of principles which is easily transferable to production on a daily basis. The basic knowledge of gelatin and its characteristics is indispensable to the aspiring culinarian.

REVIEW QUESTIONS

1. Define the terms *gelatin, sol* and *gel.*
2. Discuss how a gelatin gel is formed.
3. List and discuss the forms in which gelatin is available.
4. How is gelatin used in the kitchen?
5. What are the steps for the reconstitution of granulated dry gelatin?
6. What factors affect the strength of gelatin?
7. How much gelatin should be used?
8. Define *aspic jelly* and list the types.
9. How do the classical and quick methods for aspic jelly preparation differ?
10. Define *sauce chaud-froid.*
11. What are the steps in the preparation of a chaud-froid?
12. In what manner is aspic jelly used in preparation?
13. Discuss the tempering of aspic and gelatin.
14. How does temperature affect working with gelatin?
15. Discuss the use of aspic and gelatin in food decoration.

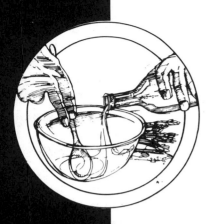

CHAPTER OBJECTIVES

- Definition of types of forcemeat and mousse.

- The contribution of the components of forcemeat and mousse.

- Methods of preparation of forcemeat and mousse.

- Handling and storage of forcemeat and mousse before, during and after production.

Forcemeat and Mousse

There are certain food preparations which are considered to be reserved only for the finest restaurants. When forcemeat and mousse are mentioned, this is often the reaction of those who do not understand what they are. There are many common items which are consumed by the general public that rely heavily on the principles involved in the preparation of forcemeat and mousse. Two of the most common which come to mind are bologna and the frankfurter. These favorites of the picnic and football crowd are applications of the principles of forcemeat and mousse preparation. As you study this chapter remember that most food production techniques have applicability in a variety of settings when you understand the basic principles.

FORCEMEAT

The general American definition of *forcemeat* is ground or pureed flesh (meat, poultry or fish) which is combined with fat and seasonings and then bound by the process of emulsification or the addition of other binders. The French term for forcemeat, *farce*, can indicate a stuffing of either meat or non-meat type. This being the case, a farce may be made of bread or vegetables.

Though most forcemeats are raw when being shaped, piped or formed, there are some which are fully cooked and then pureed prior to being used. An example of the fully cooked and pureed type is chopped liver. Forcemeats can be either fresh or cured. The designation depends upon the components of the product. Fresh indicates a forcemeat to which no nitrates have been added. The nitrates are usually added in the form of curing salts. Cured indicates a forcemeat which has curing salt as an ingredient. Forcemeats of all types are used in both the hot and cold areas of the kitchen. Uses include stuffing of various foods, such as paupiettes of sole; preparation of terrines, such as chilled terrine of rabbit, and a seemingly endless variety of sausages.

TYPES & DEFINITIONS

There are five primary types of forcemeat, each having its own distinctive ingredients and preparation. Each of the five will be discussed individually .

CAMPAGNE

Campagne is also known as *country -style* forcemeat. It was the earliest style and is traditionally made of pork. Though pork is frequently found in many forcemeat recipes, it is particularly conspicuous in country-style. This is possibly due to the historically low expense and small amount of land needed for raising pigs since their domestication some 7,000 years ago. The type of fat used in country-style forcemeat is pork fatback or jowl fat.

This forcemeat has a dense, coarse ground texture, a characteristic which resulted from the lack of sophisticated grinding equipment available when it was first developed. The earliest forcemeats were chopped with two knives, a method which resulted in the coarse textured associated with the country-style forcemeat today.

An additional bit of character resulting from the time it was developed is that of being highly seasoned. Due to the virtual non-existence of refrigeration and other preservation techniques, the heavy seasoning covered both the flavor of tainted meat and acted as a preservative for the forcemeat. The seasonings commonly used in country-style include onion, garlic, black peppercorns, juniper berries, bay leaf and nutmeg. Traditionally country-style forcemeat uses an additional binding agent to help hold some of the fat, which is rendered by cooking, in the forcemeat. The most common method to gain this extra holding power is the use of extra eggs or a panada (paste prepared from a starch product). A sample recipe for a campagne or country-style forcemeat is shown in Figure One.

STRAIGHT METHOD

This forcemeat is more refined, having a finer, less dense texture. As culinary preparations and equipment improved, the capability of producing a more refined style of forcemeat was possible. In the preparation of this style of forcemeat any type of meat can be used as the dominant meat. Commonly the combination would be a dominant meat (possibly veal, duck or rabbit) plus pork. White poultry or fish are rarely used as the dominant meat in this type of forcemeat. Ideally the type of fat will be pork fatback or jowl fat, although substitution of the fat of the dominant meat is common.

The finer, lighter texture and more delicate seasoning of this forcemeat is indicative of the refinement of many

CAMPAGNE OR COUNTRY-STYLE FORCEMEAT

INGREDIENTS	AMOUNT
1) LEAN PORK BUTT (1" CUBES)	1 LB
2) LEAN VEAL (1" CUBES)	1 LB
3) FATBACK (1" CUBES)	1 LB
4) PORK LIVER (1" CUBES)	8 OZ
5) BRANDY	5 OZ
6) SALT	1 T
7) PATE SPICE	1.5 T
8) CURING SALT	.5 TSP
9 ONION (DICED AND SWEATED)	8 OZ
10) GARLIC (MASHED AND SWEATED)	3 CLOVES
11) BLACK PEPPER (CRACKED)	1 TSP
12) PARSLEY (CHOPPED)	2 T
13) EGG	1

METHOD 1
1. COMBINE 1 THRU 11 AND ALLOW TO MARINATE OVERNIGHT.
2. GRIND THIS MIXTURE THROUGH A 1/4" DIE.
3. PUREE 1/3 OF THIS COARSE GROUND MIXTURE TO A SMOOTH PASTE.
4. COMBINE COARSE MIXTURE, SMOOTH MIXTURE, INGREDIENTS 12 AND 13. MIX WELL OVER ICE FOR 3 MINUTES.
5. THIS MIXTURE IS USUALLY COOKED IN A TERRINE LINED WITH SHEETS OF FAT BACK OR BACON.

METHOD 2
1. OMIT THE PUREEING STEP IN METHOD 1.
2. ADD 12 OZ. OF PANADA TO THE COARSE GROUND MIXTURE AND MIX WELL OVER ICE FOR 3 MINUTES.

Figure 1

culinary preparations as technological advances were made. It was no longer necessary to mask the natural flavor of the meats. It was possible to simply enhance it. The common seasonings in the straight method include shallots, wine, brandy, allspice and ground white pepper. This type of forcemeat does not typically use a panada to assist with binding. Due to the improved qualities of meat in the early part of this century and a better understanding of the importance of refrigeration during the grinding of meat, the natural binding action of the proteins in the meat can be better utilized. In some cases, a panada may be used to achieve a lighter texture in the forcemeat. An example recipe for straight method forcemeat is shown in Figure Two.

GRATIN-STYLE

The name of this forcemeat is derived from the practice of pre-cooking some (up to 100%) of the major components, such as meat and fat, prior to the grinding or pureeing process. In some cases this may entail only lightly browning the dominant meat or pork, hence the use of the term *gratin*. The contemporary interpretation of gratin style is an expansion on that of Escoffier. The classical definition of Escoffier refers to any forcemeat based on liver and including partial pre-cooking or browning of the major components. In

STRAIGHT METHOD FORCEMEAT

INGREDIENTS	AMOUNT
1) LEAN PORK BUTT (1" CUBES)	1 LB
2) LEAN DOMINANT MEAT (1" CUBES)	1 LB
3) FATBACK	1 LB
4) SHALLOTS (MINCED AND SWEATED)	2 OZ
5) BRANDY	1 OZ
6) SALT	1 T
7) PATE SPICE	1 T
8) CURING SALT	.5 TSP
9) WHITE PEPPER	1 TSP
10) EGG	1 EA

METHOD

1. COMBINE ALL INGREDIENTS EXCEPT THE EGG AND ALLOW TO MARINATE OVERNIGHT.
2. USING A WELL-CHILLED GRINDER, PROGRESSIVELY GRIND THIS MIXTURE ONCE THROUGH A LARGE DIE; THEN A MEDIUM DIE, AND FINALLY THROUGH A SMALL DIE.
3. TRANSFER THE MIXTURE TO A WELL-CHILLED FOOD PROCESSOR; ADD THE EGG, AND PUREE TO A SMOOTH PASTE.

NOTE: FOR A VERY REFINED PRODUCT IT IS OFTEN NECESSARY TO STRAIN THE FORCEMEAT THROUGH A FINE SIEVE

Figure 2

both the contemporary interpretation and that of Escoffier the preparation of the gratin-style is essentially the same as the straight method with the exception of the browning step.

As in the case of the straight method forcemeat, most types of meat (with the exception of white poultry and fish) are used in the preparation of the gratin-style. Often the liver of pork, veal or the dominant meat are used. Pork fatback or jowl fat is preferred for this style; however, fat from the dominant meat can also be substituted. The texture of this forcemeat should be very fine, ground until smooth. The density is slightly lighter than that of the straight method due to the varying degree of binding power which is lost. This loss of binding power will be relative to the amount of pre-cooking involved in the particular recipe. A panada is not normally used in this style forcemeat because of its tendency to soften the already delicate texture. To compensate for the loss of binding power, extra eggs are sometimes used.

The seasoning of this refined forcemeat is the same as that of the straight method forcemeat. A different flavor is achieved in the gratin-style by virtue of the slightly nutty flavor which is a result of the browning of the meats prior to grinding. The overall result is a very smooth, delicately flavored forcemeat. An example recipe for a gratin-style forcemeat is shown in Figure Three.

MOUSSELINE-STYLE

The most distinctive feature of this style of forcemeat is the type of fat used in its preparation. The use of cream as the source of fat, combined with the processing of the components to an ultrafine consistency, allows the production of an extremely light and smooth product. This product is in sharp contrast to that produced using the harder

GRATIN-STYLE FORCEMEAT

INGREDIENTS	AMOUNT
1) LEAN PORK BUTT (1" CUBES)	1 LB
2) LEAN DOMINANT MEAT (1" CUBES)	1 LB
3) FATBACK(1" CUBES)	1 LB
4) VEAL LIVER (1"CUBES)	8 OZ
5) SHALLOTS (MINCED)	2 T
6) GARLIC (MINCED)	1 T
7) BRANDY	1 OZ
8) WHITE WINE	.5 C
9) SALT	1 T
10) PATE SPICE	1.5 T
11) CURING SALT	.5 TSP
12) WHITE PEPPER	1 TSP
13) EGG	2 EA
14) HEAVY CREAM	4 OZ

METHOD

1. COMBINE 1 THRU 4.
2. SWEAT 1/3 OF THE MIXTURE BRIEFLY IN A SAUTE PAN WITH THE SHALLOTS AND GARLIC.
3. FLAME THE SWEATED MIXTURE WITH THE BRANDY.
4. ADD WHITE WINE AND REDUCE MIXTURE UNTIL NEARLY DRY.
5. CHILL SWEATED MIXTURE THOROUGHLY THEN COMBINE WITH REMAINING MEAT/FAT MIXTURE.
6. ADD 8 THRU 12 TO MIXTURE AND MARINATE OVERNIGHT.
7. FOLLOW THE PROGRESSIVE GRINDING METHOD AS GIVEN FOR THE STRAIGHT METHOD FORCEMEAT IN FIGURE TWO, ADDING THE EGGS AND CREAM AT THE END OF THE PUREEING PROCESS.

Figure 3

types of fats. Mousseline-style forcemeat is made using lean white or light meats and fish; including chicken, veal, rabbit, sole, shrimp and well-trimmed lean pork. Although a panada is not needed for additional binding in this style of forcemeat, one is occasionally added to achieve a lighter consistency. Due to the delicate nature of the meats and creams used in this forcemeat, the seasoning should be very delicate. Care must be taken not to overpower the flavors of the components of the forcemeat. The most common seasonings used are shallots, ground white pepper and wine. An example recipe of a mousseline-style forcemeat is shown in Figure Four.

NOTE: The term *mousseline forcemeat* is often improperly abbreviated as *mousse* in everyday use. This is a source of much confusion in the use of the respective terms. The novice culinarian must work to distinguish between the two. A mousse is a mixture of fully cooked and pureed basic ingredients bound with gelatin or fat and lightened with an aerator.

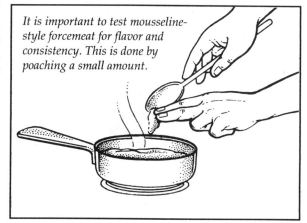

It is important to test mousseline-style forcemeat for flavor and consistency. This is done by poaching a small amount.

MOUSSELINE-STYLE FORCEMEAT

INGREDIENTS	AMOUNT
1) FLESH (MEAT OR FISH)	1 LB
2) EGG	1
3) HEAVY CREAM	1 C
4) SHALLOTS (SWEATED AND CHILLED)	1 T
5) SALT	1.5 TSP

METHOD
1. CAREFULLY CLEAN AND CUT MEAT OR FISH. IT SHOULD BE CLEANED OF ALL SINEW AND SILVERSKIN.
2. PROGRESSIVELY GRIND THROUGH MEDIUM AND SMALL DIES OF A WELL-CHILLED GRINDER.
3. COMBINE IN A WELL-CHILLED FOOD PROCESSOR, WITH THE EGG, SHALLOTS AND SALT.
4. PROCESS TO A SMOOTH PASTE, ADDING THE CREAM AT THE END OF THE PROCESS.

Figure 4

5/4/3 EMULSION FORCEMEAT

This type of forcemeat is used extensively in sausage making (frankfurters, bologna, knockwurst) and less often in the kitchens of hotels and restaurants. Its name is derived from the ratio of the components of the forcemeat. The normal ratio is five parts meat to four parts fat to three parts ice. A 5/4/3 emulsion forcemeat can be made from virtually any kind of meat. Fish is not considered suitable for this style of forcemeat. Pork jowls are the predominant choice of fat, however pork fatback is acceptable. The term *emulsion* automatically indicates that the texture of this style of forcemeat should be a perfectly smooth paste. Processing the components of the forcemeat with ice results in a very strong emulsion of meat and fat when it is cooked. The resulting blend has a moderate density, such as that of bologna.

A variety of binders are used in the production of this style of forcemeat to assist in binding and water retention. A panada is not capable of providing the type of binding power needed in the making of sausages. In this process the binders include non-fat dry milk, sodium caseinate and phosphates. The seasoning of this style of forcemeat will vary from one formulation to another. The usual intent in this style of preparation is to create a distinctive flavor for the product being produced. An example recipe for 5/4/3 emulsion forcemeat is shown in Figure Five.

COMPONENTS & THEIR CONTRIBUTION TO THE WHOLE

MEAT

Meat is the major component of a forcemeat. Its contribution to the particular character of the forcemeat will depend on the dominant meat chosen. The types of meats used include pork, lamb, beef, veal, poultry, game meats and fish.

Pork is often combined with a dominant meat in a forcemeat. This is because of the characteristics of the pork. It has a neutral flavor which easily takes on the flavor of the dominant meat. It also has a high capacity for water retention which aids in the production of a moist forcemeat and readily allows for extension of volume in the final product. Pork is also used commonly due to its traditionally lower cost in comparison to other meats.

Lamb is most commonly used in

5/4/3 EMULSION FORCEMEAT: FRANKFURTER

INGREDIENTS	AMOUNT
1) MEAT - PORK OR BEEF (CUBED)	5 LB
2) PORK JOWLS (CUBED)	4 LB
3) ICE (CRUSHED OR SHAVED)	3 LB

CURE MIXTURE

4) SALT	.36 OZ
5) CURING SALT	.04 OZ
6) SODIUM ERYTHORBATE	.01 OZ
7) DEXTROSE	.08 OZ
8) PHOSPHATE	.04 OZ
9) NON-FAT DRY MILK (N. F. D. M.)	.64 OZ

SPICE MIXTURE

10) WHITE PEPPER	.33 OZ
11) CORIANDER	.25 OZ
12) NUTMEG	.25 OZ
13) ONION POWDER	2 T
14) GARLIC POWDER	.5 TSP

METHOD

1. COMBINE MEATS (NOT JOWL FAT) WITH 4 THRU 8 AND ALLOW TO CURE OVERNIGHT.
2. PROGRESSIVELY GRIND MEAT THROUGH MEDIUM AND SMALL DIE.
3. PROGRESSIVELY GRIND JOWL FAT THROUGH MEDIUM AND SMALL DIE.
4. PLACE GROUND MEAT IN FOOD PROCESSOR.
5. PLACE ICE ON TOP OF MEAT.
6. PLACE SPICES AND N. F. D. M. ON TOP OF ICE.
7. PROCESS TO A TEMPERATURE OF 40°F.
8. ADD GROUND FAT AND PROCESS TO 58°F.
9. STUFF IN SHEEP CASING, TIE OFF AT SIX INCH LINKS. POACH AT 170°F TO AN INTERNAL TEMPERATURE OF 155°F.

NOTE: THIS FORMULA FOR FRANKFURTER IS SOMEWHAT INVOLVED, AS ARE NEARLY ALL TRADITIONAL "OLD WORLD" RECIPES. PRECISE MEASUREMENT OF SPICES AND ADDITIVES IS CRUCIAL TO A CONSISTENT PRODUCT, WHICH IS FAMILIAR TO THE CUSTOMER.

Figure 5

Middle Eastern and Indian recipes where it is valued for its strong distinctive flavor. The high cost of lamb is often a deterrent to its regular use in the preparation of forcemeats.

Beef is considered to be moderately expensive. When used in forcemeat production, the meat of the bull is preferred. Bull meat has a deep red color and good binding ability resulting from its high protein content. It is considered to be excellent for the production of forcemeat, as well as economical.

Veal is both very delicate in flavor and very expensive. It is used in the production of extremely delicate forcemeats.

Poultry is relatively inexpensive and mildly flavored. It is used most often in mousseline-style forcemeats, due to its naturally softer, lighter texture.

Game is classified as either wild or farm-raised. Wild game will have a strong, gamey flavor while farm-raised game will have milder flavor. Both types of game are considered to be expensive. They are most often used to make sausage or occasionally a paté.

Fish have a wide range of flavors and are considered expensive in relation to other meats. Fish are most often used in mousseline-style forcemeat with the exception of gefilte fish which is coarser in texture.

The functions of the meat, as the major component in the forcemeat, are extremely important to the production of a quality product. The body and structure of the product is dependent upon the meat for the matrix of protein into which the fat particles of the forcemeat are suspended. The meat is broken down into progressively smaller particles by the grinding process. This process exposes more proteins. These proteins encapsulate the smaller particles of fat. As the forcemeat cooks, the proteins surround the fat, trapping it in the forcemeat. This process results in a moist, flavorful product with a pleasing mouth feel.

The variations of color in forcemeat are a result of the coloring properties of the dominant meat. In red meat, poultry and fish the oxygen-carrying pigment of the muscle tissue, myoglobin, accounts for about eighty-five percent of the color. The hemoglobin in the blood in the tissue only accounts for twenty-five percent of the color. In red meats, they are red when fresh. When cured they appear grey due to the action of the curing salts. When fully cooked, the fresh meats appear grey, yet the cured meats retain a characteristic pink cured color, as in ham or bologna. The color difference between fresh and cured chicken, veal and other white meats is less drastic. This is a result

CUTTING STRIPS AND DICE

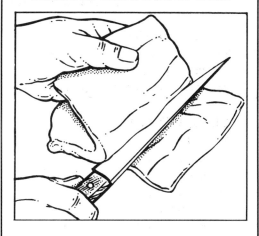

1. Remove Rind. Use a long, sharp knife to cut into end lf slab just above the rind. Slice, lifting away fat.

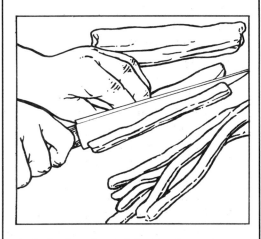

2. Cut Lardons. Cut the fatback into long strips about 1/4 inch thick.

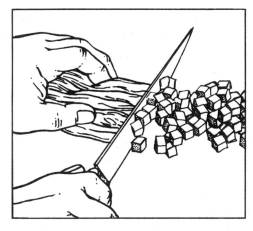

3. Prepare Dice. Hold several strips in a bundle with one hand. Slice crosswise to make 1/4 inch cubes.

of the decreased concentration of myoglobin in these meats. In fish there is virtually no difference in color between cured and uncured flesh.

FAT

Fat contributes flavor, binding power and texture to the forcemeat. The type of fat used in a forcemeat will depend upon the formulation.

Pork fat, primarily fatback and jowl fat, is considered the best type of fat for forcemeat. It has a neutral flavor and is relatively pure, meaning it contains few blood vessels or sinew which are undesirable. Pork fat has an ideal melting point for forcemeat production. It is soft enough to melt in the mouth, resulting in a good mouth feel. Yet it is hard enough to stand up to cooking temperatures. The plentiful supply of this type of fat, due to the high percentage of fat a swine produces, makes it an economical choice.

Lamb fat is limited in forcemeat production to those which contain lamb. The strong flavor and hardness of this fat makes it less desirable in forcemeats. It is particularly undesirable because of the greasy mouth feel it produces in cold forcemeats. Beef fat is very hard, having a high melting point which results in a coating effect in the mouth in cold forcemeats. Poultry fat is very soft and has a strong flavor. The low melting temperature of the fat makes it very difficult to emulsify.

The type of fat chosen for the forcemeat will have a major effect upon the flavor of the item. The mouth feel of the item is largely a result of the fat used. A higher ration of fat results in a more tender forcemeat, as well as providing a moist feel in the mouth.

PANADA

Panada, as it applies to forcemeats, indicates a paste prepared from flour, bread, rice or other starch product. It is intended to be added to the forcemeat for three primary reasons.

1. It aids in binding the fat.
2. It lightens the density of the product.
3. It contributes to the seasoning of the product.

Panadas are used less frequently in the contemporary kitchen where improved technology and equipment make it possible to create better emulsions. Even in the case of the country-style forcemeat, a portion of the meat and fat mixture may be pureed to take the place of the traditional panada. In Le Guide Culinaire, Escoffier describes five types of panadas.

1. Bread Panada.
2. Flour Panada.
3. Frangipane Panada.
4. Rice Panada.
5. Potato Panada.

These are by no means the only panadas; however, they do serve to illustrate the various components typically found in a panada. Whichever panada is utilized, it should not comprise more that twenty percent of the total weight of the forcemeat.

EGGS

The major contributions of the egg to a forcemeat are binding power and firmer texture. Both of these attributes result from the extra protein the egg brings to the mixture. Eggs are not used in sausage making.

SEASONINGS

Seasonings serve a far greater function in the forcemeat than simply addition and enhancement of flavor.

Salt is a primary binder. It facilitates the exposure of myosin, the protein largely responsible for binding a forcemeat. It also enhances water retention and adds to and enhances flavor.

Curing salt is also called *T.C.M.*, tinted cure mix and *prague powder*. It is composed of ninety-four percent salt and six percent sodium nitrate. Curing salt is tinted pink to distinguish it from ordinary salt. The two primary reasons it is used are to fix the color in a processed meat and to inhibit the growth of clostridium botulinum, the anaerobic bacteria which can be deadly. Curing salt converts to nitric oxide when it combines with many processed meats. This nitric oxide then combines with the myoglobin, the red meat pigment. This combination preserves a pink color in the meat after cooking. It is this chemical action which results in the pink color associated with cured meat products, such as ham and bologna.

Spices are primarily responsible for the distinctive flavor characteristics of the various forcemeats. The classical *paté spice* is an example of the type of spice combinations often used in forcemeat production. This mixture includes white pepper, black pepper, bay leaves, cloves, paprika, marjoram, thyme, basil, nutmeg, mace and ginger.

A few of the other flavorings often used in forcemeats are wines, brandy, garlic, onions and shallots. The components are usually cooked to some degree prior to incorporation into the forcemeat.

GARNISHES

Garnishes may be added to a forcemeat after it is completed. There is a wide range of possibilities for this purpose, including mushrooms, dried currants, nutmeats and the traditional garnish for classical paté of pistachios, smoked tongue and truffles. It should be remembered that garnishes are best at least partially cooked and cooled before being added to the forcemeat.

METHODOLOGY OF PREPARATION

The basis of successful forcemeat preparation begins, as with all products, with proper preparation. Carefully select the ingredients which are to be used and assemble them before beginning. This will save time and effort later. It is important to choose the right pieces of equipment and to prepare them properly for production. The two primary pieces of processing equipment needed are the grinder and some type of food processor. The preparation of forcemeat can be broken into three main steps: fabrication and grinding; molding, forming and stuffing; and cooking.

NOTE: When using grinding equipment, it must be kept sharp and sanitary. All grinding equipment should be chilled in ice water or the refrigerator prior to use in forcemeat production.

FABRICATION & GRINDING

Basic fabrication will include four steps. First the meats should be trimmed of fat gristle and silver skin. Second, the rind should be removed from the fatback or other fat being used. Third, the meats and fat should be cubed or cut into small strips. Fourth, the cubed meats and fat should be well chilled. Partial freezing of the fat will assist in maintaining low grinding temperatures, however freezing of the meat should be avoided.

Seasoning and curing is the next step in this part of production. Salt, curing salt (if used), and any other seasonings are distributed evenly over the meat and fat mixture. The mix is then allowed to marinate, preferably overnight.

Grinding procedure will vary with the size of the batch being prepared. A small batch (up to approximately 15 pounds) will depend greatly upon the integrity of the meat protein being kept intact until the cooking stage for the success of the emulsion. Maintaining the temperature of the meat between 35°-50°F during the grinding process prevents the denaturing of the proteins. This will minimize the loss of binding power during this stage of production. The marinated meat and fat mixture is ground through a large, 1/4-inch die on medium speed. If a smaller grind is desired for a finer textured forcemeat, the mixture is ground a second time through a smaller die. This is referred to as *progressive grinding*. For a pureed forcemeat the mixture would be transferred at this point to a well-chilled food processor and processed to a smooth paste. Caution should be exercised to prevent the temperature of the mixture from rising above 50°F.

In large-scale emulsion production, such as commercial sausage production, an alternate method is often used. When the basic fabrication, seasoning and curing steps are finished, the marinated mixture is combined in a large vertical chopper or buffalo chopper. Ice or ice water is added to the mixture to maintain the temperature during processing. In this manner the mixture is processed to the desired texture.

MOLDING, FORMING & STUFFING

Prior to filling molds, the forcemeat mixture should be tested. Poaching a small quenelle in lightly salted water will allow the determination of correctness of flavor, seasoning and binding. Forcemeats should be packed into terrines and paté molds in several layers to minimize the possibilities of air pockets in the finished product. When layering, garnishes may be added to the forcemeat. *Random* garnishes should be evenly distributed throughout the forcemeat. *Inlaid* garnishes should be carefully positioned within the terrine, paté or galantine.

The various uses of forcemeat are discussed in depth in Chapter 26. The common uses are mentioned here. When forcemeat is used to produce a terrine, it is molded into terrines lined with sheets of fatback, bacon or plastic wrap. In the production of paté it is packed into a hinged mold lined with pastry (paté) dough. In the galantine, it is wrapped in the skin of the dominant meat. This is traditionally done with poultry or game. A forcemeat used in the production of a ballottine is wrapped in the skin of a leg of poultry. A quenelle is forcemeat which is formed into an oblong shape with two spoons. Forcemeat may also be used as a farce or stuffing for poultry or larger pieces of meat, such as pork loin or breast of veal.

COOKING

Generally forcemeats are cooked at low temperatures, 150°-180°F, to internal temperatures of 140°-170°F. If a forcemeat is cooked at too high a temperature, for too long, the proteins overcook. The resulting excessive coagulation of the proteins forces out the fat, producing a dry crumbly forcemeat, which is difficult to slice. A forcemeat which is not fully cooked will be mushy and unstructured when sliced.

HANDLING & STORAGE

The nature of both the product being produced and the equipment used in production require careful attention. The preparation of a wholesome product calls for strict sanitary practices. There is the constant danger of cross contamination of the various components in the forcemeat. The meat of a healthy animal is generally sterile and relatively free of harmful levels of bacteria when first slaughtered. It must be remembered that from the point of slaughter the meat begins to deteriorate, becoming increasingly susceptible to the growth of bacteria. This is particularly true when it is exposed to temperatures in the danger zone (45°-140°). The meats and other components in the forcemeat must be held at safe temperatures both before and during processing. Once processed they should be quickly cooled and then held at safe temperatures. Even cured meat is not safe from harmful bacteria growth when mishandled. Traces of forcemeat are easily overlooked in the cleaning of processing equipment. Always fully dismantle and clean grinding and processing equipment between batches of different types of meat to avoid cross contamination from one meat to another.

If there is one BEST KNOWN SECRET in the preparation of forcemeat, it is the chilling of everything involved in the production. Forcemeats produced with strict regard for temperature are not only wholesome, they are also of superior quality. Once production is completed, always store forcemeats covered and under refrigeration.

AVAILABLE FORMS

In the past, the only recourse for a restaurant, which wished to offer the customer one of the various products made from forcemeat, was to produce it in their own kitchen. Technological developments in processing, refrigeration, packaging and transportation have changed this. There are now available to the commercial operator and homemaker a wide variety of these types of products. The selection includes the most commonly recognized forms of sausages and luncheon meats which have been available in great quantities for many years. However the number of patés and galantines which specialty purveyors provide in a ready-to-use form is growing rapidly. The decision whether to buy or produce these items will depend upon the operation, its available equipment and staff. Whether buying or making forcemeats, the goal should always be to have high quality.

CONTEMPORARY APPLICATIONS

Modern application of the principals of forcemeat production are reflected in the enormously popular seafood product known as *surimi*. This is an analog, a combining of different components to create an imitation of one of the components. This ultrafine fish paste is die-molded and cooked in various ways to imitate more expensive items, such as crab legs, lobster tails and scallops. There are currently many new types of sausages which are in the developmental stage. This classical technique will continue to evolve in the future, with the availability of previously only wished for foods from around the world and with improved kitchen technology.

MOUSSE

TYPE & DEFINITION

For the garde manger chef, mousse is a fully cooked basic ingredient which is pureed, bound with a form of gelatin or fat, and lightened with an aerator of whipped cream or egg whites. The term can be used to describe preparations which are either hot or cold. In a hot mousse the mixture is always a mousse-like forcemeat of some form. The cold mousse mixture is always as described in the basic definition. The term is also used to describe dessert preparations which are of the same basic structure as the cold mousse.

COMPONENTS AND THEIR CONTRIBUTION TO THE WHOLE

The structure of the cold mousse has three basic components: Base, binder and aeration.

1. Base of a cold mousse can be meat, fish, cheese or vegetable. This base provide flavor, color, body and character in the product.

2. Binder in the preparation provides structure to the finished product. This may be accomplished by the inclusion of gelatin or aspic jelly which will set as the finished mousse is chilled. A flavorful fat, such as butter, will also contribute to the structure of a cold mousse. As the mousse cools, the fat congeals, thereby setting the mixture.

3. Aeration, the lightening of the mousse by adding a component which has the ability to act as a vehicle for the introduction of air to the mixture. Whipped cream works well. It lightens as well as adding extra fat content, resulting in a richer mixture. Whipped egg white adds lightness without adding extra fat to the mixture. This results in a leaner mousse.

The usual proportions of the basic components would be one quart of prepared base to one ounce of gelatin dissolved in one cup of water, to one quart of prepared aeration.

METHODOLOGY OF PREPARATION

The preparation of mousse divides into seven primary steps: Molds, base, binder, aeration, whisk, fold and mold.

Molds should be prepared first to ensure that the mousse can be molded before it sets. Individual molds, such as ramekins or small timbales, should be lubricated or lined in a manner consistent with the character of the mousse. The classical method when serving mousselines (the term for individual portions of mousse) is to line the molds with a thin coating of aspic gelee. Decoration is laid on the layer of aspic gelee and the mousse mixture is poured into the molds. When the mousse is unmolded, it is a finished product, both coated and decorated. The contemporary method calls for the molds to be lined with plastic wrap or simply oiled. When the mousse is set, it is then turned out and can be decorated or coated as needed.

Base preparation is the next step. Fully cook the base product if necessary, taking care not to overcook. Overcooking the base product will result in a dry texture in the finished mousse which will have a poor mouth feel. The base product should then be pureed. The consistency of the pureed mixture can be adjusted with one or more of the following items: Velouté, mayonnaise, bechamel, sour cream, cream or some similar product. The resulting puree should have a smooth, velvety texture. If a cream is used, it must be added near the end of the puree process to avoid breaking the cream. The puree should be slightly overseasoned to allow for the aeration which will be added. For the highest quality preparation, the pureed mixture should be put through a fine sieve. This is done by working small amounts of the mixture at a time through the fine sieve with a rubber bowl scraper or spatula. Today's modern food processing equipment is thought by many to make this step unnecessary. However, for a very refined product it is still a necessity.

Binder preparation begins with the weighing of the gelatin. This weight will be contingent on the amount of base to be set. Measurement of the liquid will also be dependent on the amount of

---

MOUSSE - SALMON

INGREDIENTS	AMOUNT
1) SALMON (POACHED)	10 OZ
2) FISH VELOUTÉ	6 OZ
3) SALT AND WHITE PEPPER	TO TASTE
4) GELATIN GRANULES (DRY)	.5 OZ
5) DRY WHITE WINE	.5 C
6) WHIPPED CREAM	1 PT

METHOD

1. PUREE SALMON WITH THE VELOUTÉ, UNTIL VERY SMOOTH. PUT THROUGH A FINE SIEVE IF NECESSARY.
2. ADD SEASONING TO THE PUREED MIXTURE.
3. SPRINKLE THE GELATIN INTO THE WINE AND ALLOW TO BLOOM FOR 10 MINUTES.
4. PLACE GELATIN MIXTURE OVER HOT WATER UNTIL BLOOMED GELATIN IS DISSOLVED.
5. WHISK GELATIN INTO SALMON PUREE.
6. FOLD WHIPPED CREAM INTO THE PUREE MIXTURE AND TURN INTO MOLD.

Figure 6

base. The liquid is limited only by what is suitable to the character of the mousse and the setting power of the gelatin. To re-hydrate the dry gelatin, sprinkle it evenly into the cool liquid. Allow sufficient time for the gelatin granules to absorb the liquid (bloom). Then place the bloomed gelatin over a hot water bath until melted.

Aeration preparation will require the whipping of either cream or egg whites to a soft peak.

Whisk the binder into the base. Both the base and the binder should be at room temperature for this step.

Fold the aeration into the base/binder mixture. If the base is too thick or cold, the aeration will be deflated before it is worked into the mousse.

Mold the mousse before it starts to set. The time it takes the mousse to set will depend on the temperature of the completed product. The molded mousse should be allowed to chill overnight.

The characteristics of a well-made mousse are:

1. Velvety smooth texture.
2. Light and airy consistency which is not heavy or rubbery, no air pockets.
3. A delicate but distinctive flavor.

NOTE: If a mousse mixture is molded into multi-portion terrines or timbales, the resulting item is referred to as a mousse. If the mousse mixture is molded into single portion timbales or molds, or shaped into quenelles, the resulting item is termed a mousseline. An example recipe for a mousse is shown in Figure Six.

CONCLUSION

The principles presented in this chapter will be referred to often in Chapters 26, 27 and 28. These chapters discuss the preparation of patés, hors d'oeuvres, and sausages, to name only a few items. Forcemeats and mousse are the base preparations for these items. It is from these two types of preparations that many other culinary delights blossom.

REVIEW QUESTIONS

1. List and define the five basic types of *forcemeat.*
2. What is the function of meat in forcemeat production?
3. What is the function of fat in forcemeat production?
4. What is curing salt and what function does it serve in forcemeat production?
5. What is the importance of temperature in forcemeat production?
6. What are two definitions of the term *mousseline?*
7. What is commonly used as an aerator in mousse?
8. What types of binders are used in mousse preparation?
9. Define the term *mousse.*
10. List, in order, the seven basic steps of mousse production. State why the steps are in a particular order.
11. What are the characteristics of a high quality mousse?

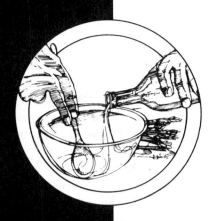

Chapter 26

CHAPTER OBJECTIVES

- **To define paté.**
- **To discuss the preparation of paté.**
- **To define terrines.**
- **To discuss the preparation of terrines.**
- **To define galantine and ballotine.**
- **To discuss the preparation of galantine and ballotine.**
- **To define mousse and mousseline.**
- **To discuss the preparation of mousse and mousseline.**
- **To define and discuss related culinary preparations.**

Patés and Terrines

This chapter discusses preparations considered to be the flagships of the garde manger department. The intent, in part, is to clarify the use of the various terms. Confusion is caused by overlapping use of terms and inconsistent classifications.

There are three basic ways the items may be classified. Some are named for their shape, such as the timbale and quenelle. Others are named for their size, such as mousse and mousseline and others for the type of mixture or ingredient used. The primary items with which this chapter will be concerned are: Patés, terrines, galantines, roullades, ballottine, parfaits, mousse and mousseline.

PATÉS

In the American kitchen, the term *paté*, used by itself, means a forcemeat baked in a crust, usually in a rectangular or oval loaf mold. This usage is acceptable, as a proper abbreviation of the French term *paté en croute*. A dictionary definition of pate would state that it is a spread of finely chopped or pureed, seasoned meat, often chicken liver.

There are a few traditional French preparations referred to as paté which are not baked in a crust, such as *paté campagne*. These preparations should more correctly be called terrines.

In a very general sense, the term paté applies to mixtures other than forcemeat baked in a crust. Pate could also apply to crusted items not baked in a mold. However, these items are normally given other names, such as the English *pork hat pie*, Cornish *pasty*, and Spanish *empanada*.

EQUIPMENT

Preparation of paté in a crust requires the use of specific pieces of equipment. These include paté molds, pastry wheels, scissors, palette knives, round cutters (1-inch and 1/2-inch in diameter) and aluminum foil.

The paté molds provide a great degree of choice. The mold selected will determine the appearance of the final product. There are three basic types of paté molds.

Hinged oval paté molds are classically styled. Ornate decoration on the sides is a distinctive characteristic of these molds. They come in either a three-piece or four-piece, hinged mold. The mold is sized by its weight capacity.

Hinged rectangular paté molds have contemporary styling. The rectangular shape allows a higher product yield and easier portioning. This is the preferred mold for large quantity production. Molds of this type have smooth or textured sides, but seldom decorative designs. Normally they are three-piece, hinged molds. Those made from

black steel are preferred because they allow better browning of the pastry. This mold is sized by weight capacity or measurements.

Tapered loaf pans give patés a colloquial or "home-style" appearance. The sides of the mold taper for easy removal.

PREPARATION

Preparation of a paté (paté en croute) is accomplished in five stages. Each needs to be executed with care to produce a high quality paté. The five stages of production are: Pre-preparation, assembling the paté, inserting the chimneys, cooking the paté and finishing the paté.

PRE-PREPARATION

1. PREPARE THE DOUGH, SEE FIGURE ONE.

2. PREPARE THE FORCEMEAT, REFER TO CHAPTER 25 FOR A REVIEW OF THE PROCEDURE AND THE BASIC RECIPE.

3. ROLL THE DOUGH ABOUT 1/8-INCH THICK AND ABOUT THE SIZE OF A SHEET PAN.

4. USING THE ASSEMBLED HINGED MOLD, MARK THE DOUGH FOR THE MAIN AND CAP PIECES.

   A) THE MAIN PIECE SHOULD BE ONE PIECE OF DOUGH LARGE ENOUGH TO COVER THE BOTTOM AND FOUR WALLS OF THE MOLD. ALLOW FOR A 1/2-INCH OVERHANG OF THE FOUR WALLS.

   B) THE CAPPING PIECE SHOULD BE THE SIZE OF THE BOTTOM PLATE OF THE MOLD, WITH AN EXTRA 1/2-INCH ON ALL FOUR SIDES.
   NOTE: THE EXTRA 1/2-INCH WILL ALLOW THE EDGES OF THE CAP PIECE TO BE TUCKED DOWN THE SIDES OF THE MOLD, FORMING A GOOD SEAL.

5. CUT 2 CHIMNEY RINGS FROM AN EXTRA PIECE OF DOUGH. USING A 1-INCH AND 1/2-INCH ROUND CUTTER.
   NOTE: THE RINGS SHOULD RESEMBLE A 1-INCH WASHER WITH A 1/2-INCH HOLE.

PATÉ DOUGH

INGREDIENTS	AMOUNT
1. FLOUR, ALL-PURPOSE	2 LB 8 OZ
2. BUTTER	5 OZ
3. SHORTENING, EMULSIFIED	7 OZ
4. BAKING POWDER	.5 OZ
5. WATER	9 OZ
6. VINEGAR	1 OZ
7. EGGS	3 EA
8. SALT	2 TSP

METHOD

1. SIFT TOGETHER FLOUR AND BAKING POWDER.
2. CUT SHORTENING AND BUTTER INTO THE FLOUR MIXTURE USING A FOOD PROCESSOR.
3. COMBINE REMAINING INGREDIENTS AND ADD TO THE MIXTURE IN THE FOOD PROCESSOR.
4. PROCESS UNTIL THE DOUGH FORMS A BALL.
5. TRANSFER DOUGH TO A MIXER AND MIX WITH DOUGH HOOK FOR 3 MINUTES.
6. REMOVE DOUGH FROM MIXER AND SHAPE INTO A THICK, FLAT RECTANGLE.
7. COVER AND REFRIGERATE OVERNIGHT.

Figure 1

ASSEMBLING THE PATÉ

1. LIGHTLY OIL THE ASSEMBLED MOLD.

2. FOLD THE MAIN PIECE OF DOUGH LENGTHWISE. IT SHOULD DROP EASILY INTO THE MOLD.

3. UNFOLD THE DOUGH COVERING THE FOUR SIDE WALLS OF THE MOLD, ALLOWING THE DOUGH TO OVERHANG THE TOPS OF THE MOLD BY ABOUT 1/2-INCH ALL AROUND.

   NOTE: THIS IS A SINGLE PIECE OF DOUGH, INTENDED TO COVER ALL FOUR WALLS AND THE BOTTOM OF THE MOLD. THE END WALLS SHOULD BE COVERED AUTOMATICALLY AND HAVE EQUAL OVERHANG.

In traditional patés a lining of thin sheets of fatback is placed between the dough and forcemeat. This is, however, an optional step we have chosen to delete here.

4. USING A SMALL BALL OF SCRAP DOUGH, CAREFULLY PRESS THE DOUGH INTO THE CORNERS OF THE MOLD.

   NOTE: THE BALL OF DOUGH PREVENTS PUNCTURING THE DOUGH WITH YOUR FINGER.

5. COVER AND REFRIGERATE THE LINED MOLD FOR ONE HOUR.

   NOTE: THIS ALLOWS THE DOUGH TO ADHERE TO THE MOLD, MAKING IT LESS LIKELY TO SLIP OR WRINKLE DURING FILLING.

6. FILL THE LINED MOLD WITH WELL-CHILLED FORCEMEAT 1/2-INCH SHORT OF THE TOP EDGE.

   NOTE: THE FORCEMEAT SHOULD BE PLACED IN THE MOLD IN SEVERAL LAYERS. USE A PALETTE KNIFE TO PRESS IT INTO PLACE. THIS REDUCES THE CREATION OF AIR POCKETS IN THE FINISHED PRODUCT.

7. FOLD THE OVERHANGING FLAPS OF DOUGH OVER THE TOP OF THE FORCEMEAT.

8. USE SCISSORS TO TRIM THE SIDE FLAPS FLUSH IN THE CENTER OF THE MOLD WITH NO OVERLAP.

   NOTE: THERE SHOULD NOW BE A SIN-

GLE THICKNESS OF DOUGH COMPLETELY ENCOMPASSING THE FORCEMEAT. THE DOUGH SHOULD MEET WITH A SEAM RUNNING LENGTHWISE DOWN THE TOP SURFACE OF THE FORCEMEAT.

9. SQUEEZE THE END FLAPS TO A SINGLE, 1/8-INCH THICKNESS AND TRIM TO A LENGTH OF 1/2-INCH. THESE END FLAPS ARE THEN FOLDED OVER ONTO THE TOP OF THE PATÉ AND EGG WASHED INTO PLACE.

10. LIGHTLY EGG WASH THE DOUGH COVERING THE TOP OF THE PATÉ.

NOTE: AVOID LETTING THE EGG WASH RUN DOWN BETWEEN THE MOLD AND THE DOUGH. THIS WILL CAUSE UNEVEN BROWNING AND POSSIBLY STICKING.

11. LIGHTLY EGG WASH THE FACE OF THE CAPPING PIECE.

12. LAY THE CAPPING PIECE, EGG WASH SIDE DOWN, ON THE TOP OF THE PATÉ.

13. THERE SHOULD BE A 1/2-INCH OVERHANG OF THE CAPPING PIECE. USING A PALETTE KNIFE, GENTLY TUCK THIS DOWN INSIDE THE MOLD, LOCKING IT BETWEEN THE MOLD AND THE DOUGH WRAPPING OF THE FORCEMEAT. THEN PRESS LIGHTLY TO SECURE.

INSERTING THE CHIMNEYS

Chimneys are placed in the paté to allow steam to escape. If chimneys are not present, the steam can crack the crust.

1. PREPARE THE CHIMNEYS BY ROLLING A 2 1/2-INCH WIDE BAND OF FOIL AROUND A SHARPENING STEEL. THIS WILL PRODUCE A 2 1/2-INCH LONG FOIL TUBE. TWO OF THESE ARE NEEDED.

2. USING THE 1/2-INCH CUTTER, CAREFULLY CUT TWO EVENLY SPACED HOLES IN THE TOP OF THE PATÉ SO THAT THE FORCEMEAT CAN BE SEEN.

3. EGG WASH THE CHIMNEY RINGS AND PLACE OVER THE HOLES TO ACT AS REINFORCEMENT.

4. PLACE ONE FOIL CHIMNEY INTO EACH REINFORCED HOLE .

NOTE: DO NOT PUSH THE CHIMNEY IN SO FAR THAT IT TOUCHES THE FORCEMEAT. THIS WILL CLOG IT UP.

5. SECURE THE CHIMNEYS IN PLACE WITH A LITTLE MORE EGG WASH.

COOKING THE PATÉ

Cooking the paté is divided into two stages termed browning and cooking.

1. BROWNING STAGE:
   A) WITHOUT EGG WASHING THE TOP OF THE PATÉ, COVER THE PATÉ WITH FOIL.
   B) PLACE IN A PREHEATED 475°F OVEN, PREFERABLY CONVECTION TYPE, FOR 10 MINUTES OR UNTIL THERE IS EVIDENCE OF LIGHT, EVEN BROWNING ON THE SURFACE.
   C) REMOVE FROM THE OVEN AND ALLOW TO REST FOR 15 MINUTES.

2. COOKING STAGE:
   A) UNCOVER AND LIGHTLY EGGWASH THE TOP OF THE PATÉ.
   B) PLACE IN A PREHEATED, 350°F OVEN UNTIL AN INTERNAL TEMPERATURE OF 150°F IS REACHED.
   NOTE: A) THE TEMPERATURE CAN BE TAKEN THROUGH THE CHIMNEY OPENING.
   B) BE SURE THE THERMOMETER PENETRATES DEEPLY ENOUGH INTO THE FORCEMEAT TO REGISTER THE CENTRAL INTERIOR TEMPERATURE, NOT JUST THAT SLIGHTLY UNDER THE SURFACE.

FINISHING THE PATÉ

The paté is not complete when it is removed from the oven. It must first be filled with aspic.

1. ALLOW THE PATÉ TO REST AT ROOM TEMPERATURE FOR 15 MINUTES, AFTER REMOVAL FROM THE OVEN.
   NOTE: THIS WILL ALLOW THE JUICES AND FAT THAT HAVE COME OUT OF THE MEAT AND RISEN UP THE CHIMNEY DURING COOKING TO BE RE-ABSORBED INTO THE MEAT.

2. CAREFULLY FILL THE CHIMNEYS WITH A GOOD QUALITY ASPIC JELLY. (SEE CHAPTER 24 FOR A DISCUSSION OF ASPIC.)
   NOTE: THE ASPIC PROCESS WILL CON-

TINUE OVER THE PERIOD OF AT LEAST AN HOUR. AS THE ASPIC IS SLOWLY ABSORBED INTO THE WARM FORCEMEAT, THE LEVEL IN THE CHIMNEY WILL LOWER AND MORE ASPIC SHOULD BE ADDED UNTIL THE CHIMNEY REMAINS FULL.

3. ALLOW THE PATÉ TO CHILL OVERNIGHT BEFORE REMOVAL AND SLICING.

NOTE: Patés can also be made using yeast doughs such as brioche.

TROUBLESHOOTING

As you can see, making a paté is an involved process. There are a variety of problems which can occur. Figure Two gives some pointers as to possible causes and solutions to these.

TERRINES

Terrines are the closest cousin of the paté. The term, as it relates to food, refers to a preparation cooked or molded in a terrine. The terrine vessel is an oblong, earthenware mold. More durable modern materials such as enameled cast iron are also used to provide even, all around cooking. The term *terrine* is from the French expression *paté en terrine*. This is a paté cooked in a terrine mold and not a crust. This term can easily confuse the novice culinarian. Care should be taken to use the proper American abbreviation, *terrine*.

Since the terrine takes its name from the vessel and not the mixture used, the variety of types is limitless. For example, the mixture used in the most common form of terrine is a forcemeat. However, a terrine can also be made using a pre-cooked paste of meat, fish or vegetable purees bound cold with gelatin or hot with eggs.

It is even possible to take freshly poached pieces of boneless chicken, still warm, and press them into a terrine. When weighted, pressed and cooled, the result is a terrine which can be removed and sliced. The only binding is the natural gelatin present in the cooked chicken.

Terrines can be served directly from the mold or removed. They are most often served cold; however, it is not inappropriate to serve them hot.

EQUIPMENT

The equipment needed in the preparation of a terrine includes: Terrine

---

TROUBLESHOOTING FOR PATÉ

PROBLEM	CAUSE	SOLUTION
Aspic runs from the bottom of the mold after cooking.	Hole or crack in the dough.	Cool paté completely, remove mold. Patch holes with cold butter or raw dough. Return paté to mold and fill with tepid aspic. Chill completely.
Excessive fat in sheet pan after cooking.	1) Same as above. 2) Poorly prepared forcemeat. The meat got too warm during processing, or processor blades were too dull, resulting in a fat smear.	1) Same as above. 2) None at this stage, forcemeat will be grainy and dry, with poor mouth feel.
Paté not brown on sides.	Oven not hot enough at browning stage.	Be sure oven is fully preheated. If using a conventional oven, raise temperature by 25° F.
Paté unevenly browned.	Poor heat distribution. Pates too closely packed in oven or foil left on too long during browning stage.	Use a convection oven. Rotate pates half way through cooking. Remove foil earlier in browning stage.

Figure 2

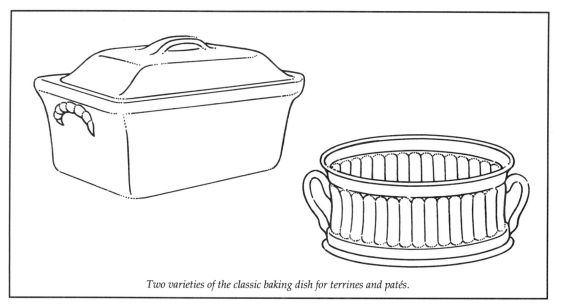

Two varieties of the classic baking dish for terrines and patés.

molds, plastic food film, palette knife and a water bath with rack. There are oval and rectangular terrine molds. All have two pieces, a lid and bottom.

Oval earthenware molds were the earliest form of molds. They can be fashioned to resemble the crust of a classical, ornate paté en croute, or have simple lines, with smooth sides. These molds are sized by weight capacity. They are available in heavily glazed pottery or white porcelain.

Rectangular terrines are contemporary in style. They allow a higher product yield and easier, more consistent portioning. They are smooth sided, and sized by weight capacity. Rectangular terrines are available in earthenware or enameled cast iron.

PREPARATION

Preparation of a terrine can be divided into four stages. Each stage is critical to the quality of the finished product. Those stages are pre-preparation, assembling the terrine, cooking the terrine and pressing the terrine.

PRE-PREPARATION

The first step in preparing a terrine is the selection of a suitable mold. For the purpose of this discussion we will use a 2 1/2-pound, rectangular, enameled cast iron mold.

1. PREPARE THE MOLD:
   A) LIGHTLY OIL MOLD.
   B) LINE MOLD WITH A SINGLE PIECE OF PLASTIC FILM, LARGE ENOUGH TO COVER THE BOTTOM AND FOUR SIDES OF THE TERRINE.
   C) SMOOTH AWAY ANY LARGE WRINKLES IN THE FILM.
2. PREPARE FORCEMEAT:
   A) FROM A FILLETED SIDE OF SALMON, CUT A RECTANGULAR BAR OF SALMON, SUITABLE IN SIZE TO RUN DOWN THE CENTER AND COVER THE BOTTOM OF THE TERRINE. THIS SERVES AS AN INLAY FOR THE TERRINE.
   B) PREPARE A SALMON MOUSSELINE FORCEMEAT FROM THE REMAINING SALMON. (REFER TO CHAPTER 25 FOR REVIEW.)
   C) MIX A RANDOM GARNISH INTO THE FORCEMEAT USING THE FOLLOWING INGREDIENTS:

FRESH BASIL, CHOPPED	2 TBS
FRESH PARSLEY, CHOPPED	1 TBS
TRUFFLES, CHOPPED	2 TBS

ASSEMBLING THE TERRINE

1. FILL THE TERRINE HALF FULL WITH FORCEMEAT, BEING CAREFUL NOT TO FORM AIR POCKETS.
2. PLACE THE BAR OF SALMON ON TOP OF THE FORCEMEAT AND GENTLY PRESS DOWN INTO POSITION.

3. FILL THE TERRINE WITH THE REMAINING FORCEMEAT TO THE SHOULDER OF THE MOLD.
4. FOLD THE OVERHANGING SIDE FLAPS OF PLASTIC WRAP OVER SO THEY REST ON THE SURFACE OF THE FORCEMEAT.
5. PLACE LID ON TERRINE.

COOKING THE TERRINE

1. ASSEMBLE THE WATER BATH:
   A) SELECT A BRAZIER OR SIMILAR POT, LARGE ENOUGH TO HOLD THE TERRINE OR TERRINES.
   B) PLACE A LOW STABLE RACK IN THE BRAZIER.
   NOTE: 1) IF A RACK IS NOT AVAILABLE, A TOWEL MAY BE PLACED UNDER THE TERRINE VESSEL INSTEAD.
   2) THE RACK OR TOWEL ACTS AS A BUFFER BREAKING THE DIRECT METAL TO METAL CONTACT BETWEEN THE BRAZIER AND THE TERRINE. THIS IMPROVES THE EVEN COOKING OBTAINED BY USING THE WATER BATH.
   C) PLACE TERRINE IN THE WATER BATH.
   D) PLACE BRAZIER, WITH THE TERRINE, IN A PREHEATED 325°F OVEN.
   E) FILL BRAZIER WITH 190°F WATER TO 1/2-INCH BELOW THE LEVEL OF THE FORCEMEAT.
   NOTE: THE WATER BATH MUST BE MAINTAINED AT BETWEEN 170-175°F. IF NEEDED, ADD SHAVED ICE PERIODICALLY TO MAINTAIN THE CORRECT TEMPERATURE.
2. COOK TO AN INTERNAL TEMPERATURE OF 140°F.
3. REMOVE FROM WATER BATH.
4. COOL AT ROOM TEMPERATURE FOR 30 MINUTES.

PRESSING TERRINES

A cooked terrine is pressed by removing the lid and placing a metal plate, cut to fit the opening of the terrine, on top of the forcemeat or filling. A moderate weight is placed on top of the plate and the terrine is refrigerated overnight.

It is not always necessary, or good, to press a terrine. Forcemeat terrines normally should not be pressed. Pressing squeezes out some of the fat in the forcemeat which can create an undesirable change in the texture of the terrine when cold.

There are terrines which benefit from pressing. Terrines made with cubed or shredded meats or vegetables may benefit by the increased contact between the individual ingredients. Pressing a terrine set with aspic will help eliminate air pockets.

COUNTRY-STYLE TERRINES

Country-style terrines use a campagne forcemeat (see Chapter 25). The general procedure for preparing a terrine of this type is similar to that previously discussed. However, there are a few differences.

There is no center inlay in a country-style terrine. A random garnish of diced tongue, peeled pistachio nuts and ham may be added to the forcemeat. Also, the terrine may be lined with sheets of fatback or strips of bacon. When this is done, the plastic wrap is not needed.

A country-style terrine is cooked to a slightly higher internal temperature of 150°F. Once it has cooled at room temperature for thirty minutes, the fat surrounding the terrine is poured off. The fat removed is replaced with a good quality aspic. There is more shrinkage in a country-style forcemeat than in a mousseline. The added aspic gives the terrine a more finished appearance when removed.

GALANTINES

Galantine, by classical definition, is a boned poultry or game animal (such as rabbit), stuffed with forcemeat. The earliest versions of these were carefully boned and trussed or reinforced with armatures to resemble the natural shape of the animal. The name galantine, rooted in the French term *gallant* refers to the elegant nature of the presentation.

Modern galantines are more often rolled into an even, elongated shape, resembling a thick sausage. The meat of the poultry or game may be left attached to the skin in its natural position. Poultry or game may also be skinned first and the prime pieces, such as the breast, used for inlays.

Once assembled, the galantine is poached and left to cool in a rich stock. The stock is usually made from the bones of the animal used. When cooled, galantines may be braised briefly.

NOTE: In recent years the definition of galantine has been expanded to include similar preparations of rolled fish.

The equipment needed for preparation of a galantine includes a boning knife, cheese cloth, kitchen twine and brazier.

PREPARATION

The preparation of a galantine is divided into three stages: Pre-preparation, assembly and cooking. In the first stage it is necessary to remove the bone from the poultry or game animal used. This must be done with precision to maintain the quality and appearance of the skin and meat. Refer to Chapter 18 for a review of these procedures.

The preparation of a Pheasant Galantine is outlined below.

PRE-PREPARATION

1. **TRIM THE PHEASANT.**
   A) **BEGIN WITH A PHEASANT WHICH HAS BEEN PLUCKED, DRESSED, WASHED AND SINGED.**
   B) **REMOVE THE WINGS AT THE SECOND JOINT AND RESERVE FOR THE STOCK POT.**
2. **SKIN THE PHEASANT.**
   A) **MAKE AN INCISION DOWN THE BACKBONE AND CAREFULLY WORK THE SKIN OFF THE MEAT, USING THE TIP OF THE KNIFE.**
   B) **TRIM THE SKIN INTO A GENERALLY RECTANGULAR SHAPE, REALIZING IT NEED NOT BE A PERFECT RECTANGLE.**
3. **REMOVE THE MEAT FROM THE BONES.**
   A) **CAREFULLY REMOVE THE BREAST MEAT FROM THE BONES LEAVING THE MEAT SECTIONS INTACT. THESE WILL BE MARINATED.**

ROLLING A GALANTINE

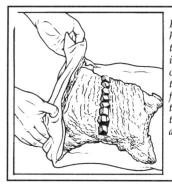
Form the roll by holding one end of the cloth and lifting one side of the chicken, folding it to center. Lift and fold the other side to meet the first at the center forming a cylinder.

Secure the roll with (3) 1 1/2 foot long cloth strips.

Place the roll on a rack in a snug fitting pot. Cover with boiling meat stock. Poach at 175°F for 1 3/4 hours or until roll feels firm.

Serve on a bed of aspic.

B) REMOVE THE BONES FROM THE LEGS AND THIGHS, RESERVING THE MEAT FOR FORCEMEAT AND THE BONES FOR STOCK.

4. MARINATE THE BREAST MEAT AND SKIN FOR THREE HOURS IN THE FOLLOWING:

BRANDY	1 TBS
WHITE WINE	1 TBS
CURING SALT	PINCH
SALT AND PEPPER	PINCH

5. PREPARE A STOCK FROM THE BONES (REFER TO CHAPTER 14).

6. PREPARE A STRAIGHT METHOD FORCEMEAT (REFER TO CHAPTER 25) USING THE MEAT OF THE LEGS AND THIGHS.

A) RATIO:

1 PART	DOMINANT (PHEASANT) MEAT
1 PART	PORK
1 PART	PORK FAT

NOTE: A) A RANDOM GARNISH OF ITEMS SUCH AS PEELED PISTACHIO NUTS, DICED TRUFFLES, SMOKED TONGUE, HAM, CURRANTS OR OTHER SIMILAR ITEMS WILL ENHANCE THE FLAVOR AND APPEARANCE OF THE FINISHED PRODUCT.

B) THE SIZE AND AMOUNT OF GARNISH IS LARGELY A MATTER OF PERSONAL TASTE.

ASSEMBLING THE GALANTINE

Assembling the galantine is simply a matter of placing and rolling. However, this too must be done with care and precision. If not, the result will be a poorly formed galantine with an uneven texture. Assembly is a series of steps, each building upon the other to produce the highest quality product.

1. LAYOUT:
A) DAMPEN A PIECE OF CHEESECLOTH, ABOUT 1 SQUARE YARD IN AREA. FOLD CLOTH IN HALF AND SPREAD ON THE WORK TABLE, CREATING A DOUBLE THICKNESS SQUARE OF CHEESE CLOTH.
B) POSITION THE RESERVED PHEASANT SKIN SO THE LENGTH OF THE RECTANGLE RUNS PARALLEL TO THE LONG SIDE OF THE CHEESE CLOTH. THE SKIN SHOULD BE PLACED OUTER SIDE DOWN.
C) DUST THE SKIN LIGHTLY WITH A PINCH OF DRY GELATIN, SALT AND PEPPER.
D) SPREAD THE FORCEMEAT ON THE SKIN ABOUT 1-INCH THICK, LEAVING A 1-INCH MARGIN OF SKIN ALL AROUND.
E) PLACE THE MARINATED BREASTS LENGTHWISE ON THE FORCEMEAT WITH THE THINNER ENDS OF THE BREASTS OVERLAPPING IN THE MIDDLE.
NOTE: OVERLAPPING THE THINNER PARTS OF THE BREAST'S MIDDLE WILL GIVE A CONSISTENT THICKNESS THROUGHOUT THE INLAY.

3. ROLL:
A) USING THE CHEESECLOTH TO ASSIST, ROLL THE GALANTINE AWAY FROM YOU SO THAT THE BREAST SECTIONS ARE WRAPPED INTO THE CENTER OF THE GALANTINE.
B) IF NECESSARY, YOU MAY LIFT THE SKIN AND SMOOTH THE SEAM IN THE FORCEMEAT WITH A PALETTE KNIFE SO THAT NO SEPARATION WILL BE VISIBLE WHEN THE GALANTINE IS SLICED.
C) IF NECESSARY, USE YOUR HANDS TO HELP FORM THE TUBULAR SHAPE.
D) PLACE THE NEAR EDGE OF THE CHEESECLOTH OVER THE GALANTINE.
E) MAKE A SNUG ROLL, FREE OF ANY LARGE WRINKLES IN THE CHEESECLOTH.

4. TIE:
A) GATHER THE CHEESECLOTH AT ONE END OF THE ROLL AND TIE USING A SLIP KNOT OF TWINE.
NOTE: DO NOT TIE TOO TIGHTLY BECAUSE THE FORCEMEAT MAY BE SQUEEZED OUT THE OPEN END.
B) GATHER THE CHEESECLOTH AT THE OPEN END OF THE GALANTINE AND REPEAT THE PROCEDURE. COMPRESS THIS END MORE TIGHTLY TO PRODUCE A SNUG, COMPACTED ROLL.
NOTE: INSTRUCTIONS WILL OFTEN SUGGEST TYING THE GALANTINE WITH LOOPS OF TWINE EVERY INCH AND A HALF ALONG THE LENGTH OF THE GALANTINE. IF THE CHEESECLOTH

HAS BEEN ROLLED CORRECTLY, THE REINFORCING ACTION OF THE TWINE LOOPS IS NOT NECESSARY. AN ADDED BONUS TO A PROPERLY ASSEMBLED GALANTINE WILL BE SMOOTH SIDES WITH NO VISIBLE TIE MARKS.

COOKING THE GALANTINE

The correct cooking method used for galantines is poaching. Faster cooking will coarsen the texture and possibly harm the appearance. It is important to monitor the temperatures of both the stock and the galantine closely.

1. PLACE THE GALANTINE IN A BRAZIER OR FISH POACHER LARGE ENOUGH TO HOLD IT *WITHOUT BENDING IT.*

2. COVER WITH THE PREPARED STOCK AND PLACE ON THE RANGE. USING MODERATE HEAT SETTING, BRING THE TEMPERATURE OF THE STOCK UP TO 190°F.

3. POACH THE GALANTINE UNTIL IT REACHES AN INTERNAL TEMPERATURE OF 170°F.

    NOTE: THE TEMPERATURE IS MOST EASILY TAKEN BY PASSING THE STEM OF A THERMOMETER THROUGH THE END OF THE GALANTINE, WHERE ALL THE CHEESECLOTH IS GATHERED. OTHERWISE A SMALL HOLE MAY BE MADE IN THE CHEESECLOTH WITH THE POINT OF A SHARP PARING KNIFE.

4. WHEN THE GALANTINE REACHES 170°F, IT IS A GOOD IDEA, THOUGH NOT VITAL, TO UNROLL IT FROM THE CHEESECLOTH AND THEN RE-ROLL IT IN THE SAME CHEESECLOTH, MAKING IT MORE SNUG. THIS ENSURES A PERFECTLY ROUND SHAPE AND GOOD ADHESION OF THE SKIN TO THE FORCEMEAT.

    NOTE: THIS IS SUGGESTED BECAUSE THE GALANTINE SHRINKS DURING COOKING.

5. RETURN THE GALANTINE TO THE STOCK AND REFRIGERATE OVERNIGHT.

NOTE: If cooled and left sealed in the gelled stock, the galantine may be stored safely for a week.

PRESENTATION

Traditionally, the galantine is sliced and served with small cubes of a delicate aspic. This aspic can be made by clarifying the cooking stock, or it can be produced as a separate item. Aspic is discussed in Chapter 24.

ROULLADES

The only criteria for a food item to be termed a *roullade* is that it be rolled. The term *roullade* can be applied to contemporary products prepared in a manner which is similar to a galantine yet do not fully satisfy the classical definition of a galantine.

An example of a roullade might be a flank steak, butterflied, pounded, spread with a chorizo or similar forcemeat and rolled in the style of a galantine. The roullade is then either roasted or poached. The item is prepared in a fashion similar to the galantine, but does not contain the ingredients required for a galantine. However, the fact that it is rolled makes it a roullade. Therefore, the variety of roullades is unlimited.

BALLOTINE

This is a smaller relative of the galantine. It is an excellent method for using the leg portions of poultry when the breasts have been used in other preparations.

The leg bones are removed leaving the skin and meat intact. Forcemeat is stuffed in the pocket formed by the removal of the bones. This preparation should be the shape of a small ball or ham.

The ballotine is normally roasted or braised. However, it can be glazed with aspic or coated with chaud-froid sauce and served cold. In either case they are a product of the garde manger department.

PARFAITS

This is the French word for *perfect*. In culinary usage it refers to two distinctly different items. One is a frozen mousse-like dessert of lightened, still frozen ice cream, which in America is served in a tall glass. The other parfait is a *savory terrine*, which, by its delicacy, is reminiscent of perfection. This parfait is discussed here. The dessert type will be discussed in a later chapter.

A savory parfait uses vegetables, fish, shellfish, poultry or other light meats. It is distinguished by its very fine texture and preparation methods.

One preparation method is based on a raw mousseline forcemeat. Whipped cream is incorporated into this mixture for lightness. This mixture is set with gelatin, not by heat. The second method is based on a puree of cooked meat or vegetable fortified with egg whites and lightened with cream. The mixture is then molded and poached.

A parfait can be cooked in a terrine mold, large timbale or loaf pan. However, a gutter mold is most often used. This results in a terrine with a gracefully curved top when it is inverted and removed. An example recipe for a parfait is provided in Figure Three.

MOUSSE & MOUSSELINE

Mousse and *mousseline*, like so many other culinary terms, have a variety of meanings. The definition of each is normally determined by the area of kitchen producing the dish.

The terms *mousse* and *mousseline* have two applications.

A) The type mixture determines the definition of the mixture. For mousse the mixture is a cooked puree, bound with gelatin and lightened with whipped cream, which is set by chilling.

The mousseline forcemeat is composed of raw pureed meat or fish combined with eggs and cream set by cooking.

B) The terms *mousse* and *mousseline* also refer to the size of a finished dish. A mousse, hot or cold, is a dish made from mousse mixture or mousseline forcemeat. It is molded in a terrine, charlotte or

---

LOBSTER PARFAIT

INGREDIENTS	AMOUNT
LOBSTER, 1 1/2 LB EA	2 EA
PIKE FILLET, DICED	1 LB
BREAD PANADA	2 OZ
EGG WHITES	3 EA
BISQUE REDUCTION	1/2 C
HEAVY CREAM	1/2 C
WHIPPED CREAM	1 C

METHOD

1. REMOVE THE TAIL AND CLAW MEAT FROM THE LOBSTERS. DICE CLAW MEAT AND RESERVE FOR GARNISH. DICE TAIL MEAT.
2. PREPARE A SMALL AMOUNT OF BISQUE, USING THE SHELLS. REDUCE TO 1/2 CUP AND COOL.
3. COMBINE TAIL MEAT AND PIKE FILLET, PREPARING A MOUSSELINE-STYLE FORCEMEAT, BY PUREEING THE FISH WITH THE PANADA, EGG WHITES AND BISQUE REDUCTION, ADDING THE CREAM LAST.
4. SIEVE THE FORCEMEAT, ADD THE DICED CLAW MEAT AND FOLD IN THE WHIPPED CREAM IN TWO PARTS.
5. MOLD IN A GUTTER MOLD, OILED AND LINED WITH PLASTIC FILM.
6. POACH IN A 170°F WATER BATH TO AN INTERNAL TEMPERATURE OF 140°F.
7. CHILL COMPLETELY BEFORE TURNING OUT.
8. THE PARFAIT MAY BE THINLY COATED WITH DELICATE FISH ASPIC, THEN SPRINKLE WITH FRESHLY CHOPPED DILL.

Figure 3

large timbale mold, suitable in size to serve two or more people.

A mousseline is a small quenelle or molded, individual portion of mousse mixture, served cold. If served hot, it is termed mousseline forcemeat. The mousseline forcemeat is also prepared in single portions.

PREPARATION

For a review of the assembly and preparation of a cold mousse see Chapter 25. The instructions for preparing a mousseline served cold are listed below.

1. PREPARE THE MOUSSE MIXTURE (REFER TO CHAPTER 25).
2. SHAPE IN ONE OF TWO WAYS:
   A) SHAPE INTO INDIVIDUAL SIZE QUENELLES USING TWO TABLESPOONS DIPPED IN WATER.
   B) PIPE INTO INDIVIDUAL SIZE TIMBALE MOLDS, MASKED WITH ASPIC JELLY OR OTHER SUITABLE LINING SUCH AS PLASTIC FILM OR THIN VEGETABLE STRIPS.
3. CHILL THOROUGHLY (2 HOURS MINIMUM) AND SERVE WITH A COLD SAUCE WHICH WILL COMPLEMENT THE FLAVOR OF THE MOUSSELINE.

To prepare a mousseline to be served hot, the steps are:

1. PREPARE A MOUSSELINE-STYLE FORCEMEAT.
2. KEEPING THE FORCEMEAT COLD, SHAPE INTO QUENELLES USING TWO TABLESPOONS DIPPED IN WATER.
3. CAREFULLY DROP THE QUENELLES INTO FLAVORFUL STOCK AND POACH. THE STOCK SHOULD BE 190-200°F.
4. REMOVE AND BLOT ON A PAPER TOWEL AND SERVE WITH A COMPLEMENTARY HOT SAUCE.
   NOTE: FOR BANQUET SERVICE THE QUENELLES CAN BE POACHED AHEAD OF TIME AND RE-HEATED IN MASS BY BATHING IN HOT STOCK, JUST BEFORE SERVICE.

CONCLUSION

The proper preparation of a paté, galantine, mousse or one of the other items discussed in this chapter can be the perfect beginning to a meal. The majority of these items are served as either appetizer or hors d'oeuvre. They are accompanied by light sauces which complement the flavors of the item. The portion size should be small in comparison to the entree. The intent is to tease the palate, preparing it for the rest of the meal. The usually mild flavor and light texture of a paté or mousse serves this purpose extremely well. These preparations represent a knowledge of refined culinary preparation and are a mark of culinary excellence.

REVIEW QUESTIONS

1. Define *paté*.
2. Discuss the type of molds used in the preparation of paté.
3. List the steps for the preparation of a paté.
4. Define *terrine*.
5. Discuss the preparation of a terrine.
6. Discuss the pressing of a terrine.
7. What is a country-style terrine?
8. How does a galantine differ from a ballotine?
9. Discuss the preparation of a galantine.
10. Define *roullades* and *parfait*.
11. What is the proper usage of the terms *mousse* and *mousseline*?
12. Discuss the preparation of a mousse.
13. Discuss the preparation of a mousseline.

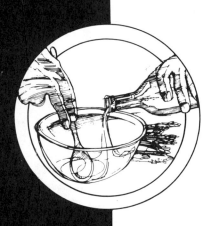

Chapter 27

CHAPTER OBJECTIVES

- **To introduce the terms hors d'oeu-vre and appetizer.**

- **To discuss the use of hors d'oeuvres.**

- **To describe vari-ous types of cold hors d'oeuvres.**

- **To discuss the preparation of various types of cold hors d'oeuvres.**

- **To describe vari-ous types of hot hors d'oeuvres.**

- **To discuss the preparation of various types of hot hors d'oeuvres.**

- **To discuss the pre-sentation of hors d'oeuvres.**

Appetizers

The terms *hors d'oeuvre* and *appetizer* often cause confusion when used. The formal definitions for these terms are given in Figures One and Two. To reduce the confusion for the novice culinarian, these definitions will be refined somewhat for this discussion. Hors d'oeuvre will be used as the term for types of preparations used at a reception or as a first course of a meal, lunch or dinner. The preparations would be in keeping with the definition in Figure One: Always small, delicate, flavorful and attractive. It is a stimulant for the appetite, in anticipation of the meal to come.

The term *appetizer* is most often used in conversation as the name of a course, not a type of preparation. Again this is in line with its definition. Our application of these terms reflects the current usage of them; however, the terms are often used interchangeably.

USING HORS D'OEUVRES

The possible variations of hors d'oeuvres are almost limitless. By definition, they always go before or at the beginning of the meal. The contents of hors d'oeuvres however, are not limited to a particular food or types of foods. They can involve preparations of marinated meats, fish or vegetables. Hot or cold finely diced mixtures or mousses may be used, or items which require little or no preparation, such as roasted nuts, brined olives, or raw, cut fruit or vegetables.

Although virtually unlimited, the selection of hors d'oeuvres served by the chef may be dictated by specific occasions. There are three major categories of hors d'oeuvres used in American menus, plus specific international applications. Almost every culture has their version of what is referred to by Americans as appetizers and the French as hors d'oeuvre.

PRE-MEAL RECEPTION

Hors d'oeuvres are most often identified with receptions. A reception is a convenient and pleasant way to allow for the varied arrival times of guests. Normally, the guest is offered hors d'oeuvres and some type of beverage in a room other than the dining room, while waiting for guests to gather. In the late 19th century the French elite popularized the Russian tradition of offering vodka, *zakuska* and *canapes a la Russe* before the main meal of the day. This custom dates back a thousand years to Scandinavia.

This type of reception is followed by a full meal. There are certain guidelines for the selection of hors d'oeuvres.

1. KEEP THE FOOD LIGHT, delicate and unsubstantial. Guests should not feel full before sitting down to the meal.
2. LIMIT THE VARIETY OF INGREDIENTS, do not overwhelm the guest's palate.
3. AVOID REPETITION OF INGREDIENTS THAT WILL BE SERVED IN THE MAIN MEAL. For example, do not serve Mushrooms a la Grecque as an hors d'oeuvre if sauteed mushrooms will be served during the meal.
4. AVOID HIGHLY SPICED OR HIGHLY ACIDIC FOODS. These will interfere with the subtleties of the meal to follow.
5. LIMIT THE AMOUNT OF HORS D'OEUVRES SERVED. This will prevent the guests from filling up on them and losing their appetites for the meal.
6. PROVIDE FOR PRACTICAL SERVICE BASED ON THE FACILITIES BEING USED. For instance, if the room is too small to provide tables or chairs for each guest, provide only finger food. Holding a plate, fork and drink at the same time presents a definite coordination problem.

FULL RECEPTION

A meal does not follow this type of reception. It is an event in and of itself and can last on average from 1 1/2 to 3 hours.

Although the character of the food should be in keeping with that of hors d'oeuvres, the full reception provides a setting for greater freedom in the menu.

1) A wider variety of both hot and cold hors d'oeuvres can be offered.
2) The range of flavors and textures used can be broader.
3) Finger foods can be accompanied on the buffet by those types requiring a fork or spoon for service and eating.

WITHIN THE MEAL

Hors d'oeuvres served within the framework of the meal, as appetizers or starters, should be planned as part of the overall balance of the meal. The colors, textures and flavors of the total menu must be considered.

As always, the portion should be small, fairly simple and with little repeating of ingredients. Finger food is not normally served within the meal. It is not suitable for the more formalized atmosphere of a sit down meal.

INTERNATIONAL

RUSSIAN zakuska are various preparations in the tradition of "Czarist" Russia. These are laid out on a table to be enjoyed by the arriving guest for an hour or so before the dinner meal.

ITALIAN antipasto means "before the pasta." A typical selection would include marinated mushrooms and artichoke hearts; sliced salami and prosciutto ham; smoked sardines; anchovies; stuffed olives; caponata, and roasted red peppers.

SPANISH tapas means "lid." The name comes from the practice of placing a piece of bread, tapas, over the wine glass to keep out the flies. Today it refers to a variety of items, including kidney beans in vinegar sauce with parsley, onion, and red pepper; boiled, sliced potatoes with garlic and mayonnaise; small meatballs in gravy, with peas; pickled cauliflower; stewed salt cod with garlic and cayenne; tripe stew, and black olives marinated with onion and oregano. This Spanish and Portuguese custom of serving tapas in bars has become popular in the United States.

ENGLISH tea sandwiches are very traditional. They can be tiny sandwiches of shrimp paste, paper thin cucumber, tomatoes or ham. These are served alongside scones with jam, tea biscuits and tea cakes.

SWEDISH smorgasbord means "bread and butter table" and is probably the forerunner of the Russian zakuskas. It includes shrimp, pickles, meatballs, herring, smoked herring, pickled herring, smoked reindeer, boiled potatoes, asparagus, mushrooms, smoked salmon, burbot (freshwater cod), caviar, beer and aquavit.

INDONESIAN rijsttafel, meaning "'rice table," is a Dutch Colonial tradition stemming from the Indonesian affinity for rice. The rijsttafel, as the Dutch knew it in colonial times, cannot be found in Indonesia today. It is, however, very popular in Holland. Here it is done in special shops called "toko." It is the service of a central dish of fluffy rice surrounded by a large number of side dishes. These include: sate (small bamboo skewers of meat, grilled); dishes of braised, spicy pork and goat; fried dumplings; spiced hard boiled eggs, and steamed vegetables.

JAPANESE sushi is considered by many to be the national dish of Japan. These are tiny portions of sliced raw fish, placed on mounds of vinegared rice. They are the snack food of Japan. Within the context of a formal Japanese menu, sushi and sashimi (slices of raw fish) are the first course.

GREEK mezes is the equivalent of appetizer. It includes such items as keftedhakia (tiny meat balls); kreatopita (triangular flaky pastry filled with ground meat); spanakopita (triangular pastries filled with spinach and feta cheese), and taramosalata (creamy pink cod roe paste).

TYPES & DEFINITIONS

The major division in categories of hors d'oeuvres is the temperature at which they are served--cold and hot. There are further classifications within these major categories.

COLD HORS D'OEUVRES

HORS D'OEUVRE A LA FRANCAISE

Hors d'oeuvre a la francaise is the general term for hors d'oeuvres presented in small oblong dishes called *raviers*. The dish is needed because the hors d'oeuvres are usually served with a marinade, sauce, relish or other accompaniment and require a fork or spoon for service and eating. Examples range from raviers of marinated vegetables to small stuffed cabbage rolls on tomato relish to bite size portions of sole roullade with an accompanying sauce. Any food can be used in this category. However, portion size is generally one to two bites per item. The normal number of varieties offered to the guest is six to eight.

FINGER FOOD

As the name implies, these are small portions of food prepared and/or portioned so that they can be picked up with the fingers. They are most appropriate for pre-meal receptions in tight quarters where plates and serviceware are not practical or wanted.

There are basic principles for proper preparation and presentation of finger foods:

1. Finger food composition should be such that the fingers are left clean after eating. This is done by:
   a. A dry base to handle it by, such as a canape.
   b. Use of skewers or toothpicks for items such as sate or attereaux.

2. They should be neat and easily handled.

3. They should be only one or two bites in size.

4. The majority of finger foods are served cold; however, a few are served hot. A toothpick, skewer, or pastry crust is usually used to keep the fingers of the guest neat and clean.

CRUDITES

Crudite, essentially, means "food eaten raw." Common usage of the term is normally limited to raw vegetables, particularly for hors d'oeuvres. This is one of the simplest hors d'oeuvres.

Vegetables often used for crudite are red, yellow, and green bell peppers; carrots; celery stalks; summer squash; red radishes; belgian endive; cucumbers, and cherry tomatoes. These are cut into finger size pieces or decorative rounds and served with one or more varieties of dip or dressing.

CANAPE

Canape, in the strict sense, refers to a toasted or fried rectangular slice of crustless bread also termed a crouton. In the category of hors d'oeuvres, however, the term *canape* refers to a small open face sandwich which may be topped with an endless variety of savory food items. This canape is comprised of four parts: Base, spread, main body and garnish.

BASE

The *base* serves as the foundation for the canape. It must be firm enough for the guest to handle with two fingers, without its topping spilling into the guest's lap.

Breads with a firmer consistency, such as pumpernickel, are preferred for the base since they may be used without toasting. A more delicate type of bread should be toasted, fried or baked (dried) in the oven. This will give it the sturdier structure needed to act as a canape base. Bases can be cut in a variety of interesting shapes before being used, such as rectangle, square, circle, oval, crescent, diamond or triangle.

SPREAD

The *spread* applied to the base has a three-fold purpose.

1. Spread adds flavor and moisture to the canape.

2. Spread acts as a glue, helping to hold all of the components of the canape together. This makes it more stable and easier to eat with the fingers.

3. Spread provides a fat barrier to prevent the base from becoming limp and soggy from the juices of the main body.

There are two primary types of spread used for canapes:

1) A basic spread made up of fifty percent butter and fifty percent cream cheese.

2) Any compound butter that is suitable for the main topping of the canape being prepared.

Either type of spread should be softened sufficiently to allow easy spreading; however, they should not be melted in any form. A melted butter will soak into the base and not form a protective layer on it.

Spread can be applied to the bases individually. A faster method, if the design allows, is to spread a whole slice of uncut bread and then cut it into the desired shapes. This technique is the basis for preparation of large numbers of banquet-style canapes as discussed later in this chapter.

MAIN BODY

This part of the canape may be almost any savory food item such as sliced cold meat; meat or seafood salad, or sliced vegetable. The main body is what gives the canape its particular flavor and character. Items of food used for the main body must be cut so that each canape has a consistent size and shape.

GARNISH

Garnish of a canape adds eye appeal. It should enhance, not overshadow, the main body. Garnish can be a small leaf of herb or piece of food which is in keeping with the canape as a whole.

STYLES OF CANAPES

Styles of canapes are categorized as either banquet or a la carte. Banquet-style are canapes of a simpler design. They can be produced in large quantities, fairly quickly and easily. They are made from less expensive foods and sometimes leftover foods. Usually they sell for lower prices. A la carte-style canapes are individually prepared. They are more complex in design and made a few at a time. Premium ingredients are used and they command a higher price. This type of canape is mainly used for special occasions.

ASSEMBLING BANQUET-STYLE CANAPES

Efficient use of time is always important in professional food production. This is particularly true in making canapes where the production time for one canape may have to be multiplied by the number of pieces being prepared. It is not unusual for 1,000 of each of a number of types of canape to be produced for a large function.

The exact approach to canape production will have to be designed for the specific items needed. What Figure Three shows are some methods of saving time. In general, *producing banquet style canapes calls for an assembly line approach. You finish step one for each item before beginning step two.*

ASSEMBLING CANAPES

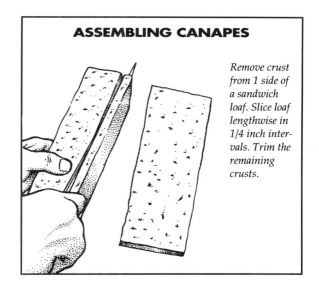

Remove crust from 1 side of a sandwich loaf. Slice loaf lengthwise in 1/4 inch intervals. Trim the remaining crusts.

Spread compound butter on each slice. Pipe sides with star tube and pastry bag. Chill for 30 minutes.

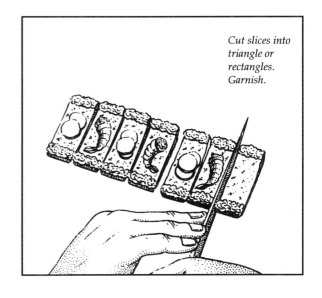

Cut slices into triangle or rectangles. Garnish.

ASSEMBLING BANQUET-STYLE CANAPES

1. USE A DENSE BREAD, SUCH AS PUMPERNICKEL OR RYE. (THIS WILL ALLOW ELIMINATION OF TOASTING.)
2. USE PULLMAN LOAVES, APPROXIMATELY 4 INCH X 4 INCH X 18 INCH. THESE SHOULD BE SLICED LENGTHWISE, NO THICKER THAN 1/4 INCH.

NOTE: A) IF BREAD IS EXTREMELY FRESH OR COARSE TEXTURED IT IS DIFFICULT TO GET EVEN, THIN SLICES.

B) FOR THIN, EVEN SLICES, SLICE THE BREAD WHEN IT IS SLIGHTLY FROZEN.

C) ALWAYS TRIM CRUST FROM THE BREAD AFTER SLICING, NOT BEFORE.

D) THE EVENESS OF SLICES CAN BE IMPROVED BY THE USE OF A BAND SAW TO SLICE THE LOAVES.

3. SOFTEN SPREAD BY LETTING IT WARM TO ROOM TEMPERATURE OR BY WHIPPING.
4. APPLY SPREAD TO PULLMAN SLICE WITH A MEDIUM-SIZE PALETTE KNIFE.
5. APPLY MAIN BODY TO PULLMAN SLICE.

NOTE: A) SELECT AN ITEM FOR THE MAIN BODY WHICH CAN BE APPLIED QUICKLY AND EASILY TO THE BREAD. IT IS BEST IF IT CAN BE APPLIED IN ONE STEP.

B) ITEMS THAT CAN BE SLICED IN LONG SHEETS ON A MEAT SLICER AND THEN LAID ON TOP OF THE PULLMAN LOAF, WORK WELL. THESE INCLUDE HAM, TURKEY, CHEESE OR SMOKED SALMON.

C) FINE TEXTURED SALADS, SUCH AS TUNA SALAD, SALMON SALAD AND CHICKEN SALAD (WHEN THE RECIPE IS ADJUSTED TO AVOID SEEPAGE OF MOISTURE.) CAN BE EASILY SPREAD ONTO THE PULLMAN SLICE.

At this point you have, essentially, a very large, open face sandwich. Banquet-style canapes can be and are often made up to this point, one to two days in advance. If you are making them in advance, the next step would be number 6. If they are to used fresh that day, you go straight to step 7. (The canape can be tightly wrapped and frozen at this point, then defrosted and finished when needed.)

6. THE PULLMAN-SIZED SLICES, SPREAD AND TOPPED WITH THE MAIN BODY, ARE COATED WITH A THIN LAYER OF ASPIC. THIS HELPS TO PRESERVE THEIR FRESHNESS AND GIVES THEM A GLISTENING FINISH.

NOTE: A) THE ASPIC CAN BE APPLIED WITH A BRUSH OR SPRITZER-TYPE SPRAY BOTTLE.

B) ASPIC SHOULD BE DELICATE, NOT RUBBERY. IT SHOULD BE PERFECTLY CLEAR, AND HAVE A GOOD FLAVOR.

7. THE PULLMAN SLICE IS NOW READY TO CUT INTO INDIVIDUAL CANAPES.

NOTE: A) SQUARES, DIAMONDS AND TRIANGLES CAN BE CUT USING STRAIGHT LINE CUTS OF A LONG FRENCH KNIFE. THIS TECHNIQUE RESULTS IN THE LEAST WASTED PRODUCT.

B) ROUNDS AND CRESCENTS CAN BE CUT USING A SHARPENED ROUND CUTTER. THIS TECHNIQUE RESULTS IN MORE WASTE.

C) SPECIAL SHAPES, SUCH AS STARS, HEARTS, SPADES AND OTHERS, CAN BE CUT FROM THE PULLMAN SLICE. THESE CUTS HAVE THE LOWEST YIELD PER PULLMAN SLICE.

D) EXACTNESS OF SIZE AND SHAPE IS CRITICAL FOR AN ELEGANT PRESENTATION.

8. INDIVIDUAL CANAPES SHOULD BE LINED UP ON A WORK TRAY IN NEAT "RANK AND FILE" ORDER. ANY MISSHAPED OR MISSIZED ITEMS CAN BE PICKED OUT EASILY.
9. GARNISH CAN BE APPLIED TO THE CANAPE.

NOTE: A) THE GARNISH SHOULD BE ONE WHICH CAN BE QUICKLY MADE AND EASILY APPLIED.

B) CHOOSE A GARNISH WHICH IS SUITABLE FOR THE MAIN BODY.

EXAMPLE: USING A PIPING BAG WITH A SMALL STAR TIP, PIPE A TINY ROSETTE OF BASIC SPREAD OR COMPOUND BUTTER ONTO THE CENTER OF EACH CANAPE. INTO EACH ROSETTE, GENTLY PUSH AN OLIVE SLICE, CAPER, LEAF OF CHERVIL OR ANY OTHER SUITABLE FOOD ITEM. THE ROSETTE WILL SERVE TO ANCHOR THE GARNISH IN PLACE.

Figure 3

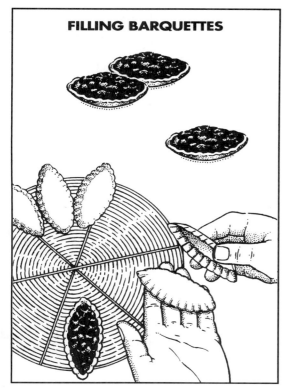

FILLING BARQUETTES

Bake barquettes in preheated 350°F oven for 15 minutes until golden. Cool, then invert pan onto your hand and lift pan off of its pastry. Cool shells and fill.

ASSEMBLING A LA CARTE-STYLE CANAPES

The basic assembly of an a la carte canape is the same as a banquet-style. The intricate designs and types of ingredients take more effort and time. Some of the more time consuming techniques usually reserved for a la carte-style are discussed in Figure Four. As with the banquet-style, if these canapes are made up a day ahead of time, they need to be coated with a thin coat of aspic. This can be applied with a brush or spray.

Rarely are canapes produced at the last minute or to the order. This is due to the numerous steps involved.

Storage of canapes should be done in a refrigerator. The completely finished canapes should be covered airtight and stored, without disturbing the carefully placed garnish, until service. Storage in deep hotel pans covered tightly with plastic wrap works best. It is possible to store them on trays with the plastic film suspended on toothpicks stuck carefully into a few canapes. Handle them as little and delicately as possible.

BARQUETTES & TARTLETS

These are miniature pie shells made from a short (high fat content) pie dough. The shells are filled with a variety of fillings. These can range from hot, finely diced mixtures to cold mousses.

Shape is the distinction in this type of hors d'oeuvre. Tartlets are round like a miniature tart. Barquettes are elongated diamond cut, similar to a marquise cut. They resemble a miniature barque, a boat of the same shape.

The fillings for tartlets and barquettes are basically interchangeable. However, traditionally the barquette-shape crust (boat-like) has been used for fish and seafood fillings. The advantage of both crusts is the ability to present more moist types of finger food. The food can have a high degree of sauce in it since the filling is held in between dry walls of crust, protecting the guest's fingers.

Figure Five gives directions for preparation of tartlet and barquette shells. As mentioned earlier, the range of fillings is nearly limitless.

SPECIAL TECHNIQUES FOR A LA CARTE-STYLE CANAPES

1. OFTEN BASES WITH SPECIAL SHAPES ARE USED. THEY COST MORE TO HANDLE AND HAVE A LOWER YIELD OF USABLE PRODUCT.
2. AN OFTEN PRODUCED ITEM IS THE CORONET. MADE FROM SALAMI, HAM, SMOKED SALMON OR SIMILAR FOOD, THESE ARE ATTACHED TO A BASE WITH A ROSETTE OF BASIC SPREAD OR COMPOUND BUTTER. THE CORONET IS FILLED WITH AN OLIVE, SOUR CREAM, CAVIAR OR OTHER SUITABLE FOOD. THIS PREPARATION HAS GREAT EYE APPEAL, BUT TAKES MORE PRODUCTION TIME.
3. GARNISHES ARE OFTEN MORE COMPLEX, SUCH AS A STRIP OF MARINATED RED PEPPER TIED IN A TINY BOW.

Figure 4

PREPARING TARTLETS & BARQUETTES

1. PREPARE AN UNSWEETENED SHORT PIE DOUGH. (THIS IS DISCUSSED IN CHAPTER 33.)
2. ROLL OUT THIN, 1/8-INCH THICK MAXIMUM.
3. ALLOW ROLLED OUT DOUGH TO REST. (RELAXING OF DOUGH IS DISCUSSED IN CHAPTER 33.)
   NOTE: FREEZING THE DOUGH BRIEFLY WILL SPEED UP THE RESTING PROCESS.
4. CUT THE ROLLED OUT DOUGH INTO SMALL CIRCLES, SQUARES OR RECTANGLES. THESE SHOULD BE LARGE ENOUGH TO LINE THE INTERIOR OF THE BARQUETTE OR TARTLET MOLD FULLY.
5. LOOSELY PLACE THE SQUARE OF DOUGH INTO THE MOLD.
   NOTE: IT IS NOT NECESSARY TO OIL OR LUBRICATE THE MOLDS WHEN USING A SHORT PIE DOUGH.
6. PLACE A SECOND MOLD ON TOP OF THE FIRST, SANDWICHING THE DOUGH BETWEEN THE TWO MOLDS. APPLY GENTLE PRESSURE BRINGING THEM TOGETHER.
7. TRIM THE EXCESS DOUGH FROM THE EDGES OF THE MOLDS WITH A PARING KNIFE.
8. PLACE THE MOLDS UPSIDE DOWN ON A SHEET PAN.
   NOTE: A SECOND SHEET PAN MAY BE PLACED ON TOP OF THE MOLDS TO REDUCE THE TENDENCY OF THE DOUGH TO DRAW BACK DURING BAKING.
9. BAKE IN A 375°F OVEN, UNTIL THE TOP MOLD FALLS OFF EASILY.
   NOTE: A) IT IS ACCEPTABLE FOR BARQUETTES AND TARTLET SHELLS TO BE PALE AND NOT "GOLDEN BROWN."
   B) BE CAREFUL NOT TO OVERBAKE. OVERBAKED SHELLS WILL SHATTER EASILY.

   IF A CUSTARD IS TO BE COOKED IN THE SHELLS, THE DOUGH SHOULD BE RAW OR JUST BLANCHED WHEN FILLED WITH THE CUSTARD.

   SHELLS CAN BE MADE UP A WEEK IN ADVANCE.

10. COAT THE INSIDE OF THE PREPARED SHELL WITH A SPREAD OR COMPOUND BUTTER IF THE BARQUETTE OR TARTLET IS TO BE SERVED COLD.
    NOTE: THIS WILL HELP KEEP THE CRUST FROM GETTING SOGGY OR WARPED.
11. FILL AND GARNISH THE SHELLS AS YOU WOULD A CANAPE.

Figure 5

Storage in the proper manner is critical to the quality of these hors d'oeuvres. Barquettes and tartlets cannot be filled as far in advance as most canapes. The crust has a more delicate property. When filled and stored in the refrigerator they draw moisture from both the filling in them and the air around them. They will become limp and soggy, and will lose their shape relatively quickly.

Before being filled, the shells should be covered and stored in a dry area, at room temperature. Once filled, store in a manner suitable for the filling used. (Ready to use barquette and tartlet shells are available from many food suppliers.)

CHOUX PUFFS & CAROLINES

Choux puffs, also called *petit choux*, and carolines are small crusts made from unsweetened chou paste, *pate a chou*. Shape is what differentiates the two. Choux puffs are shaped like little balls, miniature cream puffs. Carolines are slightly elongated like a miniature eclair. Figure Six discusses the production of these. (The chou paste used is discussed in Chapter 33.)

PREPARING CHOUX PUFFS & CAROLINES

1. A) FOR CHOUX PUFFS, USE A STRAIGHT #6 OR #7 PASTRY TUBE. PIPE THE PASTE INTO A SMALL BALL, ABOUT 3/4-INCH IN DIAMETER.
NOTE: AFTER BAKING, THE DIAMETER OF THE CHOUX PUFFS SHOULD BE NO MORE THAN 1 1/2 INCHES.
B) FOR CAROLINES, USE A STRAIGHT #5 OR #6 PASTRY TUBE. PIPE THE PASTE INTO LENGTHS OF NO MORE THAN 2 INCHES.

2. BAKE AS YOU WOULD ANY ITEM MADE FROM CHOU PASTE.
NOTE: THESE SHELLS SHOULD NOT BE PREPARED MORE THAN 3-4 DAYS IN ADVANCE.

3. PREPARE THE FILLING.
NOTE: A) FILLINGS MOST SUITED FOR CHOUX PUFFS AND CAROLINES ARE PUREES OR MOUSSES OF MEAT, FISH OR VEGETABLES.
B) THE CONTENTS OF THE FILLING, INCLUDING GARNISHES, NEED TO BE SMALL ENOUGH TO PASS THROUGH THE PASTRY TUBE.
C) BE CAREFUL NOT TO OVERCOOK THE FISH OR MEAT FOR THE PUREE. IF OVER-COOKED, IT WILL GIVE A GRAINY MOUTH FEEL TO THE FILLING. THIS CANNOT BE MASKED BY THE ADDITION OF VELOUTE OR MAYONNAISE DURING PROCESSING.

4. MAKE A SMALL HOLE IN THE BOTTOM OF THE PUFF WITH THE TIP OF A SMALL PASTRY TUBE AND PIPE IN THE FILLING.
NOTE: A) IN SOME CASES, IN ORDER TO FILL THE PUFFS, THE TOP IS SIMPLY CUT OFF. THE CAVITY WITHIN THE PUFF IS THEN FILLED WITH THE DESIRED FILLING.
B) FILL PUFFS AS CLOSE TO SERVICE AS POSSIBLE. THEY TEND TO BECOME SOGGY WHEN HELD.

5. A) CHOUX PUFFS ARE NOT USUALLY GARNISHED. THEY CAN, HOWEVER, BE GARNISHED LIKE A CANAPE.
B) CAROLINES, AFTER FILLING, ARE OFTEN TOPPED WITH A SUITABLE CHAUD-FROID SAUCE IN THE STYLE OF THE CHOCOLATE ON AN ECLAIR.

Figure 6

PIPING CHOUX PUFFS

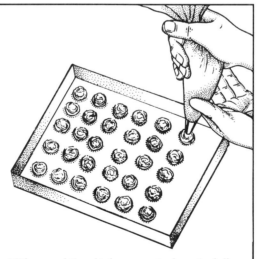

With a round-tipped tube on a pastry bag, pipe balls of choux paste 1/2 inch in diameter onto prepared baking sheet.

Bake in pre-heated 375°F oven for 20 minutes until golden. Prick with a knife and let dry in turned-off oven for 20 minutes. Slice off tops and fill. Replace tops.

Storage of choux puffs and carolines is the same as for barquettes and tartlets. They also absorb moisture in the same manner and should be made close to service.

SANDWICHES

This is the most common version of finger food. Not all sandwiches can be included in a discussion of hors d'oeuvres. The hardier, larger versions, served as a meal themselves, are discussed in Chapter 29. They do not meet the criteria of foods suitable for hors d'oeuvres. Those that do are divided into three categories: *Tea sandwiches, fancy sandwiches* and *smorrebrod.*

TEA SANDWICHES

Tea sandwiches are most often closed faced. That is, they are made with two pieces of bread. They are usually eaten at tea time and are well suited as hors d'oeuvres, being small and delicate. The fillings in these are usually very finely chopped and mixed with butter or cream cheese. The preparation of tea sandwiches is given in Figure Seven.

Size, as with any hors d'oeuvre, is important in the making of tea sandwiches. The desired size is no more than 1 1/2 inches by 3 inches, if they are rectangular. Fancier shapes should be of a similar size. The thickness of the sandwich should be 1/2-inch.

An option to finely chopping the filling for the sandwich is to use meats or vegetables sliced paper thin. Ham, chicken, cucumber and watercress are commonly used.

FANCY SANDWICHES

Fancy sandwiches are variations of those prepared as tea sandwiches. The filling used in fancy sandwiches is almost as fine as a puree. They can also be made with vegetables and meats sliced paper-thin. Pastel colored breads may be used to create interesting fancy sandwiches. The pastel colored breads are prepared from dough which is colored with edible food color prior to it being baked. The method of assembling them is the same, except for the specialized procedures added to achieve a fancier result. The method for preparing two types is given in Figure Eight.

SMORREBROD

Smorrebrod means "buttered bread." This is a Danish open-face sandwich using substantial pieces of meat, fish or vegetables. These are artfully arranged on a piece of bread. Traditionally they are sized to be a meal in themselves. However, they are easily adapt-

PINWHEEL

1. SLICE THE PULLMAN LOAF OF BREAD LENGTHWISE, AS YOU WOULD FOR CANAPES.
2. BUTTER THE SLICES.
3. SPREAD WITH FILLING CHOPPED EXTREMELY FINE OR TOP WITH PAPER THIN SLICES OF MEAT OR VEGETABLE.
   NOTE: IF THE FILLING IS THINLY SLICED MEAT OR VEGETABLE, SPREAD A SECOND LAYER OF BUTTER ON TOP OF THE FILLING. THIS WILL ENSURE THAT THE SANDWICH STICKS TOGETHER.
4. ROLL THE BREAD LIKE A ROULADE.
5. WRAP IN FOIL OR PLASTIC FILM AND LEAVE ROLLED OVERNIGHT.
6. REMOVE THE WRAPPING AND SLICE INTO 1/4-INCH ROUNDS.

LAYERED SANDWICHES

1. CHOOSE TWO OR MORE KINDS OF BREAD, SUCH AS LIGHT RYE AND DARK PUMPERNICKEL.
2. SLICE THE LOAVES LENGTHWISE, THINLY.
3. BUTTER EACH SLICE.
4. SOFTEN THE FILLING FOR THE SANDWICH.
5. SPREAD FILLING ON EACH SLICE.
6. NEATLY STACK THE SLICES, ALTERNATING THE KINDS OF BREAD.
7. WRAP SNUGLY IN PLASTIC WRAP.
8. GENTLY WEIGH DOWN THE STACKED SLICES OVERNIGHT.
9. SLICE DOWN ACROSS THE SLICES REVEALING THE STRIPED PATTERN.
10. TRIM THE CRUSTS AND SHAPE AS DESIRED FOR CANAPES.

Figure 8

ed in size to serve as hors d'oeuvres.

A typical smorrebrod would be as follows:

1. Butter a slice of rye bread.
2. Place two slices of tomato on the bread.
3. On top of the tomato and slightly off center, shingle two small fillets of smoked sardines or eel.
4. Where the tails of the sardines come together, mound a small amount of lightly scrambled eggs.
5. Top the eggs with a few capers.
6. Crisscross two small chives on top of the whole sandwich.

It is not unusual to serve an appropriate sauce with a smorrebrod. The miniature versions of these sandwiches are quite appropriate for tea service as well.

SPREADS & DIPS

Spreads and dips are not, by themselves, a finger food. However, when served with sliced baguette, croutons, crackers, breadsticks, vegetable sticks or slices, potato chips, corn chips or other similar items, they fit the bill.

The difference between spreads and dips is consistency. A DIP is a mixture that is loose or soft enough to cling to an item dipped into it. SPREADS are stiffer, harder, more solid mixtures, which need to be spread with a knife. Spreads are normally used on crackers, bread or similar foods.

SPREADS

These can be thick mixtures based on chopped or pureed meats, fish or cheese. Often, there is a high degree of fat in spreads, which gives them a smooth, rich texture.

Rillete is a popular French spread available commercially in France. It is a pork spread made by slowly stewing pork until it falls apart. The meat is then shredded by hand or machine. A quantity of the fat rendered in the cooking process is added back in during the shredding process. This yields a smooth, very rich product. Rillete is served chilled in a crock, surrounded by crackers, croutons or slices of baguette.

Cream cheese spreads are the most widely used in hors d'oeuvre service. These are based on soft cream cheeses, such as cream cheese, boursin, ricotta, petit suisse, brie and camembert. One or more of these cheeses is blended with suitable ingredients such as onion, garlic, chives, scallions, chopped or minced seafood and vegetable purees.

DIPS

Dips are made to be either hot or cold, with certain ones being served either way. They are often hot or cold sauces, thin purees of fruits or vegetables, or based on whipped cream-type cheeses, sour cream, yogurt, mayonnaise or a combination of these. Examples of dips include French onion, guacamole and hummus.

CHEESE

Cheese, in general, is a rich source for hors d'oeuvres as an ingredient; main body, or by themselves. If there is a meal to follow, their use should be limited. The high fat content of cheese is very filling. There is also a possibility of repetition in the cheese course of the dinner menu. Types and character of various cheeses are discussed below with fur-

---

TYPES OF CHEESE

UNRIPENED CHEESES are soft, white, freshly made cheeses.

NAME	DESCRIPTION
COTTAGE CHEESE	A moist, loose curd which may or may not have cream added to it. It is often described by curd size. Small curd particles are 1/8- to 1/4-inch in size. Large curd particles are up to 1/2-inch in size.
BAKERS OR POT CHEESE	Similar to cottage cheese but not as wet. It is used in cheesecakes and pastries.
RICOTTA CHEESE	Often referred to as Italian cottage cheese. It is a smoother, milder and sweeter cheese.
CREAM CHEESE	It is smooth and mild, with a high fat content. Used extensively in making spreads, dips, canapes and for baking.
NEUFCHATEL	Similar to cream cheese, but contains less fat.
MARSCAPONE	Italian cream cheese, which is very soft and rich. It resembles whipped cream and has a slightly tangy taste that goes well with fruits. It is used in desserts.
MOZZARELLA	A soft, mild cheese, made from whole or skim milk. Originally buffalo milk was used. It has a stringy texture developed by pulling and stretching during processing. A popular cheese, widely used in pizza and Italian dishes. Freshly made mozzarella is more moist and tender than the packaged type.

FETA	A crumbly cheese, made from sheep and goats' milk. Commonly used in the Balkan countries, such as Greece. Instead of being aged or cured, it is pickled in brine (highly concentrated salt water). This gives the cheese a unique salty flavor. When heated the flavor of the cheese becomes somewhat sweet.

SEMI-SOFT cheeses are more developed than unripened, but still have a generally buttery texture.

NAME	DESCRIPTION
BEL PAISE & FONTINA	Italian cheeses range in flavor from bland and buttery when young to earthy and more full flavored when a bit older. Often used as dessert or as hors d'oeuvres.
MUNSTER & BRICK	American cheeses. Similar to bel paise.
PONT L'EVEQUE & LIVAROT	French cheeses. Similar to bel paise.

SOFT-RIPENED CHEESE is ripened from the outside toward the center. When young they are firm and compact, with little flavor. As they mature with age, they soften. When fully ripe, they may be runny.

NAME	DESCRIPTION
BRIE & CAMEMBERT	French cheeses, which are ripened by mold. They are made in flat, round shapes and covered with a crust. The crust can vary in color from white to beige. Creamy and flavorful when ripe, a sharp ammonia odor develops when overripe.
LEIDERKRANZ	A Belgian cousin of limburger, which is made in the United States. Ripened by bacteria, and becomes softer with age. These cheeses are not that strong in aroma, when not overripe. They have a smooth texture and can be served as a dessert cheese.
DOUBLE & TRIPLE CREME	These include brillat savarin, boursin, and boursalt.

HARD-RIPENED CHEESES are cured cheeses which have a firm texture. They have varying degrees of mildness or sharpness of flavor, depending on their age.

NAME	DESCRIPTION
CHEDDAR	This cheese is an English variety. highly popular in America, it ranges in flavor from mild to sharp. Color varies from light yellow to orange. It can be eaten as is or used in cooking.
COLBY & MONTEREY JACK	These cheeses are similar to cheddar, and are usually sold when young.
DOMESTIC SWISS	Largest selling cheese in the United States.
SWISS or EMMENTHALER	More flavorful than the United States domestic Swiss. Swiss cheeses are firm, slightly rubbery, and have a nutty taste. The large holes are caused by gasses formed during ripening.

GRUYERE	Another Swiss-type cheese from either France or Switzerland. Has smaller holes and a sharper, earthier flavor. Gruyere and emmenthaler are widely used for sauces, souffles, fondue and gratineed items.
CONTE	Swiss-related cheese from France.
APPENZELLER & RACLETTE	Swiss-related cheese from Switzerland.
JARLSBURG	Swiss-related cheese from Norway.

BLUE VEINED CHEESES owe their flavor and appearance to blue and green mold, which is variegated throughout the cheese.

NAME	DESCRIPTION
ROUQEFORT	Comes only from the Rouqefort region of France. It is made from sheeps' milk. This type of blue veined cheese is cured in limestone caves near the town of Rouqefort.
STILTON	Product of England in the area of Stilton. It is more mellow and firm than its French counterpart.
GORGONZOLA	Italian blue-veined. It is soft, creamy and has a very pungent flavor.
BLEU DE BRESSE & SAGA BLEU	Other French blue-veined cheeses.
BLUE CASTELLO	Blue-veined from Denmark.
BAVARIN BLEU	A product of Germany.

HARD-GRATING CHEESES owe their flavor to a long aging period, and are often sold already grated.

NAME	DESCRIPTION
PARMESAN	A product of Italy. It is also referred to as grana (grating) cheese. The very best is parmigiana reggiano. It is aged at least two years and is very expensive. Parmesan is very dry, hard and grainy in texture.
ROMANO	Also an Italian grana cheese. Italian romanos are made from sheeps' milk. American romano is made from cows' milk.

ther information provided in Chapter 8.

CAVIAR

The ultimate hors d'oeuvre. Caviar is the processed roe (egg) of the sturgeon. If the roe is from a fish other than the sturgeon, the product must be qualified as such on the label. For example, prepared roe from salmon must be labeled as *salmon caviar*. The finest caviar comes from the Caspian Sea, which is bordered by Russia and Iran. The three species of sturgeon harvested in this area are the Beluga, Osetra and Sevruga. Caviar is categorized not only by the type of fish it comes from, but also by the method of processing and condition when sold.

Fresh caviar is the most perishable. The eggs make up 8-14% of the sturgeon's body weight, depending on the age of the fish and its species. Once the fish is caught, the eggs are removed as quickly as possible. In the process the skein, a connective membrane around the eggs, is left intact. They are then filtered through a coarse mesh screen to separate them from each other and the skein.

Once separated, salt in certain amounts is gently worked into the eggs by hand. Sometimes a mixture of salt and borax is used if the caviar is being produced for markets other than the United States. The amount of salt used varies from one caviar to another. For example, "malossol" means "little salt." Sometimes this term is used for Caspian caviars to indicate use of only a small amount of salt in processing.

The salted eggs are poured into a fine sieve to drain, then hand packed into tins. Fresh caviar is highly perishable, so keep it refrigerated at all times. It should never be frozen. Once opened it must be used within three days.

Pressed caviar is processed from the eggs of Osetra and Sevruga sturgeon when a high percentage of the eggs/berries are ruptured or shrunken. In this process the eggs, normally a blend of the two types, are heated to about 100°F in a saltwater solution. The caviar is put into fabric pouches and pressed to remove excess salt and oil.

It takes three pounds of eggs to yield one pound of pressed caviar. Pressed caviar is drier and spreadable. It has a consistency like jam. This caviar is highly prized.

Pasteurized caviar initially is prepared the same as fresh caviar. However, it is then pasteurized and vacuum packed. This gives it a longer shelf life, up to three months without refrigeration. It is best when used within three months. The pasteurization process is good for the shelf life, but bad for the roe's taste. This is a lesser quality caviar than fresh.

Frozen caviars are roe from non-sturgeon type fish, such as salmon, white-fish and lumpfish. The berries are tougher and can stand the rigors of freezing. However, they are of a lower quality. Of course, they are also less expensive.

Beluga caviar is from the largest species of sturgeon, the Beluga. This is the largest, most delicate berry, which bursts easily against the tongue. It ranges from light to dark gray in color. Beluga is the most expensive, highest quality caviar.

Osetra caviar, from the Osetra sturgeon, has the second largest berries. They are delicate, with a slightly fruity flavor. Ranging in color from golden to dark brown or gray, the golden color is very rare and called "royal caviar." It is the second most expensive caviar.

Sevruga caviar has smaller, delicate berries of a light to medium gray color. This caviar is very popular in Europe and is the least expensive of the Caspian varieties.

American sturgeon has a medium sized, delicate berry of light gray color. It is inexpensive compared to Caspian varieties.

Other species of caviar must be labeled as to species. Salmon is the most popular in Japan. It has a large, translucent grain and delicate berries. This caviar has a natural red to orange color and comes from Pacific Northwest and Atlantic salmon.

Lumpfish comes from Arctic waters. It has a small grain and tough berries. The caviar is dyed black or red for market. White fish has a small grain, and delicate, crunchy berries. It is a product of the northern Great Lakes. The caviar is either dyed black or sold in its natural golden hue.

Paddlefish, also called spoonbill, is unrelated to the sturgeon. It is found in the large lakes and river systems of the Mississippi, Ohio and Missouri rivers. Paddlefish roe is similar to sevruga sturgeon roe. Most of what is incorrectly labeled American Sturgeon caviar is actually processed roe from this fish.

PRESENTATION & UTILIZATION

CASPIAN VARIETIES, because of their superior qualities and delicate flavor and texture, should be served accompanied by buttered toast points, using a salted butter, lemon wedges and little else. Purists will even reject the lemon.

The caviar itself is best presented in the original tin, set on crushed ice in a "presentoir." This is a silver serving dish designed specifically for the presentation of caviar. Other elaborate presentations will involve small ice carvings designed to hold the tin.

The spoons or palettes should not be silver, because it reacts with the flavor of the caviar. Ivory, mother of pearl and gold plated spoons are all possibilities. Traditionally, caviar is accompanied by champagne or vodka.

DOMESTIC CAVIAR allows a bit more freedom in presentation and use. American caviar can be featured in the original tin and accompanied by buttered toast points; lemon; minced, rinsed sweet onion; sieved hard-cooked egg white and yolk (separately), and sour cream. Blinis, dense bread or crackers are also acceptable.

It is the opinion of many that the best use of the least expensive types is as an ingredient mixed in with sauces, toppings and sour cream. Their flavor and texture do not merit a featured presentation.

HOT HORS D'OEUVRES

Hot hors d'oeuvres are as diverse in nature and number as those served cold. Produce them with the thought in mind that they should be small and dainty. They should be items which spark the palate of the guest without satisfying the appetite. What is offered here is a sampling of the traditional classical preparations, and some better known international items.

ATTEREAUX

Attereaux are rooted deeply in the classical vein. They consist of small, identically sized slices of various food items placed on a wooden or bamboo skewer. The attereaux are coated with a reduced sauce, such as duxelle, bechamel or veloute. After chilling to allow the sauce to set, they are breaded with a standard breading of egg and bread crumbs. They are deep fried for immediate service.

Attereaux may be prepared to the breading stage up to two hours before service. They should be stored under refrigeration. Loosely cover them and top with extra loose breadcrumbs to prevent drying. This hors d'oeuvre can be frozen after breading. However, they should be of small enough size to be cooked fully from the frozen state.

Classically, the bamboo skewers of the attereaux are removed and replaced with decorative metal skewers, of the same name. They are arranged in a crown by sticking them in a large crouton or rice mold. Contemporary presentation is the arrangement of attereaux on a napkin and garnished with fried parsley.

BARQUETTES & TARTLETS

The same method of preparation used for this item in cold hors d'oeuvres can be used for hot. Bake the shells blind and fill them close to service with a puree, mousse, finely diced mixture or ragout.

BEIGNET (FRITTER)

This term describes an item or mixture of ingredients dipped in a batter and deep fried. Some examples are beignets of diced ham, potato and cod, as well as fritters of poached fish roe. These can be made from a variety of solid food items or salpicon (finely diced mixture of one or more items) or other mixtures. These are then dipped in batter and fried.

Solid items to be fried should be blotted dry and lightly dusted with flour before being dipped in batter.

BASIC BATTER FOR BEIGNETS

INGREDIENTS	AMOUNT
FLOUR	4 OZ
SALT	1 PINCH
EGG, WHOLE	1 EA
WATER, WARM	4-5 OZ
OIL	1 TBS
EGG WHITE	1 EA

METHOD
1. COMBINE FLOUR AND SALT.
2. MIX TOGETHER THE WHOLE EGG AND MOST OF THE WATER.
3. GRADUALLY WHISK THE FLOUR INTO THE EGG & WATER MIXTURE UNTIL SMOOTH.
4. ALLOW TO REST AT LEAST ONE HOUR.
5. SHORTLY BEFORE USE, BEAT EGG WHITES TO A SOFT PEAK.
6. COMBINE OIL WITH FLOUR AND EGG MIXTURE.
7. FOLD IN BEATEN EGG WHITES.

Figure 9

Salpicons and similar mixtures must be bound with a thick sauce to insure that the fritter will not break apart in frying. Once bound, the mixture should be well chilled and portioned. The portions are dusted lightly in flour, then dipped in batter. The recipe for the batter is in Figure Nine. These items should be fried golden brown in fat that is 375°F. This temperature will insure a crisp product, with the least absorption of fat.

Storage of fritters is not possible. The batter can be made a day in advance. However, dipping and deep frying is done immediately before service. Presentation of beignets or fritters should be on a napkin serviette. The traditional garnish is fried parsley. They may be served with appropriate sauces such as curry, mornay or cumberland. The sauce served will be determined by the nature of the beignet.

BOUCHEE

Bouchee means "mouth" or "mouthful." It is similar to a miniature "vol-au-vent," which is a puff paste patty shell. As with tartlets and barquettes, there is an almost limitless variety of fillings. The most popular are any type of ragout.

The size of the bouchee depends on what is needed. They can range in size from 1 1/2 to 3 inches in diameter, with anything above 3 inches being considered a vol-au-vent.

The familiar shape of the bouchee is round. They can be made in oval, square, triangle or special shapes like flowers and fish. Bouchees are baked blind and then filled. Figure Ten discusses the preparation of bouchees.

After baking, these items will keep well when wrapped airtight. They can be stored at room temperature for 5-7 days. For longer storage they should be frozen. They may be frozen with no ill effects.

Presentation of these requires reheating of them as close to service time as practical. Re-heat in a moderate oven, then fill with hot filling. If allowed to sit for more than about 15 minutes (time will depend on the filling), they are likely to become soggy.

If they are to be served buffet-style, lay them out in the chafing dish in which they are to be served. When served as a plated appetizer within the meal, re-heat; fill, and serve immediately.

BROCHETTE

The preliminary preparation of a brochette as an hors d'oeuvre is like that of attereaux; however, a brochette is not coated with a sauce or breading. The brochette is grilled or broiled instead of deep-fried. It is normally marinated meat or seafood interspersed on a skewer with colorful vegetables. Brochettes are usually served with a compound butter, piquant sauce or other light sauce suitable for a broiled item. An example of an hors d'oeuvre brochette is small pieces of beef tenderloin marinated in a teriyaki sauce, skewered with alternating pieces of red and yellow peppers, pearl onion and mushroom cap. What ever items are used on the skewer, it must be small enough to be suitable as an hors d'oeuvre.

RISSOLE

The rissole is a semicircular pocket of puff or unsweetened pastry dough, filled with a finely diced mixture or, occasionally, a forcemeat. It is deep-fried. The fillings should be flavorful enough to overcome the masking of the fried outer coating.

Rissoles freeze well, but should be defrosted unwrapped, before cooking. This hors d'oeuvre is served as finger food and is not normally accompanied by a sauce. Preparation of rissoles is discussed in Figure Eleven.

COMMON HOT HORS D'OEUVRES

Many of the more commonly used hot hors d'oeuvres are adaptations or miniaturizations of larger menu items, such as drummettes, mini-eggrolls and mini-quiche. Drummettes are the split chicken wing which is marinated and then baked, broiled or fried. The marination used may vary from a simple saltwater solution to a piquant cajun mixture. They can be served with an appropriate hot or cold sauce such as blue cheese dressing, mustard sauce or Oriental sweet and sour sauce. Mini-quiche are prepared in the same manner as standard quiche, but are baked in special miniature quiche pans. Mini-egg rolls have the same type of wrapper and filling as the larger version and are just

```
┌─────────────────────────────────────────────────────────────────┐
│                   PREPARATION OF RISSOLES                         │
│                                                                   │
│   1.  SELECT EITHER PUFF PASTRY DOUGH OR PIE PASTRY DOUGH.         │
│   2.  ROLL OUT DOUGH 1/8-INCH THICK.                              │
│   3.  USING A SHARP CUTTER, CUT INTO ROUNDS 2 1/2-INCH TO 4-INCH  │
│       IN DIAMETER. NOTE: THE SIZE OF THE FINAL PRODUCT YOU WANT,  │
│       WILL DETERMINE THE SIZE OF THE INITIAL ROUND.               │
│   4.  PLACE 2/3 TBS. OF FILLING IN THE CENTER OF EACH ROUND.      │
│   5.  BRUSH EDGE OF ROUND WITH EGG WASH; FOLD THE ROUNDS IN HALF, │
│       AND SEAL THE FILLING IN THE DOUGH.                          │
│   6.  COAT WITH BREAD CRUMBS AND DEEP FRY AT 375°F, UNTIL GOLDEN  │
│       BROWN.                                                      │
│                                                                   │
│   MANY CLASSICAL EXAMPLES OF THIS HORS D'OEUVRE CAN BE FOUND IN   │
│   THE VARIOUS WRITINGS OF ESCOFFIER.                             │
│                                                                   │
│   Figure 11                                                       │
└─────────────────────────────────────────────────────────────────┘
```

one-fourth the size.

Swedish meatballs, cocktail franks and chicken livers wrapped in bacon have long been popular hors d'oeuvres items. Cocktail franks (these may be either miniature frankfurters or smoked sausage) may be wrapped in puff pastry and baked; barbecued, or wrapped in bacon and baked. Swedish meatballs are a mixture of ground pork and beef which is seasoned with onion, cinnamon and nutmeg, then bound with egg. The mixture is formed into balls (two-bite size), baked and served with a demi-glace laced with sour cream or some other appropriate sauce. Chicken livers wrapped in bacon are just that. Many variations of this can be produced by wrapping such items as almond-stuffed dates, water chestnuts, pineapple or green olives in bacon. They are baked or broiled and then may be lightly coated with a light soy sauce and honey glaze.

Seafood is also popular as a hot hors d'oeuvre. Fried shrimp, scallops, oysters and calamari (squid) served with cocktail sauce are often used. Scallops wrapped in bacon, broiled, then glazed in the same manner as chicken livers wrapped in bacon are excellent.

The preparation of hot hors d'oeuvres is not limited to the classical preparations. It is limited only by your vision. New hors d'oeuvres are constantly being developed. Jalapeno pepper stuffed with cheese, then breaded and fried; miniature enchilada; fried cheese sticks; broiled stuffed mushroom cap, or miniature marinated tenderloin brochette, these are each an adaptation of items used in some other fashion in the menu.

PRESENTATION & LAYOUT TIPS

HORS D'OEUVRES WITHIN THE MEAL

The plated hors d'oeuvre or appetizer can be more complex in design and ingredients than those served at receptions. Components such as sauce and edible garnish can add nicely to the presentation. Care must be taken to insure that the appetizer does not become so complex that it overshadows the main course.

HORS D'OEUVRES DURING RECEPTIONS

These can be divided into buffet-style service and butler-style service. For BUFFET-STYLE service of large receptions, several buffet tables can be set up with a complete selection of hors d'oeuvres on each. Large trays are often used for these. They may last longer on the buffet, but they also lose their stylish appearance faster. They are not as easily replaced on the buffet as a smaller tray.

SERVING PIECES

For platter and tray service, the serving piece should match the character of the function. Silver is always elegant, and normally mandatory for higher priced functions. However, it is expensive to purchase and requires constant care. It is also not easily sanitized. Silver is not suitable for contact with salty and acidic foods. It is also expensive to replace.

Mirrors are a popular service piece for moderately priced parties. They are very practical, affordable and easily maintained. They can be easily sanitized. Wooden trays or planks are suitable only for banquets with a rustic theme and for picnics. They are difficult to sanitize and must be replaced more often.

Plexiglass or plastic serving pieces should only be used for super modern or futuristic themes. Although affordable, they are difficult to maintain in top condition. They scratch and lose their luster easily. However, they are easily sanitized.

The service of hot hors d'oeuvres buffet-style requires the use of chafing dishes. These are portable hot holding units which may either be made of silver or stainless steel. The amount of food in the chafing pan should be sufficient to look generous and serve the guests' needs; however, it should not be excessive. The chafing dish will not hold the dish as well as it can be maintained in the kitchen. Chafing dishes are available in a variety of sizes and shapes, which can assist in the set-up of a beautiful and interesting buffet.

A major concern in the presentation of food buffet-style is freshness. Food should be presented in sufficient quantities to allow ease of service for the guest, yet amounts small enough to insure a rapid turnover of the food. The amount of food needed to accomplish these goals will depend on the size of the function and the menu.

BUTLER-STYLE service is a good option for smaller receptions with limited space. It accomplishes the following:

1. Takes the food to the guest.

2. Lends a more elegant air to the function.

3. Gives better control of the flow of food and alcohol.

For this type of service, smaller "butler" trays are needed. These are usually silver, draped with a napkin or doily. More trays are required to keep up with the service flow. Hot hors d'oeuvres must be presented in small amounts to insure that they stay hot since no heat source is available. This takes more labor in the front and back of the house.

CONCLUSION

The preparation of hors d'oeuvres can be a very time consuming process, yet a rewarding one. As the guest's first glimpse of what is to come, hors d'oeuvres set the stage for the meal. When used for receptions, they allow the culinarian to demonstrate a great deal of creativity. Hors d'oeuvres are also items which command high prices. The guest is often willing to pay for these miniature culinary delights. Experiment with the concept of hors d'oeuvres, using the classical examples as a guidepost.

1. Define *hors d'oeuvre*.
2. Define *appetizer*.
3. List and discuss the three major categories of hors d'oeuvre use.
4. What are the basic principles for preparing and presenting finger foods?
5. Define *crudite*.
6. Discuss the four parts of a canape.
7. When is a canape a canape and not called a canape?
8. How and why does the assembly of banquet-style canapes and a la carte-style canapes differ?
9. Define *barquette* and *tartlet*. Explain why they might be used instead of a canape.
10. Choux puffs and carolines are prepared from what type of paste and differ in what manner?
11. What types of sandwiches are used for hors d'oeuvres?
12. How are pinwheel and layered sandwiches prepared?
13. What is the role of spreads and dips in hors d'oeuvres preparation?
14. Define *caviar*.
15. List and give the characteristics of six types of caviar.
16. What is the proper method for presentation of Caspian caviar?
17. What is the proper method for presentation of domestic caviar?
18. Define *attereaux*.
19. Discuss the preparation of beignet, bouchee, brochette and rissole.
20. Discuss the common hot hors d'oeuvres used today.
21. How are new hors d'oeuvres created?

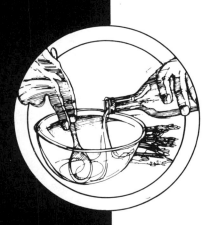

Chapter 28

CHAPTER OBJECTIVES

- **To introduce and define charcuterie.**

- **To define sausage.**

- **To discuss the components of sausage.**

- **To identify and discuss the characteristics of the major types of sausage.**

- **To introduce processed whole meats.**

- **To discuss the characteristics and manufacture of ham.**

- **To identify the major types of ham.**

- **To identify and discuss bacon varieties.**

- **To identify and discuss other specialty processed and cured meats.**

Charcuterie

Charcuterie is the art and science of making raw and cooked preparations of meat, with special emphasis on pork. Today, most of these preparations are called *processed meats*. These preparations include many forms of processed meat including hams, sausages, cold cuts, rolled shoulders, frankfurters and others.

The art and science of charcuterie has a long history. Its practice has been documented as early as the Minoan Period, 6,000 years ago. Its development continued through the ages with it becoming a recognized part of the kitchen during the height of the Roman Empire. The making and selling of charcuterie products in France during the Middle Ages was the focal point of conflict between the Rotisseurs (Roasting Chefs) and the Charcutiers (Pork Butchers). They each had separate guilds which wanted to control the business. This political struggle between the two guilds brought increased attention and popularity to the art of charcuterie. Regional specialties developed all over Europe, many of which are widely used in kitchens and homes today including (but not limited to):

1) The *frankfurter* from Frankfurt, Germany.

2) *Genoa salami* from Genoa, Italy.

3) *Bologna* from Bologna, Italy.

4) *Braunschweiger* from Brunswick, Germany.

Charcuterie shops are still common in Europe today, where they are producers of one of the mainstays of European traditional food. Austria, Germany and Switzerland eat sixty percent of their red meat in the form of sausage. The French regions of Canada still enjoy the traditional charcuterie shop as a matter of daily fare.

In the United States the charcuterie shop is a specialty shop. Few Americans are familiar with the term. Butcher shop, sausage shop and delicatessen are the more commonly used terms. There has been an increase in the number of delicatessens (deli's) in the last few years; however, most are only sellers of processed meats, few are makers of processed meats. Possibly this is because Americans only eat about thirty-five percent of their red meat in the form of sausage.

In the United States the foundation of the processed meat industry is charcuterie. It is a multi-million dollar business in which most major food conglomerates are involved. The Food Safety and Inspection Board (FSIB) of the Meat and Poultry Inspection (MPI) division of the United States Department of Agriculture (USDA) monitors these manufacturers. The wholesomeness of ingredients, hygiene, sanitation, packaging, labeling, refrigeration, weights and compliance with accepted manufacturing procedures are strictly controlled. The art and science of charcuterie in the United States has in many ways been transformed from a craft practiced by individuals in the kitchen to a manufacturing process. There are, however, still those chefs who practice this craft in their kitchen, bringing their creativity and innovation to charcuterie.

CHARCUTERIE PRODUCTS

Processed meats is the terminology used by the meat industry in the United States. It refers to meats which have been changed by cooking, canning, freezing, comminuting, seasoning, curing, drying or a combination of processes. The major purpose of processing meats is to preserve them. Normally, the processing also enhances flavor and texture, and makes the item easier to handle.

PATES, TERRINES, GALANTINES

Pates, terrines and galantines are examples of traditional European charcuterie items. These items are fully discussed in Chapter 26 and will not be dealt with further here.

SAUSAGES

Sausage is any meat that has been comminuted and seasoned. *Comminuted* means diced, ground, chopped, emulsified or otherwise reduced to minute particles by mechanical means. The USDA definition of sausage is shown in Figure One. In the simplest terms,

---
SAUSAGE

THE COARSE OR FINELY COMMINUTED MEAT PRODUCT PREPARED FROM ONE OR MORE KINDS OF MEAT OR MEAT BY-PRODUCTS; CONTAINING VARIOUS AMOUNTS OF WATER; USUALLY SEASONED WITH CONDIMENTAL SUBSTANCES, AND FREQUENTLY CURED.

SPECIFICATIONS
1) BINDERS AND EXTENDERS MUST BE PROMINENTLY LABELED.
2) THE FINISHED PRODUCT WILL CONTAIN NO MORE THAN 3.5% OF THESE ADDITIVES.
3) RAW SAUSAGE MAY CONTAIN UP TO, BUT NOT MORE THAN, 3% WATER TO FACILITATE CHOPPING, MIXING OR THE DISSOLVING OF CURING OR FLAVORING INGREDIENTS, BASED ON THE TOTAL INGREDIENTS OF THE FORMULA.
4) COOKED SAUSAGES (POLISH SAUSAGE, COTTO SALAMI, BRAUNSCHWEIGER, ETC.) MAY CONTAIN NO MORE THAN 10% ADDED WATER IN THE FINISHED PRODUCT, INTENDED TO GIVE THE PRODUCT ITS CHARACTERISTIC TEXTURE.

Figure 1

---

sausage is ground meat which has been salted for preservation and seasoned to taste. The variety is virtually endless.

TYPES & DEFINITIONS

Over five billion pounds of sausage are produced under federal inspection each year. It would be impractical to list every type of sausage manufactured. There are over 250 varieties in just the United States and 1,200 worldwide. We will discuss the major types.

FRESH SAUSAGE

Fresh sausages are made from meats which have not been cured or smoked. The meat is ground, chopped, diced, etc., and seasoned. It is used in bulk form, or stuffed into casings. This is a raw product and must be fully cooked before eating. Bockwurst, country-style sausage and Italian sausage are examples of fresh sausage.

COOKED SAUSAGES

Cooked sausages are made from uncured meats. The meats are ground, seasoned and stuffed into casings. The sausage is then cooked, normally by poaching. These sausages are not smoked. Cooked sausages are usually served cold and as purchased. Braunschweiger is an example of a cooked sausage.

COOKED-SMOKED SAUSAGES

This type of sausage is made from cured meats. The meat is ground, seasoned and stuffed into casings. The sausage is then smoked and fully cooked. Cooked-smoked sausages do not need further cooking, but some are heated before serving. Examples of this type of sausage are bologna, frankfurters, cotto salami and berliners.

UNCOOKED-SMOKED SAUSAGES

Uncooked-smoked sausage is made from cured or uncured meats. The meat is ground, seasoned and stuffed into casings. The sausage is smoked, but not cooked. This means it has to be fully cooked before being eaten. Kielbasa and mettwurst are examples of this type of sausage.

DRY AND/OR SEMI-DRY SAUSAGES

These sausages are made from cured meats, which are ground, seasoned and stuffed into casings. This sausage may or may not be smoked before drying. They are air dried under controlled conditions. The amount of time, temperature and humidity are closely regulated. These types of sausages are then fermented under controlled conditions. This gives them a slightly acidic flavor. Dry/semi-dry sausages need no further cooking. They are served as purchased. German salami, Italian salami, Lebanon bologna, pepperoni and landjaeger sausage are examples of this type of sausage.

COMPONENTS

Sausage making has three primary components: Meat ingredients, non-meat ingredients and casings. Each of these components is important to the quality of the finished product. We will discuss them individually in this section and as they relate to specific sausages later in the chapter.

MEAT INGREDIENTS

A variety of meat types are used in sausage making. Each type provides a particular flavor, texture and color in the product.

LEAN MEATS

Lean meats make up the largest proportion of sausage ingredients, providing the dominant character of the finished product. The flavor, color, texture and appearance of the sausage is determined by these meats.

Pork is the largest single species of animal processed for sausages and cured or smoked products. Bull meat is often used in sausage production because of its excellent binding properties and deep color. Beef is becoming more popular in sausage making, particularly for all beef products. Turkey is being used to produce a wide variety of sausages, particularly in the search for leaner sausages. Veal, lamb, mutton and poultry are also used in specific products, depending on the formulation.

FATTY MEATS

These are a source of fat for most sausages. Jowl fat is the most commonly used type in commercial production of charcuterie items. The fat adds flavor, texture, mouth feel and appearance to the sausage. The fat content in a finished sausage is limited by law to no more than thirty percent.

VARIETY MEATS

Variety meats are the organs, glands and other meats which are not part of the dressed carcass. These include the heart, kidney, tripe, liver, tongue and others. These meats have a low binding power. Recipes for sausage emulsions using a high ratio of variety meats usually need a binder to form a stable emulsion.

NON-MEAT INGREDIENTS

Non-meat ingredients are food additives which can legally be added to sausages or other processed meats. They enhance flavor and color; slow or prevent bacteria growth; act as a preservative, and extend the volume of the sausage. There are six types of additives: Water, curing agents, curing accelerators, sensory enhancers, stability enhancers and extenders and binders.

WATER

Water is usually added to the sausage mixture during the blending stage. It improves the mixing and helps to extract the proteins from the meat. It is used in all products.

CURING AGENTS

Curing agents are necessary to inhibit the growth of clostridium botulinum (an anaerobic bacteria which can cause death) and to improve shelf life. They also fix the color of the item. They make the frankfurter and ham pink. The two common curing agents are sodium nitrate and sodium nitrite. Nitrite is used in cured, cooked or smoked products. Sodium nitrate is used in dry sausage.

CURING ACCELERATORS

Curing accelerators, such as ascorbic acid, erythorbic acid and citric acid, are used in cured, cooked and fermented products. As their name indicates they speed up the curing process. The accelerators should not be mixed directly with the curing agents.

SENSORY ENHANCERS

The variety of items used to enhance the flavor, smell, color and feel of sausages is extensive. Many are used exclusively by the commercial manufacturers of sausage and will not be discussed here. We will concentrate on the ones most often used for sausage making in the kitchen. These are food items which are used everyday in the kitchen.

Salt is used in all charcuterie products for the enhancement of flavor and as an aid in protein extraction from meats.

Sweeteners are used in some form in all sausages. There are both nutritive and non-nutritive sweeteners used. Non-nutritive sweeteners, such as saccharin and sorbitol, are used in making bacon and cooked, cured sausages. These add sweetness and aid in peeling. Nutritive sweeteners, such as cane or beet sugar, dextrose and corn syrup are used in all products. The quantity used will be determined by the type of sweetener and the intended end product.

Flavorings for sausages include spices and spice extractives. Those used in a particular sausage will be determined by its type. Whatever type of spice is used, it should be as fresh as possible to gain maximum flavoring. Large-scale sausage production also uses hydrolized plant, vegetable and milk protein; autolyzed yeast extract, and mustard flour. These add flavor; increase volume; act as binders, and improve peeling.

Colorings for sausages include both natural and artificial. Artificial colors, certified food colors, are used in most mass produced sausages. These colors are not recommended for use by the chef. Natural colors can be obtained from paprika, saffron, turmeric and other spices; caramel, and certain plant pigments. These add not only color, but also flavor. The use of natural colors is recommended whenever possible.

Smoke, natural smoke, using a smoker or smokehouse, is the best. It will give the highest amount of flavor and color. This may be hot or cold smoking. Liquid smoke is condensed from burning wood. Although not recommended for use in place of natural smoke, it can boost the flavor of the product when properly used. Use of too much liquid smoke will give the product a bitter flavor.

Flavor enhancers are products which bring out the flavor of the other ingredients, yet have no real flavor of their own. The one used most in the kitchen is monosodium glutamate. This is a natural product, but should be used sparingly. It may cause allergic reactions in some people. Monoammonium glutamate, nucleotides and other flavor enhancers are used in mass production of sausages. They are suitable for use in all sausages, but are not widely used.

Others: There are four other groups of sensory enhancers: Bacterial cultures, enzymes, phosphates and acidulants. These serve a variety of purposes in sausage making including flavoring, softening of tissue, juice retention, etc. They are used in mass production and would rarely be seen in the commercial kitchen.

STABILITY ENHANCERS

Stability enhancers are used in sausage making to protect the flavor of the product; to slow down mold growth, and to extend and bind the product. In the kitchen, extending and binding the product are the common goals. The use of antioxidants and antimicrobials is normally confined to what are contained in the curing agents.

EXTENDERS & BINDERS

There are three classes of extenders and binders: Animal-based, fermentation-based, and cereal grain-based. Gelatin stock and non-fat dry milk solids are the animal-based ones most commonly used in the kitchen. Fermentation-based extenders and binders involve the introduction of specified types of microorganism into the sausage. As these grow they create changes within the sausage. Cereal grain-based ones include flour, oat, wheat, barley, corn and rye, as well as starches from vegetables and cereals. The purpose of these is to bind the sausage and to give stable form to the emulsion. These products can also be used to extend the volume of the sausage, what is often termed *filler*. The use of these products as extenders is far more common in mass production than in specialized kitchen preparations.

CASINGS

Casings are of vital importance in sausage making. Their primary function is that of a holder for the prepared meat mixture. They also have a major effect on the mouth feel, if edible, and appearance, both edible and inedible. The variety of casings available is broad. There are six types: Natural, collagen, peelable cellulose, fibrous cellulose, plastic and caul fat. Some casings are edible and meant to be eaten with the sausage. Other casings are non-edible. They are peeled off the sausage before it is eaten. The type of casings you need for a sausage depends to a large degree on the type of sausage.

NATURAL CASINGS

Natural casings are made from the submucosa of the intestines of hogs, sheep and cattle. The submucosa is made up mostly of collagen. The fat and inner mucosa of the intestine is removed before the submucosa is prepared as a casing.

Use of natural casings is considered by many professional sausage makers to have advantages.

1) They permit deeper smoke penetration.

2) Natural casings absorb flavors and release fats better.
3) Generally, they hold their shape better and will burst less easily in cooking.
4) They provide a snap when eaten that is not present in other casings.
5) Natural casings are fully edible, so no peeling is necessary.
6) They have a better appearance.

MANUFACTURE OF NATURAL CASINGS

The manufacture of natural casings includes cleaning and calibrating. After the intestinal tract is removed intact from the animal, it is cleaned. The tissues connecting the sections of intestine are separated and it is laid out in long strands. By a combination of flushers and rollers, all manure and foreign matter is removed from the strands of intestine. The casings are then immersed in a strong salt solution. This stops any bacterial growth.

The cleaned casing is calibrated. This allows the determination of the size casing produced. The casing is inflated with air or water until it is stretched to the same degree it would be when stuffed as sausage. Its diameter is then measured, normally in millimeters.

AVAILABLE FORMS AND PREPARATION

There is a variety of natural casings available. The most commonly used being *hog casings*. Figure Two shows where the casing comes from in the animal, the sizes and uses of the types. Casings from hogs are available in four forms: Hog casings, hog middles, hog bungs and sewed hog bungs.

Sheep casings are the highest quality small casings. They are usually preferred for some sausages because they are tender casings, yet strong enough to hold the filling. Figure Three discusses sheep casings.

Beef casings are available in four varieties: Beef rounds, beef middles,

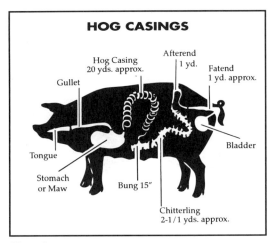

Figure 2

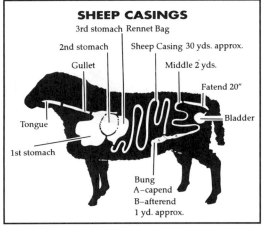

Figure 3

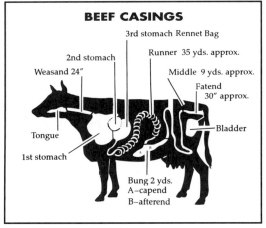

Figure 4

beef bung caps and beef bladders. The most commonly used varieties are bungs, rounds and middles. Figure Four discusses beef casings.

Laminated casings are used mainly in the manufacture of dry sausage or semi-dry sausage. The larger laminated cas-ings are often used with a netting of some type. Laminated casings are man-ufactured from pieces of sheep or hog casings. These are split open and lami-nated together over a form or mold. Laminated casings can be made in any size or shape. Once the casing is formed it is exposed to high temperatures. This kills any bacteria and seals the seams of the casing by coagulating the proteins in the casing. The casing is then cooled and removed from the form. The result is a custom made casing, which is still all natural in content. The sizes of lami-nated casings are shown in Figure Five.

Hog and sheep casings are sold in *bundles* or *hanks*. This is 100 yards or 91 meters, of casings. They are ready for sale in either salted, preflushed form, or tubed form. Beef casings are sold in *sets*. These are in salted form. A set is 100 feet for beef rounds, or 60 feet for beef middles.

PACKAGING

Natural casings are packaged in three forms: Dry salt pack, slush or pre-flushed pack and preflushed wet pack. Dry salt pack casing must be rinsed to remove the salt before using. Soak at room temperature for one hour to soft-en the casings. Preflush the casings by running water through them.

Slush or preflushed casings are prepared for use in the same manner. They will require less soaking to soft-en, since they are somewhat hydrated in the slush.

Preflushed wet pack casings come packed in a brine with a lower salt content. They need only a final flush before loading on the stuffing tube. Tubed items are often packed in this same manner.

STORAGE

Natural casings need to be protected from extreme variations in temperature. The ideal storage temperature is 40-45°F. Dry salt pack casings have the best shelf life and are least damaged in shipping.

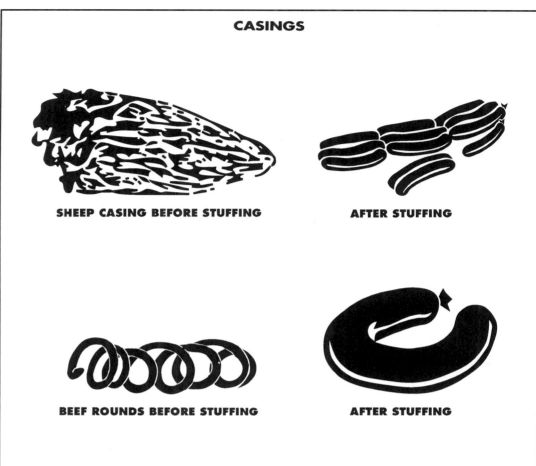

CASINGS

SHEEP CASING BEFORE STUFFING

AFTER STUFFING

BEEF ROUNDS BEFORE STUFFING

AFTER STUFFING

Figure 5

COLLAGEN CASINGS

Collagen casings are edible. They are not synthetic casings. Collagen casings are made from collagen from the hides of cattle. The fat, flesh and hair are removed from the hide and it is split into two layers by special equipment. The hair side of the hide is used for leather goods. The flesh side (corium layer) is used in producing collagen casings.

There are benefits to using collagen casings. They are consistent in diameter in each hank, ranging in size from 14 to 45 millimeters and 16 or 20 feet lengths. The consistent diameter allows better portion control. These casings also have superior machinability. They take on smoke color quickly and evenly, yet require no pre-preparation.

Collagen casings should be stored at temperatures below 50°F. This will reduce drying and development of brit-tleness. If collagen casings become too dry and brittle, dip them in water before use, but do not soak them.

PEELABLE CELLULOSE

This type of casing is not edible. It is used extensively in the commercial manufacture of frankfurters and closely related products. Forcemeat is stuffed into the casing; cooked, and possibly smoked. The casing is peeled from the finished sausage by a special machine. Skinless franks are an example of the products made with this casing.

FIBROUS CELLULOSE CASINGS

Fibrous cellulose casings are not edible. These casings are designed for strength. Fibers run the length of the casing to increase its strength and durability. An interior layer of protein is applied to the casing, causing it to shrink with the meat as it is dried.

Used mainly for dry/semi-dry sausage, the casings come in red or clear. They must be soaked in water before stuffing. Sometimes the casings are soaked in vinegar or liquid smoke. This prevents surface mold and makes it easier to peel the casing off after the finished product is sliced.

PLASTIC CASINGS

Plastic casings have become popular in the meat processing industry. They are cheaper, stronger and uniform in size. They do need to be removed before the item is served.

CAUL FAT

Caul fat is a thin membrane which surrounds the stomach of a hog. The membrane is networked, like a spider web, with streaks of fat. Caul fat is excellent for wrapping items of irregular size. It is used for loukanika (patty-shaped Greek sausage), and crepinettes.

SAUSAGE VARIETIES

There are five categories of sausage: Fresh sausage, cooked sausage, cooked-smoked sausage, uncooked-smoked sausage and dry or semi-dry sausage.

FRESH SAUSAGES

BOCKWURST is a sausage made of veal and pork. In finer types the veal content is higher than the pork. The meat is combined with milk, eggs, chives and chopped parsley. The texture of bockwurst is medium to fine and it is seasoned similarly to a frankfurter. Bockwursts are stuffed in lamb casings, normally 24-26 millimeters. They are 4- to 6-inch links, available fresh or parboiled.

COUNTRY-STYLE PORK SAUSAGE is made from pork and has a very coarse texture. It is highly seasoned with peppercorns, nutmeg and rubbed sage. This sausage is made in bulk, links or perforated patties. It is generally sold in unlinked hog casings of 32-35 millimeters. Both the link and bulk form of this sausage is considered breakfast sausage.

ITALIAN SAUSAGE is made of pork butts. It has a coarse texture and sweet or hot taste. Normally stuffed in 32-35 millimeter hog casings, forming 3- to 4-inch links. This sausage is also very popular in long spiral ropes which are placed on two long skewers and grilled whole over charcoal.

COOKED SAUSAGES

BRAUNSCHWEIGER is the best example of a cooked sausage. Made of pork livers and jowls, it has a smooth texture. It is seasoned with allspice, cloves, ginger, mustard and other spices. Braunschweiger is stuffed in regular or sewed hog bung, 3 inches long. This sausage can be smoked after cooking.

COOKED-SMOKED SAUSAGES

BOLOGNA originated in Bologna, Italy. Made of cured pork and/or beef, it is finely ground. The seasoning of bologna is similar to that of frankfurters. It is available in a variety of forms. It comes packed in large cellulose or plastic casings, beef bungs or extra wide beef rounds for ring bologna.

FRANKFURTERS originated in Frankfurt, Germany, and are made from pork and/or beef. They are seasoned with coriander, garlic, nutmeg, sugar and white pepper. Frankfurters are fully cooked and smoked, but usually served warm. They come in a wide variety of sizes from jumbo dinner size to tiny cocktail size. Frankfurters can be stuffed into natural lamb or hog casings or be skinless.

BERLINERS are made of cured, coarsely ground pork, encased in mildly cured, finely chopped beef. The only seasonings used are sugar and salt. They are available rolled or in packaged slices.

UNCOOKED-SMOKED SAUSAGES (COLD SMOKED)

KIELBASA (POLISH SAUSAGE) is made of coarsely ground pork with beef added. It is highly seasoned with garlic. The term *kielbasa* is the Polish word for sausage, not a particular type. However, in the United States it has come to mean one type.

METTWURST and TEEWURST are sausages made of cured beef and pork, which are ground fine. The meat is combined with allspice, ginger, mustard and coriander to a smooth and spreadable consistency. These sausages are usually bright red and should be cooked fully before using. They are not served hot.

DRY/SEMI-DRY SAUSAGES

SALAMI is a general classification for highly seasoned dry sausage, having a characteristic fermented flavor. Genoa salami is a prime example. This type of sausage is usually made with beef and pork, seasoned with salt, peppercorns and sugar. Most are air dried and not smoked or cooked. The cooked salamis, such as cotto salami, are not dry sausage.

CERVELAT is a general classification for mildly seasoned, smoked, semi-dry sausages. These are also called SUMMER SAUSAGES. Examples of this type of sausage include LANDJAEGER CERVELAT of Swiss origin. It is made of beef and pork and processed with heavy smoke. It has a black, wrinkled appearance. Landjaeger is formed in links the size of large franks, but pressed flat. THURINGER CERVELAT is made of beef and ham fat. It has a distinct, tangy flavor, which is mildly spicy. LEBANON BOLOGNA originated in Lebanon, Pennsylvania. Made of coarsely chopped beef, it is heavily smoked. This sausage has a tart, tangy taste and a dark surface appearance.

PROCESSED WHOLE MEATS

HAM

Ham, in the simplest terms, is the hind leg of a pig. Because of the popularity of cured pork, the term has become synonymous in many instances with the cured and often smoked preparations of the leg. Salt is always the main curing agent. However, today nitrites, both sodium- and potassium-based, play an important role in control of clostridium botulinum and color retention in cooked hams.

Once cured, hams may or may not be smoked, depending on the variety. There are both cooked and uncooked types of hams. Hams in the 12-14 pound range are considered the most tender.

As with sausage, the variety of hams is virtually limitless. There are at least 100 different traditional styles of preparation. These differ mainly in the flavoring and cure recipes involved. The basic techniques, however, are normally the same.

CURING

There are four methods of curing hams: Brine pumping, spray pumping, brining and dry curing.

Brine pumping is the curing of the ham by a combination of spray pumping and immersion. An apparatus similar to a large syringe is filled with the prepared brine. The meat is injected with the brine at several points, insuring even distribution. The ham is then immersed in the same brine for three to four days to insure the exterior portions are fully cured.

Spray pumping is accomplished by commercial processors with special pumps. This is also called *stitch pumping*. The pump has multiple needles and can deliver brine to every part of the ham's interior in one step. This does away with the need for immersion.

NOTE: Whether the ham is brine pumped or spray pumped, pumping is considered the best method for curing a ham.

Brining is immersing only. This can be done for very small hams. It is not the ideal method because of two factors:

1. It takes the brine much longer to penetrate the interior of the ham. If the ham is too large the interior may spoil before the cure has a chance to reach it.

2. If the ham is purchased from an unknown supplier it may already be very old and may spoil before the brine can reach the interior.

For *dry curing*, a dry cure mixture is rubbed thoroughly onto the ham. Several hams are normally cured at once. They are closely stacked, one on top of the other, in a barrel. The dry cure mix is basically the same as a brine without the water or other liquid. Some producers of ham will spray pump the hams and then pack the exterior with dry cure to fully cure the exterior layers of the ham.

DRYING

Certain types of hams, such as prosciutto crudo, are not cooked or smoked. They are merely dried. The drying process can take several months to a year, varying with the size of ham. For preparations of this type it is important to use "certified pork."

The term *certified pork* means pork products in which the possibility of trichinea bacteria growing is eliminated. This is accomplished by the ham being frozen according to a specified schedule. This schedule is shown in Figure Six.

SMOKING

Some types of hams are smoked for flavor, color and preservation. Before smoking, they are rinsed of excess cure or brine. They are then either slowly hot smoked or cold smoked. A slowly hot smoked ham is ready to eat when it has been fully smoked. Cold smoked hams must be cooked before eating.

VARIETIES OF HAMS

FRESH HAM is the hind leg of a pig that has not been cured or smoked. It is sold bone-in or boneless and is usually purchased in the raw form.

COUNTRY HAM is a generic term for cured hams which are not normally smoked when purchased.

KENTUCKY HAM is a heavily smoked ham and very lean.

PENNSYLVANIA HAM is brine cured. It is pickled in vinegar and sugar, then smoked over apple or hickory wood. This is a fully cooked ham.

SMITHFIELD HAM is a trade name for a variety of Virginia hams, available only from Smithfield, Virginia. They are dry cured for many months, resulting in a dense, dark red meat. Available cooked or uncooked, they are not smoked.

SUGAR CURED is a ham cured with a brine containing brown sugar or molasses.

VIRGINIA HAM is a general term for a ham made from the meat of hogs fed on acorns, peanuts and peaches. Dry cured in barrels for seven weeks, they are then coated with molasses, pepper and brown sugar. They are cured for two more weeks and then hung to dry slowly for 10-12 months. This involved process gives this ham a distinct flavor and deep reddish brown color.

WILLIAMSBURG HAM is a milder version of the Smithfield ham.

BOILED HAM is a common term for cured ham which is boned, rolled and boiled. This ham is sold fully cooked.

CERTIFIED PORK FREEZING SCHEDULE

PORK BOXED IN LAYERS 6" OR LESS:

+05°F FOR 20 DAYS

-10°F FOR 12 DAYS

-20°F FOR 6 DAYS

PORK BOXED IN LAYERS 27" OR LESS

+05°F FOR 30 DAYS

-10°F FOR 24 DAYS

-20°F FOR 12 DAYS

Figure 6

CANNED HAMS are available from Denmark, Poland and Holland. They may or may not be smoked. No refrigeration is necessary for the unopened can if it is marked "sterilized."

BAYONNE HAM originated in Bayonne, France, and is used in the same way as Prosciutto ham.

PROSCIUTTO is the Italian name for all ham. However, the term has become the popular name for "Parma Ham," which is named after the city where it was developed. Hogs are often fed on the whey of the cheese processed nearby, giving the ham a distinct sweet flavor. There are two types of prosciutto: CRUDO, a raw ham of the highest quality, which is air dried with a dry cure and eaten raw, and COTTO, a cooked version of crudo which takes far less time to produce, making it much less expensive. Either type can be purchased bone-in or boneless.

CULATELLO is an Italian raw ham. It is cured and aged in wine and eaten raw. This is a rare and expensive ham.

PRAGUE HAM is Czechoslovakian ham which is cured and smoked. It must be cooked before eating. This ham can occasionally be found canned.

PRESUNTO HAM is from Portugal. It is a cured and smoked ham similar to prosciutto.

SERRANO HAM is a raw ham from Spain. It is similar to prosciutto crudo but sweeter. This ham is cured in wine for several months, then coated with olive oil and paprika and hung to dry for several more months.

WESTPHALIAN HAM is from the Westphalia region of Germany. This is a superior quality ham. It is acorn-fed hog meat that has been dry cured, sweet pickled, and then aged for four weeks. Finally it is lightly smoked over juniper wood. The resulting ham is dense textured and dark brown in color. Westphalian is available bone-in or boneless.

YORK HAM is a famous English ham. Pale pink in color, it has a very mild flavor.

CAPACOLLA HAM is a specialty of Parma, Italy. Like the picnic ham, this is not a true ham. It is made from the shoulder of the hog, not the hind leg. It is cured and smoked.

PICNIC HAM is actually not a ham. The *picnic shoulder* comes from the shoulder of the hog, not the hind leg.

STORAGE

The undried varieties of ham have a refrigerated shelf life of eight days. The fine texture of ham is adversely affected by freezing. Hold at the temperatures recommended for fresh meats.

BACON

Bacon is the term used to describe a cured and usually smoked meat product made from the belly of pigs. The production of bacon is much the same as the one given above for ham.

VARIETIES OF BACON

SLICED BACON is from hog bellies which have been squared off. They are cured and most often smoked; sliced thin, and then packaged for retail sale. The thickness of the slice varies the slices per pound as is indicated in Figure Seven.

SLAB BACON is the unsliced version of sliced bacon. It has a longer shelf life.

SLICES OF BACON PER POUND

THIN SLICED	36 SLICES PER POUND.
REGULAR SLICED	16-20 SLICES PER POUND.
THICK SLICED	12 (APPROXIMATE) SLICES PER POUND.

Figure 7

COUNTRY-CURED BACON has a salty, very strong flavor. It is more expensive then slab bacon.

CANADIAN BACON is processed in the same manner as slab bacon, except it is made from the eye of the loin. It is fully cooked and smoked at the time of sale. This product is more like ham than bacon, and is very lean.

PEA MEAL BACON is a form of Canadian bacon that is not smoked. After curing it is dried briefly and coated with yellow cornmeal.

SCHINKENSPECK (HAM-BACON) is a German preparation, processed like bacon. However, it is comprised of a combination of pork leg meat rolled inside a pork belly; tied, and processed.

STORAGE

Smoked bacon has a refrigerated shelf life of many months. Surface mold which forms during storage may be cut away and the rest of the bacon used, as long as it has not turned rancid. Canadian bacon is much more perishable, having a refrigerated shelf life of only four days.

CORNED BEEF

The name *corned beef* is from the old English term *Corns*, a coarse salt, the size of corn kernels, used to cure beef. Corned beef is usually made from the brisket or plate of beef. Bottom rounds are sometimes used for those guests who prefer a less fatty product. This version is cheaper and easier to slice. It is also much drier and has less flavor. Corned beef is available already corned (cured) in the raw state, or fully cooked and ready to eat.

PASTRAMI

Pastrami is processed in a manner similar to corned beef. The differences are that it is made from the navel portion of the beef plate; that it is covered with black pepper and spices after it is cured, and that it is hot smoked and fully cooked.

SPECIALTY ITEMS

The products listed in this section, although closely related to some of the groups already discussed, are those products associated most closely with the art and science of charcuterie.

Zampone is a Northern Italian, Modena region, fresh pork sausage. It is highly seasoned and the casing is the boned leg section of the skin with the foot attached. It is traditionally served with lentils on New Year's Day.

Tete Presse is a cured, boneless, rolled or pressed pig's head. It is poached and served with a vinaigrette and thinly sliced onions.

Head Cheese is a loaf product made from a pig's head, tongue included. It is cured and simmered in a gelatinous stock for about three hours. The meat is then removed from the head, diced and molded with the broth in which it was cooked. (Refer to Chapter 24, Aspic.)

Sulze is a German product very similar to head cheese. The difference is that it is made from the meat of a calf's or pig's feet. This meat is combined with chopped pickles and vegetables in a tart flavored meat aspic.

Jamboneaux is cured ham shank which is fully cooked in a rich stock. The large shank bone is removed, leaving the small one in place. The skin is removed, scraped clean of excess fat, and returned to the original position. The shank is wrapped in cheese cloth, rolled into a pear shape, and returned to the stock to cool. When cooled the cheese cloth is removed. The meat is rubbed with rendered pork fat, and finally rolled in fine bread crumbs.

Rillete is essentially a cooked pork spread. Boneless pork shoulder, with the fat, is cubed. It is then braised slowly with paté-type seasonings and onions. No liquid is added and the meat is cooked until it falls apart. The meat is then shredded into coarse fibers or crushed in a mortar. This mixture is packed into a clean crock or earthenware terrine and the rendered fat is strained over the top to seal it. Rillete will keep several months sealed in this manner and refrigerated.

REVIEW QUESTIONS

1. Define the term *charcuterie*.
2. Discuss what has happened to the art and science of charcuterie in the United States.
3. Define the terms *processed meats* and *comminuted*.
4. What is sausage?
5. List and define the five major categories of sausage, giving examples of each.
6. Discuss the function of the three types of meat ingredients used in sausage making.
7. List the six classes of non-meat ingredients (additives) used in the preparation of sausage.
8. List two types of curing agents used in sausage making and discuss their function.
9. Identify and discuss the major flavor enhancers utilized in sausage making.
10. What is the advantage of using natural casings in sausage preparation?
11. How are natural casings packaged and how are they prepared for use?
12. List and discuss three types of casings other than natural.
13. Define the term *ham*.
14. Discuss the curing and drying of hams.
15. Describe the following types of ham: Fresh, Virginia, prosciutto, Westphalian, picnic.
16. Define the terms *bacon* and *sliced bacon*.
17. How do Canadian, pea-meal and country-cured bacon differ.
18. Discuss corned beef, pastrami, rillete, head cheese and zampone.

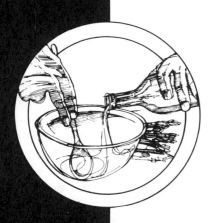

Chapter 29

CHAPTER OBJECTIVES

- **To discuss why sandwiches are so popular.**

- **To introduce the history of the sandwich.**

- **To identify the qualities of a good sandwich.**

- **To discuss various types of sandwiches.**

- **To discuss the components of the sandwich and their contributions to the whole sandwich.**

- **To identify the basic ingredients of a sandwich and their importance.**

- **To detail the guidelines for mis en place of a good sandwich station.**

- **To discuss proper service and presentation of sandwiches.**

Sandwiches

The sandwich in simplest terms is a bread-encased filling. As unimportant and lackluster as this description sounds, the sandwich is a cornerstone of cuisines the world over. It is unquestionably the most popular prepared food item in the United States. It can be made and served quickly, and is adaptable to enough variations that it satisfies practically every taste and nutritional guideline. Twenty percent (one fifth) of every consumer dollar spent in foodservice is spent on the sandwich.

The sandwich is usually in the background during any serious discussion about culinary arts. It is perceived as being too simple, too much a part of popular culture. As the backbone of many foodservice operations, country clubs, fast food operations and hotel restaurants, to mention just a few, the sandwich deserves better.

HISTORY

It is difficult to pinpoint when the sandwich actually appeared as a form of food presentation. We do know that the concept of wrapping bread around a filling for portability is ancient. It parallels the invention of bread, whether leavened or un-leavened. The sandwich in one way or another involves bread. There is a universal chain of foods worldwide which all have the connection of a filling encased in a starch product. In China there is the egg roll; in Italy the calzone; in Mexico the burrito, tamale and taco; in Israel the felafel, and in Spain the empanada...to name a few. These can all be considered variations of what is termed a sandwich.

One of the earliest recorded references to the sandwich tells of the famed Jewish teacher Rabbi Hillel (70 B.C. - 70 A.D.), a prince, who established the practice of eating sandwiches at Passover that were made of two pieces of matzoh (unleavened bread) encasing mohror (bitter herbs) and haroseth (chopped nuts and apples), to resemble the mortar of the Egyptians, as a reminder of suffering before deliverance from Egypt.

The open-faced sandwich has a slightly different history. In Old Russia the nobility came from far and wide for dinner dances. Waiting for the coaches to arrive became an event in and of itself. During this wait, the party began in the form of a reception. At first only drinks (vodka) were served, but as the wait became longer it became necessary to serve some type of food to sustain the crowd until dinner. The food was to be eaten with the fingers and served on toasted bread with cold meat, cheese, game or salads on top. This was the birth of the open-faced sandwich. The competition became intense amongst the chefs trying to outdo each other in the creativity and magnitude of these sandwiches.

During this period of Russian history there were many chefs from France working in Russia. When they returned to France they carried with them the concept of the open-faced sandwich. This is how the canape eventually evolved as is already discussed in Chapter 27. The idea also spread from Russia to the Scandinavian countries. The Danish version, the smorrebrod, is a national food. This delicacy achieves the highest level in culinary arts for the open-faced sandwich because of the multitude of available breads, toppings and beautiful garnishes.

Field workers in France have long had the custom of eating meat enclosed in two slices of brown bread. In southern France it is customary to provide those setting out on a journey with slices of cooked meat (usually pork or veal), sprinkled with its own juices sandwiched between two pieces of bread. The pan-bagnat of Nice is a definitive example of a sandwich which has been around for centuries.

The term *sandwich* came into use about two hundred years ago, close to the time of the birth of the United States. There lived a notorious gambler in the court of King George III of England whose name was John Montagu ("Jemmy Twitcher"), the Fourth Earl of Sandwich (1718-1792). The Earl's gambling affliction was such that he would enter in 24-hour betting marathons during which he would not remove himself from the table for any reason. Any eating had to be quick and not distracting to the task. The Earl asked the butler to serve bread and cheese. His chef knew of his master's intensity and so made it easy for him by placing the cheese between two slices of buttered bread, and the rest is...sandwich. Actually it became named after him in 1762.

The sandwich was little known in the United States until the latter part of the 19th Century with the invention of soft, white, sliced bread. Due to this change the sandwich was embraced by a nation. The sandwich's popularity rose until it hit its stride in the 1920's when all white bread was referred to as *sandwich bread* or *sandwich loaf*.

Today it is difficult to imagine any full-scale foodservice operation without the sandwich being a part of it. The most popular sandwich in the world is the hamburger. It has become a symbol for the expansion of the American economic system, for international diplomacy, if you will, as history and the sandwich move forward, hand on bun.

WHAT IS THE BASIC SANDWICH?

A sandwich is a balance of the same qualities that bring greatness to the other avenues of the culinary arts. In fact, through the sandwich it may be easier to see and to understand the essence of what makes cooked food set off the right bells for each individual's personal taste and enjoyment.

The sandwich, as defined, is a very simple culinary item. Yet, it relies on a perfect balance of the basic elements of culinary art to succeed. It is a balance of:

Temperature -- hot to cold.
Texture -- crunchy, chewy, unctuous, smooth, wet, dry.
Flavor -- integrity of the various components.
Appearance -- simple and correct.

It is from this balance of the basics that the wide variety of sandwiches all originate. As basic as this beginning is, the number of variations is quite remarkable. It is with the nature of these variations that we will begin our discussion of the sandwich.

TYPES & DEFINITIONS

It is really quite simple to divide the family of the sandwich. There are two main divisions -- hot and cold, and, beneath that, two secondary divisions -- open or closed. The one exception is that of tea sandwiches.

HOT SANDWICHES

There are three primary characteristics of hot sandwiches:

1. HOT SANDWICHES MUST BE HOT.

2. THEY MUST REMAIN HOT THROUGH SERVICE.
3. HOT SANDWICHES CAN HAVE A HOT SAUCE AS AN ACCOMPANIMENT.

A hot sandwich always conforms to these three basic characteristics, but there are two groups of hot sandwiches: Closed and open.

CLOSED

A *closed hot sandwich* is defined as one which has a hot filling served in bread, toast, roll or toasted roll. This sandwich combination works because of its balance of the basic culinary components. The key points are:

1. THE COOLER TEMPERATURE OF THE BREAD CASING BALANCES THE TEMPERATURE OF THE HOT FILLING.
2. THE RICHNESS OF A MEAT FILLING IN ITS OWN JUICES OR THE FRESHNESS OF A VEGETABLE FILLING ARE THE KEY TO THE SANDWICH'S FLAVOR.
3. A BALANCE OF CRUNCHY, CHEWY, UNCTUOUS (SPREAD OR SAUCE), SMOOTH, WET AND DRY TEXTURES ARE VERY IMPORTANT IN THE HOT SANDWICH. (AN ABSOLUTE TRAVESTY IS THE SERVING OF A BONE DRY STEAK ON DRY BREAD.)
4. THE PURE SIMPLICITY OF THE CASING AND FILLING CREATES A WELL-BALANCED AND APPETIZING APPEARANCE.

The closed hot sandwich can be subdivided into three basic groupings: Simple, grilled and fried.

SIMPLE CLOSED HOT SANDWICHES

A good example of this type of sandwich is a French Dip sandwich. The filling for this sandwich is cooked roast beef which is thinly sliced and dipped in au jus. It is then placed in a soft or hard roll, cut in half and served with a cup of hot au jus. A truly simple preparation, yet a balance of the basics. Other examples of this type of sandwich are given in Figure One.

Although the sandwich of this type

is simple, there are a few basic guides to its preparation.

1. THE MEATS USED IN ALL SANDWICHES SHOULD BE FRESH AND MOIST.
2. THE PORTION OF SLICED MEAT FOR A CLOSED SANDWICH IS NORMALLY 2 OUNCES.
3. A SPREAD IS OFTEN USED ON THIS TYPE OF SANDWICH BUT MAY BE ELIMINATED IF THE FILLING IS SUFFICIENTLY MOIST, AS IN THE CASE OF THE FRENCH DIP SANDWICH.
4. A CLOSED SANDWICH MAY CONTAIN COLD SECONDARY INGREDIENTS, SUCH AS LETTUCE, TOMATO AND ONION.
5. IT IS CRITICAL THAT THE CASING NOT BECOME SOGGY DUE TO MEAT JUICES OR SAUCES USED. THIS POSSIBILITY CAN BE REDUCED BY:
   A. PREPARING AND SERVING SANDWICHES QUICKLY.
   B. SELECTING CASINGS WHICH HAVE FIRMER TEXTURES AND ARE LESS LIKELY TO QUICKLY ABSORB THE MOISTURE RELEASED BY THE FILLING. EXAMPLES WOULD BE FRENCH-TYPE ROLLS AND RYE BREADS.
   C. USING LETTUCE AS A SHIELD BETWEEN THE CASING AND THE MOIST FILLING.
6. HOT SANDWICHES SHOULD NOT BE HELD FOR LONG PERIODS UNDER WARMING LIGHTS. THIS RAPIDLY DRIES OUT THE CASING AND ALSO THE FILLING IF IT IS EXPOSED. IF COLD SECONDARY INGREDIENTS ARE USED, THEY WILL BECOME WARM AND WILT, LOSING THEIR CRISP TEXTURE AND FLAVOR.

New variations on this basic sandwich are constantly being developed. These variations use different items and items prepared in different ways to create flavor variations. Currently these include the increased use of broiled fish and chicken as filling in closed sandwiches. Blackened and smoked meat, poultry and fish are broadening the sandwich selections on menus. It is pos-

---

SIMPLE CLOSED HOT SANDWICH VARIATIONS

STEAK SANDWICH -- THIS IS A 6-10 OZ STEAK COOKED TO THE GUEST'S ORDER OF DONENESS AND SERVED ON A LARGE ROLL WITH A LETTUCE, TOMATO AND ONION GARNISH. IT MAY BE ACCOMPANIED BY HORSERADISH OR MUSTARD SAUCE.

FISH SANDWICH -- THIS IS A BREADED 3-6 OZ PORTION OF BONELESS FILET OF FISH WHICH IS DEEP-FRIED AND SERVED ON A BUN, WITH A LETTUCE AND TOMATO GARNISH. IT IS NORMALLY ACCOMPANIED BY TARTAR SAUCE.

BARBECUED PORK SANDWICH -- THIS IS SLICED SMOKED PORK SERVED ON TWO SLICES OF BREAD OR A BUN. IT IS EITHER ACCOMPANIED BY, OR SERVED IN, BARBECUE SAUCE.

HOT DOG -- THIS IS THE WORLD REKNOWNED 6 TO 12 PER POUND SAUSAGE SERVED ON A SPECIAL ROLL. IT CAN BE TOPPED WITH A HOT TOPPING, SUCH AS CHILI OR CHEESE SAUCE, OR WITH COLD TOPPINGS LIKE CHEESE, SAUERKRAUT, COLE SLAW, AND ACCOMPANIED WITH RELISH, CHOPPED ONIONS AND OTHER CONDIMENTS, MOST ESPECIALLY CATSUP AND MUSTARD.

HAMBURGER -- THIS IS THE MOST POPULAR SANDWICH IN THE WORLD, 2- TO 6-OZ. PATTY OF GROUND BEEF: BROILED, FRIED, OR GRILLED TO ORDER, SERVED ON A ROUND BUN WITH A LETTUCE, TOMATO AND ONION GARNISH AND THE APPROPRIATE CONDIMENTS. A COMMON VARIATION OF THE BASIC BURGER IS THE MELTING OF A SLICE OF AMERICAN CHEESE ON TOP FOR THE BASIC CHEESEBURGER. THERE ARE AS MANY VARIATIONS AS THE MIND CAN IMAGINE.

Figure 1

sible for you to create your own signature sandwich by working within the basic guides for closed sandwiches

GRILLED CLOSED SANDWICHES

The *grilled closed sandwich*, by definition, is two slices of bread encasing a filling. The casing is buttered on the outside top and bottom and then placed on a griddle or in a pan to brown on both sides. A grilled cheese sandwich, which is an excellent example of this sandwich type, can be considered a perfect balance of the culinary basics. The browned outside is dry, yet the melted cheese inside is wet. The crunchy exterior of the sandwich is accentuated by the smooth interior. As you bite through the cooler casing you encounter the hot cheese. The attractive golden color enhances the nutty flavor of the browned butter which is complementary to the richness of the cheese. This sandwich is truly the simplest form of culinary art and science.

The basic guides for a grilled sandwich are:

1. ANY TYPE OF BREAD MAY BE USED FOR THE CASING OF THE GRILLED SANDWICH. IN FACT, DAY-OLD BREAD MAY BE USED WITHOUT LOSS OF QUALITY TO THE FINAL PRODUCT.

2. SPREAD CAN BE USED INSIDE THE BREAD, SUCH AS FLAVORED MAYONNAISE OR MUSTARDS, BUT ARE NOT REQUIRED.

3. THE SELECTED FILLING SHOULD COVER THE BREAD USED.

4. THE BUTTER OR MARGARINE USED ON THE OUTSIDE OF THE CASING MUST BE SPREAD SMOOTHLY AND EVENLY TO ENSURE PROPER BROWNING.

5. THIS TYPE OF SANDWICH MAY BE PREPPED THE DAY BEFORE IT IS USED, THEN TIGHTLY WRAPPED IN PLASTIC WRAP AND HELD UNDER REFRIGERATION.

6. A LIGHT WEIGHT CAN BE PUT ON TOP OF THE SANDWICH DURING GRILLING TO ENHANCE THE BROWNING.

Although the grilled cheese sandwich is most often prepared using American cheese, this sandwich is an example of the variations possible. This old favorite is being varied with the use of different types of cheeses and the addition of various spreads. As with the closed sandwich the variety is only as limited as your imagination. Figure Two lists a few other examples of grilled sandwiches.

FRIED CLOSED SANDWICH

By definition, *fried closed sandwiches* are two pieces of bread encasing some type of filling which have been dipped in an egg mixture (sometimes breaded) and then deep- or pan-fried till golden. They are often finished in the oven to ensure that the interior is hot. The most common example of this hot sandwich is the Monte Christo, which can also be called Croute Monsieur or Monte Carlo.

GRILLED CLOSED SANDWICH VARIATIONS

GRILLED TUNA SALAD AND CHEESE -- A VARIATION OF THE GRILLED CHEESE SANDWICH WITH THE ADDITION OF A GOOD TUNA SALAD FILLING.

GRILLED HAM AND CHEESE -- A POPULAR VARIATION OF THE GRILLED CHEESE WITH THE ADDITION OF SLICED OR SHAVED HAM. THE HAM MAY BE PLACED ON THE SANDWICH COLD OR IT MAY BE PRE-BROWNED AND THEN ADDED.

GRILLED REUBEN -- RYE BREAD, SWISS CHEESE, GRILLED CORNED BEEF OR PASTRAMI, WARM SAUERKRAUT AND THOUSAND ISLAND DRESSING.

Figure 2

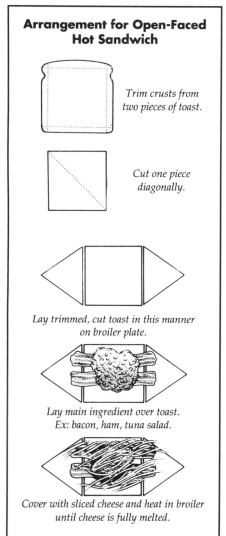

Arrangement for Open-Faced Hot Sandwich

Trim crusts from two pieces of toast.

Cut one piece diagonally.

Lay trimmed, cut toast in this manner on broiler plate.

Lay main ingredient over toast. Ex: bacon, ham, tuna salad.

Cover with sliced cheese and heat in broiler until cheese is fully melted.

This sandwich is very similar to the grilled cheese, yet, due to the coating, does not have as crisp a casing. However, it has an excellent appearance.

The Monte Christo is normally prepared with Swiss cheese, ham and Dijon mustard on a light bread. It is usually accompanied by red currant jelly which complements both the color and flavor of the sandwich.

The key points in the production of a quality fried sandwich are:

1. THE FRYER MUST BE AT THE CORRECT TEMPERATURE, NORMALLY 350-375°F. IF THE TEMPERATURE IS TOO HIGH, THE SANDWICH WILL BROWN BEFORE THE INTERIOR IS HEATED THOROUGHLY. IF THE TEMPERATURE IS TOO COOL, THE SANDWICH WILL ABSORB TOO MUCH FAT AND BE GREASY.

2. THE FILLING USED IN THE SANDWICH MUST ADHERE TO THE INSIDE OF THE CASING OR THE SANDWICH WILL LOSE ITS SHAPE WHILE FRYING.

3. THE COATING MUST SEAL THE SANDWICH TO PREVENT THE FILLING FROM SEEPING DURING FRYING.

4. THIS SANDWICH CAN BE PREPPED, WITH THE EXCEPTION OF COATING, THE DAY BEFORE IT IS TO BE USED. IT IS THEN WRAPPED TIGHTLY IN CLEAR WRAP AND HELD UNDER REFRIGERATION. WHEN THE SANDWICH IS NEEDED, IT CAN BE COATED AND FRIED QUICKLY.

The variations possible in the preparation of fried sandwichs are as great as those of the grilled type. However, the basic guides must be followed.

OPEN

Open hot sandwiches are prepared with the bread or toast laid side by side with the filling exposed on the surface of both sides. The sandwich is then heated throughout. This type of hot sandwich can be subdivided into two main categories: Grilled or broiled, and meat combination sandwiches.

GRILLED OR BROILED

A *grilled* or *broiled open faced hot sandwich* is made of trimmed or untrimmed toasted bread with a filling on top. It is heated through in a hot broiler or oven. For this sandwich the bread acts as a platform for the filling. Normally this sandwich does require the garnishment of other sandwiches. However, depending on how it is prepared, it may betray one of the basic rules of the sandwich, portability. If a great deal of topping and filling are

---

OPEN GRILLED/BROILED SANDWICH VARIATIONS

OPEN-FACED GRILLED CHEESE -- THIS IS A SANDWICH PREPARED WITH ANY TYPE OF BREAD AND A VARIETY OF FILLINGS, SUCH AS BACON AND TOMATO. IT IS TOPPED WITH CHEDDAR OR AMERICAN CHEESE. IT IS THE MOST COMMON SANDWICH OF THIS TYPE.

TUNA MELT -- THIS IS TUNA SALAD (SEAFOOD, HAM, CHICKEN OR OTHER SALADS MAY BE SUBSTITUTED FOR VARIETY.) WITH SLICES OF CHEESE ON TOP, ALL HEATED THROUGH.

HOT BROWN -- THIS IS SLICED TURKEY, BACON AND TOMATO TOPPED WITH CHEESE SAUCE AND HEATED.

Figure 3

used, it may be necessary for the guest to eat it with a fork and knife.

This sandwich makes good use of the basic culinary elements. It has a wet, soft top and dry, crisp bottom which makes for a different taste experience from the grilled cheese. If the sandwich is topped with cheese, the first taste in the mouth is that of rich cheese. This sandwich can also be a source of surprises with a wide variety of flavors and textures possible between the bread and the topping. Bacon, hot chicken salad or crunchy celery are just a few. The traditional cutting of these sandwiches and arranging them geometrically on the plate or platter can create a very pleasing and appetizing appearance.

Creativity is not a problem with this type of sandwich. The use of different fillings and toppings combined with variations of bread and shapes give wide possibilities. Examples of the more common open grilled/broiled sandwiches are given in Figure Three.

MEAT COMBINATION

A *meat combination sandwich* is two slices of trimmed or untrimmed bread with slices of hot meat on top, smothered with appropriate gravy, usually accompanied by mashed potatoes and, occasionally, bread dressing. To some culinarians this sandwich is truly a puzzle. It is one of those items which goes against many of the glorious rules and guidelines by which we create quality food.

This sandwich has little variation of texture. It is a combination of soft, gummy bread, soft overcooked meat and soft gravy. Even the accompanying items normally served with it are soft, mashed potatoes, dressing and more gravy. The appearance of the item is not normally colorful or exciting. Why, then, is it still a staple item at the majority of the smaller cafes in the midwestern United States? The key is flavor. For all of its disrespect for the finer points of culinary distinction, the guests enjoy the flavor combination. However, it is

beginning to lose ground as a popular choice primarily because of the increased health consciousness of the public.

COLD SANDWICHES

As with the hot sandwiches, cold sandwiches can be divided into two primary groupings: Closed and open.

CLOSED

Closed cold sandwiches can be defined as those having two slices of bread (toast) or two halves of a roll (toasted) which have a spread applied and are filled with a cold filling. This grouping can be subdivided into three types: Simple, combination and multi-decker.

SIMPLE CLOSED COLD SANDWICHES

These sandwiches meet the definition above, but only have one filling. In view of this, only the best, freshest ingredients should be used for this type of sandwich. The quality of the filling and the nature of the spread and bread are what can make this sandwich come to life.

The basic structure of this sandwich consists of:

1. THE BREAD SHOULD BE SELECTED TO COMPLEMENT THE TYPE OF SPREAD. IT MAY OR MAY NOT BE TOASTED DEPENDING ON THE SANDWICH DESIRED. THE USE OF UNUSUAL OR SPECIALTY BREADS ALLOWS THE CREATION OF A WIDE VARIETY OF FLAVOR COMBINATIONS. NOTE: REMEMBER, ONLY THE FRESHEST BREAD SHOULD BE USED. THERE WILL BE NO REVIVAL OF THE BREAD'S TEXTURE WITH HEAT AS THERE IS IN THE HOT SANDWICH. TO CUT IT WITHOUT FEATHERING OR TEARING THE BREAD, USE A SERRATED KNIFE. THIS IS TRUE FOR ALL SANDWICHES.

2. THE SPREAD (BUTTER, MAYONNAISE, MUSTARD OR OTHER) ASSISTS IN PROTECTING THE BREAD FROM ABSORBING MOISTURE FROM THE FILLING AND BECOMING SOGGY. IT ALSO ADDS TO

THE FLAVOR OF THE SANDWICH AND SHOULD BE CAREFULLY CHOSEN TO COMPLEMENT THE FILLING.

3. THE FILLING MAY BE: COOKED AND SLICED MEATS; COOKED AND SLICED OR SHREDDED POULTRY; COOKED FISH OR SHELLFISH; SHREDDED VEGETABLES OR VEGETABLE SPREADS; CHEESE (MANY VARIETIES ARE SUITABLE, EITHER SLICED OR AS SPREADS), MEAT, POULTRY, TUNA, EGG OR OTHER SALADS. A WIDE VARIETY OF FILLINGS MAY BE USED. THE SELECTION WILL DEPEND ON THE TASTE PREFERENCES OF THE GUEST.

4. A SECONDARY FILLING (GARNISH) MAY BE USED, SUCH AS LETTUCE, TOMATO OR PICKLE. AGAIN THIS SHOULD BE CHOSEN TO COMPLEMENT THE FLAVOR OF THE FILLING. CREATIVITY WITH THE SECONDARY FILLING IS VITAL TO DOING SOMETHING OUT OF THE ORDINARY. NOTE: THE PRIMARY FOCUS OF ANY SANDWICH SHOULD BE THE FILLING. SECONDARY FILLINGS SHOULD NOT OVERPOWER THE PRIMARY FILLING, BUT, RATHER, THEY SHOULD ENHANCE IT.

COMBINATION CLOSED COLD SANDWICHES

Combination closed cold sandwiches are those which have more than one primary filling. These types of sandwiches are a step up from the simple variety in that they have a higher level of flavor integration. The BLT (bacon, lettuce and tomato sandwich) is possibly the best example of this. The wet of the mayonnaise and tomato in conjunction with the dry toast and bacon make an interesting contrast on the palate. The flavor of the sandwich benefits by the robust flavor of the bacon and the mild taste of the lettuce. For texture, there is the crunch of the toast, bacon and lettuce and yet the smooth mouth feel of the mayonnaise and tomato. The balance is delicate and grand.

The key to this type of preparation is that each component must be assured of the retention of its own character until they all meld together on the palate. This requires great attention to detail, such as maintaining proper temperature for each item. Of vital importance is the

---

COMBINATION CLOSED COLD SANDWICH VARIATIONS

HAM AND CHEESE ON RYE -- THIS SANDWICH IS A CLASSIC EXAMPLE OF THIS TYPE. THE PRIMARY FILLINGS ARE HAM, SLICED OR SHAVED, AND SLICED CHEESE, USUALLY SWISS. IT IS NORMALLY ACCOMPANIED BY MUSTARD AND POSSIBLY LETTUCE, TOMATO AND PICKLE.

TURKEY AND PASTRAMI ON PUMPERKNICKEL - THIS IS SLICED OR SHAVED TURKEY AND PASTRAMI ON PUMPERKNICKEL BREAD GARNISHED WITH COLE SLAW. IT IS NORMALLY ACCOMPANIED BY MUSTARD AND PICKLE.

SUBMARINE -- THIS EXTREMELY POPULAR SANDWICH (ALSO CALLED A HERO, HOAGIE, GRINDER OR MUFALATA) IS A COMBINATION OF COLD CUTS, VEGETABLES AND CHEESE ON A SPECIAL BUN. IT IS USUALLY SPRINKLED WITH ITALIAN-TYPE DRESSING. MUSTARD OR MAYONNAISE IS OPTIONAL.

PEANUT BUTTER AND JELLY -- THE ALL-TIME FAVORITE WITH THE YOUNGER SET. TO BE PREPARED PROPERLY, IT MUST BE MADE WITH THE FRESHEST POSSIBLE WHITE BREAD, HIGH QUALITY PEANUT BUTTER AND THE FINEST GRAPE JELLY. (DO NOT KID YOURSELF, THERE ARE PLENTY OF OLDER FOLKS OUT THERE WHO LIKE THIS SANDWICH, TOO.)
NOTE: TO CUT IT WITHOUT FEATHERING OR TEARING THE BREAD, USE A SERRATED KNIFE. THIS IS TRUE FOR ALL SANDWICHES.

Figure 4

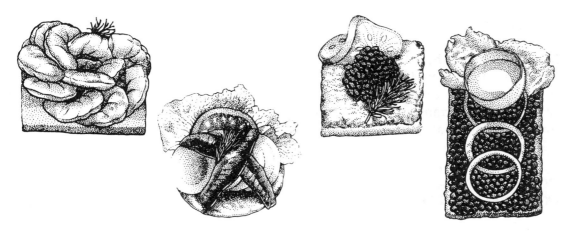

The Danish smorrebrod provides great stimulation for the eye as well as the palate in its many forms.

protection of the texture of the individual items. Limp toast and bacon will not yield the BLT we have described here. Examples of other combination sandwiches are listed in Figure Four.

MULTI-DECKER CLOSED COLD SANDWICHES

Multi-decker closed cold sandwiches have more than two slices of bread (toast) or a roll split more than once. They also have several fillings. The club sandwich is a classic example of this type of sandwich. It is composed of three pieces of toasted bread, bacon, lettuce, tomato and turkey fillings. The toast is spread with mayonnaise and layered evenly for two levels with the fillings. The sandwich is cut in quarters and normally toothpicked with fancy frilled picks.

The key points in making the club are the same as those of the BLT. Extra consideration must be given to the condition of the toast. If it is cooked too much, or is too old and dry, it will break in cutting. Extra care must be used in cutting the sandwich to maintain its appearance.

The same praise that applied to the BLT applies to the club with the exception that it is possibly a little too much to be considered perfection. However, it has an extremely impressive appearance and a high level of flavor and texture. There have been many attempts to improve on this classic sandwich; however, it is still hard to improve on the original.

OPEN

By definition, an *open cold sandwich* is a single slice of bread (toast) with attractively arranged fillings on top and garnished appropriately. These sandwiches are similar to a larger version of the canapes discussed in Chapter 27 (Hors d'oeuvre & Appetizer) of this text. This type of sandwich has not gained wide acceptance in the United States.

Examples of this type of sandwich include lox and cream cheese and open-faced seafood salad sandwiches. The Danish smorrebrod discussed briefly in Chapter 27 is another example. Meat, poultry, and seafood salads of all types are appropriate for use in making these types of sandwiches.

Though not a popularly accepted type of sandwich in the United States, culinarily it is possibly one worth pursuing. It allows a great deal of opportunity for upgraded sandwich appearance by creative garnishing and dressing. There are also greater opportunities for flavor combinations by using the layering effect.

TEA SANDWICH

Tea sandwiches do not fit exactly in the other categories. These are discussed more at length in Chapter 27. They are characterized by being fancy, light, delicate sandwiches. They are normally not associated with the heartier, entree-replacing types we have discussed up to now. They can be open, closed, rolled and cut, and are occasionally served hot.

455

Definitely portable and a finger food, they are also intended more to impress one with their daintiness. Pastel green and pink colored breads are often used and the sandwiches are always small. They are arranged in assortments on trays and plates and passed or served buffet-style.

COMPONENTS AND THEIR CONTRIBUTION TO THE WHOLE

The ingredients of a sandwich could not be too much simpler. There is the bread; a spread to go on the bread, and a filling. Because of this simplicity, it is critical that only the freshest ingredients are used and that every effort is made to maintain that freshness. The discussion of the various components of the sandwich will be heavily concerned with this charge.

BREAD

The casing, normally bread of some type, is the foundation of the sandwich. If it is not chosen and handled properly, the quality of the sandwich can not be good. The bread used for the sandwich is a major part of the balance of the basic culinary elements. Basically, bread has it all. It can be moist or dry, depending on the need and the care taken in handling it. Bread can have a full flavor or mild flavor depending on its make-up. How it is handled will determine whether its texture is crisp or smooth. The appearance of it can be as simple or intricate as desired. When well chosen and handled correctly, it makes the perfect match with a filling.

PURPOSE

The overall purpose of the bread is to act as an edible casing for the filling of the closed sandwich and a platform for the filling of the open sandwich. The finished sandwich depends as heavily on the bread as the filling for its quality. The bread must be a good match for the filling. Bread provides the following for the sandwich:

VARIETY.
TEXTURE.
FLAVOR AND AROMA.
EYE APPEAL.
BULK.
CARBOHYDRATES, VITAMINS AND
    MINERALS.

SELECTION FACTORS

The bread used for making a sandwich must be chosen carefully. As important as the flavor match between the filling and bread may be, there are some basic guides for choosing bread that go beyond the flavor component. These apply to bread as a group.

1. ALWAYS SELECT FRESH BREAD THAT HAS A CLOSE SMOOTH CRUMB AND GOOD FLAVOR AND MOISTNESS.
2. THE BREAD SHOULD BE CAPABLE OF BEING PICKED UP WITHOUT BENDING OR LOSING FILLING.
3. CHOOSE A BREAD THAT HAS A FINE GRAINED TEXTURE.
4. THE BREAD SHOULD HAVE A FIRM, NOT PASTY, TEXTURE.
5. BREAD SHOULD BE AT LEAST 12 HOURS OLD WHEN USED FOR SANDWICH MAKING, BECAUSE EXTREMELY SOFT BREAD IS NOT GOOD FOR SANDWICH MAKING.
6. BREAD IS AVAILABLE IN VARYING SLICE THICKNESSES.
    A. 1/4 " THICK -- THIN BREAD.
    B. 5/8 " THICK -- THICK BREAD.
    C. QUICK BREAD SLICED 1 " THICK.
    D. 3/8" - 5/8" IS THE THICKNESS RANGE MOST COMMONLY USED FOR SANDWICHES.

FORMS OF BREAD

There are a wide variety of bread forms. These do not necessarily relate to the flavor of the bread, although they may. It is becoming more and more common for certain shapes of bread that were once associated with a particular kind of bread (for instance, white) to be available also in whole wheat, rye or other.

The *pullman* is considered to be the sandwich loaf. It generally is a rectangular loaf with squared off sides, top and bottom. It can easily be cut in regular even slices. The pullman is normally available in white and whole wheat.

Rolls used for sandwiches include *hamburger, hot dog, submarine, croissant* and *French*. These rolls are available in white, whole wheat and other types.

French or *hard crusted bread* makes an excellent sandwich, but is best when used the same day it is baked.

Irregularly shaped loaf breads of various types are used for sandwich making. These include *rye, pumperknickel* and *Italian*. The list of these breads grows as more and more breads are experimented within the sandwich kitchen.

Quick breads are good for some specialty sandwiches. Particularly quick fruit breads. They must be cut thicker, because of their higher sugar content and lack of gluten development which reduces their firmness and elasticity, giving them a more cake-like crumb.

Pita or *pocket bread* was originally used in this country for the felafel (a Middle-Eastern sandwich variation), but has become a popular replacement for the more conventional breads.

STORAGE AND HANDLING

The first rule of good sandwich making is the use of fresh ingredients and this applies especially to the bread. The primary goal of storing and handling bread is to retain freshness. This can be done by doing the following:

1. PURCHASE ONLY THE AMOUNT OF BREAD THAT CAN BE USED IN ONE DAY.

2. IF EXCESS BREAD IS PURCHASED, OLD AND NEW SUPPLIES SHOULD BE SEPARATED EACH DAY. OLD BREAD SHOULD BE SET ASIDE FOR TOASTING, GRILLING OR PREPARATION AS FRENCH TOAST.

3. STORE SOFT CRUSTED BREAD IN ITS ORIGINAL WRAPPER OR TIGHTLY WRAPPED TO PROTECT AGAINST ODOR ABSORPTION, MOISTURE LOSS OR EXCESSIVE DAMPNESS.

4. HARD-CRUSTED BREAD MAY BE STORED WITHOUT WRAP IN AN AREA THAT HAS FREE AIR MOVEMENT; HOWEVER, THIS IS NOT RECOMMENDED FOR SANITATION REASONS.

NOTE: HARD-CRUSTED BREAD HAS A SHORTER STORAGE LIFE.

5. REFRIGERATING BREAD MAKES IT STALE. IF IT IS TO BE KEPT FOR MORE THAN ONE DAY, IT SHOULD BE FROZEN.

6. BREAD IS BEST STORED AT ROOM TEMPERATURE (68 - 80°F) AWAY FROM HEAT.

FILLINGS

The filling is the heart of the sandwich, determining its character. In most cases, it is what gives the sandwich its name. The filling also provides the primary source of protein in most sandwiches.

PURPOSE

The purpose of the sandwich's filling is to provide:

1. THE PREDOMINANT FLAVOR.

2. MOISTURE.

3. SUBSTANCE, BULK.

4. COMPLEXITY IN THE COMBINATION OF FLAVORS.

Put simply, there would be no sandwich without the filling.

SELECTION FACTORS

Accepting that the filling makes the sandwich what it is, then selection and preparation of it must be done carefully. As a general rule, most meats used as sandwich filling are pre-cooked. When meats and cold cuts are used sliced, they should be thinly sliced. They are more tender and easier to eat in this form.

Often the filling of a sandwich is in the form of a salad, chopped meat, egg or seafood mixture. These types of fillings should have a distinct flavor and texture. When the primary ingredient is soft, it should be complemented by some crisp item such as celery or green pepper. Salad fillings must not be so moist as to be messy or so dry that they fall out of the casing or crumble off the

457

platform. The proper texture of the chopped mixture is very important to the quality of the sandwich.

The basic guidelines for sandwich fillings are:

1. 1/3-1/2 OF THE TOTAL WEIGHT OF THE SANDWICH SHOULD BE FILLING.
2. FILLINGS MUST BE PLEASANTLY FLAVORED.
3. FILLINGS MUST BE TENDER IN TEXTURE.
4. FILLINGS MUST BE EASY TO EAT.
5. FILLINGS SHOULD BE RICH ENOUGH IN TASTE FOR THE SANDWICH TO ACT AS A MAIN COURSE SUBSTITUTE.
6. FILLINGS MUST NOT HANG OVER THE EDGE OF THE SANDWICH.
   NOTE: LIMP GREASY BACON OR WILTED LETTUCE CAN RUIN A GOOD SANDWICH.

TYPES

Any kind of food placed between two slices of bread or on top of a platform of bread can be considered a filling. This encompasses an almost endless variety of items. However there are those which have become standards.

MEAT

Meat is the main ingredient in most sandwiches served today. The use of the term *meat* here refers to beef, pork, poultry and sausages. Beef is popular in the form of sliced roast beef and corned beef, served hot and cold. Pastrami is another popular form of beef for deli-type sandwiches. Ground beef is, of course, used to make the ever popular hamburger. Small steaks are often used for higher priced sandwiches and beef tongue is used for specialty sandwiches.

Pork is used in a variety of forms in sandwich preparation. This includes the very popular ham, bacon, canadian bacon and roasted or smoked pork.

Sausages used in sandwiches include those made from one type of meat such as beef, pork or turkey, as well as those which combine either two or three types of meats. The sausages most commonly used include hot dogs, salami, bologna, liverwurst and luncheon meats. Fresh pork sausage is popular for breakfast-type sandwiches like the sausage and egg biscuit or croissant.

Poultry is rapidly increasing in popularity as a sandwich filling. This is partially due to the development of a variety of excellent processed turkey products, like turkey ham and pastrami. It is also due to the expansion of the use of the chicken breast (broiled or grilled) as a solid meat sandwich filler and a lower fat alternative to other meats.

SEAFOOD AND FISH

Seafood and fish have long been considered good sandwich fillings. Tuna salad in particular has long been a standard sandwich filler. It is relatively inexpensive and easy to handle in the canned form. Canned salmon, shrimp, crab meat analogs, oysters and sardines are a few of the more commonly used processed types. Fresh fish fillets have grown in popularity as sandwich fillings; however, they are typically fried. The expanded use of broiled and baked fish as a filler will be seen.

VEGETABLE

Vegetables are often not thought of as anything other than secondary sandwich fillings. While they make excellent accompaniments to meat and seafood fillings, they can also stand alone as a primary filler. Any ingredient that can go into a salad can be used as a sandwich filler. Some of the most popular ones used as secondary fillings are:

LETTUCE
TOMATO
ONION
AVOCADO
ALFALFA SPROUTS

As a primary filler (meat substitute) a mixture of soft and crunchy vegetables blended with nuts can make an excellent filling.

EGGS

Eggs may be used as a primary filler in sandwiches and often are in Italian cuisine. However, they are more often used as a primary filling in breakfast sandwiches. In luncheon or dinner sandwiches they are usually used as a secondary ingredient in a chopped filling.

CHEESE

Cheese is the second most used sandwich filler after meat. It is a basic ingredient for a variety of popular sandwiches. The most commonly used types are American, cheddar and Swiss. Cream cheese is also a popular spread for sandwiches. Reduced fat cheeses combined with a mixture of soft and crunchy vegetables make a healthful filling for a whole-wheat pita or a sliced whole-grain bread.

MAYONNAISE-BASED SALADS

Mayonnaise-based salads (chopped fillings) are also widely used for sandwich fillings. The more common ones include egg, tuna, chicken and ham. The standard ratio for these salad mixtures is one part chopped vegetable to four parts meat or other main ingredient.

MISCELLANEOUS

Some items used for sandwiches do not fit in the other groups. A prime example is peanut butter, which is one of the most popular sandwich fillings in the home, if not in the commercial operation. Although fruits are not commonly thought of as sandwich fillings, it can definitely be said to be a matter of taste. There really is such a thing as a peanut butter and banana sandwich. A little less exotic perhaps is the use of dates, grapes and raisins in salad mixtures.

STORAGE AND HANDLING

As with the bread for the sandwich, the goal of storing and handling fillings is to preserve their freshness. To accomplish this, the culinarian should follow these guidelines:

1. AVOID SLICING MEAT FILLINGS TOO FAR IN ADVANCE. THEY DRY OUT AND LOSE FLAVOR EASILY.
2. WHEN PRE-SLICING IS NECESSARY FOR MEAT FILLINGS, KEEP THE SLICES COVERED OR WRAPPED TIGHTLY.
3. ALL FILLINGS MUST BE KEPT REFRIGERATED UNTIL SERVED.
4. LEFTOVERS MAY BE USED FOR FILLINGS IF THEY ARE OF GOOD QUALITY AND HAVE BEEN PROPERLY HANDLED AND STORED.
5. MEAT OR CHEESE MAY BE PREPPED AHEAD AND KEPT UNDER REFRIGERATION UNTIL NEEDED FOR SERVICE.

SPREAD

The spread is the simplest of the three main ingredients of the sandwich. It has little affect on the appearance, unless used incorrectly. It is considered to have little effect on the flavor. In fact, it is thought by most to be simply a paste to glue the sandwich together as a final unit. However, when used correctly, it can go far beyond this mundane role in the sandwich.

PURPOSE

Spread serves three primary purposes in the sandwich, each of which is of vital importance to the quality of the sandwich. The spread acts as a sealant for the bread, forming a moisture barrier between it and the filling. It helps to reduce the absorption of moisture from the filling, which would otherwise cause the bread to become excessively soggy.

Flavor is another purpose of the spread. It has the ability to add additional flavor components to the sandwich, as well as to enhance the flavor of the filling. Good examples are pesto mayonnaise with chicken breast or horseradish with roast beef. The spread also adds moisture to the sandwich, improving its mouth feel.

QUALITIES

In order for a spread to act as more than a glue and possibly a distraction in

MAKING MAYONNAISE

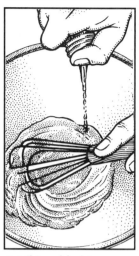

1. Oil is added to egg yolk in driplets.

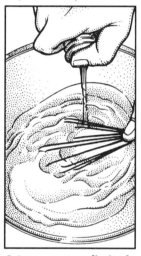

2. Increase to a limited flow as the emulsion occurs.

3. Finally, a full flow after the mixture has changed into its final form.

the sandwich, it must be of high quality, properly prepared and used.

1. **THE SPREAD MUST BE SOFT ENOUGH TO SPREAD THINLY AND EVENLY WITH A KNIFE BLADE OR A SPATULA.**
2. **THE SPREAD MUST COVER ALL FOUR CORNERS OF THE BREAD. THE PERSON EATING SHOULD FIND SOMETHING BESIDES BREAD IN EVERY BITE.**
3. **THE SPREAD SHOULD BE RICH, MOIST AND OF SUITABLE FLAVOR FOR THE FILLING.**
4. **Flavored butter, margarine or cream cheese spread should be soft and plastic.**

TYPES

Spreads used for sandwiches vary from the simple to the complex; however, the simple ones are most often used.

Mayonnaise is the most commonly used spread. It is often preferred to butter, but does not protect the bread from moisture as well as butter. Mayonnaise used as a spread should be thick.

Butter or *margarine* is softened and whipped with a spoon or spatula until creamy when it is to be used as a spread. This allows for better spreadability and greater volume.

It should be noted that flavored mayonnaise and butters should be explored to the fullest. Both are excellent mediums for the addition to a sandwich of other subtle flavors such as chervil, tarragon, basil, thyme or violet mayonnaise or butter. A lemon, lime or pineapple butter or mayonnaise will bring a slightly fruit or acid taste to the product. It is also a good way to introduce a limited taste of an item such as sardines, shrimp or lobster.

Cheese spreads such as cream cheese or processed cheese spreads bring an increased richness of flavor and texture to a sandwich.

Peanut butter and other *nut butters* may act as a filler themselves or add an interesting taste when combined with other fillings.

Cooked bean spreads are used for some regional type sandwiches.

A variety of other types of spreads are regularly used in sandwich preparation including: *mustards, tartar sauce* and *ketchup*. These do not create as effective a moisture barrier as mayonnaise or butter, but are valued for the manner in which they complement various fillings. It is also possible to combine various condiments to create interesting flavor variations.

STORAGE AND HANDLING

All spreads should be stored at proper temperatures to prevent microbial growth. The temperature will vary from one to another; however, when in doubt what temperature is best, store under refrigeration. Mayonnaise, in particular, is a potentially hazardous product due to the high egg content. Once opened it should be kept under refrigeration and items prepared with it should also be refrigerated.

METHOD OF PREPARATION

The preparation of a quality sandwich is more than the placing of a piece of meat between two pieces of bread. It is the bringing together of a number of components in a manner that will allow them to meld in the perfect balance of temperature, flavor, texture and appearance. As with everything you prepare in the kitchen, mise en place is a key to your success in this endeavor.

Normally a sandwich has to be served as quickly as possible. Speed is the main reason for the popularity of the sandwich. In order for there to be speed, there has to be proper mise en place. Speed cannot be allowed to undermine good sanitation. Ingredients must be kept cold and protected at all times.

Portion control of the sandwich components can aid in the speed and sanitation aspects of sandwich making. Meats, cheeses and fillings which are pre-portioned can be individually wrapped. This makes it possible to remove only what is needed from refrigeration. It also makes it possible to assemble a wide variety of sandwiches quickly and easily.

SETTING UP FOR PRODUCTION

When setting up for production of sandwiches you must consider four major factors:

1. A GREAT DEAL OF HAND WORK IS INVOLVED IN SANDWICH MAKING. THEREFORE WORK FLOW MUST BE SMOOTH AND EASY.
2. WHAT TYPE OF EQUIPMENT DO YOU HAVE AVAILABLE FOR USE IN THE SET UP?

TOOLS AND EQUIPMENT NEEDED FOR SANDWICH PRODUCTION

A. REFRIGERATION
  1. REACH-IN CLOSE BY WITH ALL PRIMARY INGREDIENTS
  2. REFRIGERATED TABLE WITH DRAWERS -- COLD VERSION OF STEAM TABLE -- EXCELLENT TOOL
B. HAND TOOLS
  1. VARIETY OF SPATULAS
  2. VARIETY OF SPREADS
  3. KNIVES
    A. PARING KNIFE
    B. HAM SLICER
    C. FRENCH KNIFE
    D. SERRATED KNIFE
  4. VARIETY OF SPOONS
  5. VARIETY OF SCOOPS
C. POWER TOOLS
  1. MEAT SLICER
  2. AUTOMATIC TOASTER
  3. FOOD CHOPPER AND GRINDER
D. MIXING BOWLS
E. MEASURING DEVICES -- SCALES, SCOOPS
F. CUTTING BOARDS
G. HOLDING CONTAINERS
H. PLASTIC WRAP
I. COOKING EQUIPMENT
  1. GRIDDLES
  2. GRILLS
  3. BROILER
J. LONG TABLE FOR ASSEMBLY

Figure 6

---

3. WHAT ARE THE INGREDIENTS THAT WILL BE NEEDED?
4. HOW COMPLEX ARE THE SANDWICHES BEING PREPARED?

GUIDELINES FOR PROPER MISE EN PLACE

Mise en place is everything in its place, ready for use when needed. This is incredibly important in sandwich preparation, where you are usually dealing with a limited amount of space. Everything has to be convenient, within easy reach. The set-up needs to follow a logical progression of steps in the production of the sandwich.

Tools (These are listed in Figure Six.) and materials needed should follow the sequence of production flow. In order for assembly to require as little time as possible as much pre-preparation of ingredients as possible should be done. This includes:

1. SLICE MEATS AND CHEESES AHEAD, STACKING AND WRAPPING THEM NEATLY.

2. MIX MAYONNAISE BASED SALADS AHEAD AND STORE IN AIRTIGHT CONTAINERS UNDER REFRIGERATION.

3. GATHER AND PREPARE SECONDARY FILLINGS IN ADVANCE. ORGANIZE IN SET UP TABLE IN ORDER OF USE.

4. PREPARE SPREADS AND STORE IN CONTAINERS UNDER REFRIGERATION.

Once prepared, the ingredients should be arranged by order of need during assembly. This will increase the efficiency with which the assembly can take place. Once the sandwich is assembled, it should be served immediately. If the sandwich is not to be served immediately it should be tightly wrapped and properly stored. Sandwiches lose quality quickly if not wrapped.

PRODUCTION OF QUANTITY SANDWICHES

To prepare sandwiches in quantity requires good pre-preparation and planning. The steps are as follows:

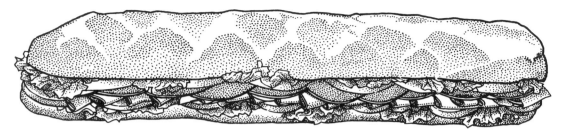

A sandwich of grand proportion – The Hero

1. PREPARE AND ASSEMBLE ALL THE NECESSARY INGREDIENTS.
2. GATHER ALL THE NECESSARY EQUIPMENT.
3. ARRANGE THE BREAD SLICES IN ROWS ON A LONG TABLE.
4. SPREAD EACH SLICE OF BREAD WITH THE CHOSEN SPREAD.
5. PLACE THE FILLINGS EVENLY AND NEATLY ON ALTERNATE SLICES OF THE BREAD.
6. TOP THE FILLED SIDE OF THE BREAD WITH THE ALTERNATE SIDE.
7. STACK TWO OR THREE SANDWICHES AND CUT THEM WITH A SHARP KNIFE
8. TO HOLD FOR FUTURE SERVICE:
   A. WRAP EACH SANDWICH WITH A PLASTIC OR WAXED PAPER SANDWICH BAG.
   B. AN ALTERNATE METHOD OF STORAGE IS TO PLACE THE SANDWICHES IN STORE PANS, THEN COVER TIGHTLY AND COVER WITH A CLEAN DAMP CLOTH. THE TOWEL MUST NOT DIRECTLY TOUCH THE SANDWICHES.
9. REFRIGERATE THE SANDWICHES UNTIL SERVICE.

PRESENTATION AND LAY-OUT

The basics of good presentation are the key to good sandwich presentation. The bread, filling and garnish should have good color and fresh appearance. The garnish should complement, not overpower, the sandwich. It should, however, enhance and improve the sandwich. In other words, it should have purpose other than just looks. Every effort should be made to present sandwiches which are evenly and smoothly cut. The sandwich should be easy to handle and should hold together well. Plates or containers used for pre-

---

NOTES ON MAKING A QUALITY SANDWICH

1. WHEN BUTTER OR MARGARINE IS MELTED AND USED, OR WHEN IT IS SOFTENED WITH ADDED MILK, THE DANGER OF IT (OR MOISTURE FROM THE FILLING) SOAKING THE BREAD IS INCREASED.
2. FRESH BREAD MUST BE CUT WITH A VERY SHARP OR SERRATED KNIFE TO PREVENT SMASHING IT.
3. DAY-OLD BREAD IS EASIER TO CUT BUT ONLY ACCEPTABLE FOR CERTAIN FUNCTIONS.
4. BREAD BEING USED TO MAKE TOAST MUST BE OF A CONSISTENT SLICE THICKNESS.
5. TOAST MUST BE EVENLY BROWNED.
6. WHITE BREAD IS OFTEN USED FOR SANDWICHES BECAUSE ITS NEUTRAL FLAVOR IS EASILY ADAPTABLE.
7. MEAT USED FOR THE MAIN FILLING MUST BE THOROUGHLY CHILLED BEFORE SLICING, UNLESS THE SANDWICH IS TO BE SERVED HOT.
8. EXCESSIVE USE OF BITTER, SWEET, TART, HARSH OR BLAND FLAVORS SHOULD BE AVOIDED.

Figure 7

sentation should be of a suitable size and type for the sandwich.

NUTRITION TIPS

The sandwich, like the salad, has become an American institution. People are seeking lighter food, reasonable prices and instant service. Although this sounds like the 1990's, this statement was made by Edgewater in the late 1920's. It may be true that the more things change the more they actually remain the same.

The sandwich is not always considered in the same nutritional breath as the salad. Yet it actually packs a greater nutritional punch. The sandwich can satisfy an appetite as well as serve as a complete meal with generally fewer calories. The meat portion in a sandwich would typically be between 1-1/2 to 3 oz. This is well below the American Heart Association guidelines to limit protein intake from meat, fish or poultry to four to six ounces per day.

If one remains true to the primary concept entered at the beginning of this chapter, it is really quite simple to take lower caloric and fat content ingredients and turn them into a magnificent sandwich. A balance of textures, temperatures and flavors that are properly wedded create an edible joy.

Is there really a great loss if Dijon mustard is used instead of mayonnaise or butter? Have we lost the battle when we substitute turkey pastrami and reduced fat and cholesterol Swiss for corned beef and Swiss? A lower fat sandwich can be made just as beautiful and delicious as the old standards. All that is required is the effort.

Really, there is not a massive amount of change or restructuring necessary for the sandwich to be "heart healthy." It is a complete meal providing complex carbohydrates, sufficient protein and substantial pleasure. America embraced this food initially for speed and portability, but may end up with a nutritional super nova that has the potential to be a culinary masterpiece.

REVIEW QUESTIONS

1. What are the three basic types of ingredients in a sandwich?
2. When did sandwiches become really popular?
3. List the components of the sandwich and their function.
4. What are the major classifications of sandwiches?
5. The sandwich should be a balance of what elements?
6. List the steps for proper mis en place of a sandwich station.
7. What types of tools and equipment are needed for sandwich production?
8. Discuss what makes a quality sandwich.
9. Discuss the nutritional value of a sandwich.
10. List three reasons why sandwiches are a popular food item.

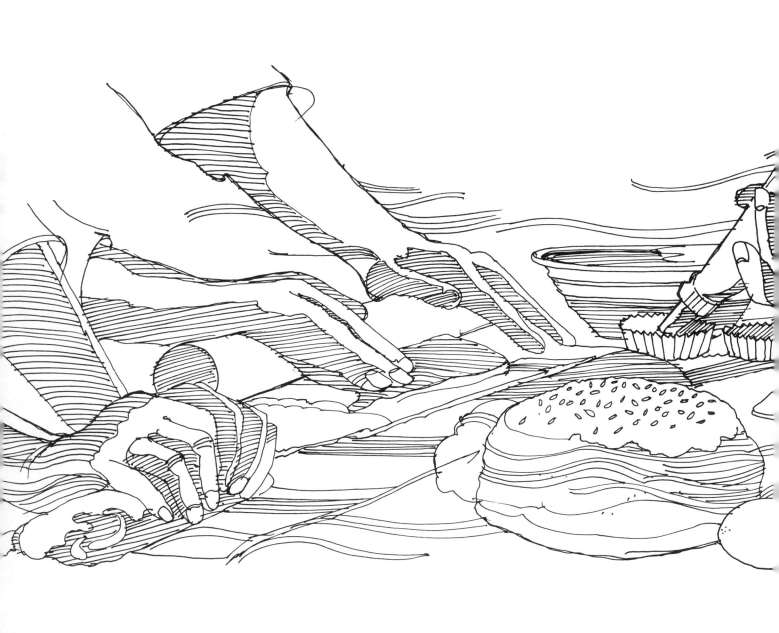

Section V
Baking

Principles of Baking

Yeast Bread & Rolls

Quick Breads

Pastry Dough

Fillings

Cakes

Frostings & Toppings

Basic Decorative Items

Sorbet, Ice Cream
  & Frozen Desserts

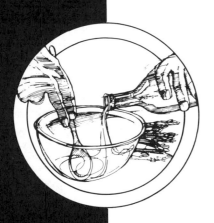

- **To discuss the historical progression leading to modern baking.**
- **To introduce baking as an art and science.**
- **To discuss ingredients and their function in the baking process.**
- **To explain temperature as a tool of the baker.**
- **To define key baking terms.**

Baking

HISTORY OF BAKING: THE SHORT VERSION

Thorough discussion of the origins of any type of food preparation leads to an investigation of the development of agriculture across the ages. This is particularly true of baking. There is no doubt that baking has always been and will continue to be one of the most important and colorful areas of culinary development. The ties of baking to agriculture lie in its quest for improved textures and refined flavors of baked goods as well as other confectioneries. The organized production of wheat by the Egyptians is considered by most historians to be the true beginning of the breads which are produced today. While it is true that the first successful bread baking is normally attributed to Asia, it was the gradual development of a better quality domestic wheat and improved harvesting and milling methods which allowed the preparation of bread to progress in the fertile valley of the Nile.

Many centuries after the Egyptians, about 400 B.C., the Greeks were preparing more than fifty different kinds of bread. All of these were being baked in a closed oven. The Romans combined the Greek and Egyptian developments in bread baking with their own improvements to begin producing bread on a large scale. This ability to mass produce bread became an asset to the Roman legions in their constant campaigns and subsequent victories. Bread was carried in large quantities as protection against an uncertain food supply in the unconquered regions of the world that would eventually become part of the Empire.

It was during the reigns of the emperors Augustus and Julius Caesar (100-44 B.C.) that public bake shops began to be established in the cities of the Empire. The owners of the bakeshops were, for the most part, prominent politicians or retired army tribunes who were able to employ slave labor. These slaves came, by virtue of Roman dominance and perseverance of the empire, from all parts of the world. The result of this blend of people from different countries and regions was an inevitable exchange of ideas and methods of culinary preparation leading to the further development of baking. This evolution was stimulated by the creation of brick ovens and mechanical means for milling flour.

The restless, demanding population of Rome was additional impetus to this development. Romans, particularly the elite, were spending a rapidly increasing amount of time and money on feasting. The sumptuous banquets lasted for days, sometimes weeks. In an attempt to satisfy the insatiable appetites of the corrupt Roman society, pastries of various kinds were created. This rush to meet the demand for the new and different resulted in many items we still make today and others which reflected the frenzied search for unusual food. These new creations, both mundane

and bizarre, were sold to the spectators during the games in the colosseum. These sweet treats were hawked by vendors much the same as popcorn and hot dogs are sold at today's football games; however, the spectators in Rome enjoyed them while watching gladiators fight to the death against both man and beast.

It was during this time of opulence and perversity, while the Roman legions and their civilization spread throughout Europe, the Middle East and North Africa, that the new profession of baking was born. Honorific titles and social status were given to members of the profession and their value to the growth and protection of the empire was acknowledged. The knowledge of baking was growing through experimentation and the influx of information from the new territories that were conquered. All of this gave birth to a new and thriving industry, baking. However, with the slow but inevitable disintegration and collapse of the Roman Empire, the new baking industry also collapsed.

Knowledge, the true legacy of Rome, which had developed was preserved in monasteries, the intellectual storehouses of Europe. The temporarily lost art of baking was practiced mainly by monks who kept their baking knowledge a well-guarded secret for many years. This reticence was encouraged by the feudal barons who gave them a monopoly on making and selling bread. These lords were pleased to accept the bread of the monks in lieu of taxes.

This was the situation at the beginning of the 13th century, when Phillip II of France granted bakers the right to build their own ovens. This movement by Phillip against the power of the nobles and the church caused an eventual division and diffusion of power resulting in the incorporation of the **PATISSIER DUBLAYERS** of Paris in 1270. These were the pastry and bread specialists, and, with a guild incorporating both, professional baking was once more firmly entrenched. The industry continued with only minor change until the discovery of America and the influx of new ingredients. When the export of sugar, in particular, became steady from the Americas, it was as if lighting had struck the pastry trays and ovens of Europe. Up until this time, honey had been the only sweetening agent. With the availability of sugar and, ah yes, another bit of magic from the Americas, *cocoa*, there was no limit to the pastry chef's art.

In 1675, this art was given another boost when a Sicilian pastry cook by the name of Procopio went to Paris and opened the first ice cream parlor. This treat, which had been enjoyed only by the rulers of nations and empires, was such a success that within five years another two hundred parlors had joined the first. Paris was mad for the cold sweetness. This success gave rise to Dublayers who roamed the streets of Paris selling the galettes and sweet breads both early in the morning and late at night. However, in the 18th century a citizen by the name of Cartouche organized a gang of outlaws who, disguised as Dublayers, robbed and murdered people. In 1721, after Cartouche's arrest, evening and night trading was stopped to protect good citizens from other brigands who might attempt to imitate the infamous Cartouche. As a result of this disruption of free enterprise, Dublayers became scarce. Many of them, unable to make a living independently, went into the service of aristocrats.

The distinction between pastry cook and baker began to become more certain at this time. Bakers and pastry makers separated generally because of arguments about proper oven temperatures. Since bread requires a much stronger heat than delicate pastries, their respective products were not compatible. In 1790, the first school of baking opened its doors in Paris. The school was created to help sustain the critically short food supply of France. It was not, however, until the French Revolution of 1789 that the pastry chef was given a real future. The revolution ruined the royal class and freed their servants, among whom were the chefs of these aristocrats. The freedom was suddenly present for these masters of the culinary arts to offer their knowledge and talent to the public. It was now that the world would see the art of which the pastry chef was capable! Among these new and free men was the maitre Antoine Careme. This brilliant individual, whose delicate creations of sugar and spectacular desserts were monuments to his ability and artistry, catapulted not just himself, but all pastry chefs to a seat of honor.

Urbain Dubois, pastry chef to the czar of Russia, was another whose skill helped to elevate the status of the pastry chef. His treatise on pastries and desserts is still valuable and inspiring today. The work of pastry chefs such as Jules and Julien Gouffe, whose pastry shop in Faubourg St. Honore became a meeting place for gourmets, helped to make the patisserie an indispensible part of French life. At last, other countries began to emulate the French. Baking schools opened on an international basis precipitating an exchange of trade secrets and continued advancement in the preparation of pastries and the baking of bread. This tradition of growth and development is the heritage of the modern baker and pastry chef. It is a field based solidly on history which must acknowledge the baker and pastry chef as scientists as well as artists and, at all times, true professionals.

THE ART & SCIENCE OF BAKING

"Bringing together a balanced quantity of various ingredients in a proper form." This is a definition of the art and science of baking. When you mix or blend many dry ingredients, liquids and leavenings together and expose the mixture to heat, a variety of actions combine as one unit. For example, butter and sugar melt; eggs coagulate; liquid makes steam; flour and starches start swelling; baking powder, baking soda, and yeast form gasses. Always remember, whatever the condition of the finished product, it is the result of the ingredients which the baker combined.

It is very important that the aspiring baker learn the performance of each ingredient used in the preparation of fillings, icings, toppings, creams and doughs. Always ask yourself the question: How can I make a better product? In the preparation of quality baked goods many things can go wrong. It is important to pay attention and follow the directions of a formula step by step. When something goes wrong, you must always find your mistake or you will repeat it. The mistake must become an opportunity to learn, improve and become more professional. It is this striving to correct errors and improve your ability to reproduce a desired product that will allow continued success for the culinarian.

INGREDIENTS AND THEIR FUNCTION

As previously stated, it is the various ingredients and how they perform that determines what type of product results from the labor of the baker. The ingredients discussed here are grouped under the headings of fats and oils; sugars and sweetners; leavening agents; flours; eggs; dairy products; spices, and chocolate. It is not possible to discuss every possible ingredient which the baker may find it necessary to use. What is offered here is a discussion of the more important and common ones. The reader will find that many of these items have been discussed elsewhere in this text in relation to other types of preparation. In baking, the function of a food item often varies somewhat from the function it may serve in other types of preparation.

FATS AND OILS

Lard: The fat of hogs has a unique flavor and makes a flaky pie crust.

Butter: Fresh butter consists of 80 to 82 percent butterfat, 13 to 15 percent water, and three to five percent milk solids. It is available salted or unsalted. It is considered irreplaceable by most bakers for the quality of its flavor.

Margarine: This product, made from a variety of vegetable and animal fats, is composed of 80 to 82 percent fat, 13 to 15 percent water and three to five percent milk solids plus salt, color and flavor. It is a shortening often used to replace butter. It must be remembered that it does have different flavor and melting properties.

Vegetable Shortening: (Specialty Food Fats) These are derived from nuts, seeds and grains. Many refining companies produce a complete line of specialty food fats. Whether your need is for whipped toppings, cake batters or doughs, there is a specialty shortening designed for the job. These shortenings are available as regular or plain, with an emulsifier or with a stabilizer for a higher or lower melting point. These shortenings have been developed to gain greater adaptability of products, improved shelf life, reduced cost and greater stability. The addition of an emulsifier, monoglycerides or lecithin, allows the formation and holding of an oil in water emulsion. The addition of stabilizers increases the body of the emulsion and prevents syneresis, water separation. It is the emulsified shortenings, which contain these emulsifiers and stabilizers that allow the preparation of high ratio cakes. These cakes have a fluffier, finer texture and lighter color because of the higher percentage of sugar in the mix. The emulsified shortening makes it possible to suspend the sugars for the finer product.

Oil: It is most often used in chiffon cakes, quick breads, breads and soft roll doughs. It is also used for deep-frying doughnuts and other pastries.

The cooking, chemical and nutritional qualities of fat and oil is discussed more fully in Chapter 7.

SUGARS AND SWEETENERS

Granulated Sugar: This sugar has been refined into crystals from either sugar cane or sugar beets. Superfine granulated sugar is preferred in baking because of its ability to dissolve faster in cake batters and other mixtures. It is often used for making meringues.

Powdered Sugar: This sugar is also known as confectioner's sugar. It has a very fine texture, the same as flour, and must always be sifted before adding to other ingredients. It should always be stored in an airtight container.

Raw Sugar: Raw sugar is less refined than other sugars, having a coarse lumpy texture. It has not been bleached and so retains its light brown to blond color.

Brown Sugar: Brown sugars are available in light and dark colors. The higher the percentage of molasses and other solids, the darker in color and more intense in flavor. It should be stored in an airtight container. To keep brown sugar soft, place a sliced apple or potato in an open plastic bag inside the container with the brown sugar.

Granulated Brown Sugar: Granulated brown sugar is not compact like brown sugar. Moisture is removed during the processing and refining, allowing the granulation. It is not possible to replace brown sugar with granulated brown sugar, because of the difference in moisture content The resulting product will have a different texture. It is used most often as a topping for pancakes and fruits.

Molasses: This is a thick, brownish liquid byproduct derived from the refining of granulated sugar. The lighter the color, the sweeter the molasses.

Maple Sugar: Maple sugar is refined maple sap and has a rich, wonderful flavor. It is a highly prized product which is very expensive. Maple sugar is a great topping for Danish pastries and special desserts and cakes.

Maple Syrup: Maple syrup is reduced maple sap. It will darken with age but retain its flavor. It is best stored under refrigeration.

Corn Syrups: Corn syrups are available with varying textures, intensities and flavors. It is used in cakes, icings, fruit fillings or toppings. The formula being used will indicate the type of corn syrup needed.

LEAVENING AGENTS

Baking Soda: Baking soda acts a leavening agent when mixed with an acid such as sour cream, sour milk, buttermilk, molasses or citrus juice. The chemical reaction of the leavening agent and acid produces gases which make the mixture rise. Baking soda is mainly used in cakes using cocoa powder or chocolate.

Baking Powder: There are three basic types of baking powder. *Double action* baking powder releases 1/3 of its carbon dioxide at room temperature and the rest during baking. *Tartrate* baking powder reacts quicker, as soon as liquid is added. *Phosphate* baking powder is slower and only heat releases its gases.

Yeast: This is a tiny living fungus which thrives on sweetness, warmth and moisture. Yeast releases gases that make bread dough rise, lightening the bread. Given sufficient time, yeast will not only make dough rise, it will also work on the gluten in the flour to give it flavor as well as texture. The primary key to effective use of yeast is control of temperature. Compressed, fresh yeast, should be dissolved in 100°-105° F milk or water. Dry yeast should be dissolved in 110°-115° F milk or water. When using the newer types of instant yeasts, follow the manufacturer's directions.

FLOURS

"Wheat contains large amounts of gluten. Gluten is the elastic, sticky, tough substance formed from the insoluble proteins of wheat flour during dough development. It is the gluten which allows expansion of air cells within the dough as it warms. This is essential to a leavened product. Consequently, wheat makes better bread than other grains. The only other grain which contains appreciable amounts of gluten is rye." This is an excerpt from Chapter 13 of this text. Flour and other cereal grain products are discussed at length in that chapter. The types listed here are those most commonly used in the bakery and pastry shop.

Cake Flour: This is selected soft wheat flour which is very finely milled. Cake flour contains more starch and less gluten than a hard wheat bread flour. It is more expensive than all-purpose flour. It makes it possible to produce a cake with a lighter smoother texture.

All-Purpose: This is a mixture or blend of hard and soft wheat flour. This type of flour is usually used in home baking because of its versatility. It can be used for cake baking and all types of soft doughs.

Bread Flour: Bread flour is made from hard wheat. It has a high gluten content and is generally used in hard rolls and bread dough. It may be used in combination with all-purpose flour in Danish or sweet doughs.

Pastry Flour: It is made from soft wheat but is not as finely milled as cake flour.

Cornmeal: It is coarsely ground kernels of corn and is available in white or yellow color.

Whole Wheat: As the name indicates, this flour contains all the ingredients of the cleaned whole-wheat grain.

EGGS

Eggs, frozen or fresh, are used in large quantities in baking. There is nothing better in taste and performance than a fresh egg. Eggs used in cakes and souffles serve as leavening agents; in sauces and custards as thickening agents, and in batters and doughs as a binding agent when they coagulate.

The egg consists of the yolk and the white. The yolk is high in fat, protein and an emulsifier called lecithin. The yolk is valued by the baker for the rich flavor and body which it contributes to the baked product. The white is primarily composed of albumin protein which is valued for its ability to act as a binder and its ability to hold air to create light products.

One of the forms in which egg whites are often used by the baker is beaten. The manner in which the egg whites are to be used in the formula determines what amount of air is incorporated into them. There are three stages of beaten egg white.

The first stage (soft peak) is when air is added to the egg whites through the beating process until they become fluffy and creamy. (This process is discussed fully in Chapter 9.) If the recipe calls for sugar, this is the point at which it should be gradually added. The second stage (glossy peak) is the beating of the egg whites until they form glossy peaks when the beater is lifted from the bowl. Egg whites at this stage hold their shape and are stiff but not dry. This stage is best for egg whites that are to be folded into a soft batter, chiffon pies, mousses, souffles, puddings, chiffon cakes and similar items. To fold beaten egg whites into a batter, pile all whites on top of the batter at once and proceed to blend gently. Cut down to the bottom of the mixture and then return in an upward motion until a perfect blending is achieved. Do not overmix. Your aim is to incorporate the air captured in the beaten egg whites. If you overfold or overmix, the tiny air pockets will be flattened.

Third stage (stiff peak) is any continued beating after the second stage. The result is stiffer, larger peaks. This stage is generally used for meringue, pie toppings, frostings and similar items. Continued beating in excess of the third stage merely yields a dry, useless egg white. Any further addition of sugar or other products into the beaten egg whites should be done gently and carefully. Fold ingredients into the egg whites with a large spatula to avoid breaking the fragile air cells which have been beaten into the whites. The cooking properties and available forms of eggs are discussed more fully in Chapter 9.

MILK

Whole Milk: This milk that contains 3.5 percent butterfat and is used in baking for the rich flavor which it provides.

Low-Fat Milk: Low-fat milk contains one to two percent butterfat. When substituted for whole milk, it may be necessary to consider the change in fat content.

Skim Milk: This milk contains 0.1-0.5 percent butterfat, and is not a suitable replacement for whole milk.

Buttermilk: This is the product remaining after sweet or sour milk has been churned and the fat removed. It has a distinctive flavor.

Cultured Buttermilk: Cultured buttermilk is the soured product produced in the making of pasteurized skim milk after treatment with a suitable lactic acid bacteria culture. This product has a distinctive flavor, texture and high acid content.

Evaporated Milk: This is whole cow's milk from which 60 percent of the water has been removed. It is homogenized, pasteurized and sealed in cans.

Sweetened Condensed Milk: This product is produced by evaporating half of the water from the whole milk and adding sufficient quantities of cane or corn sugar to act as a preservative. It is then heated, cooled and canned. This is not a suitable replacement for other milk products due to its high sugar content.

Dry Whole Milk Solids: These are the remaining dry solids after all water has been removed from whole milk.

Yogurt: Yogurt is milk which has been fermented by the introduction of a bacterium.

Heavy Cream: This product contains 35 to 40 percent butterfat. There is little which replaces the richness of heavy cream.

Light Cream: This product contains less than 30 percent butterfat.

All fresh milk and cheese products must be kept under refrigeration. It should be remembered that liquid milk products are susceptible to odors and flavors and so should be stored in tight containers. Dairy products are discussed in greater detail in Chapter 8.

SPICES

Allspice

Allspice: The flavor of this item compares to a blend of cinnamon, nutmeg and cloves. It comes from the West Indies and is used in cakes, pies and cookies.

Anise: This is a tiny oval seed of the parsley family. It has a licorice taste. It comes from Spain, the Middle East and Mexico. It is used in pastries and cookies.

Caraway: This is a tiny oval seed widely distributed throughout the world. It is used in bread, rolls, cookies and a variety of other items.

Cinnamon: This is the oldest of all the spices. It is the bark of a tree that grows in Indonesia, India and China. It is widely used in desserts, pastries and cookies.

Cloves: These are the dried flower buds of a tropical tree of the myrtle family. It is used in cookies, puddings and a variety of other preparations.

Ginger: This is the dried root of a tropical plant native to India. It is used in cakes, pies, puddings and other preparations.

Mace: The husk of nutmeg is ground to a fine powder called mace and used primarily in sweet dough preparation.

Nutmeg: The aromatic seed of a plant originally from East Africa, it is used in numerous preparations including pies, cakes and cookies.

Poppy Seed: The tiny, round, blue-black seeds of the poppy plant are used in breads, rolls and cookies.

Sesame Seeds: These small white seeds, derived from the pods of a plant which grows in the Middle East and South America, are used for bread and cookies.

Effort should be made to purchase spices only in quantities which can used in a short period of time to ensure a fresh product which can deliver its full flavor. It is recommended that premium brand spices always be purchased. They should be stored in tightly covered containers at moderate temperatures to prevent loss of flavor. Spices should be measured accurately. An excess of any spice can become unpleasant and distasteful. Spices and other flavorings are discussed at length in Chapter 5.

CHOCOLATE

It is important that you know and understand a few facts concerning the composition of chocolate. It is made from roasted cocoa beans. The nibs or meat inside the beans are rich in cocoa butter. The heat created in the grinding process causes the cocoa bean to melt into a dark mass called *chocolate liquor*.

Dark Chocolate: The most versatile chocolates are the dark, sweetened varieties: *Bitter sweet*, *semi-sweet* and *sweet chocolate*. Varying amounts of sugar are added to the chocolate liquor to create the three types of chocolate.

Milk Chocolate: This chocolate contains more cocoa butter but less chocolate liquor compared with dark chocolate. It has a milder taste and a softer texture. It must contain 12 percent dry milk solids to meet government standards.

White Cocoa Butter Coating: White cocoa coating does not contain chocolate liquor. That is why it cannot be called chocolate. This popular coating has a sweet, very mild, milk chocolate flavor and is ideal for delicate desserts and decorative work.

Compound Coatings: This product is frequently confused with white cocoa butter coatings and real chocolate. It is a flavored and colored compound which contains no cocoa butter! It is a vegetable oil-based coating which cannot be considered chocolate. It often contains palm kernel oil, sugar, dry milk solids, lecithin, flavoring, cocoa and food coloring.

Cocoa Butter: This is the natural fat contained within the cocoa bean.

Unsweetened Chocolate: This is 100 percent chocolate liquor, also called bitter or baking chocolate.

Natural Cocoa Powder: This is the dry, pulverized and nearly defatted chocolate liquor.

Dutch Processed Cocoa: Cocoa powder of this type has been treated with alkalis.

Coverture: This term means "coating." It identifies the highest quality chocolates, those containing a large percentage of cocoa butter.

TEMPERATURE AND THE BAKER

The primary type of heat used by the baker is that indicated by the name, *dry heat*. It is the manipulation of heat which will often determine success or failure. There are three important guidelines to remember in the proper use of the oven. Do not crowd your items too close together in the oven; the air flow around your product is very important. Improper loading of the oven can cause hot and cold spots within the oven and therefore uneven baking. Always preheat the oven and check it for the proper temperature. It must be remembered that the temperature at which the thermostat is set may not necessarily be the temperature actually maintained within the oven. It pays to become familiar with the idiosyncrasies of the equipment with which you are working. A guide for the major temperature settings is shown in Figure One. These settings are for a standard oven. They would need to be lowered by approximately 50° for a convection oven.

KEY BAKING TERMS

The language of the baker and that of the rest of the kitchen have a common heritage and therefore many common word usages; however, there are also differences. Many of the terms used by the baker are the same as those of the rest of the kitchen, but they are defined differently. The novice culinarian must strive to readily interpret a term as it applies to baking. The list of terms given

OVEN TEMPERATURES

FAHRENHEIT*	CELSIUS*	DESCRIPTION
250°	120°	Very Slow
300°	150°	Slow
325°	165°	Moderately Slow
350°	180°	Moderate
375°	190°	Moderately Hot
400°	205°	Hot
450°	230°	Very Hot
500°	260°	Extremely Hot

*Temperatures are approximately equivalent.

Figure 1

KNEADING DOUGH

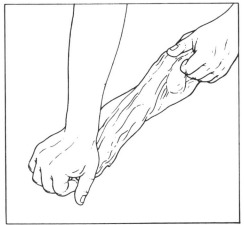 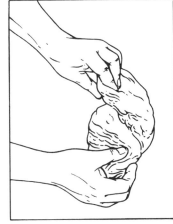

KNEADING DOUGH

1. *Dough held in one hand. Using heel of other hand push dough out with firm stroke. Work gently.*

2. *After each pull fold dough back and give a slight turn. Push, fold, turn for 10-15 minutes.*

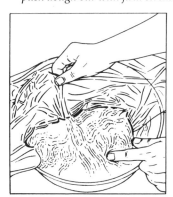 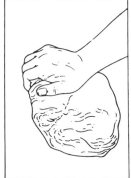 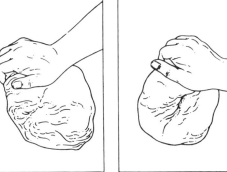

LETTING DOUGH RISE   **SHAPING FOR BAKING**

3. *Put dough in greased bowl, cover with damp cloth or plastic wrap. Set in warm place about 1 1/2 hours.*

4. *Push one corner of the dough with the heel of your hand and at the same time twist the corner back into the mass to turn it.*

5. *Push, turn and fold repeatedly until the dough is rounded.*

here is by no means complete. It is inclusive of the key terms necessary to begin mastery of the art and science of baking.

Batter: A mixture of ingredients and liquids that is thin enough to pour.

Blend: The incorporation of ingredients thoroughly, either by hand or with a machine.

Bloom: A discoloration on the surface of chocolate indicating the presence of unstable cocoa butter crystals.

Caramelize: To heat sugar slowly until it is melted and brown in color.

Chill: To cool a mixture until cold, but not frozen.

Chill Until Set: To cool a mixture until it gels.

Coat: To spread a surface with cream, flour, sugar or other substance.

Coddle: To poach gently in barely simmering liquid.

Conching: The working of the chocolate during processing which smooths out the rough edges of the sugar crystals to produce a very smooth chocolate. This process can take several days.

Combine: To mix ingredients thoroughly.

Crimp: To seal together (for example, the edges of a two crust pie) by making a decorative edge.

Cream Until Light: To mix and whip ingredients until smooth and with enough air incorporated to make a light mixture.

Cut In Shortening: Mixing shortening with dry ingredients using a pastry blender or the tips of your fingers.

Dissolve: Separating dry ingredients into particles for complete absorption in liquid.

Dot: Placing small pieces of butter, fat, cheese or other substances on top of dough or food.

Dough: A mixture of ingredients and liquids stiff enough to shape or knead with your hands.

Dust: To sprinkle lightly with flour, sugar or other substance.

Egg Wash: A mixture of egg or egg yolk with milk or water.

Flambé: To flame a dessert or other food by dousing with potable alcohol and setting alight. If the alcohol is warmed in advance, it will burn more readily.

Floured: Dusted with a thin layer of flour.

Flute: Making a decorative scalloped design on the edge of a pie crust or pastry.

Garnish: Decorating with whipped cream, buttercream, icings, fruits or other items for eye appeal.

Glaze: Applying a thick liquid over the surface of an item to give a final glossy sheen.

Hot Water Bath: The idea of preventing an item from coming into contact with direct heat. This can be done in the form of a double boiler or a bain marie, where there is a second container filled with hot water that insulates the basic mixture from direct heat which might cause scorching, curdling or burning.

Knead: Manipulating dough using the heel of your palms to achieve a smooth consistency.

Lecithin: An emulsifier used in many chocolates to reduce the viscosity

Lukewarm: Neither cool or warm, approximately body temperature.

Macerate: Tossing fruit in sugar, lemon, wine or liqueur to absorb flavors. (Same as marinate.)

Mask: Covering a surface with cream, icing, frosting, sauce or other substance.

Meringue: Egg whites and sugar beaten to a stiff consistency.

Mix: The combining of two or more ingredients.

Mold: Making an attractive shape by filling a decorative container. The product may then be baked, steamed, chilled or finished using other methods.

Pinch: A pinch is the amount you can hold between your thumb and forefinger.

Pipe: To squeeze a soft, smooth textured substance through a pastry tube, thus making a design or decoration.

Plump: Soaking dried fruit in liquid until it swells.

Poach: Simmering an item gently in syrup or liquid below the boiling point, while maintaining shape and texture.

Proof: To test yeast for potency before baking.

Refresh: To run cold water over something that has been boiled.

Roll Out: To spread the surface of a product with a rolling pin.

Scald: To scald milk is to bring it to a point when bubbles appear around the edges of the pan.

Set: Allowing an item to go from a soft or liquid state to a firmer, more solid state.

Sift: Removing possible lumps of dry ingredients through a strainer or sifter.

Soak: To soak a cake or ingredients in liquid or syrup until absorbed.

Stew: Long, slow cooking in liquid or syrup.

Sprinkle: Dusting dry ingredients onto the surface of food.

Stir: Mixing ingredients gently, using a circular motion with a spoon or whisk to ensure even cooking and to prevent sticking.

Tempering: A method used to establish proper crystallization of cocoa butter crystals in melted chocolate; to achieve a shiny, dark, hard-finished product.

Unmold: Turning a substance out of a mold so that the interior keeps its proper shape.

Whip: To lighten and increase the volume of a mixture by beating using a fork, whisk or electric beater.

Whisk: To beat with a whisk or whip until well mixed.

CONCLUSION

This brief introduction to the history, basic terms and concepts of baking has laid the foundation for what is to follow. It is intended only to be an introduction, a taste as it were of the true flavor of baking. When taken in concert with the chapters that follow, it is hoped that it will allow you, the reader, to not only feel confident in performing basic preparations in the area of baking, but to be motivated to investigate the vast body of skill and knowledge termed BAKING.

REVIEW QUESTIONS

1. What role did the Roman Empire play in the advancement of baking?
2. What was the importance of the discovery of the Americas in the advancement of baking?
3. Why are emulsifiers and stabilizers added to some fats and oils?
4. List four types of fats and oils used in baking.
5. List four types of sugars and sweeteners used in baking.
6. Discuss the three types of leavening agents.
7. What is the difference between cake flour and bread flour?
8. List and discuss the three stages of a beaten egg white.
9. List four types of dairy products used in baking.
10. Why is skim milk not a suitable substitute for whole milk or heavy cream?
11. List six spices and state their primary use in baking.
12. Discuss the process by which chocolate is made.
13. What is the difference between a chocolate, a coating and a compound?
14. List four products produced from the cocoa bean.
15. List six terms which have a different meaning for the baker than they do for the cook.

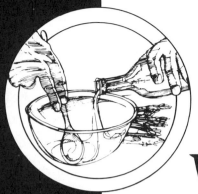

Chapter 31

Yeast Breads and Rolls

Chapter 34

CHAPTER OBJECTIVES

- To introduce and discuss the function of the primary ingredients used in yeast doughs.

- To define lean dough and rich dough.

- To introduce the straight dough method.

- To introduce the sponge dough method.

- To discuss the raising of the dough.

- To explain the process of scaling, rounding and benching.

- To discuss the proofing and baking of yeast doughs.

- To discuss the handling of baked breads.

There is a sense of mystery in watching basic ingredients like flour, water, sugar and salt respond to the power of yeast. The gluten stretches and expands as air pockets form. The sugars color with the heat and become golden. What was simply a spongy mass miraculously becomes a veritable work of art. A very edible work of art. A creation which makes the mouth water from the sight and aroma. From earliest times the human race has prized above almost all else the person who can produce good bread. Appropriately called the staff of life, good bread was so highly valued that only the bakers were excused from guard duty in Constantinople during the seige of the Fourth Crusade. This chapter is a discussion of controlling this bit of culinary magic. The master baker is thought of, by those who do not understand bread making, as a magician. However, the master baker knows that it is knowledge, understanding and experience which brings the ingredients together in a manner that allows both the ingredients and the baker to do their magic.

COMPONENTS & THEIR CONTRIBUTION TO THE WHOLE

Bread is composed of various ingredients, each playing a particular role and contributing to the flavor and texture of the finished product. To be familiar with and understand these ingredients is the first step in baking good bread. For the sake of clarity, each of these major components will be discussed individually in this chapter. It will be necessary for you, the reader, to draw upon the knowledge you have gained from previous chapters in this text. Those of greatest importance will be Chapters 5, 7, 8, 9 and 13.

YEAST

Yeast is a tiny living fungus. It thrives on sweetness, warmth and moisture. As the yeast eats, it excretes a gas of carbon dioxide and alcohol. It is this gas which causes the rise in the baked product. The alcohol evaporates during the baking process, yet helps in development of flavor in the bread. Because yeast is a living organism, it must be remembered that it can die. The baker's goal is to control the point of death of the yeast. The primary cause of death for yeast in the bakery is excessive heat.

Yeast will mature according to its own timetable. It should not be hurried to meet your schedule. Premature death of the yeast will cause your bread not to rise. Activity of the yeast should never be rushed, if it is to rise properly as well as developing good flavor and texture.

Yeast is available in two basic forms, compressed cakes or dry granular. Both, when properly used, are equally satisfactory. Compressed yeast must be stored in the refrigerator and will only keep for one to two weeks.

The advantage of dry yeast is that, under normal conditions, it has a shelf life of one year. Always watch for the expiration date on the package of yeast. Dry yeast should be stored in a cool and dry place. Manufacturers state that 1/4-ounce of dry yeast equals 3/5-ounce of compressed yeast.

Yeast, compressed or dry, is usually stirred into a small amount of warm liquid and allowed to stand for at least five minutes to dissolve. If you have any doubt about the freshness of the yeast, it should be proofed. This is a method for checking the life of the yeast. Dissolve it in 1/4-cup of warm water with one teaspoon of sugar and two tablespoons of flour. If the yeast is active, it will be spurred on by the sugar and fed by the flour. Within ten minutes it should begin to expand and foam. Proofing yeast before adding it to other ingredients will save time and expense.

The temperature of the liquid in which the yeast is dissolved is critical. Human beings do not grow and develop if the conditions are not right, and neither will yeast. If the temperature is too cold, the yeast will hibernate and not grow. If the temperature is too high, it will die. As with Goldilocks and the three bears, the temperature needs to be JUST RIGHT. The correct temperatures for both types of yeast are given in Figure One.

NOTE: There are new types of yeast being developed as this text is being written. Currently there are some available which do not require dissolving prior to use. These are mixed with the other ingredients of the dough. Some

WATER TEMPERATURE FOR YEAST	
COMPRESSED YEAST	$\pm$100° - 105°F
DRY YEAST	$\pm$105° - 115°F

Figure 1

function at lower and higher temperatures than those discussed here. As a culinarian, you must constantly be aware of the new products which become available. When using a new product with which you are not familiar, follow the manufacturer's directions. Find out all you can about a new product and then determine how it can help you in your operation.

YEAST FOODS/DOUGH CONDITIONERS

Do not be misled by the first name given to these products. They serve a far greater function than simply supplying food for yeast. Their major purposes are to condition the water and to assist in the proper fermentation of the dough. Improperly fermented dough will not rise properly. This is caused by improper generation of yeast and sugar interaction with the flour. It may rise too rapidly, not allowing proper development of the gluten. This can result in an overly soft texture. Or it may yield bread which has a strong, yeasty flavor and heavy texture.

Yeast foods contain three types of functional ingredients:

Ammonium salts supply yeast with the nitrogen they need for growth.

Calcium salts produce the correct amount of hardness in the dough water to firm the gluten.

Oxidizing agents result in a firmer, less sticky dough.

The use of yeast foods is determined by the strength of the flour and the fermentation period desired. These are products used mainly in large quantity bread and roll production. They help to give breads a better grain, texture and appearance. Yeast food must be used with caution. An excessive amount will produce inferior products which are low in volume and coarse in texture.

FLOUR

One of the most important ingredients in bread is flour. Wheat flour, with its rich protein called *gluten*, gives doughs their strength and elasticity. Gluten is capable of expanding greatly. This expansion creates a network of hundreds of little pockets. These pockets trap the gases produced by the yeast, which would otherwise escape.

As discussed in Chapter 13, whole-wheat flour contains all of the wheat kernel, including the bran and germ. All-purpose white flour is made from the inner part of the wheat kernel, known as the endosperm. It is the endosperm which yields the highest quantity of gluten. Bread dough formulas that use yeast must contain at least some white or whole wheat flour which provide gluten. Gluten rich wheat flour produces a good eating bread, except that it is lacking in fat. (Possibly this is why we spread bread with butter.)

The hard *winter wheat* flour used in bread making has the highest gluten content. This flour is also known as *winter patent* flour in many areas. The commonly used *hi-gluten*, or *bread* flour is high in gluten content, yet not as high as winter wheat flour. It is used in many kitchens for bread making and produces a good product. *All-purpose* flour was originally formulated to accommodate the home kitchen for all-around cooking. It is also widely used in both commercial and home baking. All-purpose flour produces a satisfactory loaf. The unbleached flours have more food value, yet do not produce as white a bread as the bleached variety.

Flours vary considerably and react in different ways. This makes it hard to specify the exact amount of flour needed in a bread recipe. Even the most reputable and dependable supplier of flour will have variations in the flour they sell from one time of year to another. The flour is affected by soil and weather conditions beyond the control of the grower, processor or supplier. It is best, when possible, to choose and consistently use one particular brand of flour. Most processors purchase from specified areas of the country and specify particular types of wheat in order to limit variations in the flour. Switching brands can require adjustment of formulas. For this reason, we suggest holding back the final cup of flour in the formula. This is then kneaded in only as necessary to gain the correct consistency.

There are special flours, such as rye, corn, barley, graham, soybean, rice and buckwheat, which are used in breads for variation of flavor and texture. Meals such as oat, corn, barley and rice are also used for this purpose. All of these products lack sufficient gluten content for the yeast to react effectively. For this reason they <u>must</u> be <u>used</u> <u>in</u> <u>combination</u> <u>with</u> <u>white</u> <u>or</u> <u>whole-wheat</u> <u>flour</u>. Bran, wheat germ, whole-wheat kernels and wheat berries will add both texture and nutrients to your bread. Stone-ground flours retain more of the germ and bran. They are more nutritious and give a coarser texture to your bread. With the growing health consciousness in the United States, you will need to consider use of more of these special flours in the future. The list of special flours and grains is lengthy, yet, as you become more experienced, you will want to seek them out and try them. For the master baker they are part of the magic!

LIQUID

It is the liquid in the dough which turns into steam during baking. This steam helps create the texture of the bread. Water, potato water, milk or even beer can be used as the liquid. Each of these will provide the moisture needed to create the dough and the steam. The difference in the breads will stem from the other components within the liquid.

An example is milk. Milk will produce a richer bread with a more tender crust, and less grainy taste. The natural fat content of the milk shortens and softens the strands of gluten and enriches the bread. The natural sugars in the milk also add to the richness.

The proportion of liquid to flour and yeast will vary greatly from formulation to formulation. The variation is caused by the composition of the flour used and the liquid. The proportions shown in Figure Two are intended only as a rule of thumb, not as an absolute.

SWEETENERS

Sugar makes the dough rise quickly and helps brown the crust. The baker should not assume that "if a little bit is good, then a whole lot is better." Sugar should be used sparingly. Too much sugar will inhibit the action of the yeast. It is always best to follow your formula carefully. Remember, baking is a science as well as an art. Though granulated sugar is the most commonly used sweetener, there are others which will add variety in flavor, texture and color. Honey, molasses, corn syrup or brown sugar can be used to sweeten bread, as can raisins and dates.

SALT

Salt has three primary functions in bread doughs. Its greatest function is the improvement of the bread's flavor. It adds its own characteristic flavor and enhances the flavors of the other ingredients in the bread.

The second function of salt in the

PROPORTION FOR LIQUID IN BREAD	
LIQUID	1#
YEAST	3/5 OZ COMPRESSED OR 1/4 OZ DRY
FLOUR	1# 8 OZ

Figure 2

dough has both positive and negative aspects. Salt has an inhibiting effect on the fermentation process of the yeast and other ingredients in the dough. This is a beneficial attribute when the temperatures used for proofing the bread are not well controlled. The salt reduces the gassing power of the yeast, allowing the development of a more uniform rise in the product. While in some situations the lessening of rise caused by salt may be helpful, when too much salt is used in the dough, the results will be disastrous. The amount of salt in the dough must be balanced to achieve proper fermentation of the dough. An excessive amount of salt will result in a bread which is dense, with an underdeveloped volume. Too little salt can yield a dough which has too much volume and a shape lacking uniformity. The best range of salt content in a dough is one and a half to four percent of the flour weight.

The third function of salt in the dough is the strengthening and tightening of the gluten. As the dough ferments, the proteolytic proteins (enzymes) in the flour begin to react with the gluten in the flour, restricting the gluten's formation. The formation of the gluten is critical to the texture and flavor of the bread. Salt inhibits the enzyme action, allowing the gluten to develop properly.

SHORTENING

Shortening is often added to enrich bread; however, it is not essential to any formula. Shortening does give flavor to the bread and make it tender. Breads made with shortening also keep longer and better. Again, the baker must use restraint when adding shortening to bread dough. Sometimes, when a dough is too rich with fat, the yeast may act slowly.

There are many fats which can be used in bread baking. Many people feel that the finest bread they ever ate was made by their mother on the farm during the Depression, using fine hog lard.

However, today, the preferred fats are vegetable shortening and fresh butter. Vegetable shortening gives a good, crisp texture to non-sweet breads. Many chefs prefer butter for rich, sweet doughs.

EGGS

Eggs are not required in the making of bread, yet they contribute many desirable characteristics. They provide richness, flavor and improve texture. A bread made with eggs has an improved keeping quality (longer shelf life). As discussed earlier, the qualities stem from the composition of the egg itself. Its fat and sugar content are the main components which improve bread. Eggs are best used in the production of sweet doughs.

METHODS OF PREPARATION

The formula (*recipe* in cook's language) is the basis for all bread making. The proper development of the formula itself is the first step to a good finished product. There are many good formulas readily available, or you may create your own. Whichever, once the formula is chosen it should be carefully followed.

There are many different formulas for bread and yeast-raised products. Some of these contain few or no enriching ingredients. These are called *lean dough*. Others have a high percentage of ingredients like eggs, fat and sugar. These are called *rich dough*. Figure Three discusses the difference between lean and rich dough. Whichever type of dough is being prepared, there are certain steps which will be used.

STRAIGHT DOUGH METHOD

Most small retail bakeries use the straight dough method. In this method the yeast is combined with a portion of the water. The remainder of the water, salt, sugar and non-fat dry milk is placed in a mixing bowl. The flour is then added, and the mixture is mixed for one minute. The yeast solution is then added, and the mixture is mixed

WHAT IS A LEAN DOUGH? WHAT IS A RICH DOUGH?

THERE ARE MANY DIFFERENT FORMULAS FOR BREAD, YEAST-RAISED PRODUCTS, CAKES AND ICINGS. SOME OF THESE FORMULAS CONTAIN FEW OR NO ENRICHING INGREDIENTS. THESE ARE TERMED *LEAN* DOUGHS, CAKES, ICINGS, ETC. OTHER FORMULAS HAVE A HIGH PERCENTAGE OF THESE ENRICHING INGREDIENTS: EGGS, BUTTER, FAT, SUGAR, CREAM, ETC. THESE ARE TERMED *RICH*. REDUCING OR INCREASING THE PERCENTAGES OF THE VARIOUS INGREDIENTS REDUCES OR MAGNIFIES THE CHARACTERISTICS THAT THEY CONTRIBUTE TO THE PRODUCT.

A DOUGH MADE FROM WATER, SALT, FLOUR AND YEAST IS A LEAN DOUGH USING LEAN INGREDIENTS. A DOUGH MADE WITH FLOUR, YEAST, MILK, CREAM, BUTTER, EGGS, SUGAR AND SALT IS A RICH DOUGH, CONTAINING A NUMBER OF ENRICHING INGREDIENTS. A BUTTER COOKIE USES RICHER INGREDIENTS THAN A PLAIN CRACKER.

THE MOST ACCURATE WAY TO DETERMINE THE LEAN AND RICH CHARACTERISTICS OF A FORMULA IS BY TRUE PERCENTAGE. WHAT PERCENTAGE OF THE RECIPE'S TOTAL INGREDIENTS DO THEY REPRESENT? THE FOLLOWING EXAMPLE IS GIVEN NOT AS A FORMULA BUT AS AN EXAMPLE OF USING THIS TECHNIQUE FOR DETERMINING WHETHER A FORMULA IS RICH OR LEAN.

LEAN DOUGH

INGREDIENT	LBS	OZS	PERCENT
FLOUR, BREAD	12		60
WATER	7	8	37.5
YEAST		4	1.25
SALT		4	1.25
TOTAL WEIGHT 20		TOTAL PERCENT	100

RICH DOUGH

INGREDIENT	LBS	OZS	PERCENT
FLOUR, BREAD	8		40
MILK	3		15
YEAST		8	2.5
SALT		4	1.25
BUTTER	4		20
SUGAR	2		10
EGGS	2	4	11.25
TOTAL WEIGHT 20		TOTAL PERCENT	100

THE RICH DOUGH CONTAINS 41.25 PERCENT ENRICHING INGREDIENTS IN COMPARISON TO THE LEAN DOUGH WHICH CONTAINS 0 PERCENT ENRICHING INGREDIENTS.

Figure 3

for one minute. The shortening is added last, and you mix for 10 to 15 minutes or until the dough is smooth and elastic.

At this point, two things need to be pointed out. First, the shortening is added last to prevent its interference with incorporation of the yeast and to help produce a good blend of all the ingredients. Secondly, the last mixing stage allows the gluten in the dough to stretch and develop. It must develop enough elasticity to allow the yeast to do its work later.

In making straight dough, after the dough has been mixed, it is customary to let the fermentation (*rising*) to proceed until the mass has expanded to nearly full capacity. This should be done before it has risen to the point where it begins to sag near the center of the dough. Once the dough has been punched, it is then folded. The cooler portion of the dough is folded toward the center and the warm portion is pulled up and over. This process equalizes the temperature of the dough, retarding the continued fast action of the yeast for a short period. The dough is now ready to be benched and formed.

GLUTEN MOLECULES

A gluten molecule has kinks in it.

When you knead bread dough the kinks are stretched out.

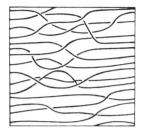

Gluten associations are formed throughout the dough providing a smooth, fine texture to the bread.

SPONGE DOUGH METHOD

Sponge dough is used extensively for large quantity bread production. It produces a very tightly textured, sponge bread. The sponge dough method is done in two stages.

A. The yeast is dissolved using the full amount of liquid. Then part of the sugar and flour are also added to this mixture. This combination is mixed to a thick batter or very soft dough. The mixture is covered and allowed to ferment until at least double in size.

B. The mixture is then punched. (This is the pushing of the dough/mixture down to release part of the carbon dioxide which has developed.) The remaining ingredients are added, making a uniform smooth dough. (There are several ways to ferment your dough. A long fermentation of five to six hours at a controlled temperature of 75°F or lower improves the flavor and texture of your final product greatly. As with the straight dough, this dough is punched and folded when fermentation is completed. It is then ready to bench and form.)

For both dough methods, control of fermentation is the key. Otherwise you can make a young or underripe dough, or an overripe old dough. There must be a proper balance of ingredients, mixing, temperature and time.

RAISING DOUGH

The dough should never be disturbed during the rising period. At that time the yeast is producing the little gas bubbles that stretch the gluten in the flour and make the dough expand. Most bakers test the dough to determine when it is ready, by pressing the dough lightly with the fingertips. When the finger is removed, the dough may recede slightly around the area pressed or the imprint made may simply close. If the imprint recedes slightly, the dough is ready to be punched and folded. If the imprint closes and the dough does not recede, it is not ready to be punched. When it is ready, the dough is punched down. This releases large quantities of carbon dioxide.

The time required for dough to rise will vary considerably, depending on a number of factors. These factors include the type of yeast, fat content and temperature. If you over-proof your dough, the bread may have a yeasty flavor and aroma. It may lack good flavor and texture or have a separation between the crumb and the crust. If your product has over-risen in the final phase, most likely it will sink (fall) in the oven. If you do not give your dough sufficient time to rise, the product will be too moist and heavy.

Always let your product rise to the desired bulk in a warm and humid place. The best environment is ± 80°F, away from drafts. Depress the raised dough with your fingers, and if the indentation remains, the dough has fully risen.

FORMING LOAVES

After the dough has developed properly, it is then benched and formed. Benching simply means the handling of the dough on the baker's table. There are three steps which lead to a properly formed loaf or roll. These are *scaling, rounding* and *make-up*. Benching must be done rapidly to prevent overfermenting the dough. Additional rise in the dough on the table can result in a poor finished product. If it is not possible to bench the dough rapidly enough to prevent further rise, a portion of the dough should be retarded. It can then be benched as time allows. Retarding the dough means the placement of it in a cooler place. This slows down the action of the yeast.

Scaling is the division of the dough into the size pieces needed. It is done twice in the benching of the dough. First, the dough is divided into large pieces to allow it to rest before final make-up. Secondly, it is divided into the size pieces needed for the final product. This is usually done by weight and is called scaling. Begin by cutting your dough with a baker's knife (metal scraper) into the size pieces needed. For the sizing of the final piece, you should weigh each piece on a scale to insure correct portioning. Once you have done this several times, it should be possible for you to estimate the size piece needed with a degree of accuracy; however, even the experienced baker should have a scale close at hand to spot check the weight of the pieces cut. As with all production in the kitchen, consistency is

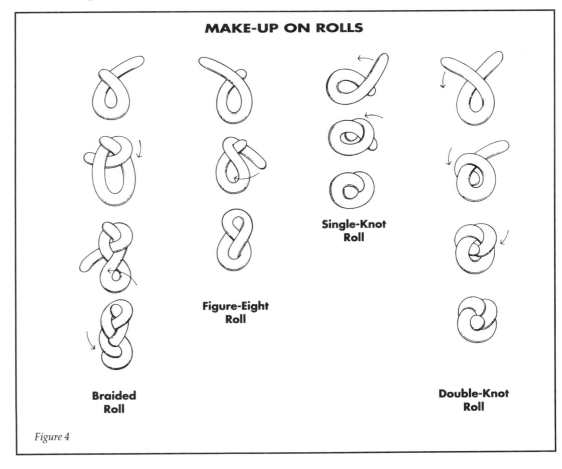

MAKE-UP ON ROLLS

Single-Knot Roll

Figure-Eight Roll

Braided Roll

Double-Knot Roll

Figure 4

important in bread baking. This includes the sizing (scaling) of loaves and rolls. Correct scaling of the final piece assures even cooking of the pans of bread and rolls.

Rounding is the preliminary step in shaping the loaf or roll. Each scaled piece of dough is shaped into a smooth, round ball. This is done by rolling the piece of dough between your two hands. Your hands will need to be slightly cupped to achieve the round shape. Press the dough gently down between your hands and rotate it a few times back and forth in a circular motion. The piece is then placed seam down on the table. It is then covered with a cloth to prevent formation of a crust. Let the pieces rest for 15-20 minutes. This allows the gluten to relax prior to final make-up. If the gluten is not allowed to relax, the final shape of the product will be distorted as the gluten relaxes. Proper make-up will yield an evenly balanced product. When not done properly, rolls begin to resemble footballs and basketballs with hernias.

You can produce many shapes and forms using a variety of make-up techniques. With any of these techniques, however, it is necessary to place the scaled and shaped piece of dough seam down on the baking sheet or bread pan. The piece must be properly molded to avoid splitting during the final proofing and baking. A piece with creases, cracks and seams in its surface will not proof or bake well. Your goal is a piece with a smooth, even surface.

Once the product has been made up, it is placed in the prepared pans (lined with parchment paper, oiled or sprayed with non-stick vegetable oil spray) in which it will bake. You are now ready to proof the final product.

PROOFING

Previously in this chapter we discussed proofing the yeast prior to mixing the bread dough. The proofing we will discuss here has a somewhat differ-

ent purpose. This proofing is done to allow the yeast one last time to inflate the formed piece with gas. The dough will adjust and relax itself in this final stage. The length of time for final proofing varies from 50 to 75 minutes. This standard applies when the proofing is done in a proofing box or room which is 90°F. Final proofing requires close attention to two things. First, is the temperature. We have already discussed proper temperatures for yeast activity. Second, is the function of humidity in the proofing process.

Relative humidity refers to the amount of moisture in the air. Air that is 100 percent humid will not take moisture from an object placed in it. At 100 percent humidity the air is not able to hold more moisture. If the air is less saturated and only contains 50 percent of its total moisture capacity, it will remove moisture from an object containing more than 50 percent moisture. What this has to do with you, the baker, is very simple. Raw dough, ready to be proofed, is high in moisture content. This moisture will be absorbed by the air unless the air is equally saturated by moisture. For this reason, to prevent drying of the product in proofing, the relative humidity of the proofing atmosphere should be 85 to 90 percent.

There are types of proofing chambers available today which have humidity settings. If you are working with one which does not have this feature, remember to set the air vents on closed and the water pan vents on open. The best proofing temperature and relative humidity will vary from one product to another. However, a general rule is a temperature of 90 to 95°F and 85 to 90 percent relative humidity.

NOTE: Loaves and rolls which have been proofed for baking are very tender. They must be handled gently when being transferred from the proofing cabinet to the oven. Rough handling can cause the item to fall. (A release of the trapped gases, similar to a balloon

OVEN TEMPERATURES FOR BREAD	
LEAN BREADS	385-420°F
RICH BREADS	350-400°F
FRENCH BREADS	415-465°F

Figure 5

bursting.) This will result in an unacceptable finished product.

BAKING

The actual baking of the product requires consideration of the desired finished product. What crust texture do you want your product to have? Hard crusted breads are baked with steam injected into the oven during the first part of baking. The amount of steam must be controllable to avoid excess amounts. Too much steam tends to produce a shiny, excessively tough crust. During the baking process, steam, whether injected or naturally created by the product, vaporizes at oven temperatures. As the moisture on the surface of the baked product vaporizes, it causes caramelization of sugars, starches and other ingredients. This provides the golden, crisp crust that is so highly valued in breads.

The oven temperature and time required to bake a loaf of bread or pan of rolls will vary depending on several factors. The primary factor in loaf bread is the size and shape of the loaf. If the loaf is large, the temperature of the oven must be regulated so the surface of the loaf will not burn before the interior of the loaf is baked. For a small loaf the temperature must be raised so the loaf will brown before the loaf is overbaked and dried out. The same is true for rolls.

The type of bread dough also affects the temperature and time required for proper baking. Rich dough formulas are usually baked at lower oven temperatures. This prevents excessive browning of the crust. Lean dough requires a longer baking time at higher temperatures. This

will result in a thick, hard crust. Extremely lean doughs, such as that for French breads, need even higher temperatures. Recommended temperatures for breads are shown in Figure Five.

WASHES

Most yeast products are brushed with a wash before baking. This is done to improve the finished appearance of the baked bread. The type of wash used will depend upon the intended use of the final product. The wash must be appropriate for the product it is being used on.

Water is often used for hard crusted breads, if no or little steam is available. This assists in the production of the browning and formation of the texture of the crust. It is applied immediately prior to placing the item in the oven.

Egg wash is also applied immediately before placing an item in the oven. This wash must be applied very evenly to prevent the item browning with streaks and highlights. The egg wash is mainly used for Danish, coffee cakes and soft rolls. Two types of egg wash may be used, whole egg or egg white. When using the whole egg the normal mixture is one egg to one cup of water. A wash prepared of egg whites only brings less cholesterol and fat to the finished product. The normal mixture is three egg whites to one cup of water.

Sugar-based glazes are applied after baking. They give the product a high shine and help to seal in moisture. Examples of these would be honey or sugar syrup glazes and fruit puree-based glazes, such as a thin apricot glaze on a Danish or other sweet dough product.

VARIETY IN BREAD BAKING

The principles of bread baking are the same for most types of bread. Do not be afraid to experiment and try new and different formulas; however, always remember to read the formula carefully and follow directions. A partial list of the bread varieties which are waiting for your magical touch are listed in Figure Six.

CURRENT TRENDS

Not every foodservice operation has the equipment, space or staff needed to produce bread from scratch. You, as a culinarian, should be aware of the variety of quality convenience products available. There are several companies which have developed and formulated a line of frozen bread and roll items. The selection is no longer limited to pre-baked frozen breads. These products are made from young bread dough that has been through only the first rise. The dough is cut into pieces appropriate for the intended final product and are individually quick frozen (IQF). The pieces are packed and then stored in holding freezers. Many of products require proofing before baking. These are called "proof & bake." There are frozen breads available which are pre-proofed and only require baking. For best results the manufacturer's directions should be followed.

Many will argue that these products do not deliver the quality of finished product that is made by a good baker from scratch; however, these products are a part of our industry. You should be aware of them as a possible answer to questions of space, time and staff expertise. When handled properly, many produce excellent finished products. It is up to you as the user to give them your personal signature by topping them with such items as sesame seeds or herb butter, as you determine the needs of your establishment.

STORAGE AND HANDLING

COOLING BAKED BREADS

Proper cooling is as important to the production of a good bread as is proper mixing. Once the bread or rolls are baked, they should be removed from the pan. The pans retain heat after removal from the oven. The result is what is termed *carry-over* cooking. The heat from the pans is transferred to the bread resulting in drying. A perfectly baked bread can be ruined by carry-over cooking.

After removal from the pan, place your bread in a cool area free from drafts. Breads will dry out more quickly if the air is either too warm or too dry.

Any bread is best served within eight hours of being baked; however, for longer storage, wrap your bread in a moisture-proof plastic bag. It is a popularly held belief that storing bread under refrigeration will extend its shelf life. While it is true that it will retard molding, even well-wrapped bread will undergo staling reactions much faster when refrigerated. Remember that

---

BREAD VARIETIES

RYE BREAD	WHOLE WHEAT BREAD	FRENCH BREAD
WHITE BREAD	CRACKED WHEAT BREAD	RAISIN BREAD
WATER BREAD	PUMPERNICKEL BREAD	GARLIC BREAD
BRIOCHE BREAD	GERMAN CARAWAY BREAD	CHEESE BREAD
OATMEAL BREAD	BRAN AND HONEY BREAD	HERB BREAD
CORNELL BREAD	RAISIN AND NUT BREAD	COLONIAL BREAD
GRAHAM BREAD	CHRISTMAS STOLLEN	SWEDISH BREAD

Figure 6

refrigeration works by the circulation of cold air. This circulation has the same effect as drafts when cooling bread. The circulating air removes moisture more rapidly from the bread. If it is necessary to store bread for longer periods of time, it is best to freeze them. Otherwise store your bread in a cool area of the kitchen or stock room. Molding is a problem with breads produced from scratch in the foodservice kitchen. These breads will not hold as long as the commercially produced breads. The breads produced at the large commercial bakeries have mold inhibitors and moisturizing agents added to them which extend their shelf life.

CONCLUSION

Bread baking is uniquely satisfying. It is an art and science involving patience, creativity and an intuitive feeling for the constantly changing texture of the dough. There is a sense of mystery in watching basic ingredients like flour, water, sugar and salt respond to the magical power of the yeast to lift and expand, maturing according to its own timetable, not yours. If you are baking your own bread, produce it in small quantities which can be used each day. Not only does this relieve the problem of waste due to drying and molding, it will also insure that your customers have the pleasure of eating freshly baked bread. This is truly the _magic_ in any great meal.

REVIEW QUESTIONS

1. What is _yeast?_
2. Discuss the handling of yeast in the making of bread.
3. List three types of yeast foods or dough conditioners.
4. What is the difference between hard and soft flour?
5. What is _gluten_ and why is gluten important in bread making?
7. Discuss the contributions of liquid, sweeteners, shortening, salt and eggs in bread making.
8. Discuss the straight and sponge dough methods of bread preparation.
9. What is raising the dough and how does it differ from proofing dough?
10. How can you tell when dough has fermented or developed fully?
11. Discuss the three steps in the forming of loaves and rolls.
12. What is the importance of consistent sizing of loaves and rolls?
13. What is relative humidity and how does it relate to bread baking?
14. List and discuss two types of washes used in bread baking.
15. Why are different temperatures used for lean dough and rich dough?
16. Why is temperature important in handling dough?
17. Where and how should bread be stored?

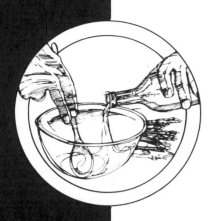

Chapter 32

CHAPTER OBJECTIVES

- **To introduce quick breads as a versatile culinary preparation.**

- **To delineate between pour batter, drop batter and dough.**

- **To discuss the ingredients used in making quick breads and their function.**

- **To introduce the mixing methods used in making quick breads.**

Quick Breads

Quick breads are valued for the ease and speed with which they can be made. They are made without yeast from doughs and batters. A quick bread does not have to rise (proof) before going into the oven. They rise quickly once they are in the oven. Baking powder, baking soda, beaten eggs and egg whites, or other combinations of leavening agents provide the steam, air and carbon dioxide gases to leaven the product. The quick breads have a cake-like appearance and a lighter texture than yeast bread and they are frequently embellished with fruits, nuts and other seasonings.

TYPES OF MIXTURES

Quick breads are grouped according to the type of mixture from which they are produced. The two main groupings are batter and dough. Batters are termed as either a *pour* batter or a *drop* batter. The amount of liquid in the mixture will determine the category in which the batter is classified.

Pour batters are thin enough to pour directly from your mixing bowl into the baking pan or onto a griddle. An example of a pour batter is griddle cakes.

Drop batters are thick enough to require spooning into your baking pan. Muffins are a good example of a drop batter.

The other main grouping for quick breads is comprised of those produced from dough. Dough is defined as a mixture which is stiff enough to roll out. This includes the soft dough, such as that used for baking powder biscuits, and the stiffer dough, such as that for what are termed cake doughnuts.

INGREDIENTS

Batters or doughs for quick breads are made with dry mixtures of flour, baking powder, baking soda, salt and sugar. Fats, eggs and liquid are used as needed to produce the type of item desired. As mentioned earlier there are a number of flavorings which can also be added to the mixture.

Flour of many different types can be used to make quick breads. Normally an all-purpose flour, or mixture of hard and soft wheat flour, is used. The hard wheat flours are rarely used in large concentration in quick breads. They contain too much gluten and produce a tough product. Quick breads normally should have more of a cake-type texture. This requires a softer flour.

The *liquid* used can be water, milk or other source of moisture. Your choice of liquid will have an effect on the flavor of the finished product. When water is the liquid used, it should be remembered that there is no additional flavor or richness gained. Non-fat dry milk solids are often used with the dry mixture and water as the liquid. This enhances the richness of the mixture without excessive expense.

Leavening in most quick breads is either baking powder or baking soda. You should be careful to scale baking powder accurately. Too much baking powder produces a coarse grain and the color will be darker and yellowish. A quick bread which contains too much baking powder will also have a salty and bitter taste. When using baking soda as the leavening agent, it must have an acid to react with to create gas. The source of acid most commonly used for quick breads is buttermilk. The baking soda as an alkaline reacts with the acid in the buttermilk to create the gas which causes the product to rise.

Fat content in the quick bread mixture acts the same as it does in the yeast dough. It both shortens the strands of gluten and softens them. Fat also adds richness and flavor. The type of fats and oils commonly used in quick breads are hydrogenated shortenings, vegetable oils and butter.

Eggs are an important ingredient in quick breads. Fresh whole eggs add flavor and color, and improve the mouth feel. In addition to the richness which eggs provide, they also act as a leavening agent.

Sugars are not considered a required ingredient in a quick bread. When included, however, they assist in browning; crust and crumb formation, and flavor of the item.

There are a number of other possible ingredients which can be used in quick breads. Salt, for example, aids in flavor development in the mixture. Spices, fruits and nuts (grated, whole or chopped); seeds or cereals such as bran oatmeal, and cornmeal add to the variety of flavor and texture possible in quick breads.

MIXING METHODS

How you mix ingredients together determines to a large extent the structure and texture of the finished product. When making quick breads, all ingredients should be evenly mixed together at one time. Development of the gluten in the flour is controlled in mixing quick breads. It is the stirring and kneading (working a dough by hand or machine) that develops (stretches) the gluten. Normally in the preparation of quick breads stirring and kneading should be kept to a minimum, while for yeast breads a great deal of kneading is needed. (Remember, from Chapter 31, the 10 to 15 minutes recommended for development of the yeast dough on the mixer.) The amount that you develop the gluten will depend on what the texture of the finished product is to be. The gluten should, however, be sufficient in any mixture to keep the loss of leavening gas to a minimum during the baking process.

The degree of mixing varies with the kind of ingredients and their proportions. For example, a product containing a high percentage of fat and sugar may be mixed longer with less harm to the quality of the finished product. Quick breads leavened with baking powder generally call for limited mixing.

METHODS OF PREPARATION

The variety of quick breads is almost limitless. It seems to be primarily a matter of the creativity of the baker. The types we discuss here are only a small representative grouping of the broader variations. Included in those used often in the kitchen are muffins of all types, biscuits, cornbread, griddle cakes, popovers, gingerbread and various fruit and nut breads (datenut, orange, banana).

MUFFINS

Ingredients for muffins cover a wide range of products. However, the basic ingredients are flour, fat (normally shortening or butter), eggs, liquid, baking soda, salt and baking powder. To this basic mixture can be added fruits such as blueberries, dates, raisins or bananas, and nut meats, such as pecans, walnuts or almonds. Other items often added to muffin mixes are poppy seeds, cooked bacon bits and many types of cereals.

MIXING PROCEDURE

Muffins are easy and quick to make. Mix the flour, baking powder, salt and sugar in a large mixing bowl. Blend together the milk, soft or melted butter and eggs. (If an acid liquid (such as buttermilk) and baking powder are being used, combine them a short time before blending in the other moist ingredients.) Make a well in the center of the dry mixture and pour the liquid mixture into it. Mix the ingredients only enough to dampen the flour.

The mixing time is more limited for muffins than for other products. Usually the batter should appear quite lumpy. The batter should not be smooth. If overmixed, tunnels will form in the product during baking. The result will be a product with a tough texture and the yield will be of low volume. For an explanation of this phenomenon, refer to the discussion of gluten earlier in this chapter and in Chapters 31 and 13.

If the muffins are to be flavored with an additional ingredient, such as fruit, it should be folded into the batter just before panning. If the folding is done properly, the additional ingredients will provide an interesting flavor and texture. (For information on folding refer to Chapter 30.)

To bake the muffins, scoop the batter into greased muffin pans, filling each cup in the pan two-thirds full. When a standard muffin pan is used, this will yield a muffin of 3/4 ounce to 1 1/4 ounce scaled weight. When baked at 360°-385°F, a muffin of this size will bake in fifteen to twenty minutes. The scaled weight of the muffin and the baking time will vary depending on the ingredients used. It is important to use the correct temperature when baking muffins. Too low a temperature will cause the muffin to have a low volume and poor color quality. Too high a temperature will cause the muffin to rise too quickly creating a cone shape. High temperatures will also cause excessive browning. As with any baked product, you must experiment to find the best temperature for your oven. Remember that all ovens are not created equal and thermostats from time to time do lie! Test the heat of your oven and adjust accordingly.

Some of the more common varieties of muffins are listed below.

BASIC MUFFINS, BLUEBERRY MUFFINS, PECAN MUFFINS, BACON MUFFINS, WHOLE-WHEAT MUFFINS, BRAN MUFFINS, RAISIN MUFFINS, DATE NUT MUFFINS, BANANA MUFFINS.

BAKING POWDER BISCUITS

Baking powder biscuits are made from a dough which contains more flour than liquid. It is of a kneaded consistency, yet is mixed only enough to yield a homogeneous dough. Baking powder biscuits are one of the easiest quick breads to make. The basic ingredients are flour, salt, leavening, fat and liquid. Though it is an extremely simple product, it is one which requires close attention to handling. Overhandling the biscuit dough can ruin it.

The first step in making biscuits is the thorough blending together of the dry ingredients. This ensures an even distribution of the leavening agent and salt. The next stage in making biscuits is the cutting of the fat (normally shortening or butter) into the dry ingredients. Whether this is done with a pastry blender or on a mixer, when completed, the fat should be in small pieces. The mixture will be the consistency of coarse cornmeal; however, be careful not to blend the flour and shortening completely. This will not allow development of the structure of the biscuit for rising. When the flour and fat are blended to the point of being a unified mass, the biscuits will be short and heavy, not flaky and light.

Once the shortening has been cut into the dry ingredients, you add the liquid. The proportion of liquid to dry ingredients is important. Sometimes the recipe will call for the gradual addition of water or other liquid until the dough is formed. This is because of the variations in the flour; moisture in the air, and the speed of mixing. All of these can alter the amount of liquid which needs to be used. Your goal is to use the minimum amount needed for the dry ingredients to form a soft dough while working the mixture as little as possible.

The soft dough is placed on a floured bench and folded into itself two to three times, until it feels soft but not sticky. The folding action develops the gluten just enough to give the biscuit a slightly firm texture. If the dough is not kneaded the finished biscuit will have a much lighter, more crumbly, texture, which, while an acceptable texture for biscuits, makes the biscuit hard to handle in a commercial food operation. Overkneading must be avoided, it will result in a tough product with low volume.

After the dough is properly folded, it should be gently rolled out to approximately 1/2-inch thick. You can then cut it into the desired shape: Round, square or rectangular. Place each biscuit on a greased or parchment-lined baking pan about a 1/2-inch apart. Brush the tops lightly with oil or egg wash. Biscuits should be baked as soon as possible after mixing. At a scaled weight of 1 to 1 1/4 ounce the biscuits should be baked for fifteen to twenty minutes in a 400°-425°F standard oven. A few of the possible variations for biscuits are shown in Figure One.

CORNBREAD

Cornbread is a quick bread which is popular in both the northern and southern parts of the United States. The basic ingredients for cornbread are cornmeal (white or yellow), flour, sugar, baking powder, eggs, fat and liquid. The mixing method is the same as that for muffins. As with muffins, it is important not to overmix cornbread batter. The batter can be baked either in a muffin pan or a sheet pan. The baking temperature and time for cornbread is the same as that for muffins.

YEAST DOUGHNUTS

Yeast doughnuts are made using a simple straight dough mixing procedure. All the ingredients are combined in the mixing bowl. It is similar to a regular bun or sweet dough; however, it is not as rich, using less sugar, fat and eggs. Doughnut formulas can contain different percentages of sugar, shortening and eggs. The variations of richness for yeast-raised doughnuts does not extend over as wide a range as that of cake doughnuts. The sugar percentage in yeast raised doughnuts controls the

---

YEAST-RAISED DOUGHNUTS
YIELD: 8 DOZ. 1 1/2OZ DOUGHNUTS

INGREDIENT	AMOUNT
SUGAR	8.5 OZ
SALT	1 OZ
SHORTENING	6 OZ
EGGS	6
MILK, FRESH WHOLE	1.5 LB
VANILLA	1 OZ
MACE	2 TSP
YEAST, DRY	4 OZ (VARIABLE)
WATER	8 OZ
FLOUR, ALL-PURPOSE	2 LB
FLOUR, BREAD	1.5 OZ

METHOD
MIX USING STRAIGHT DOUGH METHOD (CHAPTER 31). BENCH, CUT AND FRY AS DISCUSSED ON FOLLOWING PAGES.

Figure 2

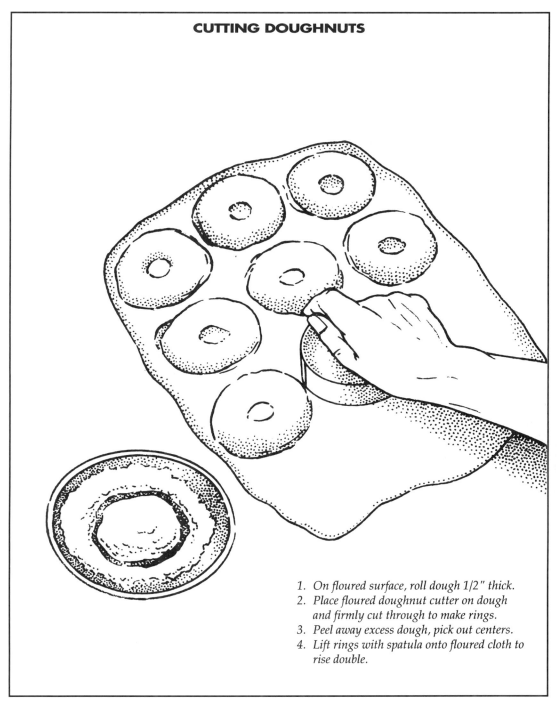

CUTTING DOUGHNUTS

1. On floured surface, roll dough 1/2" thick.
2. Place floured doughnut cutter on dough and firmly cut through to make rings.
3. Peel away excess dough, pick out centers.
4. Lift rings with spatula onto floured cloth to rise double.

amount of browning and fat absorption during frying.

A blend of soft and hard wheat flour makes a more tender doughnut than using 100 percent hard wheat flour. It should also be noted that the fermentation time is shorter when a combination of soft and hard wheat flour is used. An example recipe for yeast-raised doughnuts is shown in Figure Two.

MIXING

A major problem in preparing good doughnuts is keeping fat absorption to a minimum during frying. The temperature of the ingredients when mixed has a definite effect on the amount of fat absorbed during frying. The mixing temperature should be controlled so that the dough leaves the mixer at 78 to 82°F. Mixing time should be limited to 10 minutes. The dough produced should be medium soft with a smooth elastic texture.

FERMENTATION AND MAKE UP

Mixed dough should be taken to the bench at once. You then divide it into uniform pieces, the size of which depend on the weight of the entire batch being made up. The bulk pieces of dough should be allowed one to one and one-half hours for fermentation.

CUTTING

It is best to follow the formula directions for rolling and cutting. Remember that the thickness of the dough and the uniformity of the doughnut size are important for proper frying. Doughnut cutters should be used carefully to prevent overlapping the cuts and wasting dough. Reworked dough does not give cut doughnuts a smooth surface and greatly influences the frying time and evenness of brown color. Once the doughnuts are cut into the shape needed (round without centers, long johns, crullers or twists), let the units rest for about 15 to 20 minutes. This allows the gluten to relax before frying. If this relaxation does not take place, the result will be a tough doughnut with poor expansion.

PLAIN CAKE DOUGHNUTS
YIELD: 8 DOZ. 1 1/2 OZ DOUGHNUTS

INGREDIENTS	AMOUNT
SUGAR	15 OZ
SALT	.5 OZ
SHORTENING	8 OZ
CINNAMON	2 TSP
EGGS	10
MILK, FRESH 2%	2 LB
VANILLA	1 TBSP
BAKING POWDER	3 OZ
CAKE FLOUR	2.33 OZ
BREAD FLOUR	2 LB

METHOD

1. USING LOW SPEED ON AN ELECTRIC MIXER, BLEND SUGAR, SHORTENING, SALT AND CINNAMON UNTIL SMOOTH IN AN APPROPRIATE SIZE BOWL.
2. GRADUALLY ADD EGGS, DEVELOPING A SMOOTH MIXTURE.
3. ADD COMBINED MILK AND VANILLA ALTERNATELY WITH BLENDED AND SIFTED FLOURS AND BAKING POWDER TO FORM A SMOOTH DOUGH. (DO NOT OVERMIX.)
4. PLACE DOUGH ON FLOURED BENCH AND ALLOW TO REST 10 TO 15 MINUTES.
5. ROLL OUT DOUGH TO 3/8-INCH THICK AND CUT WITH DOUGHNUT CUTTER. (AVOID CREATING EXCESSIVE SCRAPS. THE REWORKED SCRAPS WILL YIELD A TOUGH DOUGHNUT.)
6. REST THE CUT DOUGHNUTS AN ADDITIONAL 15 MINUTES, THEN FRY IN PREHEATED (375° TO 380°F) FRENCH OR DONUT FRYER FOR APPROXIMATELY ONE MINUTE ON EACH SIDE.
7. DIP DOUGHNUTS IN GRANULATED SUGAR OR DONUT GLAZE WHILE WARM OR ALLOW TO COOL THEN ICE WITH FUDGE ICING OR ROLL IN CONFECTIONERY SUGAR AND STARCH.
   (FOUR PARTS CONFECTIONERY SUGAR TO ONE PART CORN STARCH.)

Figure 3

FRYING

The temperature of the frying fat must be correct to keep fat absorption to a minimum. Improper temperature can also result in the doughnuts browning before they are done. The recommended temperature is 375°F for raised doughnuts and 360°-375°F for cake doughnuts. To allow for the expansion of the doughnuts, place them one and a half inches apart on the frying screen.

If a proper formula is used, doughnuts will absorb minimal amounts of fat during frying. Normal fat absorption should be 2 to 2 1/2 ounces per dozen. This amount is both desirable and necessary to have high quality products. A fat soaked doughnut is heavy, greasy tasting and stales rapidly. Doughnuts removed from the fat should be thoroughly drained either on screens or brown paper and cooled to 160°F for glazing.

CAKE DOUGHNUTS

The quality of a cake doughnut depends on the recipe balance and the type of ingredients. Techniques of mixing, rolling and cutting also affect quality. Operations that produce cake doughnuts in large volume use equipment that forms the dough and drops it directly in hot fat.

Cake doughnuts are usually made from a combination of soft and hard wheat flour. A flour with a high gluten content such as hard wheat flour makes a tough product. The amount of moisture absorbed also depends on the type of flour used. If the dough is too stiff, the cake doughnut will have a poor expansion. This will result in a tight, dry texture and deep cracks. Insufficient mixing produces a coarse, hard texture, while overmixing yields a compact, tough product. An example recipe for cake doughnuts is shown in Figure Three.

The major difference between a cake and a yeast doughnut is in the leavening agent used. Cake doughnuts are normally leavened with baking powder. The result is a product which, as with a muffin, requires no fermentation period. Frying procedures are the same as for yeast-raised doughnuts, except for the use of a slightly lower temperature.

DOUGHNUT ICING

The icing used for doughnuts is a flow icing. It is a combination of blended syrup, salt, powdered sugar, boiling water, egg whites and flavoring. It can be used as a spread over coffee cakes, sweet rolls or doughnuts.

GRIDDLE CAKES AND WAFFLES

For griddle cakes or pancakes and waffles, it is important that the proportion of liquids (including eggs) to dry ingredients is adequate. The proportion should produce either a hearty, porous, thick cake, or a thin, moist, tight-grained cake.

The basic ingredients for griddle cakes and waffles are flour (all-purpose), sugar, baking powder, salt, eggs, fat and milk or cream. You should try to have the milk at room temperature, yet take care not to overheat the mixture.

MIXING PROCEDURE

Beat the egg, milk and melted butter lightly in a mixing bowl. Mix the flour, baking powder, sugar and salt together. Combine the two mixtures, stirring just enough to dampen the mixture. (You can make a lighter, fluffier product by separating the eggs; beating the egg whites, and folding it last.)

BAKING GRIDDLE CAKES

Baking griddle cakes should proceed as soon as the ingredients have been mixed. A hot, well-seasoned griddle is essential to the production of a high quality product. (A non-stick skillet/cooking surface can be used, if less fat is desired in the final product.) Make sure that the griddle maintains 375°, if it is thermostatically controlled. An overheated surface causes uneven browning and a lack of volume.

If you are making small griddle

cakes, drop about two tablespoons of batter onto the griddle. For larger pancakes pour about 1/4 cup onto the griddle. Bake the cakes on the griddle until they are full of bubbles on the top and the undersides are lightly browned. Turn over with a spatula and brown the other side. Place on a warm plate and serve immediately.

GRIDDLE CAKE AND WAFFLE MIX

When preparation time is limited, there are a number of time saving commercial mixes available. All of the ingredients are pre-measured, except the liquid. Simply follow the manufacturer's directions. Many of these mixes are of high quality and worth consideration for use.

VARIATIONS

As with muffins, there are a wide variety of possible additional ingredients for griddle cakes and waffles. We list only some of the most common ones. We encourage you to create your own griddle cake specialty.

WAFFLES

A waffle mixture is often considered to be richer than a pancake mixture. This is done by including cream in the recipe and increasing the oil content by approximately ten percent. The beating of the egg whites is often done separately to make waffles somewhat lighter and crisper.

BUTTERMILK GRIDDLE CAKES

This is a very popular variation. Use buttermilk, sour cream or yogurt instead of milk. Substitute 1/2 teaspoon of baking soda for two teaspoons of baking powder. The flavor of a buttermilk griddle cake is distinctive and good.

WHOLE-WHEAT GRIDDLE CAKES

Replace one third of your white flour with whole-wheat flour. To give this variation a really unique flavor sweeten the batter with molasses or honey, instead of white sugar.

OATMEAL GRIDDLE CAKES

Heat milk and stir in quick-cooking oatmeal. Let the oatmeal cool and add your remaining ingredients with reduced flour. This gives the cakes both a different flavor and texture.

BUCKWHEAT GRIDDLE CAKES

For this variation, simply replace half your white flour with buckwheat flour.

APPLE GRIDDLE CAKES

Using your standard pancake batter, stir thin slices of tart apple into it.

BLUEBERRY GRIDDLE CAKES

This all-time favorite is so simple to make. Gently fold well drained blueberries into your standard pancake batter and bake as usual.

The possible variations are endless. Bananas. Pineapple. Strawberries. Peaches. It is your choice.

CONCLUSION

Quick breads offer the opportunity to create much needed variety and versatility in menus during any part of the day. The majority can be made in a very short period of time, allowing the service of hot fresh breads at any meal. Quick breads adapt themselves well to even the most basic kitchen equipment and, in most cases, require no special work space. These breads, whether the muffin, griddle cake or fruit bread, are an invaluable product in the kitchen.

REVIEW QUESTIONS

1. Define the term *quick bread*?
2. List and define the two batter types for making quick breads.
3. How does the handling of a quick bread dough or batter differ from that of a yeast dough?
3. What is the primary mixing method for quick breads?
4. Discuss the preparation of muffins.
5. Discuss the preparation of baking powder biscuits.
7. List the basic ingredients used in making cornbread.
8. Discuss what makes a yeast-raised doughnut different from a cake doughnut.
9. How is absorption of fat during frying minimized in doughnut making?
10. List the basic ingredients used in making griddle cakes.
11. How can you tell when a product has too much baking powder in it?
12. How does a waffle differ from a griddle cake?
13. Why is baking soda added to a mix which contains buttermilk?
14. Discuss the importance of quick bread as a menu item.

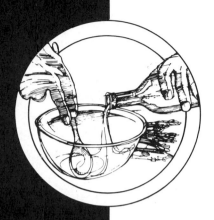

Chapter 33

CHAPTER OBJECTIVES

- **To introduce the four primary types of pastry dough.**

- **To delineate the ingredients and discuss the preparation and handling of sweet dough.**

- **To delineate the ingredients and discuss the preparation and handling of puff pastry dough.**

- **To delineate the ingredients and discuss the preparation and handling of pie dough.**

- **To delineate the ingredients and discuss the preparation and handling of cookie dough.**

- **To introduce tart and tartlet dough.**

Pastry Dough

This chapter will discuss the primary types of doughs used in making pastries. Although there are a wide variety of pastry doughs, there are four basic types. These are sweet dough, pie pastry dough, puff pastry dough and cookie dough. This chapter is divided into these four areas. The other types of doughs are simply variations of these four basic preparations. In discussing pastry doughs we will also discuss the preparation of items produced with these doughs. This is in no way intended to suggest that what is discussed here is the total of what can be made with pastry doughs. What information is presented here is only an introduction to the world of pastry making, without a doubt one of the most enjoyable areas of culinary preparation.

SWEET DOUGH

Among the many types of yeast-raised doughs made in the bakery, sweet dough is the most common. It is a type of dough which should be sweet, as its name implies. It is made from a formula high in sugar, shortening, eggs and other rich ingredients. This rich, succulent type of dough is used to make a wide variety of breakfast rolls and coffee cakes.

INGREDIENTS

Flour: Sweet dough or Danish pastry dough is made from hard wheat flour. This type of flour requires a longer fermentation period, yet has a better tolerance for extended work on the bench. This tolerance is important in those sweet doughs, such as Danish, which require multiple rolls and folds.

Sugar: The most common sugar used is white granulated sugar. This yields the finest product. The sugar content of the dough has an effect on the character of the dough and the final product. The percentage of sugar in sweet dough formulas ranges from nine to 20 percent, depending on the product being made.

When rolls are made using only nine percent sugar, they are similar to a bun or soft roll. This dough will have a good tolerance and be easy to make up. It will yield a good volume*; however, this type of roll will be lacking in sweetness and richness.

*NOTE: References in baking to *volume* concern the increase in size expected from a product as it is leavened. This is important to the commercial baker, particularly since consumers buy with their eyes. A one ounce piece of dough or a scoop of batter which doubles in size during the leavening process will look like a better deal to the person buying it. This is true when that piece is compared to a one ounce piece of dough or scoop of batter which only increases one and one-half times in size. The baker will be called upon often to choose between the eating quality of an item and the bulk developed by that item in the leavening and baking process. Ultimately, the decision of the baker must be based upon the expectations of the customer being served.

Rolls or buns made with a higher percentage of sugar have a shorter tolerance for bench work. This means that the baker has less time to make up the product. This dough also needs a longer fermentation and yields a smaller volume. The result is a product which costs more to produce. Products produced from this dough, however, will be sweeter, more tender and will have a longer shelf life.

Shortening: The most desirable sweet dough is made from a formula containing 16 to 24 percent fat. This percentage will yield a roll which is tender and short in texture, yet it will not have a greasy feel in the mouth. Too much fat content will cause a low volume. The dough with 16 to 24 percent fat will yield a good volume.

Eggs: Eggs improve the handling and quality of the dough. However, too high an egg content will unnecessarily increase the cost of the item. Ideally use whole eggs in amounts ranging from 16-22%, depending on the type used and the product desired. Eggs contribute little to the color of the dough, unless the percentage is very high.

Milk: Fresh milk is acceptable for use in any sweet dough formula. However, due to cost and handling, non-fat dry milk is often used. Non-fat dry milk in an amount of three to six percent yields a good product.

Yeast: Yeast content is increased in sweet doughs because the high sugar content in the dough inhibits the work of the yeast. Sugar slows down yeast action by increasing the viscosity of the dough, making it more difficult for the yeast-produced gases to raise. Though a greater amount of yeast is needed, it must be a balanced amount. Too high a percentage of yeast will shorten the fermentation and bench tolerance of the dough. It can also result in old dough. The amount of yeast ranges between three to six percent depending on the richness of the formula.

Spices: These add variety and flavor to the baked product, such as mace in Danish dough. However, as with any product, you must remember that an excess amount of extracts or spices can create an undesirable flavor.

PREPARATION OF SWEET DOUGHS

There are two basic types of sweet dough: *Regular sweet dough* and *Danish pastry dough*. Products made from either of these doughs may be similar in size, shape and weight, but will differ considerably in texture. The fine, even texture and grain of regular sweet dough items are quite different from the flaky texture of Danish pastry products. Both kinds of sweet dough may be handled either as dough with normal fermentation and make-up, or as retarded sweet dough.

SPECIAL POINTS IN MIXING SWEET DOUGH

The mixing of sweet dough is no more complex than the mixing of any other yeast-raised dough. Mix Danish pastry and regular sweet doughs, using the straight dough method, until the dough is smooth and elastic. As in bread production, the yeast is dissolved in water before being added to the mix. Sweet doughs normally have a higher egg content than many other yeast doughs. You should remember that eggs improve the handling character of the dough; however, sweet dough containing eggs can appear very slack, without being sticky. The finished dough temperature should range between 78 to 82°F.

FERMENTATION OF SWEET DOUGH

The normal fermentation for regular sweet dough and Danish pastry differs. The fermentation tolerance of sweet

---

SWEET DOUGH
YIELD: APPROX. 9 DOZ (1 1/4OZ UNITS)

INGREDIENTS	AMOUNT
SUGAR	14 OZ
SALT	1 OZ
SHORTENING	14 OZ
MACE	1.25 OZ
EGGS	12 OZ
MILK, FRESH WHOLE	1.75 LB
YEAST	5 OZ
WATER, 80°F	4 OZ
BREAD FLOUR	3 LB
CAKE FLOUR	1 LB

METHOD
1. MIX INGREDIENTS USING STRAIGHT DOUGH METHOD (REFER TO CHAPTER 31). TEMPERATURE OF FINISHED DOUGH SHOULD BE 80°F.
2. GIVE 1 1/2 HR (APPROX.) FERMENTATION PERIOD. CHECK FOR PUNCHING AND PUNCH WHEN READY. (TAKE THIS DOUGH YOUNG, DO NOT DOUBLE PUNCH, THIS WILL ALLOW FOR BENCH RISE DURING MAKE-UP.)

THIS DOUGH CAN BE MADE UP IN A VARIETY OF SWEET PASTRIES.

Figure 1

doughs is less critical than that of bread doughs. It is a common practice to adjust the fermentation time. This adjustment is based on the time needed for make-up, turning the dough into various rolls, coffeecakes and other pastries. Realizing that the time for make-up will vary greatly for different types of sweet rolls and coffee cakes, it is better to keep the dough on the young side because of its longer bench tolerance. (For a review of the problems of product rising on the bench, refer to Chapter 31.)

Regular sweet dough is usually given a normal fermentation. This means that it is allowed one full rise before make-up, proofing and baking. (See Figure One for a sample formula.) Regular sweet dough may be retarded, but it is not mandatory. The fermentation of Danish pastry dough is retarded. The dough is chilled after mixing; then the dough is chilled, and the butter or margarine is rolled and folded into layers in the dough. (See Figure Two for a sample formula.) The dough is chilled again before make-up proofing and baking. The chilling period is necessary to keep the fat from melting and soaking into the layers of dough.

RETARDING SWEET DOUGHS

Retarded dough is yeast dough that is refrigerated for a time before proofing and baking. This is done to lengthen the amount of time the product may be held before being baked. If left at room temperature, the yeast will continue to be highly active and the product may overrise before it is to be baked. Refrigeration temperatures retard the fermentation process, but do not affect the quality of the product.

Temperature is the key factor in control of retarded sweet dough fermentation. The ideal refrigerator holding temperature for retarded sweet dough is 35°F. Doughs that are to be held as long as 24 hours <u>must</u> be kept below 40°F. Temperatures above 40°F shorten the holding life of the dough because the yeast remains too active in the dough.

Refrigeration of the sweet or Danish dough can cause the exterior of the dough to form a crust and dry out. It is possible to control the humidity within some refrigerators. If you have this capability, the best relative humidity for the dough is 85 percent. If you cannot control the humidity in the refrigerator, lightly oil the dough and wrap it in plastic film to prevent the drying. When a crust is allowed to form, it will crack as the dough is rolled out, creating small dry spots throughout the dough. In the case of sweet dough, these spots will cause the made-up item to brown unevenly when baked. These spots will also make Danish brown unevenly and can cause greasy spots in the roll due to ruptures releasing melted roll-in fat.

The baker's time is as valuable as the ingredients used in making a product. Savings in the time needed for production of sweet dough by utilizing retardation of doughs at various stages of production instead of normal fermentation can be as great as 60 percent. Use of the retarded method allows the production of larger quantities of sweet rolls because the need to mix numerous small batches is removed.

When using this method, keep your dough young, allow it to rise only three-fourths in the first rise. Make-up the dough in the desired roll shapes, pan and immediately refrigerate. If the make-up of the dough is progressing slowly, retard the dough not being currently benched by placing it in the refrigerator until you are ready. One of the major dangers in benching any yeast product in any small kitchen is that when we get distracted by other necessary activities, we allow the dough to rise too much on the bench before it gets made-up. The result is a product with poor volume, highly yeasty flavor and poor texture. When you are ready to bake the made-up items give them a normal pan proofing in a proofing cabinet with 85 percent to 90 percent

DANISH PASTRY DOUGH
YIELD: APPROX 11 DOZ (1.25 OZ UNITS)

INGREDIENTS	AMOUNT
SUGAR	1 LB
SHORTENING	9 OZ
NON-FAT MILK POWDER	5 OZ
FLAVORING OR SPICES	TO TASTE
WATER	1.25 LB
EGGS	1 LB
YEAST	4 OZ
WATER	12 OZ
BREAD FLOUR	4 LB
CAKE FLOUR	8 OZ
ROLL-IN BUTTER	2 LB

METHOD

1. COMBINE ALL INGREDIENTS USING STRAIGHT DOUGH METHOD (REFER TO CHAPTER 31) TO CREATE WELL DEVELOPED DOUGH.
2. ROLL THE BUTTER INTO THE DOUGH IN THE SAME MANNER AS DESCRIBED FOR PUFF PASTRY IN FIGURE THREE AND SHOWN IN FIGURE FOUR.

THIS DOUGH CAN BE MADE-UP INTO A VARIETY OF SWEET PASTRIES.

Figure 2

humidity and 90 to 95°F. The products may take slightly longer to proof due to their lower temperature, but they will proof properly when given time. After proofing, they are ready to bake. The storage of made-up units saves and makes better use of the baker's time.

RETARDING DANISH PASTRY

Danish dough may be retarded for the reasons previously discussed; however, there is an additional reason for retarding Danish dough. A key factor in making excellent Danish pastry is the temperature of the dough when the butter is rolled in. It should be cold enough to keep the roll-in butter firm. Cool dough (retarded dough) will also roll out with less effort. The dough temperature should be about 65°F. It is also important that the dough be kept cool during the rest periods between each rolling and folding which makes the layers in the dough. Under the described conditions, Danish dough will keep for 72 or more hours. Before make-up, bring the dough to room temperature, not above.

PROOFING DANISH PASTRY

The correct degree of proofing will yield a flaky, buttery Danish pastry. Under-proofed dough will not be flaky. Overproofed dough will cause the roll-in butter to leak out. It is important that the oven temperature is not too low. Too low a temperature will cause the roll-in butter to be absorbed improperly into the dough. This creates a product which is heavy and greasy, instead of light and flaky.

BAKING SWEET DOUGH PRODUCTS

All sweet dough products need a full proofing period before baking. Sweet dough, as with Danish dough products, should not be baked slowly. Most varieties of sweet rolls may be topped with nuts, streusel, fruit or other toppings before being baked. (Fruit placed on rolls before baking should be of the no-bake-out type. These are formulated to withstand exposure to high temperatures without the sugars breaking down.) The sweet rolls should be washed with an appropriate egg wash before proofing. And most baked sweet dough products are glazed or iced while warm.

PUFF PASTRY DOUGH

Puff pastry dough is referred to as the pastry of a thousand leaves. Its many rich, crisp layers are light enough to be all but airborn. Its a flaky miracle of levitation. This is a rolled-in dough like croissant and Danish dough. It is one of the most difficult to make. The rising of puff pastry is truly a magical performance which requires a number of steps. The process of rolling, folding and turning will create hundreds of alternating sheets of fat and dough. The heat of the oven melts the butter and creates steam which puffs the dough into flaky layers. The various ingredients in this bit of magic intertwine to create the finest of pastries. Puff pastry is like many marriages, it unites separate identities into a compatible relationship.

INGREDIENTS

Flour used in puff pastry must be from hard wheat bread flour. Two factors require that this type of flour be used. Puff pastry contains a very high percentage of fat in relation to the flour content. A minimum fat content is 50 percent and it can be as high as 100 percent of the weight of the flour. The amount of rolling which the dough must withstand requires a flour higher in gluten content. A softer flour will break down during the rolling process, yielding a short greasy paste instead of the high flaky paste desired.

Shortening is used in relatively small quantities in the dough from which puff pastry is made. The reason for incorporating such a small amount (3.65 percent

of the total dough weight before roll-in fat is added compared to a Danish dough which contains nine percent shortening) is the great amount of roll-in fat which will be incorporated into the dough. The shortening incorporated into the dough during mixing assists in lubricating the gluten, allowing the gluten in the dough to develop properly.

Acid of some type (cream of tartar, lemon juice, vinegar) is used by many bakers in the preparation of puff paste dough. The acid does not affect the flaking properties of the dough; however, it does assist in the relaxing of the gluten in the dough. This relaxing of the gluten makes the dough easier to roll out without having to use an excessive amount of pressure.

Salt is included in some puff pastry doughs for improvement of flavor.

Eggs function in the puff dough in two ways. The fat of yolk lubricates the gluten in the dough. The egg white contributes to the volume of the dough in baking and to the fine flakiness of the finished product. Some bakers delete the shortening in the dough and rely on the lubrication of the egg yolk in the preparation of the dough.

Roll-in fat is crucial to the quality of the finished puff pastry. The percentage of fat to flour in the finished dough must be high. A low fat percentage dough, less than 50 percent, will not rise high even when baked. Roll-in fat should be of the same consistency as the dough itself. The fats most often used are butter, margarine, shortening or *puff paste* (a fat specially blended for use in puff pastry preparation). The consistency of the fat may be adjusted by adding a small amount of flour to it or by blending a firmer fat, such as an animal fat (oleo stearin), with shortening which has greater plasticity. When the fat is at the right consistency and its temperature is equal to that of the puff dough, it is possible to distribute the fat in the dough evenly without tearing the dough. It should be noted that butter is

PUFF PASTRY DOUGH
YIELD: APPROX. 100 PIECES

BASE DOUGH

INGREDIENTS	AMOUNT
BREAD FLOUR	5 LB
LEMON JUICE, FRESH	4 OZ
SALT	.75 OZ
SHORTENING	6 OZ
EGGS	6 OZ
WATER, COLD	2 LB 4 OZ

METHOD
1. BLEND FLOUR, SALT, LEMON JUICE AND SHORTENING IN APPROPRIATE SIZE BOWL.
2. MIX EGGS AND WATER TOGETHER.
3. ADD EGG AND WATER MIXTURE TO FLOUR MIXTURE AND DEVELOP INTO A WELL-FORMED DOUGH.

FINISHING THE DOUGH

INGREDIENTS	
ROLL-IN FAT:	
BUTTER, UNSALTED	4 LB
SHORTENING, VEGETABLE	10 OZ

METHOD
1. PLACE THE DEVELOPED DOUGH ON A FLOURED BENCH AND ROUND INTO A SMOOTH BALL. ALLOW THE DOUGH TO REST FOR 15 TO 20 MINUTES (THIS LETS THE GLUTEN RELAX.).
2. USING SUFFICIENT FLOUR TO PREVENT THE DOUGH FROM STICKING TO THE BENCH, ROLL THE DOUGH OUT INTO A RECTANGULAR SHAPE, 1/2-INCH THICK.
3. SPREAD OR DOT BLENDED ROLL-IN FAT ON TWO THIRDS OF THE DOUGH.
4. FOLD THE THIRD OF THE DOUGH WHICH HAS NO FAT ON IT OVER ON TOP OF THE MIDDLE THIRD OF DOUGH, THEN FOLD THE REMAINING THIRD WHICH HAS FAT ON TOP OF THE FOLDED DOUGH. THIS CREATES THREE LAYERS OF DOUGH AND FAT. (REFER TO THE DIAGRAM IN FIGURE FOUR.) SEAL THE ENDS OF THE DOUGH TO PREVENT THE FAT FROM BEING PUSHED OUT BY SUBSEQUENT ROLLING.
5. TURN THE DOUGH AND, USING ONLY THE PRESSURE NECESSARY TO ROLL OUT THE DOUGH (EXCESSIVE PRESSURE WILL UNITE THE FAT LAYER AND DOUGH LAYER AND THE POCKETS IN WHICH THE STEAM BUILDS WILL NOT FORM AND THE DOUGH WILL NOT RISE.), ROLL OUT IN A RECTANGULAR SHAPE 1/2-INCH THICK. (BE SURE YOU HAVE ENOUGH FLOUR TO PREVENT THE DOUGH FROM STICKING TO THE BENCH. TEARS IN THE DOUGH WILL CAUSE THE FAT TO LEAK, RESULTING IN A GREASY PASTRY WHICH DOES NOT HAVE GOOD VOLUME.)
6. DUST OFF ANY EXCESS FLOUR FROM THE TOP OF THE DOUGH AND FOLD BOTH ENDS OF THE RECTANGLE TOWARD THE MIDDLE AND THEN FOLD IN HALF.
7. PLACE DOUGH IN REFRIGERATOR AND LET REST FOR 30 MINUTES. REPEAT STEPS 5 AND 6 THREE TIMES, CHILLING AND RELAXING THE DOUGH BETWEEN EACH TIME.
8. LIGHTLY OIL THE FINISHED DOUGH, PLACE ON SHEET PAN, WRAP WITH PLASTIC FILM AND PLACE IN REFRIGERATOR.
9. ALLOW DOUGH TO REST FOR 12-24 HOURS BEFORE MAKE-UP. THIS ALLOWS THE GLUTEN TO RELAX AND THE DOUGH TO BLEND.

PUFF PASTRY DOUGH IS USED FOR THE MAKE-UP OF NAPOLEONS, VOL-AU-VENT PATTY SHELLS, CREAM HORNS AND TURNOVERS, TO MENTION ONLY A FEW. THE MAKE-UP OF TURNOVERS IS DIAGRAMMED IN FIGURE SIX.

Figure 3

often preferred because of its low melting point. Fats with higher melting points may not leak out of the pastry as readily (achieving an extremely high volume and fine flake); however, they can leave a greasy feel in the mouth.

Leavening agents are not used in this dough. It is the fat which raises the layers. The fats for roll-in must contain a small amount of moisture. As the dough is folded and rolled with the fat, multiple layers of dough sealed around fat are formed. When the dough is placed in the hot oven, the fat begins to melt, enriching and lubricating the dough surrounding it. The fat thereby creates a small pocket in the dough. The moisture released by the fat evaporates as it is heated, creating steam. This steam pushes up the pocket that has been formed. This same action is created in hundreds of pockets within the pastry, creating the volume, a minimum of eight times its original thickness, and forming the flaky texture which makes this such a grand pastry.

PREPARATION OF PUFF PASTRY

The goal in making puff pastry is the building of separate, distinct and even layers of dough and fat. This starts with the proper preparation of the base dough into which the roll-in fat will be rolled. A sample formula and the procedure for puff pastry dough are shown in Figure Three.

Proper rolling of the dough is a key factor in the preparation of quality puff pastry. You must remember that it is the fat which creates the cavity for the steam. At temperatures above 75°F, the roll-in fat will soften too quickly making it almost impossible to gain the proper layering. You should not try to make puff pastry dough when the room temperature is greater than 75°F. The dough must be somewhat chilled before you begin rolling it out. While rolling the dough, lift and move it constantly. To prevent it from sticking to the bench top, dust the surface lightly with flour as needed. Any excess flour should be brushed from the dough

---

FOLDING PUFF PASTRY

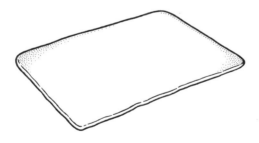

1. *Roll dough out on floured bench in rectangular shape, 1/2-inch thick.*

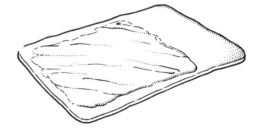

2. *Spread roll-in fat on two thirds of dough.*

3. *Fold end of dough not covered with fat onto center.*

4. *Fold remaining third on top of already folded two thirds.*

Figure 4

before folding it. It is important to let the dough and gluten relax and cool in the refrigerator between rolling out. This allows the dough to lose some of its elasticity and firm up. The rolling and folding of puff pastry dough is shown in Figure Four.

There are two basic rules which will help you produce a high quality puff pastry dough.

1. NEVER TRY TO LOOSEN UP YOUR DOUGH. Doing this by giving it a few whacks with the rolling pin in different places is absolutely out! By doing this you smash all of the formed butter and dough layers, making a blended dough. If the dough is too cold when you take it out of the refrigerator, leave it at room temperature for a few minutes.

2. If your dough becomes too warm and smeary during rolling, STOP IMMEDIATELY. Wrap it in plastic and return it to the refrigerator.

A few pointers for the make-up and baking of puff pastry dough are given in Figure Five. Making puff pastry sounds very complicated. Yet, when you do make it according to the directions in your formula and the guidelines given here, you will find that you can create magic!

PASTRY AND PIES

Pie, a favorite American dessert, is a light brown flaky crust holding fresh fruit, custard or cream. A good pie is the result of high quality ingredients and skill in mixing and handling. All too often materials are less to blame for a poor quality pie than the baker. Production of a quality pie crust is a matter of technique and understanding the ingredients. A professional baker must have a knowledge of the reactions that take place when flour, shortening, salt and water are brought together in a pie crust mixture. Likewise, careful preparation of fillings is required; however, the filling is much less responsible for poor quality pie crust than improperly prepared pie crust. With this in mind, we will begin by discussing the ingredients used in pie crust.

PIE CRUST

INGREDIENTS

Hard wheat bread flour is normally used in pie crust formulas. This type of flour is less likely to absorb fat than soft wheat flour, thereby yielding a pie dough that is easier to roll and pan. A common practice in many kitchens is the use of a combination of sifted hard wheat and soft wheat flour, or all-purpose flour for pie dough. Although the fat absorption may increase slightly,

---

GUIDELINES FOR MAKE-UP AND BAKING OF PUFF PASTRY DOUGH

1. Puff pastry dough should be cooled and wrapped.
2. If the dough is too soft, layers may stick together at the cuts, preventing proper rising.
3. Use sharp cutting tools or knives. Cut straight and firm.
4. Avoid touching cut edges with your tool or fingers.
5. Avoid allowing egg wash to run down and over cut edges.
6. Place made-up products into refrigerator or very cool area for at least 30 minutes prior to baking. This allows the fat to set, assuring a flaky texture.
7. Puff pastry needs a higher baking temperature for the formation of steam. 400°-430°F is recommended in a standard oven.

Figure 5

the result will be more tender. (For a discussion of hard and soft flours refer to Chapter 30.)

Shortening is responsible for the tenderness, taste and shelf life of pie crust. The essential quality factor for fats used in pie crust is freshness. Fat which has been stored improperly, allowing it to absorb odors from other foods, or rancid fat should not be used.

Solid fat yields flakier pie crust than melted or soft fat. A solid fat will not blend as readily with the flour, allowing the development of layers in the rolled dough, similar to those in Danish and puff pastry. Soft shortening cannot be used for pie dough. Instead of being coated by the flour, soft shortening soaks into it. When this happens there is no flour left to absorb moisture, and no structure is created when the crust is baked.

Your goal is to have the shortening cover enough flour to make the pie crust tender, yet leave enough uncoated flour to combine with the water to form a gluten structure. The shortening should be plastic at room temperature; neutral in flavor, and stable under normal conditions. The plasticity, or workability, of hydrogenated shortenings at room temperature makes them desirable types of fat to use.

Liquid is the most critical ingredient in pie dough. The quantity used and the method of mixing it into the flour, salt and shortening mixture can make the difference between a tough, rubbery crust or a tender crust. When the water comes into contact with the flour the dough formed has an elastic property from the development of gluten, the protein in the flour.

The quantity of water used should be adequate to form a dough that handles well; that is, one which is not too sticky or wet and not so dry that it crumbles from the dough mass. The amount of water which a pie dough mixture will need depends on how thoroughly the flour and shortening are blended. The more thoroughly blended the flour and fat, the less water the dough will take because there is no flour left free to absorb it. A dough that is undermixed and wet will shrink as it bakes, and may be difficult to brown. If too small a quantity of liquid is used, the result will be a flour and shortening mixture which is too crumbly and too difficult to handle. What happens in such a mixture is practically no development of the gluten. Some gluten development is necessary for a good pie dough.

Salt has a desirable binding effect upon the dough. It also helps the development of flavor and enhances the flavor of other ingredients.

Variations: There are a wide variety of other ingredients which may be added to pie dough to create different flavors, textures and colors. Sugar may be be added if a sweeter crust is desired. A crust with sugar added will brown more readily; however, it has a shorter shelf life. Cheese, such as coarse ground cheddar cheese, may be added. Spices which will complement whatever filling is going to be used are sometimes added. These types of additions must be done in a manner which will complement the intended end use of the dough.

MIXING PIE CRUST

The method and amount of mixing, as well as the kind and quality of ingredients used, are responsible for the type of crust produced. There are three basic types of pie crust: *Mealy, medium-flaky*, and *long-flaky*. Each of these types are produced from the same basic ingredients. They differ in the degree of blending which occurs between the fat and the flour. Mealy pie crust is prepared by blending the flour and fat until the flour is almost completely incorporated with the fat. This crust will be very tight and dense and will require little water in the mix. The most common type of pie crust in America is the medium-flaky. For this type of crust, the fat is rubbed into the flour until walnut-size pieces of fat are formed. When baked, this dough yields a flaky crust. Long-flaky crust is prepared by rubbing the fat into the flour only enough to break it into long pieces. The dough is then rolled and folded two to three times in the manner of a puff pastry or Danish dough, forming similar layers of fat and dough. The result, when baked, is a crust with larger, longer flakes.

The technique used in mixing the fat and flour to lubricate the flour particles is an extremely important step in pie crust production. Steps for mixing a flaky pie crust are given in Figure Seven. Your goal in following these guidelines is to produce crispy, flaky pie crust. Pay close attention to the temperature of your ingredients and to the amount of mixing.

MAKE-UP OF THE DOUGH

When mixing is complete, roll pieces of the dough into three-inch thick cylinders. Allow the dough to rest for at least four or more hours under refrigeration. Resting the dough increases its stretching properties, so that it handles much more easily when it is rolled out and made-up.

Dividing the dough. When you are ready to make a pie, cut the dough into the size pieces needed for tops and bottoms. For a normal pie the top piece should be seven ounces and the bottom piece eight ounces. This weight of dough is suitable for a nine-inch pie plate.

Rolling the dough. Dust each chilled pie dough piece lightly with flour. Flatten each piece with the palm of your hand before rolling with a dusted rolling pin. When rolling, use quick strokes. Start rolling from the center of the piece and roll towards the edges in all directions. Roll, do not force the dough out, making a circular shape. Forcing or stretching will cause the dough to shrink during baking.

Dough should be rolled into a circle about one to two inches larger than the size needed. It should be rolled approximately 1/8-inch thick. Your pie crust is now ready to pan. Do not grease pie pans. Pie dough has enough fat to prevent sticking.

Fold the rolled dough in half; lift to the pie pan, and unfold it carefully. It is important to avoid stretching the dough during this process. This will cause shrinkage during the baking process. Fit the dough carefully so that there are no air spaces between the pan and the dough. Gently push the dough down into the bottom of the pan and pat out any air pockets that form.

ONE-CRUST PIE

If you are making a pie shell for a single crust or open-face pie, form the shell in the pan as follows.

1. Fold the extra 3/4's of an inch of dough under along the rim of the pie

---

MIXING PROCEDURES FOR PIE DOUGH

1. Refrigerate ingredients to improve the handling of pie dough, particularly if store rooms are warm. Flour and shortening should be about 60°F for best mixing. Water, however, should be 40°-45°F.

2. Blend all the flour and all the fat using a pastry blender, cutting fat into small pieces until it resembles a coarse cornmeal.

3. Dissolve salt in the water and add it to the flour and fat mixture. Mix lightly until the desired consistency is obtained. Overmixing will produce a tough crust with considerable shrinkage.

Figure 7

plate so that it is double in thickness.

2. Crimp using your two forefingers. Press and pleat at intervals to make a stand-up scalloped edge.

TWO-CRUST PIE

For a two-crust pie, first fold the extra 3/4's of an inch of dough of the bottom crust under; fill the shell with appropriate filling; egg wash the edge, then carefully place the top crust on top. Crimp the two pieces of crust together as you did for the edge of the one-crust pie. However, be sure to seal the pie well all the way around. A two-crust pie is usually washed to remove excess dusting flour and to give it a high sheen. The wash can be either water, milk, melted butter, egg wash or other washes. Allow the wash to dry on the crust before baking. This will eliminate dark spots.

LATTICE-TOP CRUST

Lattice-top crust makes a beautiful finish, especially for shiny berry pies. Roll out your dough as for top crust. Cut it into strips 1/2- to 3/4-inch wide. Place the strips on the filled pie, weaving them in and out of each other. If you prefer, just lay them across each other at right angles. Trim the strips even with the overhanging bottom crust. Fold the edge of the bottom crust up over the ends of the strips and press together. Lattice strips may also be twisted to give a spiral effect.

COBBLERS

Cobblers are sheet-type pies. The bottom and top crust are made of regular pie dough or a cookie or tartlet dough. The fillings are usually fruit. Make-up for a cobbler is the same as for a two-crust pie.

NOVELTY PIE CRUST

In addition to regular pie dough, graham crackers, vanilla cookies, ginger snaps or other dry cake or cookie crumbs, may be used in making a crust for cream-type fillings. These items are crushed and blended with butter or margarine and nuts or spices then molded into a pie pan. This type of pie crust should be chilled before using, or may be baked if a firmer crust is desired.

TURNOVER

Pie dough or puff pastry dough may be used to make turnovers. Turnover fillings are like those used for regular pies. The dough is rolled into rectangular sheets, then cut into six-inch squares. The edges of each square are brushed with water or egg wash (this helps to insure a tight seal of the turnover). About two ounces of filling is placed in the center of a square of dough. The edges are then folded, forming a triangular shape, and sealed. You should then cut a vent to allow the steam from the filling to escape during cooking. The method for assembling turnovers is diagrammed in Figure Six.

STORAGE

Unbaked pie dough will keep in the refrigerator, tightly wrapped for about four days. It may be frozen for at least three months if tightly wrapped and sealed.

FILLED PIES AND FILLED PIE SHELLS

Pies and pie shells with fruit or similar mixtures will keep well in the freezer for at least two to three months. We find that unbaked pies remain crisper and more tender after freezing than baked pies.

Frozen unbaked pies should not be thawed before baking. Unwrap frozen pies and place directly into a preheated 425°F standard oven for about 15 to 20 minutes and then lower the oven temperature to 350°F for the remainder of the baking time. Usually total baking time for a frozen pie will be about 20 minutes longer than for an unfrozen pie.

Baked pies should be frozen only when necessary. Let a baked frozen pie

TURNOVER MAKE-UP

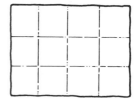

1. *Rolled cut dough in 4" squares.*

2. *Place crumb mixture and then fruit in the center of the dough square.*

3. *Paint two edges lightly with egg-wash, fold to form triangle, and seal with pastry wheel or fork.*

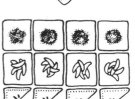

4. *Summary of turnover make-up process.*

Figure 6

defrost unwrapped at room temperature for about three hours, then crisp it in a preheated oven for about 15 or more minutes.

PIE TOPPINGS

The list of toppings for pies is a long one. In addition to the customary preparation of a baked pie, here is an opportunity for an imaginative individual to add more glory to his or her creations. Pie toppings have two functions:

1. Garnish or provide eye appeal.
2. Add flavor and texture contrast to the product.

Applying topping at the right time is

FILLINGS

There is a wide variety of types of fillings used in pies. The list given below includes the most common. Recipes for the various fillings can be found in many cook books.

FRUIT PIE FILLING	CUSTARD PIE FILLING	CREAM PIE FILLING
APPLE/DUTCH APPLE	CUSTARD	VANILLA CREAM
BLUEBERRY	COCONUT CUSTARD	COCONUT CREAM
CHERRY	PUMPKIN	BANANA CREAM
PEACH	SWEET POTATO	CHOCOLATE CREAM
APRICOT	SQUASH	STRAWBERRY CHIFFON
STRAWBERRY	PECAN	LEMON CHIFFON
RHUBARB	COTTAGE CHEESE	BLACK BOTTOM
PRUNE	LEMON CRUMB	RASPBERRY CHIFFON
RAISIN	LEMON MERINGUE	PINEAPPLE CHIFFON
APPLE CRANBERRY		CHOCOLATE CHIFFON
PINEAPPLE		ORANGE CHIFFON
MINCEMEAT		PUMPKIN CHIFFON
		BUTTERSCOTCH

important. Streussle topping, for example, should be applied to the pie before it is placed in the oven for baking. Fresh whipped cream should be placed on a pie after it has been baked and cooled. Meringue topping is usually placed on an already baked pie, and placed again in the oven for browning the surface.

COOKIE DOUGH

Cookies are often referred to as small, sweet cake items. They are very similar to cakes in the type of ingredients used and the methods to mix them. They differ from cakes in the proportion of ingredients and panning methods. The primary difference between cakes and cookies is the amount of moisture in the mixture. A balance of the other ingredients is needed to accommodate the lack of other moisture in the mix.

INGREDIENTS

Sugar is a major ingredient in most cookie mixtures. The type of sugar used and the quantity both affect the spread of the cookie as it cooks. (Spread is a major concern in the production of cookies, particularly those which are to have a particular design.) A coarse sugar will cause a creamed cookie to spread a great deal in cooking. An extremely fine sugar, confectioner's sugar, may restrict the spread of the cookie too much and may also cause the fat to separate from the mix if the cookie is to be bagged (pressed from a pastry bag). Finely granulated sugar is the best for most cookies.

Fat is also a major ingredient in many cookies. It is the fat that gives the cookie its richness. The type of fat chosen can affect the flavor and handling characteristics of the cookie dough. Butter gives the best flavor; however, it has a low melting point and may not stand up to the handling. For a rolled cookie dough, shortening has a better plasticity at normal temperatures. Shortening has a higher melting point and acceptable flavor, but not the rich flavor of butter.

The best results will be achieved with the use of a blend of butter and shortening.

Eggs are important to the structure and flavor of the cookie. Increased egg content will reduce spread and increase flavor. They also assist in holding the sugar in the mixture.

Flour is the primary source of structure in the cookie. The majority of cookie formulas require a blend of hard and soft wheat flour. The high fat and sugar content of the cookie formula cannot be properly contained by a soft flour, such as a cake flour, causing excessive spread; however, use of strictly hard wheat flour can yield a tough cookie. The gluten in the flour should not be developed when the cookie dough is mixed. When it is, the result will be a tough cookie. The exception to the use of hard wheat flour is in the preparation of cookie doughs with egg whites. These require the use of the soft wheat cake flour.

Milk or *water* are the liquids most commonly used in cookie doughs. When water is used, a non-fat milk powder is normally added to the formula. The flavor of the cookie benefits from the milk. Liquids must be used cautiously. A slack mixture will have greater spread.

TYPES OF COOKIE DOUGHS

Cookie doughs are classified according to the method by which they are mixed. They are placed in three categories.

1. STIFF DOUGH.
2. SOFT DOUGH.
3. REFRIGERATOR DOUGH.

Formulas of *stiff dough* contain less liquid, eggs and flour than soft cookies. These cookies are often referred to as sliced or roll cookies. The desirable finished product is crisp. When humidity becomes excessive, this cookie becomes moist and tends to soften up, loosing its crispness. This type of cookie includes peanut butter cookies and sugar cookies. Crisp cookies keep best when stored in a container with a loose fitting cover.

Soft dough batter has a high moisture content and requires a greater percentage of eggs to build structure. The desired finished product is a soft, moist cookie. It is best stored or packed in a container with a tight fitting cover. Cookies in this category are drop cookies of all sorts, such as butterscotch and chocolate.

Refrigerator doughs are mixed in the same manner as other doughs except the dough is very stiff. The resulting cookie is very brittle. After the mixing is completed, the dough is weighed off into pieces of convenient size. The dough is then formed into rolls which may be wrapped and refrigerated to be cut into cookies as needed. The roll of dough may be sliced into individual cookies which are panned, wrapped and then refrigerated, ready to be placed directly into the oven when needed or the cut cookies can be stored in bulk and panned as needed. The advantage of this dough is that it can be made and stored in the refrigerator until needed. This eliminates waste and provides a ready source of dessert at short notice.

MIXING

Mixing methods for cookies are similar to that for batter cakes. (Refer to Chapter 35.) The primary factors in making a quality cookie is proper mixing and temperature control. Although cookie dough is often chilled after mixing to facilitate shaping, the ingredients should be approximately 65 to 70°F when mixing.

The conventional or creaming method is the one most commonly used for cookies. (For a discussion of creaming refer to Chapter 35.) Cookie doughs should be mixed just enough to blend the ingredients thoroughly. The longer the creaming of the shortening and sugar, the less spread the final product will have, because the sugar will be more finely distributed throughout the mix. When the mix is overcreamed, the cookies will not spread as much, due to the dissolving of the sugar crystals.

Undercreaming will give the cookies a coarse structure and will result in a baked product that has spread. It is important to achieve the correct balance in the creaming process. Not only does it affect the spread of the cookie, but also the baking quality. If lumps of sugar are left in the dough during mixing, sticking is likely to occur. The syrup, formed during baking, becomes hard and solidifies on the baking pan.

Once the creaming is complete, the flour is added to the mixture. Here again you have the opportunity to determine the quality of your cookie. Overmixing develops the gluten in the dough. This retards the spread of the cookie in baking. The longer the mixing after blending the flour and water, the more developed the structure. A highly developed structure reduces the spread of the cookie in baking.

BAKING COOKIES

Proper baking is a major factor in the production of a quality cookie. Unless care is taken to bake the cookies at the right temperature (385°-400°F) for the correct length of time, poor flavor, eating qualities and appearance may result. A cool oven produces a pale color, while a hot oven may produce too dark a color. Too hot an oven will set a cookie before it has a chance to spread to any extent. Steam has a softening effect upon the cookies in the oven, giving them a greater chance to spread before they become set. Cookies should be on the soft side when removed from the oven, the heat in the cookie and the pan will continue to cook (dry) the cookie during the cooling period. Overbaking dries out the cookie and reduces flavor and taste. Many cookies prepared from high quality ingredients in a diligent manner are reduced to a stale nature by overcooking.

TART AND TARTLET DOUGH

A tart is a small or large shell without a top crust. Often, the sides are fluted and the tart is removed from the baking form prior to service. However, the molds may also have straight or sloping sides. A tartlet is a miniature version of a tart. Individual tartlet molds come in many shapes and sizes, such as plain, round, fluted, rectangular, boat-shaped and others, both large and small.

Tarts and tartlet shells are both made from either pie dough or cookie dough. However, since tarts contain less filling than pies, the flavor of the tartlet dough or sweet dough is important. The fillings which can be put in them is limited only by your imagination. A baked fruit tart is nothing more than a baked shell, which can be filled with bavarian cream or pastry cream; topped with fresh fruits, and glazed. Another variation would be to fill the shell with frangipane before topping with fruit. A number of variations are possible.

CONCLUSION

Delicious, delectable Danishes, cinnamon rolls, napoleons, cherry pies and chocolate chip cookies. This chapter truly has introduced you to some of the prides of the pastry shop. The combination of basic ingredients creates what dreams are made of; however, when assembled in the wrong manner, they are enjoyable for no one. The discussions of the role of the various ingredients in these basic doughs are guides to your future pastry production. When experimenting, as you should, bear in mind the relationship of the basic ingredients. By doing this you will be able to create what has not yet been dreamed of.

REVIEW QUESTIONS

1. What is the significance of volume in baking?
2. What is the relationship of the sugar, yeast and flour in a sweet dough?
3. Define *retarded dough*.
4. How does the retarding of a sweet dough differ from the retarding of a Danish dough?
5. Why must a Danish dough be oiled before being refrigerated?
6. What are the characteristics of an overproofed Danish dough?
7. Discuss the process by which puff pastry is leavened.
8. List the steps in rolling the roll-in fat into puff pastry. How does this differ from rolling the roll-in fat into Danish pastry?
9. Describe the relationship between the fat and the flour in pie dough.
10. Discuss the three types of pie dough.
11. List and discuss four uses of pie dough.
12. List three major ingredients in cookie dough and their effect on the cookie.
13. Discuss the difference between the three categories of cookies dough.
14. What is tart and tartlet dough and how is it used?

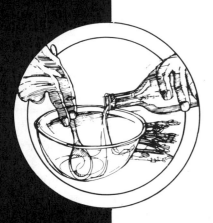

Fillings

The preparation of a delicious pastry or pie requires more than just a high quality dough. It is the filling which gives the pie or pastry a large share of its character or flavor. What would a cherry pie be without cherries? What would cheese Danish be without cheese? It is this dependence upon the filling which requires that you, the baker, know and understand the basics of filling preparation. We will begin our discussion of fillings with the types of ingredients used.

INGREDIENTS

THICKENING AGENTS

Although it is possible to put plain raw fruit into a crust and bake it, the result would not be satisfactory. Most pie fillings require thickeners of one sort or another. These binding agents not only help to form the fruit, they also develop the flavor and texture. They provide the means for the transference of flavors. The thickness created reduces loss of juices and absorption of juices by the dough. In the case of a filling such as one made of cheese, they prevent the complete meltdown and spread of the cheese. The two major binding agents used in pie fillings are various forms of starch and egg. Many kinds of pie fillings, like fruit or cream fillings, depend upon starch for their thickness. Egg thickened filling, such as pumpkin pie, sometimes also contains starch. The starch acts as a stabilizer and reduces cost by allowing for a lower egg content.

STARCHES

Cornstarch is often used for cream pies, because it sets up firm, holding its shape when sliced. It may also be used for fruit pies; however, *waxy maize* or *modified starches* are the best for fruit pie fillings. Waxy maize is genetically engineered to be 100 percent amylopectin, a starch which yields a less viscous cooked mixture. It forms a gel similar to cornstarch. Modified starch has been chemically altered to have better stability in the freezing and thawing process; greater stability with acidity, and a slower rate of syneresis (releasing the water held in the gel). In general these starches yield a clear gel which has a softer paste texture instead of a firm, rubbery gel.

Instant/pre-gelatinized starch is also used in thickening pie fillings. It needs no cooking, because it is cooked in processing. This allows the production of a fruit filling with a fresher, brighter appearance. The fruit does not have to be exposed to additional heat.

Although starches are easy to use, there are a few basic guidelines. To avoid lumping, starches must be mixed with cold liquid or with sugar before being added to a hot liquid. The instant and pre-gelatinized starches must be blended with sugar prior to being mixed with a cold liquid. Sugar and acids, such as lemon and pineapple juice, reduce the thickening power of starch. When possible, add part of the sugar and acid after the starch has been thickened. Acid and heat can break down the starch into its constituent sugars resulting in a loss of thickness (viscosity). This may also occur without the presence of heat if the acid content is too high.

EGG

Egg contributes flavor, richness and thickness to cream filling and custard. The thickness is a benefit of the coagulation of the protein in the egg. In the case of the custard (standard proportions are one egg or two egg yolks to one cup of milk) this thickening will result in either a sol or a gel. When the custard mixture containing the egg is stirred as it is cooked, the protein in the egg forms a sol, the soft form of a gel. When stirred constantly the protein molecules in the mixture do not have sufficient opportunity to interlock as the gel forms. The result is a soft custard. When the custard is not stirred as it cooks, as in a baked custard, a more solid gel is formed by the coagulation of the egg protein. Eggs incorporated into cream filling also contribute to the thickness, but are stabilized and assisted by starch in some form.

Egg whites have a particular value in the preparation of certain pie fillings. In chiffons and Bavarians they are whipped prior to being incorporated, providing a lightening effect for the mixture. The proper method for whipping egg whites and the various stages of whipped egg whites are discussed in Chapter 30.

FRESH FRUITS

There is nothing better than using fresh fruit in pies, especially when they are at their seasonal peak. Many fresh fruits require a lot of labor, but, when successful, it is very rewarding. Fruits are available year-round in varieties and forms that meet all requirements. In the broadest sense, fruits are technically known as a part of plants used for food. They are nutritional necessities in a well balanced meal. Not only do they provide important vitamins, minerals and other nutrients, but they also offer pleasant contrasts in texture and flavor.

Fruits are those parts of a plant consisting of a ripened seed, surrounded by some edible tissue that is pulpy and juicy. The flavors of fruits vary from sour to sweet. Seeds may or may not be present.

CANNED FRUITS

Canned fruits are cooked in the canning process and are handled differently than fresh fruits. More effort must be taken to protect the texture of the canned fruit in preparing the filling. However, these fruits are comparable nutritionally to fresh fruits. The major factor in selection of canned fruits is the packing style and canning medium. Fruits are canned primarily three ways. They are packed in syrup or water, or canned in what is termed solid pack.

Water packed fruit are used almost exclusively for pie making. They are referred to as pie peaches, pie apples, etc. This pack contains no added sugar and normally less than 10 percent added water. The most commonly purchased fruits of this type are sliced apples, blueberries, peaches and sour red cherries.

Solid packed fruit is also used almost exclusively for pie making. In this type of canned fruit there is no added water or sugar. Any juice which is present in the can came from the fruit itself as it was cooked in the can. The most commonly purchased pie fruits of this type are sliced apples and peaches.

Syrup packed fruits are used in many ways in the kitchen, such as salads, breakfast fruit, desserts and, in some cases, pies. These fruits are more expensive than water or solid pack because of the high sugar content. However, the texture, color and flavor is superior because of the preservative effect of the sugar. They are convenient to use and permit year-round service of a variety of fruits, which is not always possible with fresh fruits.

FROZEN FRUITS

Frozen fruits are used primarily in pie fillings or desserts. A wide variety of *frozen syrup pack* fruits are available. These are often packed with a designation of the weight of sugar to fruit. For example, a four-to-one frozen pie cherry would contain one pound of sugar for every four pounds of cherries. As with syrup packed canned fruits these fruits do not need to be sweetened when making a filling. This pack of fruit is sold in a 30-pound tin and require two to three days under refrigeration to thaw.

I.Q.F. fruits are ones which have been *individually quick frozen*. Each individual piece of fruit is frozen separately. This yields a free flowing product when handled properly. This type of frozen fruit is extremely susceptible to temperature changes. To maintain its I.Q.F. form it must be kept at freezing temperatures at all times. When allowed to rise above freezing, the pieces will stick together. The advantage of this product is the ability to remove from the package exactly what is needed at a particular time. I.Q.F. fruit also has a fresher appearance and greater eye appeal. Sugar must be added to this fruit when preparing filling. There is a wide variety of types of fruit available in this form, such as blueberries, peaches, boysenberries, strawberries and others.

PREPARATION OF FILLINGS

FRUIT FILLINGS

One category of fillings includes all forms of fruit. Whether produced from fresh, frozen or canned fruit, attention to detail is necessary for good results. Fruit fillings are solid fruit pieces bound together by a gel. The gel consists of fruit juice, water, sugar, spices and cooked starch. As explained earlier, modified starch such as waxy maize, is preferred by some bakers. Other starches like corn starch, tapioca or potato starch may be used.

Solid fruit is an important part of the filling. For a good fruit pie filling, you should have two to three pounds of drained fruit to each pound of liquid. The functions of the gel are to bind the solid fruit pieces together and to help carry the flavors of spices and sweetness of the sugar. Gel also improves the appearance by giving a shine or gloss to the fruit. Figure One shows a sample recipe for basic fruit filling.

CREAM FILLINGS

The cream fillings used for pies and cakes are variations of plain puddings. Plain pudding is broadly defined as pastry cream. We can add flavor such as

---

APPLE PIE FILLING
YIELD: APPROX. 7 (10-INCH) PIES

INGREDIENTS	AMOUNT
APPLES, SOLID PACK CANNED	6.5 LB
WATER OR JUICE	1.5 LB
SUGAR	1 LB
CORNSTARCH	3 OZ
(OR MODIFIED STARCH)	(2.5 OZ)
WATER	8 OZ
SUGAR	8 OZ
SALT	2 TSP
CINNAMON	4.5 TSP
NUTMEG	1 TSP

METHOD

1. IN AN APPROPRIATE SIZE HEAVY BOTTOM PAN COMBINE 1.5 LB WATER/JUICE AND 1 LB SUGAR, THEN BRING TO A BOIL.
2. DISSOLVE 3 OZ CORNSTARCH (OR 2.5 OZ MODIFIED STARCH) IN 8 OZ OF COOL WATER AND STIR INTO BOILING SYRUP.
3. ADD 8 OZ SUGAR AND 2 TSP SALT TO MIXTURE AND RETURN TO A BOIL. WHEN MIXTURE CLEARS, REMOVE FROM HEAT.
4. BLEND 4.5 TSP CINNAMON AND 1 TSP NUTMEG INTO COOKED GEL AND THEN GENTLY FOLD IN APPLES. (BE CAREFUL NOT TO BREAK FRUIT INTO PIECES WHEN FOLDING IT INTO THE GEL.)
5. STORE MIXTURE UNDER REFRIGERATION IN APPROPRIATE CONTAINER.

THIS BASIC RECIPE CAN BE ADAPTED FOR USE WITH PEACHES, PINEAPPLES AND CHERRIES. FOR PEACHES, THE WATER CONTENT SHOULD BE INCREASED BY ONE CUP. CHERRY FILLING WILL REQUIRE AN INCREASE IN STARCH OF 1 OZ AND IN SUGAR OF 6 OZ. THE CINNAMON AND SUGAR SHOULD BE OMITTED FOR CHERRY FILLING. REPLACE THEM WITH LEMON JUICE.

Figure 1

BASIC CREAM FILLING
YIELD: APPROX. 6 (10-INCH PIES)

INGREDIENTS	AMOUNT
MILK	8 LB
CORNSTARCH	10.5 OZ
SUGAR	3 LB
EGG YOLKS, BEATEN (MED)	14
EGGS, WHOLE, BEATEN (MED)	4
BUTTER	8 OZ
VANILLA	1 OZ

METHOD
1. BLEND CORNSTARCH, SUGAR AND SALT.
2. BRING MILK TO 200°F AND GRADUALLY WHISK INTO MILK. WHISK CONSTANTLY UNTIL SMOOTHED AND THICKENED. (THIS IS BEST DONE IN A DOUBLE BOILER OR STEAM-JACKETED KETTLE.)
3. COMBINE BEATEN EGG YOLKS AND EGGS; TEMPER WITH THICKENED MILK, THEN SLOWLY ADD TEMPERED EGGS TO THICKENED MILK.
4. COOK 2-3 MINUTES THEN REMOVE FROM HEAT.
5. WHISK IN BUTTER AND VANILLA.
6. COOL AND THEN POUR INTO PREPARED PIE CRUSTS OR PLACE IN APPROPRIATE CONTAINER AND STORE UNDER REFRIGERATION.

NOTE: DUE TO THE POSSIBILITY OF SALMONELLA CONTAMINATION, THE CREAM FILLING MUST BE THOROUGHLY COOKED AND, ONCE COOKED, CONSTANTLY KEPT UNDER REFRIGERATION.

Figure 2

vanilla, coconut, chocolate or fruit. A sample recipe for cream filling is shown in Figure Two. To make a lemon pie filling, simply substitute water and lemon juice in place of milk. Your goal in making cream filling is the development of a product which is silky in texture and firm, but not rubbery.

There are divided opinions as to whether pie shells should be filled with warm or cold pie filling. For the best looking slices, fill your pie shell with warm cream filling. Make sure, however, that you use a good mealy pie dough that resists soaking to prevent a soggy bottom crust.

BAKED CUSTARD

Basic baked custard is a combination of sweetened milk and eggs. As previously mentioned, it is the coagulation of the protein in the egg which forms a gel to thicken the mixture. It should be noted that little actual thickening is contributed by the milk itself; however, it does provide mineral salts necessary for the coagulation of the egg protein. Without these salts the gel would not form.

How long it takes for a gel to form in a custard and how much heat is required varies with the number of additional ingredients incorporated into the custard. Due to this variation, it is important that custards be carefully checked during the baking process to determine the correct point to remove them from the oven. Baked custards continue to be affected by carry-over heat after removal from the oven. A baked custard which is cooked to a complete gel in the oven will continue

CUSTARD PUMPKIN PIE FILLING
YIELD: APPROX. 8 (10-INCH PIES)

INGREDIENTS	AMOUNT
SUGAR, GRANULATED	1.25 LB
SUGAR, BROWN	1 LB
SALT	.75 OZ
CINNAMON	.5 OZ
NUTMEG	1 TSP
GINGER	1 TSP
CLOVES	1 TSP
ALLSPICE	1 TSP
EGG, WHOLE	1.25 LB
BUTTER, MELTED	6 OZ
PUMPKIN	6.66 LB
MILK, FRESH, WHOLE	6 LB

METHOD
1. BLEND ALL DRY INGREDIENTS TOGETHER.
2. LIGHTLY WHISK EGGS.
3. IN APPROPRIATE SIZE BOWL COMBINE DRY INGREDIENTS, EGGS, MELTED BUTTER AND PUMPKIN, WHISK UNTIL THOROUGHLY BLENDED.
4. BLEND IN MILK AND ALLOW TO STAND ONE HOUR (UNDER REFRIGERATION), STIRRING OCCASIONALLY, BEFORE PANNING.

NOTE: PUMPKIN IS SLOW TO ABSORB AND, IF NOT ALLOWED TO STAND BEFORE BEING PANNED AND BAKED, BEADING OF OILS AND SUGARS CAN OCCUR ON THE SURFACE OF THE BAKED PIE.

Figure 3

to cook sufficiently after removal from the oven to cause premature syneresis and a porous texture. This not only affects the eating quality of the pie, but also shortens its shelf life. Check baked custard by inserting a knife halfway between the outer edge of the pie and the center. When the knife is removed with a clean blade, sufficient heat has transferred to that point to coagulate the egg protein and there will be sufficient carry-over heat to finish cooking the center of the pie after removal from the oven. Figure Three shows a sample baked custard recipe.

CHIFFON PIE FILLINGS

A chiffon type of pie filling has a light, fluffy texture. This is created by folding beaten egg whites and whipped cream into the cream filling with gelatin. The folding in of the egg whites and whipped cream must be done before the gelatin sets. After the pie is chilled and the gelatin has set, the filling should be firm enough to hold a clean slice; however, it should not have a rubbery consistency.

BAVARIAN CREAM PIE FILLINGS

Bavarian cream is a mixture of approximately 50 percent custard and approximately 50 percent whipped cream folded together. Dissolved gelatin is used as a gum holding both together. On average, gelatin equaling one to one-and-a-half percent of the total ingredients is sufficient. For example 100 ounces of Bavarian cream would call for one to one-and-a-half ounces of gelatin.

Gelatin should always be accurately measured. Not enough gelatin will

---

BAVARIAN CREAM

1. ALWAYS ADD YOUR DISSOLVED GELATIN TO YOUR HOT BASE.
2. COOL THE MIXTURE UNTIL THICK AND ALMOST SET.
3. FOLD IN YOUR WHIPPED CREAM.
4. RAPIDLY POUR THE BAVARIAN CREAM INTO YOUR PIES OR MOLDS.
5. CHILL UNTIL SET.

Figure 4

---

yield a soft Bavarian which will lose its shape and texture. Too much gelatin makes a stiff and rubbery Bavarian cream. (Always remember those flavored gelatin molds that they fed you in elementary school. Yes, those ones you used as rubber balls on the playground!) The steps for producing a Bavarian cream are shown in Figure Four.

Fruit Bavarians can be made two ways. They can be made like regular custard Bavarians, using fruit puree and water instead of milk. They can also be made by simply folding fruit puree into your custard base. Bavarian creams can be used to make elaborate and elegant desserts, or as a fancy cake filling for special cakes. They are extremely versatile and easily prepared products which are always well received.

REVIEW QUESTIONS

1. What is the difference between cornstarch, waxy maize and modified starch?
2. Discuss the interaction of starch and acid.
3. How does the egg contribute to cream filling and custard?
4. Define *soft custard* and *baked custard*.
5. Discuss the use of fresh, canned and frozen fruits in pie preparation.
6. What are the basic amounts of liquid and fruit for a good fruit pie filling?
7. Define *syneresis*.
8. State the proper method for checking the doneness of a baked custard.
9. How is a chiffon pie filling prepared?
10. How is a Bavarian cream pie filling prepared?
11. Discuss why cream filling must be thoroughly cooked and kept chilled once cooked.

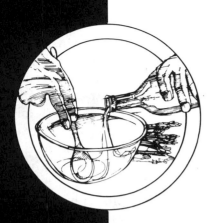

Chapter 35

Cakes

Baking is no more difficult than other kinds of cooking, but it is different. There are special techniques, like folding and whipping, and there are basic rules of chemistry to obey. It is important to follow a recipe exactly; to measure accurately, and to use well regulated ovens and well prepared baking pans. Once you accept these facts, you will find that it does not take long to acquire a feeling for baking procedures. You cannot help but gain an appreciation for the wondrous process by which butter, sugar, eggs, flour, leavening, liquid and spices transform into sweet, light, tempting arrays of confections called *cake*. This word has brought audible sounds of delight from the mouths of even the most conservative people.

INGREDIENTS

The ingredients used in most cakes are flour, sugar, shortening or butter, eggs, salt, liquid and leavening. The ingredients may vary in kind, quantity and method used. Again, it is important that you, as the baker, understand and recognize the function of the ingredients in various cake formulas.

Formula balance is the key to producing a good cake of any type. For balancing a cake formula the ingredients can be categorized according to four functions: *Tough, tender, moist* or *dry*. The ingredients used in cake-making can contribute these characteristics to the finished product. The idea is to find the proper balance suitable to the product we are looking for. Keep in mind that new ingredients and procedures are frequently developed. Have an open mind to new ideas and be willing to try them out.

FLOUR

Most cake formulas call for bleached soft wheat flour. This flour produces fine cell structure, fine grain and smooth texture. The low protein, soft wheat flour is essential to quality production. It reduces the possibility of toughness developing. Hard wheat flour by contrast, contains more gluten and produces a coarser textured cake. (For a more complete discussion of flour, see Chapters 13 and 30.)

SUGAR

Sugar serves three purposes in the cake mixture. It sweetens; tenderizes, and moistens. Sugar tenderizes by softening the flour protein and starches in the cake mix. It helps retain moisture in baked cakes, making them moist and edible after several days. The types of sugars used most often in cake recipes are granulated sugar, brown sugar and molasses. Molasses is used in gingerbread or spice cakes to add flavor and moisture. Brown sugar enhances flavor and, like molasses, increases moisture retention.

FAT

Cakes may contain butter, margarine, hydrogenated shortening compounds (with or without emulsifiers added) or oil. The function of shortenings and other types of fat or oil, in cake is to lubricate its internal structure. They aid the incorporation and holding of air and moisture, allowing production of a tender product. To fulfill this function, fats must be thoroughly mixed and dispersed throughout the batter.

Butter and hydrogenated shortening compounds are easily mixed and yield cakes of maximum volume. Hydrogenated shortening may contain an ingredient known as an emulsifier. This aids the distribution of fat in a mixture, enabling the baker to obtain a cake that is of large volume, fine grain and pleasing moistness. More importantly, the emulsifier aids in the creating of an even texture with less effort and skill. A cake made with emulsified shortenings does not require as much creaming action because the fat is dispersed more efficiently. This type of shortening is mandatory for what are termed *high-ratio cakes*. These are cakes which contain a greater percentage of sugar than flour. (For a complete discussion of fats and oils see Chapter 7.)

SALT

The main purpose of salt in cake baking is its effect on the taste and flavor of the baked product. It brings out the flavor of all other ingredients. Too high a level of salt content will create an unpleasant flavor.

EGG

The egg used in cake baking serves a number of purposes. It contributes to cake structure by working with the gluten in the flour. Egg binds and helps stabilize the batter. Whipped egg holds air and allows it to expand during baking, supplying some leavening action. Egg also acts as an emulsifying agent, because of the lecithin in the yolks, a natural emulsifier. (Refer to Chapter 4 for a discussion of emulsifiers and their importance.) Moisture, color, flavor and eating quality are all contributions of the egg in cake baking.

Because eggs are a major ingredient in cake baking, it is important that the quality and quantity be consistently precise. Although fresh eggs are best, they vary in size. The yield of a given amount of fresh eggs can differ greatly. Always weigh the fresh eggs broken out of the shell for use in cakes. Frozen whole eggs should be properly thawed; thoroughly stirred, and then weighed.

LIQUID

Liquid is needed to combine and activate other ingredients. It is the primary control for the consistency of the finished cake batter. Milk, water, juice, liqueurs or coffee can be used as the liquid in cake baking.

LEAVENING

Cakes are leavened in three ways: Incorporation of air during mixing; chemical leavening agents, such as baking powder, or vapor pressure created in the oven. The kind of leavening used depends on the richness of the formula, consistency of the batter and the baking temperature. All three leavening agents produce the lightness or porousness which gives cakes their characteristic texture.

INCORPORATED AIR

Air is naturally incorporated into the cake batter during mixing. How much air is incorporated will depend on many factors. How many times the flour is sifted, the speed of hand or machine mixing, the mixing method and tools used, all affect the incorporation of air. Another factor is the temperature of the cake batter. You should carefully follow formula directions, paying close attention to mixing times and ingredient temperatures. Cakes low in moisture, those made with rich ingredi-

ents, such as pound cake, obtain most of their leavening from mixing. Due to this incorporation of air they require less or no chemical leavening.

CHEMICAL LEAVENING AGENTS

Baking powder is the most common chemical leavening agent used in cake baking. It liberates carbon dioxide gas when it comes in contact with a liquid. The amount and speed with which it releases gas depends on the type of baking powder used. (Refer to Chapter 30 for a complete discussion of leavening agents.)

Baking soda is used in many cake formulas. It is used to generate carbon dioxide gas and contributes to the lightness of the cake. When baking soda is the only leavening used, the formula must also contain a moist acid ingredient. It is the combination of soda and moist acid which produces carbon dioxide gas. Sour milk, vinegar, buttermilk, sour cream and molasses are commonly used in this manner.

Cakes made from lean formulas, high in moisture, require more leavening ingredients.

NOTE: Because soda is used in the production of baking powder, use extreme care in measuring or weighing baking powder and soda. An excess or shortage of either will produce undesirable results in cake production.

VAPOR (WATER OR STEAM)

Some leavening action is produced by steam or water vapor given off by the liquid in the cake batter during baking. As the steam is released, it expands the cells developed in the cake's structure, pushing the cake up.

CHOCOLATE

Possibly the most popular cake flavor is chocolate. The types of chocolate used in cake baking vary from the unsweetened to the sweet. The choice of chocolate will depend on the final product desired. You must be cautious when

CHOCOLATE HANDLING

1. Remember chocolate burns easily. It should be melted over simmering water or in a bain marie.
2. Keep and store chocolate well wrapped in a cool place.
3. When chocolate is exposed to air over a long period it sometimes takes on a harmless white discoloration and becomes crumbly. This does not mean that it is stale, it is perfectly usable.

Figure 1

substituting one type of chocolate for another called for in a formula. The variance in sugar, milk solid and oil content can change the texture of the end product. (For a complete discussion of the characteristics and types of chocolate see Chapter 30.) A few hints for good chocolate handling are listed in Figure One.

DRIED FRUIT AND NUTS

The contribution of dried fruit and nuts to cake is variety of flavor and texture. However, dried fruit that is old and hard will not soften during baking. Soften dried fruit by boiling it in water for five to ten minutes, then drain thoroughly and pat dry. Both dried fruit and nuts are often floured before being added to cake batter. This helps to keep them from settling to the bottom of the cake during handling and baking. When grinding nuts for tortes, keep them light and fluffy. Do not overgrind them. For the best flavor and texture, nuts should be stored in the freezer or refrigerator.

POUND CAKE
YIELD: APPROX. 3 (2-LB LOAVES)

INGREDIENTS	AMOUNT
SUGAR	1.66 LB
SHORTENING, EMULSIFIED	8 OZ
BUTTER	8 OZ
FLOUR, CAKE	1.66 LB
BAKING POWDER	1 TBSP
SALT	2 TSP
NUTMEG	PINCH
MILK, FRESH, 2%	1 LB
EGGS, WHOLE, SEPARATED	1 LB
VANILLA	TO TASTE

METHOD
1. CREAM SHORTENING AND BUTTER, THEN ADD SUGAR (RESERVE 2 OZ) AND SALT GRADUALLY, CREAMING UNTIL LIGHT.
2. WHISK EGG YOLKS UNTIL LIGHT AND ADD TO CREAMED MIXTURE. ALLOW THEM TO INCORPORATE.
3. SIFT TOGETHER FLOUR, NUTMEG AND BAKING POWDER.
4. BLEND MILK AND VANILLA.
5. ALTERNATE ADDING THE DRY INGREDIENTS AND THE MILK MIXTURE TO CREATE A SMOOTH BATTER. DO NOT OVERBEAT.
6. BEAT EGG WHITES TO SECOND STAGE AND BEAT IN RESERVED SUGAR. CAREFULLY FOLD BEATEN EGG WHITES INTO BATTER. IMMEDIATELY SCALE AND BAKE.

Figure 2 – continued on next page

PLAIN LAYER CAKE
YIELD: 9 .66 LB

INGREDIENTS	AMOUNT
SUGAR	2 .5 LB
SALT	4 TSP
SHORTENING, EMULSIFIED	12 OZ
BUTTER	8 OZ
FLOUR, CAKE	2.75 LB
BAKING POWDER	2 OZ
MILK, FRESH, 2 %	1.5 LB
EGG WHITES	1.5 LB
VANILLA	TO TASTE

METHOD

1. CREAM SHORTENING, BUTTER AND VANILLA UNTIL LIGHT.

2. ADD SUGAR AND SALT GRADUALLY, CREAMING UNTIL LIGHT.

3. SIFT CAKE FLOUR AND BAKING POWDER TOGETHER, THEN ALTERNATE ADDING DRY INGREDIENTS AND MILK TO CREAMED MIXTURE, BLENDING ONLY ENOUGH TO FORM SMOOTH BATTER.

4. ADD EGG WHITES TO BATTER IN THREE STAGES TO FORM BLENDED BATTER.

CHOCOLATE CAKE
YIELD: 9.25 LB

INGREDIENTS	AMOUNT
SUGAR	2.5 LB
ALMOND EXTRACT	TO TASTE
SALT	2 TSP
SHORTENING, EMULSIFIED	8 OZ
BUTTER	8 OZ
CHOCOLATE, UNSWEETENED, MELTED	8 OZ
EGGS, WHOLE	1.25 LB
FLOUR, CAKE	2 LB
BAKING POWDER	1 TBSP
MILK, FRESH, 2%	2 LB

METHOD

1. CREAM BUTTER, SHORTENING AND VANILLA UNTIL LIGHT.

2. GRADUALLY ADD SUGAR AND SALT TO CREAMED FAT UNTIL LIGHT.

3. ADD MELTED CHOCOLATE, FORMING A SMOOTH BLEND.

4. ADD EGGS IN THREE PARTS, ALLOWING TO INCORPORATE WELL.

5. SIFT CAKE FLOUR AND BAKING POWDER TOGETHER, THEN ALTERNATE ADDING DRY INGREDIENTS AND MILK TO CREAMED MIXTURE TO FORM SMOOTH BATTER. DO NOT OVERMIX.

Figure 2

527

TYPES

In order to produce good cakes you must understand the principles, techniques and ingredients for making cakes. This understanding begins with a knowledge of the basic types of cakes. The proportion and type of ingredients used serve as the basis for dividing cakes into three separate groups: *Batter cakes, foam cakes* and *chiffon cakes.*

BATTER CAKES

There are many subdivisions of the three main groups of cakes. These subdivisions are based on the ingredients in the mix and the way in which they are added to the basic formula. Batter cakes include:

Pound cake which contains a high percentage of fat as can be seen in the formula shown in Figure Two.

Plain layer cake which contains a smaller percentage of fat as can be seen in the formula in Figure Two.

Chocolate cakes which are layer cakes incorporating chocolate cocoa powder and soda. Again, this can be seen in the formula in Figure Two.

FOAM CAKES

Foam cakes contain very little or no fat. This class of cake is leavened by air whipped into the egg portion of the mix. The expansion of air and the vapor pressure created by heat in the baking process causes the mix to rise. Foam cakes include:

Angel food cake in which egg whites are used for foam.

Sponge cake in which the whole eggs, egg yolks or a combination of the two are used for foam.

A sample formula for a foam cake is shown in Figure Three.

CHIFFON CAKES

Chiffon cakes contain both foam and batter. The two components are mixed separately and folded together for the final mixture as shown in the formula in Figure Four.

SPONGE CAKE
YIELD: 9.66 LB

INGREDIENTS	AMOUNT
SUGAR	3 LB
EGGS, WHOLE	2.8 LB
VANILLA	TO TASTE
SALT	1 TSP
MILK, FRESH, WHOLE	1.25 LB
BUTTER	5 OZ
FLOUR, CAKE	2.25 LB
BAKING POWDER	1 OZ

METHOD
1. WHISK TOGETHER EGGS, VANILLA, SALT AND SUGAR. HEAT IN DOUBLE BOILER TO 110°F, STIRRING CONSTANTLY.
2. BEAT ON HIGH SPEED APPROXIMATELY 10 MINUTES UNTIL LEMON COLORED. VOLUME SHOULD TRIPLE.
3. HEAT MILK AND BUTTER UNTIL BUTTER MELTS.
4. SIFT TOGETHER FLOUR AND BAKING POWDER.
5. ALTERNATELY FOLD DRY AND WET INGREDIENTS INTO BEATEN EGG AND SUGAR MIXTURE TO FORM BATTER. SCALE AND BAKE IMMEDIATELY.

Figure 3

CHIFFON YELLOW CAKE
YIELD: 7.6 LBS

INGREDIENTS	AMOUNT
SUGAR	1.5 LB
SALT	2 TSP
BAKING POWDER	1.75 OZ
FLOUR, CAKE	1 LB, 14 OZ
OIL, VEGETABLE	1 LB
EGG YOLKS	1 LB
WATER	1 LB, 10 OZ
VANILLA	.5 OZ
LEMON JUICE	.5 OZ
EGG WHITES	2 LB
SUGAR	14 OZ
CREAM OF TARTAR	1/2 TSP

METHOD

1. SIFT TOGETHER SUGAR, SALT, BAKING POWDER AND CAKE FLOUR.
2. BLEND TOGETHER EGG YOLKS, WATER (1 LB) AND OIL, THEN ADD TO DRY INGREDIENTS IN A STEADY STREAM AND BLEND SMOOTH. SCRAPE DOWN THE BOWL AND BLEND FOR TWO MINUTES.
3. BLEND VANILLA LEMON JUICE AND WATER (10 OZ) AND ADD TO MIXTURE, MIXING JUST UNTIL SMOOTH. SCRAPE BOWL.
4. BEAT EGG WHITES TO SECOND STAGE AND BEAT IN SUGAR AND CREAM OF TARTAR. FOLD BEATEN EGG WHITES INTO BATTER. SCALE AND BAKE IMMEDIATELY.

PREPARATION OF CAKES

PREPARING THE CAKE PAN

It is important that you use the size pan called for in the formula. For most cakes the pan should be greased and lightly floured. This prevents the cake from sticking to the pan. Cakes in general have a delicate texture and are easily broken. If the cake sticks to the baking pan, it will normally break when removed from the pan. This makes it useless for proper finishing. Pans and molds with designs in them need special care.

There are certain types of cakes which do not require greased and floured pans. The most prominent one is angel food cake. The beaten egg whites that leaven angel food cake will rise better and higher on an ungreased surface. Another type which does not traditionally use a greased pan is jelly roll. Traditionally jelly roll pans are lined with a paper liner or waxed paper. This makes it easier to handle them after baking.

MIXING CAKE BATTERS

The selection of good, high quality ingredients is absolutely necessary to produce a good, high quality finished product. The ingredients alone, however, will not guarantee a fine product. It is the balance of ingredients, the mixing procedure, the gravity, batter or dough final temperature and finally the baking process.

The goal, the majority of the time, is to combine several ingredients into a homogeneous mixture. This can be complicated by the nature of the ingredients being combined. For example, liquid and fat do not readily mix. It is for this reason that close attention must be given to the mixing procedure.

To mix a cake properly you must be organized (mis en place). As with any other type of preparation in the kitchen, you should first gather and measure all the ingredients called for in the formula. Try to get in the habit of turning on the oven to preheat while you assemble and mix the scaled ingredients according to your formula. It is best when making cakes to have all ingredients at room temperature. This allows you to produce a batter which is at the best temperature for the ingredients to interact. The preferred temperature of most batters is 70°F.

It is almost impossible to state the exact amount of time to mix a cake batter. The time will vary, according to the formula and the type of beater used. Needless to say, if you are beating a cake by hand, it will take more time and the ingredients should be added more gradually. Normally, cake batter should be beaten only long enough to combine all ingredients thoroughly.

The procedure for mixing cakes will vary with the type of cake being produced. Mixing the batter for batter cakes differs considerably from the technique used for foam cakes.

MIXING BATTER CAKES

Batter cakes normally require that the butter or shortening be softened or creamed first. This allows it to blend more readily with the other ingredients. The sugar should then be added gradually and beaten in well. Butter or shortening and sugar, when properly creamed together, will get light in color and creamy or fluffy in consistency.

The eggs or egg yolks are added next, with vanilla or other flavorings. Be careful to add the eggs one at a time or very gradually. Given the opportunity, the eggs will act as an emulsifying agent, suspending the fat and sugar, so that the final mix is a smooth blend. When the eggs are added too quickly, or the sugar and fat are improperly creamed, the fat will separate from the rest of the mixture. The result will be a cake with a poor texture and uneven browning. If the batter cake formula calls for separated eggs, the egg whites should be beaten separately at the end and folded in just before baking.

After the eggs have been added, the flour is added. Remember that, at this point, you only want to mix enough to combine the ingredients. If the cake batter is overbeaten, the cake will have a coarse, tough texture with large tunnels. Once the mix is complete, scale or measure the batter into prepared baking pans.

MIXING FOAM CAKES

Foam cakes, more specifically sponge cakes, are very delicate, and their ingredients must be combined carefully. The egg yolks are beaten first, and then the sugar and other flavorings are added. The egg whites, which do the leavening, should be carefully beaten, not overbeaten. This should be done just before they are folded in. It is best to beat a little sugar into the beaten egg whites to help them hold the air.

Next, stir a little of the beaten egg whites into the egg yolk mixture to lighten it. Fold the remaining whites alternately with the sifted flour gently into the mixture. Be sure to use a gentle hand and mix only enough to blend the mixture.

FILLING CAKE PANS

Most cake pans should be filled no more than two-thirds full. This allows the cake to have room to rise. Be sure to spread the batter up against the sides of the pan and into the corners of a square pan. The filling of pans with cake batter is termed *scaling*. This refers to the need for accuracy and uniformity in the amount of batter placed in pans. Figure Five shows the standard scaling weights for cakes based on the more common pan sizes. Figure Six lists the most common baking temperatures for cakes.

SCALING CAKES

PAN SIZE	PAN TYPE	WEIGHT OF BATTER
6-INCH	LAYER	10 OZ
7-INCH	LAYER	14 OZ
8-INCH	LAYER	18 OZ
9-INCH	LAYER	22 OZ
10-INCH	LAYER	26 OZ
12-INCH	LAYER	38 OZ
2.25 X 2.5 X 8 INCHES	LOAF	16 OZ
18 X 26 INCHES	SHEET	7 LB
18 X 13 INCHES	SHEET	3.5 LB

WHEN SCALING FOAM CAKES, REDUCE THE WEIGHT OF BATTER IN THE PAN BY 35%.

Figure 5

BAKING CAKES

Always bake your cakes in a pre-heated oven unless the formula says otherwise. Many cakes have been ruined by a slow start in a cold oven. Make sure that your oven temperature is accurate. You can use an oven thermometer to check it out, but the best test is your own experience. If your cake bakes unevenly or it consistently takes more time than the formula suggests, have your oven checked. Even when familiar with the ovens being used and comfortable with their accuracy, remember that the times and temperatures in any formula or recipe are guidelines based on the equipment used in development.

Glass or dark-colored pans will retain more heat than shiny ones. When using these types of pans, use the same amount of baking time but reduce the oven temperature by 25°F. Also, remember to adjust the oven temperature if the formula calls for a standard oven and you are using a convection oven. If the formula does not state standard or convection oven, it normally is based on a standard oven. You should reduce a standard oven temperature by 50°F when using a convection oven.

Crowding the oven will cause uneven baking of your cakes. Allow room for the heat to circulate. Do not overcrowd the oven or let pans touch each other. If the cake is baking unevenly, turn the baking pans several times during baking.

Any discussion of when a cake is done must consider carry-over cooking. The heat remaining in a cake pan after it is removed from the oven will continue

BAKING TIMES AND TEMPERATURES FOR CAKES

SIZE	TEMPERATURE	APPROXIMATE TIME
6-8 INCHES	365°F	18-25 MINUTES
9-12 INCHES	350°F	25-40 MINUTES
14 INCHES	350°F	35-45 MINUTES
2.25 X 2.5 X 8 INCHES	350°F	45-55 MINUTES
18 X 26 INCHES	365°F	20-25 MINUTES

Figure 6

to be transferred to the interior of the cake until the pan is completely cooled. To retain the proper moisture level in your baked cake requires that you remove it from the oven at the right time. It also needs to be removed from the pan at the right time. Begin to test a cake five to 10 minutes before it is supposed to be done. This is done by pressing lightly with your fingertips on the center of the cake. Most cakes, unless they are very rich, will spring back, leaving little depression when done. Additionally, a cake that is done will shrink a bit away from the sides of the baking pan.

HIGH ALTITUDE BAKING

A change in altitude is a real problem in making any type of leavened product. We give you here only the most basic guidelines for high altitude baking. At an altitude of 3,500 feet or higher, the amount of leavening in a cake must be reduced. Also the oven temperature is raised. If these changes are not made, your cake will be dry, coarse and crumbly. Decrease the amount of baking powder or baking soda by one-third at 3,500 feet; by one-half at 5,000 feet, and by two-thirds above 5,000 feet. Raise the oven temperature by 25°F and do not beat the eggs or egg whites quite as much as usual. The agriculture departments in many states issue books of recipes especially adapted for high altitudes.

COOLING CAKES

As previously stated, timely removal of the cake from its baking pan is important to the quality of the cake. Let batter cakes cook and shrink in their pans for about five minutes after removal from the oven. Then turn them out on a wire rack to cool completely. If the cake should stick to the pan, use a spatula to loosen it gently.

Sponge cakes, angel food cakes and chiffon cakes should be allowed to cool upside down in their pans. This is done by inverting the tube pans in which they were baked. If the pan does not have little feet to raise it above the surface on which

it rests, set the pan over the neck of a bottle. Air must be able to freely circulate around the cake while it is cooling. When the cake is cooled, it can be unmolded.

STORAGE OF CAKES

As with most baked products, cakes taste better when they are fresh, no more than a day or two old. However, if you plan to keep a cake for several days, wrap it well in foil or plastic wrap. A cake, even when well covered, should only be stored for a few days in the refrigerator. Not only will it absorb odors and flavors, it will also dry out.

For long term storage of cakes, freezing is best. Almost all cakes freeze well. They should be wrapped tight before freezing to prevent the "freezer burn" that results when air gets into the wrapping. Cakes can be frozen with or without frosting. However, it is easier to freeze them without frosting.

Defrost cakes at room temperature for one to two hours. If they are unfrosted, let them thaw completely before unwrapping. This will prevent drying caused by exposure to the air. However, if the cake is frosted, it is best to unwrap it before thawing. This will prevent unnecessary build-up of moisture between the wrapping and the frosting.

CONCLUSION

The preparation of quality cakes requires attention to details. The function of the various ingredients, the method of bringing the mixture together and the temperature at which the cake is baked are each crucial factors in cake preparation. When the details are properly handled, the results can be marvelous for both you and your guests. The variety of textures, light as air to sinfully rich and heavy, bring enrichment to a meal. The simplicity or complexity of the flavors are exciting to the mind and palate. Possibly the only thing that is better than a finely prepared cake is a finely prepared cake topped with an appropriate icing. These, however, are the subject of Chapter 36.

SHEET CAKES
Standard 18 x 26" Cake

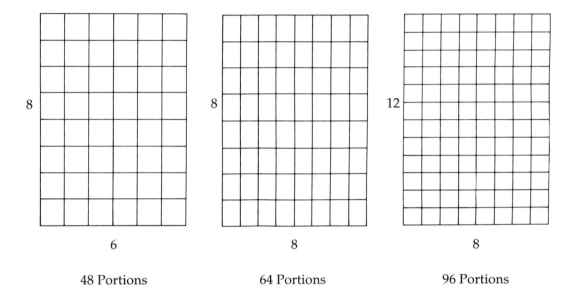

8   8   12

6   8   8

48 Portions   64 Portions   96 Portions

ROUND CAKES

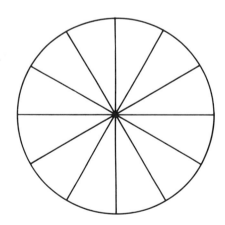   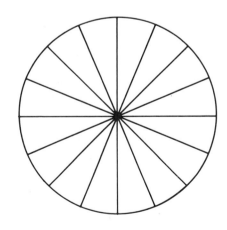

8 - 10" Layer Cake   10 - 12" Layer Cake
12 Portions   16 Portions

REVIEW QUESTIONS

1. What are the four functions of the ingredients in cake?
2. What type of flour is used in cakes and why?
3. What are the functions of sugar in cake preparation?
4. Discuss the leavening of cakes.
5. What is the function of fat in cake preparation and what types are used?
6. List the types of batter cakes.
7. List the types of foam cakes and discuss how they differ from batter cakes.
8. Discuss the preparation of chiffon cakes.
9. How are cake pans prepared for the batter?
10. What are the key points in mixing cake batters?
11. Discuss the baking of cakes and checking for doneness.
12. How should cakes be stored?

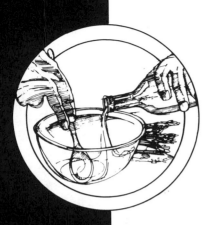

Chapter 36

- **To delineate the ingredients used in frostings and toppings, and to discuss their function.**
- **To delineate the basic types of frostings and toppings.**
- **To discuss the preparation of the basic frostings and toppings.**
- **To discuss the application of frosting.**

Frostings

It is often said that children eat the cake to get the frosting. Truthfully, this is also the reason most adults eat cake. Sweet, creamy frostings and toppings give the sought after flavor to your cake. However, they contribute more than this. The frosting or topping adds eye appeal, gives the baker the chance to garnish, and, in many cases, acts as an edible wrapper for the cake or other baked good. The key to a well-finished cake or sweet good is a well-made, complementary frosting or topping.

INGREDIENTS

The variety which can be created in baked sweet goods by the addition of frostings and toppings is broad. When combined with well-made fillings, the varieties appear to be almost limitless. To make the best use of this important tool for creativity you must know the basic ingredients and their function. Once these are understood and the basic types of frostings and toppings are known, you can begin to create your own combinations.

FRESH WHIPPING CREAM

Fresh whipping cream is highly perishable. It will turn to butter if overwhipped and it will separate if held too long before serving. The most important factor in making whipping cream is temperature. The cream should be whipped in a very cold mixing bowl. Fresh whipping cream must remain cold during whipping and service. Although it is not a stable topping, fresh whipped cream is the best tasting topping you can use. There is nothing which can match its flavor and texture.

PASTEURIZED WHIPPING CREAM

Pasteurized whipping cream has been processed to extend its holding quality. Pasteurized heavy whipping cream is intended for whipping. It produces a stiff and stable whip, like fresh cream. Pasteurized cream should be handled the same as fresh whipping cream, always kept cold and whipped until stiff peaks form. Whipped cream prepared from pasteurized fresh whipping cream is often stabilized with powdered sugar.

DEHYDRATED AND FROZEN NON-DAIRY TOPPINGS

These types of products have improved greatly in the last few years. They produce a very stable topping which has a good flavor. Although they do not taste the same as fresh whipped cream, they are a valuable replacement for it when temperature and time are a problem. Follow the manufacturer's directions when using these products.

Dehydrated and frozen non-dairy toppings normally give the best volume when handled cold. When you are concerned about the holding life of a topping, it may be possible to use a combination of fresh cream and a manufactured product. This combination, when done carefully, can yield a rich flavor, yet good holding life. These products are best produced using high speed on your mixer.

EGG WHITE

Egg white acts as a structure builder in cooked frostings, such as marshmallow and fluffy frostings. It is often used to achieve the texture desired in buttercream frostings. Egg white is the primary ingredient in the preparation of meringue. It is also mixed with powdered sugar in royal icing, which is used solely for decorations.

SUGAR

Sugar, or some substance high in sugar, is the basis of all frostings. The principal sugars used are granulated sugar, powdered sugar and syrup. Powdered sugar is the preferred sugar in uncooked frostings. Its properties of fine granulation and rapid blending are valuable in making smooth, silky frostings and toppings. Granulated sugar is normally used in the preparation of syrups for use in frostings such as the fudge type.

SYRUP

Bakers often use either a simple syrup they prepare (equal amounts of sugar and water) or blended syrups which are purchased. (The cooking of sugars is discussed more fully in Chapter 38.) Glucose or invert sugar (blended sugars) are preferred for making cooked frostings. These blended syrups prevent the formation of large, hard crystals in the frosting. The amount of syrup a mixture can tolerate depends on the grind of the sugar and the amount of fat in the frosting. Remember that too much syrup will keep the frosting from hardening.

LIQUID

Liquids are necessary in frostings to make them soft enough to spread. The amount of liquid in a frosting dictates the consistency of the product and the drying time that it will require. The most common liquids used in frosting formulas are milk, water, coffee, various juices, flavorings and egg white.

FAT

Butter, margarine and emulsified shortening are all suitable for cream frosting. The fat used will depend on the intended use of the frosting and the storage and handling intended for the final product. The temperatures the finished product will be exposed to must also be considered in your decision. Emulsified shortening is far more stable at higher temperatures than butter; however, flavor and mouth feel are also a factor. Butter will give a more pleasant flavor and mouth feel than shortening. A possible solution to the dilemma of stability and flavor is using a combination. If desired, emulsified shortening may be substituted for part of the butter in a frosting formula.

SALT

The function of salt in frostings is that of flavor. As in most other foods, it brings out the other flavors. It should, however, be used sparingly in making frostings.

COLORING AGENTS

There is no substitute for the attractive natural color of frosting. If, however, a particular color of frosting is needed, it can be manufactured using either natural or U.S. Food and Drug Administration-approved artificial food colors. It is always preferable to use natural colors when possible. This can often be achieved by infusing the color of a fruit or vegetable into a syrup or liquid to be used in the frosting. Care must be used when coloring with these types of preparations since they contain not only color but flavor. The quantity needed to achieve the desired color may not equal the flavor desired. Artificial colors do not flavor the frosting; however, when too much is used, an undesirable flavor may occur. Whether using natural or artificial coloring agents, the level of color and the color itself should have a natural appearance with the food. Delicacy of color is the mark of a master baker. An excess of color is always undesirable. Strive for soft pastel tones.

CREAM OF TARTAR

Cream of tartar in frostings changes the chemical form of the sugar, creating small crystals. This gives a creamy texture to the frosting. Cream of tartar and cornstarch act as drying agents, assisting the frosting in forming a thin, dry shell on the outside of the frosting. This helps to retain moisture in the iced item.

TYPES OF FROSTINGS & TOPPINGS

There are a wide variety of frostings and toppings used to cover cakes and other baked sweet goods. Those discussed here are by no means a complete listing. They are the basic ones used in today's bakery.

WHIPPED-TYPE TOPPINGS

Whipped toppings may be prepared from fresh whipping cream, pasteurized whipping cream and dehydrated or frozen non-dairy toppings. For best results, follow your formula for whatever whipped topping you are preparing. The temperature of the product being whipped determines to a great extent how it responds to whipping. Other points to consider are the beater speed and the manner of adding flavorings. To gain maximum volume in a whipped topping, it should be handled cold and

Plain

Open Star

Leaf

Rose Petal

Drop Leaf

whipped quickly. Electric mixers are best for the production of whipped toppings. All whipped toppings can be varied by the addition of fruit, flavorings, coconut, spices or chocolate. These additions are made after the whipped cream has formed a peak.

FONDANT

Fondant is a cooked sugar syrup comprised of eight ounces of glucose (corn syrup), five pounds of granulated sugar and one pound of water, which has been cooked to 240°F, between the firm ball and hard ball stage. The cooked mixture is placed on a wet marble slab and allowed to cool to approximately 110°F. It is then worked with a baker's knife bringing the outer edges to the center. This results in a more even cooling, preventing the outer edges from becoming hard while forming the mixture into a consistently smooth, creamy, white paste. The ingredients are simple, as is the method of preparation for fondant. However, temperature and proper handling are critical to production of a quality fondant. The preparation of fondant is time consuming and it can be difficult to achieve a consistent texture and quality. For this reason, most bakeries today rarely make fondant. It is normally purchased in a ready to use (R.T.U.) form or as a powdered base to which water is added. The quality of the R.T.U. fondants on the market vary widely. You will need to experiment to find the one which works best for you.

It is used both as a frosting and as an additive or base for other frostings. As a frosting, fondant is used for frosting cakes, petit fours, napoleons, coffee cakes and other items. Whether using an R.T.U. or a fondant which you have prepared as a frosting, it is applied in a semi-liquid state which will set up into a shiny, non-sticky coating. This is achieved by heating the desired amount of fondant over a hot water bath to 98°F to 100°F. If the temperature raises too much above 100°F, the fondant will lose its shine. Fondant which is still too thick after reaching the proper temperature can be thinned with a small quantity of simple syrup. The fondant may also be colored or flavored as it is heated. The fondant should be stirred, not whipped, if it is to be used as a dipping or coating frosting. Whipping will cause the devel-

---

SIMPLE BUTTER CREAM
YIELD: 11 LB 5 OZ

INGREDIENT	AMOUNT
BUTTER	3 LB
SHORTENING, EMULSIFIED	1.5 LB
SUGAR, POWDERED	6 LB
EGG WHITES	8 OZ
VANILLA	1 OZ
WATER	4 OZ

METHOD
1. CREAM BUTTER AND SHORTENING TOGETHER ON MEDIUM SPEED.
2. USING LOW SPEED, ADD POWDERED SUGAR GRADUALLY AND CONTINUE MIXING TO ACHIEVE SMOOTH PASTE.
3. GRADUALLY ADD EGG WHITE AND VANILLA, CHANGE TO MEDIUM SPEED AND MIX TO DESIRED CONSISTENCY.
4. ADD WATER AS NEEDED TO ACHIEVE DESIRED TEXTURE.

Figure 1

opment of air bubbles which will create an unattractive appearance on the surface of the finished item.

Fondant used as a base or additive for other items may be handled in the same basic manner. It may, in some cases, be creamed with fat or other ingredients without being heated. Be diligent in following the method given in the formula you are using.

BUTTER CREAMS

Butter cream frostings are light, smooth mixtures of butter, margarine or shortening with sugar and liquid. The goal in a good butter cream frosting is to create a balance between the fat and the sugar. Too much fat, or the wrong type of fat, will create a frosting which leaves a greasy feel in the mouth when eaten. Too high a sugar content will produce a cloyingly sweet taste when eaten. A good butter cream frosting is sweet tasting and not greasy.

This frosting should be creamed enough to give a light, fluffy product.

When properly made, it is a popular frosting for many types of cakes and pastries. There are a number of variations of this frosting which are created by changing the form of the sugar, method of preparation and the handling of the egg whites, plus the addition of flavorings, spices or pureed fruit.

Basic butter cream is simply a mixture of fat; shortening or butter, and sugar. This basic butter cream is often lightened by the addition of egg white or enriched with egg yolks. Figure One shows a formula for *simple butter cream* which is lightened with egg white.

Meringue-type butter creams are mixtures of butter and meringue. These are very light frostings which have a shorter shelf life. *French butter creams* are mixtures prepared by beating a boiling syrup into beaten egg yolks and then whipping the mixture to a light foam. Soft butter is then whipped in to finish the frosting. A recipe for French butter cream is shown in Figure Two. *Pastry cream butter cream* is made of equal parts

---

FRENCH BUTTER CREAM
YIELD: 9 LB 1 OZ

INGREDIENT	AMOUNT
SUGAR, GRANULATED	3 LB
WATER	12 OZ
EGG YOLKS	8 OZ
BUTTER, SWEET UNSALTED	3.75 OZ
VANILLA	1 OZ

METHOD
1. COMBINE SUGAR AND WATER AND BOIL TO 240°F.
2. WHIP EGG YOLKS TO A LIGHT AND THICK TEXTURE.
3. REDUCE MIXER SPEED TO MEDIUM SPEED AND POUR IN SYRUP IN A THIN STEADY STREAM.
4. RETURN MIXER TO WHIPPING SPEED AND WHIP UNTIL MIXTURE IS COMPLETELY COOL.
5. SLOWLY ADD SOFT BUTTER AND VANILLA AND BLEND WELL.

NOTE: SYRUP CAN BE ADDED WITH MIXER ON A HIGH WHIPPING SPEED. HOWEVER, CRYSTAL THREADS FORM ON THE SIDES OF THE BOWL. REDUCING THE SPEED WHEN ADDING THE SYRUP WILL PREVENT THIS FROM HAPPENING.

Figure 2

MARSHMALLOW FROSTING
YIELD: 10.3 LBS

INGREDIENT	AMOUNT
GELATIN (GRANULAR PLAIN)	3 OZ
WATER, COLD	2 LB
GLUCOSE (CORN SYRUP)	15 OZ
SUGAR, POWDERED	6 LB 9 OZ
SALT	1 TSP
VANILLA	1 OZ
EGG WHITES	8 OZ

METHOD
1. SOAK GELATIN IN WATER FOR 10 MINUTES AND THEN HEAT UNTIL DISSOLVED.
2. PLACE MELTED GELATIN IN APPROPRIATE SIZE MIXING BOWL AND ADD SUGAR, GLUCOSE, SALT AND VANILLA. THEN MIX AT MEDIUM SPEED UNTIL WELL BLENDED.
3. ADD EGG WHITES AND WHIP TILL LIGHT AND FLUFFY.
4. USE IMMEDIATELY.

THIS FROSTING MAY BE MADE MORE TENDER BY THE ADDITION OF 2 TO 3 OZ OF EMULSIFIED SHORTENING PER POUND OF FROSTING.

Figure 3

of butter, pastry cream and powdered sugar. Sweet unsalted butter is preferred because of its flavor and melting point when consumed.

Butter cream should be covered in the refrigerator. However, it should be used at room temperature. Butter cream which has been stored in the refrigerator should not be thinned until it has returned to room temperature. When a cold butter cream is thinned, it will be too thin when it becomes warm.

FOAM-TYPE FROSTING

Foam-type frostings are boiled frostings like meringue or marshmallow. Although gelatin is often used to set them and hold their shape, they are not stable. This type of frosting is used when the product will be served in a short period of time. Figure Three shows a sample formula for a marshmallow frosting.

FUDGE-TYPE FROSTINGS

Fudge-type frostings are heavy and rich. Many of them look and taste like candy. They are stable frostings which hold their shape well on cakes and cupcakes. There are a wide variety of premade fudge frosting bases available which may be worthy of your consideration. These types of convenience products greatly reduce the time needed to produce a wide variety of baked sweet goods. Figure Four shows two formulas for fudge-type frosting.

FLAT FROSTING

Flat frosting is a simple mixture of five pounds of powdered sugar, 10 ounces of water, nine ounces of corn syrup and flavoring as desired. The water content of the frosting is variable depending on the consistency needed. Egg white may also be added to lighten the frosting. This simple frosting is commonly used warm to ice coffee cakes, sweet rolls and Danish pastry.

ROYAL ICING

Royal icing is a decorative frosting, made from powdered sugar, egg

PLAIN FUDGE FROSTING
YIELD: 5 LB 2.5 OZ

INGREDIENT	AMOUNT
FONDANT	3.75 LB
GLUCOSE (CORN SYRUP)	6 OZ
BUTTER	8 OZ
SHORTENING, EMULSIFIED	8 OZ
SALT	1 TSP

METHOD
1. WARM FONDANT OVER HOT WATER BATH TO 98°F.
2. IN APPROPRIATE SIZE MIXING BOWL COMBINE WARM FONDANT, GLUCOSE, BUTTER, SHORTENING AND SALT. BLEND THOROUGHLY AT MEDIUM SPEED WITH PADDLE UNTIL DESIRED CONSISTENCY IS ACHIEVED.

CHOCOLATE FUDGE FROSTING
YIELD: 8 LB 11 OZ

INGREDIENT	AMOUNT
SUGAR, GRANULATED	3 LB
GLUCOSE (CORN SYRUP)	1 LB
WATER	12 OZ
BUTTER	1 LB
SUGAR POWDERED	2 LB
COCOA POWDER	14 OZ
VANILLA	1 OZ

METHOD
1. COMBINE GRANULATED SUGAR, GLUCOSE AND WATER IN APPROPRIATE SAUCE POT AND BOIL TO 240°F.
2. SIFT POWDERED SUGAR AND COCOA TOGETHER. ON MEDIUM SPEED, CREAM SUGAR/COCOA MIX THOROUGHLY WITH BUTTER.
3. ADD SYRUP IN SLOW STEADY STREAM WHILE CONTINUING TO MIX ON MEDIUM SPEED. ADD VANILLA AND BLEND WELL.
4. USE IMMEDIATELY WHILE WARM OR STORE IN TIGHTLY SEALED CONTAINER AND RE-HEAT IN DOUBLE BOILER WHEN READY TO USE.

Figure 4

whites and cream of tartar. It has a creamy texture and is used to make decorative ornaments placed on wedding and other specialty cakes. This frosting is not intended to be eaten. When dry, it is hard and brittle. As a man once said, you would break your teeth on it. It is of great value for the preparation of decorative and ornamental pieces.

APPLICATION OF FROSTING & TOPPING

You can add a complex blend of flavor and texture to a plain cake by using a special filling between the layers and a contrasting frosting on the sides and top of the cake. Normally, however, the filling and frosting of the cake are the same frosting. The choice is yours. Whichever you choose, you must properly prepare

ASSEMBLING AND FROSTING A CAKE

Cut layers for desired thickness. Note: Cake layers are easier to frost when chilled.

Make buttercream dam around outer edge of layer. Spread fruit or other type of filling inside dam. Note: If filling is the same as the frosting, a dam is not needed.

Place a quantity of frosting in center of top layer and spread to outer edges without contacting cake. Note: When a very fine finish is needed, pre-coat (crumb coat) with slightly thinned icing and let dry. Then apply final coat.

Comb sides of frosted cake and decorate if desired.

Figure 6

Finished cake without decoration.

your cake for frosting. If a cake is lop-sided or uneven, do not hesitate to reshape it before you frost it. Use a sharp knife and slice off whatever is necessary to make a cake regular or cake layers uniform. For example, if you are making a three-layer cake and the middle layer has a rounded top, slice off the raised portion so that the layers fit together evenly. Figure Six illustrates the frosting of a cake.

Whenever possible, spread uncooked frosting on cakes at room temperature. A cooked frosting, such as fondant, may need to be warmed slightly before being applied to the cake. In general 1 1/2 to 2 cups of frosting will fill and cover two eight- to nine-inch layers. This amount will vary depending on the thickness of the frosting. Again, as a general rule, one-half to three-quarters of a cup of filling will fill a two layer cake eight to nine inches in diameter. Thin frostings can be thickened by stirring in powdered sugar. Any frosting which is too thick can be thinned by gradually beating in a few drops of water. However, this should only be done when the frosting is at the temperature at

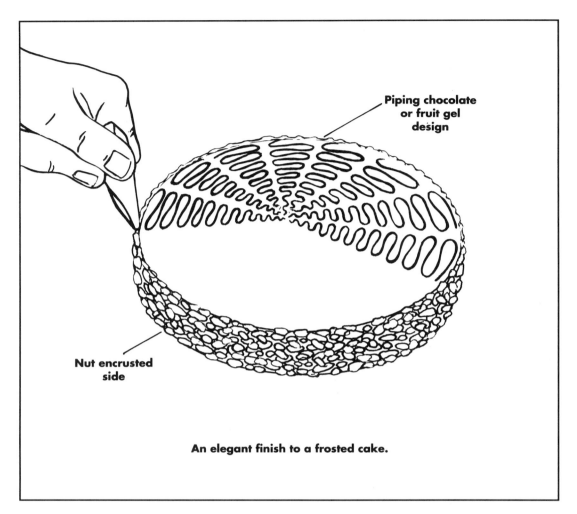

Piping chocolate or fruit gel design

Nut encrusted side

An elegant finish to a frosted cake.

which it will be used. Otherwise it will be too thin when it does reach service temperature.

The stand-up endurance of whipped toppings is short lived. Every precaution must be taken to prevent an early or premature breakdown of the foam structure. Therefore, products being topped with whipped toppings should be thoroughly chilled before the toppings are applied. If possible, whipped topping should be placed on individual desserts just prior to service. The same is true for pies being served with whipped topping and in particular, fresh whipping cream.

Frostings made with eggs or butter should be refrigerated if you are not serving the cake until the next day. Frostings, in general, will keep very well refrigerated. It is not necessary to freeze them.

CONCLUSION

The frosting or topping chosen for a cake or pastry can change its character. The refined petit four with its thin coating of perfectly smooth and glistening fondant is a stark contrast to the cupcake topped with chocolate fudge frosting. Both items are prepared with cake and frosting, yet perceived by the guest and often the preparer as separate entities. Choose your frosting and toppings in accordance with the meal being served; who it is being served to, and how long the item will have to stand before service. These considerations do not limit the creativity of the cake baker, rather, they make it more meaningful. In addition to these considerations you may wish to dress up the petit four or the cupcake for presentation to the guest. The use of frostings and toppings to pipe designs and create ornaments for cakes and other items is discussed in Chapter 37.

REVIEW QUESTIONS

1. Discuss the preparation of whipped cream.
2. How are non-dairy toppings used in the bakery?
3. What function does egg white serve in the preparation of frosting?
4. Discuss the types and forms used in frosting and topping preparation.
5. How does liquid affect a frosting?
6. What types of fat are used in making frostings and why?
7. Discuss the use of coloring agents in frostings.
8. What is the function of cream of tartar and cornstarch in frosting?
9. What is fondant?
10. Discuss the preparation and use of fondant.
11. What are the basic components of butter cream frosting?
12. Discuss the preparation of three butter cream frosting variations.
13. What is a foam-type frosting?
14. Discuss the preparation and use of fudge-type frosting.
15. Define *flat icing* and *royal icing*.
16. State how frosting is applied to a cake.

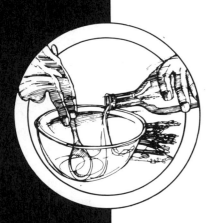

Chapter 37

CHAPTER OBJECTIVES

• **To introduce decorative work as an expressive and useful medium.**

• **To introduce cake decorating as a decorative form.**

• **To discuss the production of decorated cakes.**

• **To introduce showpieces and decorative centerpieces as culinary work.**

• **To discuss a variety of showpiece mediums.**

Decorative Items

The decoration of food has long been regarded as an ultimate form of expression for the chef, baker or pastry chef. It is the ice carving, the tiered cake and the cocoa painting which intrigue and awe the public. Yet, this is possibly the least understood part of the art and science of culinary preparation. Pursue this type of endeavor only after conquering the basics of good food preparation.

Remember that the production of beautiful food is not enough. It must be backed up by good taste! This is true whether the decorative work is part of an item to be eaten, or designed only to be looked at. However, decorative work coupled with well prepared food is truly grand. With this in mind we will discuss basic decorative items.

Decorative items associated with the baker or pastry chef normally fall into two categories. The item is either intended to be eaten or only for display. In either case, toxic paints and sprays, or artificial materials and decorations, should be avoided. The exception to this is when the material is used to create a support structure for a sculpture or similar creation; however, even then the use of non-food materials should be kept at a minimum.

This chapter will divide decorative items into two basic areas. The primary decorative work intended to be eaten is that of cake decorating. The primary decorative work intended not to be eaten is termed showpiece. We will discuss each of these divisions.

CAKE DECORATING

Cake decorating is a fine art, part painting and part sculpture. For large cakes, decorating even becomes part architectural design. A decorated cake offers the customer a truly edible art form. When done properly, it is as pleasing to see as it is to eat. In recent years, customers have increasingly recognized this. The result is the rapid growth of demand for decorated cakes.

CHOOSING THE FROSTING

The first important step in decorating is to choose a frosting of the type and consistency suitable for making the desired shapes. Royal icing and cream frostings are commonly used. However, frostings used for decorating should be stiffer than those for spreading, yet not too stiff.

Heavy, stiff frostings cannot be dropped from a pastry tube. Thin frostings will not hold their shape. You need to find the best consistency for the work you are doing. For simple borders, frosting should be of a medium consistency. Flowers and leaves require a frosting stiff enough to make the petals stand up.

For writing on the cake, the icing should be somewhat thinner than medium consistency, but sufficiently stiff to draw out properly. The frosting lines should not break as they are drawn onto the cake. Frosting for writing may be thinned with a small amount of syrup or water to flow more smoothly.

DECORATING THE CAKE

One of the simplest, yet effective, ways to decorate a cake is with chopped or whole nuts, coconut, candied fruit or other items. These can be arranged in patterns or sprinkled at random over the cake. If you wish to do something more elaborate, there are many ways. The most common of these is pushing the frosting through a pastry bag.

Figure One shows 11 tips for decorating cakes. If you follow these guidelines and develop good techniques for handling the pastry bag, you will be surprised at just how good the results are.

A pastry bag can be bought with a set of tips, or each tip can be purchased separately. Each is cut in a special way to make specific patterns. When using more than one color for decorating, you will need one bag for each color. Because of this, you may wish to make your own pastry bags from parchment paper. This is really quite simple. Fold each sheet into a tight cornucopia with a sharp point. Then fasten it with scotch tape or by folding it inside the tube. It takes practice, but is easy once you get the hang of it. See Figure Two for an illustration of how it is done.

If you are interested in arts and crafts, you likely are a good candidate for cake decorating. As with learning any skill, you need help. Art classes are helpful background in mixing colors and designing patterns. They also provide a learned perspective on proportions and sizes. Regardless of how you choose to learn, the main element in progressing is to **PRACTICE, PRACTICE, PRACTICE!**

Experiment to develop your own style and practice to develop it. Figure

TIPS FOR CAKE DECORATING

1. A CLEAN WORK AREA, CLEAN EQUIPMENT, CLEAN HANDS AND A CLEAN UNIFORM ARE ALL MAJOR FACTORS IN PRODUCING A BEAUTIFULLY DECORATED CAKE. USE A HIGH QUALITY SOAP TO ENSURE GREASE REMOVAL FROM DECORATING TUBES AND TOOLS. BE SURE THESE ARE WELL RINSED. BOTH GREASE AND SOAP CAN CAUSE DISCOLORATION, SEPARATION OF COLORS AND OFF FLAVORS IN ICING.

2. TAKE PROPER CARE OF YOUR DECORATING EQUIPMENT. MANY OF THESE ITEMS ARE SMALL AND DELICATE. IT IS BEST TO HAVE SPECIAL PLACES TO STORE THEM.

3. APPLY A FEW STROKES OF ICING BENEATH THE CAKE ON A DOLLIED BOARD. THIS HELPS TO KEEP THE CAKE FROM SLIDING AND SHIFTING.

4. ENSURE THAT THE ICING ON THE CAKE IS SMOOTH AND CRUMB-FREE BEFORE DECORATING. REMEMBER, THIS IS YOUR BLANK CANVAS UPON WHICH YOU ARE TO PAINT A PICTURE. CAKE LAYERS HANDLE BEST WHEN CHILLED. AN INITIAL THIN COAT OF ICING HELPS TO SEAL IN CRUMBS, AND ALLOWS FOR A BEAUTIFUL FINISH COAT.

5. WHEN FILLING CAKES WITH SOFT JAMS, PUDDING-TYPE FILLINGS, OR OTHER FILLINGS, SQUEEZE A DAM OF BUTTER CREAM AROUND THE TOP EDGE OF THE LOWER LAYER, THEN FILL. ADD THE TOP LAYER. DO THIS BETWEEN EACH LAYER TO PREVENT LEAKING FILLING OR HAVING THE FILLING BLEED INTO THE OUTER COAT OF ICING.

6. USE ONLY PURE F.D.A.-APPROVED FOOD COLORS, WHETHER LIQUID, PASTE OR POWDERED. WHEN DIPPING INTO THESE, USE ONLY A CLEAN SPATULA OR WOODEN STICK (E.G. TONGUE DEPRESSOR).

7. LEARN COLOR USAGE. A COLOR WHEEL, WHICH IS AVAILABLE FROM AN ART STORE, IS HELPFUL. REMEMBER THAT MOST COLORS DARKEN AS THEY DRY. USE COLORS SPARINGLY, BECAUSE, WHILE TOO MUCH COLOR IS NOT UNATTRACTIVE, IT CAN CREATE OFF FLAVORS.

8. SELECT YOUR FLAVORS CAREFULLY. USE ONLY PURE, GOOD TASTING FLAVORS. ALWAYS START WITH A SMALL AMOUNT FIRST, BECAUSE SOME FLAVORS BECOME STRONGER WITH AGE. DO NOT TRY TO FLAVOR EACH COLORED ICING IN DECORATING, THE RESULT CAN EASILY BE AN ODD FLAVORED CAKE.

9. USE A VARIETY OF DESIGNS AND FLOWERS. THESE SHOULD VARY WITH THE SEASONS. CONSTANTLY WORK TO UPGRADE YOUR SKILLS IN CREATING NEW AND DIFFERENT DESIGNS.

10. WRITE OR PRINT THE MESSAGE ON CAKES CLEARLY AND LEGIBLY. THE MESSAGE IS IMPORTANT TO THE CUSTOMER. SEEK YOUR CUSTOMER'S IDEAS TO HELP MAKE THE CAKE A SPECIAL, ORIGINAL DESIGN.

11. UPDATE YOUR SKILLS BY PRACTICING; READING; OBSERVING DEMONSTRATIONS, AND ATTENDING MEETINGS, CULINARY SHOWS AND CONVENTIONS. REMEMBER, YOU NEVER STOP LEARNING!

Figure 1

ASSEMBLING A PAPER PASTRY BAG

Cut a square piece of parchment paper diagonally in half, making two triangles.

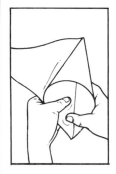  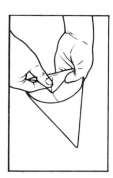 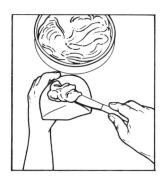 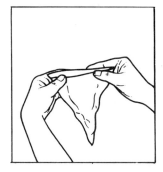

Curl triangle to
begin cone.

Wrap paper to
form cone.

Fold in flap

Fill the bag (not more than
halfway) with frosting or cream.

Fold open end several times.
Before using, snip off tip of bag.

Figure 2

Three illustrates a few basic decorative designs which can act as a guide to design. Always remember that a simple, yet neatly decorated, cake will

*Decorating ornaments for cakes
piped from a pastry bag.*

Figure 3

outdo an elaborate, but sloppy, cake every time. Be creative and original. Ideas are everywhere. The curlicues on a building, a design in nature or a border on a piece of cloth can each be combined with your own special creative ingenuity. Doing this will yield a constant stream of ideas.

Keep yourself and your work area clean and efficient for the best results. By practicing self-discipline you will earn a sense of pride and satisfaction when you realize your creation is the center of attention at a special function. Most importantly, ENJOY YOUR CAKE DECORATING. If you do, it will show.

SHOWPIECE

The primary reason for a pastry chef to make a decorative center or showpiece is pure pleasure. There is little, however, which is as impressive when properly done. These works bring to the attention of the guest the skills and artistry of the chef, baker and pastry chef. Decorative showpieces allow the theme of a function to be tastefully and dramatically emphasized in a form consistent with the food presented. It is far preferable to decorate a food display with a food centerpiece than with non-food artwork. All the items used for these pieces are edible, but showpieces are made for display only. Although these items are time consuming and sometimes expensive to produce, they often can be stored and used many times. When considering the expense of preparing these items, the fact that they can be reused and the impact they have on the guest must be considered. Decorative showpieces can be useful and profitable.

Any form of decorative or artistic display made from legitimate food materials can be considered a showpiece. The most commonly used materials include the following: Sugar, chocolate, pastillage, marzipan, cakes, cocoa paintings, almond paste, nougat, vegetables, ice, salt, tallow, wax, butter, shortening, fat, bread dough, spices, gumpaste, fruit, salt dough and plastic chocolate. We will discuss here only the most prominent types of showpiece work done by the pastry chef. Due to the complexity and intricacies of making these types of items, this is only intended to be an introduction. It will require specialized instruction and a great deal of practice for

you to be able to handle these well, but the effort will be most rewarding for you and your customers.

PASTILLAGE (GUMPASTE)

Pastillage (gumpaste) is a powdered sugar dough made from water-dissolved gelatin. Sometimes it is made with glucose or cornstarch.

The type of pastillage or gumpaste formula chosen will depend on the project. You can make a *hard drying paste* (An example formula is shown in Figure Four.); a *soft keeping paste* (As shown in Figure Five.), or one in between. A hard drying paste will contain a high level of cornstarch, which acts as a drying agent. It dries quickly and is brittle. Hard drying pastillage must be handled very quickly, yet is best for making pieces for construction of miniature buildings or plaques for cocoa paintings. A soft keeping pastillage contains little or no cornstarch, and will stay soft and pliable longer. It is best for sculpting. Beautiful centerpieces can be made from any variation of the two extremes. Again, it all depends on the subject and decorations of your particular piece.

HARD DRYING PASTILLAGE PASTE
YIELD: 3 LB 4OZ

INGREDIENT	AMOUNT
GELATIN (PLAIN GRANULAR)	.5 OZ
WATER, COLD	6 OZ
SUGAR, POWDERED	2.5 LB
CORNSTARCH	5.5 OZ
CREAM OF TARTAR	1/2 TSP

METHOD
1. SOAK GELATIN IN COLD WATER AND LET STAND FOR FIVE TO SIX MINUTES, THEN HEAT UNTIL GELATIN IS DISSOLVED.
2. SIFT DRY INGREDIENTS TOGETHER.
3. PLACE DISSOLVED GELATIN IN APPROPRIATE SIZE STAINLESS STEEL MIXING BOWL.
4. USING DOUGH HOOK, MIX ON LOW SPEED WHILE GRADUALLY ADDING DRY INGREDIENTS, FORMING A SMOOTH, FIRM BUT WORKABLE PASTE.
5. REMOVE PASTE FROM MACHINE AND KEEP COVERED WITH CLEAN DAMP CLOTH AT ALL TIMES.

Figure 4

SOFT KEEPING PASTILLAGE PASTE
YIELD: 2 LB 13 OZ

INGREDIENTS	AMOUNT
GELATIN (PLAIN GRANULAR)	.5 OZ
WATER, COLD	4 OZ
SUGAR, POWDERED	2.5 LB

METHOD
1. SOAK GELATIN IN COLD WATER FOR FIVE TO SIX MINUTES, THEN HEAT UNTIL GELATIN IS DISSOLVED.
   NOTE: THE AMOUNT OF WATER USED MAY BE VARIED TO ACHIEVE THE TEXTURE NEEDED FOR THE WORK BEING DONE.
2. PLACE DISSOLVED GELATIN IN AN APPROPRIATE SIZE STAINLESS STEEL BOWL.
3. USING DOUGH HOOK ON LOW SPEED, MIX GELATIN AND GRADUALLY ADD SUGAR, MIXING INTO A SMOOTH, FIRM BUT WORKABLE PASTE.
4. REMOVE PASTE FROM MACHINE AND KEEP COVERED WITH CLEAN DAMP CLOTH AT ALL TIMES.

Figure 5

Production of a quality pastillage piece requires that all work surfaces, equipment and hands that come into contact with the paste be spotlessly clean. Mise en place is critical to working with pastillage dough. Although keeping the paste, particularly hard drying paste, covered with clean damp clothes will help prevent drying, the work must progress quickly. All necessary tools and equipment should be readily available to speed the process. A marble slab is preferred for rolling out the paste because of the smooth surface it will give the worked piece. Use cornstarch to sprinkle on the paste and marble when rolling. The paste is rolled to the desired thickness and the shapes needed are cut out using paper patterns to ensure accuracy. The pieces can then be dried flat or molded around cylinders of various sizes to achieve the necessary shape for the dried piece. The finished pieces are assembled using either egg white or royal icing as an adhesive. This should be applied with small brush to create as close a seam as possible. It is possible to work food color into the piece to achieve particular shades of color. However, there is little more dramatic or impressive than the natural tone of the pastillage paste when properly rolled, cut and formed.

MARZIPAN

Marzipan is one the most popular mediums for decorative work in the bake shop. Almond marzipan is an off-white, cream-colored paste made from blanched ground almonds, powdered sugar and corn syrup. It is used in fillings or for decorating. Marzipan is impressive, delicious and easy to work with. Because of its texture and malleability, it can be fashioned into whatever your imagination and dexterity will allow. It is great for centerpieces, bouquets of flowers, miniature objects, figures and more. The list is endless.

Marzipan also has many culinary uses, other than decoration. Cake and cookie formulas use marzipan because it provides a richness and flavor not available otherwise. It makes an excellent covering for cakes, which can then be covered with fondant for a wonderful finish. It is also used to make flowers, borders and inlays for cakes. Or it can be formed into individual fruit-shaped candies which can be eaten separately.

The production of your own marzipan is fairly simple. It is the addition of powdered sugar to almond paste. Almond paste is available from manufacturers in the United States and Europe. Ready-to-use marzipan is also available. Both of these products come primarily from California or Europe.

PULLED AND BLOWN SUGAR

Pulled and blown sugar work is the most intricate type of decorative work. By cooking granulated sugar with water or glucose and cream of tartar to 315°F, we are able to make a hot sugar mass. At this point almost all water content is evaporated. The hot sugar dough can then be pulled or blown, depending on the technique used, into beautiful shapes and designs. Mastery of this art form requires a great deal of practice. Once mastered, the pieces produced can only be described as stunning.

NOUGAT

Nougat is a candy made of caramelized sugar and almonds. It looks similar to peanut brittle, but is more attractive because of the sliced almonds. A well-made nougat has a clear amber color and is not cloudy. When the sugar is hot and pliable it can be rolled and cut into various shapes, creating attractive centerpieces.

CHOCOLATE

Chocolate is useful for making many types of decorations; however, it is difficult to work with. Melting and cooling must be done with extreme care. When handled properly, it is possible to carve figures from blocks of tempered chocolate or to pipe out thin, elegant decorations using a pastry bag. Chocolate is one of the most widely used decorating mediums.

DECORATED CAKES

Decorated cakes themselves can become showpieces. The use of a very simple, but elegant, design can create a stunning centerpiece for a reception or dessert table. A decorated cake should have not only eye appeal, but also a story to tell.

MODELING AND SCULPTURES

Modeling and sculptures are two of the most creative art forms. Most likely after craftsmen found that they could obtain clay from river banks, they realized that it could be modeled or sculpted into forms and shapes. The pastry chef can do the same thing, only using a different medium. You will create your art using ice, bread and salt dough, wax, shortening or others. By using techniques that are often the same as those used by woodcarvers and stone sculptors, you can produce reproductions of figures or any fascinating subject. You have the ability to use several combinations of mediums to produce a single centerpiece. This will bring added dimension and interest to your piece. Combinations of marzipan and pastillage or of plastic chocolate and royal icing can be very beautiful.

CONCLUSION

Although much of what we have discussed here is difficult, do not let that stop you from working at it. Once conquered, you will be amazed at the beauty you can create. Before you start anything, get a good idea first. Put it on paper and work out all the details and dimensions. Only by doing this and looking at it several times, can you determine if its a project worth starting. Stay away from showing political or religious expressions in your display. You may hurt yourself or someone else. Always make and show your talents in a RESPECTABLE AND HONORABLE MANNER. Remember that a showpiece is a reflection of the industry you are part of. Represent it well.

REVIEW QUESTIONS

1. What should be avoided in the production of decorative centerpieces and showpieces?
2. What type of frosting is used for cake decorating?
3. Discuss the filling and preparation of a cake for decoration.
4. How is a pastry bag made out of parchment paper?
5. List a minimum of five tips for decorating cakes.
6. Draw five basic decorative designs that can be used in cake decorating.
8. Why do chefs, bakers and pastry chefs produced showpieces and decorative centerpieces?
9. What is pastillage paste?
10. How is pastillage paste used?
11. What is marzipan?
12. How is marzipan used?
13. Discuss pulled and blown sugar, nougat, chocolate, decorated cakes and sculpture as expressive, useful mediums in culinary preparation.

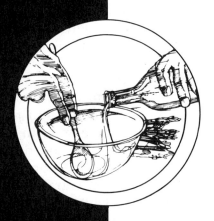

Chapter 38

CHAPTER OBJECTIVES

• **To delineate the primary types of frozen desserts.**

• **To list the basic ingredients of frozen desserts and discuss their function.**

• **To discuss the preparation of frozen desserts.**

• **To discuss the available forms of frozen desserts.**

• **To discuss the storage and handling of frozen desserts.**

Frozen Desserts

Those luscious frozen taste treats, so popular and often so mystifying, have long been a favorite culinary creation. Long before Marco Polo brought back the recipe for sharbat from Persia, the emperors of Rome sent runners to the mountains to bring snow. This snow was flavored with fruit juices and wines and enjoyed at state dinners.

This ancient version of the snowcone gradually evolved, with the help of ideas introduced from travelers to other parts of the world, into a variety of items. These items include the immensely popular ice cream of today.

TYPES & DEFINITIONS

Ices is a general term used in culinary preparation to identify the group of frozen desserts that includes *sherbets* and *ice creams*. The term *ice*, is also used in America for the preparation known to the French as *granite*. For clarity, in this chapter, the term *ice*, when referring to a culinary preparation, will include the general group of frozen desserts as discussed. The term *granite* will be used to identify the specific dessert preparation, which is part of the sherbet group.

SHERBETS

Up to the present century, *sherbet* was regarded as an iced drink. The earliest and simplest forms of frozen desserts were cracked ice or snow covered with fruit juices. This is the description of the Persian *sharbat* from which the present day term *sherbet* derived. The modern versions of this early dessert are the snowcone and water ices.

Marco Polo is credited with bringing back to Italy the idea of a sherbet-like mixture on his return from the Orient. It was during the 17th century that a flavored ice known as *sorbetto* was exported from the kitchens of Catherine de Medici to France. The French called this frozen dessert *sorbet*. Sherbet is the closest translation of the term *sorbet*.

WHAT IS SHERBET?

The basic mixture for all sherbets is a combination of sugar syrup and fruit or, possibly, fruit juice alone. It is the lower fat content and higher acidity level (0.35 percent acidity is specified for commercial sherbet, but not for ice milk or ice cream) that distinguishes the sherbet from ice creams. Many individuals consider sherbet to be an essentially fat-free mixture; however, when produced in the kitchen this may not be true, due to the addition of cream or milk. Commercially produced sherbets also contain milk solids, but normally no milk fat. The result is a product which can vary widely in texture and flavor, depending on the components used in its production.

We can identify several variations of the sherbet family, such as sherbets proper, granite, *spoom* and *punches*. These represent differences in smoothness, flavor, density and degree of hardness due to the comparative degrees of sugar concentrations and the inclusion of egg white and/or milk fat in the basic mixtures.

Sherbets (sorbets) and granite (ices) make a suitable light dessert course; however, they are used most as a palate refresher in formal dinners. This intermezzo is served between the fish course and entree, or between the entree and roast beef course, depending upon the complexity and style of the menu. The sherbet refreshes the palate by helping to cleanse it of the flavors of the previous dish, preparing it for the enjoyment of the dish to come.

Escoffier suggests that as a palate refresher, the consistency of the sherbet should be such that it can almost be drunk from the glass. Sherbets served as palate refreshers in modern foodservice are often more frozen than this. However, they are usually not as firm as a dessert sherbet. This difference in consistency is largely due to the inclusion of wine or liquor in the mix or the pouring of a small amount of liquor or wine over the sherbet just at service. When served as an intermezzo, the portion should be very small, normally around 3.5 ounces or less. When served as the dessert course, the consistency of the sherbet is usually firm. The portion size of the sherbet served in this manner should be consistent with that of a dessert.

SHERBET TYPES

GRANITE

Granite, also termed *granolata*, *granita* and *ice*, is the simplest form of sherbet. It is made with fruit juice, champagne or wine with very little sugar added. This mixture is not extremely sweet. It has a somewhat tart, but highly refreshing taste. The low sugar content, as well as the method of freezing (this mixture is frozen without agitation) allows the formation of larger ice crystals. This yields its characteristic *icy* texture similar to crushed ice. It is this texture which gives the mixture its name.

SHERBET(SORBET)

Sherbet (sorbet) is based on fruit juices, as in the granite, or in some cases fruit purees. However, the typical sherbet has a finer grain than the granite. The refined texture of the sherbet is a product of the egg whites, a component in most recipes.

Egg whites inhibit the formation of very large ice crystals. Additionally, the egg white is most often beaten before being added to the mix. This gives an even smoother feel to the sherbet. Purees of fruit, when used in the mix, also contribute to a finer textured sherbet. This is true even if egg whites are not present in the mix, probably due to the higher natural sugar content.

Sherbets may also be based on a wine such as champagne, sauterne or port. When this is done, they are often served with a spoonful of the same wine poured over them at service. As previously mentioned, this type of sherbet is often used as an intermezzo. Alcohol does not freeze and, when included in the sherbet, yields a softer texture. The higher the level of alcohol included in the mix the less firm the mixture will freeze.

On occasion an element of cream may be introduced to the sherbet mixture. This creates a variation of flavor and texture. An excess of cream will inhibit the fruity, light nature of the sherbet and should be avoided. The addition of the cream also adds fat to the product, which may be unnecessary.

SPOOM (SPUMA)

Spoom (Spuma) differ from sherbets primarily in the amount of egg whites in the mix. A spoom contains approximately twice the egg whites found in sherbet. Also, the egg whites, in the form of a meringue, are usually folded into the mixture after it has been partially frozen.

The addition of the egg whites as a meringue at the end of the preparation, yields a very light, refreshing and always soft consistency. Although they can be made with fruit juices, spoom are most often made using a wine, such as champagne, muscat or sauterne. They may be presented in the same manner as a sherbet.

PUNCHES

Punches, for the most part, are sherbets made using a dry white wine and citrus juice. Into the mixture, a rum or similar liquor is mixed just prior to service.

ICE CREAM

Ice creams, by the nature of their mixture, are richer than sherbets. This is due to the presence of fat in the basic mixture. This usually comes in the form of cream, egg yolks or, in particular varieties, chocolate.

WHAT IS ICE CREAM?

The U.S. Food and Drug Administration requires that any product sold as *ice cream* contain a minimum of 10 percent milkfat/butterfat. Frozen dairy dessert products containing two to seven percent milkfat are called *ice milk*. The outstanding factor that distinguishes ice creams from sherbets is the relative richness and fine, creamy smooth texture of the product. While sherbets are based primarily on fruit juices, ice creams are based on custards or creams which are flavored with fruit and other flavorings. When the major component in the basic mixture is a custard or cream, the frozen concoction is no longer considered a sherbet, but rather an ice cream. In addition, ice cream and frozen custards contain saturated fats while sherbets, if containing any fat,

MAKING AN ICE CREAM BOMBE

1. Place a chilled bombe mold in ice. Line mold with 3/4-inch layer of softened ice cream, ensuring total coverage of interior of mold. Place in freezer temporarily.

2. Sprinkle liqueur and sugar over soft fruit, then toss gently. Fruit can be used whole or puréed.

3. Remove mold from freezer. Put back in ice. Fill center with fruit halfway. Then top fruit with a parfait mixture, and add another layer of fruit on parfait. Seal the bombe with more softened ice cream. Smooth and cover with a circle of waxed paper. Cover tightly with foil and freeze for four hours.

4. Warm exterior of mold with hot towel to remove. Let soften one half hour in refrigerator before cutting for service.

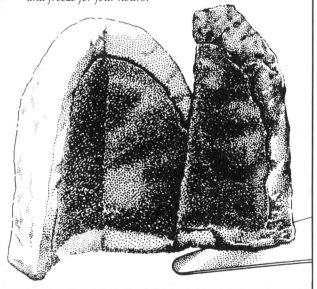

generally contain unsaturated fats.

It is worth noting that currently the ice cream industry is petitioning the FDA to eliminate the ice milk designation. They are recommending that ice cream be sold under four designations utilizing nutrition labeling to explain the difference to the consumer. The four suggested designations are:

1) Ice cream, high fat version.
2) Reduced fat ice cream.
3) Low fat ice cream.
4) Non-fat ice cream.

ICE CREAM TYPES

REGULAR ICE CREAM

Regular ice cream is churned during freezing. The churning of ice cream as it freezes is one of the reasons that it develops a smooth, creamy texture. As the mixture freezes, the constant mixing action keeps the forming ice crystals small. The smaller the ice crystals, the smoother the ice.

Regular ice cream is the foundation of many frozen dessert variations. The most well known of these dessert variations is ICE CREAM itself without adornment. To many purists, ice cream needs no adornment. Simply a scoop or two of well-made ice cream is all that is necessary to fill the requirements of dessert. There are those who feel that a well prepared ice cream deserves an appropriate crowning touch. Some of the desserts prepared from regular ice cream include sundaes, baked Alaska and profiteroles.

Sundaes are desserts made with scoops of one or more flavors of regular ice cream and accompanied by a sauce. They can be garnished with a wide variety of fruits, candies and nuts. In French, these are called *coupes*.

Baked Alaska is a definitely American dessert creation. A version of a Norwegian omelet, this very festive dessert is composed of slightly softened ice cream mounded on top of a round or oval base of sponge cake. The entire assembly is coated with a layer of meringue and quickly browned under a hot flame.

Profiteroles are puff shells, made from choux paste, which are then filled with ice cream. The flavor of ice cream used is normally vanilla and the profiterole is served with a complementary sauce. These may also be prepared using pastry cream instead of ice cream.

LIGHTENED ICE CREAM

Lightened ice cream is a *still* frozen ice cream. The term *lightened ice cream* is used in a culinary sense here. This usage should not be confused with the marketing term *light/lite*, which indicates a product lower in calories that must contain less than 40 calories per serving.

Still frozen means that the mixture is not churned during freezing. It is the introduction of many tiny air bubbles that provide a smooth texture and light airy consistency. These bubbles are incorporated in the form of whipped cream or meringue. This very smooth, airy ice cream is the base for many frozen desserts.

BOMBE

Bombe, *ice bombe*, is potentially the most dramatic of frozen desserts. Different flavors of lightened ice cream, also referred to as *bombe mixture* or *parfait*, are layered into the bombe mold. The mold is often in the shape of a hemisphere. More ornate molds in the shape of a half melon or turreted molds are also used. When completed, the bombe is turned out of the mold and decorated with whipped cream, small meringues, wafer cookies or chocolate.

PARFAIT

The term *parfait* originally referred specifically to the coffee-flavored dessert *parfait au cafe*. In a short time, it evolved as a name used to describe desserts made in a similar manner, but using a wide variety of flavors. Parfait mixtures are comparable to bombe mixtures, but usually only a single flavor is used when making the parfait.

The European-style of presentation for the parfait is molded in oblong parfait molds, or rectangular terrine molds. The molded mixture is then sliced and served accompanied by a sauce and possibly a suitable garnish.

The version of parfaits that most Americans are familiar with is served in a tall narrow glass. The lightened ice cream, or often regular ice cream, is layered with various fruits, sauces or liqueurs and topped with whipped cream.

FROZEN SOUFFLES

Frozen souffles are parfait mixtures, molded and presented in souffle dishes. The souffle mixture is most often based on a whipped egg yolk and sugar syrup foundation. This is flavored and then lightened with whipped cream. A small band of paper is used to allow the mold to be filled above its top. When this band of paper is removed, the frozen souffle resembles its hot counterpart.

FROZEN MOUSSE

A frozen mousse can be made either from a creme anglaise base or from a syrup as are most types. In either case, the mixtures are whipped to a frothy state after being assembled. The mixture is then still frozen.

BISCUITS GLACE

Biscuits glace are molded in loaf pans. Different flavors of lightened ice cream are layered in the mold. These normally contain three or more flavors. The most familiar version of this dessert in America is *Neapolitan* ice cream. When sliced, the marked contrast of the various flavors is displayed in the slice.

COMPONENTS & THEIR CONTRIBUTION TO THE WHOLE

There are a variety of components that come together to make the sum of what we think of as ice cream or sherbet. The part that each of these plays within

---

STAGES IN SUGAR COOKERY

STAGE*	BAUME*	BOILING POINT
SUGAR SYRUP	28°	220°F
THREAD		223°F
FIRM BALL		224°F
HARD BALL		257°F
SOFT CRACK		275°F
HARD CRACK		305°F
LIGHT CARAMEL		320°F
DARK CARAMEL		356°F

*NOTE: The names given to the stages of the syrup are general indicators of the hardness with which the syrup will set when cooled. These names vary from one source to another and are meant only as indicators, not as absolutes. It is also important to remember that the syrup magically shifts from one stage to another. It is changing constantly throughout the cooking process. For this reason the best indicator of the hardness with which the syrup will set (and of the concentration of sugar within it) is the temperature of the syrup.

*NOTE: Baume indicates the specific density of something relative to water at a temperature of 60°F. In this case it indicates the density of the sugar relative to the water in the syrup at his stage. Due to its density, the syrup boils at 220°F. As the density of the sugar in relation to the water rises, the temperature at which it boils increases.

Figure 1

the mixture is integral to the final product. By understanding the individual parts, it is possible to manipulate more easily the quality of the whole.

BOILING SUGAR

Not all ice cream or sherbet mixtures are based on syrup, but many are. Those based on sugar generally utilize granulated sugar. Boiling sugar to make syrup is a process that brings water and sugar together in the desired concentration. It is first necessary to mix the sugar with the prescribed amount of water before bringing the mixture to a boil. As the water evaporates during boiling, the proportion of sugar to water rises. The greater the concentration of sugar, the thicker the syrup. As the syrup continues to boil, the temperature of the mixture continues to rise. The rise of the temperature is directly related to the concentration of sugar in the syrup. It is therefore possible to attach a specific temperature to each stage of the boiling of sugar (at sea level). Figure One shows these designations.

EGG

In most ice creams, whole eggs or egg yolks can be found in the custard. The egg in the base inhibits the formation of large ice crystals during the freezing process. This results in a smoother, more richly textured prod-

---

FRUIT SAUCES FOR FROZEN DESSERTS

ORANGE SAUCE

INGREDIENTS	AMOUNT
FRESH SQUEEZED ORANGE JUICE	1 C
ORANGE RIND, CUT IN STRIPS	1 EA
GRAND MARNIER	2 OZ
ARROWROOT	AS NEEDED.

METHOD
1. COMBINE JUICE AND RIND.
2. REDUCE, OVER MEDIUM HEAT, BY 1/4.
3. ADD GRAND MARNIER.
4. SLIGHTLY THICKEN SAUCE WITH A SMALL AMOUNT OF ARROWROOT.
5. COOL AND SERVE.
NOTE: THIS IS A LOW CALORIE, HIGH FLAVOR FORMULA.

APRICOT SAUCE

INGREDIENTS	AMOUNT
APRICOTS	1 LB
SUGAR SYRUP, LIGHT	3 OZ
LIME JUICE	4 TSP
APRICOT BRANDY	1/4 C
BRANDY	4 TSP

METHOD
1. BLANCH, SKIN AND PIT APRICOTS.
2. PUREE APRICOTS IN A LARGE BLENDER.
3. STIR REMAINING INGREDIENTS INTO PUREED FRUIT.
4. CHILL AND SERVE.

Figure 2

---

uct. Whipped egg whites are often incorporated into ice cream mixtures prior to still freezing. It is this whipped meringue which holds air in the mix, allowing for a light and airy product.

Sherbets sometimes contain egg whites. Usually these are recipes where mechanical churning is called for in the freezing process. As with ice cream, the egg whites inhibit the formation of large ice crystals.

MILK/CREAM

The milk or cream present in ice cream contributes to the richness and flavor of the mixture. It also assists in the development of a smooth texture. In the Americanized versions of traditional sherbet found in American markets, milk or cream is often used. As an ingredient in sherbet, it helps to keep the product from becoming icy and hard over long periods of storage.

FRUITS

Fruits are the main source of flavoring for ice cream and sherbet. They are also the source for many sauces and accompanying garnishes. As a flavoring they can be used in a variety of forms, such as purees, juices or pieces of whole fruit. Sample recipes for fruit sauces are given in Figure Two.

NUTS

Nuts contribute to the flavor and texture of ice cream. They are used in ground praline mixtures as a flavoring mixed into the ice cream base, or as a garnish sprinkled onto the completed ice cream. Nut butters are a major constituent of ice cream bases for some ice creams.

It is best to remove the papery skin found between the nut shell and nut meat. This often has a bitter taste and undesirable texture. This can be quickly removed by roasting or blanching the nutmeats and rubbing them briskly in a towel.

SPICES AND FLAVORINGS

There are a number of spices and flavorings that are used to bring character and distinction to the various frozen dessert mixtures. The manner in which the flavor of these is extracted and added to the base varies. The simplest method is *straight addition*. The flavoring is simply added or poured into the basic mixture. *Powdering* is the reduction of the spice to a powder form which is then added to the base. This is used for spices like nutmeg and cinnamon.

Two slightly more complicated methods are infusion and decoction. *Infusion* is the steeping of the flavoring agent in liquid which has been brought to a boil, but is no longer boiling. The solid particles are strained out and the flavored liquid is then incorporated into the product. *Decoction* is similar to infusion except that the liquid is allowed to continue to boil or simmer during the decoction process. This method, decoction, can form bitter compounds due to the long heating, but can do a superior job in the extraction of flavors.

Puree is a method of flavor addition that is often used. The flavor and character of tender leaves of herbs can be incorporated by pureeing them with some portion of the sugar in the recipe. The flavored sugar puree can be dissolved into the cooled majority of the base, avoiding the heat that would likely destroy the color or flavor of the herb.

METHODOLOGY OF PREPARATION

There are three distinct stages in the preparation of sherbets and ice creams:

A) PREPARATION OF THE BASIC MIXTURE.
B) FREEZING.
C) MOLDING.

BASIC PREPARATION

For basic preparation there are three primary components: Sugar syrup, basic custard and meringues.

Sugar syrup is the predominant ingredient in a sherbet base. When preparing

BLUEBERRY & SAGE SHERBET
YIELD: 1 QUART

INGREDIENTS	AMOUNT
BLUEBERRIES	4 C
WATER	2 T
28° SUGAR SYRUP	1/2 C
FRESH SAGE LEAVES	8 EA
LEMON JUICE	1/2 C
BRANDY	1 T

METHOD

1. PREPARE BLUEBERRIES:
   A) RINSE AND PICK OVER BERRIES.
   B) PLACE IN POT WITH WATER, COVER AND SIMMER, ALLOWING BERRIES TO BURST.
   C) PUREE BERRIES AND STRAIN TO REMOVE TINY SEEDS.
2. INFUSE SAGE:
   A) COMBINE SYRUP AND SAGE IN POT, COVER, THEN BRING TO A SIMMER.
   B) REMOVE FROM HEAT AND ALLOW TO INFUSE APPROXIMATELY 10 MINUTES.
   C) DISCARD LEAVES.
3. FINISH SHERBET BASE, COMBINING PUREE WITH SYRUP AND THEN ADDING REMAINING INGREDIENTS.
4. FREEZE:
   A) FREEZE IN AN ICE CREAM FREEZER ACCORDING TO MANUFACTURER'S INSTRUCTIONS OR,
   B) FREEZE IN A METAL BOWL; BREAK INTO PIECES, AND PROCESS IN A FOOD PROCESSOR OR BLENDER, AND REFREEZE.

Figure 3

sherbets and ice creams, it is the understanding of sugar syrup that is most important. An instrument used in the preparation of sugar syrup is a *saccharometer*. This measures the syrup on the Baume scale, with the ideal syrup being 28° Baume which boils at about 220°F.

The basic mixture for sugar syrup is two cups of water with two cups of white granulated sugar. The mixture is boiled for approximately one minute. The thermometer should read 220°F. This 28° syrup is the ideal consistency for the production of ice creams and sherbets. It may be prepared in large quantities and diluted to the concentration needed for each recipe.

Basic custard constitutes the predominant portion of most ice cream bases. The basic formula for custard is:

1 QT MILK + 8 EA EGGS + 10 TO 12 OZ SUGAR.

The ratios this formula represents may vary slightly in regard to the fat content. This will be a matter of individual preference.

Meringues prepared for ice creams and sherbets follow a basic method. The egg whites are whisked in a grease-free bowl until soft peaks form. Super fine or confectioner's sugar is added and the whisking is continued until stiff peaks form.

FREEZING

Freezing is the second step in the preparation of sherbet or ice cream. The type of equipment used, affects the texture of the end product. To freeze the

RHUBARB SPOOM
YIELD: 1 QT

INGREDIENTS	AMOUNT
WATER	1 C
SUGAR	.5 C
BRANDY	1 TSP
LIME JUICE	3 OZ
RHUBARB WINE	3 C
EGG WHITES	3 EA
CONFECTIONER'S SUGAR	.25 C

METHOD
1. PREPARE SYRUP:
   A) COMBINE WATER, SUGAR, BRANDY AND LIME JUICE. BRING TO A BOIL.
   B) COOL.
2. FINISH SPOOM BASE BY COMBINING SYRUP WITH WINE.
3. FREEZE IN AN ICE CREAM FREEZER FOR SMOOTHEST PRODUCT, ALLOWING TO FREEZE FIRMER THAN A SHERBET.
4. FINISH WITH MERINGUE:
   A) PREPARE A MERINGUE FROM THE EGG WHITES AND SUGAR. THIS SHOULD HAVE A STIFF PEAK.
   B) FOLD THE MERINGUE INTO THE SPOOM BASE AND PIPE INTO SERVING GLASSES WITH A PASTRY BAG AND RETURN TO FREEZER UNTIL SOFTLY SET.

Figure 4

mixtures correctly, you must understand the various types of equipment available.

Churning ice cream freezers come in three types: Ice cooled, self contained or fully electric.

Ice cooled freezers can be hand-cranked or electric, and are cooled by ice and rock salt. They are used for small batches, from one to four quarts.

Self-contained coolant-type freezers have a double walled bowl which is filled with a super coolant. The bowl is placed in the freezer for a number of hours prior to use. This type unit is only suitable for very small batches of one quart or less.

Fully electric churning freezers are both churned and cooled by electricity. These freezers are capable of producing from one quart to many gallons for commercial manufacture.

Non-churning equipment falls into two categories, stir freezing and blending/processing.

The *stir freezing* method is for the production of more coarsely textured granite and ices. All that is needed is a standard freezer, a metal mixing bowl and a whisk. This is explained in the discussion of granite.

The *blender/food processor* method requires one or the other of the two pieces of equipment. A sherbet base is frozen in ice cube trays, reserving a small portion of the mixture unfrozen. The frozen cubes are then placed in a chilled blender or food processor with the reserved, unfrozen base. The mixture is blended until a smooth and icy mixture is obtained.

As previously, stated the technique of freezing used will determine the texture of the final product. Specifically, a product which is constantly churned during the freezing process will have a smooth texture. In addition, incorporation of fat or air into the mixture will change the texture of the product. The technique

COFFEE PARFAIT
YIELD: 1QT

INGREDIENT	AMOUNT
COFFEE, GROUND	1.5 TSP
MILK	1 C
SUGAR, GRANULATED	1 C
INSTANT COFFEE	3 T
EGG YOLKS	6 EA
HEAVY CREAM	.5 C

METHOD

1. PREPARE THE BASIC CUSTARD USING THE COFFEE, MILK, SUGAR, INSTANT COFFEE AND EGG YOLKS. REFER TO THE RECIPE FOR VANILLA ICE CREAM FOR METHOD OF CUSTARD PREPARATION.

2. COOL THE CUSTARD BASE BY STRAINING THE COOKED CUSTARD INTO THE BOWL OF AN ELECTRIC MIXER FITTED WITH A WHIP, AND WHIP UNTIL THE CUSTARD IS COOL AND THE CONSISTENCY OF SPONGE CAKE BATTER (A RIBBON SHOULD FORM AS THE BASE FALLS FROM A SPOON.). THIS WILL TAKE APPROXIMATELY 15 MINUTES. THEN REFRIGERATE FOR 1 HOUR.
   NOTE: THE VOLUME OF THE BASE WILL INCREASE SUBSTANTIALLY DURING THIS PROCESS.

3. AERATE THE PARFAIT:
   A) WHIP THE HEAVY CREAM TO A MEDIUM PEAK AND FOLD INTO THE BASE.
   B) WHEN THE MIXTURE IS HOMOGENEOUS IT IS READY TO BE MOLDED.

4. MOLD THE PARFAIT:
   A) THE PARFAIT SHOULD BE MOLDED AS SOON AFTER BEING ASSEMBLED AS POSSIBLE.
   B) POUR INTO A CLEAN METAL MOLD.
   C) STILL FREEZE TO HARDEN.

Figure 5

used for freezing will be decided by the type of product that is desired.

SHERBET requires constant churning during the freezing process, if the typically smooth texture is desired. This is normally accomplished by the use of either an electric or hand-cranked ice cream freezer.

Granite can be partially still frozen in a metal bowl. The mixture is periodically stirred during the freezing process to break up the forming ice crystals and then is left to rest again, continuing to freeze. This process is repeated until the granite has reached the desired firmness. It should have a flaky, crystalline texture.

Spoom is frozen in the same manner as a sherbet. However, it is frozen slightly firmer than desirable for a sherbet. After freezing, a stiff meringue is folded into the mixture, smoothing the texture.

Regular ice cream is made by churning the mixture constantly during freezing. This is done with either an electric or a hand-crank ice cream freezer.

Lightened ice cream is still frozen, after the mixture is aerated with whipped cream or meringue. Bombe, parfait and frozen souffle mixtures are all still frozen.

AVAILABLE FORMS

The variety of ice creams and sherbets available commercially has

```
╔══════════════════════════════════════════════════════════════╗
║                                                                ║
║                     VANILLA ICE CREAM                          ║
║                       YIELD: 1QT                               ║
║                                                                ║
║  INGREDIENTS                              AMOUNT               ║
║  MILK                                     2 C                  ║
║  VANILLA BEAN, SPLIT                      1 EA                 ║
║  GRANULATED SUGAR                         1 C                  ║
║  EGG YOLKS                                6 EA                 ║
║  HEAVY CREAM                              1 EA                 ║
║                                                                ║
║  METHOD                                                        ║
║   1. FLAVOR THE MILK:                                          ║
║      A) PLACE THE MILK, VANILLA BEAN AND HALF THE SUGAR IN A SAUCE PAN  ║
║         AND BRING TO A BOIL.                                   ║
║      B) REMOVE FROM HEAT AND ALLOW TO STEEP FOR 10 MINUTES.    ║
║      NOTE: IN MANY RECIPES USING FLAVORS WITH VOLATILE CHARACTERISTICS, THE ║
║      FLAVORINGS ARE OFTEN ADDED AFTER THE CUSTARD HAS BEEN COOKED, ║
║      WHETHER STILL WARM OR COMPLETELY COOLED.                  ║
║   2. PREPARE THE EGG & SUGAR MIXTURE BY COMBINING THE YOLKS WITH THE ║
║      REMAINING SUGAR AND WHISKING BRIEFLY TO COMBINE THOROUGHLY. ║
║   3. TEMPER THE EGGS:                                          ║
║      A) RETURN THE MILK MIXTURE TO A BOIL AND POUR A SMALL AMOUNT OVER ║
║         THE EGG & SUGAR MIXTURE, WHISKING CONSTANTLY.          ║
║      B) ADD THE MILK & EGG MIXTURE BACK INTO THE MILK AND LOWER HEAT. ║
║   4. COOK THE CUSTARD:                                         ║
║      A) COOK THE CUSTARD OVER LOW HEAT TO A TEMPERATURE OF 185°F. ║
║      B) REMOVE FROM HEAT AND CONTINUE TO STIR FOR APPROX. 4 MINUTES. ║
║   5. COOL THE CUSTARD:                                         ║
║      A) REMOVE THE VANILLA BEAN AND POUR THE CUSTARD INTO A BOWL SET ║
║         IN ICE WATER.                                          ║
║      B) STIR IN THE HEAVY CREAM TO IMMEDIATELY LOWER THE TEMPERATURE OF ║
║         THE CUSTARD, THEN CONTINUE TO STIR UNTIL THE CUSTARD IS COLD TO THE ║
║         TOUCH.                                                 ║
║      NOTE: THE CUSTARD MUST BE COMPLETELY COOLED BEFORE THE    ║
║      FREEZING PROCESS IS BEGUN, OTHERWISE SMALL PARTICLES OF   ║
║      BUTTERFAT MAY APPEAR IN THE FINISHED PRODUCT.             ║
║   6. FREEZE THE MIXTURE IN AN ICE CREAM FREEZER UNTIL FIRM AND SMOOTH. ║
║                                                                ║
║  Figure 6                                                      ║
╚══════════════════════════════════════════════════════════════╝
```

increased dramatically in the last five years. Ice cream is available frozen prepackaged in a wide variety of sizes. Additionally there are mixes available to which milk is added and then the mixture is churn frozen. Liquid ice cream bases are offered by many suppliers. These mixes are packaged in cartons, pasteurized and shelf stable. They are ready to flavor and freeze. Sherbets are also available prepackaged frozen. The primary advantages to these products is consistency of quality; convenience, and a reduction in labor and, possibly, equipment expense.

With any of these products, quality becomes a major issue. The fat content of ice cream can vary widely. Premium brands contain 12 to 15 percent milkfat/butterfat. This gives these products a dense, rich, smooth sensation when eaten. They will not leave a buttery feel or coating sensation on the roof of the mouth or the tongue.

Overrun is another factor in the quality of ice cream. This is the amount of air incorporated into the mix during freezing. Federal regulations require that ice cream weigh a <u>minimum</u> of four and one-half pounds per gallon, this allows for approximately 90 percent overrun. This is the manner in which the amount of overrun is regulated. The key word in this regulation is minimum. Most high quality ice creams run in the range of 60 percent. The lower the overrun, the denser and richer the product. Ice creams with a high overrun feel *warmer* on the tongue.

Smoothness is another important quality indicator. There should be a completely smooth feel to the ice cream. This excludes, of course, the incorporation of nuts, whole fruits or other forms of garnish. There should also be no evidence of tiny ice crystals or refreezing.

HANDLING & STORAGE

Proper service of ice creams and sherbets requires that molded ice creams and sherbets be allowed to soften slightly after unmolding. If being served in scoops, they should be softened slightly in the container.

This is best done by placing the product in the refrigerator an average of 30 minutes before service. The gentle warming action of the refrigerator allows the dessert to soften evenly all the way through. Softening at room temperature would cause the outside of the product to melt before the center was softened. Remember, sherbets and ice creams are only good for about 20 minutes after they are removed from the refrigerator or freezer.

The worst enemy of a high quality sherbet or ice cream is improper storage. They should be stored in tightly sealed, tall containers of two-to-four quart capacity. Ice creams need to be stored at 0°F or lower. High temperatures will allow the formation of coarse ice crystals. Sherbets should be stored at 10 to 20°F.

The maximum storage time for ice cream is three weeks and for sherbet and parfaits two weeks. Ice filled fruits such as oranges or lemons should be stored no longer than 48 hours.

CONCLUSION

Frozen desserts have long been a popular and profitable menu item. With the introduction of frozen yogurts and frozen desserts manufactured with fat replacements (These cannot be marketed as ice cream currently, because they do not meet the standards for fat content.), these types of desserts have taken on a new look. The opportunity exists to apply classical, traditional presentation techniques to the various less fattening products now becoming available. This has increased the desirability of these types of desserts for the health-conscious consumer.

The traditional preparations are not going to become obsolete, they are simply going to be joined by new selections. As a culinarian, you will find it to your benefit to master the preparation of the traditional frozen desserts. This mastery will bring with it an understanding and appreciation of the methods which can be applied effectively to new products that appear. This will make it possible for you to offer your guest a truly sumptuous selection of desserts that will suit every taste.

REVIEW QUESTIONS

1. Define the term *ices*.
2. What is sherbet?
3. How does sherbet differ from ice cream?
4. What is the function of egg white in the preparation of sherbet?
5. What does *still frozen* mean and how is product prepared in this manner different?
6. What effect does the inclusion of alcohol have on a frozen dessert?
7. Define *granite, spoom* and *punch*.
8. What is ice cream?
9. What is regular ice cream and what types of desserts are prepared with it?
10. Define *bombe, parfait, frozen souffle, frozen mousse* and *biscuit glace*, including a description of their preparation.
11. Define *Baume* and *sacchrometer*.
12. Discuss the preparation of syrup.
13. What is the function of egg in the preparation of frozen desserts?
14. Discuss the use of nuts and fruits in the preparation of frozen desserts.
15. How are spices and flavorings added to frozen dessert mixtures?
16. Define *infusion* and *decoction*.
17. What are the advantages and disadvantages of decoction?
18. What are the stages of sherbet and ice cream preparation?
19. What are the primary components in sherbet and ice cream preparation?
20. Discuss the types of equipment used in preparing frozen desserts.
21. Discuss the preparation of lightened ice cream.
22. What is overrun and how does it affect the quality of ice cream?
23. How should sherbet and ice cream be stored?

Glossary

Aging - Allowing the natural tenderization of meats over time under controlled environmental conditions.

Á la - A French phrase used in menu writing to indicate a style of preparation, such as A la King.

Á la Carte - Items prepared to order or served without accompaniments.

Al Dente - A French phrase meaning firm to the bite, not soft or mushy. Normally refers to the doneness of pasta or vegetables.

Allemande - German-style, also a sauce prepared with veal (or other) velouté sauce and an egg yolk and heavy cream liaison finished with lemon juice.

Allumette - French term for "matchstick." In the bakery, this refers to a variety of puff pastries made in thin strips or sticks. In the other areas of the kitchen it refers to items cut into matchstick shapes, usually potatoes.

Almond Paste - Finely ground almonds mixed with sugar.

Amandine - French term meaning served or prepared with almonds.

A. P. Weight - As purchased; indicates the weight of an item before trimming.

Au Gratin - French phrase meaning food cooked with a topping of buttered bread crumbs, often mixed with grated parmesan or other cheeses.

Au Jus - French phrase meaning served with natural juices or gravy without a thickening agent.

Au Sec - French phrase meaning to cook until dry.

Bake - To cook food by surrounding it with hot dry air. This term usually refers to breads, rolls, cakes and pastries.

Barbecue - To cook food on a grill or spit over hot coals, or in an enclosed pit. Depending on the type of barbecue, the item may be seasoned or marinated before cooking.

Bard - To cover a piece of meat with salt pork or slices of bacon prior to cooking. A method of adding additional moisture and flavor.

Baste - To pour drippings or other fat over a food before or during cooking in order to prevent drying or to glaze the item. Basting of meats should not be done with liquid such as stock. This washes away the fats which protect the meat from drying.

Batter - Semiliquid mixture of flour and other starchy ingredients and liquids, which has a pouring consistency.

Beat - To move a whip or spoon rapidly back and forth to blend products together to achieve a smooth texture.

Bind - To cause two or more items to cohere, unite or hold together; such as to bind a croquette mixture.

Blanc - French for white.

Blanch - To cook a food item partially and very briefly in boiling liquid or hot oil. Usually this is a technique for the pre-preparation of a food item for finishing later.

Blend - To mix two or more ingredients so completely that they lose their separate identities.

Bloom - A measure of the strength of gelatin; also a whitish layer that forms on chocolate due to the separation of the cocoa butter.

Boil - To cook a food item in a boiling liquid. Very few items are actually boiled due to the drying which can occur in this method of preparation.

Boiling - To raise the temperature of a liquid to the point where it bubbles rapidly with the bubbles breaking above the surface of the liquid. At sea level and normal pressure the temperature will be 212° Fahrenheit.

Bouquet Garni - Fresh herbs of various types, tied together and used as a flavoring agent.

Bouquetiere - French term meaning to serve with a bouquet of vegetables.

Braise - This preparation method has two meanings in the kitchen. 1) The food item is browned and then cooked covered in a small amount of liquid. 2) The cooking of unbrowned vegetables slowly in a small amount of liquid.

Breaded - Coating a food item with bread or cracker crumbs. The food item is then usually fried, broiled or baked.

Break - When a liquid such as milk, or a mixture such as a sauce, loses its ability to hold the particles or oils it contains in suspension. This is normally caused by exposure to a rapid temperature change or excess heat. This may also be referred to as curdling.

Broil - The cooking of a food item with radiant heat.

Butter cream Icing - A combination of powdered sugar and/or sugar syrup with butter and/or shortening and possibly other ingredients to form an icing.

Calorie - The amount of heat needed to raise one kilogram of water by 10° Celsius. This term is used as a measure of food energy.

Caramelization - The browning of sugars when exposed to 300°F+ heat.

Carbohydrates - Any of various neutral compounds of carbon, hydrogen and oxygen which combine in the form of sugar, starches and cellulose. These constitute energy food.

Carry-over Cooking - The continued conduction of heat from the outside of an item to the inside after removal from the oven. This occurrence must be taken into consideration in cooking time in order to avoid unnecessary drying of the item.

Casserole - A heavy dish suitable for food to be baked in and food baked in a casserole dish.

Celsius - The thermometric scale on which 0°C is the freezing point of water and 100°C is the boiling point of water.

Centi - The prefix used in the metric system which means "one-hundredth."

Clarify - To clear a liquid, such as consomme, by adding slightly beaten egg white. The protein in the egg white coagulates, attracting the particles in the liquid which can then be removed.

Coagulation - The process of becoming thick or solidifying. In the kitchen, it usually refers to the firming of protein as food is exposed to some type of heat.

Coat - To cover with a layer, usually thin, of some substance, such as flour, aspic or oil.

Collagen - A type of connective tissue which dissolves when cooked in a moist environment.

Complementary Protein - A combination of two or more foods which, when eaten together, provide all the amino acids necessary for proper human nutrition.

Complete Protein - A protein that provides all the amino acids necessary for proper human nutrition. Complete proteins are found only in meat, dairy and egg products.

Consistency - The degree of density, firmness or solidity of a mixture.

Convenience Food - Any food which has been partially or fully prepared by the manufacturer.

Course - A food or group of foods served at one time or intended to be eaten together.

Cross Contamination - The transfer of bacteria from one food to another; from one work surface to another, or from a work surface to a food.

Danger Zone - 45° F to 140° F The range of temperature in which bacteria multiply the most rapidly.

Deep - Fry - To cook food by submerging it in hot fat or oil.

Deglaze - The removal of caramelized sugars and other food particles from a pan by swirling with liquid.

Degrease - To skim the fat from the top of a liquid such as a sauce or a stock.

Dredging - Coating a food with flour or other substance without use of a batter.

Elastin - A type of connective tissue in meat which does not dissolve in cooking.

Emulsion - The combination of two incompatible liquids, such as oil and water.

E. P. Weight - Edible Portion; the weight of the item after trimming and preparation is done.

Fermentation - The interaction of yeast and carbohydrates which develops carbon dioxide gas and alcohol.

Fiber - Indigestible carbohydrates found in fruits and vegetables.

Florentine - Garnishing a dish with spinach.

Fold - The gentle mixing of one ingredient with another.

Fondant - Finely crystallized sugar syrup worked into a smooth, creamy frosting or candy.

Food Cost - The cost of the ingredients used in the preparation of the food .

Fry - To cook in hot fat.

Garni - To add a garnish or decoration to a finished item.

Garnish - The artistic complementing of a food item with other food items.

Garniture - The act of garnishing items.

Gelatinization - The process of converting into a jelly. This is the process by which starch granules swell due to absorption of water.

Gluten - The protein-based substance in wheat flour which builds structure in baked goods.

Gram - The basic unit of weight in the metric measurement system. One gram equals approximately 1/30 of an ounce.

Granité - A frozen dessert which contains coarse crystals.

Griddle - The cooking of food on a flat, solid surface.

Grill - The cooking of food over an open heat source on a screen or grid.

Gross Piece - The centerpiece of a buffet platter.

Herb - A wide variety of aromatic plants used for seasoning and garnishing foods. These plants also have medicinal uses.

Kosher Style - Foods which have been blessed by a rabbi or prepared in accordance with Jewish dietary laws.

Jardiniere - French term meaning the serving of a food item garnished with vegetables.

Jus Lie - French meaning the thickened juices from a roast.

Kilo - The prefix used in the metric measurement system meaning 1,000.

Lard - The soft, white, solid/semisolid fat rendered from the fatty tissue of the hog.

Lard/Larding - To insert strips of fat into a piece of meat prior to cooking.

Liaison - A binding and enriching agent used in the finishing of sauces, usually composed of egg and cream, or raw butter.

Liter - The basic unit of volume measurement in the metric system. It is equal to slightly more than one quart.

Marbling - The rivulets of fat which run through the skeletal muscle of animals.

Marinate - To soak food in a flavorful liquid to add flavor and to tenderize.

Mask - To cover a food item completely with a sauce.

Meter - The basic unit of length in the metric measurement system. It is equal to slightly more than one yard.

Microwave - The electromagnetic wave used to cook food.

Mise en Place - French meaning everything in place. The key to efficient kitchen preparation.

Mirepoix - A combination of vegetables (normally celery, carrot and onion) used for imparting flavor to dishes.

Mix - To combine ingredients in such a way that the parts of each ingredient are evenly dispersed in the total product.

Nouvelle Cuisine - A modern style of cooking that emphasizes light sauces and seasoning and shortened cooking time, sometimes combined with new types of food items.

Nutrient - Anything having food value. It is that which is in food that supports the life system.

Pan-Fry - To cook a food item in a moderate amount of fat or oil.

Papillote - Normally prefixed by "en," this is a French term denoting the cooking of an item wrapped in paper or possibly foil.

Parboil - To partially cook in simmering or boiling liquid.

Par-cook - To cook partially by any method.

Pasteurized - Partial sterilization of a substance, particularly a liquid, at a temperature and for a length of time sufficient to kill harmful bacteria, but without substantial effect on the flavor of the substance. This is the process used to ensure the wholesomeness of milk and other products.

Pathogen - A bacteria or virus that causes disease.

Portion Control - The measurement of a food item to ensure that the standard amount is served to the customer. This action is primary to control of food cost.

Protein - Extremely complex combinations of amino acids which occur naturally in different food items. Proteins are essential constituents of all living cells.

Puree - To mash a product to a fine pulp, usually by forcing it through a sieve or putting it into a blender.

Recipe - A list of ingredients and set of instructions for the preparation of a dish.

Reduce - To boil or simmer a liquid to a small volume. Usually this is done to concentrate flavors.

Roast - To cook food by surrounding it with dry heat.

Rough Prep - The preliminary preparation of ingredients to the point of being ready to cook.

Roux - A combination of fat and flour (usually a one-to-one ratio) used to thicken sauces.

Royal Icing - The combination of egg white, powdered sugar and cream of tartar used as a decorative frosting.

Sachet - Herbs and spices tied in a cheesecloth/muslin bag, used for the flavoring of stocks, sauces and soups.

Sauce - A flavorful liquid, usually thickened, which is used to enhance the flavor and give moisture to food.

Sauté - To brown a food item quickly in very little fat or oil.

Scald - To bring a liquid to a temperature just below the boiling point.

Scaling - The weighing of ingredients or prepared food mixtures for use, such as the scaling of cake batter.

Score- To cut narrow gashes in crossbar or straight patterns across the outer surface of a food item.

Sear - To brown the surface of a food item by a short application of high heat. This process is used to develop flavor and color.

Season - (1) To enhance flavor by the addition of salt or other ingredients. (2) To mature and bring to a proper condition by aging or special preparation, this usually applies to the processing of beef.

Simmer - To cook food in liquid which is just below the boiling point. The temperature of the liquid will be 200°F at sea level and normal pressure and the bubbles will break gently below the surface of the liquid.

Short - Description of a product which is very crumbly and tender due to a high fat content. This term normally refers to doughs for pastry and quick breads.

Sift - To put flour, sugar or other similar substance through a sieve to ensure a fine grain.

Smother - To cook in a covered kettle until tender.

Spice - (1) Any of a number of aromatic vegetable products used to season or flavor food. For the culinarian these are normally considered to be the parts of the plant other than the leaves. (2) The addition of zest or flavor to a dish.

Standardized Recipe - The established method of preparation for a dish in a particular establishment.

Straight Flour - Flour milled from all parts of the wheat kernel except the bran.

Strong Flour - Flour with a high gluten content such as winter patent flour.

Sweat - To cook in a small amount of fat or oil over low heat.

Syneresis - The release of liquid from a gel.

Temper - The gradual raising of the temperature of a cold liquid by the addition of a hot liquid. This is done to avoid breaking the cold liquid.

Turntable - A rotating platform which is on a pedestal, used for holding cakes which are being iced and decorated.

Variety Meat - The non-skeletal meats of the dressed carcass. These include liver, tongue, kidneys, heart, sweet breads and feet, as well as others

Vitamin - Any of a variety of groups of compounds present in foods in small quantities which are necessary for regulating body functions.

Wash - (1) Brushing or coating a food item with a liquid such as egg white, milk or egg wash. (2) The liquid used to coat the item. (3) The applying of the coating to the item.

Whip - To beat with a rapid lifting motion to incorporate air into a product.

Weak Flour - Flour which has a low gluten content, such as cake flour.

Whitewash - A thin mixture of starch, such as flour or cornstarch, and cold liquid used to thicken sauces and other liquid items.

Zest - The colored portion of the peel of citrus fruit.

Bibliography

Amendola, J. (1972).
   The Baker's Manual for Quantity Baking and Pastry Making (3rd Ed.). Rochelle Park, NJ: Hayden Book Company, Inc.

Amendola, J. and D. E. Lundberg (1972).
   Understanding Baking. Chicago: Institutions Magazine.

American Culinary Federation Educational Institute (1982).
   Manual for Culinarians, Volumes I and II. St. Augustine, FL: A.C.F.E.I.

American Egg Board (1989).
   The Incredible Edible Egg. Park Ridge, Ill: American Egg Board.

Amerine, M., Pangborn, R. M. and Roessler, E. (1965).
   Principles of Sensory Evaluation of Food. New York: Academic Press.

Belitz, H.D. and W. Grosch (1987).
   Food Chemistry. (Translated from 2nd Ed.) New York: Springer-Verlag.

Bianchini, F. (1976).
   Fruits and Vegetables. New York: Crown Publishers, Inc.

Bickel, W., Ed. (1987).
   Hering's Dictionary of Classical and Modern Cookery. London: Virtue.

Bloch, B. (1977).
   The Meat Board Meat Book. New York: McGraw-Hill Book Company

Bryan, F. L. (1990).
   Application to HAACP to Ready-To-Eat Chilled Foods. Food Technology. 44, (7).

Charley, H. (1982).
   Food Science. New York: John Wiley & Sons.

Chesser, J. W. and V. Grimes (1976).
   Food Service: Production and Service. Stillwater, OK: State Department of Vocational Technical Education.

Dziezak, J. D. (1989).
   "Spices." Food Technology, January, p.102-116.

Ehlert, F.W. (1984).
   Pates and Terrines. New York: Hearst Books.

Escoffier, A. (1985).
   The Complete Guide to the Art of Modern Cookery: Le Guide Culinaire. New York: William Heinemann, Ltd.

Escoffier, A. (1921).
   Le Guide Culinaire (Trans. H.L. Cracknell and R.J. Kaufmann). New York: Mayflower Books.

Famularo, J. and L. Imperiale (1983).
   The Joy of Pasta. Hauppage, New York: Barrons.

Fennema, O. R. (1985).
   Food Chemistry (2nd Ed.) New York: Marcel Dekker, Inc.

Fennema, O. R., M. Karel and D. B. Lund (1975).
   Principles of Food Science - Part II, Physical Principles of Food Preservation. New York: Marcel Dekker, Inc.

Folsom, L.A. (1974).
   The Professional Chef (4th Ed.). Boston: CBI Publishing Company, Inc.

Gisslen, W. (1985).
   Professional Baking. New York: John Wiley & Sons.

Gisslen, W. (1989).
   Professional Cooking (2 nd Ed.) New York: John Wiley & Sons.

Haines, R.G. (1988).
   Food Preparation. Homewood, Ill: American Technical Publishers.

Harper, J. C. (1976).
   Elements of Food Engineering. Westport, Conn: AVI Publishing Inc.

Hauff, S. (1982).
   The Native Game. Winnipeg, Canada: Gateway Publishing Co. Ltd.

Hazelton, N. (1980).
   Cook's Ingredients. New York: William Morrow & Company, Inc.

Heath, H. B. (1985).
   "Tasteful Developments." Food, Flavoring, Ingredients, Processes, and Packages 7(2), p. 17.

Heath, H.B. and G. Reineccius (1986).
   Flavor Chemistry and Technology. New York: AVI.

Igoe, R.S. (1989).
   Dictionary of Food Ingredients. New York: Van Nostrand Rheinhold.

Journal of Gastronomy
   Journal of Gastronomy. San Francisco: CA,

Kotschevar, L. H. (1988).
   Standards, Principles, and Techniques in Quantity Food Production (4th Ed.). New York: Van Nostrand Reinhold

Kotschevar, L. H. and C. Levinson (1988).
   Quantity Food Purchasing (3rd Ed.) New York: Macmillan Publishing Co.

Kramer, M. (1975).
   Illustrated Guide to Foreign and Fancy Foods. Fullerton, CA: Plycon Press.

Kutas, R. (1987).
   Great Sausage Recipes and Meat Curing. New York: Macmillan Publishing Co.

Lenotre, G. (1979).
   Lenotre's Ice Creams and Candies. New York: Barrons.

Leto, B. (1975).
   The Larder Chef (2nd Ed.). North Pomfret, VT: William Heinemann Ltd.

Levie, A. (1981).
   Meat Handbook (4th Ed.). New York: AVI Publishing Company, Inc.

Lundberg, D. and Kotschevar, L. (1968).
   Understanding Cooking (Rev.). Amherst, MA: University of Massachusetts

Mariani, J.F. (1983).
   Dictionary of American Food and Drink. New York: Ticknor and Fields.

Mario, T. (1978).
   Quantity Cooking. New York: AVI Publishing Co.

McClane, A.J. (1977).
   The Encyclopedia of Fish. New York: Holt, Rinehart & Winston.

McGee, H. (1984).
On Food and Cooking. New York: Scribners.
McWilliams, M. (1989)
Foods: Experimental Perspectives. New York:
Macmillan Publishing Company.
Mengelatte, P. (1980).
Buffets and Receptions. LaMesa, CA: Virtue
& Co.
Mizer, D.A., M. Porter, and B. Sonnier (1987).
Food Preparation for the Professional (2nd
Ed.). New York: John Wiley & Sons.
Montagne, P. (1988).
Larousse Gastronomique (New American
Edition). New York: Crown Publishers.
Morgan, W.J. (1988).
Supervision and Management of Quantity
Food Preparation: Principles and Procedures
(3rd Ed.). Berkeley, CA: McCutchan
Publishing Corporation.
Moyer, W. C. (1976).
The Buying Guide (6th Ed.). California: Blue
Goose Inc.
National Association of Meat Purveyors. (1988).
The Meat Buyer's Guide. McLean, VA: The
National Association of Meat Purveyors.
National Livestock and Meat Board. (In Process).
The Meat Board's Lesson on Meats. Chicago:
The National Livestock and Meat Board.
Oakley, H. (1980).
The Buying Guide for Fresh Fruits,
Vegetables, Herbs and Nuts (7th Ed.) Blue
Goose, Inc.: Hagerstown, MD.
Organization for Economic Cooperation and
Development (1978).
Multilingual Dictionary of Fish and Fish
Products. Surrey, England: Fishing News
Books Limited.
Pauli, E. (1988).
Classical Cooking the Modern Way (2nd Ed.)
New York: Van Nostrand Rheinhold
Company, Inc.
Peckhams, G. C. and J. H. Freeland-Graves (1987).
Foundations of Food Preparation. New York:
Macmillian.
Produce Marketing Association (1988).
Fresh Produce Workshop. Newark, NJ:
Produce Marketing Association.
Riley, E. (1986).
The Chefs Companion. New York: Van
Nostrand Rheinhold.
Root, W. (1980).
Food. New York: Simon and Schuster.
Saulnier, L. (1977).
Le Repertoire de la Cuisine. New York:
Barrons.
Schneider, E. (1990).
Uncommon Fruits and Vegetables: A
Common Sense Guide from Arugula to Yucca:
an Encyclopedic Cookbook of America's New
Produce. New York: Harper & Row.
Shircliffe, A. (1975).
The Edgewater Sandwich and Hors
D'oeuvres Book. New York: Dover
Publications, Inc.
Shugart, G. and Molt, M. (1989).
Food for Fifty (8th Ed.). New York: Macmillan
Publishing Company.

Sinkeldam, C. (1991).
The Art of Marzipan Modeling. New York:
Van Nostrand Rheinhold.
Sokolov, R. (1976).
The Saucier's Apprentice: A Modern Guide to
Classic French Sauces for the Home. New
York: Knopf.
Sonnenschmidt, F. H. and J. J. Nicolas (1988).
The Professional Chef's Art of Garde Manger
(4th Ed.). New York: Van Nostrand
Rheinhold.
Spear, R. (1985).
The Classic Vegetable Cookbook. New York:
Harper & Row.
Steffanelli, J.M. (1985).
Purchasing: Selection and Procurement for
the Hospitality Industry (2nd Ed.). New York:
John Wiley & Sons.
Stuart, M. (1979).
The Encyclopedia of Herbs and Herbalism.
New York: Crescent Books.
Sultan, W. J. (1983).
The Pastry Chef. Westport, Conn: AVI
Publishing Co.
Sultan, W. J. (1987).
Practical Baking. (4th Ed.). Westport, Conn:
AVI Publishing, Company, Inc.
Sylvester, J. and J. Planche. (1969).
Fundementals of French Cookery. Paris:
Librairie Jacques Lanore.
Tannahill, R. (1989).
Food in History. New York: Stein and Day.
Tarantino, J. (1988).
Sorbets!. Freedom, CA: The Crossing Press.
Terrell, M.E. and Headlund, D.B. (1989).
Large Quantity Recipes (4th Ed.). New York:
Van Nostrand Rheinhold.
Teubner, C. (1983).
The Great Dessert Book. New York: Hearst
Books.
Time-Life Books (1980).
Snacks and Sandwiches: The Good Cook
Series. New York: Time-Life Books.
Time-Life Books (1981).
The Good Cook Techniques and Recipes.
Alexandria, VA: Time-Life Books.
Tuer, D. F. & P. Russell (1987).
The Nutrition and Health Encyclopedia. New
York: Van Nostrand Rheinhold Company, Inc.
Von Welanetz, P. (1982).
The Von Welanetz Guide to Ethnic
Ingredients. Los Angeles: J.P. Tarcher, Inc.
Wells, J. and R. Johnson (1986).
The Noble Spud. New York: Penguin Books.
Willan, A. (1989).
La Varenne Practique: The Complete
Illustrated Guide to the Techniques,
Ingredients and Tools of Classic Modern
Cooking. New York: Crown Publishers, Inc.
World Health Organization. (1989).
Health Surveillance and Management
Procedures For Food-handling Personnel.
(Technical Report: Series 785). Geneva: The
World Health Organization.

Index

A

A la carte canapes, 418
A la minute reductions, 232-233
Acids
    emulsions and, 43
    fruit and, 96
    marinades and, 59
    milk and, 82
    puff pastry dough and, 504
Active carbon, 166
Adipose tissue, 239-340
Aeration of a mousse, 396, 397, 398
Agar, 42
Agar-agar, 367
Aging process of meats, 244-245
Al dente, 153
Albedo, 99
Albumin, 88, 89, 163, 164
Alexander the Great, 2
Alimentary pastes, 150
Alkaloids in potatoes, 137
All-purpose flour, 470, 479
All-purpose shortening, 72
Allemande Sauce, 222
Allspice, 471
Alsatian cookery, 156
Aluminum cookware, 128, 205
Amber savory jelly, 368, 369
American cheese, 84
American cookery, 5, 8, 9, 10, 191-193
American Culinary Federation
    Educational Institute (ACFEI), 7-8
American Heart Association, 57, 76, 463
Amino acids, 149
Ammonium salts, 479
Angel food cake, 528
Anise, 471
Anisette liqueur, 129
Anthocyanin pigment, 119
Antibuse, 116
Antipasto, 413
Apicius, 3, 4, 172, 274
Appetizers, 411-412. See also Hors
    d'oeuvres
Apple griddle cakes, 497
Apple orange salad, 360
Apple pie filling, 518
Apple seeds, 98
Aquaculture, 286
Aroma of foods, 36
Aromatics in stock, 164
Arrowroot, 206
Artichokes, 117, 128
Artificial fats, 77

Asparagus, 107
Aspic jelly
    characteristics of, 370-371
    commercial mixes, 368-369
    culinary applications, 371-383, 378-
    379, 402-403
    decorative techniques, 379-383
    handling/storage, 371
    preparation methods, 167-168, 368,
    376-378
    types, 369, 370
Aspic mirror, 382
Attereaux, 427
Au sec, 100
Augustus, Emperor, 466
Austrian cookery, 193
Avgolemono soup, 194
Axis deer, 280

B

Bacon, 318-321, 444-445
Bacteria, 18, 83
Baked Alaska, 557
Baked custard pie filling, 519-520
Baker, 7
Baker's percentage, 23
Baker's shortening, 72
Baking. See also Bread; Dough, bread;
    Dough, pastry
    art/science of, 467-468
    cakes, 531-532
    cookies, 513
    definition, 39
    fish, 301
    griddle cakes, 496-497
    history, 465-467
    ingredients/functions, 468-472
    oven temperatures, 472, 473
    potatoes, 136-137
    terminology of, 472, 474-475
    vegetables, 123-124
Baking powder, 469, 525
Baking powder biscuits, 492
Baking soda, 469, 525
Ballottines, 395, 399, 408
Banquet-style canapes, 416-417
Barbecue sauces, 233
Barbecuing, 300-301
Barding meats, 256
Barquettes, 418-419, 427
Base sauces, 203
Bases
    canapes, 415
    convenience, 169

mousse, 396, 397
Basic beurre blanc, 226-227
Basic butter cream frosting, 539
Basic custard, 561
Basic French dressing, 328-331
Basic liaison, 208
Basic sandwich, 449
Batonette, 24
Batter, 490, 529-530
Batter cakes, 530, 538
Bavarian cream pie fillings, 520-521
Bayonne ham, 444
Bean spreads, 460
Bean sprouts, 110
Bean thread noodles, 154
Beans, 110-111
Bear, 280
Bearnaise sauce, 227-228, 230
Beating egg whites, 88, 92, 470, 536
Bechamel sauce, 218, 219
Beef
    aging process, 244-245
    cuts of, 247-250
    history, 236-237
    quality grading, 243-244
Beef broth, 174, 175
Beef fat, 71-72
Beefalo, 281
Beets, 128
Beignets, 427-428
Belgium endive, 109
Bell peppers, 113
Bercy blanche, 224
Bercy butter, 231
Berliners, 441
Bernard, Emile, 4, 5
Beurre sauces, 226-227, 230-232
Binders
    mousse, 396, 397-398
    sausages, 437-438
Birds, game, 276-279
Biscuits, 322, 492, 493
Biscuits, glace, 558
Bisques, 182, 184-185
Bitter sensations (tongue), 48
Bivalves, 296, 307-308, 359
Black bean salad, 352
Blackbuck antelope, 280
Blanching, 121-122, 135, 256
Blond roux, 204
Bloom number, 364
Blue cheese dressing, 332
Blue veined cheese, 84, 425
Blueberry and sage sherbert, 561

Blueberry griddle cakes, 497
Boar, 280
Bockwurst, 441
Boiled dressing, 333, 334
Boiled eggs, 312-313
Boiled ham, 443
Boiled rice, 142, 143
Boiling
    definition, 39
    potatoes, 135
    sugar, 558, 559
    vegetables, 122, 123
Bok choy, 108
Bologna, 441
Bolognese fennel, 129
Bombe, 556, 557
Bone tissue, 240
Boning knife, 23
Bony fish, 291
Bordelaise sauce, 221
Borscht, 195
Boston bibb lettuce, 109
Bouchees, 428-429
Bouillabaisse Marseillaise, 194
Bouillon, 168-169, 173-175
Braising
    definition 37
    meats, 259
    potatoes, 135
    vegetables, 123, 124
Bran layer of wheat, 148
Braunschweiger, 441
Bread. See also Quick breads
    baking, 486
    components, 478-481
    definition, 477
    forming loaves, 484-485
    handling/storage, 487-488
    kneading dough, 473
    preparation methods/dough, 481-484
    proofing, 485-486
    sandwiches, 456-457
    variety/trends, 487
    washes, 486
Bread flour, 470
Breading of fried foods, 75-76
Breads, breakfast, 323-324
Breakfast cookery
    breads, 323-324
    cereals and, 318
    definition, 311-312
    eggs, 312-318
    fruit/juices, 324
    meats and, 318-321
    mise en place/preparation, 312
    pancakes/waffles/French toast, 323

potatoes, 321, 323
Brigade, Classical. See Classical Brigade
    system
Brillat-Savarin, 48, 236
Brine pumping, 442
Brining, 442-443
British cookery. See English cookery
British Thermal Unit (BTU), 29-30
Broccoli, 106
Broccoli soup, cream of, 188
Brochettes, 429
Broiled sandwiches, 452-453
Broiler-cook, 6-7
Broiling, 37, 135
    fish, 300-301
    meats, 257
    poultry, 266-267
Broth, 173-176
Brown rice, 141
Brown roux, 204
Brown sauces, 213-218, 220
Brown stock, 160, 162
Brown sugar, 469, 551
Browning reactions, 35
Brussels sprouts, 104-105
Buckwheat griddle cakes, 497
Buffalo, 280-281
Buffet-style service, 8, 9, 430-431
Bulb vegetables, 114-115
Burnt bones, 166
Butter, 69, 72-73, 75, 83
    in baking, 468
    in sandwiches, 460
    in sauces, 207
Butter cream frosting, 529-540, 538
Butter sauces, 45, 230-232
Butterfat, 81
Butterhead lettuce, 109
Buttermilk, 81, 471
Buttermilk griddle cakes, 497

C

Cabbage soup, 193
Cabbage turnip, 106, 129
Cabbages, 104-106
Caesar, Julius, 466
Cake decorating
    definition, 546
    frostings for, 546
    mediums for, 549-551
    techniques, 546-549
Cake doughnuts, 495, 496
Cake flour, 470
Cake pans, 529, 530
Cakes
    assembling/frosting, 541-542
    baking, 531-532

cooling/storage, 532
cutting of, 533
definition, 523
ingredients/functions, 524-527
preparation methods, 529-530
types, 526, 527, 528-529
Calcium salts, 479
California long white potatoes, 133
Calories, 76
Campagne forcemeat, 386, 387
Canadian bacon, 445
Canapes, 415-418
Canned fruits, 517
Canned hams, 444
Canned vegetables, 122
Capacolla ham, 444
Caramelization, 35, 39, 162
Caraway, 471
Carbohydrates, 242
Carbon steel cookware, 97
Carcass cuts, 245-246
Carcass fat, 71
Careme, Antoine, 4, 5, 9, 202, 467
Carob, 42
Carolines, 419-421
Carotene, 120, 146
Carotene pigment, 150
Carpaccio, 354
Carrageenan, 42
Carrots, 128-129
Carry-over heat, 487, 519, 531
Cartouche, 467
Carving knife, 23
Carving meats, 260-261
Casings for sausages, 438-441
Caspian caviar, 427
Caul fat casings, 441
Cauliflower, 105-106
Caviar, 425-427
Celeriac, 129
Celery, 107-108
Cellulose, 96, 118
Cepe mushrooms, 116-117
Cephalopods, 294, 296, 308, 309
Cereals, breakfast, 318
Cereals and grains
    cooking methods, 148-149
    definition, 145-146
    nutritional aspects, 149
    types, 146-148
Certified pork, 443
Cervelat, 442
Chalazae, 88, 89
Champignon de Paris muchrooms, 115-116
Chanterelle mushrooms, 116
Charcuterie

casings, 438-441
components, 436-438
definition, 433-434, 435
products, 434-435
types, 435-436, 441-445
United States, 434
Charlemagne, 3, 4
Chartreuse liqueur, 129
Chaud-froid sauce
    handling/storage, 376
    mirrors with, 382
    preparation methods,
        classical/contemporary, 372-373
    preparation methods, steps of, 373-375
    quality indicators for, 375-376
    types/definition, 371-372, 378
Cheddar cheese, 85
Cheese
    cooking with, 85
    hors d'oeuvres, 423-425
    in sandwiches, 459, 460
    storage/service, 85
    types, 83-84, 423-425
Cheese spreads, 85, 460
Chef salad, 343
Chefs, 4, 6, 7-8. See also Careme,
    Antoine; Escoffier, Auguste;
    Executive chefs
Chefs de partie, 6
Chevre, 84
Chicken, 266, 268, 272
Chicken consomme, 179
Chicken salad with raspberry
    vinaigrette, 354
Chiffon cakes, 529, 538
Chiffon pie fillings, 520
Chimneys in paté, 402
Chinese artichokes, 128
Chinese cabbage, 104
Chinese cookery, 10, 100, 147
Chinese egg noodles, 154
Chinese snow peas, 110
Chives, 115
Chlorophyll pigment, 120
Chocolate, 46, 472, 525-526, 551
Chocolate cakes, 527, 528
Chocolate fudge frosting, 541
Cholesterol, 73, 76-77, 92, 336
Chop, 26
Choux puffs, 419-421
Chowders, 190-192
Chutney, 100
Cider vinegar, 57
Cinnamon, 471
Citric acid, 96, 97
Citrus juices, 43

Clams, 309
Clarification of consomme, 176-177, 178
Clarification of stock, 163-164
Clarified butter, 75, 83, 204
Classic cuisine, 9
Classical Brigade system, 5, 6, 7
Classical cuts, 24-26
Classical garniture, 64, 65
Classical menus, 12-13
Cleaning of sauces, 210-211
Clear soups, 173-182
Closed sandwiches, cold, 453-455
Closed sandwiches, hot, 449-452
Cloves, 471
Club cheese, 85
Club sandwiches, 455
Cobblers, 510
Cocktail sauce, 335
Cocoa butter/powder, 472
Cod, 290-291
Coffee parfait, 563
Cold foods, safe temperatures for, 17,
    18, 62, 200
Cold mousses/mousselines, 378
Cold pack cheese, 85
Cold sandwiches, 453-455
Cold sauces
    commercially produced, 337
    definition, 327-328
    function of, 327
    handling/storage, 337-338
    nutritional aspects, 336-337
    types, 328-336
Cold smoked sausages, 441-442
Cold soups, 195-197
Cole slaw, 106
Collagen casings (sausages), 440-441
Collards, 108-109
Collees, 376
Color of foods, 63, 119-120
Coloring agents, 437, 537
Columbus, 47
Combination closed sandwiches, cold,
    454-455
Combination salads, 341
Commis, 6
Communication. See Language of the
    kitchen
Compound butters, 230-232
Compound coatings, 472
Compound sauces, 218, 220, 222-224
Compound shortening, 72
Concentrated flavoring agents, 56
Condensed milk, 82
Condiments, 100, 328, 460
Conduction, 29, 31-32
Consomme, 176-180, 180-181. See also

Jellied consomme
Consumer Reports magazine, 74
Convection, 29
Convection ovens, 259
Convenience bases and glazes, 169
Converted rice, 141
Converting
    recipes, 22
    weights and measures, 21
Cook, 7
Cooked marinades, 59
Cooked sausages, 435, 441
Cookie dough
    baking, 513
    definition, 499
    ingredients, 512
    mixing, 513
    types, 512-513
Cooking methods
    types/terminology, 36-39
Cooking oils as flavoring agents, 56
Cook's helper, 6, 7
Cook's helper assistant, 6
Cooling of foods, 32-34, 532
Copper cookware, 31
Corn, 111, 146-147
Corn syrup, 469
Cornbread, 492-493
Corned beef, 445
Cornish pastry, 400
Cornmeal, 146-147, 470
Cornstarch, 147, 206, 516, 537
Cos lettuce, 109
Cotto, 444
Coulis, 182-185
Country-cured bacon, 445
Country ham, 443
Country-style forcemeat, 386, 387
Country-style pork sausage, 441
Countey-style terrines, 405
Court bouillon, 168-169
Coverture, 472
Crab, 294, 304, 305-306
Crayfish, 294, 306-307
Cream, 80-81, 207-208, 209, 560
Cream cheese spreads, 423
Cream of tartar, 92, 537
Cream pie fillings, 518-519, 520-521
Cream sauce, 222
Cream soups, 186-188
Creaming of cookie dough, 513
Creole cookery, 112
Crisphead lettuce, 109
Croutes, 198
Croutons, 198, 382-383
Crudites, 415
Crudo, 444

Crustaceans, 293, 294, 359-360
Crusts, pie, 508-509
Cucumbers, 111-112
Cuisine development, 9-11
Culatello, 444
Culinary preparation. *See also*
    Decoration of food; Language of the
    kitchen; Presentation of food
    art/science of, 1-2
    history, 2-6
    kitchen organization and, 6-8
    menu planning, 11-13
    sanitation and, 16-18
    type of cuisine and, 9-11
    type of service and, 8-9
Cumberland sauce, 335
Curdling of milk, 82-83
Curing agents
    forcemeats, 394-395
    hams, 442-443
    sausages, 436-437
Curing salt, 393
Curly endive, 109
Curried rice salad, 351
Custard, 233-234, 561
Custard pie fillings, 519-520
Cutting techniques
    cakes, 533
    doughnuts, 494, 495
    fish, 297
    strips and dice, 392
    terminology/types, 24-26
    vegetables, 121

D

Dairy products
    cooking with, 82-83, 85
    definition, 79
    storage/service of, 85
    types, 80-82, 83-85
Danish pastry dough, 501, 503
Dark chocolate, 472
Dark-fleshed fish, 293
Daube de veau en gelée, 377-378
David, Elizabeth, 149
Decoction of spices, 560
Decoration of food, 545. *See also* Cake
    decorating
Deep fat frying
    definition, 37-38
    doughnuts, 496
    fish, 301
    potatoes, 136
    poultry, 269-270
    protecting fats/oils, 75-76
    vegetables, 124-125
Deer, 280

Dehydrated non-dairy toppings, 536
Demi-glace sauce, 213-216, 221
Dent corn, 146
Depouillage, 164, 210-211
Deuxieme commis, 6
Diat, Louis, 196
Dice, 26
Dipping method, 374-375
Dips, 423
Disodium phophate, 150
Distillation of flavoring agents, 56
Distilled vinegar, 57
Domestic caviar, 427
Doneness, testing for. *See* Testing for
    doneness
Double consomme, 176
Dough, bread
    baking, 486
    forming loaves, 484-485
    ingredients/functions, 478-479
    kneading, 473
    preparation methods, 481-483
    proofing, 485-486
    raising of, 483-484
    washes, 486
Dough, pastry. *See also* Cookie dough;
    Pie pastry dough; Puff pastry
    dough; Sweet dough
    definition, 499
Dough conditioners, 479
Doughnut icing, 496
Doughnuts, 493-496
Dressings, salad. *See* Salad dressings
Dried eggs, 91
Dried fruit, 526
Dried herbs, 55
Dried milk, 82
Drop batter, 490
Dry aging process, 245
Dry and semi-dry sausages, 435-436,
    442
Dry curing, 442, 443
Dry rendering, 71
Dry whole milk solids, 471
Drying of hams, 443
Dubois, Urbain, 4, 5, 467
Duck, 266, 276, 278
Durum wheat, 148
Dutch East India Company, 141
Dutch processed cocoa, 472
Dutch yellow and red long potatoes,
    133

E

Earl of Sandwich, 448
Early summer carrots, 128
Edgewater, 463

Edible fungi, 115-117
Edible pods. *See* Seeds, edible pods,
    young shoots
Egg royale, 198
Egg washes, 486
Egg whites, 88, 92, 470, 536
Eggplant, 112
Eggs
    available forms, 90-91
    in baking, 470-471
    in bread baking, 481
    in cakes, 524
    composition, 88
    in cookie dough, 512
    definition, 87
    in forcemeat, 393
    in frozen desserts, 559-560
    grading/sizing criteria, 88-90
    handling/storage, 92
    for making pasta, 150, 151
    nutritional aspects, 92
    in pie fillings, 516
    preparation, 91-92, 312-318
    in puff pastry dough, 504
    in quick bread baking, 490
    in sandwiches, 459
    in sweet dough, 500
Electric slicers, 24
Emincer, 26
Empanada, 400
Emulsified French dressing, 330-331
Emulsified sauces, 225-230
Emulsified shortening, 72
Emulsions
    breakdown of, 43-45
    definition, 41-42
    importance of, 45-46
    stabilization of, 42-43
Endive, 109
English cookery, 3, 8, 335-336, 414
Enoki mushrooms, 116
Enriched rice, 141
Entremetier, 6
Enzymatic browning, 35, 97-98
Escoffier, Auguste, 5, 6, 9, 12, 62, 159,
    172, 202, 211, 214, 339, 387-388, 393,
    554
Espagnole sauce, 213-215, 221
Essences, 166, 180-181
Essential oils, 56
Evaporated mlik, 82, 471
Executive chefs, 6, 7, 8
Exotic game, 279, 282
Extenders for sausages, 437-438
Extra virgin olive oil, 71
Extraction of flavoring agents, 56
Eye appeal in food presentation, 63

F

Fabrication of forcemeats, 394-395
Factory mass-produced pasta, 150, 152-153
Family-style service, 9
Farina, 140, 145
Farinaceous cookery
    definition, 139-140
    grains/cereals, 145-149
    pasta/noodles, 149-157
    rice, 140-145
Farmstyle vegetable soup, 190
Fat fish, 287, 302
Fats. *See also* Oils
    in baking, 468
    in cakes, 524
    chemical makeup of, 68-70
    in cookie dough, 512
    definition, 67
    filtering, 75-76
    in forcemeat, 393
    in frostings/toppings, 537
    in meat, 241-242
    in puff pastry dough, 504, 506
    in quick bread baking, 490
    temperature effects on, 73-75
    types, 77
    types/extraction methods, 71-73
Fatty acids, 68-70, 76, 77
Fava beans, 110
Feathered game, 274, 276-279
Fennel, 129
Fermentation of dough, 495, 501
Fermented milk products, 81
Field corn, 146
Filled pasta, 152
Fillings, pie, 510-512
Fillings, sandwiches, 457-458
Filtering of stock, 166
Finger food, 414-415
Finish, 240
Firm white fish, 289-290
First-in-First-out (FIFO), 17
Fish
    available forms, 296-297
    composition/structure, 286
    definition, 285-286
    fat/lean, 287
    preparation methods, 168-169, 297-303
    preparation methods, specialized, 303-309
    in sandwiches, 458
    types, 286, 287-296
Fish chowder, New England style, 191
Fish consomme, 180
Fish essence, 165

Fish oils, 69, 77
Fish salads, 360-361
Fish stock, 160-161, 163
5/4/3 emulsion forcemeat, 390, 391
Flaky white fish, 290
Flambe desserts, 100
Flash point of fats, 74
Flat frosting, 540
Flatfish, 287-288
Flavones pigment, 119
Flavor
    cooked vegetables and, 119
    development of, 35-36
    food presentation and, 62
Flavored marinades, 59
Flavored milk, 80
Flavored salt, 49
Flavored vinegar, 58
Flavoring agents, 51-59, 98-99. *See also* Seasoning and flavoring
Flint corn, 146
Florentine fennel, 129
Flour
    in baking, 469-470
    in bread baking, 479-480
    in cakes, 524
    in cookie dough, 512
    in pasta, 150, 151
    in pie pastry dough, 507-508
    in puff pastry dough, 504
    in quick breads, 490
    in sweet dough, 500
Flow icing, 496
Foam cakes, 528, 530
Foam-type frosting, 540
Foie gras, 208
Fond, 159-161
Fondant, 538-539
Food calories, 76
Food contamination, 519
Food preparation, sanitary, 16-18
Food processors, 24
Food Safety and Inspection Board (FSIB), 434
Forcemeats
    available forms, 396
    components, 390-394
    definition, 385-386
    handling/storage, 395-396
    preparation methods, 394-395
    types, 386-390
Foresaddles and hindsaddles, veal and lamb, 246, 250-252
Formal meals and menu planning, 12-13
Forming forcemeats, 395
Formula balance, 524

Formulas. *See* Recipes
Fortified milk, 80
Fortified wine, 57
Foundation sauces, 203
Frankfurters, 390, 391, 441
Freezing, 33-34, 443, 561-563
French butter cream frosting, 539
French cookery, 3, 4-5, 8, 9, 193, 202
French Dip sandwich, 449
French dressing, 328-331
French knife, 23
French onion soup gratinee, 193-194
French School of Culinary Arts – La Cuisine Classique, 5
French toast, 323
Fresh fruit
    cooking methods, 99-100
    pie fillings, 517
    preparation methods, 97-99, 324
    salads, 360, 361-362
Fresh ham, 443
Fresh herbs, 55
Fresh meat, 255
Fresh pasta, 150-153
Fresh sausages, 435, 441
Fresh shell eggs, 90
Fresh vegetables, 121
Fresh whipping cream, 536
Fresh whole milk, 80
Freshwater fish, 292-293
Fricasseeing, 268, 270
Fried closed sandwiches, 451
Fried eggs, 313-314
Fritters, 427-428
Frostings and toppings
    application of, 541-543
    for cake decorating, 546-551
    definition, 535
    ingredients, 536-537
    types, 537-541
Frozen desserts
    available forms, 563-565
    components, 558-560
    definition, 553, 554
    freezing/equipment for, 561-563
    fruit sauces for, 559
    handling/storage, 565
    preparation methods, 560-563
    types, 554-558
Frozen eggs, 91
Frozen fruits, 517
Frozen herbs, 55
Frozen meat, 255
Frozen mousse, 558
Frozen non-dairy toppings, 536
Frozen souffles, 558
Frozen vegetables, 121-122

Fruit
  characteristics/texture of, 96
  as condiments, 99-100
  cooking methods, 99-100
  definition, 95-96
  in frozen desserts, 560
  in pie fillings, 517, 518
  preparation methods, 96-99, 324
  selection/handling/storage, 100-101
Fruit, dried, 526
Fruit-flavored vinegar, 333
Fruit juices, 324
Fruit salads, 360, 361-362
Fruit sauces, 233, 559
Fruit soups, 197
Frying. *See also* Deep fat frying
  chicken, 268
  potatoes, 135-136
  poultry, 268, 269-270
  shortening for, 72
  vegetables, 123
Fudge frosting, 540, 541
Fume de poisson, 160-161, 163
Fungi. *See* Edible fungi
Furred game, 274, 276, 280-283
Fusion, heat of, 30

G

Galantines, 378-379, 395, 399, 405-408, 434
Game
  coulis of, 184
  definition, 273-274
  handling/storage, 283-284
  hanging of, 274-275
  marinades for, 59
  preparation methods, feathered, 276-279
  preparation methods, furred, 280-283
  selection of, 275-276
Game consomme, 179
Garde manger, 6
Garden beets, 128
Garden turnips, 130
Garlic, 115, 124
Garni, 64
Garnishes
  canapes, 416
  consomme, 177
  definition, 64-65
  forcemeats, 394
  sauces, 221
  soups, 197-199
Garniture, 64, 378-379
Gazpacho, 196, 197
Gel, 364

Gelatin
  available forms, 365
  culinary applications, 43, 365
  handling/storage, 365, 367-368
  properties/formation of, 363-364
  recommended concentrations of, 366-367
  reconstitution of dry granulated, 366
  tempering, 380
  types/definition, 364-365
Gelation, 148
Geography and cuisine development, 10
George III, King of England, 448
Giblets, 270-271
Ginger, 471
Glazes/glace, 166-167
Glazing, 382
Gluten, 147, 479, 483
Gnocchi, 155-156
Goat cheese, 84
Golden heart celery, 107
Goose, 276-278
Gouffe, Jules and Julien, 467
Goulash soup, 194
Grading
  eggs, 89
  meat, 243-244
  poultry, 264
Graham flour, 148
Grand jus lie, 218
Grande sauces, 203
Granite, 554, 563
Granular gelatin, 365, 366
Granulated cornmeal, 146
Granulated sugar, 469
Grapefruit seeds, 98
Gratin-style forcemeat, 387-388, 389
Grating cheese, 84
Gravy, 232
Greek cookery, 2, 194, 414
Green onions, 115
Griddle cakes, 320, 323, 496-497
Grillardin, 6
Grilled closed/open sandwiches, 451, 452-453
Grilling, 37, 135, 268
Grinding, 394-395
Ground spices, 51
Grouper, 58
Grouse, 278
Guar gum, 42
Guillaume of Tirel, 4, 172
Gulya's leves (goulash soup), 194
Gumbo, 112, 192-193
Gumpaste, 549-551

H

Half and half, 80, 81
Ham, 318-321
  curing/drying/smoking, 442-443
  fresh, 252
  storage, 444
  types, 443-444
Ham-bacon, 445
Handwashing technique, 17
Hanging game, 274-275
Hard drying pastillage paste, 549
Hard-grating cheese, 84, 425
Hard-ripened cheese, 84, 424-425
Hard wheat, 147
Hare, 281, 282
Haricot beans, 110
Hasenpfeffer, 281
Hazard analysis critical control points (HACCP), 18
Head cabbage, 104
Head cheese, 445
Health and culinary preparation. *See* Nutritional aspects
Heart disease, 69, 76-77
Heat capacity, 31
Heat transfer, 28-30
Heating of foods, 29, 34-36
Heavy cream, 80, 81, 471
Henin, Roland, 19
Henry II, King of France, 4, 237
Herb broth, 176
Herb-infused oil, 333
Herbs. *See also* Spices
  cuisine development and, 10
  handling/storage, 56
  listing of, 52-54
  types/characteristics, 55-56
  uses, 2
High-altitude baking, 532
High-ratio cakes, 524
Hillel, Rabbi, 448
Hollandaise, 229-230. *See also* Emulsions
Homemade pasta. *See* Fresh pasta
Homogenization, 42, 80
Honey yogurt dressing, 336
Hors d'oeuvre a la Francaise, 414
Hors d'oeuvres
  definition, 411-412, 414
  development of, 430
  international variations, 413-414
  presentation/service of, 430-431
  types, cold, 414-427
  types, hot, 429-430
  uses of, 412-413
Horseradish sauce, 336

Hot foods, safe temperatures for, 17, 18, 62, 200
Hot/pungent peppers, 113
Hot sandwiches, 449-453
Hotel kitchens. *See* Kitchens (hotel/restaurant)
Hungarian cookery, 194
Hydrogenation, 73-74
Hydrolysis of fats, 74, 75
Hygiene, personal, 16-17

I

Ice cream, 554, 555, 556, 557, 563
Iceberg lettuce, 109
Ices, 554
Icing, doughnut, 496
Idaho potatoes, 132
Illness, food-borne, 18, 270, 519
Immiscible liquids, 41
Incorporated air in cakes, 525
Indian chutney, 100
Indian cookery, 194
Individually-quick frozen foods, 487, 517
Indonesian cookery, 414
Infusion of spices, 560
Ingredient proportions, calculation of, 22-23
Instant dried milk, 82
Instant marinades, 59
Instant pre-gelatinized starch, 516
Institutional Meat Purchasers Specifications (IMPS), 245
International cuisine, 10, 51
Iron, 92
Italian cookery, 144-145, 195, 413
Italian sausage, 441

J

Jamboneaux, 445
Jams, 100
Japanese artichokes, 128
Japanese cookery, 414
Jeanne, Queen of France, 4
Jellied consomme, 181-182, 195, 376
Jellied soups, 181-182
Jellies, 100, 167-168. *See also* Aspic jelly
Jerusalem artichokes, 128
Joseph, Franz, Emperor, 237
Juices, fruit, 324
Julienne, 24
Jus de veau lie, 215-216

K

Kale, 108
Katahdin potatoes, 133
Kentucky ham, 443

Kidney beans, 110
Kielbasa, 355, 441-442
Kill step, 18
Kitchens (hotel and restaurant), 6-8. *See also* Language of the kitchen
Kneading dough, 473
Knives, 23-24, 97
Kohl suppe (cabbage soup), 193
Kohlrabi, 106, 129
Kosher foods, 10
Kosher gelatin, 42

L

"La Cuisine Classique," 9
Ladling method, 374
Lamb
    cuts of, 254-255
    history, 237-238
    quality grading, 244
Language of the kitchen
    definition, 18-19
    mise en place, 19-20
    recipes, 21-23
    terminology, 23-26
    weights/measures, 19, 20-21
Lard, 71, 468
Larding meat, 256
Large white oval potatoes, 133
Larousse, 159
Lattice-top crust pies, 510
Layered sandwiches, 422
Le Cuisinier Francois, 4
Le Guide Culinaire, 5, 172, 214, 393
Le Viandier, 4, 172
Leaf fat/lard, 71
Leaf gelatin, 365
Leaf lettuce, 109
Leafy vegetables, 108-109
Lean dough, 481, 482
Lean fish, 287, 302
Leavening agents
    in cakes, 525
    functions, 469
    in puff pastry dough, 506
    in quick breads, 490
Lebanon bologna, 442
Lecithin, 42, 44, 45
Leeks, 115
Legume salads, 352-353
Lemon-lime French dressing, 330
Lettuces, 109
Liaison finale, 206-207, 208
Light cream, 80, 81, 471
Lightened ice cream, 557, 563
Lima beans, 111
Lining molds, plates and platters with aspic, 381-382

Linoleic fatty acid, 76, 149
Linolenic fatty acid, 76
Liquids
    in bread baking, 480
    in cakes, 525
    in cookie dough, 512
    in frostings/toppings, 537
    in pie pastry dough, 508
    in quick breads, 490
    types for sauces, 203-204
Lobster, 294, 303-305
Lobster parfait, 409
Lobster salad, 358
Locust bean gum, 42
Long-bodied fish, 293
Long-flaky pie crust, 508
Long grain rice, 140
Low-fat milk, 471
Low temperature rendering, 71
Lucullus, 3
Lyonnaise potatoes, 319, 323

M

Macaroni products, 150
Mace, 471
Magellan, 47
Maillard browning, 35, 39
Maitre d'hotel butter, 231
Make-up of dough, 484, 485, 507
Malic acid, 96
Malt vinegar, 57
Mango rice salad, 350
Maple sugar/syrup, 469
Marbling, 240, 243, 244
Margarine, 73, 468
Marinades, 59
Marinated meats, 256
Marinated salads, 359-361
Marshmallow frosting, 540
Martino of Como, 4
Marzipan, 550-551
Masking, 379, 381-382
Master chefs, 8
Mayonnaise, 331-332, 334, 459, 460. *See also* Emulsions
Mealy pie crust, 508
Mealy potatoes, 134
Meat and Poultry Inspection (MPI), 434
Meat combination sandwich, 453
Meat glaze, 167
Meat Inspection Act (1906), 242
Meat salads, 353-356
Meats. *See also* Game
    aging process, 244-245
    basic cuts, 245-255
    breakfast, 318-321
    composition, chemical, 240-242

composition, physical, 239-240
cooking methods, 256-259
definition/history, 235-237
in forcemeat, 390-393
grading, quality/yield, 243-244
handling/storage, 255
inspection of, 242-243
preparation methods, 255-256
in sandwiches, 458
in sausages, 436
selection of, 242-245
Meaty fish, 288-289
Medici, Catherine de, 4, 149, 237, 554
Medium-flaky pie crust, 508
Menu planning, 4-5, 11-13
Meringue-type butter cream frosting, 539
Merinques, 561
Metric weights and measures, 20, 21
Mettwurst, 442
Mezes, 414
Microwaves, 28, 29
Microwaving potatoes, 136-137
Middle Eastern cookery, 81
Mild/sweet peppers, 113
Milk
    in baking, 471
    cooking with, 82-83
    fermented/processed products, 81-82
    in frozen desserts, 560
    in sauces, 209
    in sweet dough, 500
    types, 80
Milk chocolate, 472
Milk fats, 69
Mince, 26
Minerals, 242
Minestrone, 195
Mint sauce, 335
Mirepoix in stock, 164, 166
Mise en place
    breakfast cookery, 312
    definition, 19-20
    sandwiches, 461
Mixed salads, 341, 342, 360, 361-362
Modeling and sculptures, 551
Molasses, 469
Molding
    forcemeats, 395
    mousses, 397, 398
    paté, 400
    terrines, 403-404
Molds, 143, 381-382
Mollusks, 294, 295-296, 359
Monkfish, 289
Monosodium glutamate (MSG), 49, 50

Monounsaturated fatty acids, 69, 74, 77
Montagu, John, 448
Morel mushrooms, 116
"Mother" formation (vinegar), 58
Mother sauces, 45, 203
    accessory elements, 220-221
    making, 209-210
    preparation methods, 213-218
    types of, 211-212
Mousse
    components, 396
    definition, 385, 389, 396, 399, 409-410
    frozen, 558
    preparation methods, 397
    types, 396
Mousseline
    cold, 378
    definition, 398, 399, 409-410
    preparation methods, 410
Mousseline-style forcemeat, 388-389, 390
"Mouth feel," 76
Muffins, 322, 491-492
Mulligatawny soup, 194
Multi-decker sandwiches, 455
Multiplier, determination of, 22
Muscle (meat), 239
Mushrooms, 115-117, 346
Mussel salad with saffron dressing, 357
Mussels, 309
Mutton, 238, 244
Mutton broth, 195

N
National Association of Meat
    Purveyors (NAMP), 245
Natural casings (sausages), 438-439
Natural gelatin, 365
Neapolitan ice cream, 558
Neutral stock, 160
New Larousse Gastronamique, 201, 327
New potatoes, 133-134
Newburg sauce, 225
Non-meat ingredients in sausages, 436-438
Nonfat dry milk solids, 82
Nonfat milk, 80
Noodles
    cooking methods, 155-157
    definition, 149
    types, 154-155
Norgold russet potatoes, 133
Norland potatoes, 133
North American bighorn sheep, 281
Nougat, 551
Novelty pie crusts, 510
Nut butters, 460

Nut sauces, 233
Nutmeg, 471
Nutritional aspects
    cereals/grains, 149
    chicken, 272
    deer, 280
    eggs, 92
    fats/oils, 76-77
    MSG, 50
    poultry, 271-272
    salads, 345
    salt, 50
    sandwiches, 463
    sauces, cold, 336-337
    spices, 56
    vegetables, 120-121, 125
    wine, 57
Nuts, 526, 560

O
Oatmeal griddle cakes, 497
Oil-based marinades, 59
Oils. See also Fats
    in baking, 468
    chemical makeup of, 68-70
    deep fat frying and, 38
    filtering, 75-76
    for making pasta, 151-152
    temperature effects on, 73-75
    types/extraction methods, 70-71
Oily fish, 292, 293
Okra, 112
Oleic fatty acid, 149
Oleoresins, 56
Olestra, 77
Olive oil, 70-71
Omega-3-fatty acids, 69, 77
Omelets, 315, 316-317
One-crust pies, 509-510
1000 island dressing, 332
Onions, 114-115
Open sandwiches, cold, 455
Open sandwiches, hot, 452-453
Orange seeds, 98
Oranges, peeling, 101
Oven baked fried potatoes, 136
Oven baked rice, 144
Oxidation of fats, 73-74
Oxidizing agents, 479
Oyster plant, 130
Oysters, 308-309

P
Paddy rice, 141
Palate cleansers, 13
Pan-frying
    fish, 298, 299

poultry, 269
    vegetables, 123
Panada, 393
Panbroiling of meats, 258
Pancakes, 320, 323
Pancakes, potato, 135-136
Pantry cook, 7
Parboiling potatoes, 135
Parfair (frozen dessert), 557-558, 563
Parfait (savory terrine), 399, 408-409
Paring fruits, 98-99
Paring knife, 23
Parmesan cheese, 85
Parsnips, 129
Partial carcass cuts, 246
Partridge, 278
Pascal celery, 107
Pasta
    categories by use, 152
    definition, 149
    preparation/cooking methods, 152,
       153-154
    types, 150-153
Pasta salads, 349-351
Pasteurization, 18, 80
Pasteurized cream, 536
Pastillage paste, 549-550
Pasting of cereal/grain starches, 148
Pastrami, 445
Pastry bag, paper, 548
Pastry chef/cook, 7, 8
Pastry cream, 518
Pastry cream butter cream frosting, 539-
    540
Pastry dough. *See* Dough, pastry
Pastry flour, 470
Paté
    aspic jelly in, 379
    definition, 399-400, 434
    equipment, 400
    preparation methods, 400-403
    troubleshooting, 403
Paté dough, 401
Paté spice, 394
Patissier, 6, 7
Patissier Dublayers, 466-467
Pea meal bacon, 445
Peanut butter, 460
Pears, poached in red raspberry juice,
    99-100
Peas, 110
Pectin, 42, 96, 100, 118
Peeling techniques, 101, 121
Pennsylvania ham, 443
Peppers, 113
Percentages in recipes, 22-23
Perigord truffles, 117

Petit choux, 419-421
Phase changes of compounds, 31
Pheasant, 278
Phillip II, King of France, 466
Pickled herbs, 55
Picnic ham, 444
Pie fillings
    definition, 515
    ingredients, 516-517
    preparation methods,
       cream/custard/chiffon, 518-521
    preparation methods, fruit, 518
    types, 511-512
Pie pastry dough
    crust types, 508, 509-510
    definition, 499
    fillings/toppings, 510-512
    ingredients, 507-508
    make-up/rolling, 509
    mixing, 508-509
    storage, 510
Pie toppings, 511-512
Piedmontese truffles, 117
Pigeon, 278-279
Pigments in vegetables, 119-120
Pilaf, rice, 143-144
Pineapples, sectioning of, 96
Pinwheel sandwiches, 422
Piping
    choux puffs, 420
    tubes for frosting, 537
Pita bread, 457
Pith, 99
Plain fudge frosting, 541
Plain layer cake, 527, 528
Plastic casings (sausages), 441
Plates and platters, 65-66, 382
Poaching
    eggs, 317
    fish, 298-300
    fruits, 99-100
    meats, 257
    poultry, 267-268
Pocket bread, 457
Pods. *See* Seeds, edible pods, young
    shoots
Poissoner, 6
Polenta, 155
Polish sausage, 441-442
Polished rice, 141
Polo, Marco, 149, 553, 554
Polysaccharide, 149
Polysaccharide gums, 42-43
Polyunsaturated fatty acids, 69, 74
Poppy seed, 471
Pork
    cuts of, 252-254

freezing of, 443
history, 238
quality grading, 244
Pork fat, 71
Pork hat pie, 400
Pot roasting of meats, 259
Potage a la fermiere, 189
Potager, 6
Potato pancakes, 136
Potatoes
    available forms, 133, 134
    definition, 127, 131
    nutritional aspects, 137
    preparation methods, 134-136, 319,
    321, 323
    starch content, 134
    storage, 137-138
    types, 130-134
Poultry
    classification of, 264-265, 266
    cutting of, 268
    definition, 263-264
    handling/storage, 270
    nutritional aspects, 271-272
    preparation methods, 265-271
    refrigeration of, 265
    selection of, 264-265
Poultry fat, 72
Poultry giblets, 270-271
Poultry Product Inspection Act (1957),
    242
Poultry salads, 352-353
Pound cake, 526, 528
Pour batter, 490
Powder gelatin, 365
Powdered sugar, 469
Powdering of spices, 560
Prague ham, 444
Prague powder, 393
Prawn, 294-295
Premier commis, 6
Presentation of food
    basic factors of, 62-66
    definition, 61
    hors d'oeuvres, 430-431
Preserves, 100
Pressing terrines, 405
Presunto ham, 444
Primal cuts, 246-249
Primary seasoning agent, 49
Processed cheese, 84-85
Processed meats. *See also* Charcuterie
    definition, 433-434
    whole, 442-445
Processed milk products, 82
Procurement grades, poultry, 264
Profiteroles, 198, 557

Progressive grinding, 395
Proofing, 478, 485-486, 503
Prosciutto, 444
Protein, meat, 240-241
Puff pastry dough, 499, 504-507
Pulled sugar, 551
Pullman bread loaf, 456-457
Pumpkin, 114
Pumpkin custard pie filling, 520
Punches, 554, 555
Purees, 182-185

Q

Quail, 279
Quenelles, 198, 395, 398, 399
Quick beef broth, 175
Quick breads
    definition, 489
    ingredients, 490
    mixing methods, 490-491
    mixture types, 490
    types/preparation methods, 491-497
Quick-cooking rice, 141
Quick demi-glace sauce, 215-216
Quinine, 48

R

Rabbit, 282
Radetsky, Marshal, 237
Radiation, 28, 29
Radish, 129-130
Raft, 177
Raising dough, 483-484
Rancidity of fats, 73-75
Raviers, 414
Raw fish, 303
Raw marinades, 58, 59
Raw milk, 80
Raw sugar, 469
Ray, 288
Receptions, hors d'oeuvres for, 412-413
Recipes
    converting, 22
    determining percentages, 22-23
    structure, 21-22
Red butter, 232
Red cabbage, 104
Red pontiac potatoes, 133
Red raspberry juice, poached pears
    and, 99-100
Red round potatoes, 133
Reduction of sauces, 209, 223-224
Refined olive oil, 71
Refrigerator cookie dough, 512, 513
Regional cuisine, 10, 51, 55, 190-195,
    413-414
Regular dried milk, 82

Regular ice cream, 557, 563
Religion and cuisine development, 10,
    238
Remontage of broken sauces, 226
Remouillage, 166
Rennet, 83
Reptiles as exotic game, 282
Restaurant kitchens. See Kitchens
    (hotel/restaurant)
Retarded dough, 502-503
Rhubarb, 117-118
Rhubarb spoom, 562
Rice
    boiled/pilaf/risotto, 141-145
    composition/struction, 140-141
    processing methods/types, 141
Rice salads, 350, 351-352
Rice vinegar, 58
Rich dough, 481, 482
Richard II, King of England, 274
Rijsttafel, 414
Rillette, 423, 445
Ripening of cheeses, 84
Risotto, 144-145
Rissoles, 429, 430
Roasting
    definition, 39
    game birds, 279
    goose, 277-278
    meats, 258-261
    potatoes, 135
    poultry, 267
Rock salt, 49
Roll-in fat, 504, 506
Rolls, sandwich, 457
Romaine lettuce, 109
Roman Cookery Book, The, 3
Romanae Artis Coquinariae Leber, 3
Root plants, 127
Rossini, 236
Rotisseur, 6
Roullades, 399, 408
Round cakes, 533
Round white potatoes, 133
Rounding, 484, 485
Roux
    composition/types of, 204
    preparation methods, 205
    uses of, 206
Royal icing, 540-541
Royale garnish, 198
Russet potatoes, 132, 133
Russian cookery, 4-5, 8, 195, 413
Rutabaga, 130

S

Safety practices, 16-18, 23

Saffron dressing, 357
Salad dressings, 328-336, 341, 347
Salad greens, 109, 344
Salads
    definition, 339-340
    handling/storage, 348-349
    layout, 345
    mayonnaise-based, in sandwiches,
    459
    parts of, 340-341
    preparation methods, 345-348
    produce selection for, 348
    selection/presentation of, 343, 345
    types, 341-343, 345, 349, 351-362
Salami, 442
Salmon, 69, 77, 291-292
Salmon mousse, 397
Salmonella, 519
Salsify, 130
Salt
    in bread baking, 480-481
    in cakes, 524
    in food preparation, 2, 49-50, 97
    in forcemeats, 393-394
    in frostings/toppings, 537
    in pie pastry dough, 508
    in puff pastry dough, 504
    types, 49
Salty sensations (tongue), 48
Sandwiches
    components, 456-460
    definition, 447, 449
    history, 448
    as hors d'oeuvres, 421, 422
    nutritional aspects, 463
    preparation methods, 460-461
    production of/mise en place, 461-
    462
    quality/layout, 462-463
    types, 449-456
Sanitary food handling, 16-18
Saturated fats, 69-70, 74, 92
Saturation of emulsions, 44
Sauce Allemande, 222
Sauce Supreme, 223
Sauces. See also Chaud-froid sauce;
    Cold sauces
    accessory elements/garnish, 220-221
    brown, 213-218
    butter/compound butters, 230-232
    components, 203-204
    compound, 218-224
    depouillage/cleaning, 210-211
    emulsified, 225-230
    essentials of, 203
    function of, 201-203
    miscellaneous, 232-234

for pasta, 154
physical properties of, 210
reduction of, 209, 223-224
seasoning/flavoring agents, 208-209
shellfish, 224-225
straining, 211
thickening agents/roux, 204-208
types/classification of, 211-213
white, 218
Saucier, 6
Sauerkraut, 104
Sausage
  breakfast, 318-321
  casings, 438-441
  components, 436-438
  definition, 434-435
  types, 435-436, 441-442
Sauteing
  definition, 36-37
  fish, 298, 299
  fruits, 100
  poultry, 268
  vegetables, 123
Savory, 167
Savory fruit sauces, 233
Savory sabayon, 233
Savory terrine, 408, 409
Savoy cabbage, 104
Scaling, 484-485, 530, 531
Scallion, 115
Scallops, 309
Scampi, 294-295
Scandinavian fruit soup, 197
Scappi, Bartolomeo, 4
Schinkenspeck, 445
Scorzonera, 130
Scottish cookery, 195
Scrambled eggs, 314, 315
Sculptures. See Modeling and
  sculptures
Sea salt, 49
Seafood gumbo, 192
Seafood salads, 356-359
Seafood sandwiches, 458
Seasoning and flavoring
  definition, 47-48
  forcemeats, 393-394, 394
  frozen desserts, 560
  handling/storage, 50-51
  sauces, 208
  sausages, 437
  taste and, 48-49
  types/characteristics, 49-50
Second chef/cook, 6, 7
Seeding fruits, 98
Seeds, edible pods, young shoots, 109-
  111

Semi-soft cheese, 84, 424
Serrano ham, 444
Service
  of hors d'oeuvres, 430-431
  of soups, 199-200
  types of, 4-5, 8-9
Serving amounts. See Yields
Sesame seeds, 471
Seviche, 356
Shad roe, 292
Shallots, 115
Shape and food presentation, 63
Shark, 288
Sharpening knives, 24
Sheet cakes, 533
Sheet gelatin, 365
Shellfish, 293-296
Shellfish butters, 231, 232
Shellfish sauces, 224-225
Shells, egg, 88, 90
Sherbets, 13, 560-561
  definition, 554
  freezing, 563
  types, 554-555
Shirataki, 154
Shirred eggs, 317-318
Shoots. See Seeds, edible pods, young
  shoots
Shot fat, 71-72
Short grain rice, 140
Short-order cook, 6-7
Shortening
  baking and, 468
  bread baking and, 481
  definition, 72, 73
  in pie pastry dough, 508
  in puff pastry dough, 504
  in sweet dough, 500
Showpieces, decorative, 548-549, 551
Shred, 26
Shrimp, 294-295, 306
Shrimp bisque, 185
Shrimp noodles, 154-155
Shrimp remoulade, 358
Sides and quarters, beef, 246
Simmering stock, 162, 165-166
Simple butter cream frosting, 538, 539
Simple closed sandwiches, cold, 453-
  454
Simple closed sandwiches, hot, 449-451
Simple salads, 341
Simplesse, 77
Sizing of eggs, 90
Skate, 288
Skeletal tissue, 240
Skim milk, 80, 471
Skimming stock, 164

Slab/sliced bacon, 444
Slice, 26
Slicers, electric, 24
Small brown and white sauces, 218, 220
Smithfield ham, 443
Smoke point of fats, 74, 75
Smoked sausages, 435
Smoking of hams, 443
Smorgasbord, 414
Smorrebrod, 421-422
Snails, wild, 306, 307
Snipe, 279
Snow peas, 110
Soba noddles, 155
Soft cookie dough, 512-513
Soft fruit, 97
Soft keeping pastillage paste, 549, 550
Soft-ripened cheese, 84, 424
Soft-shell crab, 305
Soft wheat, 147
Sol, 364
Solid packed fruit, 517
Somen noodles, 155
Sorbet, 13, 554, 555
Sorrel, 109
Souffles, frozen, 558
Soups
  clear, 173-182
  cold, 195-197
  definition, 171-172
  garnishes/toppings, 197-199
  pastas for, 152
  service of, 200
  specialty/regional, 190-195
  thick, 182-188
  types, 172
  vegetable, 188-190
Sour cream, 81
Sour cream dressing, 335, 336
Sour sensations (tongue), 48
Soured milk, 81
Sous chef, 6, 7
Soy, 49
Soybeans, 110
Spaetzle, 156-157
Spaghetti squash, 114
Spanish cookery, 413-414
Spices. See also Herbs
  baking, 471-272
  definition, 47
  forcemeats, 394
  frozen desserts, 560
  handling/storage, 52
  listing of, 52-54
  sweet dough, 500
  types/characteristics, 51-52
Spinach, 108

Split pea soup, 183
Sponge cake, 528
Sponge dough method, 483
Spoom, 554, 555, 562, 563
Spray pumping, 442
Spreads
    canapes, 415
    hors d'oeuvres, 422-423
    sandwiches, 459-460
Spuma, 554, 555, 562, 563
Square cut chuck, 249
Squash, 113-114
Squid, 309
Stainless steel cookware, 32, 97, 205
Stalk vegetables, 106-108
Starches
    in pie fillings, 516
    potatoes, content of, 134
    in sauces, 206
Station cook, 6
Steaming
    definition, 30, 39
    fish, 300
    potatoes, 135
    poultry, 270
    vegetables, 122, 123
Steel (sharpening), 24
Stewing
    meats, 256-257
    potatoes, 135
    poultry, 268, 270
Stiff cookie dough, 512
Still frozen ice cream, 557
Stir-frying poultry, 268
Stitch pumping, 442
Stock
    definition, 159-160
    preparation methods, 161-166
    for sauces, 203-204
    types/elements of, 160-161
    uses of, 166-169
Stone ground cornmeal, 146
Straight dough method, 481-482
Straight forcemeat method, 386-387, 388
Straining sauces, 211
String beans, 110-111
Stroganoff, Count, 236
Stuffing
    forcemeats, 395
    meats, 259-260
Sturgeon, 288
Sublimation, 33
Suckling pig, 261
Suet, 71
Sugar
    in baking, 469
    boiling, 558, 559

in cakes, 524
cookie dough, 512
frostings/toppings, 536
quick bread baking, 490
sweet dough, 500
Sugar-based glazes, 486
Sugar cured ham, 443
Sugar syrup, 560
Sulze, 445
Summer sausages, 442
Summer squash, 113
Sundaes, 557
Superior potatoes, 133
Supreme Sauce, 222
Surimi, 396
Sushi, 414
Swedish cookery, 414
Sweet butter, 83
Sweet dough
    baking of, 503-504
    definition, 499
    fermentation of, 501-502
    ingredients, 500-501
    preparation methods, 501
    retarding, 502-503
Sweet fruit sauces, 233
Sweet potatoes, 130-131
Sweet sensations (tongue), 48
Sweetened condensed milk, 471
Sweeteners in baking, 469, 480
Swiss chard, 108
Swiss cheese, 85
Syneresis, 516, 520
Synthetic fats, 77
Syrup packed fruit, 517
Syrups in frostings, 536-537

T
Table beets, 128
Table wines, 56-57
Taillevent, 4
Talleyrand, 202
Tapas, 413-414
Tapioca starch, 206
Tartar sauce, 334
Tartaric acid, 96
Tartlets, 418-419, 427, 514
Tarts, 514
Taste sensations, 48-49
T.C.M., 393
Tea sandwiches, 414, 421, 455-456
Teewurst, 442
Temperature
    baking and, 472, 473
    bread baking, 486
    cake baking, 531
    emulsions and, 44-45

fats/oils and, 73-75
flavor development and, 35-36
food preparation and, 17, 18, 62, 200, 270
forcemeat preparation, 395-396
gelatin and, 379
heat transfer, 28-30
internal of meats, 258
taste and, 48-49
yeast and, 478
Tempering
    aspic jelly, 379, 380
    chaud-froid sauce, 373-374
Tenderizing meats, 255-256
Teodoric, Prince of Ravenna, 149
Terrines, 379, 395, 398, 400, 403-405, 434
Testing for doneness
    baked custard, 520
    cakes, 531-532
    fish, 302, 303
    meats, 259
Tete presse, 445
Texture and food presentation, 63-64
Thawing foods, 33-34
Thermal conductivity, 31-32
Thick soups, 182-188
Thickening agents
    pie fillings, 516
    roux and, 204, 206
Thin-bodied fish, 291
Timbales, 143, 398, 399
Tinted cure mix, 393
Tomato sauce, 212, 213
Tomatoes, 112-113
Tongue, 48
Tooth of a sauce, 370, 375
Toppings. See Frostings and toppings;
    Pie toppings
Tossed salads, 342
Tournant, 6
Townsend, Lord Turnip, 236
Trimmed beef loin, 248
Triumph potatoes, 133
Troisieme commis, 6
Tropical oils, 69
Trout, 291-292
True percentage, 23
True suet, 71
Truffles, 117
Trumpet mushrooms, 116
Trussing a bird, 277
Tubers, See also Potatoes
    defined, 127
    types, 128-131
Turkey, 266
Turnips, 130
Turnovers, 510, 511

Twitcher, Jemmy, 448
Two-crust pies, 510
Type A and Type B gelatin, 364

U

Udon noodles, 155
Unbleached flour, 148
Uncooked salads, 359-361
Uncooked-smoked sausages, 435, 441-442
United States. *See* American cookery
U.S. Dept. of Agriculture, 88, 242, 243, 244, 264, 434
U.S. Dept. of Labor, 8
U.S. Food and Drug Administration, 150
U.S. Standard weights and measures, 19, 21
Univalves, 295
Universal solvent, 30
Unripened cheese, 84, 423-424
Unsalted butter, 83
Unsaturated fatty acids, 69-70
Unsweetened chocolate, 472

V

Vacuum-pack aging process, 245
Vanilla ice cream, 563
Vapor as leavening agent, 525
Vaporization, heat of, 30
Varenne Francois Pierre de la, 4
Veal
    cuts of, 250-252
    history, 237
    quality grading, 244
Veal kidney fat, 72
Vegetable bouillon, 175
Vegetables fats, 69
Vegetable fruits, 111-114
Vegetable gelatin, 367
Vegetable oyster, 130
Vegetable salds, 342, 345-348
Vegetable soups, 188-190
Vegetable stock, 160
Vegetables
    cooking methods, 123-125
    definition, 103-104
    handling fresh/frozen/canned, 121-122
    nutritional aspects, 120-121, 125
    Preparation methods, 118-221
    in sandwiches, 458
    types/descriptions, 114-118
Velouté, 72
Velouté sauces, 217, 218
Velouté soups, 186-188
Vinison, 280

Vichyssoise, 196
Vinegar
    emulsions and, 43, 44
    as flavoring agents, 57-58
    fruit-flavored, 333
Virgin olive oil, 71
Virginia ham, 443
Vitamin A, 80, 92, 120, 137, 146
Vitamin B complex, 92, 137, 141, 146, 149
Vitamin C, 120, 137, 146
Vitamin D, 80, 92
Vitamin E, 76, 92
Vitamin K, 92
Vitamins, 242
Volatile elements of spices, 51-52
Volume of leavened product, 500

W

Waffles, 321, 323, 496-497
Waldorf salad, 360
Washes in bread baking, 486
Water, properties of, 30-31
Water chestnuts, 129
Water packed fruit, 517
Waxy maize cornstarch, 516
Waxy potatoes, 134
Weight loss, 76
Weights and measures, 19-21
Westphalian ham, 444
Wet rendering, 71
Wheat, 147-148
Whey, 82, 83
Whipped butter, 83
Whipped-style toppings, 537-538
Whipping cream, 46, 80, 81, 536
Whisking of emulsions, 44, 45
White asparagus, 107
White aspic jelly (fish), 370
White butter sauces, 226-227
White chaud-froid sauce, 372, 373
White cocoa butter coating, 472
White corn, 146
White fish, firm and flaky, 289-290
White House muffins, 322
White mustard cabbage, 108
White rice, 140-141
White roux, 204
White sauces, 203, 218, 219, 220
White stock, 160, 161
Whites, egg, 88, 92, 470, 536
Whole carcass cuts, 245-246
Whole milk, 471
Whole rice, 141
Whole spices, 51, 52
Whole wheat flour, 148, 470
Whole wheat griddle cakes, 497

Wholesale cuts, 246
Wild rice, 145
Williamsburg ham, 443
Willoof chicory, 109
Wine vinegar, 58
Wines
    in aspic jelly, 370
    as flavoring agents, 56-57, 208-209
Winter carrots, 128
Winter square, 113-114
Winter wheat, 479
Winterized fat, 72
Woodcock, 279
Working chef, 7
World Health Organization, 16

X

Xanthan gum, 42

Y

Yams, 130-131
Yeast, 469, 478-479, 500
Yeast doughnuts, 493-496
Yellow chiffon cake, 529
Yellow corn, 146
Yields
    of bacon, 444
    of fish, 297
    of rice, 143
Yogurt, 81, 336
Yolks, egg, 42, 44, 45, 88
York ham, 444
Young shoots. *See* Seeds, edible pods, young shoots

Z

Zakuska, 413
Zampone, 445
Zucchini, 113